THE PICKERING MASTERS

THE WORKS OF ELIZABETH GASKELL
VOLUME 3

THE PICKERING MASTERS
THE WORKS OF ELIZABETH GASKELL

Volumes 1–5

General Editor:	Joanne Shattock
Volume Editors:	Linda K. Hughes
	Charlotte Mitchell
	Joanne Shattock
	Alan Shelston
	Joanne Wilkes
Advisory Editor:	Angus Easson

THE WORKS OF
ELIZABETH GASKELL

VOLUME 3

Novellas and Shorter Fiction II

Round the Sofa,
and
Tales from *Household Words* (1852–9)

Edited by
Charlotte Mitchell

LONDON
PICKERING & CHATTO
2005

Published by Pickering & Chatto (Publishers) Limited
21 Bloomsbury Way, London WC1A 2TH

2252 Ridge Road, Brookfield, Vermont 05036-9704, USA

www.pickeringchatto.com

BRITISH LIBRARY CATALOGUING IN PUBLICATION DATA
Gaskell, Elizabeth Cleghorn, 1810–1865
   The works of Elizabeth Gaskell
   Vols. 1–3, 5, 7. – (The Pickering masters)
   1. Gaskell, Elizabeth Cleghorn, 1810–1865 – Criticism and interpretation
   I. Title II. Shattock, Joanne
   823.8
ISBN-10: 185196777X

LIBRARY OF CONGRESS CATALOGING-IN-PUBLICATION DATA
A catalogue record for this title is available from the Library of Congress.

This publication is printed on acid-free paper that conforms to the American
National Standard for the Permanence of Paper for Printed Library Materials

New material typeset by
P&C

Printed by Cromwell Press,
Trowbridge, Wiltshire.

CONTENTS

Acknowledgements — vii
Introduction — ix
Bibliography — xxvii
Abbreviations — xxxv

'The Old Nurse's Story' — 1
'Morton Hall' — 21
'My French Master' — 53
'The Squire's Story' — 73
'Right at Last' — 89
'The Manchester Marriage' — 107

Round the Sofa — 131
  'My Lady Ludlow' — 143
  'An Accursed Race' — 295
  'The Doom of the Griffiths' — 311
  'Half a Life-Time Ago' — 343
  'The Poor Clare' — 383
  'The Half-Brothers' — 429

Explanatory Notes — 441
Textual Notes — 481

ACKNOWLEDGEMENTS

I have incurred many debts in preparing this edition. In particular, when compiling the explanatory notes I called on the help of experts in a wide variety of disciplines including heraldry, legal history, theology and Welsh: it is my hope that their learning has enabled me effectively to conceal my ignorance of these subjects. I would like to thank warmly the many friends and strangers who responded so obligingly to my emails, especially Edward Clive, Patric Dickinson, Rosemary Dunhill, Graham Handley, Timothy Hochstrasser, Steve Holmes, Michael Lobban, Hugh Massingberd, Paul Matthews, Charles Mitchell, John Mullan, Roger Llewellyn, Richard North, John Geoffrey Sharps, Alison Shell, Alan Shelston, Anthony Strugnell, John Styles and Michael Wheeler. I am immensely grateful to Joanne Shattock, the General Editor of this edition, for her unfailing encouragement, patience and good humour. I should also like to thank Marian Olney of Pickering & Chatto and the staff of the University of London Library, the British Library and the London Library.

INTRODUCTION

The eleven stories and one article (non-fiction) included in this volume were all initially published in periodicals, mainly in Charles Dickens's *Household Words*, between December 1852 and December 1858. One story appeared in an American journal, and another in a provincial almanac. All twelve pieces were republished in volume form shortly afterwards. Four stories were collected in volume form, with others, in *Lizzie Leigh and Other Tales* (1855). Two stories were collected in *Right at Last and Other Tales* (1860) and the remaining five stories (and the non-fiction article) were published, with a frame story, as *Round the Sofa* (1859), which is here printed in its entirety.

The publication of these works belongs therefore to the hectic period in Elizabeth Gaskell's life which saw the completion of *Ruth* (December 1852) and the anxiety about its publication (January 1853) and its reception; the composition and occasional publication of *Cranford* (December 1851–May 1853) and its volume publication (June 1853); the composition (from March 1854) and serial publication of *North and South* (September 1854–January 1855) and its rewriting for publication in volume form (April 1855); the research and writing of *The Life of Charlotte Brontë* (July 1855–February 1857), its publication (March 1857), its rewriting in response to legal action and the publication of the revised third edition (November 1857). During this period she also supported her second daughter through the difficult period of her ultimately abortive engagement. Not surprisingly, Gaskell was frequently exhausted during the mid-1850s and many of her short stories were published to buy her and her family holidays to recover from the strain and exhaustion of her literary, parochial and domestic work and from the heat and pollution of Manchester life. Edgar Wright describes her recuperating from the furore over *The Life of Charlotte Brontë* and as turning 'only occasionally to her fiction, partly to earn money for holidays and travel, partly in response to pressures from publishers and editors'.[1] Not only did she write stories in order to get the money to travel, but particular places stimulated her to write stories, places whose topographical precision is often

---

1. Edgar Wright, Preface to *My Lady Ludlow and Other Stories* (Oxford: Oxford University Press, 1989), p. x.

surprising in a writer notoriously careless with names and dates. Through-out this period she showed a striking enthusiasm for escaping from Manchester.[1] Among other places she went to the Lake District, Essex, Worcestershire, Gloucestershire, Hampshire, Yorkshire, Staffordshire, Lancashire, Scotland, Wales, France, Italy and Germany, and some of this experience undoubtedly fed into the composition of the stories in this volume.

It is uncertain, all the same, how many of them were entirely written during this period. 'The Doom of the Griffiths' is the clearest case of a story which seems definitely to have been composed, in some version, much earlier than its date of publication, since Gaskell mentions in a letter that it had been begun 'when Marianne was a baby', that is, in about 1834.[2] But it may well be the case that others had a similar history, which happens not to have been mentioned in any of the surviving correspondence. As Jenny Uglow observes, 'by the late 1840s and 1850s, when her work was much in demand, she produced her stories suspiciously quickly, even for someone who wrote at speed.'[3] 'The Poor Clare' may perhaps have partly existed in 1845–6, if Ellen M. Laun is correct in associating it with the story set 'more than a century ago ... on the borders of Yorkshire'[4] begun after Willie Gaskell's death, even if John Chapple has proved that in its present form it cannot have been written before 1855.[5] The case of 'Half a Life-Time Ago' is an interesting one in this connection. It has long been known that it reworks features of 'Martha Preston', a story published in 1850 (included in Volume 1 of this edition); it is usually described as a revision, but in fact the rewriting is very extensive, involving significant changes in characterisation and plot.[6] Of course there is no way of knowing whether or not this was typical of Gaskell's practice, but it certainly suggests that, even if she did reuse her own work, she may have done more than fish old manuscripts out of a drawer. We know little about the genesis of 'The Old Nurse's Story', 'The Squire's Story' or 'The Half-Brothers', and it is quite possible that they represent work begun in the 1840s or even earlier. On the other hand, there are sound reasons for believing that 'Morton Hall' was composed after Gaskell's

---

1. As she wrote to Eliza Fox at the height of the *Ruth* controversy in early 1853: 'Oh how I should like to be wafted out of this England full of literal and metaphorical nipping east wind to Constantinople for a month – a long sail along the Mediterranean, slowly and lazily floating' (*Letters*, p. 224).

2. *Letters*, p. 488.

3. *Uglow*, p. 127.

4. Ellen M. Laun, 'A Missing Gaskell Tale Found', *Studies in Short Fiction*, 15 (1978), pp. 177–83. *MB*, 'Preface', p. vi.

5. J. A. V. Chapple, 'Elizabeth Gaskell's "Morton Hall" and "The Poor Clare"', *BST*, 20 (1990), pp. 47–9.

6. The two stories are compared by Larry K. Uffelman, 'From "Martha Preston" to "Half a Life-Time Ago": Elizabeth Gaskell rewrites a story', *GSJ*, 17 (2003), pp. 92–103.

first visit to Haworth in September 1853, and 'My French Master' after her visits to Paris and the New Forest in May and July 1853. Much of 'My Lady Ludlow' was evidently written week-by-week as it came out in *Household Words*. 'Right at Last' and 'The Manchester Marriage' seem definitely to have been written in Heidelberg in autumn 1858.[1]

The stories in this volume thus vary widely in genre, in length and in the circumstances of composition and of publication. Three ('The Old Nurse's Story', 'Half a Life-time Ago' and 'The Half-Brothers') are set in Cumberland and Westmorland, and the second and third of these strongly recall the shorter narrative poems of Wordsworth, which, as Stephen Gill says, Gaskell found 'enabling models for a certain kind of moral fable'.[2] All three show the remote north-west as a setting in which domestic tragedies are played out against a backdrop of magnificent scenery and menacing weather. Tragedy also dominates 'The Doom of the Griffiths', 'The Poor Clare' and 'The Squire's Story', which also all have a strong sense of place, though variously set in Wales, Lancashire and Derbyshire, and all feature cross-class marriages. 'My French Master', 'A Manchester Marriage' and 'Right at Last' have in common more cheerful endings, but are equally dominated by issues of class, in employer/servant relationships as well as marriage. 'Morton Hall' and 'My Lady Ludlow', which, though of different lengths, have some interesting common features, are frame stories of mixed genre, in which, once again, history, tragedy and class feature strongly. But though such generalisations can be made, the many gaps in our knowledge of the process of composition do make it rather risky to advance any elaborate theory of the relationships among them, though it is possible to identify persistent concerns and common features. Most obviously, as has been pointed out repeatedly, Dickens's Scheherazade was interested in tale-telling: in the narrative act itself.

There is some awkwardness in discussing *Round the Sofa* in this connection, since the stories were first published separately, and only ascribed to the particular speakers when the frame and links were written. But it remains true that the illusion of oral narration seems to have been fundamental to Gaskell's concept of the short story, though within this group there are some tales in which an authorial persona is used and some which are recounted by an individualised speaker. In many of them the bias of the narrator exists in a playful tension with prejudices attributed to the reader as well as to the characters: there is persistent irony about story-telling and, its close relative, history-making. Single and childless women, both as story-

---

1. 'When at Heidelberg we wished to go on to Dresden … I wrote two stories for Household Words, & asked for immediate payment, in order to obtain money to gratify this wish' (*Letters*, p. 534).

2. Stephen Gill, *Wordsworth and the Victorians* (Oxford: Oxford University Press, 1997), p. 133.

tellers and as protagonists, recur; in their mortality and volubility they represent the human desire to make connections between past and future.
Marginal as they are, chroniclers of small beer, they are destined to be forgotten. Susan in 'Half a Life-Time Ago' is so moving because she stands for
the peculiar virtues of one phase of country life, something of which the loss
is inevitable. The existence of the story saves a memory of her, just as Lady
Ludlow is preserved by being handed on from Miss Galindo to Margaret
Dawson to Miss Greatorex, and Phillis Morton by being handed on from
Bridget Sidebotham to Cordelia Manisty. Yet though the stories are so
obsessed with loss, they are also preoccupied with the power of history to
affect the present. The living are haunted by the dead, not only in ghost sto-
ries like 'The Old Nurse's Tale' and 'The Poor Clare', but in all these stories.
And this is shown happening not only to individuals but to nations, in
France as well as England.

Several of these stories are animated by the pathos of the narrator's own,
partly-told story, and by a tension between their interpretation of their material and the reader's response. Some of the horror in 'The Old Nurse's Tale'
derives from the situation of Hester, the nurse. Scarcely more than a child
herself, isolated from all her friends, not privy to the house's secrets, not the
legal guardian but the only real friend of the helpless orphan child, she is a
version of the deserted wife and child of the ghost story, who also lack
money and power and status to escape from the Furnival family.[1] The narrative is set safely in the long ago and the old nurse has served many years with
Rosamond and her children (so that she stands, as old nurses do, for comfort, security and changelessness) yet she tells a Gothic tale of male tyranny,
female cruelty, class antagonism and gender inequality. Bridget Sidebotham,
the narrator of 'Morton Hall', is a comic reactionary, yet her tales of the
Mortons reveal their cruelty, their oppression of their women, their unfit-
ness for the romantic roles assigned them in the Sidebotham mythology.
That mythology has cheered the meagre existence of Bridget and her sister,
yet it has also deformed their lives. Like both of the above, the narrator of
'My French Master' is an onlooker, a spinster; she experiences romance at
second-hand; she subsequently becomes an exile, the counterpart of M. de
Chalabre, whose life is spent in exile from the military and chivalrous life he
was trained for. He plays in fact, a woman's part, self-denying, domesticated.
Like his historian, he is rewarded with the satisfactions of romance and restoration at second-hand. 'The Half-Brothers' combines the point of view of
the adult speaker and his child self so that the two motherless orphans
yearning for family affection are almost merged into a single figure, though

1. The point is made by Carol A. Martin, 'Gaskell's Ghosts: Truths in Disguise', *Studies in the Novel*, 21 (1989), pp. 27–40, 34.

one died young long ago of exposure, and the other is looking back after a long and prosperous adulthood.

One might think of Bridget Sidebotham as an extreme version of Gaskell's typical surrogate; her conservatism and worship of the gentry is echoed by Margaret Dawson, and even faintly by the dull stick who recounts 'The Poor Clare' and the loyal retainer who recounts 'The Old Nurse's Story'. Like these narrators Gaskell was in some ways drawn to the romance of the past, to rural tranquillity, to the traditional and the unchanging: 'I like dearly to call up pictures, – & thoughts suggested by so utterly different a life to Manchester … I like Kings & Queens, & nightingales and mignionettes & roses.'[1] To read 'My Lady Ludlow', 'My French Master' or 'Morton Hall' is to be invited, not insincerely, to share these pleasures. But equally characteristic is the subversion of this harmonious mood by the content of the story.[2] Both 'The Old Nurse's Tale' and 'The Poor Clare' turn out to be savage tales of patriarchal violence and class antagonism. Both 'Morton Hall' and 'My Lady Ludlow' expose the inequality and gender bias of gentry society: its charms are lingered over, but they are exposed to mockery, and ultimately the virtues it encourages in women are shown to be outweighed by the selfishness it encourages in men.[3]

This obliquity also emerges in tales not narrated by one of the characters. Several are told in an authorial voice which is privy to the inner thoughts and motives of the characters, but it is common for emphasis to be laid on the teller's voice and the implied reactions of the audience. A relationship is being set up which is akin to the convivial space 'Round the Sofa' of Margaret Dawson. Even in the probably early and certainly uneven 'The Doom of the Griffiths' the narrator dramatises herself making the tale more melodramatic, creating a spooky atmosphere like one of the witches in *Macbeth*. The narrator of 'The Squire's Story' is a self-consciously modern speaker, telling a tale ironically at the expense of the old-fashioned 'good people of Barford'. That story, like 'Right at Last', ends with the narrator authenticating the tale with reference to physical reality: 'I saw the White House not a month ago', 'The last time I was in London, I saw a brass-plate'. In an anonymous story appearing in *Household Words*, such a device may even have left readers genu-

---

1. Describing to Charles Eliot Norton a visit to Oxford, *Letters*, p. 492.

2. Julian Wolfreys, *Being English: Narratives, Idioms and Performances of National Identity from Coleridge to Trollope* (Albany: State University of New York Press, 1994), p. 82, argues that 'Gaskell's metalanguage is usually sympathetic to [the] speaker. Thus, at different moments, the text appears Tory, Whig or radical in its polemical undercurrent.' However, sympathetic as this view is to Gaskell's interest in the exploration of contradictory positions, it is much more characteristic of her to attribute the Tory sentiments to the narrator and to leave the reader to see the radical implications than the other way round.

3. In contrast, 'The Manchester Marriage', which is the only one of these tales to focus clearly on a member of the commercial middle class, specifically stresses his delicacy in personal relationships and his egalitarian attitude to matrimonial finances.

inely confused about whether the tale was fiction or fact; it roots it in an exchange of personal experience, as do the Welsh place names and the chatty introduction in 'The Doom of the Griffiths'. 'The Manchester Marriage' is a tale told to southerners by someone familiar with Manchester life, apparently ready enough to make jokes at the expense of the provinces, though telling a story which creates an unlikely hero. The appalling events described in 'An Accursed Race' are also mediated through a dry, humorous, authorial persona whose assumption that such prejudices are safely in the past raises the distinct possibility that they are not. In 'Half a Life-Time Ago' the narrator, who is probably the closest of all these to the authorial voice of Gaskell's major novels, adopts the persona of a tourist visiting the Lake District which is gradually abandoned, as the reader's sympathies are engaged, for a narrative dominated by Susan's consciousness, so that the concluding line, re-establishing the relationship between speaker and listener, comes as a slight shock.

It is not surprising, then, that Gaskell seems to have found the time-honoured idea of connecting stories together by means of a frame and links a congenial one. *Round the Sofa* was a compilation of previously published tales of unequal length and varying character. In weaving the collection of tales into a whole, Gaskell excused their variety by attributing them to a very mixed group of narrators. The slightly unexpected inclusion of the non-fiction cuckoo, 'An Accursed Race', supports the view that she had some idea of unifying the book round a theme of tolerance and the conquest of prejudice. 'The Poor Clare', for example, addresses itself to the penal laws against Catholics, finally repealed, after intense public debate, in 1829. Far more obviously than the other historical tales, it describes an England in which several faiths (Catholicism, Anglicanism and Presbyterianism) exist side by side, and in which they compound the class conflicts and personal antagonisms of the characters. Generically it is very unlike 'My Lady Ludlow', but it shares its underlying sense of the direction of reform: Bridget Fitzgerald's heroic compassion and self-sacrifice is the tragic version of Lady Ludlow's socially mixed tea party: both express fictionally what is made explicit in 'An Accursed Race', that prejudice and cruelty were worse in the hidebound past than they are now. 'The Doom of the Griffiths' and 'Half a Life-Time Ago', also hinge on prejudice (mental handicap, class), although, like 'The Half-Brothers' they focus more on unchanging problems of domestic life than on cultural change. There is some warrant, therefore, for seeing *Round the Sofa* as a celebration of heterogeneous voices engaged in actively sharing the listening space, a celebration of story-telling itself (and hence, fiction-reading) as a moral activity. As Julian Wolfreys observes: 'all the characters gathered together speak an accented English … [which] suggests a community of identity founded on difference and a respect for, and enunciation of, that difference.'[1] However, since tolerance and forgiveness are omnipresent in

Gaskell's work, it is perhaps unwise to press this argument too far. The stories had, after all, been written and published separately before they were welded together in one volume. The frame and links may well tell us more about the first and longest story than about the others.

'My Lady Ludlow', the first and most substantial work in the volume, has never achieved the popularity of *Cranford*, which had appeared five years earlier. But there is little doubt that its conception was shaped by the huge contemporary success of *Cranford*, both as an occasional series of sketches in *Household Words* and on its publication in volume form. Once again, Gaskell offered Dickens a picture of provincial life in a community consisting mainly of women, looking back to the recent past, within living memory, and humorously comparing the gains and losses involved in progress towards the present. Whereas *Cranford* had grown haphazardly, and was shaped into a coherent whole retrospectively, 'My Lady Ludlow' was written and published over a much shorter period, and it seems likely that its overall scheme was established fairly quickly. Yet it is the latter which has always been found wanting in design and unity; it had no special success either in periodical or volume form, added little to Gaskell's reputation, and critics of all persuasions have continued to find it in varying degrees unsatisfactory.[1]

Like the earlier and shorter 'Morton Hall', it is a tripartite frame story (though it was soon to be itself incorporated within a second frame story, *Round the Sofa*). As in the case of 'Morton Hall', the narrator partly describes her own experience, and partly hears tales from others. There are in fact a significant number of parallels between the two, enough to support the view that Gaskell had a continuing interest in evolving a new kind of form for women's stories about women and history.[2] In each case one story recounts the speaker's own experience and one story is a historical one, involving civil war and social revolution. Both collections involve a series of misshapen families worthy of Dickens. In each case two dark stories are followed by a comic story, and by a swift resolution of the plot with a marriage. The almost absurdly casual way in which these marriages are offered to us underlines the fact that they are pure symbols of harmony between opposed forces; neither 'Morton Hall' nor 'My Lady Ludlow' can be read as a love story: each disrupts generic expectations by its formal oddity and main focus on elderly

---

1. Wolfreys, *Being English*, p. 84.

1. A. W. Ward, for instance, comments that she 'either attempted too much, or allowed herself insufficient space and time for harmonising all that she attempted' (*Knutsford*, vol. v, p. xvi). A summary of later critics is given by Edgar Wright, *'My Lady Ludlow*: Forms of Social Change and Forms of Fiction', *GSJ*, 3 (1989), pp. 29–41, 30–1.

2. It is illuminating to think about 'Morton Hall' in the light of the reading of 'My Lady Ludlow' as a new model of women's history, an 'eccentric narrative ... to disrupt centered narrative' offered by Christine L. Krueger, ('The "Female Paternalist" as Historian: Elizabeth Gaskell's *My Lady Ludlow*' in *Rewriting The Victorians: Theory, History and the Politics of Gender*, ed. by Linda M. Shires (London: Routledge, 1992), pp. 166–183, 170).

and childless women. Comparison between them emphasises how connections between the three stories which are explicit in 'Morton Hall' remain implicit in 'My Lady Ludlow'. The Morton heroines are all from the same family, their experiences happen in the same place, the underlying theme of the tension between tradition and change is explored in a variety of plots and moods. In 'My Lady Ludlow', though, connections between the three stories are much more obviously artificial, and the reader is left to make sense of their juxtaposition. The apparently loose construction of both collections is undoubtedly partly attributable to their being written for anonymous serial publication in a weekly magazine. Where the modern reader seeks consistency, the Victorian editor, and the reader of *Household Words,* probably welcomed variety. But even if we allow for a gulf between the conventions of a mid-Victorian magazine story and the expectations of a modern reader familiar with later incarnations of the form, we may feel that Gaskell stretches herself to bring revolutionary Paris into Hanbury, as she had not done in bringing the Civil War to Morton Hall.[1] A connected problem is that the characterisation of Clément and Virginie is slight and the villainous Morin, though his feelings are more convincingly portrayed, is stagy; there is also something less than satisfactory about the duplication of faithful retainers. The Revolution is evidently essential to the design, but it is a source of strain.

The *Round the Sofa* frame story can, I think, legitimately be used to shed some light on 'My Lady Ludlow' in particular. The story's sale as a serial to *Household Words* and as a volume to Sampson Low were both arranged in the summer of 1858, and were associated with Gaskell's plan to take her daughters to Germany that September.[2] It occupies the whole of the first volume of *Round the Sofa* and was also the most recent of the stories to be republished in that work. There is therefore every reason to suppose that the frame and links were primarily designed to accommodate it. It may follow then that we are entitled to use the frame to interpret it in a way which would be less appropriate with the other stories in the collection. The most striking fact is that the retrospective narrative of Margaret Dawson, published in 1858, opens with a reference to the pre-railway age, and therefore implies that it is written by an adult in the 1850s about her childhood in the 1800s. But the *Round the Sofa* opening of 1859 pushes the voice of the narrator back in time, since Miss Greatorex, the narrator of the frame, writes as an adult about her own childhood. The frame scenes should logically date no earlier than 1845 (the year the railway from London reached Edinburgh) or

---

1. Angus Easson describes the French episode as 'introduced on the flimsiest grounds' (*Easson*, p. 214).

2. The letter to Louis Hachette (16 August 1858) in *Further Letters,* p. 189, seems to imply that the frame story was already being conceived of in August 1858, shortly after 'My Lady Ludlow' had been written.

thereabouts. The Margaret Dawson who was sixteen at the time of meeting Lady Ludlow could have been sixty in 1845. But Gaskell was not pedantic about chronology, and the implication is that Miss Greatorex's childhood visits to Mrs Dawson took place rather earlier, 'long ago', perhaps about 1830, a period for which Gaskell could draw on memory of her own early visits to the city, not much earlier, because Margaret Dawson has become old.

Within a few months of composing 'My Lady Ludlow', therefore, Gaskell had taken the decision to associate it with Edinburgh, with a society cosmopolitan yet provincial, professional, intellectual, liberal, ethnically diverse. The special character of post-Enlightenment Scotland is notorious; Scottish education, cheap, broad and egalitarian in comparison with English, had created an educated class in Edinburgh both more intellectual and more diverse in social origin than elsewhere, where a lively and intellectual salon culture flourished.[1] Without any apparent warrant from the stories she was compiling, Gaskell chose to associate her tales with this setting. Why set the frame in Edinburgh? During her own stay there social reform had been the subject of urgent public debate. The Catholic Emancipation Act had been passed in 1829; starving farm labourers took part in the Captain Swing riots in 1830; the Reform Bill was first read in 1831: related issues do arise in 'My Lady Ludlow'. Its debates, however, are carefully sited in a different historical context, in the aftermath of 'the famine in seventeen hundred and ninety-nine and eighteen hundred' (p. 159). Another possibility may be that Edinburgh was associated for her with the period in the early 1800s her own parents had spent living there before she was born, following the failure of William Stevenson's farming venture, which John Chapple tentatively attributes to the very same famine.[2] It is generally agreed that *Cranford* may be seen as, on one level, a fictionalisation of her Knutsford childhood, and of the experience of women of her aunt's generation. It may be possible to see 'My Lady Ludlow' as, to some extent, an exploration of the intellectual world inhabited by the shadowy William Stevenson, who, although doubtless less dear and less influential than Hannah Lumb, could have played a larger part in forming his daughter's mind than the surviving evidence suggests (he could hardly play a smaller one).

'My Lady Ludlow' associates itself firmly with early nineteenth-century debates about agriculture, economics and political theory. It sketches a dispute in the management of an agricultural estate between those who conceive of it in seignorial terms and those who want to run it as a business. This cultural conflict is aligned with a debate about the education of the

---

1. Arthur Herman, *The Scottish Enlightenment: The Scots' Invention of the Modern World* (London: Fourth Estate, 2001), p. 227.

2. *Early Years*, p. 61.

working classes. In Lady Ludlow's rank-ordered universe individual destiny is properly determined by genetics, and gentility is revealed by the inherited ability to smell the scent of decaying strawberry leaves. This view is controverted by Mr Gray, for whom education is a necessity for spiritual development, and by Harry Gregson, whose cleverness enables him to escape the miserable circumstances he was born in. Law, government, inheritance, class, tradition, progress, debt, investment and the relationship between land and power are the constant preoccupations of the story. Early on Mr Gray wins a significant victory when he persuades Lady Ludlow to rescue Job Gregson from being unfairly treated by local magistrates out of class solidarity. She makes a significant remark to the boorish Harry Lathom:

> A pretty set you and your brother magistrates are to administer justice throughout the land! I always said a good despotism was the best form of government; and I am twice as much in favour of it now I see what a quorum is! (p. 166)

Complicated ironies are at work here. Lady Ludlow's position is inherently contradictory, since she has earlier defended the magistrates' customary practices to Mr Gray. She becomes even less logical in admonishing Lathom for his folly and unfairness, by suggesting that they are attributable to the fact that the decision has been a collective one. (There is a pun on 'quorum' which means both 'a bench of magistrates' and 'a sufficient number of people to act with authority'.) In claiming to believe that 'a good despotism' is the most efficient government she alludes to a position held by a particular school of mid-eighteenth-century French thinkers, now known as the Physiocrats, but then known as the Economists, who were also notorious for having argued that the land, rather than trade, was the basic wealth of a nation.[1] There is thus a possible connection between this passage and that in the last chapter in which Miss Galindo declares that 'all those trades where iron and steel do the work ordained to man at the Fall, are unlawful' (p. 000), and with the book's general concern about the change from a primarily agricultural to a primarily industrial society. Whether Gaskell's acquaintance with the doctrines of the Physiocrats was superficial or profound, she is attributing to Lady Ludlow some attempt to evolve a theoretical underpinning for her paternalist rule. Adherence to this discredited *ancien régime* theory suggests the weakness of her position, and thus looks forward to the

---

1. Ronald L. Meek, *The Economics of Physiocracy: Essays and Translations* (London: George Allen & Unwin, 1962), p. 32 and p. 20: 'Agriculture was the supreme occupation, not only because it was morally and politically superior to others … but also … because it alone yielded a disposable surplus.' Adam Smith, *The Wealth of Nation*, 3 vols (Dublin, 1776), vol. iii, p. 7, specifically rebutted the claim of what he called 'the Œconomists' that 'the class of artificers, manufacturers, and merchants [is] altogether barren and unproductive.' EG is known to have read *The Wealth of Nations*: *Letters*, p. 148.

compromises she eventually makes with commercial forces, running her estate more progressively, entertaining the dissenting middle class, and paying her debts with an inheritance from a snobbish businessman. The passage thus, like the account of Virginie de Créquy's connections with the Encylopédistes, places its political theory with some precision in a particular intellectual context. It seems more than coincidental that William Stevenson had specialised in the history of economics, as well as in a subject which is another of the story's themes, the developing science of farming that brought about what we call the Agricultural Revolution.

Students of Gaskell's work are no longer as ready as they once were to accept the lady-like profession of ignorance she offers in the 'Preface' to *Mary Barton*: 'I know nothing of Political Economy, or the theories of trade.'[1] She had at least as much reason to be aware of economic and political theory as any other major Victorian novelist of either sex. Her father, as Chapple has shown, had made such matters his life's work 'the bent of my inclination … is to subjects that require & admit methodical & close reasoning – such as Political Economy – the general principles of Politics – the Philosophy of the human mind &c.'[2] Though William Stevenson does not seem to have been close to his daughter, he was not so distant that it is reasonable to believe that she was wholly unaware of his activities, his publications, or his views, and she was nearly nineteen when he died. Trained as a Unitarian minister, Stevenson worked variously as a tutor, lecturer, farmer, journalist, writer and civil servant. His first book, *Remarks on the Very Inferior Utility of Classical Learning* (1796), argued that forward-looking studies in politics and science should be substituted for the traditional grounding in Latin and Greek literature.[3] The series of articles on the history of economics which he wrote for *Blackwood's*, although so long-winded and dull that the editor seems to have discontinued their publication, give further indication of the character of his opinions, which can be supplemented from what is known of his education and associates.[4] He appears to have been influenced by the philosopher Dugald Stewart, and therefore would have known the latter's view of the Physiocrats, which was not antagonistic, except in the one article of their enthusiasm for the benevolent despot.[5] Stevenson's most substantial and

1. *MB*, 'Preface', p. vii.

2. William Stevenson to William Blackwood (October/November 1823) (MS, National Library of Scotland), quoted in *Early Years*, p. 265.

3. *Early Years*, p. 38. At the risk of overstating the case, one could point out that, in 'My Lady Ludlow', Margaret Dawson's brother and Harry Gregson get a classical education at Christ's Hospital thanks to Lady Ludlow's patronage.

4. 'The Political Economist', *Blackwoods*, 15 (May 1824), pp. 522–31; (June 1824), pp. 643–5; 16 (July 1824), pp. 34–45; (August 1824), pp. 202–14; 17 (February 1825), pp. 207–20.

5. On Stevenson's association with Dugald Stewart see *Early Years*, pp. 216, 218; on Stewart's view of the Physiocrats see *The Collected Works of Dugald Stewart*, ed. by Sir William Hamilton, 11 vols (Edinburgh: Constable, 1854–60), vol. ii, p. 240n.; vol. x, p. 97.

attractive work, *Historical Sketch of the Progress of Discovery, Navigation and Commerce* (1824) winds up by arguing that democracy, education, advances in technology (like Miss Galindo, he takes the cotton industry as his example) and the availability of capital are the key to Britain's economic success: 'without political freedom, the mass of the people never can be intelligent'.[1] It is not a strikingly original observation, but it does touch on the issues with which 'My Lady Ludlow' is most closely concerned: the change from a rank-ordered society to a more meritocratic one with more individual responsibility, the shift of power from the landed to the manufacturing interest, and the investment required to keep up with the rapid progress of science and technology. Stevenson's other main publications, *General View of the Agriculture of the County of Surrey* (1809) and *General View of the Agriculture of the County of Dorset* (1812), were reports prepared for the Board of Agriculture, a body set up to promote the kind of farming practices which Mr Baker and Captain James learnt from the example of Thomas Coke of Holkham and the writings of Arthur Young. Stevenson, Chapple emphasises, was on the side of science and modernisation rather than tradition and old associations.[2] He had links with those, like Lord Lauderdale and Sir John Sinclair, who were trying to introduce scientific agriculture to Scotland's peasant economy; he would have approved of Lady Ludlow's decision to mortgage her English estates to improve her husband's barren Scots acres. There is, incidentally, no mention in 'My Lady Ludlow' of whether there were clearances for sheep on that Scots property, but quite enough was known in Victorian England about the effects of the Highland Clearances to make it conceivable that Gaskell implicitly includes them in her consideration of the complex responsibilities of the landlord and the impact of scientific progress on the individual.

'My Lady Ludlow', then, represents an attempt on Gaskell's part to embody in fictional form some ideas about the cultural shifts which had taken place in the generation before her birth, as she had already done, with particular relation to women's lives, in *Cranford*. In 'My Lady Ludlow' one can see her trying to incorporate politics, economics and education into her picture of social change. Hence, one suspects, the necessary but troublesome inclusion of the French Revolution. It seems likely that, for her, some aspects of this were associated with her father's intellectual career and areas of interest. No doubt, of course, she drew on many other sources in forming her picture of British life at the turn of the century. In the explanatory notes to this volume I have offered evidence that her evocation of Lady Ludlow's world owed something to the published journal of the novelist Frances Bur-

---

1. William Stevenson, *Historical Sketch of the Progress of Discovery, Navigation and Commerce, From the Earliest Records to the Beginning of the Nineteenth Century* (Edinburgh: Blackwood and London: Cadell, 1824), p. 505. The reference to 'cotton machinery' is on p. 506.

2. *Early Years*, pp. 71, 80.

ney. The *Diary and Letters of Madame D'Arblay* (1842–6), which came out just
before Gaskell embarked on her own career as a novelist, would have been
one of the few available to her to depict with intimacy the life of a professional woman writer; its other themes include loyalty to the Crown, the
stifling pressures of court life, motherhood, bereavement, patronage, money,
the contrast between French and English political models and the effects of
the French Revolution on private individuals. Another influence on people
of Gaskell's generation (the importance of which is hard to exaggerate) is the
novels of Walter Scott. In 'My Lady Ludlow' and elsewhere she draws on his
main legacy to the novel, the realisation that relationships between individuals may express the poignant mutual incomprehension of opposed parties
caught up in inexorable historical change. And, vastly different as their experiences and their political affiliations were, she, like Scott, often leaves it
deliberately ambiguous where her loyalties lie, whether to past or future,
tradition or progress.

Throughout these tales Gaskell expects the reader to know a good deal of
history, but her use of it is frequently oblique. To annotate her allusions is to
be forcibly reminded that she saw England and its political-religious establishment from the standpoint of the Unitarian, and that in so doing she was
at odds with the dominant voice of her culture. Her heroines are normally
Church of England (one exception is the heroine of 'The Poor Clare'),
though she was not.[1] R. K. Webb observes, 'Anglican clergymen are portrayed by her as kindly and well-meaning, perhaps, but without great
conviction, serving a kind of civic religion, compromising and excusing
themselves in a way inescapable in an established church.'[2] There is little in
her fiction to startle the Anglican reader into opposition, but these stories,
several of which deal incidentally with post-Reformation English history,
show a recurrent preoccupation with the successive political settlements
which set up the relationship between the Established Church, the social
hierarchy and educational institutions.[3] It is not the Reformation which
appears as the key event in England's past, but the struggle to institutionalise
the Church of England as the established church, the story which leads from
the Gunpowder Plot (1605), through the Civil War to the Glorious Revolution, the Battle of the Boyne and the Jacobite rebellions of 1715 and 1745.
This is the historical background not only to those parts of 'Morton Hall'
and 'The Poor Clare' which deal directly with the English Civil War, the
defeat and exile of James II and the Jacobite rebellions, but also to the class

1. Valentine Cunningham, *Everywhere Spoken Against: Dissent in the Victorian Novel* (Oxford:
Clarendon Press, 1975), p. 141.
2. R. K. Webb, 'The Gaskells as Unitarians', p. 159, in *Dickens and Other Victorians*, ed. by
Joanne Shattock (London: Macmillan, 1988), pp. 144–71.
3. 'An Accursed Race' too can be seen as an oblique comment on English institutions: as
Wolfreys, *Being English*, p. 85, points out, 'We start from England and return to it …'

struggles of 'The Squire's Story' and 'My Lady Ludlow'. In 'My French Master' and 'My Lady Ludlow' the great image of social disorder is the French Revolution. The latter story emphasises the Revolution's effect in polarising English society along old lines of class and religion, so that it too becomes metaphorically a version of the old struggle. And both the English and the French Revolutions become nightmare versions of the revolution Gaskell herself is living through, the one in which the landowning interest learns to accommodate the scientific, forward-looking manufacturing interest, as the conclusions of both 'Morton Hall' and 'My Lady Ludlow' imply.

In none of her fiction, anonymous or otherwise, does she acknowledge herself a Unitarian, or use the word; Webb suggests this decision was made for commercial reasons; it no doubt smoothed her path to the market and contributed to her contemporary success and subsequent canonisation.[1] Yet apparently innocent allusions to the triumphalist version of the history of the Church of England recur in these stories and remind the reader that Gaskell had been accustomed from childhood to textbooks and fiction in which Anglicanism was normal, and her own sect was not. Though she created new fictions, in which Anglicanism also ostensibly appears the normal condition, she contrives destabilising moments. The toast 'Church and King and Down with the Rump', for example, seems to have been for her a kind of mental shorthand for dyed-in-the-wool Toryism. The Rump Parliament of 1648–53, which condemned Charles I to death and created the Commonwealth of England, here symbolises reform and progressive causes in general. The expression implies that any dissent from the Church of England involves disloyalty to the Crown. Gaskell may well have known it from a nursery rhyme of her childhood.[2] In *North and South*, Chapter V, it evokes the mental world of Mrs Hale, clinging to the social status deriving from the connection between Church and State:

> Though of course, if your father leaves the Church, we shall not be admitted into society anywhere. It will be such a disgrace to us! Poor dear Sir John! It is

1. Webb, 'The Gaskells as Unitarians', p. 159.
2. It occurs in a rhyme about the town of Middlewich, not far from Knutsford, collected from oral tradition by Egerton Leigh, *Ballads & Legends of Cheshire* (London: Longmans, 1867), p. 60:

> Middlewych is a pretty town,
> Seated in a valley,
> With a church and market cross
> And eke a bowling alley.
> All the men are loyal there;
> Pretty girls are plenty;
> Church and King, and down with the Rump,
> There's not such a town in twenty.

well he is not alive to see what your father has come to! Every day after dinner,
when I was a girl … Sir John used to give for the first toast – 'Church and
King, and down with the Rump'

In 'The Squire's Story' the phrase is the undoing of the murderer:

On the other side there is some allusion to a race-horse, I conjecture,
though the name is singular enough; "Church-and-king-and-down-with-
the-Rump."

  Miss Pratt caught at this name immediately; it had hurt her feelings as a dissenter only a few months ago, and she remembered it well.   (pp. 85–6)

The story turns on the willingness of the local elite to accept Higgins as one
of their own on the basis of his participation in their boisterous sports and
revels; and Miss Pratt's dissent from the consensus of opinion: 'She did not
hunt … She did not drink … She could not bear comic songs …' Just as
the act of making the toast obliges those present to pay lip service to the
political and sectarian affirmation it makes, so the naming of the horse forces
those referring to it to make a statement with which they may have no sympathy. There is clearly a parallel here. In *North and South* the contrast
between Mr Hale's painful doubts and his wife's sense of humiliation
emphasises her muddle-headed conflation of religious and social obligation,
his appreciation of where his real duty lies. In 'The Squire's Story' the distinction between Higgins's real and assumed characters is detected by
someone not inclined to confuse gentry manners with Christianity. The
phrase recurs in 'My Lady Ludlow' with reference to a Church of England
parson of the pre-evangelical old school:

Mr. Mountford was true blue, as we call it, to the back-bone; hated the dissenters and the French; and could hardly drink a dish of tea without giving out
the toast of 'Church and King and down with the Rump'.   (p. 155)

His character exists to contrast with the painfully conscientious Mr Gray, the
new model of Anglican clergyman for whom spiritual authority and secular
power have a more problematic relation to each other. The contexts in
which Gaskell uses the phrase, then, associate it with both unthinking con-
formism and the uncomfortable payment of lip service. But, fascinatingly,
she makes nothing of its Jacobite associations.[1] It passes in the stories as a
reactionary slogan, annoying perhaps, but scarcely sinister. Yet the resonance
it held for Gaskell, her husband, his congregation, her family, the Unitarian
community, and dissenters generally in her audience, was probably stronger

    1. Paul K. Monod, *Jacobitism and the English People, 1688–1788* (Cambridge: Cambridge
University Press, 1989), pp. 183–5, 201, 203, 205, 236, makes clear its use in anti-Hanoverian
rhetoric, and mentions also, p. 293, its association with hunting, and its use in Jacobite toasts, p.
295.

than this. The Cross Street Unitarian Chapel, in which William Gaskell officiated and his wife and family worshipped, had been wrecked by a Jacobite mob in 1715, on 10 June, the Old Pretender's birthday.[1] The event is recorded in a verse history of Manchester, published in 1822:

> And the mob-cry – a religio-political lump, –
> Was 'Church and King,' (James, Sirs!) 'and down with the rump.'[2]

As late as 1792, at the height of the reactionary response to the French Revolution, the Cross Street Chapel was attacked with a battering ram by Tories objecting to the fact that dissenters were campaigning against the legal disabilities they suffered under the Test and Corporation Acts:

> A 'Church and King Club' was formed in Manchester, the members of which wore uniforms with the representation of the Old Church engraved on their buttons, and at their usual convivial meetings the standing toast was 'Church and King, and down with the Rump.' The dominant party called a meeting on the King's birthday, 4th June 1792, to agree upon a loyal address … They proceeded to tear up several … trees … one was carried with great triumph to Cross-street Chapel, and with it the mob attempted to force open the gates, at the same time crying out 'Church and King,' 'Down with the Rump,' 'Down with it,' &c.[3]

When the newly married Gaskells came to Manchester in 1832 the congregation must have included many people who remembered these events. In any case Gaskell is likely to have been exceptionally well aware of the controversy surrounding the various campaigns against the legal disabilities of non-Anglicans, which were at their height during her childhood and teens. Her early friend the Revd William Turner, the father-in-law of William Gaskell's fellow minister, had agitated strenuously against the Test and Corporation Acts,[4] which were finally repealed in 1828, just before Gaskell's stay with him in Newcastle; the Catholic Emancipation Act was finally passed in the following year.

Anniversaries, as these anecdotes illustrate, were often the occasion for outbreaks of religious violence. It is in this light that we should see the surprisingly frequent references in these stories to the Church of England services and public festivals commemorating events in the civil and religious history of England. Such collective celebrations, hallowed by their associa-

1.   Richard Wade, *The Rise of Nonconformism in Manchester with a Brief Sketch of the History of Cross Street Chapel* (Manchester: The Unitarian Herald Printing Office, 1880), p. 32.
2.   Joseph Aston, *Metrical Records of Manchester in which its History is Traced (currente calamo) from the Days of the Ancient Britons to the Present Time* (London: Longman and Manchester: Aston, 1822), p. 13, cited in Wade, *The Rise of Nonconformism*, as above.
3.   Wade, *The Rise of Nonconformism*, p. 47.
4.   Cunningham, *Everywhere Spoken Against*, p. 129.

tion with innocent jollification, have a sinister side which Gaskell repeatedly chooses to underline. They existed to reinforce the link between religious and political prejudice. The Feast of King Charles the Martyr (30 January) is referred to both in 'Morton Hall' and 'My Lady Ludlow'; Restoration or Oak Apple Day (29 May) in 'Morton Hall'; and Guy Fawkes Day (5 November) is referred to once in 'Morton Hall', twice in 'My Lady Ludlow' and once in 'An Accursed Race'. The politicised special church services, abolished in 1859, served, as Gaskell's allusions to them emphasise, to enforce acceptance of a version of history in which Catholics and Dissenters are disloyal and dangerous; and as public demonstrations, akin to the Church-and-King toast, of loyalty to the state church as the spiritual seat of secular authority. When Lady Ludlow misunderstands Mr Gray's allusion to a higher power and mentions the village celebrations of the birthday of George III on 4 June precisely the same ironic distinction between state authority and religious authority is being made by the author. Critics have made much of Gaskell's interest in the communal, but the character of her references to these events is a reminder that though the world she grew up in was shaped by this calendar of festivals, her family's participation in them must often have involved silent reservation if not public dissent. And this must have continued to be partly true throughout her life, as, surely, is implied in the letter to her sister-in-law of late 1852:

> Not having a tree. Our Xmas days are always very quiet, principally a jollifica-tion for the servants.[1]

She participated in the Victorian commercialisation of Christmas, as a con-tributor of stories to Dickens's Christmas numbers, and the author of Christmas books, but her private practice was not to observe it. This seems highly characteristic. These stories remind us of how equivocal her voice is even when she is at her most charming.

---

1. *Letters*, p. 217.

BIBLIOGRAPHY

I have omitted from this bibliography the following periodicals: *The Times*, the *Spectator*, the *Tatler*, the *Gentleman's Magazine*, the *Annual Register* and *Boyle's Court Guide*.

Altick, R. D., *The English Common Reader: A Social History of the Mass Reading Public, 1800–1900* (Chicago and London: Phoenix Books, 1957)

Anon., 'The Half-Brothers', *Dublin University Magazine*, 52 (November 1858), pp. 587–98

Aston, Joseph, *Metrical Records of Manchester in which its History is Traced (currente calamo) from the Days of the Ancient Britons to the Present Time* (London: Longman and Manchester: Aston, 1822)

Bailey, Nathan, *An Universal Etymological English Dictionary* (London: Bell, 1721)

Bates, Alan (ed.), *Directory of Stage Coach Services 1836* (Newton Abbot: David and Charles, 1969)

Beeton, Isabella, *Beeton's Book of Household Management* (London: Beeton, 1861)

Blackburn, B. and L. Holford-Strevens, *The Oxford Book of Days* (Oxford: Oxford University Press, 2000)

Boase, Frederick, *Modern English Biography*, 6 vols (Truro: Netherton, 1892–1926)

Boswell, James, *A Tour to the Hebrides* (London: Dilly, 1785)

Buchan, William, *Domestic Medicine, or, The Family Physician* (Edinburgh: Balfour, Auld and Smellie, 1769)

Bunyan, John, *The Pilgrim's Progress from this World to That Which is to Come* (London: Ponder, 1678)

Burn, Richard, *The Justice of the Peace and Parish Officer*, 23rd edition (London: Cadell, 1820)

Butler, Samuel, *Hudibras* (London: Marriot, et al, 1663–78)

Carlyle, Thomas, *The French Revolution: A History*, 3 vols (London: Fraser, 1837)

Cassell's Household Guide, 4 vols (London: Cassell, 1869–71)

Chapone, Hester, *Letters on the Improvement of the Mind*, 2 vols (London: Walter, 1773)

Chapple, J. A. V., 'Elizabeth Gaskell's "Morton Hall" and "The Poor Clare"', *BST*, 20 (1990), pp. 47–9

Chesterfield, Earl of, *Letters written by the late Right Honourable Philip Dormer Stanhope, Earl of Chesterfield, to his Son*, 4 vols (London: Dodsley, 1774)

Cocker, Edward, *The Tutor to Writing and Arithmetic* (London: Rooks, 1664)

Cunningham, Valentine, *Everywhere Spoken Against: Dissent in the Victorian Novel* (Oxford: Clarendon Press, 1975)

Cuthbertson, Catharine, *Santo Sebastiano, or, The Young Protector*, 5 vols (London: Robinson,1806)

Danican, François-André, known as Philidor, *L'analyze des échecs* (London: 1749)

Daniel Defoe, *A True Relation of the Apparition of One Mrs. Veal, the Next Day After Her Death* (London: Bragg, 1706)

David, Elizabeth, *English Bread and Yeast Cookery* (London: Allen Lane, 1979)

Davidson, Alan, *The Oxford Companion to Food* (Oxford: Oxford University Press,1999)

De Staël, Anne-Louise-Germaine, *Corinne* (Paris: Nicolle, 1807)

Dickens, Charles, *The Life and Adventures of Nicholas Nickleby* (London: Chapman and Hall, 1839)

Dodwell, Henry, the Elder, *An Epistolary Discourse Proving from the Scriptures and the First Fathers, that the Soul is a Principle Naturally Mortal* (London: Smith, 1706)

Dodwell, Henry, the Younger, *Christianity Not Founded on Argument* (London: Cooper, 1742)

Duthie, Enid, 'Echoes of the French Revolution in the Work of Elizabeth Gaskell', *GSJ*, 2 (1988), pp. 34–40

Easson, Angus, *Elizabeth Gaskell* (London: Routledge, 1979)

L'Encyclopédie, ou Dictionnaire raisonné des sciences, des Arts et des Métiers, 28 vols (Paris: 1751–72)

Fletcher, Eliza, *Autobiography of Mrs. Fletcher, of Edinburgh* (Carlisle: privately printed, 1874)

Fox, William, *An Address to the People of Great Britain on the Propriety of Abstaining from West India Sugar and Rum* (London: Bell, 1791)

Fuchs, Max, *Lexique des troupes de comédiens au XVIIIe siècle* (Paris: Droz, 1944)

Gaskell, Elizabeth, *Cousin Phillis and Other Tales*, ed. by Angus Easson (Oxford: Oxford University Press, 1981)

—, *Gothic Tales*, ed. by Laura Kranzler (Harmondsworth: Penguin, 2000)

—, *My Lady Ludlow and Other Stories*, ed. by Edgar Wright (Oxford: Oxford University Press, 1989)

—, *The Moorland Cottage and Other Stories*, ed. by Suzanne Lewis (Oxford: Oxford University Press, 1995)

Gaskell, William, *Two Lectures on the Lancashire Dialect* (London: Chapman and Hall, 1854)

Gessner, Salomon, *The Death of Abel*, trans. by Mary Collyer (London: Dodsley, 1761)

Gibbon, Edward, *The History of the Decline and Fall of the Roman Empire*, 6 vols (London: Strahan, Cadell, 1776–88)

Gill, Stephen, *Wordsworth and the Victorians* (Oxford: Oxford University Press, 1997)

Goldsmith, Oliver, *An History of England*, 2 vols (London: Newberry, 1764)

Graves, Richard, *The Spiritual Quixote, or, The Summer's Ramble of Mr Geoffry-Wildgoose: A Comic Romance*, 3 vols (London: Dodsley, 1772)

Green, Henry, *Knutsford, Its Traditions and History* (London: Smith, Elder & Co., 1859)

Gregory, John, *A Father's Legacy to his Daughters* (London: Strahan, Cadell, 1774)

Hamilton, Sir William (ed.) *The Collected Works of Dugald Stewart*, 11 vols (Edinburgh: Constable, 1854–60)

Hardy, Thomas, *The Mayor of Casterbridge*, 2 vols (London: Smith, Elder & Co., 1886)

Herman, Arthur, *The Scottish Enlightenment: The Scots' Invention of the Modern World* (London: Fourth Estate, 2001)

Holland, Robert, *Glossary of Words Used in the County of Chester,* English Dialect Society, 16 (London: Trubner, 1886)

Hopkins, Annette, 'Dickens and Mrs. Gaskell', *Huntington Library Quarterly*, 9 (1946), pp. 354–5

Houghton, W., et al (eds), *The Wellesley Index to Victorian Periodicals*, 5 vols (Toronto: University of Toronto Press and London: Routledge, 1966–1989)

James, Louis, *Fiction for the Working Man, 1830–1850* (London: Oxford University Press, 1963)

Jerdan, William, *The Autobiography of William Jerdan*, 4 vols (London: Hall, 1852–3)

Johnson, Samuel, *A Dictionary of the English Language*, 2 vols (London: W. Strahan, 1755)

Kinsley, James (ed.) *The Poems and Fables of John Dryden* (London: Oxford University Press, 1962)

Krueger, Christine L., 'The "Female Paternalist" as Historian: Elizabeth Gaskell's *My Lady Ludlow*' in *Rewriting The Victorians: Theory, History and the Politics of Gender*, ed. by Linda M. Shires (London: Routledge, 1992), pp. 166–183

La Motte Fouqué, Friedrich, Baron de, *Undine: eine Erzählung* (Berlin: Hitzerg, 1811)

Laun, Ellen M., 'A Missing Gaskell Tale Found', *Studies in Short Fiction*, 15 (1978), pp. 177–83

Leigh, Egerton, *Ballads & Legends of Cheshire* (London: Longmans, 1867)

Lewis, Donald M. (ed.), *The Blackwell Dictionary of Evangelical Biography 1730–1860*, 2 vols (Oxford: Blackwell, 1995)

Luke, Jemima, *The Female Jesuit, or, The Spy in the Family: A True Narrative of Recent Intrigues in a Protestant Household* (London: Partridge & Oakey, 1851)

Lyonnet, Henri, *Dictionnaire des comédiens français* (Paris: Librairie d'art du téatre, 1910)

Martin, Carol A., 'Gaskell's Ghosts: Truths in Disguise', *Studies in the Novel*, 21 (1989), pp. 27–40

Mather, Cotton, *The Wonders of the Invisible World: Being an Account of the Tryals of Several Witches, Lately Executed in New-England* (London and Boston: Dunton, 1693)

Meek, Ronald L., *The Economics of Physiocracy: Essays and Translations* (London: George Allen & Unwin, 1962)

Milton, John, *The Complete Poems*, ed. by Alastair Fowler, et al (London: Longman, 1968)

Monod, Paul K., *Jacobitism and the English People, 1688–1788* (Cambridge: Cambridge University Press, 1989)

Moorhouse, Sydney, *The Forest of Bowland* (London: Saint Catherine Press, 1948)

Murray, Lindley, *English Grammar* (York: Wilson, Spence and Mawman, 1795)

Murray's Handbook for Modern London (London: Murray, 1851)

Ricks, Christopher (ed.), *The Poems of Tennyson* (London: Longmans, 1969)

Rollin, Charles, *Histoire ancienne*, 13 vols (Paris: Estienne, 1730–8)

Rousseau, Jean-Jacques, *Discours qui a remporté le prix à l'Academie de Dijon. En l'année 1750: sur cette question proposée par la même Académie: Si le rétablissement des sciences & des arts a contribué à épurer les moeurs sur les sciences et les arts* (Paris: Pissot, 1750)

Scott, H. M. (ed.), *Enlightened Absolutism: Reform and Reformers in Later Eighteenth-century Europe* (London: Macmillian, 1990)

Scott, Walter, *The Antiquary*, 3 vols (Edinburgh: Constable, 1816)

—, *Minstrelsy of the Scottish Border* (Kelso: Ballantyne, 1802–3)

—, *Redgauntlet* (Edinburgh: Constable, 1824)

Shakespeare, William, *The Riverside Shakespeare*, ed. by G. Blakemore Evans, et al (Boston: Houghton Mifflin, 1974)

Smith, Adam, *An Inquiry into the Nature and Causes of the the Wealth of Nations*, 2 vols (London: Strahan, Cadell, 1776)

Souvestre, Émile, 'Industrie et commerce de la Bretagne', *Revue des deux mondes*, 4:4 (1835), p. 400

Stevenson, Burton, *Book of Proverbs* (London: Routledge, 1949)

Stevenson, William, *General View of the Agriculture of the County of Surrey* (London: Phillips, 1809)

—, *General View of the Agriculture of the County of Dorset* (London: Nicol, 1812)

—, *Historical Sketch of the Progress of Discovery, Navigation and Commerce, From the Earliest Records to the Beginning of the Nineteenth Century* (Edinburgh: Blackwood and London: Cadell, 1824)

—, 'The Political Economist', *Blackwood's Edinburgh Magazine*, 15 (May 1824), pp. 522–31; (June 1824), pp. 643–5; 16 (July 1824), pp. 34–45; (August 1824), pp. 202–14; 17 (February 1825), pp. 207–20

—, *Remarks on the Very Inferior Utility of Classical Learning* (Manchester: Nicholson, 1796)

Sturm, Christoph Christian, *Reflections on the Works of God and of His Providence Throughout All Nature for Every Day in the Year*, 3 vols (Edinburgh: Cheyne, 1788)

Swift, Jonathan, *Travels into Several Remote Nations of the World: In Four Parts, by Lemuel Gulliver*, 2 vols (London: Motte, 1726)

Taylor, Henry, *Autobiography of Henry Taylor 1800–1875*, 2 vols (London: Longmans, 1885)

Turner, Joseph Horsfall, *Haworth Past and Present* (Brighouse: Jowett, 1879)

Uffelman, Larry K., 'From "Martha Preston" to "Half a Life-Time Ago": Elizabeth Gaskell Rewrites a Story', *Gaskell Society Journal*, 17 (2003), pp. 92–103

Upham, Charles, *Lectures on Witchcraft: Comprising a History of the Delusion in Salem in 1692* (Boston: Carter, Hendee and Babcock, 1831)

Vaughan, John Lloyd, *Glyndwr: A Poem* (Ruthin: Robert Jones, 1826)

Vicinus, Martha, and Bea Nergaard (eds), *Ever Yours, Florence Nightingale* (London: Virago, 1989)

Wade, Richard, *The Rise of Nonconformism in Manchester with a Brief Sketch of the History of Cross Street Chapel* (Manchester: the Unitarian Herald Printing Office, 1880)

Watts, Isaac, *Divine Songs Attempted in Easy Language for the Use of Children* (London: Lawrence, 1715)

Webb, R. K., 'The Gaskells as Unitarians', in *Dickens and Other Victorians*, ed. by Joanne Shattock (London: Macmillan, 1988), pp. 144–71

Welding, J. D., *Leicestershire in 1777* (Leicester: Leicester Libraries, 1984)

Wesley, John, *The Journal of the Rev. John Wesley A. M.* (London: Bennett, 1830)

Wheeler, Michael, 'Mrs Gaskell's Reading and the Gaskell Sale Catalogue in Manchester Central Library', *Notes and Queries* (January–February 1977), pp. 25–30

Whitaker, T. D., *An History of the Original Parish of Whalley and Honor of Clithe-roein the Counties of Lancaster and York*, 2 vols (Blackburn: Hemingway and Crook, 1800, 1801)

—, *The History and Antiquities of the Deanery of Craven in the County of York* (London: Nichols, 1805)

White, Florence, *Good Things in England* (London: Cape, 1932)

Wilson, F. P. (ed.), *The Oxford Dictionary of English Proverbs* (Oxford: Oxford University Press, 1970)

Wolfreys, Julian, *Being English: Narratives, Idioms and Performances of National Identity from Coleridge to Trollope* (Albany: State University of New York Press, 1994)

Wordsworth, William, *Poetical Works*, ed. by Ernest de Selincourt (Oxford: Oxford University Press, 1936)

Wright, Edgar, '*My Lady Ludlow*: Forms of Social Change and Forms of Fiction', *GSJ*, 3 (1989), pp. 29–41

Yonge, Charlotte M., *History of Christian Names*, 2 vols (London: Parker, 1863)

Young, Arthur, *A Six Months' Tour Through the North of England*, 4 vols (London: Strahan, Nicoll, 1770)

—, *A Six Weeks' Tour Through the Southern Counties of England and Wales* (London: Nicoll, 1768)

—, *A Tour in Ireland*, 2 vols (London: Cadell, 1780)

—, *The Farmer's Tour Through the East of England*, 4 vols (London: W. Strahan, 1771)

ABBREVIATIONS

Brontë Letters   *The Letters of Charlotte Brontë*, ed. by Margaret Smith, 3 vols (Oxford: Oxford University Press, 1995–2000)

BST   *Brontë Society Transactions*

CD Letters   *The Pilgrim Edition of the Letters of Charles Dickens*, ed. by M. House, G. Storey, et al, 12 vols (Oxford: Oxford University Press, 1965–2002)

Chadwick   Ellis H. Chadwick, *Mrs Gaskell: Haunts, Homes and Stories* (London: Pitman, 1910)

D'Arblay   Frances Burney, *Diary and Letters of Madame D'Arblay,* 7 vols (London: Colburn, 1842, 1846)

DNB   *Dictionary of National Biography*

Early Years   J. A .V. Chapple, *Elizabeth Gaskell: The Early Years* (Manchester: Manchester University Press, 1997)

Easson   Angus Easson, *Elizabeth Gaskell* (London: Routlege and Kegan Paul, 1979)

EG   Elizabeth Gaskell

Further Letters   *Further Letters of Mrs Gaskell*, ed. by John Chapple and Alan Shelston (Manchester: Manchester University Press, 2000)

Gérin   Winifred Gérin, *Elizabeth Gaskell: A Biography* (Oxford: Clarendon Press, 1976)

GSJ   *Gaskell Society Journal*

Harper's   *Harper's New Monthly Magazine*

Knutsford   *The Works of Mrs Gaskell*, ed. by A. W. Ward, The 'Knutsford' Edition, 8 vols (London: Smith, Elder & Co., 1906)

Letters   *The Letters of Mrs Gaskell*, ed. by J. A. V. Chapple and Arthur Pollard (Manchester: Manchester University Press, 1966, new edn 1997)

MB   *Mary Barton*

Michel   Francisque Michel, *Histoire des races maudites de la France et de l'Espagne*, 2 vols (Paris: A. Franck, 1847)

OED   *Oxford English Dictionary*

Sharps   J. G. Sharps, *Mrs Gaskell's Observation and Invention: A Study of her Non-Biographic Works* (Fontwell: Linden Press, 1970)

Smith   Walter E. Smith, *Elizabeth C. Gaskell: A Bibliographical Catalogue of First and Early Editions* (Los Angeles: Heritage Bookshop Inc., 1998)

Uglow   Jenny Uglow, *Elizabeth Gaskell: A Habit of Stories* (London: Faber and Faber, 1993)

WG   William Gaskell

'THE OLD NURSE'S STORY'

'The Old Nurse's Story' first appeared in 'A Round of Stories by the Christmas Fire', the Extra Christmas Number of *Household Words* (1852), pp. 11–20. It was reprinted in *Lizzie Leigh and Other Tales* (London: Chapman and Hall, 1855), pp. 69–85. It also appeared in *Lizzie Leigh and Other Tales* (1865). The text in 1855 follows the *HW* text closely; the discrepancies, which are not numerous, are mainly punctuation, the 1859 text being rather more lavish with commas. In accordance with editorial policy, in this, and in other stories, EG's careless use of different names for the same character has been regularised and annotated.

For Dickens's attempts to get EG to change the end of this story see *CD Letters*, vol. vi, pp. 799–823. For discussion of the extent to which EG altered her story in response to Dickens's comments, see Annette B. Hopkins 'Dickens and Mrs. Gaskell', *Huntington Library Quarterly*, 9 (1946), pp. 354–5; *Sharps*, pp. 143–4; and Laura Kranzler's notes in her edition of Elizabeth Gaskell, *Gothic Tales* (Harmondsworth: Penguin, 2000), pp. 344–5. Dickens argued that only Rosamond should see the ghosts, and EG resisted; she evidently made some changes but their precise nature is uncertain.

THE OLD NURSE'S STORY.

———•———

YOU know, my dears, that your mother was an orphan, and an only child; and I dare say you have heard that your grandfather was a clergyman up in Westmoreland,[1] where I come from. I was just a girl in the village school, when, one day, your grandmother came in to ask the mistress if there was any scholar there who would do for a nurse-maid; and mighty proud I was, I can tell ye, when the mistress called me up, and spoke to my being a good girl at my needle, and a steady honest girl, and one whose parents were very respectable, though they might be poor. I thought I should like nothing better than to serve the pretty young lady, who was blushing as deep as I was, as she spoke of the coming baby, and what I should have to do with it. However, I see you don't care so much for this part of my story, as for what you think is to come, so I'll tell you at once I was engaged and settled at the parsonage before Miss Rosamond (that was the baby, who is now your mother) was born. To be sure, I had little enough to do with her when she came, for she was never out of her mother's arms, and slept by her all night long; and proud enough was I sometimes when missis trusted her to me. There never was such a baby before or since, though you've all of you been fine enough in your turns; but for sweet, winning ways, you've none of you come up to your mother. She took after her mother, who was a real lady born; a Miss Furnivall, a granddaughter of Lord Furnivall's, in Northumberland. I believe she had neither brother nor sister, and had been brought up in my lord's family till she had married your grandfather, who was just a curate, son to a shopkeeper in Carlisle – but a clever, fine gentleman as ever was – and one who was a right-down hard worker in his parish, which was very wide, and scattered all abroad over the Westmoreland Fells. When your mother, little Miss Rosamond, was about four or five years old, both her parents died in a fortnight – one after the other. Ah! that was a sad time. My pretty young mistress and me was looking for another baby, when my master came home from one of his long rides, wet, and tired, and took the fever he died of; and then she never held up her head again, but just lived to see her dead baby, and have it laid on her breast before she sighed away her life. My mistress had asked me, on her death-bed, never to leave Miss Rosamond; but if she had never spoken a word, I would have gone with the little child to the end of the world.

The next thing, and before we had well stilled our sobs, the executors and guardians came to settle the affairs. They were my poor young mistress's own cousin, Lord Furnivall, and Mr. Esthwaite, my master's brother, a shopkeeper in Manchester; not so well to do then, as he was afterwards,[2] and with a large family rising about him. Well! I don't know if it were their settling, or because of a letter my mistress wrote on her death-bed to her cousin, my lord; but somehow it was settled that Miss Rosamond and me were to go to Furnivall Manor House, in Northumberland, and my lord spoke as if it had been her mother's wish that she should live with his family, and as if he had no objections, for that one or two more or less could make no difference in so grand a household. So, though that was not the way in which I should have wished the coming of my bright and pretty pet to have been looked at – who was like a sunbeam in any family, be it never so grand – I was well pleased that all the folks in the Dale should stare and admire, when they heard I was going to be young lady's maid at my Lord Furnivall's at Furnivall Manor.

But I made a mistake in thinking we were to go and live where my lord did. It turned out that the family had left Furnivall Manor House fifty years or more. I could not hear that my poor young mistress had ever been there, though she had been brought up in the family; and I was sorry for that, for I should have liked Miss Rosamond's youth to have passed where her mother's had been.

My lord's gentleman,[3] from whom I asked as many questions as I durst, said that the Manor House was at the foot of the Cumberland Fells, and a very grand place; that an old Miss Furnivall, a great-aunt of my lord's,[4] lived there, with only a few servants; but that it was a very healthy place, and my lord had thought that it would suit Miss Rosamond very well for a few years, and that her being there might perhaps amuse his old aunt.

I was bidden by my lord to have Miss Rosamond's things ready by a certain day. He was a stern proud man, as they say all the Lords Furnivall were; and he never spoke a word more than was necessary. Folk did say he had loved my young mistress; but that, because she knew that his father would object, she would never listen to him, and married Mr. Esthwaite; but I don't know. He never married at any rate. But he never took much notice of Miss Rosamond; which I thought he might have done if he had cared for her dead mother. He sent his gentleman with us to the Manor House, telling him to join him at Newcastle that same evening; so there was no great length of time for him to make us known to all the strangers before he, too, shook us off; and we were left, two lonely young things (I was not eighteen), in the great old Manor House. It seems like yesterday that we drove there. We had left our own dear parsonage very early, and we had both cried as if our hearts would break, though we were travelling in my lord's carriage, which I thought so much of once. And now it was long past noon on a September day, and we stopped to change horses for the last time at a little smoky town, all full of colliers and miners. Miss Rosamond had fallen asleep, but Mr. Henry told me to waken her, that she might see the park and the Manor House as we drove up. I thought it rather a pity; but I did what he bade me, for fear he should complain of me to my lord. We had left all signs of a town, or even a village, and were then inside the gates of a large wild park – not like the parks here in the south, but with rocks, and the noise of running water, and gnarled thorn-trees, and old oaks, all white and peeled with age.

The road went up about two miles, and then we saw a great and stately house, with many trees close around it, so close that in some places their branches dragged against the walls when the wind blew; and some hung broken down; for no one seemed to take much charge of the place; – to lop the wood, or to keep the moss-covered carriage-way in order. Only in front of the house all was clear. The great oval drive was without a weed; and neither tree nor creeper was allowed to grow over the long, many-windowed front; at both sides of which a wing projected, which were each the ends of other side fronts; for the house, although it was so desolate, was even grander than I expected. Behind it rose the Fells, which seemed unenclosed and bare enough; and on the left hand of the house, as you stood facing it, was a little, old-fashioned flower-garden, as I found out afterwards. A door opened out upon it from the west front; it had been scooped out of the thick dark wood for some old Lady Furnivall; but the branches of the great forest trees had grown and overshadowed it again, and there were very few flowers that would live there at that time.

When we drove up to the great front entrance, and went into the hall I thought we should be lost – it was so large, and vast, and grand. There was a chandelier all of bronze, hung down from the middle of the ceiling; and I had never seen one before, and looked at it all in amaze. Then, at one end of the hall, was a great fire-place, as large as the sides of the houses in my country, with massy andirons and dogs to hold the wood; and by it were heavy old-fashioned sofas. At the opposite end of the hall, to the left as you went in – on the western side – was an organ built into the wall, and so large that it filled up the best part of that end. Beyond it, on the same side, was a door; and opposite, on each side of the fire-place, were also doors leading to the east front; but those I never went through as long as I stayed in the house, so I can't tell you what lay beyond.

The afternoon was closing in and the hall, which had no fire lighted in it, looked dark and gloomy, but we did not stay there a moment. The old servant, who had opened the door for us bowed to Mr. Henry, and took us in through the door at the further side of the great organ, and led us through several smaller halls and passages into the west drawing-room, where he said that Miss Furnivall was sitting. Poor little Miss Rosamond held very tight to me, as if she were scared and lost in that great place, and as for myself, I was not much better. The west drawing-room was very cheerful-looking, with a warm fire in it, and plenty of good, comfortable furniture about. Miss Furnivall was an old lady not far from eighty, I should think, but I do not know. She was thin and tall, and had a face as full of fine wrinkles as if they had been drawn all over it with a needle's point. Her eyes were very watchful, to make up, I suppose, for her being so deaf as to be obliged to use a trumpet. Sitting with her, working at the same great piece of tapestry, was Mrs. Stark, her maid and companion, and almost as old as she was. She had lived with Miss Furnivall ever since they both were young, and now she seemed more like a friend than a servant; she looked so cold and grey, and stony, as if she had never loved or cared for any one; and I don't suppose she did care for any one, except her mistress; and, owing to the great deafness of the latter, Mrs. Stark treated her very much as if she were a child. Mr. Henry gave some message from my lord, and then he bowed good-bye to us all, – taking no notice of my sweet little Miss Rosamond's out-stretched hand – and left us standing there, being looked at by the two old ladies through their spectacles.

I was right glad when they rung for the old footman who had shown us in at first, and told him to take us to our rooms. So we went out of that great drawing-room, and into another sitting-room, and out of that, and then up a great flight of stairs, and along a broad gallery – which was something like a library, having books all down one side, and windows and writing-tables all down the other – till we came to our rooms, which I was not sorry to hear were just over the kitchens; for I began to think I should be lost in that wilderness of a house. There was an old nursery, that had been used for all the little lords and ladies long ago, with a pleasant fire burning in the grate, and the kettle boiling on the hob, and tea things spread out on the table; and out of that room was the night-nursery, with a little crib for Miss Rosamond close to my bed. And old James called up Dorothy, his wife, to bid us welcome; and both he and she were so hospitable and kind, that by and by Miss Rosamond and me felt quite at home; and by the time tea was over, she was sitting on Dorothy's knee, and chattering away as fast as her little tongue could go. I soon found out that Dorothy was from Westmoreland, and that bound her and me together, as it were; and I would never wish to meet with kinder people than were old James and his wife. James had lived pretty nearly all his life in my lord's family, and thought there was no one so grand as they. He even looked down a little on his wife; because, till he had married her, she had never lived in any but a farmer's household. But he was very fond of her, as well he might be. They had one servant under them, to do all the rough work. Agnes they called her;[5] and she and me, and James and Dorothy, with Miss Furnivall and Mrs. Stark, made up the family; always remembering my sweet little Miss

Rosamond. I used to wonder what they had done before she came, they thought so much of her now. Kitchen and drawing-room, it was all the same. The hard, sad Miss Furnivall, and the cold Mrs. Stark, looked pleased when she came fluttering in like a bird, playing and pranking hither and thither, with a continual murmur, and pretty prattle of gladness. I am sure, they were sorry many a time when she flitted away into the kitchen, though they were too proud to ask her to stay with them, and were a little surprised at her taste; though to be sure, as Mrs. Stark said, it was not to be wondered at, remembering what stock her father had come of. The great, old rambling house, was a famous place for little Miss Rosamond. She made expeditions all over it, with me at her heels; all, except the east wing, which was never opened, and whither we never thought of going. But in the western and northern part was many a pleasant room; full of things that were curiosities to us, though they might not have been to people who had seen more. The windows were darkened by the sweeping boughs of the trees, and the ivy which had overgrown them: but, in the green gloom, we could manage to see old China jars and carved ivory boxes, and great heavy books, and, above all, the old pictures!

Once, I remember, my darling would have Dorothy go with us to tell us who they all were; for they were all portraits of some of my lord's family, though Dorothy could not tell us the names of every one. We had gone through most of the rooms, when we came to the old state drawing-room over the hall, and there was a picture of Miss Furnivall; or, as she was called in those days, Miss Grace, for she was the younger sister.[6] Such a beauty she must have been! but with such a set, proud look, and such scorn looking out of her handsome eyes, with her eyebrows just a little raised, as if she wondered how any one could have the impertinence to look at her; and her lip curled at us, as we stood there gazing. She had a dress on, the like of which I had never seen before, but it was all the fashion when she was young: a hat of some soft white stuff like beaver,[7] pulled a little over her brows, and a beautiful plume of feathers sweeping round it on one side; and her gown of blue satin was open in front to a quilted white stomacher.

'Well, to be sure!' said I, when I had gazed my fill. 'Flesh is grass,[8] they do say; but who would have thought that Miss Furnivall had been such an out-and-out beauty, to see her now?'

'Yes,' said Dorothy. 'Folks change sadly. But if what my master's father used to say was true, Miss Furnivall, the elder sister, was handsomer than Miss Grace. Her picture is here somewhere; but, if I show it you, you must never let on, even to James, that you have seen it. Can the little lady hold her tongue, think you?' asked she.

I was not so sure, for she was such a little sweet, bold, open-spoken child, so I set her to hide herself; and then I helped Dorothy to turn a great picture, that leaned with its face towards the wall, and was not hung up as the others were. To be sure, it beat Miss Grace for beauty; and, I think, for scornful pride, too, though in that matter it might be hard to choose. I could have looked at it an hour, but Dorothy seemed half frightened at having shown it to me, and hurried it back again, and bade me run and find Miss Rosamond, for that there were some ugly places about the house, where she should like ill for the child to go. I was a brave, high-spirited girl, and thought little of what the old woman said, for I liked hide-and-seek as well as any child in the parish; so off I ran to find my little one.

As winter drew on, and the days grew shorter, I was sometimes almost certain that I heard a noise as if some one was playing on the great organ in the hall. I did not hear it every evening; but, certainly, I did very often; usually when I was sitting with Miss Rosamond, after I had put her to bed, and keeping quite still and silent in the bed-room. Then I used to hear it booming and swelling away in the distance. The first night, when I went down to my supper, I asked Dorothy who had been playing music, and James said very shortly that I was a gowk to take the wind soughing among the trees for music: but I saw Dorothy look at him very fearfully, and Agnes, the kitchen-maid,[9] said something beneath her breath, and went quite white. I saw they did not like my question, so I held my peace till I was with Dorothy alone, when I knew I could get a good deal out of her. So, the next day, I watched my time, and I coaxed and asked her who it was that played the organ; for I knew that it was the organ and not the wind well enough, for all I had kept silence before James. But Dorothy had had her lesson I'll[a] warrant, and never a word could I get from her. So then I tried Agnes, though I had always held my head rather above her, as I was evened to James and Dorothy, and she was little better than their servant. So she said I must never, never tell; and if I ever told, I was never to say *she* had told me; but it was a very strange noise, and she had heard it many a time, but most of all on winter nights, and before storms; and folks did say, it was the old lord playing on the great organ in the hall, just as he used to do when he was alive; but who the old lord was, or why he played, and why he played on stormy winter evenings in particular, she either could not or would not tell me. Well! I told you I had a brave heart; and I thought it was rather pleasant to have that grand music rolling about the house, let who would be the player; for now it rose above the great gusts of wind, and wailed and triumphed just like a living creature, and then it fell to a softness most complete; only it was always music, and tunes, so it was nonsense to call it the wind. I thought at first, that it might be Miss Furnivall who played, unknown to Agnes; but, one day when I was in the hall by myself, I opened the organ and peeped all about it and around it, as I had done to the organ in Crosthwaite Church[10] once before, and I saw it was all broken and destroyed inside, though it looked so brave and fine; and then, though it was noon-day, my flesh began to creep a little, and I shut it up, and ran away pretty quickly to my own bright nursery;

and I did not like hearing the music for some time after that, any more than James and Dorothy did. All this time Miss Rosamond was making herself more, and more beloved. The old ladies liked her to dine with them at their early dinner; James stood behind Miss Furnivall's chair, and I behind Miss Rosamond's all in state; and, after dinner, she would play about in a corner of the great drawing-room, as still as any mouse, while Miss Furnivall slept, and I had my dinner in the kitchen. But she was glad enough to come to me in the nursery afterwards; for, as she said, Miss Furnivall was so sad, and Mrs. Stark so dull; but she and I were merry enough; and, by-and-by, I got not to care for that weird rolling music, which did one no harm, if we did not know where it came from.

That winter was very cold. In the middle of October the frosts began, and lasted many, many weeks. I remember, one day at dinner, Miss Furnivall lifted up her sad, heavy eyes, and said to Mrs. Stark, 'I am afraid we shall have a terrible winter,' in a strange kind of meaning way. But Mrs. Stark pretended not to hear, and talked very loud of something else. My little lady and I did not care for the frost; not we! As long as it was dry we climbed up the steep brows, behind the house, and went up on the Fells, which were bleak, and bare enough, and there we ran races in the fresh, sharp air; and once we came down by a new path that took us past the two old gnarled holly-trees, which grew about half-way down by the east side of the house. But the days grew shorter, and shorter; and the old lord, if it was he, played away more and more stormily and sadly on the great organ. One Sunday afternoon, – it must have been towards the end of November – I asked Dorothy to take charge of little Missey when she came out of the drawing-room, after Miss Furnivall had had her nap; for it was too cold to take her with me to church, and yet I wanted to go. And Dorothy was glad enough to promise, and was so fond of the child that all seemed well; and Agnes and I set off very briskly, though the sky hung heavy and black over the white earth, as if the night had never fully gone away; and the air, though still, was very biting and keen.

'We shall have a fall of snow,' said Agnes to me. And sure enough, even while we were in church, it came down thick, in great large flakes, so thick it almost darkened the windows. It had stopped snowing before we came out, but it lay soft, thick and deep beneath our feet, as we tramped home. Before we got to the hall the moon rose, and I think it was lighter then, – what with the moon, and what with the white dazzling snow – than it had been when we went to church, between two and three o'clock. I have not told you that Miss Furnivall and Mrs. Stark never went to church: they used to read the prayers together, in their quiet gloomy way; they seemed to feel the Sunday very long without their tapestry-work to be busy at.[11] So when I went to Dorothy in the kitchen, to fetch Miss Rosamond and take her up-stairs with me, I did not much wonder when the old woman told me that the ladies had kept the child with them, and that she had never come to the kitchen, as I had bidden her, when she was tired of behaving pretty in the drawing-room. So I took off my things and went to find her, and bring her to her supper in the nursery. But when I went into the best drawing-room, there sat the two old ladies, very still and quiet, dropping out a word now and then, but looking as if nothing so bright and merry as Miss Rosamond had ever been near them. Still I thought she might be hiding from me; it was one of her pretty ways; and that she had persuaded them to look as if they knew nothing about her; so I went softly peeping under this sofa, and behind that chair, making believe I was sadly frightened at not finding her.

'What's the matter, Hester?' said Mrs. Stark sharply. I don't know if Miss Furnivall had seen me, for, as I told you, she was very deaf, and she sat quite still, idly staring into the fire, with her hopeless face. 'I'm only looking for my little Rosy-Posy,' replied I, still thinking that the child was there, and near me, though I could not see her.

'Miss Rosamond is not here,' said Mrs. Stark. 'She went away more than an hour ago to find Dorothy.' And she too turned and went on looking into the fire.

My heart sank at this, and I began to wish I had never left my darling. I went back to Dorothy and told her. James was gone out for the day, but she and me and Bessy took lights and went up into the nursery first, and then we roamed over the great large house, calling and entreating Miss Rosamond to come out of her hiding place, and not frighten us to death in that way. But there was no answer; no sound.

'Oh!' said I at last, 'Can she have got into the east wing and hidden there?'

But Dorothy said it was not possible, for that she herself had never been in there; that the doors were always locked, and my lord's steward had the keys, she believed; at any rate, neither she, nor James had ever seen them: so, I said I would go back, and see if, after all, she was not hidden in the drawing-room, unknown to the old ladies; and if I found her there, I said, I would whip her well for the fright she had given me; but I never meant to do it. Well, I went back to the west drawing-room, and I told Mrs. Stark we could not find her anywhere, and asked for leave to look all about the furniture there, for I thought now, that she might have fallen asleep in some warm hidden corner; but no! we looked, Miss Furnivall got up and looked, trembling all over, and she was no where there; then we set off again, every one in the house, and looked in all the places we had searched before, but we could not find her. Miss Furnivall shivered and shook so much, that Mrs. Stark took her back into the warm drawing-room; but not before they had made me promise to bring her to them when she was found. Well-a-day! I began to think she never would be found, when I bethought me to look out into the great front court, all covered with snow. I was up-stairs when I looked out; but, it was such clear moonlight, I could see quite plain two little footprints, which might be traced from the hall door, and round the corner of the east wing. I don't know how I got down, but I tugged open the great, stiff hall door; and, throwing the skirt of my gown over my head for a cloak, I ran out. I turned the east corner, and there a black shadow fell on the snow; but when I came again into the moonlight, there were the little footmarks going up – up to the Fells. It was bitter cold; so cold that the air almost took the skin off my face as I ran, but I ran on, crying to think how my poor little darling must be perished, and frightened. I was within sight of the holly-trees, when I saw a shepherd coming down the hill, bearing something in his arms wrapped in his maud.[12] He shouted to me, and asked me if I had lost a bairn; and, when I could not speak for crying, he bore towards me, and I saw my wee bairnie lying still, and white, and stiff, in his arms, as if she had been dead. He told me he had been up the Fells to gather in his sheep, before the deep cold of night came on, and that under the holly-trees (black marks on the hill-side, where no other bush was for miles around) he had found my little lady – my lamb – my queen – my darling – stiff, and cold, in the terrible sleep which is frost-begotten. Oh! the joy, and the tears of having her in my arms once again! for I would not let him carry her; but took her, maud and all, into my own arms, and held her near my own warm neck, and heart, and felt the life stealing slowly back again into her little gentle limbs. But she was still insensible when we reached the hall, and I had no breath for speech. We went in by the kitchen door.

'Bring the warming-pan,' said I; and I carried her up-stairs and began undressing her by the nursery fire, which Agnes had kept up. I called my little lammie all the sweet and playful names I could think of, – even while my eyes were blinded by my tears; and at last, oh! at length she opened her large blue eyes. Then I put her into her warm bed, and sent Dorothy down to tell Miss Furnivall that all was well; and I made up my mind to sit by my darling's bedside the live-long night. She fell away into a soft sleep as soon as her pretty head had touched the pillow, and I watched by her till morning light; when she wakened up bright and clear – or so I thought at first – and, my dears, so I think now.

She said, that she had fancied that she should like to go to Dorothy, for that both the old ladies were asleep, and it was very dull in the drawing-room; and that, as she was going through the west lobby, she saw the snow through the high window falling – falling – soft and steady; but she wanted to see it lying pretty and white on the ground; so she made her way into the great hall; and then, going to the window, she saw it bright and soft upon the drive; but while she stood there, she saw a little girl, not so old as she was, 'but so pretty,' said my darling, 'and this little girl beckoned to me to come out; and oh, she was so pretty and so sweet, I could not choose but go.' And then this other little girl had taken her by the hand, and side by side the two had gone round the east corner.

'Now you are a naughty little girl, and telling stories,' said I. 'What would your good mamma, that is in heaven, and never told a story in her life, say to her little Rosamond, if she heard her – and I dare say she does – telling stories!'

'Indeed, Hester,' sobbed out my child, 'I'm telling you true. Indeed I am.'

'Don't tell me!' said I, very stern. 'I tracked you by your foot-marks through the snow; there were only yours to be seen: and if you had had a little girl to go hand-in-hand with you up the hill, don't you think the footprints would have gone along with yours?'

'I can't help it, dear, dear Hester,' said she, crying, 'if they did not; I never looked at her feet, but she held my hand fast and tight in her little one, and it was very, very cold. She took me up the Fell-path, up to the holly trees; and there I saw a lady weeping and crying; but when she saw me, she hushed her weeping, and smiled very proud and grand, and took me on her knee, and began to lull me to sleep; and that's all, Hester – but that is true; and my dear mamma knows it is,' said she, crying. So I thought the child was in a fever, and pretended to believe her, as she went over her story – over and over again, and always the same. At last Dorothy knocked at the door with Miss Rosamond's breakfast; and she told me the old ladies were down in the eating parlour, and that they wanted to speak to me. They had both been into the night-nursery the evening before, but it was after Miss Rosamond was asleep; so they had only looked at her – not asked me any questions.

'I shall catch it,' thought I to myself, as I went along the north gallery. 'And yet,' I thought, taking courage, 'it was in their charge I left her; and it's they that's to blame for letting her steal away unknown and unwatched.' So I went in boldly, and told my story. I told it all to Miss Furnivall, shouting it close to her ear; but when I came to the mention of the other little girl out in the snow, coaxing and tempting her out, and wiling her up to the grand and beautiful lady by the holly-tree, she threw her arms up – her old and withered arms – and cried aloud, 'Oh! Heaven, forgive! Have mercy!'

Mrs. Stark took hold of her; roughly enough, I thought; but she was past Mrs. Stark's management, and spoke to me, in a kind of wild warning and authority.

'Hester! keep her from that child! It will lure her to her death! That evil child! Tell her it is a wicked, naughty child.' Then, Mrs. Stark hurried me out of the room; where, indeed, I was glad enough to go; but Miss Furnivall kept shrieking out, 'Oh! have mercy! Wilt Thou never forgive! It is many a long year ago –'

I was very uneasy in my mind after that. I durst never leave Miss Rosamond, night or day, for fear lest she might slip off again, after some fancy or other; and all the more, because I thought I could make out that Miss Furnivall was crazy, from their odd ways about her; and I was afraid lest something of the same kind (which might be in the family, you know) hung over my darling. And the great frost never ceased all this time; and, when-ever it was a more stormy night than usual, between the gusts, and through the wind, we heard the old lord playing on the great organ. But, old lord, or not, wherever Miss Rosamond went, there I followed; for my love for her, pretty helpless orphan, was stronger than my fear for the grand and terrible sound. Besides, it rested with me to keep her cheerful and merry, as beseemed her age. So we played together, and wandered together, here and there, and everywhere; for I never dared to lose sight of her again in that large and rambling house. And so it happened, that one afternoon, not long before Christmas day, we were playing together on the billiard-table in the great hall (not that we knew the right way of playing, but she liked to roll the smooth ivory balls with her pretty hands, and I liked to do whatever she did); and, by-and-by, without our noticing it, it grew dusk indoors, though it was still light in the open air, and I was thinking of taking her back into the nursery, when, all of a sudden, she cried out:

'Look, Hester! look! there is my poor little girl out in the snow!'

I turned towards the long narrow windows, and there, sure enough, I saw a little girl, less than my Miss Rosamond – dressed all unfit to be out-of-doors such a bitter night – crying, and beating against the window-panes, as if she wanted to be let in. She seemed to sob and wail, till Miss Rosamond could bear it no longer, and was flying to the door to open it, when, all of a sudden, and close upon us, the great organ pealed out so loud and thunder-ing, it fairly made me tremble; and all the more, when I remembered me that, even in the stillness of that dead-cold weather, I had heard no sound of little battering hands upon the window-glass, although the Phantom Child had seemed to put forth all its force; and, although I had seen it wail and cry, no faintest touch of sound had fallen upon my ears. Whether I remembered all this at the very moment, I do not know; the great organ sound had so stunned me into terror; but this I know, I caught up Miss Rosamond before she got the hall-door opened, and clutched her, and carried her away, kicking and screaming, into the large bright kitchen, where Dorothy and Agnes were busy with their mince-pies.

'What is the matter with my sweet one?' cried Dorothy, as I bore in Miss Rosamond, who was sobbing as if her heart would break.

'She won't let me open the door for my little girl to come in; and she'll die if she is out on the Fells all night. Cruel, naughty Hester,' she said, slap-ping me; but she might have struck harder, for I had seen a look of ghastly terror on Dorothy's face, which made my very blood run cold.

'Shut the back kitchen door fast, and bolt it well,' said she to Agnes. She said no more; she gave me raisins and almonds to quiet Miss Rosamond: but she sobbed about the little girl in the snow, and would not touch any of the good things. I was thankful when she cried herself to sleep in bed. Then I stole down to the kitchen, and told Dorothy I had made up my mind. I would carry my darling back to my father's house in Applethwaite; where, if we lived humbly, we lived at peace. I said I had been frightened enough with the old lord's organ-playing; but now, that I had seen for myself this little moaning child, all decked out as no child in the neighbourhood could be, beating and battering to get in, yet always without any sound or noise – with the dark wound on its right shoulder; and that Miss Rosamond had known it again for the phantom that had nearly lured her to her death (which Dorothy knew was true); I would stand it no longer.

I saw Dorothy change colour once or twice. When I had done, she told me she did not think I could take Miss Rosamond with me, for that she was my lord's ward, and I had no right over her; and she asked me, would I leave the child that I was so fond of, just for sounds and sights that could do me no harm; and that they had all had to get used to in their turns? I was all in a hot, trembling passion; and I said it was very well for her to talk, that knew what these sights and noises betokened, and that had, perhaps, had something to do with the Spectre-Child while it was alive. And I taunted her so, that she told me all she knew, at last; and then I wished I had never been told, for it only made me more afraid than ever.

She said she had heard the tale from old neighbours, that were alive when she was first married; when folks used to come to the hall sometimes, before it had got such a bad name on the country side: it might not be true, or it might, what she had been told.

The old lord was Miss Furnivall's father – Miss Grace, as Dorothy called her, for Miss Maude was the elder, and Miss Furnivall by rights. The old lord was eaten up with pride. Such a proud man was never seen or heard of; and his daughters were like him. No one was good enough to wed them, although they had choice enough; for they were the great beauties of their day, as I had seen by their portraits, where they hung in the state drawing-room. But, as the old saying is, 'Pride will have a fall;' and these two haughty beauties fell in love with the same man, and he no better than a foreign musician, whom their father had down from London to play music with him at the Manor House. For, above all things, next to his pride, the old lord loved music. He could play on nearly every instrument that ever was heard of: and it was a strange thing it did not soften him; but he was a fierce dour old man, and had broken his poor wife's heart with his cruelty, they said. He was mad after music, and would pay any money for it. So he got this foreigner to come; who made such beautiful music, that they said the very birds on the trees stopped their singing to listen. And, by degrees, this foreign gentleman got such a hold over the old lord, that nothing would serve him but that he must come every year; and it was he that had the great organ brought from Holland, and built up in the hall, where it stood now. He taught the old lord to play on it; but many and many a time, when Lord Furnivall was thinking of nothing but his fine organ, and his finer music, the dark foreigner was walking abroad in the woods with one of the young ladies; now Miss Maude, and then Miss Grace.

Miss Maude won the day and carried off the prize, such as it was; and he and she were married, all unknown to any one; and before he made his next yearly visit, she had been confined of a little girl at a farm-house on the Moors, while her father and Miss Grace thought she was away at Doncaster Races. But though she was a wife and a mother, she was not a bit softened, but as haughty and as passionate as ever; and perhaps more so, for she was jealous of Miss Grace, to whom her foreign husband paid a deal of court – by way of blinding her – as he told his wife. But Miss Grace triumphed over Miss Maude, and Miss Maude grew fiercer and fiercer, both with her husband and with her sister; and the former – who could easily shake off what was disagreeable, and hide himself in foreign countries – went away a month before his usual time that summer, and half-threatened that he would never come back again. Meanwhile, the little girl was left at the farm-house, and her mother used to have her horse saddled and gallop wildly over the hills to see her once every week, at the very least – for where she loved, she loved; and where she hated, she hated. And the old lord went on playing – playing on his organ; and the servants thought the sweet music he made had soothed down his awful temper, of which (Dorothy said) some terrible tales could be told. He grew infirm too, and had to walk with a crutch; and his son – that was the present Lord Furnivall's father –[13] was with the army in America,[14] and the other son at sea; so Miss Maude had it pretty much her own way, and she and Miss Grace grew colder and bitterer to each other every day; till at last they hardly ever spoke, except when the old lord was by. The foreign musician came again the next summer, but it was for the last time; for they led him such a life with their jealousy and their passions, that he grew weary, and went away, and never was heard of again. And Miss Maude, who had always meant to have her marriage acknowledged when her father should be dead, was left now a deserted wife – whom nobody knew to have been married – with a child that she dared not own, although she loved it to distraction; living with a father whom she feared, and a sister whom she hated. When the next summer passed over and the dark foreigner never came, both Miss Maude and Miss Grace grew gloomy and sad; they had a haggard look about them, though they looked handsome as ever. But by-and-by Miss Maude brightened; for her father grew more and more infirm, and more than ever carried away by his music; and she and Miss Grace lived almost entirely apart, having separate rooms, the one on the west side, Miss Maude on the east – those very rooms which were now shut up. So she thought she might have her little girl with her, and no one need ever know except those who dared not speak about it, and were bound to believe that it was, as she said, a cottager's child she had taken a fancy to. All this, Dorothy said, was pretty well known; but what came afterwards no one knew, except Miss Grace, and Mrs. Stark, who was even then her maid, and much more of a friend to her than ever her sister had been. But the servants supposed, from words that were dropped, that Miss Maude had triumphed over Miss Grace, and told her that all the time the dark foreigner had been mocking her with pretended love – he was her own husband; the colour left Miss Grace's cheek and lips that very day for ever, and she was heard to say many a time that sooner or later she would have her revenge; and Mrs. Stark was for ever spying about the east rooms.

One fearful night, just after the New Year had come in, when the snow was lying thick and deep, and the flakes were still falling – fast enough to blind any one who might be out and abroad – there was a great and violent noise heard, and the old lord's voice above all, cursing and swearing awfully, – and the cries of a little child, – and the proud defiance of a fierce woman, – and the sound of a blow, – and a dead stillness, – and moans and wailings dying away on the hill-side! Then the old lord summoned all his servants, and told them, with terrible oaths, and words more terrible, that his daughter had disgraced herself, and that he had turned her out of doors, – her, and her child, – and that if ever they gave her help, – or food – or shelter, – he prayed that they might never enter Heaven. And, all the while, Miss Grace stood by him, white and still as any stone; and when he had ended she heaved a great sigh, as much as to say her work was done, and her end was accomplished. But the old lord never touched his organ again, and died within the year; and no wonder! for, on the morrow of that wild and fearful night, the shepherds, coming down the Fell side, found Miss Maude sitting, all crazy and smiling, under the holly-trees, nursing a dead child, – with a terrible mark on its right shoulder. 'But that was not what killed it,' said Dorothy; 'it was the frost and the cold; – every wild creature was in its hole, and every beast in its fold, – while the child and its mother were turned out to wander on the Fells! And now you know all! and I wonder if you are less frightened now?'

I was more frightened than ever; but I said I was not. I wished Miss Rosamond and myself well out of that dreadful house for ever; but I would not leave her, and I dared not take her away. But oh! how I watched her, and guarded her! We bolted the doors, and shut the window-shutters fast, an hour or more before dark, rather than leave them open five minutes too late. But my little lady still heard the weird child crying and mourning; and not all we could do or say, could keep her from wanting to go to her, and let her in from the cruel wind and the snow. All this time, I kept away from Miss Furnivall and Mrs. Stark, as much as ever I could; for I feared them – I knew no good could be about them, with their grey hard faces, and their dreamy eyes, looking back into the ghastly years that were gone. But, even in my fear, I had a kind of pity – for Miss Furnivall, at least. Those gone down to the pit can hardly have a more hopeless look than that which was ever on her face. At last I even got so sorry for her – who never said a word but what was quite forced from her – that I prayed for her; and I taught Miss Rosamond to pray for one who had done a deadly sin; but often when she came to those words, she would listen, and start up from her knees, and say, 'I hear my little girl plaining and crying very sad – Oh! let her in, or she will die!'

One night – just after New Year's Day had come at last, and the long winter had taken a turn, as I hoped – I heard the west drawing-room bell ring three times, which was the signal for me. I would not leave Miss Rosamond alone, for all she was asleep – for the old lord had been playing wilder than ever – and I feared lest my darling should waken to hear the spectre child; see her I knew she could not. I had fastened the windows too well for that. So, I took her out of her bed and wrapped her up in such outer clothes as were most handy, and carried her down to the drawing-room, where the old ladies sat at their tapestry work as usual. They looked up when I came in, and Mrs. Stark asked, quite astounded, 'Why did I bring Miss Rosamond there, out of her warm bed?' I had begun to whisper, 'Because I was afraid of her being tempted out while I was away, by the wild child in the snow,' when she stopped me short (with a glance at Miss Furnivall), and said Miss Furnivall wanted me to undo some work she had done wrong, and which neither of them could see to unpick. So, I laid my pretty dear on the sofa, and sat down on a stool by them, and hardened my heart against them, as I heard the wind rising and howling.

Miss Rosamond slept on sound, for all the wind blew so; and Miss Furnivall said never a word, nor looked round when the gusts shook the windows. All at once she started up to her full height, and put up one hand, as if to bid us listen.

'I hear voices!' said she. 'I hear terrible screams – I hear my father's voice!'

Just at that moment, my darling wakened with a sudden start: 'My little girl is crying, oh, how she is crying!' and she tried to get up and go to her, but she got her feet entangled in the blanket, and I caught her up; for my flesh had begun to creep at these noises, which they heard while we could catch no sound. In a minute or two the noises came, and gathered fast, and filled our ears; we, too, heard voices and screams, and no longer heard the winter's wind that raged abroad. Mrs. Stark looked at me, and I at her, but we dared not speak. Suddenly Miss Furnivall went towards the door, out into the ante-room, through the west lobby, and opened the door into the great hall. Mrs. Stark followed, and I durst not be left, though my heart almost stopped beating for fear. I wrapped my darling tight in my arms, and went out with them. In the hall the screams were louder than ever; they sounded to come from the east wing – nearer and nearer – close on the other side of the locked-up doors – close behind them. Then I noticed that the great bronze chandelier seemed all alight, though the hall was dim, and that a fire was blazing in the vast hearth-place, though it gave no heat; and I shuddered up with terror, and folded my darling closer to me. But as I did so, the east door shook, and she, suddenly struggling to get free from me, cried, 'Hester! I must go! My little girl is there; I hear her; she is coming! Hester, I must go!'

I held her tight with all my strength; with a set will, I held her. If I had died, my hands would have grasped her still, I was so resolved in my mind. Miss Furnivall stood listening, and paid no regard to my darling, who had got down to the ground, and whom I, upon my knees now, was holding with both my arms clasped round her neck; she still striving and crying to get free.

All at once, the east door gave way with a thundering crash, as if torn open in a violent passion, and there came into that broad and mysterious light, the figure of a tall old man, with grey hair and gleaming eyes. He drove before him, with many a relentless gesture of abhorrence, a stern and beautiful woman, with a little child clinging to her dress.

'Oh Hester! Hester!' cried Miss Rosamond. 'It's the lady! the lady below the holly-trees; and my little girl is with her. Hester! Hester! let me go to her; they are drawing me to them. I feel them – I feel them. I must go!'

Again she was almost convulsed by her efforts to get away; but I held her tighter and tighter, till I feared I should do her a hurt; but rather that than let her go towards those terrible phantoms. They passed along towards the great hall-door, where the winds howled and ravened for their prey; but before they reached that, the lady turned; and I could see that she defied the old man with a fierce and proud defiance; but then she quailed – and then she threw up her arms wildly and piteously to save her child – her little child – from a blow from his uplifted crutch.

And Miss Rosamond was torn as by a power stronger than mine, and writhed in my arms, and sobbed (for by this time the poor darling was growing faint).

'They want me to go with them on to the Fells – they are drawing me to them. Oh, my little girl! I would come, but cruel, wicked Hester holds me very tight.' But when she saw the uplifted crutch she swooned away, and I thanked God for it. Just at this moment – when the tall old man, his hair streaming as in the blast of a furnace, was going to strike the little shrinking child – Miss Furnivall, the old woman by my side, cried out, 'Oh, father! father! spare the little innocent child!' But just then I saw – we all saw – another phantom shape itself, and grow clear out of the blue and misty light that filled the hall; we had not seen her till now, for it was another lady who stood by the old man, with a look of relentless hate and triumphant scorn. That figure was very beautiful to look upon, with a soft white hat drawn down over the proud brows, and a red and curling lip. It was dressed in an open robe of blue satin. I had seen that figure before. It was the likeness of Miss Furnivall in her youth; and the terrible phantoms moved on, regardless of old Miss Furnivall's wild entreaty, – and the uplifted crutch fell on the right shoulder of the little child, and the younger sister looked on, stony and deadly serene. But at that moment, the dim lights, and the fire that gave no heat, went out of themselves, and Miss Furnivall lay at our feet stricken down by the palsy – death-stricken.

Yes! she was carried to her bed that night never to rise again. She lay with her face to the wall, muttering low but muttering alway: 'Alas! alas! what is done in youth can never be undone in age! What is done in youth can never be undone in age!'

'MORTON HALL'

'Morton Hall' was first published in two parts in *Household Words*, 8 (19 and 26 November 1853), pp. 265–72, 293–302, one chapter in each part. It was collected in *Lizzie Leigh and Other Tales* (London: Chapman and Hall, 1855), pp. 97–127. It had previously been published in the Boston periodical *Littell's Living Age*, 2:4 (2 January 1854), pp. 31–45. It was also reprinted in *Lizzie Leigh and Other Tales* (1865). The text in 1855 follows the *HW* text closely; differences are mainly punctuation.

For the origin of the story in a conversation between Gaskell and Tabitha Aykroyd (c. 1770–1855), an old servant of the Brontës, see J. A. V. Chapple, 'Elizabeth Gaskell's "Morton Hall" and "The Poor Clare"', *BST*, 20 (1990), pp. 47–9. Chapple discovered an extract from a letter from EG to Caroline, Lady Hatherton preserved in the notebook of Jane Adeane in the Brotherton Library, Leeds; it is reproduced in *Further Letters*, p. 105 and in *Brontë Letters*, vol. iii, p. 216. EG seems to have written in answer to a query as to whether she had based her story on Little Moreton Hall in Cheshire (which now belongs to the National Trust). She replied denying any knowledge of that house, and adding:

> And about the 'poor starving people' the whole story originated in two little graphic sentences from the old Servant (aged 93) at Haworth; I asked her why a certain field was called the Balcōny Field … and she told me that when she was a girl 'while the Farmers were still about the country & before they had begun to plague the land with their Mills &c' there had been a grand House with Balcōnies in that field, that she remembered seeing Miss — (I forget the name) get into the Carriage with her hair all taken up over a cushion, and in a blue sattin open gown, but Oh! she came to sore want, for her Nephew gambled away the property and then she lent him money, and at last he & she had nowhere to hide their heads but an old tumbledown Cottage (shewn to me) where folk do say she was clemmed to death, and many a one in Haworth remembered him going to Squire (name forgotten again) to offer a bit of old plate for sale to bury his Aunt rather than that the Parish should do it. The 'Blue sattin gown' and the 'clemming to death' were a striking contrast, were they not?

Joseph Horsfall Turner, *Haworth Past and Present* (Brighouse: Jowett, 1879), p. 30, has '*Balcony*, a farmstead near the Church has been rebuilt. The Horsfalls had it some time.' According to Margaret Smith, *Brontë Letters*, vol. iii, p. 217n, the Horsfalls had been preceded by the Gaukrogers, and the story might relate to either family.

MORTON HALL.

CHAPTER I.

OUR old Hall is to be pulled down, and they are going to build streets on the site. I said to my sister, 'Ethelinda! if they really pull down Morton Hall, it will be a worse piece of work than the Repeal of the Corn Laws.'[1] And, after some consideration she replied, that if she must speak what was on her mind, she would own that she thought the Papists had something to do with it; that they had never forgiven the Morton who had been with Lord Monteagle[2] when he discovered the Gunpowder Plot; for we knew that somewhere in Rome there was a book kept, and which had been kept for generations, giving an account of the secret private history of every English family of note, and registering the names of those to whom the Papists owed either grudges or gratitude.

We were silent for some time; but I am sure the same thought was in both our minds; our ancestor, a Sidebotham, had been a follower of the Morton of that day; it had always been said in the family that he had been with his master, when he went with the Lord Monteagle, and found Guy Fawkes and his dark lantern under the Parliament House; and the question flashed across our minds, Were the Sidebothams marked with a black mark in that terrible mysterious book which was kept under lock and key by the Pope and the Cardinals in Rome?[3] It was terrible; yet, somehow, rather pleasant to think of. So many of the misfortunes which had happened to us through life, and which we had called 'mysterious dispensations,' but which some of our neighbours had attributed to our want of prudence and foresight, were accounted for at once, if we were objects of the deadly hatred of such a powerful order as the Jesuits; of whom we had lived in dread ever since we had read the Female Jesuit.[4] Whether this last idea suggested what my sister said next I can't tell; we did know the Female Jesuit's second cousin,[5] so might be said to have literary connections, and from that the startling thought might spring up in my sister's mind, for, said she, 'Biddy!' (my name is Bridget, and no one but my sister calls me Biddy) 'suppose you write some account of Morton Hall; we have known much in our time of the Mortons, and it will be a shame if they pass away completely from men's memories while we can speak or write.' I was pleased with the notion, I confess; but I felt ashamed to agree to it all at once, though even as I objected for modesty's sake, it came into my mind how much I had heard of the old place in its former days, and how it was perhaps all I could now do for the Mortons, under whom our ancestors had lived as tenants for more than three hundred years. So at last I agreed; and, for fear of mistakes, I showed it to Mr. Swinton, our young curate, who has put it quite in order for me.

Morton Hall is situated about five miles from the centre of Drumble.[6] It stands on the outskirts of a village, which, when the Hall was built, was probably as large as Drumble in those days; and even I can remember when there was a long piece of rather lonely road, with high hedges on either side, between Morton village and Drumble. Now it is all street, and Morton seems but a suburb of the great town near. Our farm stood where Liverpool Street runs now;[7] and people used to come snipe-shooting just where the Baptist Chapel is built. Our farm must have been older than the Hall, for we had a date of 1460[a] on one of the cross-beams. My father was rather proud of this advantage, for the Hall had no date older than 1554; and I remember his affronting Mrs. Dawson, the housekeeper, by dwelling too much on this circumstance one evening when she came to drink tea with my mother, when Ethelinda and I were mere children. But my mother, seeing that Mrs. Dawson would never allow that any house in the parish could be older than the Hall, and that she was getting very warm, and almost insinuating that the Sidebothams had forged the date to disparage the Squire's family, and set them selves up as having the older blood, asked Mrs. Dawson to tell us the story of old Sir John Morton before we went to bed; I slily reminded my father that Jack, our man, was not always so careful as might be in housing the Alderney in good time in the autumn evenings. So he started up, and went off to see after Jack; and Mrs. Dawson and we drew nearer the fire to hear the story about Sir John.

Sir John Morton had lived some time about the Restoration.[8] The Mortons had taken the right side, so when Oliver Cromwell came into power he gave away their lands to one of his Puritan followers – a man who had been but a praying, canting, Scotch pedlar, till the war broke out; and Sir John had to go and live with his royal master at Bruges. The upstart's name was Carr, who came to live at Morton Hall; and, I'm proud to say, we – I mean our ancestors – led him a pretty life. He had hard work to get any rent at all from the tenantry, who knew their duty better than to pay it to a Roundhead. If he took the law to them, the law officers fared so badly, that they were shy of coming out to Morton – all along that lonely road I told you of – again. Strange noises were heard about the Hall, which got the credit of being haunted but as those noises were never heard before or since that Richard Carr lived there, I leave you to guess if the evil spirits did not know well over whom they had power – over schismatic rebels, and no one else. They durst not trouble the Mortons, who were true and loyal, and were faithful followers of King Charles in word and deed. At last Old Oliver died, and folks did say that on that wild and stormy night his voice was heard high up in the air, where you hear the flocks of wild geese skirl, crying out for his true follower Richard Carr to accompany him in the terrible chase the fiends were giving him before carrying him down to hell. Anyway Richard Carr died within a week – summoned by the dead or not, he went his way down to his master, and his master's master.

Then his daughter Alice came into possession. Her mother was somehow related to General Monk,[9] who was beginning to come into power about that time. So when Charles the Second came back to his throne, and many of the sneaking Puritans had to quit their ill-gotten land, and turn to the right about, Alice Carr was still left at Morton Hall to queen it there. She was taller than most women, and a great beauty I have heard. But, for all her beauty, she was a stern, hard woman. The tenants had known her to be hard in her father's lifetime, but now that she was the owner and had the power, she was worse than ever. She hated the Stuarts worse than ever her father had done; had calves' head for dinner every thirtieth of January;[10] and when the first twenty-ninth of May[11] came round, and every mother's son in the village gilded his oak leaves, and wore them in his hat, she closed the windows of the great hall with her own hands, and sate throughout the day in darkness and mourning. People did not like to go against her by force, because she was a young and beautiful woman. It was said the King got her cousin, the Duke of Albemarle, to ask her to court just as courteously as if she had been the Queen of Sheba, and King Charles, Solomon,[12] praying her to visit him in Jerusalem. But she would not go; not she! She lived a very lonely life, for now the King had got his own again, no servant but her nurse would stay with her in the Hall; and none of the tenants would pay her any money for all that her father had purchased the lands from the Parliament, and paid the price down in good red gold.

All this time, Sir John was somewhere in the Virginian plantations;[13] and the ships sailed from thence only twice a year: but his royal master had sent for him home; and home he came that second summer after the restoration. No one knew if Mistress Alice had heard of his landing in England or not; all the villagers and tenantry knew and were not surprised, and turned out in their best dresses and with great branches of oak to welcome him as he rode into the village one July morning, with many gay-looking gentlemen by his side, laughing and talking and making-merry, and speaking gaily and pleasantly to the village people. They came in on the opposite side to the Drumble Road; indeed Drumble was nothing of a place then, as I have told you. Between the last cottage in the village and the gates to the old Hall, there was a shady part of the road, where the branches nearly met overhead, and made a green gloom. If you'll notice, when many people are talking merrily out of doors in sunlight, they will stop talking for an instant, when they come into the cool green shade, and either be silent for some little time, or else speak graver and slower and softer. And so old people say those gay gentlemen did; for several people followed to see Alice Carr's pride taken down. They used to tell how the cavaliers had to bow their plumed hats in passing under the unlopped and drooping boughs. I fancy Sir John expected that the lady would have rallied her friends, and got ready for a sort of battle to defend the entrance to the house; but she had no friends. She had no nearer relations than the Duke of Albemarle, and he was mad with her for having refused to come to court, and so save her estate according to his advice.

Well, Sir John rode on, in silence; the tramp of the many horses' feet, and the clumping sound of the clogs of the village people were all that was heard. Heavy as the great gate was, they swung it wide on its hinges, and up they rode to the Hall steps, where the lady stood, in her close plain Puritan dress, her cheeks one crimson flush, her great eyes flashing fire, and no one behind her, or with her, or near her, or to be seen, but the old trembling nurse catching at her gown in pleading terror. Sir John was taken aback; he could not go out with swords and warlike weapons against a woman; his very preparations for forcing an entrance made him ridiculous in his own eyes, and he well knew in the eyes of his gay scornful comrades too; so he turned him round about, and bade them stay where they were, while he rode close to the steps, and spoke to the young lady; and there they saw him, hat in hand, speaking to her; and she, lofty and unmoved, holding her own as if she had been a sovereign queen with an army at her back. What they said, no one heard; but he rode back, very grave and much changed in his look, though his grey eye showed more hawk-like than ever, as if seeing the way to his end, though as yet afar off. He was not one to be jested with before his face; so when he professed to have changed his mind, and not to wish to disturb so fair a lady in possession, he and his cavaliers rode back to the village inn, and roystered there all day, and feasted the tenantry, cutting down the branches that had incommoded them in their morning's ride, to make a bonfire of on the village green, in which they burnt a figure, which some called. Old Noll,[14] and others Richard Carr: and it might do for either, folks said, for unless they had given it the name of a man, most people would have taken it for a forked log of wood. But the lady's nurse told the villagers afterwards that Mistress Alice went in from the sunny Hall steps into the chill house shadow, and sate her down and wept as her poor faithful servant had never seen her do before, and could not have imagined her proud young lady ever doing. All through that summer's day she cried; and if for very weariness she ceased for a time, and only sighed as if her heart was breaking, they heard through the upper windows – which were open because of the heat – the village bells ringing merrily through the trees, and bursts of choruses to gay cavalier songs, all in favour of the Stuarts. All the young lady said was once or twice, 'Oh God! I am very friendless!' – and the old nurse knew it was true, and could not contradict her; and always thought, as she said long after, that such weary weeping showed there was some great sorrow at hand.

I suppose it was the dreariest sorrow that ever a proud woman had; but it came in the shape of a gay wedding. How the village never knew. The gay gentlemen rode away from Morton the next day as lightly and carelessly as if they had attained their end and Sir John had taken possession; and, by-and-by, the nurse came timorously out to market in the village, and Mistress Alice was met in the wood walks just as grand and as proud as ever in her ways, only a little more pale and a little more sad. The truth was, as I have been told, that she and Sir John had each taken a fancy to each other in that parley they held on the Hall steps; she, in the deep wild way in which she took the impressions of her whole life, deep down, as if they were burnt in. Sir John was a gallant-looking man, and had a kind of foreign grace and courtliness about him. The way he fancied her was very different – a man's way, they tell me. She was a beautiful woman to be tamed, and made to come to his beck and call; and perhaps he read in her softening eyes that she might be won, and so all legal troubles about the possession of the estate come to an end in an easy pleasant manner. He came to stay with friends in the neighbourhood; he was met in her favourite walks with his plumed hat in his hand pleading with her, and she looking softer and far more lovely than ever; and lastly, the tenants were told of the marriage then nigh at hand.

After they were wedded he stayed for a time with her at the Hall, and then off back to court. They do say that her obstinate refusal to go with him to London was the cause of their first quarrel; but such fierce strong wills would quarrel the first day of their wedded life. She said that the court was no place for an honest woman; but surely Sir John knew best, and she might have trusted him to take care of her. However, he left her all alone; and at first she cried most bitterly, and then she took to her old pride, and was more haughty and gloomy than ever. By-and-by she found out hidden conventicles; and, as Sir John never stinted her of money, she gathered the remnants of the old Puritan party about her, and tried to comfort herself with long prayers, snuffled through the nose, for the absence of her husband, but it was of no use. Treat her as he would she loved him still with a terrible love. Once, they say, she put on her waiting-maid's dress, and stole up to London to find out what kept him there; and something she saw or heard that changed her altogether, for she came back as if her heart was broken. They say that the only person she loved with all the wild strength of her heart, had proved false to her; and if so, what wonder! At the best of times she was but a gloomy creature, and it was a great honour for her father's daughter to be wedded to a Morton. She should not have expected too much.

After her despondency came her religion. Every old Puritan preacher in the country was welcome at Morton Hall. Surely that was enough to disgust

Sir John. The Mortons had never cared to have much religion, but what they had, had been good of its kind hitherto. So, when Sir John came down wanting a gay greeting and a tender show of love, his lady exhorted him, and prayed over him, and quoted the last Puritan text she had heard at him; and he swore at her, and at her preachers; and made a deadly oath that none of them should find harbour or welcome in any house of his. She looked scornfully back at him, and said she had yet to learn in what county of England the house he spoke of was to be found; but in the house her father purchased, and she inherited, all who preached the Gospel should be welcome, let kings make what laws, and kings' minions swear what oaths they would. He said nothing to this; the worst sign for her; but he set his teeth at her; and in an hour's time he rode away back to the French witch[15] that had beguiled him.

Before he went away from Morton he set his spies. He longed to catch his wife in his fierce clutch, and punish her for defying him. She had made him hate her with her Puritanical ways. He counted the days till the messenger came, splashed up to the top of his deep leather boots, to say that my lady had invited the canting Puritan preachers of the neighbourhood to a prayer-meeting, and a dinner, and a night's rest at her house. Sir John smiled as he gave the messenger five gold pieces for his pains; and straight took post-horses, and rode long days till he got to Morton; and only just in time; for it was the very day of the prayer-meeting. Dinners were then at one o'clock in the country. The great people in London might keep late hours, and dine at three in the afternoon or so; but the Mortons they always clung to the good old ways, and, as the church bells were ringing twelve when Sir John came riding into the village, he knew he might slacken bridle; and, casting one glance at the smoke which came hurrying up as if from a newly-mended fire, just behind the wood, where he knew the Hall-kitchen chimney stood, Sir John stopped at the smithy, and pretended to question the smith about his horse's shoes; but he took little heed of the answers, being more occupied by an old serving-man from the Hall, who had been loitering about the smithy half the morning, as folk thought afterwards to keep some appointment with Sir John. When their talk was ended, Sir John lifted himself straight in his saddle; cleared his throat, and spoke out aloud: –

'I grieve to hear your lady is so ill.' The smith wondered at this, for all the village knew of the coming feast at the Hall; the spring-chickens had been bought up, and the cade-lambs[16] killed; for the preachers in those days, if they fasted they fasted, if they fought they fought, if they prayed they prayed, sometimes for three hours at a standing; and if they feasted they feasted, and knew what good eating was, believe me.

'My lady ill?' said the smith, as if he doubted the old prim serving-man's word. And the latter would have chopped in with an angry asseveration (he had been at Worcester[17] and fought on the right side), but Sir John cut him short.

'My lady is very ill, good Master Fox. It touches her here,' continued he, pointing to his head. 'I am come down to take her to London, where the King's own physician shall prescribe for her.' And he rode slowly up to the hall.

The lady was as well as ever she had been in her life, and happier than she had often been – for in a few minutes some of those whom she esteemed so highly would be about her; some of those who had known and valued her father – her dead father, to whom her sorrowful heart turned in its woe, as the only true lover and friend she had ever had on earth. Many of the preachers would have ridden far – was all in order in their rooms, and on the table in the great dining parlour? She had got into restless hurried ways of late. She went round below, and then she mounted the great oak staircase to see if the tower bed-chamber was all in order for old Master Hilton, the oldest among the preachers. Meanwhile, the maidens below were carrying in mighty cold rounds of spiced beef, quarters of lamb, chicken pies, and all such provisions, when, suddenly, they knew not how, they found themselves each seized by strong arms, their aprons thrown over their heads, after the manner of a gag, and themselves borne out of the house on to the poultry green behind, where with threats of what worse might befall them, they were sent with many a shameful word – (Sir John could not always command his men, many of whom had been soldiers in the French wars) – back into the village. They scudded away like frightened hares. My lady was strewing the white-headed preacher's room with the last year's lavender, and stirring up the sweet-pot on the dressing-table, when she heard a step on the echoing stairs. It was no measured tread of any Puritan; it was the clang of a man of war coming nearer and nearer, with loud rapid strides. She knew the step; her heart stopped beating, not for fear, but because she loved Sir John even yet; and she took a step forward to meet him, and then stood still and trembled, for the flattering false thought came before her that he might have come yet in some quick impulse of reviving love, and that his hasty step might be prompted by the passionate tenderness of a husband. But when he reached the door, she looked as calm and indifferent as ever.

'My lady,' said he, 'you are gathering your friends to some feast; may I know who are thus invited to revel in my house? Some graceless fellows, I see, from the store of meat and drink below: wine-bibbers and drunkards, I fear.'

But, by the working glance of his eye she saw that he knew all; and she spoke with a cold distinctness:

'Master Ephraim Dixon, Master Zerubbabel Hopkins, Master Help-me-or-I-perish Perkins, and some other godly ministers, come to spend the afternoon in my house.'

He went to her, and in his rage he struck her. She put up no arm to save herself, but reddened a little with the pain, and then drawing her neckerchief on one side, she looked at the crimson mark on her white neck.

'It serves me right,' she said. 'I wedded one of my father's enemies; one of those who would have hunted the old man to death. I gave my father's enemy house and lands, when he came as a beggar to my door; – I followed my wicked, wayward heart in this, instead of minding my dying father's words. Strike again, and avenge him yet more!'

But he would not, because she bade him. He unloosed his sash, and bound her arms tight, tight together, and she never struggled or spoke. Then pushing her so that she was obliged to sit down on the bed side:

'Sit there,' he said, 'and hear how I will welcome the old hypocrites you have dared to ask to my house – my house and my ancestors' house, long before your father – a canting pedlar – hawked his goods about, and cheated honest men.'

And, opening the chamber window right above those Hall steps where she had awaited him in her maiden beauty scarce three short years ago, he greeted the company of preachers as they rode up to the Hall with such terrible hideous language, (my lady had provoked him past all bearing, you see,) that the old men turned round aghast, and made the best of their way back to their own places.

Meanwhile Sir John's serving-men below had obeyed their master's orders. They had gone through the house, closing every window, every shutter, and every door, but leaving all else just as it was: – the cold meats on the table, the hot meats on the spit, the silver flagons on the side-board – all just as if it were ready for a feast; and then Sir John's head-servant, he that I spoke of before, came up and told his master all was ready.

'Is the horse and the pillion all ready? Then you and I must be my lady's tire-women:' and as it seemed to her in mockery, but in reality with a deep purpose, they dressed the helpless woman in her riding things all awry, and, strange and disorderly, Sir John carried her down stairs; and he and his man bound her on the pillion; and Sir John mounted before. The man shut and locked the great house-door, and the echoes of the clang went through the empty Hall with an ominous sound. 'Throw the key,' said Sir John, 'deep into the mere yonder. My lady may go seek it if she lists, when next I set her arms at liberty. Till then I know whose house Morton Hall shall be called.'

'Sir John! it shall be called the Devil's House, and you shall be his steward.'

But the poor lady had better have held her tongue; for Sir John only laughed, and told her to rave on. As he passed through the village, with his serving-men riding behind, the tenantry came out and stood at their doors, and pitied him for having a mad wife, and praised him for his care of her, and of the chance he gave her of amendment by taking her up to be seen by the King's physician. But somehow the Hall got an ugly name; the roast and boiled meats, the ducks, the chickens had time to drop into dust, before any human being now dared to enter in; or, indeed, had any right to enter in, for Sir John never came back to Morton; and as for my lady, some said she was dead, and some said she was mad and shut up in London, and some said Sir John had taken her to a convent abroad.

'And what did become of her?' asked we, creeping up to Mrs. Dawson.

'Nay, how should I know?'

'But what do you think?' we asked pertinaciously.

'I cannot tell. I have heard that after Sir John was killed at the battle of the Boyne[18] she got loose and came wandering back to Morton, to her old nurse's house; but, indeed, she was mad then out and out, and I've no doubt Sir John had seen it coming on. She used to have visions and dream dreams: and some thought her a prophetess; and some thought her fairly crazy. What she said about the Mortons was awful. She doomed them to die out of the land, and their house to be razed to the ground, while pedlars and huxters such as her own people, her father, had been should dwell where the knightly Mortons had once lived. One winter's night she strayed away, and the next morning they found the poor crazy woman frozen to death in Drumble meeting-house yard; and the Mr. Morton who had succeeded to Sir John had her decently buried where she was found, by the side of her father's grave.'

We were silent for a time. 'And when was the old Hall opened, Mrs. Dawson, please?'

'Oh! when the Mr. Morton, our Squire Morton's grandfather, came into possession. He was a distant cousin of Sir John's, a much quieter kind of man. He had all the old rooms opened wide, and aired, and fumigated; and the strange fragments of musty food were collected and burnt in the yard; but somehow that old dining-parlour had always a charnel-house smell, and no one ever liked making merry in it – thinking of the grey old preachers, whose ghosts might be even then scenting the meats afar off, and trooping unbidden to a feast, that was not that of which they were baulked. I was glad for one when the Squire's father built another dining-room; and no servant in the house will go an errand into the old dining-parlour after dark, I can assure ye.'

'I wonder if the way the last Mr. Morton had to sell his land to the people at Drumble had anything to do with old Lady Morton's prophecy,' said my mother, musingly.

'Not at all,' said Mrs. Dawson, sharply. 'My lady was crazy, and her words not to be minded. I should like to see the cotton-spinners of Drumble offer to purchase land from the Squire. Besides, there's a strict entail now.[19] They can't purchase the land if they would. A set of trading pedlars indeed!'

I remember Ethelinda and I looked at each other at this word 'pedlars;' which was the very word she had put into Sir John's mouth when taunting his wife with her father's low birth and calling. We thought, 'We shall see.'

Alas! we have seen.

Soon after that evening our good old friend Mrs. Dawson died. I remember it well, because Ethelinda and I were put into mourning for the first time in our lives. A dear little brother of ours had died only the year before, and then my father and mother had decided that we were too young; that there was no necessity for their incurring the expense of black frocks. We mourned for the little delicate darling in our hearts, I know; and to this day I often wonder what it would have been to have had a brother. But when Mrs. Dawson died it became a sort of duty we owed to the Squire's family to go into black, and very proud and pleased Ethelinda and I were with our new frocks. I remember dreaming Mrs. Dawson was alive again, and crying, because I thought my new frock would be taken away from me. But all this has nothing to do with Morton Hall.

When I first became aware of the greatness of the Squire's station in life, his family consisted of himself, his wife (a frail delicate lady), his only son, 'little master,' as Mrs. Dawson was allowed to call him, 'the young Squire,' as we in the village always termed him. His name was John Marmaduke. He was always called John; and after Mrs. Dawson's story of the old Sir John, I used to wish he might not bear that ill-omened name. He used to ride through the village in his bright scarlet coat, his long fair curling hair falling over his lace collar, and his broad black hat and feather shading his merry blue eyes. Ethelinda and I thought then, and I always shall think, there never was such a boy. He had a fine high spirit too of his own, and once horse-whipped a groom twice as big as himself, who had thwarted him. To see him and Miss Phillis go tearing through the village on their pretty Arabian horses, laughing as they met the west wind, and their long golden curls flying behind them, you would have thought them brother and sister, rather than nephew and aunt; for Miss Phillis was the Squire's sister, much younger than himself; indeed at the time I speak of, I don't think she could have been above seventeen, and the young Squire, her nephew, was nearly ten. I remember Mrs. Dawson sending for my mother and me up to the Hall that we might see Miss Phillis dressed ready to go with her brother to a ball given at some great lord's house to Prince William of Gloucester, nephew to good old George the Third.[20]

When Mrs. Elizabeth, Mrs. Morton's maid, saw us at tea in Mrs. Dawson's room, she asked Ethelinda and me if we would not like to come into Miss Phillis's dressing-room, and watch her dress; and then she said, if we could promise to keep from touching anything she would make interest for us to go. We would have promised to stand on our heads, and would have tried to do so too, to earn such a privilege. So in we went, and stood together hand-in-hand up in a corner out of the way, feeling very red, and shy, and hot, till Miss Phillis put us at our ease by playing all manner of comical tricks, just to make us laugh, which at last we did outright in spite of all our endeavours to be grave, lest Mrs. Elizabeth should complain of us to my mother. I recollect the scent of the *maréchale* powder with which Miss Phillis's hair was just sprinkled; and how she shook her head, like a young colt, to work the hair loose which Mrs. Elizabeth was straining up over a cushion. Then Mrs. Elizabeth would try a little of Mrs. Morton's rouge; and Miss Phillis would wash it off with a wet towel, saying that she liked her own paleness better than any performer's colour; and when Mrs. Elizabeth wanted just to touch her cheeks once more, she hid herself behind the great arm-chair, peeping out with her sweet merry face, first at one side and then at another, till we all heard the Squire's voice at the door, asking her, if she was dressed, to come and show herself to Madam, her sister-in-law; for, as I said, Mrs. Morton was a great invalid, and unable to go out to any grand parties like this. We were all silent in an instant; and even Mrs. Elizabeth thought no more of the rouge, but how to get Miss Phillis's beautiful blue dress on quick enough. She had cherry-coloured knots in her hair, and her breast-knots were of the same ribbon. Her gown was open in front, to a quilted white silk skirt. We felt very shy of her as she stood there fully dressed – she looked so much grander than anything we had ever seen; and it was like a relief when Mrs. Elizabeth told us to go down to Mrs. Dawson's parlour, where my mother was sitting all this time.

Just as we were telling how merry and comical Miss Phillis had been, in came a footman. 'Mrs. Dawson,' said he, 'the Squire bids me ask you to go with Mrs. Sidebotham into the west parlour, to have a look at Miss Morton before she goes.' We went too, clinging to my mother. Miss Phillis looked rather shy as we came in, and stood just by the door. I think we all must have shown her that we had never seen anything so beautiful, as she was, in our lives before; for she went very scarlet at our fixed gaze of admiration, and to relieve herself she began to play all manner of antics, whirling round, and making cheeses[21] with her rich silk petticoat, unfurling her fan (a present from Madam to complete her dress), and peeping first on one side and then on the other, just as she had done upstairs; and then catching hold of her nephew, and insisting that he should dance a minuet with her until the carriage came, which proposal made him very angry, as it was an insult to his manhood (at nine years old) to suppose he could dance. 'It was all very well for girls to make fools of themselves,' he said, 'but it did not do for men.' And Ethelinda and I thought we had never heard so fine a speech before. But the carriage came before we had half-feasted our eyes enough; and the Squire came from his wife's room to order the little master to bed, and hand his sister to the carriage.

I remember a good deal of talk about royal dukes and unequal marriages that night. I believe Miss Phillis did dance with Prince William; and I have often heard that she bore away the bell at the ball, and that no one came near her for beauty and pretty merry ways. In a day or two after I saw her scampering through the village, looking just as she did before she had danced with a royal duke. We all thought she would marry some one great, and used to look out for the lord who was to take her away. But poor Madam died, and there was no one but Miss Phillis to comfort her brother, for the young Squire was gone away to some great school down south; and Miss Phillis grew grave, and reined in her pony to keep by the Squire's side, when he rode out on his steady old mare in his lazy careless way.

We did not hear so much of the doings at the hall now Mrs. Dawson was dead; so I cannot tell how it was; but by-and-by there was a talk of bills that were once paid weekly, being now allowed to run to quarter-day; and then, instead of being settled every quarter-day, they were put off to Christmas; and many said they had hard enough work to get their money then. A buzz went through the village that the young Squire played high at college, and that he made away with more money than his father could afford. But when he came down to Morton, he was as handsome as ever; and I, for one, never believed evil of him; though I'll allow others might cheat him, and he never suspect it. His aunt was as fond of him as ever; and he of her. Many is the time I have seen them out walking together, sometimes sad enough, sometimes merry as ever. By-and-by, my father heard of sales of small pieces of land, not included in the entail; and at last, things got so bad, that the very crops were sold yet green upon the ground, for any price folks would give, so that there was but ready money paid. The Squire at length gave way entirely, and never left the house; and the young master in London; and poor Miss Phillis used to go about trying to see after the workmen and labourers, and save what she could. By this time she would be above thirty; Ethelinda and I were nineteen and twenty-one when my mother died, and that was some years before this. Well, at last the Squire died; they do say of a broken heart at his son's extravagance; and, though the lawyers kept it very close, it began to be rumoured that Miss Phillis's fortune had gone too. Any way the creditors came down on the estate like wolves. It was entailed, and it could not be sold; but they put it into the hands of a lawyer who was to get what he could out of it, and have no pity for the poor young Squire, who had not a roof for his head. Miss Phillis went to live by herself in a little cottage in the village, at the end of the property, which the lawyer allowed her to have because he could not let it to any one, it was so tumbledown and old. We never knew what she lived on, poor lady, but she said she was well in health, which was all we durst ask about. She came to see my father just before he died; and he seemed made bold with the feeling that he was a dying man; so he asked, what I had longed to know for many a year, where was the young Squire; he had never been seen in Morton since his father's funeral. Miss Phillis said he was gone abroad; but in what part he was then, she herself hardly knew; only she had a feeling that, sooner or later, he would come back to the old place; where she should strive to keep a home for him whenever he was tired of wandering about, and trying to make his fortune.

'Trying to make his fortune still?' asked my father, his questioning eyes saying more than his words. Miss Phillis shook her head with a sad meaning in her face; and we understood it all. He was at some French gaming-table, if he was not at an English one.

Miss Phillis was right. It might be a year after my father's death when he came back, looking old and grey and worn. He came to our door just after we had barred it one winter's evening. Ethelinda and I still lived at the farm, trying to keep it up and make it pay; but it was hard work. We heard a step coming up the straight pebble-walk; and then it stopped right at our door, under the very porch, and we heard a man's breathing, quick and short.

'Shall I open the door?' said I.

'No, wait!' said Ethelinda; for we lived alone, and there was no cottage near us. We held our breaths. There came a knock.

'Who's there?' I cried.

'Where does Miss Morton live – Miss Phillis?'

We were not sure if we would answer him; for she, like us, lived alone.

'Who's there?' again said I.

'Your master,' he answered, proud and angry. 'My name is John Morton. Where does Miss Phillis live?'

We had the door unbarred in a trice, and begged him to come in; to pardon our rudeness. We would have given him of our best as was his due from us; but he only listened to the directions we gave him to his aunt's, and took no notice of our apologies.

CHAPTER II.

UP to this time we had felt it rather impertinent to tell each other of our individual silent wonder as to what Miss Phillis lived on; but I know in our hearts we each thought about it, with a kind of respectful pity for her fallen low estate. Miss Phillis, that we remembered like an angel for beauty, and like a little princess for the imperious sway she exercised, and which was such sweet compulsion that we had all felt proud to be her slaves; Miss Phillis was now a worn, plain woman, in homely dress, tending towards old age; and looking – (at that time I dared not have spoken so insolent a thought, not even to myself) – but she did look as if she had hardly the proper nourishing food she required. One day, I remember Mrs. Jones the butcher's wife – (she was a Drumble person) – saying in her saucy way, that she was not surprised to see Miss Morton so bloodless and pale, for she only treated herself to a Sunday's dinner of meat, and lived on slop and bread-and-butter[22] all the rest of the week. Ethelinda put on her severe face – a look that I am afraid of to this day – and said, 'Mrs. Jones, do you suppose Miss Morton can eat your half-starved meat? You do not know how choice and dainty she is, as becomes one born and bred like her. What was it we had to bring for her only last Saturday from the grand new butcher's in Drumble, Biddy?' – (We took our eggs to market in Drumble every Saturday, for the cotton-spinners would give us a higher price than the Morton people; the more fools they!)

I thought it rather cowardly of Ethelinda to put the story-telling on me; but she always thought a great deal of saving her soul; more than I did, I am afraid, for I made answer, as bold as a lion, 'Two sweat-breads, at a shilling a-piece; and a fore-quarter of house-lamb,[23] at eighteen-pence a pound.' So off went Mrs. Jones in a huff, saying 'their meat was good enough for Mrs. Donkin the great mill-owner's widow, and might serve a beggarly Morton any day.' When we were alone, I said to Ethelinda, 'I'm afraid we shall have to pay for our lies at the great day of account,' and Ethelinda answered very sharply – (she's a good sister in the main) – 'Speak for yourself, Biddy. I never said a word. I only asked questions. How could I help it if you told lies? I'm sure I wondered at you, how glib you spoke out what was not true.' But I knew she was glad I told the lies in her heart.

After the poor Squire came to live with his aunt, Miss Phillis, we ventured to speak a bit to ourselves. We were sure they were pinched. They looked like it. He had a bad hacking cough at times; though he was so dignified and proud he would never cough when any one was near. I have seen him up before it was day, sweeping the dung off the roads, to try and get enough to manure the little plot of ground behind the cottage, which Miss Phillis had let alone, but which her nephew used to dig in and till; for, said he, one day, in his grand slow way, 'he was always fond of experiments in agriculture.' Ethelinda and I do believe that the two or three score of cabbages he raised were all they had to live on that winter, besides the bit of meal and tea they got at the village shop.

One Friday night I said to Ethelinda, 'It is a shame to take these eggs to Drumble to sell, and never to offer one to the Squire, on whose lands we were born.' She answered, 'I have thought so many a time; but how can we do it? I, for one, dare not offer them to the Squire; and as for Miss Phillis it would seem like impertinence.' 'I'll try at it,' said I.

So that night I took some eggs – fresh yellow eggs from our own pheasant hen,[24] the like of which there were not for twenty miles round – and I laid them softly after dusk on one of the little stone seats in the porch of Miss Phillis's cottage. But, alas! when we went to market at Drumble, early the next morning, there were my eggs all shattered and splashed, making an ugly yellow pool in the road just in front of the cottage. I had meant to have followed it up by a chicken or so; but I saw now that it would never do. Miss Phillis came now and then to call on us; she was a little more high and distant than she had been when a girl, and we felt we must keep our place. I suppose we had affronted the young Squire, for he never came near our house.

Well! there came a hard winter, and provisions rose; and Ethelinda and I had much ado to make ends meet. If it had not been for my sister's good management, we should have been in debt I know; but she proposed that we should go without dinner, and only have a breakfast and a tea, to which I agreed, you may be sure.

One baking day I had made some cakes for tea – potato-cakes we called them. They had a savoury hot smell about them; and, to tempt Ethelinda, who was not quite well, I cooked a rasher of bacon. Just as we were sitting down Miss Phillis knocked at our door. We let her in. God only knows how white and haggard she looked. The heat of our kitchen made her totter, and for a while she could not speak. But all the time she looked at the food on the table as if she feared to shut her eyes lest it should all vanish away. It was an eager stare like that of some animal, poor soul! 'If I durst,' said Ethelinda, wishing to ask her to share our meal, but being afraid to speak out. I did not speak, but handed her the good hot buttered cake; on which she seized, and putting it up to her lips as if to taste it, she fell back in her chair, crying.

We had never seen a Morton cry before; and it was something awful. We stood silent and aghast. She recovered herself, but did not taste the food; on the contrary, she covered it up with both her hands, as if afraid of losing it. 'If you'll allow me,' said she, in a stately kind of way to make up for our having seen her crying, 'I'll take it to my nephew.' And she got up to go away; but she could hardly stand for very weakness, and had to sit down again; she smiled at us, and said she was a little dizzy, but it would soon go off; but as she smiled, the bloodless lips were drawn far back over her teeth, making her face seem somehow like a death's head. 'Miss Morton,' said I, 'do honour us by taking tea with us this once. The Squire, your father, once took a luncheon with my father, and we are proud of it to this day.' I poured her out some tea, which she drank; the food she shrank away from as if the very sight of it turned her sick again. But when she rose to go she looked at it with her sad wolfish eyes, as if she could not leave it; and at last she broke into a low cry, and said, 'Oh, Bridget, we are starving! we are starving for want of food! I can bear it; I don't mind; but he suffers, oh, how he suffers! Let me take him food for this one night.'

We could hardly speak; our hearts were in our throats, and the tears ran down our cheeks like rain. We packed up a basket, and carried it to her very door, never venturing to speak a word, for we knew what it must have cost her to say that. When we left her at the cottage, we made her our usual deep courtesy, but she fell upon our necks, and kissed us. For several nights after she hovered round our house about dusk; but she would never come in again, and face us in candle or fire light, much less meet us by daylight. We took out food to her as regularly as might be, and gave it to her in silence, and with the deepest courtesies we could make, we felt so honoured. We had many plans now she had permitted us to know of her distress. We hoped she would allow us to go on serving her in some way as became us as Sideboth-ams. But one night she never came; we stayed[a] out in the cold bleak wind looking into the dark for her thin worn figure; all in vain. Late the next after-noon the young Squire lifted the latch, and stood right in the middle of our house-place.[25] The roof was low overhead, and made lower by the deep beams supporting the floor above; he stooped as he looked at us, and tried to form words, but no sound came out of his lips. I never saw such gaunt woe; no, never! At last he took me by the shoulder, and led me out of the house.

'Come with me!' he said, when we were in the open air, as if that gave him strength to speak audibly. I needed no second word. We entered Miss Phillis's cottage; a liberty I had never taken before. What little furniture was there, it was clear to be seen were cast-off fragments of the old splendour of Morton Hall. No fire. Grey wood ashes[26] lay on the hearth. An old settee, once white and gold, now doubly shabby in its fall from its former estate. On it lay Miss Phillis, very pale; very still; her eyes shut.

'Tell me!' he gasped. 'Is she dead? I think she is asleep; but she looks so strange – as if she might be –' He could not say the awful word again. I stooped, and felt no warmth; only a cold chill atmosphere seemed to sur-round her.

'She is dead!' I replied at length. 'Oh, Miss Phillis! Miss Phillis!' and, like a fool, I began to cry. But he sate down without a tear, and looked vacantly at the empty hearth. I dared not cry any more when I saw him so stony sad. I did not know what to do. I could not leave him; and yet I had no excuse for staying. I went up to Miss Phillis, and softly arranged the grey ragged locks about her face.

'Aye!' said he. 'She must be laid out. Who so fit to do it as you and your sister, children of good old Robert Sidebotham.'

'Oh! my master,' I said, 'this is no fit place for you. Let me fetch my sister to sit up with me all night; and honour us by sleeping at our poor little cottage.'

I did not expect he would have done it; but after a few minutes' silence he agreed to my proposal. I hastened home, and told Ethelinda, and both of us crying, we heaped up the fire, and spread the table with food, and made up a bed in one corner of the floor. While I stood ready to go I saw Ethelinda open the great chest in which we kept our treasures; and out she took a fine Holland shift that had been one of my mother's wedding shifts; and, seeing what she was after, I went upstairs and brought down a piece of rare old lace, a good deal darned to be sure, but still old Brussels point, bequeathed to me long ago by my god-mother, Mrs. Dawson. We huddled these things under our cloaks, locked the door behind us, and set out to do all we could now for poor Miss Phillis. We found the Squire sitting just as we left him; I hardly knew if he understood me when I told him how to unlock our door, and gave him the key; though I spoke as distinctly as ever I could for the choking in my throat. At last he rose and went; and Ethelinda and I composed her poor thin limbs to decent rest, and wrapped her in the fine Holland shift; and then I plaited up my lace into a close cap to tie up the wasted features. When all was done we looked upon her from a little distance.

'A Morton to die of hunger!' said Ethelinda solemnly. 'We should not have dared to think that such a thing was within the chances of life; do you remember that evening, when you and I were little children, and she a merry young lady peeping at us from behind her fan?'

We did not cry any more; we felt very still and awe-struck. After a while I said, 'I wonder if after all the young Squire did go to our house. He had a strange look about him. If I dared I would go and see.' I opened the door; the night was black as pitch; the air very still. 'I'll go,' said I; and off I went, not meeting a creature, for it was long past eleven. I reached our house; the window was long and low, and the shutters were old and shrunk. I could peep between them well, and see all that was going on. He was there sitting over the fire, never shedding a tear; but seeming as if he saw his past life in the embers. The food we had prepared was untouched. Once or twice, during my long watch (I was more than an hour away), he turned towards the food, and made as though he would have eaten it, and then shuddered back; but at last he seized it, and tore it with his teeth, and laughed and rejoiced over it like some starved animal. I could not keep from crying then. He gorged himself with great morsels; and when he could eat no more it seemed as if his strength for suffering had come back; he threw himself on the bed, and such a passion of despair I never heard of, much less ever saw. I could not bear to witness it. The dead Miss Phillis lay calm and still; her trials were over. I would go back and watch with Ethelinda.

When the pale grey morning dawn stole in, making us shiver and shake after our vigil, the Squire returned. We were both mortal afraid of him, we knew not why. He looked quiet enough – the lines were worn deep before – no new traces were there. He stood and looked at his aunt for a minute or two. Then he went up into the loft above the room where we were; he brought a small paper parcel down; bade us keep on our watch yet a little time. First one and then the other of us went home to get some food. It was a bitter black frost; no one was out, who could stop indoors; and those who were out cared not to stop to speak. Towards afternoon the air darkened, and a great snow-storm came on. We durst not be left, only one alone; yet at the cottage where Miss Phillis had lived there was neither fire nor fuel. So we sate and shivered and shook till morning. The Squire never came that night nor all next day.

'What must we do?' asked Ethelinda, broken down entirely. 'I shall die if I stop here another night. We must tell the neighbours and get help for the watch.'

'So we must,' said I, very low and grieved. I went out and told the news at the nearest house, taking care, you may be sure, never to speak of the hunger and cold Miss Phillis must have endured in silence. It was bad enough to have them come in, and make their remarks on the poor bits of furniture; for no one had known their bitter straits even as much as Ethelinda and me, and we had been shocked at the bareness of the place. I did hear that one or two of the more ill-conditioned had said, it was not for nothing we had kept the death to ourselves for two nights; that to judge from the lace on her cap there must have been some pretty pickings. Ethelinda would have contradicted this, but I bade her let it alone; it would save the memory of the proud Mortons from the shame that poverty is thought to be; and as for us, why we could live it down. But on the whole people came forward kindly; money was not wanting to bury her well, if not grandly as became her birth; and many a one was bidden to the funeral who might have looked after her a little more in her life-time. Among others was Squire Hargreaves from Bothwick Hall over the Moors. He was some kind of far-away cousin to the Mortons. So when he came he was asked to go chief mourner in Squire Morton's strange absence, which I should have wondered at the more if I had not thought him almost crazy when I watched his ways through the shutter that night. Squire Hargreaves started when they paid him the compliment of asking him to take the head of the coffin.

'Where is her nephew?' asked he.

'No one has seen him since eight o'clock last Thursday morning.'

'But I saw him at noon on Thursday,' said Squire Hargreaves with a round oath. 'He came over the moors to tell me of his aunt's death; and to ask me to give him a little money to bury her, on the pledge of his gold shirt-buttons. He said I was a cousin, and could pity a gentleman in such sore need. That the buttons were his mother's first gift to him; and that I was to keep them safe, for some day he would make his fortune and come back to redeem them. He had not known his aunt was so ill, or he would have parted with these buttons sooner, though he held them as more precious than he could tell me. I gave him money; but I could not find in my heart to take the buttons. He bade me not tell of all this; but when a man is missing it is my duty to give all the clue I can.'

And so their poverty was blazoned abroad! But folk forgot it all in the search for the Squire on the moor side. Two days they searched in vain; the third, upwards of a hundred men turned out hand-in-hand, step to step, to leave no foot of ground unsearched. They found him stark and stiff, with Squire Hargreaves' money, and his mother's gold buttons, safe in his waist-coat pocket.

And we laid him down by the side of his poor Aunt Phillis.[a]

After the Squire, John Marmaduke Morton, had been found dead in that sad way, on the dreary moors, the creditors seemed to lose all hold on the property; which indeed, during the seven years they had had it, they had drained as dry as a sucked orange. But for a long time no one seemed to know who rightly was the owner of Morton Hall and lands. The old house fell out of repair; the chimneys were full of starlings' nests; the flags in the terrace in front were hidden by the long grass; the panes in the windows were broken, no one knew how or why, for the children of the village got up a tale that the house was haunted. Ethelinda and I went sometimes in the summer mornings, and gathered some of the roses that were being strangled by the bind-weed that spread over all; and we used to try and weed the old flower-garden a little; but we were no longer young, and the stooping made our backs ache. Still we always felt happier, if we cleared but ever such a little space. Yet we did not go there willingly in the afternoons, and left the garden always long before the first slight shade of dusk.

We did not choose to ask the common people – many of them were weavers for the Drumble manufacturers, and no longer decent hedgers, and ditchers – we did not choose to ask them, I say, who was squire now, or where he lived. But one day, a great London lawyer came to the Morton Arms, and made a pretty stir. He came on behalf of a General Morton, who was squire now, though he was far away in India. He had been written to, and they had proved him heir, though he was a very distant cousin; farther back than Sir John, I think. And now he had sent word they were to take money of his that was in England, and put the house in thorough repair: for that three maiden sisters of his, who lived in some town in the north, would come and live at Morton Hall till his return. So the lawyer sent for a Drumble builder, and gave him directions. We thought it would have been prettier if he had hired John Cobb, the Morton builder, and joiner, he that had made the Squire's coffin, and the Squire's father's before that. Instead, came a troop of Drumble men, knocking, and tumbling about in the Hall, and making their jests up and down all those stately rooms. Ethelinda and I never went near the place till they were gone, bag, and baggage. And then what a change! the old casement windows, with their heavy leaded panes half over-grown with vines and roses, were taken away, and great staring sash windows were in their stead. New grates inside; all modern, new-fangled, and smoking, instead of the brass dogs which held the mighty logs of wood in the old Squire's time. The little square Turkey carpet under the dining table, which had served Miss Phillis, was not good enough for these new Mortons; the dining-room was all carpeted over. We peeped into the old dining-parlour;

that parlour where the dinner for the Puritan preachers had been laid out; the flag parlour as it had been called of late years. But it had a damp earthy smell, and was used as a lumber-room. We shut the door quicker than we had opened it. We came away disappointed. The Hall was no longer like our own honoured Morton Hall.

'After all, these three ladies are Mortons,' said Ethelinda to me. 'We must not forget that: we must go and pay our duty to them as soon as they have appeared in church.'

Accordingly we went. But we had heard, and seen a little of them before we paid our respects at the Hall. Their maid had been down in the village; their maid as she was called now; but a maid-of-all-work she had been until now, as she very soon let out when we questioned her. However, we were never proud; and she was a good honest farmer's daughter out of Northumberland. What work she did make with the Queen's English! The folk in Lancashire are said to speak broad; but I could always understand our own kindly tongue, whereas when Mrs. Turner told me her name, both Ethelinda and I could have sworn she said Donagh, and were afraid she was an Irishwoman. Her ladies were what you may call past the bloom of youth; Miss Sophronia – Miss Morton, properly – was just sixty; Miss Annabella, three years younger; and Miss Dorothy (or Baby, as they called her, when they were by themselves), was two years younger still. Mrs. Turner was very confidential to us, partly because I doubt not she had heard of our old connexion with the family, and partly because she was an arrant talker, and was glad of anybody who would listen to her. So we heard the very first week how each of the ladies had wished for the east bed-room; that which faced the north-east; which no one slept in in the old Squire's days; but there were two steps leading up into it, and said Miss Sophronia, she would never let a younger sister have a room more elevated than she had herself. She was the eldest, and she had a right to the steps. So she bolted herself in for two days while she unpacked her clothes, and then came out looking like a hen that has laid an egg, and defies any one to take that honour from her.

But her sisters were very deferential to her in general; that must be said. They never had more than two black feathers in their bonnets; while she had always three. Mrs. Turner said that once, when they thought Miss Annabella had been going to have an offer of marriage made her, Miss Sophronia had not objected to her wearing three that winter; but when it all ended in smoke, Miss Annabella had to pluck it out as became a younger sister. Poor Miss Annabella! she had been a beauty (Mrs. Turner said), and great things had been expected of her. Her brother, the General, and her mother had both spoilt her, rather than cross her unnecessarily, and so spoil her good looks; which old Mrs. Morton had always expected would make the fortune of the family. Her sisters were angry with her for not having married some great rich gentleman; though, as she used to say to Mrs.

Turner, how could she help it. She was willing enough, but no rich gentleman came to ask her. We agreed that it really was not her fault; but her sisters
thought it was: and now that she had lost her beauty, they were always casting it up what they would have done if they had had her gifts. There were
some Miss Burrells they had heard of,[27] each of whom had married a lord;
and these Miss Burrells had not been such great beauties. So Miss Sophronia used to work the question by the rule of three,[28] and put it in this way –
If Miss Burrell, with a tolerable pair of eyes, a snub nose, and a wide mouth,
married a baron, what rank of peer ought our pretty Annabella to have
espoused? And the worst was, Miss Annabella – who had never had any
ambition – wanted to have married a poor curate in her youth; but was
pulled up by her mother and sisters, reminding her of the duty she owed to
her family. Miss Dorothy had done her best – Miss Morton always praised
her for it. With not half the good looks of Miss Annabella, she had danced
with an honourable[29] at Harrogate three times running; and, even now, she
persevered in trying; which was more than could be said of Miss Annabella,
who was very broken-spirited.

I do believe Mrs. Turner told us all this before we had ever seen the
ladies. We had let them know, through Mrs. Turner, of our wish to pay them
our respects; so we ventured to go up to the front door, and rap modestly.
We had reasoned about it before, and agreed that if we were going in our
every-day clothes, to offer a little present of eggs, or to call on Mrs. Turner
(as she had asked us to do), the back door would have been the appropriate
entrance for us. But going, however humbly, to pay our respects and offer
our reverential welcome to the Miss Mortons, we took rank as their visitors,
and should go to the front door. We were shown up the wide stairs, along
the gallery, up two steps, into Miss Sophronia's room. She put away some
papers hastily as we came in. We heard afterwards that she was writing a
book, to be called 'The Female Chesterfield, or Letters from a Lady of Quality to her niece.'[30] And the little niece sate there in a high chair, with a flat
board tied to her back, and her feet in stocks on the rail of the chair, so that
she had nothing to do but listen to her aunt's letters; which were read aloud
to her as they were written, in order to mark their effect on her manners. I
was not sure whether Miss Sophronia liked our interruption; but I know
little Miss Cordelia Mannisty did.

'Is the young lady crooked?' asked Ethelinda, during a pause in our conversation. I had noticed that my sister's eyes would rest on the child;
although by an effort she sometimes succeeded in looking at something else
occasionally.

'No! indeed, ma'am,' said Miss Morton. 'But she was born in India, and
her backbone has never properly hardened. Besides I and my two sisters
each take charge of her for a week; and, their systems of education – I might
say non-education – differ so totally and entirely from my ideas, that when

Miss Mannisty comes to me, I consider myself fortunate if I can undo the – hem! – that has been done during a fortnight's absence. Cordelia, my dear, repeat to these good ladies the geography lesson you learnt this morning.'

Poor little Miss Mannisty began to tell us a great deal about some river in Yorkshire of which we had never heard, though I dare say we ought to, and then a great deal more about the towns that it passed by, and what they were famous for; and all I can remember – indeed could understand at the time – was that Pomfret was famous for Pomfret cakes,[31] which I knew before. But Ethelinda gasped for breath before it was done, she was so nearly choked up with astonishment; and when it was ended, she said, 'Pretty dear! it's wonderful!' Miss Morton looked a little displeased, and replied, 'Not at all. Good little girls can learn any thing they choose, even French verbs. Yes, Cordelia, they can. And to be good is better than to be pretty. We don't think about looks here. You may get down, child, and go into the garden, and take care you put your bonnet on, or you'll be all over freckles.' We got up to take leave at the same time, and followed the little girl out of the room. Ethelinda fumbled in her pocket.

'Here's sixpence, my dear, for you. Nay, I am sure you may take it from an old woman like me, to whom you've told over more geography than I ever thought there was out of the Bible.' For Ethelinda always maintained that the long chapters in the Bible which were all names, were geography; and though I knew well enough they were not, yet I had forgotten what the right word was,[32] so I let her alone; for one hard word did as well as another. Little Miss looked as if she was not sure if she might take it; but I suppose we had two kindly old faces, for at last the smile came into her eyes – not to her mouth – she had lived too much with grave and quiet people for that; and looking wistfully at us, she said:

'Thank you. But won't you go and see Aunt Annabella?' We said we should like to pay our respects to both her other aunts if we might take that liberty; and perhaps she would show us the way. But, at the door of a room, she stopped short, and said sorrowfully, 'I mayn't go in; it is not my week for being with Aunt Annabella;' and then she went slowly and heavily towards the garden-door.

'That child is cowed by somebody,' said I to Ethelinda.

'But she knows a deal of geography' – Ethelinda's speech was cut short by the opening of the door in answer to our knock. The once beautiful Miss Annabella Morton stood before us, and bade us enter. She was dressed in white, with a turned up velvet hat, and two or three short drooping black feathers in it. I should not like to say she rouged, but she had a very pretty colour in her cheeks; that much can do neither good nor harm. At first she looked so unlike anybody I had ever seen, that I wondered what the child could have found to like in her; for like her she did, that was very clear. But, when Miss Annabella spoke, I came under the charm. Her voice was very sweet and plaintive, and suited well with the kind of things she said; all about charms of nature, and tears, and grief, and such sort of talk, which reminded me rather of poetry – very pretty to listen to; though I never could understand it as well as plain comfortable prose. Still I hardly know why I liked Miss Annabella. I think I was sorry for her; though, whether I should have been if she had not put it in my head, I don't know. The room looked very comfortable; a spinnet in a corner to amuse herself with, and a good sofa to lie down upon. By-and-by, we got her to talk of her little niece, and she too had her system of education. She said she hoped to develop[a] the sensibilities, and to cultivate the tastes. While with her, her darling niece read works of imagination, and acquired all that Miss Annabella could impart of the fine arts. We neither of us quite knew what she was hinting at at the time; but afterwards, by dint of questioning little Miss, and using our own eyes and ears, we found that she read aloud to her aunt while she lay on the sofa; Santo Sebastiano, or the Young Protector,[33] was what they were deep in at this time; and, as it was in five volumes and the heroine spoke broken English – which required to be read twice over to make it intelligible – it lasted them a long time. She also learned to play on the spinnet; not much – for I never heard above two tunes; one of which was God save the King, and the other was not. But I fancy the poor child was lectured by one aunt, and frightened by the other's sharp ways and numerous fancies. She might well be fond of her gentle, pensive (Miss Annabella told me she was pensive, so I know I am right in calling her so) aunt with her soft voice, and her never ending novels, and the sweet scents, that hovered about the sleepy room.

No one tempted us towards Miss Dorothy's apartment when we left Miss Annabella; so we did not see the youngest Miss Morton this first day. We had each of us treasured up many little mysteries to be explained by our dictionary, Mrs. Turner.

'Who is little Miss Mannisty?' we asked in one breath, when we saw our friend from the Hall. And then we learnt that there had been a fourth – a younger Miss Morton, who was no beauty, and no wit, and no anything; so Miss Sophronia, her eldest sister, had allowed her to marry a Mr. Mannisty, and ever after spoke of her as 'my poor sister Jane.' She and her husband had gone out to India; and both had died there; and the General had made it a sort of condition with his sisters that they should take charge of the child, or else none of them liked children except Miss Annabella.

'Miss Annabella likes children!' said I. 'Then that's the reason children like her.'

'I can't say she likes children; for we never have any in our house but Miss Cordelia; but her she does like dearly.'

'Poor little Miss!' said Ethelinda, 'does she never get a game of play with other little girls?' And I am sure from that time Ethelinda considered her in a diseased state from this very circumstance, and that her knowledge of geography was one of the symptoms of the disorder; for she used often to say, 'I wish she did not know so much geography! I'm sure it is not quite right.'

Whether or not her geography was right I don't know; but the child pined for companions. A very few days after we had called – and yet long enough to have passed her into Miss Annabella's week – I saw Miss Cordelia in a corner of the church green, playing with awkward humility, along with some of the rough village girls, who were as expert at the game as she was unapt and slow. I hesitated a little, and at last I called to her.

'How do you, my dear?' I said. 'How come you here, so far from home?'

She reddened, and then looked up at me with her large serious eyes.

'Aunt Annabel sent me into the wood to meditate – and – and – it was very dull – and I heard these little girls playing and laughing – and I had my sixpence with me, and – it was not wrong, was it, ma'am? – I came to them and told one of them I would give it to her if she would ask the others to let me play with them.'

'But my dear, they are – some of them – very rough little children, and not fit companions for a Morton.'

'But, I am a Mannisty, ma'am!' she pleaded, with so much entreaty in her ways that, if I had not known what naughty bad girls some of them were, I could not have resisted her longing for companions of her own age. As it was, I was angry with them for having taken her sixpence; but, when she had told me which it was, and saw that I was going to reclaim it, she clung to me, and said: –

'Oh! don't, ma'am – you must not. I gave it to her quite of my own self.'

So I turned away; for there was truth in what the child said. But to this day I have never told Ethelinda what became of her sixpence. I took Miss Cordelia home with me while I changed my dress to be fit to take her back to the Hall. And on the way, to make up for her disappointment, I began talking of my dear Miss Phillis and her bright pretty youth. I had never named her name since her death to any one but Ethelinda – and that only on Sundays and quiet times. And I could not have spoken of her to a grown-up person; but somehow to Miss Cordelia it came out quite natural. Not of her latter days, of course; but of her pony, and her little black King Charles's dogs, and all the living creatures that were glad in her presence when first I knew her. And nothing would satisfy the child but I must go into the Hall garden and show her where Miss Phillis's garden had been. We were deep in our talk, and she was stooping down to clear the plot from weeds, when I heard a sharp voice cry out, 'Cordelia! Cordelia! Dirtying your frock with kneeling on the wet grass! It is not my week: but I shall tell your Aunt Annabella of you.'

And the window was shut down with a jerk. It was Miss Dorothy. And I felt almost as guilty as poor little Miss Cordelia: for I had heard from Mrs.

Turner that we had given great offence to Miss Dorothy by not going to call on her in her room that day on which we had paid our respects to her sisters; and I had a sort of an idea that seeing Miss Cordelia with me was almost as much of a fault as the kneeling down on the wet grass. So I thought I would take the bull by the horns.

'Will you take me to your Aunt Dorothy, my dear?' said I.

The little girl had no longing to go into her aunt Dorothy's room, as she had so evidently had at Miss Annabella's door. On the contrary, she pointed it out to me at a safe distance, and then went away in the measured step she was taught to use in that house; where such things as running, going upstairs two steps at a time, or jumping down three, were considered undignified and vulgar. Miss Dorothy's room was the least prepossessing of any. Somehow it had a north-east look about it, though it did face direct south; and, as for Miss Dorothy herself, she was more like a 'Cousin Betty' than anything else; if you know what a Cousin Betty is, and perhaps it is too old-fashioned a word to be understood by any one who has learnt the foreign languages: but when I was a girl, there used to be poor crazy women rambling about the country, one or two in a district. They never did any harm that I know of; they might have been born idiots, poor creatures! or crossed in love, who knows? But they roamed the country, and were well known at the farm-houses; where they often got food and shelter for as long a time as their rest-less minds would allow them to stay in any one place; and the farmer's wife would, maybe, rummage up a ribbon, or a feather, or a smart old breadth of silk, to please the harmless vanity of these poor crazy women; and they would go about so bedizened sometimes that, as we called them always 'Cousin Betty,' we made it into a kind of proverb for any one dressed in a fly-away showy style, and said they were like a Cousin Betty. So now you know what I mean that Miss Dorothy was like. Her dress was white, like Miss Annabella's; but, instead of the black velvet hat her sister wore, she had on, even in the house, a small black silk bonnet. This sounds as if it should be less like a Cousin Betty than a hat;[34] but wait till I tell you how it was lined – with strips of red silk, broad near the face, narrow near the brim; for all the world like the rays of the rising sun, as they are painted on the public-house sign. And her face was like the sun; as round as an apple; and with rouge on, without any doubt: indeed, she told me once, a lady was not dressed unless she had put her rouge on. Mrs. Turner told us she studied reflections a great deal; not that she was a thinking woman in general, I should say; and that this rayed lining was the fruit of her study. She had her hair pulled together, so that her forehead was quite covered with it; and I won't deny that I rather wished myself at home, as I stood facing her in the door-way. She pretended she did not know who I was, and made me tell all about myself; and then it turned out she knew all about me, and she hoped I had recovered from my fatigue the other day.

'What fatigue?' asked I, immovably. Oh! she had understood I was very much tired after visiting her sisters; otherwise, of course, I should not have felt it too much to come on to her room. She kept hinting at me in so many ways, that I could have asked her gladly to slap my face and have done with it, only I wanted to make Miss Cordelia's peace with her for kneeling down and dirtying her frock. I did say what I could to make things straight; but I don't know if I did any good. Mrs. Turner told me how suspicious and jealous she was of every body, and of Miss Annabella in particular, who had been set over her in her youth because of her beauty; but, since it had faded, Miss Morton and Miss Dorothy had never ceased pecking at her; and Miss Dorothy worst of all. If it had not been for little Miss Cordelia's love, Miss Annabella might have wished to die; she did often wish she had had the smallpox as a baby. Miss Morton was stately and cold to her, as one who had not done her duty to her family, and was put in the corner for her bad behaviour. Miss Dorothy was continually talking at her, and particularly dwelling on the fact of her being the older sister. Now she was but two years older; and was still so pretty and gentle looking, that I should have forgotten it continually but for Miss Dorothy.

The rules that were made for Miss Cordelia! She was to eat her meals standing, that was one thing! Another was, that she was to drink two cups of cold water before she had any pudding; and it just made the child loathe cold water. Then there were ever so many words she might not use; each aunt had her own set of words which were ungenteel or improper for some reason or another. Miss Dorothy would never let her say 'red;' it was always to be pink, or crimson, or scarlet. Miss Cordelia used at one time to come to us, and tell us she had a 'pain at her chest' so often, that Ethelinda and I began to be uneasy, and questioned Mrs. Turner to know if her mother had died of consumption; and many a good pot of currant jelly have I given her, and only made her pain at the chest worse; for – would you believe it? – Miss Morton told her never to say she had got a stomach-ache, for that it was not proper to say so. I had heard it called by a worse name still[35] in my youth, and so had Ethelinda; and we sat and wondered to ourselves how it was that some kinds of pain were genteel and others were not. I said that old families, like the Mortons, generally thought it showed good blood to have their complaints as high in the body as they could – brain-fevers and headaches had a better sound, and did perhaps belong more to the aristocracy. I thought I had got the right view in saying this, when Ethelinda would put in that she had often heard of Lord Toffey having the gout and being lame, and that nonplussed me. If there is one thing I do dislike more than another, it is a person saying something on the other side when I am trying to make up my mind – how can I reason if I am to be disturbed by another person's arguments?

But though I tell all these peculiarities of the Miss Mortons, they were good women in the main: even Miss Dorothy had her times of kindness, and really did love her little niece, though she was always laying traps to catch her doing wrong. Miss Morton I got to respect, if I never liked her. They would ask us up to tea; and we would put on our best gowns; and taking the house-key in my pocket, we used to walk slowly through the village, wishing that people who had been living in our youth could have seen us now, going by invitation to drink tea with the family at the Hall – not in the housekeeper's room, but with the family, mind you. But since they began to weave in Morton, everybody seemed too busy to notice us; so we were fain to be content with reminding each other how we should never have believed it in our youth that we could have lived to this day. After tea, Miss Morton would set us to talk of the real old family, whom they had never known; and you may be sure we told of all their pomp and grandeur and stately ways; but Ethelinda and I never spoke of what was to ourselves like the memory of a sad, terrible dream. So they thought of the Squire in his coach-and-four as High Sheriff, and Madam lying in her morning-room in her Genoa velvet wrapping-robe, all over peacock's eyes (it was a piece of velvet the Squire brought back from Italy, when he had been the grand tour), and Miss Phillis going to a ball at a great lord's house and dancing with a royal duke. The three ladies were never tired of listening to the tale of the splendour that had been going on here, while they and their mother had been starving in genteel poverty up in Northumberland; and as for Miss Cordelia, she sate on a stool at her Aunt Annabella's knee, her hand in her aunt's, and listened, open-mouthed and unnoticed, to all we could say.

One day, the child came crying to our house. It was the old story; Aunt Dorothy had been so unkind to Aunt Annabella! The little girl said she would run away to India, and tell her uncle the General, and seemed in such a paroxysm of anger, and grief, and despair, that a sudden thought came over me. I thought I would try and teach her something of the deep sorrow that lies awaiting all at some part of their lives, and of the way in which it ought to be borne, by telling her of Miss Phillis's love and endurance for her wasteful, handsome nephew. So from little, I got to more, and I told her all; the child's great eyes filling slowly with tears, which brimmed over and came rolling down her cheeks unnoticed as I spoke. I scarcely needed to make her promise not to speak about all this to any one. She said, 'I could not – no! not even to Aunt Annabella.' And to this day she never has named it again, not even to me; but she tried to make herself more patient, and more silently helpful in the strange household among whom she was cast.[36]

By-and-by, Miss Morton grew pale and grey, and worn, amid all her stiffness. Mrs. Turner whispered to us that for all her stern, unmoved looks, she was ill unto death; that she had been secretly to see the great doctor at Drumble; and he had told her she must set her house in order. Not even her sisters knew this; but it preyed upon Mrs. Turner's mind and she told us. Long after this, she kept up her week of discipline with Miss Cordelia; and walked in her straight, soldier-like way about the village, scolding people for having too large families, and burning too much coal, and eating too much butter. One morning she sent Mrs. Turner for her sisters; and, while she was away, she rummaged out an old locket made of the four Miss Mortons' hair when they were all children; and, threading the eye of the locket with a piece of brown ribbon, she tied it round Cordelia's neck, and kissing her, told her she had been a good girl, and had cured herself of stooping; that she must fear God and honour the King; and that now she might go and have a holiday. Even while the child looked at her in wonder at the unusual tenderness with which this was said, a grim spasm passed over her face, and Cordelia ran in affright to call Mrs. Turner. But when she came, and the other two sisters came, she was quite herself again. She had her sisters in her room alone when she wished them goodbye; so no one knows what she said, or how she told them (who were thinking of her as in health) that the signs of near-approaching death, which the doctor had foretold, were upon her. One thing they both agreed in saying – and it was much that Miss Dorothy agreed in anything – that she bequeathed her sitting-room up the two steps, to Miss Annabella as being next in age. Then they left her room crying, and went both together into Miss Annabella's room, sitting hand in hand, (for the first time since childhood I should think,) listening for the sound of the little hand-bell which was to be placed close by her, in case, in her agony, she required Mrs. Turner's presence. But it never rang. Noon became twilight. Miss Cordelia stole in from the garden with its long, black, green shadows, and strange eerie sounds of the night wind through the trees, and crept to the kitchen fire. At last Mrs. Turner knocked at Miss Morton's door, and hearing no reply, went in and found her cold and dead in her chair.

I suppose that sometime or other we had told them of the funeral the old Squire had; Miss Phillis's father, I mean. He had had a procession of tenantry half-a-mile long to follow him to the grave. Miss Dorothy sent for me to tell her what tenantry of her brother's could follow Miss Morton's coffin; but what with people working in mills, and land having passed away from the family, we could but muster up twenty people, men and women and all; and one or two were dirty enough to be paid for their loss of time.

Poor Miss Annabella did not wish to go into the room up two steps; nor yet dared she stay behind; for Miss Dorothy, in a kind of spite for not having had it bequeathed to her, kept telling Miss Annabella it was her duty to occupy it; that it was Miss Sophronia's dying wish, and that she should not wonder if Miss Sophronia were to haunt Miss Annabella, if she did not leave her warm room, full of ease and sweet scent, for the grim north-east chamber. We told Mrs. Turner we were afraid Miss Dorothy would lord it sadly over Miss Annabella, and she only shook her head; which, from so talkative a woman, meant a great deal. But, just as Miss Cordelia had begun to droop, the General came home, without any one knowing he was coming. Sharp and sudden was the word with him. He sent Miss Cordelia off to school; but not before she had had time to tell us that she loved her uncle dearly, in spite of his quick hasty ways. He carried his sisters off to Cheltenham;[37] and it was astonishing how young they made themselves look before they came back again. He was always here, there, and everywhere; and very civil to us into the bargain; leaving the key of the Hall with us whenever they went from home. Miss Dorothy was afraid of him, which was a blessing, for it kept her in order; and really I was rather sorry when she died, and, as for Miss Annabella, she fretted after her till she injured her health, and Miss Cordelia had to leave school to come and keep her company. Miss Cordelia was not pretty; she had too sad and grave a look for that; but she had winning ways, and was to have her uncle's fortune some day, so I expected to hear of her being soon snapt up. But the General said her husband was to take the name of Morton; and what did my young lady do but begin to care for one of the great mill-owners at Drumble, as if there were not all the lords and commons to choose from besides? Mrs. Turner was dead; and there was no one to tell us about it; but I could see Miss Cordelia growing thinner and paler every time they came back to Morton Hall; and I longed to tell her to pluck up a spirit, and be above a cotton-spinner. One day, not half a year before the General's death, she came to see us, and told us, blushing like a rose, that her uncle had given his consent; and so, although 'he' had refused to take the name of Morton, and had wanted to marry her without a penny, and without her uncle's leave, it had all come right at last, and they were to be married at once; and their house was to be a kind of home for her Aunt Annabella, who was getting tired of being perpetually on the ramble with the General.

'Dear old friends!' said our young lady, 'You must like him. I am sure you will; he is so handsome, and brave, and good. Do you know, he says a relation of his ancestors lived at Morton Hall in the time of the Commonwealth.'

'His ancestors?' said Ethelinda. 'Has he got ancestors? That's one good point about him, at any rate. I didn't know cotton spinners had ancestors.'

'What is his name?' asked I.

'Mr. Marmaduke Carr,' said she, sounding each r with the old Northumberland burr, which was softened into a pretty pride and effort to give distinctness to each letter of the beloved name.

'Carr,' said I, 'Carr and Morton! Be it so! It was prophesied of old!' But she was too much absorbed in the thought of her own secret happiness to notice my poor sayings.

He was and is a good gentleman; and a real gentleman too. They never lived at Morton Hall. Just as I was writing this, Ethelinda came in with two pieces of news. Never again say I am superstitious! There is no one living in Morton that knows the tradition of Sir John Morton and Alice Carr; yet the very first part of the Hall the Drumble builder has pulled down is the old stone dining-parlour where the great dinner for the preachers mouldered away – flesh from flesh, crumb from crumb! And the street they are going to build right through the rooms through which Alice Carr was dragged in her agony of despair at her husband's loathing hatred is to be called Carr Street!

And Miss Cordelia has got a baby; a little girl; and writes in pencil two lines at the end of her husband's note, to say she means to call it Phillis.

Phillis Carr! I am glad he did not take the name of Morton. I like to keep the name of Phillis Morton in my memory very still and unspoken.

'MY FRENCH MASTER'

'My French Master' was first published in two parts in *Household Words*, 8 (17 and 24 December 1853), pp. 361–5, 388–93, one chapter in each part. It was collected in *Lizzie Leigh and Other Tales* (London: Chapman and Hall, 1855). It had previously been published in the Boston periodical *Littell's Living Age*, 2:4 (4 February 1854), pp. 270–78; and in *Harper's New Monthly Magazine*, 8 (February 1854), pp. 382–91. It was also reprinted in *Lizzie Leigh and Other Tales* (1865). The texts in *HW* and 1855 are very close; the differences are mainly punctuation.

Enid Duthie, 'Echoes of the French Revolution in the Work of Elizabeth Gaskell', *GSJ*, 2 (1988), pp. 34–40, 34, following *Chadwick*, p. 32, argues that M. de Chalabre is based on M. Rogier, an émigré who taught French and dancing in Knutsford; she is followed by *Uglow*, pp. 28–9. However, what is known about M. Rogier (Henry Green, *Knutsford, Its Traditions and History* (London: Smith, Elder & Co., 1859), pp. 134–6) makes this seem rather unlikely, and émigré teachers abounded in early nineteenth-century England. In May 1853, a few months before this story was published in December, EG had paid her first visit to Paris. Her hostess caught measles, and she went to stay with Mary Mohl (1793–1883), an Englishwoman who had long lived in Paris and who maintained a well-known literary salon. Several points in 'My French Master' seem to draw on this experience, and it is possible that it had its origin in an anecdote she heard at the Mohls. In July 1853 she stayed some days with William Duckworth (1795–1876) at Beechwood, Eling, Hampshire, on the edge of the New Forest, which also seems to be evoked by the story.

MY FRENCH MASTER.

———•———

CHAPTER I.

MY father's house was in the country, seven miles away from the nearest town. He had been an officer in the navy; but, as he had met with some accident that would disable him from ever serving again, he gave up his commission, and his half-pay.[1] He had a small private fortune, and my mother had not been penniless; so he purchased a house, and ten or twelve acres of land, and set himself up as an amateur farmer on a very small scale. My mother rejoiced over the very small scale of his operations; and when my father regretted, as he did very often, that no more land was to be purchased in the neighbourhood, I could see her setting herself a sum in her head, 'If on twelve acres he manages to lose a hundred pounds a year, what would be our loss on a hundred and fifty?' But when my father was pushed hard on the subject of the money he spent in his sailor-like farming, he had one constant retreat:

'Think of the health, and the pleasure we all of us take in the cultivation of the fields around us! It is something for us to do, and to look forward to every day.' And this was so true that as long as my father confined himself to these arguments, my mother left him unmolested: but to strangers he was still apt to enlarge on the returns his farm brought him in; and he had often to pull up in his statements when he caught the warning glance of my mother's eye, showing him that she was not so much absorbed in her own conversation as to be deaf to his voice. But as for the happiness that arose out of our mode of life – that was not to be calculated by tens or hundreds of pounds. There were only two of us, my sister, and myself; and my mother undertook the greater part of our education. We helped her in her household cares during part of the morning; then came an old-fashioned routine of lessons, such as she herself had learnt when a girl: – Goldsmith's 'History of England,' Rollin's 'Ancient History,' Lindley Murray's Grammar, and plenty of sewing, and stitching.[2]

My mother used sometimes to sigh, and wish that she could buy us a piano, and teach us what little music she knew; but many of my dear father's habits were expensive – at least for a person possessed of no larger an income than he had. Besides the quiet, and unsuspected drain of his agricultural pursuits, he was of a social turn; enjoying the dinners to which he was

invited by his more affluent neighbours; and especially delighted in returning them the compliment, and giving them choice little entertainments,
which would have been yet more frequent in their recurrence than they
were, if it had not been for my mother's prudence. But we never were able
to purchase the piano; it required a greater outlay of ready money than we
ever possessed. I dare say we should have grown up ignorant of any language
but our own if it had not been for my father's social habits, which led to our
learning French in a very unexpected manner. He, and my mother went to
dine with General Ashburton, one of the forest rangers,[3] and there they met
with an emigrant gentleman, a Monsieur de Chalabre, who had escaped in a
wonderful manner, and at terrible peril to his life: and was, consequently, in
our small forest-circle, a great lion, and a worthy cause of a series of dinner
parties. His first entertainer, General Ashburton, had known him in France,
under very different circumstances; and he was not prepared for the quiet,
and dignified request made by his guest, one afternoon after M. de Chalabre
had been about a fortnight in the forest, that the General would recommend
him as a French teacher, if he could conscientiously do so.

To the General's remonstrances M. de Chalabre smilingly replied, by an
assurance that his assumption of his new occupation could only be for a
short time; that the good cause would – *must* triumph. It was before the fatal
21st of January, 1793;[a] and then, still smiling, he strengthened his position
by quoting innumerable instances out of the classics, of heroes, and patriots,
generals and commanders, who had been reduced by Fortune's frolics to
adopt some occupation far below their original one. He closed his speech
with informing the General that, relying upon his kindness in acting as refe-
ree, he had taken lodgings for a few months at a small farm which was in the
centre of our forest circle of acquaintances. The General was too thoroughly
a gentleman to say anything more than that he should be most happy to do
whatever he could to forward M. de Chalabre's plans; and as my father was
the first person whom he met with after this conversation, it was announced
to us, on the very evening of the day on which it had taken place, that we
were forthwith to learn French; and I verily believe that, if my father could
have persuaded my mother to join him, we should have formed a French
class of father, mother, and two head of daughters, so touched had my father
been by the General's account of M. de Chalabre's present desires, as compared with the high estate from which he had fallen. Accordingly, we were
installed in the dignity of his first French pupils. My father was anxious that
we should have a lesson every other day, ostensibly that we might get on all
the more speedily, but really that he might have a larger quarterly bill to pay;
at any rate until M. de Chalabre had more of his time occupied with instruction. But my mother gently interfered and calmed her husband down into
two lessons a-week, which was, she said, as much as we could manage.
Those happy lessons! I remember them now, at the distance of more than

fifty years. Our house was situated on the edge of the forest; our fields were, in fact, cleared out of it. It was not good land for clover; but my father would always sow one particular field with clover seed, because my mother was so fond of the fragrant scent in her evening walks, and through this a foot-path ran which led into the forest.

A quarter of a mile beyond – a walk on the soft fine springy turf, and under the long low branches of the beech-trees, and we arrived at the old red-brick farm where M. de Chalabre was lodging. Not that we went there to take our lessons; that would have been an offence to his spirit of polite-ness; but as my father and mother were his nearest neighbours, there was a constant interchange of small messages and notes, which we little girls were only too happy to take to our dear M. de Chalabre. Moreover, if our lessons with my mother were ended pretty early, she would say – 'You have been good girls; now you may run to the high point in the clover field, and see if M. de Chalabre is coming; and if he is you may walk with him; but take care and give him the cleanest part of the path, for you know he does not like to dirty his boots.'

This was all very well in theory; but, like many theories, the difficulty was to put it in practice. If we slipped to the side of the path where the water lay longest, he bowed and retreated behind us to a still wetter place, leaving the clean part for us; yet when we got home his polished boots would be with-out a speck, while our shoes were covered with mud.

Another little ceremony which we had to get accustomed to, was his habit of taking off his hat as we approached, and walking by us holding it in his hand. To be sure, he wore a wig, delicately powdered, frizzed, and tied in a queue behind; but we had always a feeling that he would catch cold, and that he was doing us too great an honour, and that he did not know how old or rather how young we were, until one day we saw him (far away from our house) hand a countrywoman over a style with the same kind of dainty courteous politeness, lifting her basket of eggs over first; and then, taking up the silk-lined lapel of his coat, he spread it on the palm of his hand for her to rest her fingers upon; instead of which, she took his small white hand in her plump vigorous gripe, and leant her full weight upon him. He carried her basket for her as far as their roads lay together; and from that time we were less shy in receiving his courtesies, perceiving that he considered them as deference due to our sex, however old or young, or rich or poor. So, as I said, we came down from the clover-field in rather a stately manner, and through the wicket gate that opened into our garden, which was as rich in its scents of varied kinds as the clover-field had been in its one pure fragrance. My mother would meet us here; and somehow – our life was passed as much out of doors as in-doors, both winter and summer – we seemed to have our French lessons more frequently in the garden than in the house; for there was a sort of arbour on the lawn near the drawing-room window, to which we always found it easy to carry a table and chairs, and all the rest of the lesson paraphernalia, if my mother did not prohibit a lesson al fresco.

M. de Chalabre wore, as a sort of morning costume, a coat, waistcoat, and breeches all made of a kind of coarse grey cloth, which he had bought in the neighbourhood; his three-cornered hat was brushed to a nicety, his wig sat as no one else's did. (My father's was always awry.) And the only thing wanting to his costume when he came was a flower. Sometimes I fancied he purposely omitted gathering one of the roses that clustered up the farmhouse in which he lodged, in order to afford my mother the pleasure of culling her choicest carnations and roses to make him up his nosegay, or 'posy,' as he liked to call it; he had picked up that pretty country word, and adopted it as an especial favourite, dwelling on the first syllable with all the languid softness of an Italian accent. Many a time have Mary and I tried to say it like him; we did so admire his way of speaking.

Once seated round the table, whether in the house or out of it, we were bound to attend to our lessons: and somehow he made us perceive that it was a part of the same chivalrous code that made him so helpful to the helpless, to enforce the slightest claim of duty to the full. No half-prepared lessons for him! The patience, and the resource with which he illustrated, and enforced every precept; the untiring gentleness with which he made our stubborn English tongues pronounce, and mispronounce, and repronounce certain words; above all, the sweetness of temper which never varied, were such as I have never seen equalled. If we wondered at these qualities when we were children, how much greater has been our surprise at their existence since we have been grown up, and have learnt that, until his emigration, he was a man of rapid and impulsive action, with the imperfect education implied in the circumstance that at fifteen he was a sous-lieutenant in the Queen's regiment, and must, consequently, have had to apply himself hard, and[a] conscientiously to master the language which he had in after-life to teach.

Twice we had holidays to suit his sad convenience. Holidays with us were not at Christmas, and Midsummer, Easter and Michaelmas. If my mother was unusually busy, we had what we called a holiday; though, in reality, it involved harder work than our regular lessons; but we fetched, and carried, and ran errands, and became rosy, and dusty, and sang merry songs in the gaiety of our hearts. If the day was remarkably fine, my dear father – whose spirits were rather apt to vary with the weather – would come bursting in with his bright, kind, bronzed face, and carry the day by storm with my mother. 'It was a shame to coop such young things up in a house,' he would say, 'when every other young animal was frolicking in the air and sunshine. Grammar! – what was that but the art of arranging words? – and he never knew a woman but could do that fast enough. Geography! – he would undertake to teach us more geography in one winter evening, telling us of the countries where he had been, with just a map before him, than we could learn in ten years with that stupid book, all full of hard words. As for the French – why that must be learnt, for he should not like M. de Chalabre to think we slighted the lessons he took so much pains to give us; but surely we could get up the earlier to learn our French.' We promised by acclamation; and my mother – sometimes smilingly, sometimes reluctantly – was always compelled to yield. And these were the usual occasions for our holidays. But twice we had a fortnight's entire cessation of French lessons; once in January, and once in October.[4] Nor did we even see our dear French master during those periods. We went several times to the top of the clover-field, to search the dark green outskirts of the forest with our busy eyes; and if we could have seen his figure in that shade, I am sure we should have scampered to him, forgetful of the prohibition which made the forest forbidden ground. But we did not see him.

It was the fashion in those days to keep children much less informed than they are now on the subjects which interest their parents. A sort of hieroglyphic or cypher talk was used in order to conceal the meaning of much that was said if children were present. My mother was a proficient in this way of talking, and took, we fancied, a certain pleasure in perplexing my father by inventing a new cypher, as it were, every day. For instance, for some time, I was called Martia,[5] because I was very tall of my age; and just as my father had begun to understand the name – and, it must be owned, a good while after I had learnt to prick up my ears whenever Martia was named – my mother suddenly changed me into the 'buttress,' from the habit I had acquired of leaning my languid length against a wall. I saw my father's perplexity about this 'buttress' for some days, and could have helped him out of it, but I durst not. And so, when the unfortunate Louis the Sixteenth was executed, the news was too terrible to be put into plain English, and too terrible also to be made known to us children, nor could we at once find the clue to the cypher in which it was spoken about. We heard about 'the Iris[6] being blown down;' and saw my father's honest loyal excitement about it, and the quiet reserve which always betokened some secret grief on my mother's part.

We had no French lessons; and somehow the poor, battered, storm-torn Iris was to blame for this. It was many weeks after this before we knew the full reason of M. de Chalabre's deep depression when he again came amongst us: why he shook his head when my mother timidly offered him some snowdrops on that first morning on which we began lessons again: why he wore the deep mourning of that day, when all of the dress that could be black was black, and the white muslin frills and ruffles were unstarched and limp, as if to bespeak the very abandonment of grief. We knew well enough the meaning of the next hieroglyphic announcement – 'The wicked cruel boys had broken off the White Lily's[7] head!' That beautiful queen, whose portrait once had been shown to us, with her blue eyes, and her fair resolute look, her profusion of lightly-powdered hair, her white neck adorned with strings of pearls. We could have cried, if we had dared, when we heard the transparent mysterious words. We did cry at night, sitting up in bed, with our arms round each other's necks, and vowing, in our weak, passionate, childish way, that if we lived long enough, that lady's death avenged should be. No one who cannot remember that time can tell the shudder of horror that thrilled through the country at hearing of this last execution. At the moment, there was no time for any consideration of the silent horrors endured for centuries by the people who at length rose in their madness against their rulers. This last blow changed our dear M. de Chalabre. I never saw him again in quite the same gaiety of heart as before this time. There seemed to be tears very close behind his smiles for ever after. My father went to see him when he had been about a week absent from us – no reason given, for did not we, did not every one know the horror the sun had looked upon! As soon as my father had gone, my mother gave it in charge to us to make the dressing-room belonging to our guest-chamber as much like a sitting-room as possible. My father hoped to bring back M. de Chalabre for a visit to us; but he would probably like to be a good deal alone; and we might move any article of furniture we liked, if we only thought it would make him comfortable.

I believe General Ashburton had been on a somewhat similar errand to my father's before; but he had failed. My father gained his point, as I afterwards learnt, in a very unconscious and characteristic manner. He had urged his invitation on M. de Chalabre, and received such a decided negative that he was hopeless, and quitted the subject. Then M. de Chalabre began to relieve his heart by telling him all the details; my father held his breath to listen—at last, his honest heart could contain itself no longer, and the tears ran down his face. His unaffected sympathy touched M. de Chalabre inexpressibly; and in an hour after we saw our dear French master coming down the clover-field slope, leaning on my father's arm which he had involuntarily offered as a support to one in trouble – although he was slightly lame, and ten or fifteen years older than M. de Chalabre.

For a year after that time M. de Chalabre never wore any flowers; and after that, to the day of his death, no gay or coloured rose or carnation could tempt him. We secretly observed his taste and always took care to bring him white flowers for his posy. I noticed, too, that on his left arm, under his coat sleeve (sleeves were made very open then), he always wore a small band of black crape. He lived to be eighty-one, but he had the black crape band on when he died.

M. de Chalabre was a favourite in all the forest circle. He was a great acquisition to the sociable dinner parties that were perpetually going on; and though some of the families piqued themselves on being aristocratic, and turned up their noses at any one who had been engaged in trade, however largely, M. de Chalabre, in right of his good blood, his loyalty, his daring 'preux chevalier'[8] actions, was ever an honoured guest. He took his poverty, and the simple habits it enforced, so naturally and gaily, as a mere trifling accident of his life, about which neither concealment nor shame could be necessary, that the very servants – often so much more pseudo-aristocratic than their masters – loved and respected the French gentleman, who, perhaps, came to teach in the mornings, and in the evenings made his appearance dressed with dainty neatness as a dinner guest. He came lightly prancing through the forest mire; and, in our little hall, at any rate, he would pull out a neat minute case containing a blacking-brush and blacking, and re-polish his boots, speaking gaily, in his broken English, to the footman all the time. That blacking case was his own making; he had a genius for using his fingers. After our lessons were over, he relaxed into the familiar house friend, the merry play-fellow. We lived far from any carpenter or joiner; if a lock was out of order M. de Chalabre made it right for us. If any box was wanted, his ingenious fingers had made it before our lesson day. He turned silk winders for my mother, made a set of chessmen for my father, carved an elegant watch-case out of a rough beef-bone – dressed up little cork dolls for us–in short, as he said, his heart would have been broken but for his joiner's tools. Nor were his ingenious gifts employed for us alone. The farmer's wife where he lodged had numerous contrivances in her house which he had made. One particularly which I remember was a paste-board, made after a French pattern, which would not slip about on a a dresser, as he had observed her English paste-board do. Susan, the farmer's ruddy daughter, had her work-box too, to show us; and her cousin-lover had a wonderful stick, with an extraordinary demon head carved upon it; – all by M. de Chalabre. Farmer, farmer's wife, Susan, Robert, and all were full of his praises.

We grew from children into girls – from girls into women; and still M. de Chalabre taught on in the forest; still he was beloved and honoured; still no dinner-party within five miles was thought complete without him, and ten miles' distance strove to offer him a bed sooner than miss his company. The pretty merry Susan of sixteen had been jilted by the faithless Robert; and was now a comely demure damsel of thirty-one or two; still waiting upon M. de Chalabre, and still constant in respectfully singing his praises. My own poor mother was dead; my sister was engaged to be married to a young lieutenant, who was with his ship in the Mediterranean. My father was as youthful as ever in heart, and indeed in many of his ways; only his hair was quite white, and the old lameness was more frequently troublesome than it had been. An uncle of his had left him a considerable fortune, so he farmed away to his heart's content, and lost an annual sum of money with the best grace and the lightest heart in the world. There were not even the gentle reproaches of my mother's eyes, to be dreaded now.

Things were in this state when the peace of 1814[9a] was declared. We had heard so many and such contradictory rumours that we were inclined to doubt even the 'Gazette'[10] at last, and were discussing probabilities with some vehemence, when M. de Chalabre entered the room unannounced and breathless:

'My friends, give me joy!' he said. 'The Bourbons' – he could not go on; his features, nay, his very fingers, worked with agitation, but he could not speak. My father hastened to relieve him.

'We have heard the good news (you see, girls, it is quite true this time). I do congratulate you, my dear friend. I *am* glad.' And he seized M. de Chalabre's hand in his own hearty gripe, and brought the nervous agitation of the latter to a close by unconsciously administering a pretty severe does of wholesome pain.

'I go to London. I go straight this afternoon to see my sovereign. My sovereign holds a court to-morrow at Grillon's Hotel;[11] I go to pay him my devoirs. I put on my uniform of Gardes du Corps,[12] which have laid by these many years; a little old, a little worm-eaten; but never mind; they have been seen by Marie Antoinette, which gives them a grace for ever.' He walked about the room in a nervous, hurried way. There was something on his mind, and we signed to my father to be silent for a moment or two and let it come out. 'No!' said M. de Chalabre, after a moment's pause. 'I cannot say adieu; for I shall return to say, dear friends, my adieux. I did come a poor emigrant; noble Englishmen took me for their friend, and welcomed me to their houses. Chalabre is one large mansion, and my English friends will not forsake me; they will come and see me in my own country; and, for their sakes, not an English beggar shall pass the doors of Chalabre without being warmed and clothed, and fed. I will not say adieu. I go now but for two days.'

CHAPTER II.

MY father insisted upon driving M. de Chalabre in his gig to the nearest town through which the London mail passed; and, during the short time that elapsed before my father was ready, he told us something more about Chalabre. He had never spoken of his ancestral home to any of us before; we knew little of his station in his own country. General Ashburton had met with him in Paris, in a set where a man was judged of by his wit, and talent for society, and general brilliance of character, rather than by his wealth and hereditary position. Now we learned for the first time that he was heir to considerable estates in Normandy; to an old Château Chalabre; all of which he had forfeited by his emigration, it was true, but that was under another regime.

'Ah! if my dear friend – your poor mother – were alive now, I could send her such slips of rare and splendid roses from Chalabre. Often when I did see her nursing up some poor little specimen, I longed in secret for my rose garden at Chalabre. And the orangerie! Ah! Miss Mary,[13] the bride must come to Chalabre who wishes for a beautiful wreath.' This was an allusion to my sister's engagement – a fact well known to him, as the faithful family friend.

My father came back in high spirits; and began to plan that very evening how to arrange his crops for the ensuing year so as best to spare time for a visit to Château Chalabre; and, as for us, I think we believed that there was no need to delay our French journey beyond the autumn of the present year.

M. de Chalabre came back in a couple of days; a little damped, we girls fancied, though we hardly liked to speak about it to my father. However, M. de Chalabre explained it to us by saying, that he had found London more crowded and busy than he had expected: that it was smoky and dismal after leaving the country, where the trees were already coming into leaf; and, when we pressed him a little more respecting the reception at Grillon's, he laughed at himself for having forgotten the tendency of the Count de Provence in former days to become stout, and so being dismayed at the mass of corpulence which Louis the Eighteenth presented, as he toiled up the long drawing-room of the hotel.

'But what did he say to you?' Mary asked. 'How did he receive you when you were presented?'

A flash of pain passed over his face, but it was gone directly.

'Oh! his majesty did not recognise my name. It was hardly to be expected he would; though it is a name of note in Normandy; and I have – well! that is worth nothing. The Duc de Duras[14] reminded him of a circumstance or two, which I had almost hoped his majesty would not have forgotten; but I myself forgot the pressure of long years of exile; it was no wonder he did not remember me. He said he hoped to see me at the Tuileries. His hopes are my laws. I go to prepare for my departure. If his majesty does not need my sword, I turn it into a ploughshare at Chalabre.[15] Ah! my friend, I will not forget there all the agricultural science I have learned from you!'

A gift of a hundred pounds would not have pleased my father so much as this last speech. He began forthwith to inquire about the nature of the soil, &c., in a way which made our poor M. de Chalabre shrug his shoulders in despairing ignorance.

'Never mind!' said my father. 'Rome was not built in a day. It was a long time before I learnt all that I know now. I was afraid I could not leave home this autumn, but I perceive you'll need some one to advise you about laying out the ground for next year's crops.'

So M. de Chalabre left our neighbourhood, with the full understanding that we were to pay him a visit in his Norman château in the following

September; nor was he content until he had persuaded every one who had shown him kindness to promise him a visit at some appointed time. As for his old landlord at the farm, the comely dame, and buxom Susan – they, we found, were to be franked there and back, under the pretence that the French dairy-maids had no notion of cleanliness, any more than that the French farming men were judges of stock; so it was absolutely necessary to bring over some one from England to put the affairs of the Château Chala-bre in order; and Farmer Dobson and his wife considered the favour quite reciprocal.

For some time we did not hear from our friend. The war had made the post between France and England very uncertain; so we were obliged to wait, and we tried to be patient; but, somehow, our autumn visit to France was silently given up; and my father gave us long expositions of the disor-dered state of affairs in a country which had suffered so much as France, and lectured us severely on the folly of having expected to hear so soon. We knew, all the while, that the exposition was repeated to soothe his own impa-tience, and that the admonition to patience was what he felt that he himself was needing.

At last the letter came. There was a brave attempt at cheerfulness in it, which nearly made me cry, more than any complaints would have done. M. de Chalabre had hoped to retain his commission as Sous-Lieutenant in the Garde du Corps – a commission signed by Louis the Sixteenth himself, in 1791.[a] But the regiment was to be remodelled or reformed, I forget which; and M. de Chalabre assured us that his was not the only case where appli-cants had been refused. He had then tried for a commission in the Cent Suisses, the Gardes du Porte, the Mousquetaires,[16] but all were full. 'Was it not a glorious thing for France to have so many brave sons ready to fight on the side of honour and loyalty?' To which question Mary replied, 'that it was a shame;' and my father, after a grunt or two, comforted himself by saying, 'that M. de Chalabre would have the more time to attend to his neglected estate.'

That winter was full of incidents in our home. As it often happens when a family has seemed stationary, and secure from change for years, and then at last one important event happens, another is sure to follow. Mary's lover returned, and they were married, and left us alone – my father and I. Her husband's ship was stationed in the Mediterranean, and she was to go and live at Malta,[17] with some of his relations there. I know not if it was the agi-tation of parting with her, but my father was stricken down from health into confirmed invalidism, by a paralytic stroke, soon after her departure; and my interests were confined to the fluctuating reports of a sick-room. I did not care for the foreign intelligence which was shaking Europe[18] with an uni-versal tremor. My hopes, my fears were centred in one frail human body – my dearly beloved, my most loving father. I kept a letter in my pocket for days from M. de Chalabre, unable to find the time to decipher his French hieroglyphics; at last I read it aloud to my poor father, rather as a test of his power of enduring interest, than because I was impatient to know what it contained. The news in it was depressing enough, as everything else seemed to be that gloomy winter. A rich manufacturer of Rouen had bought the Château Chalabre; forfeited to the nation by its former possessor's emigration. His son, M. du Fay, was well-affected towards Louis the Eighteenth – at least as long as his government was secure, and promised to be stable, so as not to affect the dyeing and selling of Turkey-red wools; and so the natural legal consequence was, that M. du Fay, Fils,[19] was not to be disturbed in his purchased and paid-for property. My father cared to hear of this disappointment to our poor friend–cared just for one day, and forgot all about it the next. Then came the return from Elba –[20] the hurrying events of that spring–the battle of Waterloo; and to my poor father, in his second childhood, the choice of a daily pudding was far more important than all.

One Sunday, in that August of 1815,[a] I went to church. It was many weeks since I had been able to leave my father for so long a time before. Since I had been last there to worship, it seemed as if my youth had passed away; gone without a warning; leaving no trace behind. After service, I went through the long grass to the unfrequented part of the churchyard where my dear mother lay buried. A garland of brilliant yellow immortelles lay on her grave; and the unwonted offering took me by surprise. I knew of the foreign custom, although I had never seen the kind of wreath before. I took it up, and read one word in the black floral letters; it was simply 'Adieu.' I knew, from the first moment I saw it, that M. de Chalabre must have returned to England. Such a token of regard was like him, and could spring from no one else. But I wondered a little that we had never heard or seen anything of him; nothing, in fact, since Lady Ashburton had told me that her husband had met with him in Belgium, hurrying to offer himself as a volunteer to one of the eleven generals appointed by the Duc de Feltre[21] to receive such applications. General Ashburton himself had since this died at Brussels, in consequence of wounds received at Waterloo. As the recollection of all these circumstances gathered in my mind, I found I was drawing near the field-path which led out of the direct road home, to farmer Dobson's; and thither I suddenly determined to go, and hear if they had learnt anything respecting their former lodger. As I went up the garden-walk leading to the house, I caught M. de Chalabre's eye; he was gazing abstractedly out of the window of what used to be his sitting-room. In an instant he had joined me in the garden. If my youth had flown, his youth and middle-age as well had vanished altogether. He looked older by at least twenty years than when he had left us twelve months ago. How much of this was owing to the change in the arrangement of his dress, I cannot tell. He had formerly been remarkably dainty in all these things; now he was careless, even to the verge of slovenliness. He asked after my sister, after my father, in a manner which evinced the deepest, most respectful, interest; but, somehow, it appeared to me as if he hurried question after question rather to stop any inquiries which I, in my turn, might wish to make.

'I return here to my duties; to my only duties. The good God has not seen me fit to undertake any higher. Henceforth I am the faithful French teacher; the diligent, punctual French teacher: nothing more. But I do hope to teach the French language as becomes a gentleman and a Christian; to do my best. Henceforth the grammar and the syntax are my estate, my coat of arms.' He said this with a proud humility which prevented any reply. I could only change the subject, and urge him to come and see my poor sick father. He replied:

'To visit the sick, that is my duty as well as my pleasure. For the mere society – I renounce all that. That is now beyond my position, to which I accommodate myself with all my strength.'

Accordingly, when he came to spend an hour with my father, he brought a small bundle of printed papers, announcing the terms on which M. Chala-bre (the 'de' was dropped[22] now and for evermore) was desirous of teaching French, and a little paragraph at the bottom of the page solicited the patron-age of schools. Now this was a great coming-down. In former days, non-teaching at schools had been the line which marked that M. de Chalabre had taken up teaching rather as an amateur profession, than with any intention of devoting his life to it. He respectfully asked me to distribute these papers where I thought fit. I say 'respectfully' advisedly; there was none of the old deferential gallantry, as offered by a gentleman to a lady, his equal in birth and fortune – instead, there was the matter-of-fact request and statement which a workman offers to his employer. Only in my father's room, he was the former M. de Chalabre; he seemed to understand how vain would be all attempts to recount or explain the circumstances which had led him so decidedly to take a lower level in society. To my father, to the day of his death, M. de Chalabre maintained the old easy footing; assumed a gaiety which he never even pretended to feel anywhere else; listened to my father's childish interests with a true and kindly sympathy for which I ever felt grate-ful, although he purposely put a deferential reserve between him and me, as a barrier to any expression of such feeling on my part.

His former lessons had been held in such high esteem by those who were privileged to receive them, that he was soon sought after on all sides. The schools of the two principal county towns[23] put forward their claims, and considered it a favour to receive his instructions. Morning, noon, and night he was engaged: even if he had not proudly withdrawn himself from all merely society engagements, he would have had no leisure for them. His only visits were paid to my father, who looked for them with a kind of child-ish longing. One day, to my surprise, he asked to be allowed to speak to me for an instant alone. He stood silent for a moment, turning his hat in his hand.

'You have a right to know – you, my first pupil; next Tuesday I marry myself to Miss Susan Dobson – good, respectable woman, to whose happiness I mean to devote my life, or as much of it as is not occupied with the duties of instruction.' He looked up at me, expecting congratulations perhaps; but I was too much stunned with my surprise. The buxom, red-armed, apple-cheeked Susan who, when she blushed, blushed the colour of beet-root; who did not know a word of French; who regarded the nation (always excepting the gentleman before me) as frog-eating Mounseers, the national enemies of England! I afterwards thought, that perhaps this very ignorance constituted one of her charms. No word, nor allusion, nor expressive silence, nor regretful sympathetic sighs, could remind M. de Chalabre of the bitter past, which he was evidently striving to forget. And, most assuredly, never man had a more devoted and admiring wife than poor Susan made M. de Chalabre. She was a little awed by him, to be sure; never quite at her ease before him; but I imagine husbands do not dislike such a tribute to their Jupiter-ship.[24] Madame Chalabre received my call, after their marriage, with a degree of sober, rustic, happy dignity, which I could not have foreseen in Susan Dobson. They had taken a small cottage on the borders of the forest; it had a garden round it, and the cow, pigs, and poultry, which were to be her charge, found their keep in the forest. She had a rough country servant to assist her in looking after them; and in what scanty leisure he had, her husband attended to the garden and the bees. Madame Chalabre took me over the neatly furnished cottage with evident pride. 'Moussire,' as she called him, had done this; Moussire had fitted up that. Moussire was evidently a man of resource. In a little closet of a dressing-room belonging to Moussire, there hung a pencil drawing, elaborately finished to the condition of a bad pocket-book engraving. It caught my eye, and I lingered to look at it. It represented a high narrow house of considerable size, with four pepper-box turrets at each corner; and a stiff avenue formed the foreground.

'Château Chalabre?' said I, inquisitively.

'I never asked,' my companion replied. 'Moussire does not always like to be asked questions. It is the picture of some place he is very fond of, for he won't let me dust it for fear I should smear it.'

M. de Chalabre's marriage did not diminish the number of his visits to my father. Until that beloved parent's death, he was faithful in doing all he could to lighten the gloom of the sick room. But a chasm, which he had opened, separated any present intercourse with him from the free unreserved friendship that had existed formerly. And yet for his sake I used to go and see his wife. I could not forget early days, nor the walks to the top of the clover-field, nor the daily posies, nor my mother's dear regard for the emigrant gentleman; nor a thousand little kindnesses which he had shown to my absent sister and myself. He did not forget either in the closed and sealed chambers of his heart. So, for his sake, I tried to become a friend to his wife; and she learned to look upon me as such. It was my employment in the sick chamber to make clothes for the little expected Chalabre baby; and its mother would fain (as she told me) have asked me to carry the little infant to the font, but that her husband somewhat austerely reminded her that they ought to seek a *marraine*[25] among those of their own station in society. But I regarded the pretty little Susan as my god-child nevertheless in my heart; and secretly pledged myself always to take an interest in her. Not two months after my father's death, a sister was born; and the human heart in M. de Chalabre subdued his pride; the child was to bear the pretty name of his French mother, although France could find no place for him, and had cast him out. That youngest little girl was called Aimée.

When my father died, Mary and her husband urged me to leave Brook-field, and come and live with them at Valetta.[26] The estate was left to us; but an eligible tenant offered himself; and my health, which had suffered mate-rially during my long nursing, did render it desirable for me to seek some change to a warmer climate. So I went abroad, ostensibly for a year's resi-dence only; but, somehow, that year has grown into a lifetime. Malta and Genoa have been my dwelling places ever since. Occasionally, it is true, I have paid visits to England, but I have never looked upon it as my home since I left it thirty years ago. During these visits I have seen the Chalabres. He had become more absorbed in his occupation than ever; had published a French grammar on some new principle, of which he presented me with a copy, taking some pains to explain how it was to be used. Madame looked plump and prosperous; the farm which was under her management had thriven; and as for the two daughters, behind their English shyness, they had a good deal of French piquancy and *esprit*.[27] I induced them to take some walks with me, with a view of asking them some questions which should make our friendship an individual reality, not merely an hereditary feeling; but the little monkeys put me through my catechism, and asked me innu-merable questions about France, which they evidently regarded as their country. 'How do you know all about French habits and customs?' asked I. 'Does Monsieur de – does your father talk to you much about France?'

'Sometimes, when we are alone with him – never when any one is by,' answered Susan, the elder, a grave, noble-looking girl, of twenty or therea-bouts. 'I think he does not speak about France before my mother, for fear of hurting her.'

'And I think,' said little Aimée, 'that he does not speak at all, when he can help it; it is only when his heart gets too full with recollections, that he is obliged to talk to us, because many of the thoughts could not be said in English.'

'Then I suppose you are two famous French scholars?'

'Oh yes! Papa always speaks to us in French; it is our own language.'

But with all their devotion to their father and to his country, they were most affectionate dutiful daughters to their mother. They were her companions, her comforts in the pleasant household labours; most practical, useful young women. But in a privacy not the less sacred, because it was understood rather than prescribed, they kept all the enthusiasm, all the romance of their nature for their father. They were the confidantes of that poor exile's yearnings for France; the eager listeners for what he chose to tell them of his early days. His words wrought up Susan to make the resolution that, if ever she felt herself free from home duties and responsibilities, she would become a Sister of Charity,[28] like Anne-Marguérite[a] de Chalabre, her father's great-aunt, and model of woman's sanctity. As for Aimée, come what might, she never would leave her father; and that was all she was clear about in picturing her future.

Three years ago I was in Paris. An English friend of mine who lives there– English by birth, but married to a German professor,[29] and very French in manners and ways – asked me to come to her house one evening. I was far from well, and disinclined to stir out.

'Oh, but come!' said she. 'I have a good reason; really a tempting reason. Perhaps this very evening a piece of poetical justice will be done in my *salon*. A living romance! Now, can you resist?'

'What is it?' said I; for she was rather in the habit of exaggerating trifles into romances.

'A young lady is coming; not in the first youth, but still young, very pretty; daughter of a French *émigré*, whom my husband knew in Belgium, and who has lived in England ever since.'

'I beg your pardon, but what is her name?' interrupted I, roused to interest.

'De Chalabre. Do you know her?'

'Yes; I am much interested in her. I will gladly come to meet her. How long has she been in Paris? Is it Susan or Aimée?'

'Now I am not to be baulked of the pleasure of telling you my romance; my hoped-for bit of poetical justice. You must be patient, and you will have answers to all your questions.'

I sank back in my easy chair. Some of my friends are rather long-winded, and it is as well to be settled in a comfortable position before they begin to talk.

'I told you a minute ago, that my husband had become acquainted with M. de Chalabre in Belgium, in 1815. They have kept up a correspondence ever since; not a very brisk one, it is true, for M. de Chalabre was a French master in England, and my husband a professor in Paris; but still they managed to let each other know how they were going on, and what they were doing, once, if not twice every year. For myself, I never saw M. de Chalabre.'

'I know him well,' said I. 'I have known him all my life.'

'A year ago his wife died (she was an Englishwoman); she had had a long and suffering illness; and his eldest daughter had devoted herself to her with the patient sweetness of an angel, as he told us, and I can well believe. But after her mother's death, the world, it seems, became distaseful to her: she had been inured to the half-lights, the hushed voices, the constant thought for others required in a sick room, and the noise and rough bustle of healthy people jarred upon her. So she pleaded with her father to allow her to become a Sister of Charity. She told him that he would have given a welcome to any suitor who came to offer to marry her, and bear her away from her home, and her father and sister; and now, when she was called by Religion, would he grudge to part with her? He gave his consent, if not his full approbation; and he wrote to my husband to beg me to receive her here, while we sought out a convent into which she could be received. She has been with me two months, and endeared herself to me unspeakably; she goes home next week unless' –

'But, I beg your pardon; did you not say she wished to become a Sister of Charity?'

'It is true; but she was too old to be admitted into their order. She is eight-and-twenty. It has been a grievous disappointment to her; she has borne it very patiently and meekly, but I can see how deeply she has felt it. And now for my romance. My husband had a pupil some ten years ago, a M. du Fay, a clever, scientific young man, one of the first merchants of Rouen. His grandfather purchased M. de Chalabre's ancestral estate. The present M. du Fay came on business to Paris two or three days ago, and invited my husband to a little dinner; and somehow this story of Suzette Chalabre came out, in consequence of inquiries my husband was making for an escort to take her to England. M. du Fay seemed interested with the story; and asked my husband if he might pay his respects to me, some evening when Suzette should be in, – and so is coming to-night, he, and a friend of his, who was at the dinner party the other day; will you come?'

I went, more in the hope of seeing Susan Chalabre, and hearing some news about my early home, than with any expectation of 'poetical justice.' And in that I was right; and yet I was wrong. Susan Chalabre was a grave, gentle woman, of an enthusiastic and devoted appearance, not unlike that portrait of his daughter which arrests every eye in Ary Scheffer's sacred pictures.[30] She was silent and sad; her cherished plan of life was uprooted. She talked to me a little in a soft and friendly manner, answering any questions I asked; but, as for the gentlemen, her indifference and reserve made it impossible for them to enter into any conversation with her; and the meeting was indisputably 'flat.'

'Oh! my romance! my poetical justice! Before the evening was half over, I would have given up all my castles in the air for one well-sustained conversation of ten minutes long. Now don't laugh at me, for I can't bear it to-night.' Such was my friend's parting speech. I did not see her again for two days. The third she came in glowing with excitement.

'You may congratulate me after all; if it was not poetical justice, it is prosaic justice; and, except for the empty romance, that is a better thing!'

'What do you mean?' said I. 'Surely M. du Fay has not proposed for Susan?'

'No! but that charming M. de Frez, his friend, has; that is to say, not proposed but spoken; no, not spoken, but it seems he asked M. du Fay – whose confidant he was – if he was intending to proceed in his idea of marrying Suzette; and on hearing that he was not, M. de Frez said that he should come to us, and ask us to put him in the way of prosecuting the acquaintance, for that he had been charmed with her; looks, voice, silence, he admires them all; and we have arranged that he is to be the escort to England; he has business there, he says; and as for Suzette (she knows nothing of all this, of course, for who dared tell her?), all her anxiety is to return home, and the first person travelling to England will satisfy her, if it does us. And, after all, M. de Frez lives within five leagues of the Château Chalabre, so she can go and see the old place whenever she will.'

When I went to bid Susan good bye, she looked as unconscious and dignified as ever. No idea of a lover had ever crossed her mind. She considered M. de Frez as a kind of necessary incumbrance for the journey. I had not much hopes for him; and yet he was an agreeable man enough, and my friends told me that his character stood firm and high.

In three months, I was settled for the winter in Rome. In four, I heard that the marriage of Susan Chalabre had taken place. What were the intermediate steps between the cold, civil indifference with which I had last seen her regarding her travelling companion, and the full love with which such a woman as Suzette Chalabre must love a man before she could call him husband, I never learnt. I wrote to my old French master to congratulate him, as I believed I honestly might, on his daughter's marriage. It was some months before I received his answer. It was: –

'Dear friend, dear old pupil, dear child of the beloved dead, I am an old man of eighty, and I tremble towards the grave. I cannot write many words; but my own hand shall bid you come to the home of Aimée and her husband. They tell me to ask you to come and see the old father's birthplace, while he is yet alive to show it to you. I have the very apartment in Château Chalabre that was mine when I was a boy, and my mother came in to bless me every night. Susan lives near us. The good God bless my sons-in-law, Bertrand de Frez and Alphonse du Fay, as He has blest me all my life long. I think of your father and mother, my dear; and you must think no harm when I tell you I have had masses said for the repose of their souls. If I make a mistake, God will forgive.'

My heart could have interpreted this letter, even without the pretty letter of Aimée and her husband which accompanied it; and which told how, when M. du Fay came over to his friend's wedding, he had seen the younger sister, and in her seen his fate. The soft, caressing, timid Aimée was more to his taste than the grave and stately Susan. Yet little Aimée managed to rule imperiously at Château Chalabre; or rather, her husband was delighted to indulge her every wish: while Susan, in her grand way, made rather a pomp of her conjugal obedience. But they were both good wives, good daughters.

This last summer, you might have seen an old, old man, dressed in grey, with white flowers in his button-hole (gathered by a grand-child as fair as they), leading an elderly lady about the grounds of Château Chalabre, with tottering, unsteady eagerness of gait.

'Here!' said he to me, 'just here my mother bade me adieu when first I went to join my regiment. I was impatient to go; I mounted – I rode to yonder great chestnut, and then, looking back, I saw my mother's sorrowful countenance. I sprang off, threw the reins to the groom, and ran back for one more embrace. 'My brave boy!' she said; 'my own! Be faithful to God and your king!' I never saw her more; but I shall see her soon; and I think I may tell her I have been faithful both to my God and my king.'

Before now, he has told his mother all.

'THE SQUIRE'S STORY'

'The Squire's Story' was first published in *Another Round of Stories by the Christmas Fire,* the extra Christmas number of *Household Words* (December 1853), pp. 19–25. It was collected in *Lizzie Leigh and Other Tales* (London: Chapman and Hall, 1855), pp. 146–158 and in *Lizzie Leigh and Other Tales* (1865). It also appeared in a pirated edition of *Dickens' New Stories* (Philadelphia: T. B. Peterson, n.d.).

The story is based on the life of a historical character, Edward Higgins (d. 1767), a highwayman who inhabited a house in Knutsford next door to the one in which EG was brought up (*Sharps*, p. 187, and Henry Green, *Knutsford*, pp. 119–30). She probably knew of his exploits from oral tradition, since Green indicates that the inhabitants of Knutsford were able to recognise the story when it appeared in *Household Words.* She may have referred to the *Annual Register* (1767), pp. 67, 128, since the Gaskells are known to have owned a run of the periodical.

The events of the story, however, are transposed from Cheshire to Derbyshire, somewhere in the region of Aston-on-Trent, perhaps in order to distinguish it from the Cranford stories. Laura Kranzler, in her edition of *Elizabeth Gaskell, Gothic Tales* (Harmondsworth: Penguin, 2000), p. 345, also suggests that she drew on memories of her schooldays in 1821–4 at Barford House, just outside Warwick. Angus Easson finds Higgins's character inconsistent: if he 'made merry on the old lady's ginger-wine before doing her in, it seems improbable he would succumb to remorse as he does' (*Easson*, p. 216). It is perhaps fair to say that the story's interest is not in its characterisation but in its picture of the life of the upper class around a provincial town: here as elsewhere EG expresses her sense of the subtle social effects of improvements in travel, transport and communications over the previous fifty years.

THE SQUIRE'S STORY.

IN the year 1769,[a] the little town of Barford was thrown into a state of great excitement by the intelligence that a gentleman (and 'quite the gentleman,' said the landlord of the George Inn), had been looking at Mr. Clavering's old house. This house was neither in the town nor in the country. It stood on the outskirts of Barford, on the road-side leading to Derby.[1] The last occupant had been a Mr. Clavering – a Northumberland gentleman of good family – who had come to live in Barford while he was but a younger son; but when some elder branches of the family died, he had returned to take possession of the family estate. The house of which I speak was called the White House, from its being covered with a greyish kind of stucco. It had a good garden to the back, and Mr. Clavering had built capital stables, with what were then considered the latest improvements. The point of good stabling was expected to let the house, as it was in a hunting county; otherwise it had few recommendations. There were many bed-rooms; some entered through others, even to the number of five, leading one beyond the other; several sitting-rooms of the small and poky kind, wainscotted round with wood, and then painted a heavy slate colour; one good dining-room, and a drawing-room over it, both looking into the garden, with pleasant bow-windows.

Such was the accommodation offered by the White House. It did not seem to be very tempting to strangers, though the good people of Barford rather piqued themselves on it, as the largest house in the town; and as a house in which 'townspeople' and 'county people'[2] had often met at Mr. Clavering's friendly dinners. To appreciate this circumstance of pleasant recollection, you should have lived some years in a little country town, surrounded by gentlemen's seats. You would then understand how a bow or a courtesy from a member of a county family elevates the individuals who receive it almost as much, in their own eyes, as the pair of blue garters fringed with silver, did Mr. Bickerstaff's ward.[3] They trip lightly on air for a whole day afterwards. Now Mr. Clavering was gone, where could town and county mingle?

I mention these things that you may have an idea of the desirability of the letting of the White House in the Barfordites' imagination; and to make the mixture thick and slab,[4] you must add for yourselves, the[b] bustle, the mystery, and the importance which every little event either causes or assumes in a small town; and then, perhaps, it will be no wonder to you that twenty ragged little urchins accompanied the 'gentleman'[a] aforesaid to the door of the White House; and that, although he was above an hour inspecting it under the auspices of Mr. Jones, the agent's clerk, thirty more had joined themselves on to the wondering crowd before his exit, and awaited such crumbs of intelligence as they could gather before they were threatened or whipped out of hearing distance. Presently out came the 'gentleman'[b] and the lawyer's clerk. The latter was speaking as he followed the former over the threshold. The gentleman was tall, well-dressed, handsome; but there was a sinister cold look in his quick-glancing, light blue eye, which a keen observer might not have liked. There were no keen observers among the boys, and ill-conditioned gaping girls. But they stood too near; inconveniently close; and the gentleman, lifting up his right hand, in which he carried a short riding-whip, dealt one or two sharp blows to the nearest, with a look of savage enjoyment on his face as they moved away whimpering and crying. An instant after, his expression of countenance had changed.

'Here!' said he, drawing out a handful of money, partly silver, partly copper, and throwing it into the midst of them. 'Scramble for it! fight it out, my lads! come this afternoon, at three, to the George, and I'll throw you out some more.' So the boys hurrahed for him as he walked off with the agent's clerk. He chuckled to himself, as over a pleasant thought. 'I'll have some fun with those lads,' he said; 'I'll teach 'em to come prowling and prying about me. I'll tell you what I'll do. I'll make the money so hot in the fire-shovel that it shall burn their fingers. You come and see the faces and the howling. I shall be very glad if you will dine with me at two; and by that time I may have made up my mind respecting the house.'

Mr. Jones, the agent's clerk, agreed to come to the George at two, but, somehow, he had a distaste for his entertainer. Mr. Jones would not like to have said, even to himself, that a man with a purse full of money, who kept many horses, and spoke familiarly of noblemen – above all, who thought of taking the White House – could be anything but a gentleman; but still the uneasy wonder as to who this Mr. Robinson Higgins could be, filled the clerk's mind long after Mr. Higgins, Mr. Higgins's servants, and Mr. Higgins's stud had taken possession of the White House.

The White House was re-stuccoed (this time of a pale yellow colour), and put into thorough repair by the accommodating and delighted landlord; while his tenant seemed inclined to spend any amount of money on internal decorations, which were showy and effective in their character, enough to make the White House a nine days' wonder to the good people of Barford. The slate-coloured paints became pink, and were picked out with gold; the old-fashioned bannisters were replaced by newly gilt ones; but, above all, the stables were a sight to be seen. Since the days of the Roman Emperor[5] never was there such provision made for the care, the comfort, and the health of horses. But every one said it was no wonder, when they were led through Barford, covered up to their eyes, but curving their arched and delicate necks, and prancing with short high steps, in repressed eagerness. Only one groom came with them; yet they required the care of three men. Mr. Higgins, however, preferred engaging two lads out of Barford; and Barford highly approved of his preference. Not only was it kind and thoughtful to give employment to the lounging lads themselves, but they were receiving such a training in Mr. Higgins's stables as might fit them for Doncaster or Newmarket.[6] The district of Derbyshire in which Barford was situated, was too close to Leicestershire[7] not to support a hunt and a pack of hounds. The master of the hounds was a certain Sir Harry Manley, who was *aut* a huntsman *aut nullus*.[8] He measured a man by the 'length of his fork,'[9] not by the expression of his countenance, or the shape of his head. But as Sir Harry was wont to observe, there was such a thing as too long a fork, so his approbation was withheld until he had seen a man on horseback; and if his seat there was square and easy, his hand light, and his courage good, Sir Harry hailed him as a brother.

Mr. Higgins attended the first meet of the season, not as a subscriber but as an amateur.[10] The Barford huntsmen piqued themselves on their bold riding; and their knowledge of the country came by nature; yet this new strange man, whom nobody knew, was in at the death, sitting on his horse, both well breathed and calm, without a hair turned on the sleek skin of the latter, supremely addressing the old huntsman as he hacked off the tail of the fox;[11] and he, the old man, who was testy even under Sir Harry's slightest rebuke, and flew out on any other member of the hunt that dared to utter a word against his sixty years' experience as stable-boy, groom, poacher, and what not – he, old Isaac Wormeley, was meekly listening to the wisdom of this stranger, only now and then giving one of his quick, up-turning, cunning glances, not unlike the sharp o'er-canny looks of the poor deceased Reynard,[12] round whom the hounds were howling, unadmonished by the short whip, which was now tucked into Wormeley's well-worn pocket. When Sir Harry rode into the copse – full of dead brushwood and wet tangled grass – and was followed by the members of the hunt, as one by one they cantered past, Mr. Higgins took off his cap and bowed – half deferentially, half insolently – with a lurking smile in the corner of his eye at the discomfited looks of one or two of the laggards. 'A famous run, sir,' said Sir Harry. 'The first time you have hunted in our country; but I hope we shall see you often.'

'I hope to become a member of the hunt, sir,' said Mr. Higgins.

'Most happy – proud, I'm sure, to receive so daring a rider among us. You took the Cropper-gate,[13] I fancy; while some of our friends here' – scowling at one or two cowards by way of finishing his speech. 'Allow me to introduce myself – master of the hounds,' he fumbled in his waistcoat pocket for the card on which his name was formally inscribed. 'Some of our friends here are kind enough to come home with me to dinner; might I ask for the honour?'

'My name is Higgins,' replied the stranger, bowing low. 'I am only lately come to occupy the White House at Barford, and I have not as yet presented my letters of introduction.'

'Hang it!' replied Sir Harry; 'a man with a seat like yours, and that good brush in your hand, might ride up to any door in the county (I'm a Leicestershire man!), and be a welcome guest. Mr. Higgins, I shall be proud to become better acquainted with you over my dinner table.'

Mr. Higgins knew pretty well how to improve the acquaintance thus begun. He could sing a good song, tell a good story, and was well up in practical jokes; with plenty of that keen worldly sense, which seems like an instinct in some men, and which in this case taught him on whom he might play off such jokes, with impunity from their resentment, and with a security of applause from the more boisterous, vehement, or prosperous. At the end of twelve months Mr. Robinson Higgins was, out-and-out, the most popular member of the Barford[a] hunt; had beaten all the others by a couple of lengths, as his first patron, Sir Harry, observed one evening, when they were just leaving the dinner-table of an old hunting squire in the neighbourhood.

'Because, you know,' said Squire Hearn, holding Sir Harry by the button – 'I mean, you see this young spark is looking sweet upon Catherine; and she's a good girl, and will have ten thousand pounds down, the day[b] she's married, by her mother's will; and – excuse me, Sir Harry – but I should not like my girl to throw herself away.'

Though Sir Harry had a long ride before him, and but the early and short light of a new moon to take it in, his kind heart was so much touched by Squire Hearn's trembling, tearful anxiety, that he stopped and turned back into the dining-room to say, with more asseverations than I care to give:

'My good Squire, I may say, I know that man pretty well by this time; and a better fellow never existed. If I had twenty daughters he should have the pick of them.'

Squire Hearn never thought of asking the grounds for his old friend's opinion of Mr. Higgins; it had been given with too much earnestness for any doubts to cross the old man's mind as to the possibility of its not being well founded. Mr. Hearn was not a doubter, or a thinker, or suspicious by nature; it was simply his love for Catherine, his only child,[14] that prompted his anxiety in this case; and, after what Sir Harry had said, the old man could totter with an easy mind, though not with very steady legs, into the drawing-room, where his bonny, blushing daughter Catherine and Mr. Higgins stood close together on the hearth-rug – he whispering, she listening with downcast eyes. She looked so happy, so like her dead mother had looked when the Squire was a young man, that all his thought was how to please her most. His son and heir was about to be married, and bring his wife to live with the Squire; Barford and the White House were not distant an hour's ride; and, even as these thoughts passed through his mind, he asked Mr. Higgins if he could not stay all night – the young moon was already set – the roads would be dark – and Catherine looked up with a pretty anxiety, which, however, had not much doubt in it, for the answer.

With every encouragement of this kind from the old Squire, it took everybody rather by surprise when one morning it was discovered that Miss Catherine Hearn was missing; and when, according to the usual fashion in such cases, a note was found, saying that she had eloped with 'the man of her heart,' and gone to Gretna Green,[15] no one could imagine why she could not quietly have stopped at home and been married in the parish church. She had always been a romantic, sentimental girl; very pretty and very affectionate, and very much spoiled, and very much wanting in common sense. Her indulgent father was deeply hurt at this want of confidence in his nevervarying affection; but when his son came, hot with indignation from the Baronet's (his future father-in-law's house, where every form of law and of ceremony[16] was to accompany his own impending marriage), Squire Hearn pleaded the cause of the young couple with imploring cogency, and protested that it was a piece of spirit in his daughter, which he admired and was proud of. However, it ended with Mr. Nathaniel Hearn's declaring that he and his wife would have nothing to do with his sister and her husband. 'Wait till you've seen him, Nat!' said the old Squire, trembling with his distressful anticipations of family discord, 'He's an excuse for any girl. Only ask Sir Harry's opinion of him.' 'Confound Sir Harry! So that a man sits his horse well, Sir Harry cares nothing about anything else. Who is this man – this fellow? Where does he come from? What are his means? Who are his family?'

'He comes from the south – Surrey or Somersetshire, I forget which; and he pays his way well and liberally. There's not a tradesman in Barford but says he cares no more for money than for water; he spends like a prince, Nat. I don't know who his family are, but he seals with a coat of arms, which may tell you if you want to know – and he goes regularly to collect his rents from his estates in the south. Oh, Nat! if you would but be friendly, I should be as well pleased with Kitty's marriage as any father in the county.'

Mr. Nathaniel Hearn gloomed, and muttered an oath or two to himself. The poor old father was reaping the consequences of his weak indulgence to his two children. Mr. and Mrs. Nathaniel Hearn kept apart from Catherine and her husband; and Squire Hearn durst never ask them to Levison Hall, though it was his own house. Indeed, he stole away as if he were a culprit whenever he went to visit the White House; and if he passed a night there, he was fain to equivocate when he returned home the next day; an equivocation which was well interpreted by the surly, proud Nathaniel. But the younger Mr. and Mrs. Hearn were the only people who did not visit at the White House. Mr. and Mrs. Higgins were decidedly more popular than their brother and sister-in-law. She made a very pretty, sweet-tempered hostess, and her education had not been such as to make her intolerant of any want of refinement in the associates who gathered round her husband. She had gentle smiles for townspeople as well as county people; and unconsciously played an admirable second in her husband's project of making himself universally popular.

But there is some one to make ill-natured remarks, and draw ill-natured conclusions from very simple premises, in every place; and in Barford this bird of ill-omen was a Miss Pratt. She did not hunt – so Mr. Higgins's admirable riding did not call out her admiration. She did not drink – so the well-selected wines, so lavishly dispensed among his guests, could never mollify Miss Pratt. She could not bear comic songs, or buffo stories –[17] so, in that way, her approbation was impregnable. And these three secrets of popularity constituted Mr. Higgins's great charm. Miss Pratt sat and watched. Her face looked immoveably grave at the end of any of Mr. Higgins's best stories; but there was a keen, needle-like glance of her unwinking little eyes, which Mr. Higgins felt rather than saw, and which made him shiver, even on a hot day, when it fell upon him. Miss Pratt was a dissenter,[18] and, to propitiate this female Mordecai,[19] Mr. Higgins asked the dissenting minister whose services she attended, to dinner; kept himself and his company in good order; gave a handsome donation to the poor of the chapel. All in vain – Miss Pratt stirred not a muscle more of her face towards graciousness; and Mr. Higgins was conscious that, in spite of all his open efforts to captivate Mr. Davis, there was a secret influence on the other side, throwing in doubts and suspicions, and evil interpretations of all he said or did. Miss Pratt, the little, plain old maid, living on eighty pounds a-year, was the thorn in the popular Mr. Higgins's side, although she had never spoken one uncivil word to him; indeed, on the contrary, had treated him with a stiff and elaborate civility.

The thorn – the grief to Mrs. Higgins was this. They had no children! Oh! how she would stand and envy the careless, busy motion of half-a-dozen children; and then, when observed, move on with a deep, deep sigh of yearning regret. But it was as well.

It was noticed that Mr. Higgins was remarkably careful of his health. He ate, drank, took exercise, rested, by some secret rules of his own; occasionally bursting into an excess, it is true, but only on rare occasions – such as when he returned from visiting his estates in the south, and collecting his rents. That unusual exertion and fatigue – for there were no stage-coaches within forty miles of Barford,[20] and he, like most country gentlemen of that day, would have preferred riding if there had been – seemed to require some strange excess to compensate for it; and rumours went through the town, that he shut himself up, and drank enormously for some days after his return. But no one was admitted to these orgies.

One day – they remembered it well afterwards – the hounds met not far from the town; and the fox was found in a part of the wild heath, which was beginning to be enclosed[21] by a few of the more wealthy townspeople, who were desirous of building themselves houses rather more in the country than those they had hitherto lived in. Among these, the principal was a Mr. Dudgeon, the attorney of Barford, and the agent for all the county families about. The firm of Dudgeon had managed the leases, the marriage settlements, and the wills, of the neighbourhood for generations. Mr. Dudgeon's father had the responsibility of collecting the land-owners' rents just as the present Mr. Dudgeon had at the time of which I speak: and as his son and his son's son have done since. Their business was an hereditary estate to them; and with something of the old feudal feeling, was mixed a kind of proud humility at their position towards the squires whose family secrets they had mastered, and the mysteries of whose fortunes and estates were better known to the Messrs. Dudgeon than to themselves.

Mr. John Dudgeon had built himself a house on Wildbury Heath; a mere cottage as he called it: but though only two stories high, it spread out far and wide, and workpeople from Derby had been sent for on purpose to make the inside as complete as possible. The gardens too were exquisite in arrangement, if not very extensive; and not a flower was grown in them, but of the rarest species. It must have been somewhat of a mortification to the owner of this dainty place when, on the day of which I speak, the fox after a long race, during which he had described a circle of many miles, took refuge in the garden; but Mr. Dudgeon put a good face on the matter when a gentleman hunter, with the careless insolence of the squires of those days and that place, rode across the velvet lawn, and tapping at the window of the dining-room with his whip-handle, asked permission – no! that is not it – rather, informed Mr. Dudgeon of their intention – to enter his garden in a body, and have the fox unearthed. Mr. Dudgeon compelled himself to smile assent, with the grace of a masculine Griselda;[22] and then he hastily gave orders to have all that the house afforded of provision set out for luncheon, guessing rightly enough that a six hours' run would give even homely fare an acceptable welcome. He bore without wincing the entrance of the dirty boots into his exquisitely clean rooms; he only felt grateful for the care with which Mr. Higgins strode about laboriously and noiselessly moving on the tip of his toes, as he reconnoitred the rooms with a curious eye.

'I'm going to build a house myself, Dudgeon; and, upon my word, I don't think I could take a better model than yours.'

'Oh! my poor cottage would be too small to afford any hints for such a house as you would wish to build, Mr. Higgins,' replied Mr. Dudgeon, gently rubbing his hands nevertheless at the compliment.

'Not at all! not at all! Let me see. You have dining-room, drawing-room,' – he hesitated, and Mr. Dudgeon filled up the blank as he expected.

'Four sitting-rooms and the bed-rooms. But allow me to show you over the house. I confess I took some pains in arranging it, and, though far smaller than what you would require, it may, nevertheless, afford you some hints.'

So they left the eating gentlemen with their mouths and their plates quite full, and the scent of the fox overpowering that of the hasty rashers of ham; and they carefully inspected all the ground-floor rooms. Then Mr. Dudgeon said:

'If you are not tired, Mr. Higgins – it is rather my hobby, so you must pull me up if you are – we will go upstairs, and I will show you my sanctum.'

Mr. Dudgeon's sanctum was the centre room, over the porch, which formed a balcony, and which was carefully filled with choice flowers in pots. Inside, there were all kinds of elegant contrivances for hiding the real strength of all the boxes and chests required by the particular nature of Mr. Dudgeon's business: for although his office was in Barford, he kept (as he informed Mr. Higgins) what was the most valuable here, as being safer than an office which was locked up and left every night. But, as Mr. Higgins reminded him with a sly poke in the side, when next they met, his own house was not over-secure. A fortnight after the gentlemen of the Barford hunt lunched there, Mr. Dudgeon's strong-box, – in his sanctum upstairs, with the mysterious spring-bolt to the window invented by himself, and the secret of which was only known to the inventor and a few of his most intimate friends, to whom he had proudly shown it; – this strong-box, containing the collected Christmas rents of half-a-dozen landlords, (there was then no bank nearer than Derby,) was rifled; and the secretly rich Mr. Dudgeon had to stop his agent in his purchases of paintings by Flemish artists, because the money was required to make good the missing rents.

The Dogberries and Verges[23] of those days were quite incapable of obtaining any clue to the robber or robbers; and though one or two vagrants were taken up and brought before Mr. Dunover and Mr. Higgins, the magistrates who usually attended in the court-room at Barford, there was no evidence brought against them, and after a couple of nights' durance in the lock-ups they were set at liberty. But it became a standing joke with Mr. Higgins to ask Mr. Dudgeon, from time to time, whether he could recommend him a place of safety for his valuables; or, if he had made any more inventions lately for securing houses from robbers.

About two years after this time – about seven years after Mr. Higgins had been married – one Tuesday evening, Mr. Davis was sitting reading the news in the coffee-room of the George Inn. He belonged to a club of gentlemen who met there occasionally to play at whist,[24] to read what few newspapers and magazines were published in those days, to chat about the market at

Derby, and prices all over the country. This Tuesday night, it was a black frost; and few people were in the room. Mr. Davis was anxious to finish an article in the 'Gentleman's Magazine;'[25] indeed, he was making extracts from it, intending to answer it, and yet unable with his small income to purchase a copy. So he staid late; it was past nine, and at ten o'clock the room was closed. But while he wrote, Mr. Higgins came in. He was pale and haggard with cold; Mr. Davis, who had had for some time sole possession of the fire, moved politely on one side, and handed to the new comer the sole London newspaper which the room afforded. Mr. Higgins accepted it, and made some remark on the intense coldness of the weather; but Mr. Davis was too full of his article, and intended reply, to fall into conversation readily. Mr. Higgins hitched his chair nearer to the fire, and put his feet on the fender, giving an audible shudder. He put the newspaper on one end of the table near him, and sat gazing into the red embers of the fire, crouching down over them as if his very marrow were chilled. At length he said:

'There is no account of the murder at Bath in that paper?' Mr. Davis, who had finished taking his notes, and was preparing to go, stopped short, and asked:

'Has there been a murder at Bath? No! I have not seen anything of it – who was murdered?'

'Oh! it was a shocking, terrible murder!' said Mr. Higgins not raising his look from the fire, but gazing on with his eyes dilated till the whites were seen all round them. 'A terrible, terrible murder! I wonder what will become of the murderer? I can fancy the red glowing centre of that fire – look and see how infinitely distant it seems, and how the distance magnifies it into something awful and unquenchable.'

'My dear sir, you are feverish; how you shake and shiver!' said Mr. Davis, thinking privately that his companion had symptoms of fever, and that he was wandering in his mind.

'Oh, no!' said Mr. Higgins. 'I am not feverish. It is the night which is so cold.' And for a time he talked with Mr. Davis about the article in the 'Gentleman's Magazine,' for he was rather a reader himself, and could take more interest in Mr. Davis's pursuits than most of the people at Barford. At length it drew near to ten, and Mr. Davis rose up to go home to his lodgings.

'No, Davis, don't go. I want you here. We will have a bottle of port together, and that will put Saunders into good humour. I want to tell you about this murder,' he continued, dropping his voice, and speaking hoarse and low. 'She was an old woman, and he killed her, sitting reading her Bible by her own fireside!' He looked at Mr. Davis with a strange searching gaze, as if trying to find some sympathy in the horror which the idea presented to him.

'Who do you mean, my dear sir? What is this murder you are so full of? No one has been murdered here.'

'No, you fool! I tell you it was in Bath!' said Mr. Higgins, with sudden passion; and then calming himself to most velvet-smoothness of manner, he laid his hand on Mr. Davis's knee, there, as they sat by the fire, and gently detaining him, began the narration of the crime he was so full of; but his voice and manner were constrained to a stony quietude: he never looked in Mr. Davis's face; once or twice, as Mr. Davis remembered afterwards, his grip tightened like a compressing vice.

'She lived in a small house in a quiet old-fashioned street, she and her maid. People said she was a good old woman; but for all that she hoarded and hoarded, and never gave to the poor. Mr. Davis, it is wicked not to give to the poor – wicked – wicked, is it not? I always give to the poor, for once I read in the Bible that "Charity covereth a multitude of sins."[26] The wicked old woman never gave, but hoarded her money, and saved, and saved. Some one heard of it; I say she threw a temptation in his way, and God will punish her for it. And this man – or it might be a woman, who knows? – and this person – heard also that she went to church in the mornings, and her maid in the afternoons; and so – while the maid was at church, and the street and the house quite still, and the darkness of a winter afternoon coming on – she was nodding over the Bible – and that, mark you! is a sin, and one that God will avenge sooner or later; and a step came in the dusk up the stair, and that person I told you of stood in the room. At first he – no! At first, it is supposed – for, you understand, all this is mere guess work – it is supposed that he asked her civilly enough to give him her money, or to tell him where it was; but the old miser defied him, and would not ask for mercy and give up her keys, even when he threatened her, but looked him in the face as if he had been a baby – Oh, God! Mr. Davis, I once dreamt when I was a little innocent boy that I should commit a crime like this, and I wakened up crying; and my mother comforted me – that is the reason I tremble so now – that and the cold, for it is very very cold!'

'But did he murder the old lady?' asked Mr. Davis. 'I beg your pardon, sir, but I am interested by your story.'

'Yes! he cut her throat; and there she lies yet in her quiet little parlour, with her face upturned and all ghastly white, in the middle of a pool of blood. Mr. Davis, this wine is no better than water; I must have some brandy!'

Mr. Davis was horror-struck by the story, which seemed to have fascinated him as much as it had done his companion.

'Have they got any clue to the murderer?' said he. Mr. Higgins drank down half a tumbler of raw brandy before he answered.

'No! no clue whatever. They will never be able to discover him, and I should not wonder – Mr. Davis – I should not wonder if he repented after all, and did bitter penance for his crime; and if so – will there be mercy for him at the last day?'

'God knows!' said Mr. Davis, with solemnity. 'It is an awful story,' continued he, rousing himself; 'I hardly like to leave this warm light room and go
out into the darkness after hearing it. But it must be done,' buttoning on his
great coat – 'I can only say I hope and trust they will find out the murderer
and hang him. – If you'll take my advice, Mr. Higgins, you'll have your bed
warmed, and drink a treacle-posset just the last thing; and, if you'll allow
me, I'll send you my answer to Philologus before it goes up to old Urban.'[27]

The next morning Mr. Davis went to call on Miss Pratt, who was not very
well; and by way of being agreeable and entertaining, he related to her all he
had heard the night before about the murder at Bath; and really he made a
very pretty connected story out of it, and interested Miss Pratt very much in
the fate of the old lady – partly because of a similarity in their situations; for
she also privately hoarded money, and had but one servant, and stopped at
home alone on Sunday afternoons to allow her servant to go to church.

'And when did all this happen?' she asked.

'I don't know if Mr. Higgins named the day; and yet I think it must have
been on this very last Sunday.'

'And to-day is Wednesday. Ill news travels fast.'

'Yes, Mr. Higgins thought it might have been in the London newspaper.'

'That it could never be. Where did Mr. Higgins learn all about it?'

'I don't know, I did not ask; I think he only came home yesterday: he had
been south to collect his rents, somebody said.'

Miss Pratt grunted. She used to vent her dislike and suspicions of Mr.
Higgins in a grunt whenever his name was mentioned.

'Well, I shan't see you for some days. Godfrey Merton has asked me to go
and stay with him and his sister; and I think it will do me good. Besides,'
added she, 'these winter evenings – and these murderers at large in the
country – I don't quite like living with only Peggy to call to in case of need.'

Miss Pratt went to stay with her cousin, Mr. Merton. He was an active
magistrate, and enjoyed his reputation as such. One day he came in, having
just received his letters.

'Bad account of the morals of your little town here, Jessy!' said he, touching one of his letters. 'You've either a murderer among you, or some friend
of a murderer. Here's a poor old lady at Bath had her throat cut last Sunday
week; and I've a letter from the Home Office, asking to lend them "my very
efficient aid," as they are pleased to call it, towards finding out the culprit. It
seems he must have been thirsty, and of a comfortable jolly turn;[28] for
before going to his horrid work he tapped a barrel of ginger wine the old
lady had set by to work;[29] and he wrapped the spigot round with a piece of
a letter taken out of his pocket, as may be supposed; and this piece of a
letter was found afterwards; there are only these letters on the outside, "*ns,
Esq., —arford, —egworth*," which some one has ingeniously made out to
mean Barford, near Kegworth.[30] On the other side there is some allusion to

a racehorse, I conjecture, though the name is singular enough; "Church-and-King-and-down-with-the-Rump."[31]

Miss Pratt caught at this name immediately; it had hurt her feelings as a dissenter only a few months ago, and she remembered it well.

'Mr. Nat Hearn has – or had (as I am speaking in the witness-box, as it were, I must take care of my tenses), a horse with that ridiculous name.'

'Mr. Nat Hearn,' repeated Mr. Merton, making a note of the intelligence; then he recurred to his letter from the Home Office again.

'There is also a piece of a small key, broken in the futile attempt to open a desk – well, well. Nothing more of consequence. The letter is what we must rely upon.'

'Mr. Davis said that Mr. Higgins told him –' Miss Pratt began.

'Higgins!' exclaimed Mr. Merton, '*ns*. Is it Higgins, the blustering fellow that ran away with Nat Hearn's sister?'

'Yes!' said Miss Pratt. 'But though he has never been a favourite of mine –'

'*ns*.' repeated Mr. Merton. 'It is too horrible to think of; a member of the hunt – kind old Squire Hearn's son-in-law! Who else have you in Barford with names that end in *ns*?'

'There's Jackson, and Higginson, and Blenkinsop, and Davis and Jones. Cousin! One thing strikes me – how did Mr. Higgins know all about it to tell Mr. Davis on Tuesday what had happened on Sunday afternoon?'

There is no need to add much more. Those curious in lives of the high-waymen may find the name of Higgins as conspicuous among those annals as that of Claude Duval.[32] Kate Hearn's husband collected his rents on the highway, like many another 'gentleman' of the day; but, having been unlucky in one or two of his adventures, and hearing exaggerated accounts of the hoarded wealth of the old lady at Bath, he was led on from robbery to murder, and was hung for his crime at Derby, in 1775.[a]

He had not been an unkind husband; and his poor wife took lodgings in Derby to be near him in his last moments – his awful last moments. Her old father went with her everywhere but into her husband's cell; and wrung her heart by constantly accusing himself of having promoted her marriage with a man of whom he knew so little. He abdicated his squireship in favour of his son Nathaniel. Nat was prosperous, and the helpless silly father could be of no use to him; but to his widowed daughter the foolish fond old man was all in all; her knight, her protector, her companion – her most faithful loving companion. Only he ever declined assuming the office of her counsellor – shaking his head sadly, and saying –

'Ah! Kate, Kate! if I had had more wisdom to have advised thee better, thou need'st not have been an exile here in Brussels, shrinking from the sight of every English person as if they knew thy story.'

I saw the White House not a month ago; it was to let, perhaps for the twentieth time since Mr. Higgins occupied it; but still the tradition goes in

Barford that once upon a time a highwayman lived there, and amassed untold treasures; and that the ill-gotten wealth yet remains walled up in some unknown concealed chamber; but in what part of the house no one knows.

Will any of you become tenants, and try to find out this mysterious closet? I can furnish the exact address to any applicant who wishes for it.

'RIGHT AT LAST'

'Right at Last' was first published as 'The Sin of a Father' in *Household Words*, 18 (27 November 1858), pp. 553–561. It was collected in *Right at Last and Other Tales* (London: Sampson Low, 1860), pp. 1–34. It was also reprinted in the Boston periodical *Littell's Living Age*, 3:4 (29 January 1859), pp. 301–10. The text in the first collected edition is close to that in *HW*; such differences as there are are mainly punctuation and are as likely to represent the publisher's style as EG's preferences.

Ward, in *Knutsford*, vol. vii, p. xxvii, points out that Dr Brown's father anticipates Magwitch in Dickens's *Great Expectations* (1860–1) in being a forger who makes a fortune in Australia; he also objects that if Margaret knew about the father's crime before the marriage, it was dense of her not to understand her husband's despondency. Though the story is not regarded as one of EG's most successful, its focus on the servant–employer relationship, like that of 'The Manchester Marriage', gives it some interest in relation to her exploration of that theme.

RIGHT AT LAST.[a]

DOCTOR BROWN was poor, and had to make his way in the world. He had gone to study his profession in Edinburgh,[1] and his energy, ability, and good conduct had entitled him to some notice on the part of the professors. Once introduced to the ladies of their families, his prepossessing appearance and pleasing manners made him a universal favourite, and perhaps no other student received so many invitations to dances and evening[b] parties, or was so often singled out to fill up an odd vacancy at the last moment at the dinner-table. No one knew particularly who he was, or where he sprang from; but then he had no near relations, as he had once or twice observed; so he was evidently not hampered with low-born or low-bred connections. He had been in mourning for his mother when he first came to college.

All this much was recalled to the recollection of Professor Frazer by his niece Margaret, as she stood before him one morning in his study, telling him, in a low, but resolute voice, that the night before Doctor James Brown had offered her marriage – that she had accepted him, – and[c] that he was intending to call on Professor Frazer (her uncle and natural guardian)[2] that very morning, to obtain his consent to their engagement. Professor Frazer was perfectly aware, from Margaret's manner, that his consent was regarded by her as a mere form, for that her mind was made up: and he had more than once had occasion to find out how inflexible she could be. Yet he too was of the same blood, and held to his own opinions in the same obdurate manner. The consequence of which frequently was, that uncle and niece had argued themselves into mutual bitterness of feeling, without altering each other's opinions one jot. But Professor Frazer could not restrain himself on this occasion of all others.

'Then, Margaret, you will just quietly settle down to be a beggar, for that lad Brown has little or no money to think of marrying upon: you that might be my Lady Kennedy, if you would.'

'I could not, uncle.'[d]

'Nonsense, child. Sir Alexander is a personable and agreeable man, – middle aged, if you will – well, a wilful woman maun have her way; but if I had had a notion that this youngster was sneaking into my house to cajole you into fancying him, I would have seen him far enough before I had ever let your aunt invite him to dinner. Ay![e] you may mutter; but I say no gentleman would ever have come into my house to seduce my niece's affections, without first informing me of his intentions, and asking my leave.'

'Doctor Brown is a gentleman, Uncle Frazer, whatever you may think of him.'

'So you think – so you think. But who cares for the opinion of a love-sick girl? He is a handsome, plausible young fellow, of good address. And I don't mean to deny his ability. But there is something about him I never did like, and now it's accounted for. And Sir Alexander – Well, well! your aunt will be disappointed in you, Margaret. But you were always a headstrong girl. Has this Jamie Brown ever told you who or what his parents were, or where he comes from? I don't ask about his forbears, for he does not look like a lad who has ever had ancestors: and you a Frazer of Lovat![3] Fie, for shame, Margaret! Who is this Jamie Brown?'

'He is James Brown, Doctor of Medicine of the University of Edinburgh: a good, clever young man, whom I love with my whole heart,' replied Margaret, reddening.

'Hoot! is that the way for a maiden to speak? Where does he come from? Who are his kinsfolk? Unless he can give a pretty good account of his family and prospects, I shall just bid him begone, Margaret, and that I tell you fairly.'

'Uncle' (her eyes were filling with hot indignant tears), 'I am of age; you know he is good and clever; else why have you had him so often to your house? I marry him, and not his kinsfolk. He is an orphan. I doubt if he has any relations that he keeps up with. He has no brothers nor sisters. I don't care where he comes from.'

'What was his father?' asked Professor Frazer, coldly.

'I don't know. Why should I go prying into every particular of his family, and asking who his father was, and what was the maiden name of his mother, and when his grandmother was married?'[a]

'Yet, I think I have heard Miss Margaret Frazer speak up pretty strongly in favour of a long line of unspotted ancestry.'

'I had forgotten our own, I suppose, when I spoke so. Simon Lord Lovat is a creditable great-uncle[4] to the Frazers! If all tales be true, he ought to have been hanged for a felon, instead of beheaded like a loyal gentleman.'

'O! if you're determined to foul your own nest, I have done. Let James Brown come in; I will make him my bow, and thank him for condescending to marry a Frazer.'

'Uncle,' said Margaret, now fairly crying, 'don't let us part in anger. We love each other in our hearts. You have been good to me, and so has my aunt. But I have given my word to Doctor Brown, and I must keep it. I should love him if he was the son of a ploughman. We don't expect to be rich; but he has a few hundreds to start with, and I have my own hundred a year –'

'Well, well, child, don't cry. You have settled it all for yourself, it seems; so I wash my hands of it. I shake off all responsibility. You will tell your aunt what arrangements you make with Doctor Brown about your marriage, and I will do what you wish in the matter. But don't send the young man in to me to ask my consent. I neither give it nor withhold it. It would have been different if it had been Sir Alexander.'

'O! Uncle Frazer, don't speak so. See Dr. Brown, and at any rate – for my sake – tell him you consent. Let me belong to you that much. It seems so desolate at such at time, to have to dispose of myself as if nobody owned or cared for me.'

The door was thrown open, and Doctor James Brown was announced. Margaret hastened away; and, before he was aware, the Professor had given a sort of consent, without asking a question of the happy young man, who hurried away to seek his betrothed; leaving her uncle muttering to himself.

Both Doctor and Mrs. Frazer were so strongly opposed to Margaret's engagement, in reality, that they could not help showing it by manner and implication; although they had the grace to keep silent. But Margaret felt even more keenly than her lover that he was not welcome in the house. Her pleasure in seeing him was destroyed by her sense of the coldness with which he was received; and she willingly yielded to his desire of a short engagement; which was contrary to their original plan of waiting until he should be settled in practice in London, and should see his way clear to such an income as would render their marriage a prudent step. Doctor and Mrs. Frazer neither objected nor approved. Margaret would rather have had the most vehement opposition than this icy coldness. But it made her turn with redoubled affection to her warm-hearted and sympathizing lover. Not that she had ever discussed her uncle and aunt's behaviour with him. As long as he was apparently unaware of it, she would not awaken him to a sense of it. Besides, they had stood to her so long in the relation of parents, that she felt she had no right to bring in a stranger to sit in judgment upon them.

So it was with rather a heavy heart that she arranged their future ménage with Doctor Brown; unable to profit by her aunt's experience and wisdom. But Margaret herself was a prudent and sensible girl. Although accustomed to a degree of comfort in her uncle's house that almost amounted to luxury, she could resolutely dispense with it when occasion required. When Doctor Brown started for London, to seek and prepare their new home, she enjoined him not to make any but the most necessary preparations for her reception. She would herself superintend all that was wanting when she came. He had some old furniture, stored up in a warehouse, which had been his mother's. He proposed selling it, and buying new in its place. Margaret persuaded him not to do this; but to make it go as far as it could. The household of the newly-married couple was to consist of a Scotch-woman long connected with the Frazer family, who was to be the sole female servant; and of a man whom Doctor Brown picked up in London, soon after he had fixed on a house, – a man named Crawford, who had lived for many years with a gentleman now gone abroad, but who gave him the most excellent character, in reply to Doctor Brown's inquiries. This gentleman had employed Crawford in a number of ways; so that in fact he was a kind of Jack-of-all-trades; and Doctor Brown, in every letter to Margaret, had some new accomplishment of his servant's to relate, which he did with the more fulness and zest, because Margaret had slightly questioned the wisdom of starting in life with a man-servant; but had yielded to Doctor Brown's arguments on the necessity of keeping up a respectable appearance, making a decent show, &c., to any one who might be inclined to consult him, but be daunted by the appearance of old Christie out of the kitchen, and unwilling to leave a message with one who spoke such unintelligible English. Crawford was so good a carpenter that he could put up shelves, adjust faulty hinges, mend locks, and even went the length of constructing a box out of some old boards that had once formed a packing-case. Crawford one day, when his master was too busy to go out for his dinner, improvised an omelette as good as any Doctor Brown had ever tasted in Paris, when he was studying there. In short, Crawford was a kind of Admirable Crichton[5] in his way, and Margaret was quite convinced that Doctor Brown was right in his decision that they must have a man-servant; even before she was respectfully greeted by Crawford as he opened the door to the newly-married couple, when they came to their new home after their short wedding tour.

Doctor Brown was rather afraid lest Margaret should think the house bare and cheerless in its half-furnished state; for he had obeyed her injunctions and bought as little furniture as might be, in addition to the few things he had inherited from his mother. His consulting-room (how grand it sounded!) was completely arranged, ready for stray patients; and it was well calculated to make a good impression on them. There was a Turkey carpet on the floor, that had been his mother's, and was just sufficiently worn to give it the air of respectability which handsome pieces of furniture have, when they look as if they had not just been purchased for the occasion, but are in some degree hereditary. The same appearance pervaded the room: the library-table (bought second-hand, it must be confessed), the bureau – that had been his mother's – the leather chairs (as hereditary as the library-table), the shelves Crawford had put up for Doctor Brown's medical books, a good engraving or two on the walls, gave altogether so pleasant an aspect to the apartment that both Doctor and Mrs. Brown thought, for that evening at any rate, that poverty was just as comfortable a thing as riches. Crawford had ventured to take the liberty of placing a few flowers about the room, as his humble way of welcoming his mistress – late autumn flowers, blending the idea of summer with that of winter suggested by the bright little fire in the grate. Christie sent up delicious scones for tea; and Mrs. Frazer had made up for her want of geniality as well as she could by a store of marmalade and mutton hams.[6] Doctor Brown could not be easy even in this comfort until he had shown Margaret, almost with a groan, how many rooms were as yet unfurnished, – how much remained to be done. But she laughed at his alarm, lest she should be disappointed in her new home; declared that she should like nothing better than planning and contriving; that, what with her own talent for upholstery and Crawford's for joinery, the rooms should be furnished as if by magic, and no bills – the usual consequences of comfort – be forthcoming. But with the morning and daylight Doctor Brown's anxiety returned. He saw and felt every crack in the ceiling, every spot on the paper, not for himself, but for Margaret. He was constantly in his own mind, as it seemed, comparing the home he had brought her to, with the one she had left. He seemed constantly afraid lest she had repented, or would repent having married him. This morbid restlessness was the only drawback to their great happiness; and, to do away with it, Margaret was led into expenses much beyond her original intention. She bought this article in preference to that because her husband, if he went shopping with her, seemed so miserable if he suspected that she denied herself the slightest wish on the score of economy. She learnt to avoid taking him out with her when she went to make her purchases, as it was a very simple thing to her to choose the least expensive thing, even though it were the ugliest, when she was by herself, but not a simple painless thing to harden her heart to his look of mortification when she quietly said to the shopman that she could not afford this or that. On coming out of a shop after one of these occasions, he had said –

'O, Margaret, I ought not to have married you. You must forgive me – I have so loved you.'

'Forgive you, James!' said she. 'For making me so happy! What should make you think I care so much for rep in preference to moreen?[7] Don't speak so again, please.'

'O, Margaret! but don't forget how I ask you to forgive me.'

Crawford was everything that he had promised to be, and more than could be desired. He was Margaret's right hand in all her little household plans, in a way which irritated Christie not a little. This feud between Christie and Crawford was indeed the greatest discomfort in the household. Crawford was silently triumphant in his superior knowledge of London, in his favour up stairs, in his power of assisting his mistress, and in the consequent privilege of being frequently consulted. Christie was for ever regretting Scotland, and hinting at Margaret's neglect of one who had followed her fortunes into a strange country, to make a favourite of a stranger, and one who was none so good as he ought to be, as she would sometimes affirm. But, as she never brought any proof of her vague accusations, Margaret did not choose to question her, but set them down to a jealousy of her fellow-servant, which the mistress did all in her power to heal. On the whole, however, the four people forming this family lived together in tolerable harmony. Doctor Brown was more than satisfied with his house, his servants, his professional prospects, and most of all with his little bright energetic wife. Margaret, from time to time, was taken by surprise by certain moods of her husband's; but the tendency of these moods was not to weaken her affection, rather to call out a feeling of pity for what appeared to her morbid sufferings and suspicions – a pity ready to be turned into sympathy, as soon as she could discover any definite cause for his occasional depression of spirits. Christie did not pretend to like Crawford; but, as Margaret quietly declined to listen to her grumblings and discontent on this head, and as Crawford himself was almost painfully solicitous to gain the good opinion of the old Scotch woman, there was no open rupture between them. On the whole, the popular, successful Doctor Brown was apparently the most anxious person in his family. There could be no great cause for this as regarded his money affairs. By one of those lucky accidents which sometimes lift a man up out of his struggles, and carry him on to smooth unencumbered ground, he made a great step in his professional progress, and their income from this source was likely to be fully as much as Margaret and he had ever anticipated in their most sanguine moments, with the likelihood, too, of a steady increase as the years went on.

I must explain myself more fully on this head.

Margaret herself had rather more than a hundred a year; sometimes, indeed, her dividends had amounted to a hundred and thirty or forty pounds; but on that she dared not rely. Doctor Brown had seventeen hundred remaining of the three thousand left him by his mother; and, out of this, he had to pay for some of the furniture, the bills for which had not been sent in at the time, in spite of all Margaret's entreaties that such might be the case. They came in about a week before the time when the events I am going to narrate took place. Of course they amounted to more than even the prudent Margaret had expected, and she was a little dispirited to find how much money it would take to liquidate them. But, curiously and contradictorily enough – as she had often noticed before – any real cause for anxiety or disappointment did not seem to affect her husband's cheerfulness. He laughed at her dismay over her accounts, jingled the proceeds of that day's work in his pockets, counted it out to her, and calculated the year's probable income from that day's gains. Margaret took the guineas, and carried them up stairs to her own secrétaire[a] in silence; having learnt the difficult art of trying to swallow down her household cares in the presence of her husband. When she came back she was cheerful, if grave. He had taken up the bills in her absence, and had been adding them together.

'Two hundred and thirty-six pounds,' he said, putting the accounts away to clear the table for tea, as Crawford brought in the things. 'Why, I don't call that much. I believe I reckoned on their coming to a great deal more. I'll go into the City[a] to-morrow, and sell out some shares, and set your little heart at ease. Now don't go and put a spoonful less tea in tonight to help to pay these bills. Earning is better than saving, and I am earning at a famous rate. Give me good tea, Maggie, for I have done a good day's work.'

They were sitting in the doctor's consulting-room, for the better economy of fire. To add to Margaret's discomfort, the chimney smoked this evening. She had held her tongue from any repining words; for she remembered the old proverb about a smoky chimney and a scolding wife;[8] but she was more irritated by the puffs of smoke coming over her pretty white work than she cared to show; and it was in a sharper tone than usual that she spoke, in bidding Crawford take care and have the chimney swept. The next morning all had cleared brightly off. Her husband had convinced her that their money matters were going on well; the fire burned briskly at breakfast time, and the unwonted sun shone in at the windows. Margaret was surprised when Crawford told her that he had not been able to meet with a chimney-sweeper that morning, but that he had tried to arrange the coals in the grate so that, for this one morning at least, his mistress should not be annoyed, and, by the next, he would take care to secure a sweep. Margaret thanked him, and acquiesced in all his plans about giving a general cleaning to the room, the more readily because she felt that she had spoken sharply the night before. She decided to go and pay all her bills, and make some distant calls on the next morning; and her husband promised to go into the City and provide her with the money.

This he did. He showed her the notes that evening, locked them up for the night in his bureau; and, lo, in the morning they were gone! They had breakfasted in the back parlour, or half-furnished dining-room. A charwoman was in the front room, cleaning after the sweeps. Doctor Brown went to his bureau, singing an old Scotch tune as he left the dining-room. It was so long before he came back, that Margaret went to look for him. He was sitting in the chair nearest to the bureau, leaning his head upon it, in an attitude of the deepest despondency. He did not seem to hear Margaret's step, as she made her way among rolled-up carpets and chairs piled on each other. She had to touch him on the shoulder before she could rouse him.

'James, James!' she said in alarm.

He looked up at her almost as if he did not know her.

'O, Margaret!' he said, and took hold of her hands, and hid his face in her neck.

'Dearest love, what is it?' she asked, thinking he was suddenly taken ill.

'Some one has been to my bureau since last night,' he groaned, without looking up or moving.

'And taken the money,' said Margaret, in an instant understanding how it stood. It was a great blow; a great loss, far greater than the few extra pounds by which the bills had exceeded her calculations: yet it seemed as if she could bear it better. 'O, dear!' she said, 'that is bad; but after all – Do you know,' she said, trying to raise his face, so that she might look into it, and give him the encouragement of her honest loving eyes, 'at first I thought you were deadly ill, and all sorts of dreadful possibilities rushed through my mind, – it is such a relief to find that it is only money –'

'Only money!' he echoed, sadly, avoiding her look, as if he could not bear to show her how much he felt it.

'And after all,' she said, with spirit, 'it can't be gone far. Only last night here. The chimney-sweeps – we must send Crawford for the police directly. You did not take the numbers of the notes?' ringing the bell as she spoke.

'No; they were only to be in our possession one night,' he said.

'No, to be sure not.'

The charwoman now appeared at the door with her pail of hot water. Margaret looked into her face, as if to read guilt or innocence. She was a pro-tégée of Christie's, who was not apt to accord her favour easily, or without good grounds; an honest, decent widow, with a large family to maintain by her labour, – that was the character in which Margaret had engaged her; and she looked it. Grimy in her dress – because she could not spare the money or time to be clean – her skin looked healthy and cared for; she had a straightforward, business-like appearance about her, and seemed in no ways daunted nor surprised to see Doctor and Mrs. Brown standing in the middle of the room, in displeased perplexity and distress. She went about her business without taking any particular notice of them. Margaret's suspicions settled down yet more distinctly upon the chimney-sweeper; but he could not have gone far, the notes could hardly have got into circulation. Such a sum could not have been spent by such a man in so short a time, and the res-toration of the money was her first, her only object. She had scarcely a thought for subsequent duties, such as prosecution of the offender, and the like consequences of crime. While her whole energies were bent on the speedy recovery of the money, and she was rapidly going over the necessary steps to be taken, her husband 'sat all poured out into his chair,' as[a] the Ger-mans say;[9] no force in him to keep his limbs in any attitude requiring the slightest exertion; his face sunk, miserable, and with that foreshadowing of the lines of age which sudden distress is apt to call out on the youngest and smoothest faces.

'What can Crawford be about?' said Margaret, pulling the bell again with vehemence. 'O, Crawford!' as the man at that instant appeared at the door.

'Is anything the matter?' he said, interrupting her, as if alarmed into an unusual discomposure by her violent ringing. 'I had just gone round the corner with the letter master gave me last night for the post, and when I came back Christie told me you had rung for me, ma'am. I beg your pardon, but I have hurried so,' and, indeed, his breath did come quickly, and his face was full of penitent anxiety.

'O, Crawford! I am afraid the sweep has got into your master's bureau, and taken all the money he put there last night. It is gone, at any rate. Did you ever leave him in the room alone?'

'I can't say, ma'am; perhaps I did. Yes! I believe I did. I remember now, – I had my work to do; and I thought the charwoman was come, and I went to my pantry; and some time after Christie came to me, complaining that Mrs. Roberts was so late; and then I knew that he must have been alone in the room. But, dear me, ma'am, who would have thought there had been so much wickedness in him?'

'How was it he got into the bureau?' said Margaret, turning to her husband. 'Was the lock broken?'

He roused himself up, like one who wakens from sleep.

'Yes! No! I suppose I had turned the key without locking it last night. The bureau was closed, not locked, when I went to it this morning, and the bolt was shot.' He relapsed into inactive, thoughtful silence.

'At any rate, it is no use losing time in wondering now. Go, Crawford, as fast as you can, for a policeman. You know the name of the chimney sweeper, of course,' she added, as Crawford was preparing to leave the room.

'Indeed, ma'am, I'm very sorry, but I just agreed with the first who was passing along the street. If I could have known –'

But Margaret had turned away with an impatient gesture of despair. Crawford went without another word to seek a policeman.

In vain did his wife try and persuade Doctor Brown to taste any breakfast; a cup of tea was all he would try to swallow, and that was taken in hasty gulps, to clear his dry throat, as he heard Crawford's voice talking to the policeman whom he was ushering in.

The policeman heard all, and said little. Then the inspector came. Doctor Brown seemed to leave all the talking to Crawford, who apparently liked nothing better. Margaret was infinitely distressed and dismayed by the effect the robbery seemed to have on her husband's energies. The probable loss of such a sum was bad enough, but there was something so weak and poor in character, in letting it affect him so strongly – to deaden all energy and destroy all hopeful spring, that, although Margaret did not dare to define her feeling, nor the cause of it, to herself, she had the fact before her perpetually, that, if she were to judge of her husband from this morning only, she must learn to rely on herself alone in all cases of emergency. The inspector repeatedly turned from Crawford to Doctor and Mrs. Brown for answers to his inquiries. It was Margaret who replied, with terse, short sentences, very different from Crawford's long involved explanations.

At length the inspector asked to speak to her alone.

She followed him into the next room, past the affronted Crawford and her despondent husband. The inspector gave one sharp look at the char-woman, who was going on with her scouring with stolid indifference, turned her out, and then asked Margaret where Crawford came from, – how long he had lived with them, and various other questions, all showing the direction his suspicions had taken. This shocked Margaret extremely; but she quickly answered every inquiry; and, at the end, watched the inspector's face closely, and waited for the avowal of the suspicion.

He led the way back to the other room without a word, however. Craw-ford had left, and Doctor Brown was trying to read the morning's letters (which had just been delivered), but his hands shook so much that he could not see a line.

'Doctor Brown,' said the inspector, 'I have little doubt that your man-servant has committed this robbery. I judge so from his whole manner; and from his anxiety to tell the story, and his way of trying to throw suspicion on the chimney-sweeper, neither whose name nor dwelling can he give; at least he says not. Your wife tells us he has already been out of the house this morning, even before he went to summon a policeman; so there is little doubt that he has found means for concealing or disposing of the notes; and you say you do not know the numbers. However, that can probably be ascertained.'

At this moment Christie knocked at the door, and, in a state of great agita-tion, demanded to speak to Margaret. She brought up an additional store of suspicious circumstances, none of them much in themselves, but all tending to criminate her fellow-servant. She had expected to find herself blamed for starting the idea of Crawford's guilt, and was rather surprised to find herself listened to with attention by the inspector. This led her to tell many other little things, all bearing against Crawford, which, a dread of being thought jealous and quarrelsome, had led her to conceal before from her master and mistress. At the end of her story the inspector said:

'There can be no doubt of the course to be taken. You, sir, must give your man-servant in charge. He will be taken before the sitting magistrate directly; and there is already evidence enough to make him be remanded for a week; during which time we may trace the notes, and complete the chain.'

'Must I prosecute?'[10] said Doctor Brown, almost lividly pale. 'It is, I own, a serious loss of money to me; but there will be the further expenses of the prosecution – the loss of time – the –'

He stopped. He saw his wife's indignant eyes fixed upon him; and shrank from their look of unconscious reproach.

'Yes, inspector,' he said, 'I give him in charge. Do what you will. Do what is right. Of course, I take the consequences. We take the consequences. Don't we, Margaret?' He spoke in a kind of wild low voice; of which Marga-ret thought it best to take no notice.

'Tell us exactly what to do,' she said, very coldly and quietly, addressing herself to the policeman.

He gave her the necessary directions as to their attending at the police-office, and bringing Christie as a witness, and then went away to take measures for securing Crawford.

Margaret was surprised to find how little hurry or violence needed to be used in Crawford's arrest. She had expected to hear sounds of commotion in the house, if indeed Crawford himself had not taken the alarm and escaped. But, when she had suggested the latter apprehension to the inspector, he smiled, and told her that when he had first heard of the charge from the policeman on the beat, he had stationed a detective officer within sight of the house, to watch all ingress or egress; so that Crawford's whereabouts would soon have been discovered if he had attempted to escape.

Margaret's attention was now directed to her husband. He was making hurried preparations for setting off on his round of visits, and evidently did not wish to have any conversation with her on the subject of the morning's event. He promised to be back by eleven o'clock; before which time, the inspector had assured them, their presence would not be needed. Once or twice Doctor Brown said, as if to himself, 'It is a miserable business.' Indeed, Margaret felt it to be so; and now that the necessity for immediate speech and action was over, she began to fancy that she must be very hard-hearted – very deficient in common feeling; inasmuch as she had not suffered like her husband, at the discovery that the servant – whom they had been learning to consider as a friend, and to look upon as having their interests so warmly at heart – was, in all probability, a treacherous thief. She remembered all his pretty marks of attention to her, from the day when he had welcomed her arrival at her new home by his humble present of flowers, until only the day before, when, seeing her fatigued, he had, unasked, made her a cup of coffee, – coffee such as none but he could make. How often had he thought of warm dry clothes for her husband; how wakeful had he been at nights; how diligent in the mornings! It was no wonder that her husband felt this discovery of domestic treason acutely. It was she who was hard and selfish, and thinking more of the recovery of the money than of the terrible disappointment in character, if the charge against Crawford were true.

At eleven o'clock her husband returned with a cab. Christie had thought the occasion of appearing at a police-office worthy of her Sunday clothes, and was as smart as her possessions could make her. But Margaret and her husband looked as pale and sorrow-stricken as if they had been the accused, and not the accusers.

Doctor Brown shrank from meeting Crawford's eye, as the one took his place in the witness-box, the other in the dock. Yet Crawford was trying – Margaret was sure of this – to catch his master's attention. Failing that, he looked at Margaret with an expression she could not fathom. Indeed, the whole character of his face was changed. Instead of the calm smooth look of attentive obedience, he had assumed an insolent, threatening expression of defiance; smiling occasionally in a most unpleasant manner, as Doctor Brown spoke of the bureau and its contents. He was remanded for a week; but, the evidence as yet being far from conclusive, bail for his appearance was taken. This bail was offered by his brother, a respectable tradesman, well known in his neighbourhood, and to whom Crawford had sent on his arrest.

So Crawford was at large again, much to Christie's dismay; who took off her Sunday clothes, on her return home, with a heavy heart, hoping, rather than trusting, that they should not all be murdered in their beds before the week was out. It must be confessed, Margaret herself was not entirely free from fears of Crawford's vengeance; his eyes had looked so maliciously and vindictively at her and at her husband, as they gave their evidence.

But his absence in the household gave Margaret enough to do to prevent her dwelling on foolish fears. His being away made a terrible blank in their daily comfort, which neither Margaret nor Christie – exert themselves as they would – could fill up; and it was the more necessary that all should go on smoothly, as Doctor Brown's nerves had received such a shock, at the discovery of the guilt of his favourite, trusted servant, that Margaret was led at times to apprehend a serious illness. He would pace about the room at night, when he thought she was asleep, moaning to himself – and in the morning would require the utmost persuasion to induce him to go out and see his patients. He was worse than ever, after consulting the lawyer whom he had employed to conduct the prosecution.

There was, as Margaret was brought unwillingly to perceive, some mystery in the case; for he eagerly took his letters from the post, going to the door as soon as he heard the knock, and concealing their directions from her. As the week passed away, his nervous misery still increased.

One evening – the candles were not lighted – he was sitting over the fire in a listless attitude, resting his head on his hand, and that supported on his knee, – Margaret determined to try an experiment, to see if she could not probe, and find out the nature of the sore that he hid with such constant care. She took a stool and sat down at his feet, taking his hand in hers.

'Listen, dearest James, to an old story I once heard. It may interest you. There were two orphans, boy and girl in their hearts, though they were a young man and young woman in years. They were not brother and sister, and by-and-by they fell in love; just in the same fond silly way you and I did, you remember. Well, the girl was amongst her own people, but the boy was far away from his, – if indeed he had any alive. But the girl loved him so dearly for himself, that sometimes she thought she was glad that he had no one to care for him but just her alone. Her friends did like him as much as she did; for, perhaps, they were wise, grave, cold people, and she, I dare say, was very foolish. And they did not like her marrying the boy; which was just stupidity in them, for they had not a word to say against him. But, about a week before the marriage day was fixed, they thought they had found out something – my darling love, don't take away your hand – don't tremble so, only just listen! Her aunt came to her and said: – 'Child, you must give up your lover: his father was tempted, and sinned, and if he is now alive he is a transported convict. The marriage cannot take place.' But the girl stood up and said: – 'If he has known this great sorrow and shame, he needs my love all the more. I will not leave him, nor forsake him, but love him all the better. And I charge you, aunt, as you hope to receive a blessing for doing as you would be done by, that you tell no one!' I really think that girl awed her aunt, in some strange way, into secrecy. But, when she was left alone, she cried long and sadly, to think what a shadow rested on the heart she loved so dearly, and she meant to strive to lighten the life, and to conceal for ever that she had heard of the burden; but now she thinks – O, my husband! how you must have suffered –' as he bent down his head on her shoulder and cried terrible man's tears.

'God be thanked!' he said at length. 'You know all, and you do not shrink from me. O, what a miserable, deceitful coward I have been! Suffered! Yes – suffered enough to drive me mad; and if I had but been brave, I might have been spared all this long twelve months of agony. But it is right I should have been punished. And you knew it even before we were married, when you might have drawn back!'

'I could not: you would not have broken off your engagement with me, would you, under the like circumstances, if our cases had been reversed?'

'I do not know. Perhaps I might, for I am not so brave, so good, so strong as you, my Margaret. How could I be? Let me tell you more: We wandered about, my mother and I, thankful that our name was such a common one, but shrinking from every allusion – in a way which no one can understand, who has not been conscious of an inward sore. Living in an assize town was torture: a commercial one was nearly as bad. My father was the son of a dignified clergyman, well known to his brethren: a cathedral town was to be avoided, because there the circumstance of the Dean of Saint Botolph's son having been transported, was sure to be known. I had to be educated; therefore we had to live in a town; for my mother could not bear to part from me, and I was sent to a day-school. We were very poor for our station – no! we had no station; we were the wife and child of a convict, – for my poor mother's early habits, I should have said. But, when I was about fourteen, my father died in his exile, leaving, as convicts in those days sometimes did, a large fortune. It all came to us. My mother shut herself up, and cried and prayed for a whole day. Then she called me in, and took me into her counsel. We solemnly pledged ourselves to give the money to some charity, as soon as I was legally of age. Till then the interest was laid by, every penny of it: though sometimes we were in sore distresses for money, my education cost so much. But how could we tell in what way the[a] money had been accumu-lated?' Here he dropped his voice. 'Soon after I was one-and-twenty, the papers rang with admiration of the unknown munificent donor of certain sums. I loathed their praises. I shrank from all recollection of my father. I remembered him dimly, but always as angry and violent with my mother. My poor, gentle mother! Margaret, she loved my father; and, for her sake, I have tried, since her death, to feel kindly towards his memory. Soon after my mother's death, I came to know you, my jewel, my treasure!'

After a while, he began again. 'But, O Margaret! even now you do not know the worst. After my mother's death, I found a bundle of law papers – of newspaper reports about my father's trial. Poor soul! why she had kept them, I cannot say. They were covered over with notes in her handwriting; and, for that reason, I kept them. It was so touching to read her record of the days spent by her in her solitary innocence, while he was embroiling himself deeper and deeper in crime. I kept this bundle (as I thought so safely!) in a secret drawer of my bureau; but that wretch Crawford has got hold of it. I missed the papers that very morning. The loss of them was infinitely worse than the loss of the money; and now Crawford threatens to bring out the one terrible fact, in open court, if he can; and his lawyer may do it, I believe. At any rate, to have it blazoned out to the world, – I who have spent my life in fearing this hour! But most of all for you, Margaret! Still – if only it could be avoided! Who will employ the son of Brown, the noted forger? I shall lose all my practice. Men will look askance at me as I enter their doors. They will drive me into crime. I sometimes fear that crime is hereditary! O Mar-garet! what am I to do?'

'What can you do?' she asked.

'I can refuse to prosecute.'

'Let Crawford go free, you knowing him to be guilty?'

'I know him to be guilty.'

'Then, simply, you cannot do this thing. You let loose a criminal upon the public.'

'But if I do not, we shall come to shame and poverty. It is for you I mind it, not for myself. I ought never to have married.'

'Listen to me. I don't care for poverty; and, as for shame, I should feel it twenty times more grievously, if you and I had consented to screen the guilty, from any fear or for any selfish motives of our own. I don't pretend that I shall not feel it, when first the truth is known. But my shame will turn into pride, as I watch you live it down. You have been rendered morbid, dear husband, by having something all your life to conceal. Let the world know the truth, and say the worst. You will go forth a free, honest, honourable man, able to do your future work without fear.'

'That scoundrel Crawford has sent for an answer to his impudent note,' said Christie, putting in her head at the door.

'Stay! May *I* write it?' said Margaret.

She wrote: –

Whatever you may do or say, there is but one course open to us. No threats
can deter your master from doing his duty.

MARGARET BROWN.

'There!' she said, passing it to her husband; 'he will see that I know all,
and I suspect he has reckoned something on your tenderness for me.'

Margaret's note only enraged, it did not daunt, Crawford. Before a week
was out, every one who cared knew that Doctor Brown, the rising young
physician, was son of the notorious Brown the forger. All the consequences
took place which he had anticipated. Crawford had to suffer a severe sentence; and Doctor Brown and his wife had to leave their house and to go to a
smaller one; they had to pinch and to screw, aided in all most zealously by
the faithful Christie. But Doctor Brown was lighter-hearted than he had
ever been before in his conscious life-time. His foot was now firmly planted
on the ground, and every step he rose was a sure gain. People did say, that
Margaret had been seen, in those worst times, on her hands and knees cleaning her own door-step. But I don't believe it, for Christie would never have
let her do that. And, as far as my own evidence goes, I can only say that, the
last time I was in London, I saw a brass-plate with Doctor James Brown
upon it, on the door of a handsome house in a handsome square. And as I
looked, I saw a brougham drive up to the door, and a lady get out, and go
into that house, who was certainly the Margaret Frazer of old days – graver,
more portly, more stern I had almost said. But, as I watched and thought, I
saw her come to the dining-room window with a baby in her arms, and her
whole face melted into a smile of infinite sweetness.

'THE MANCHESTER MARRIAGE'

'The Manchester Marriage' was first published in the extra Christmas number of *Household Words* (7 December 1858), pp. 6–17. It was collected in *Right at Last and Other Tales* (London: Sampson Low, 1860), pp. 35–84. It was also reprinted in *Littell's Living Age*, 3:4 (5 February 1859), pp. 339–352 and, under Dickens's name, in a pirated edition of *A House to Let* (Philadelphia: Peterson, 1859), pp. 29–51. As in the case of 'Right at Last' the *HW* text is similar to 1860, with slightly heavier punctuation, but in addition a few phrases linking 'The Manchester Marriage' to the frame story were deleted.

Like 'Right at Last' the story was written for immediate cash needs, under some pressure of time, in Heidelberg. As has often been observed, its main plot anticipates Alfred Tennyson's *Enoch Arden* (1864) and Thomas Hardy's *The Mayor of Casterbridge* (1886). *Uglow,* p. 85, points out that the Manchester setting is relatively uncharacteristic of EG's work of this period.

THE MANCHESTER MARRIAGE.

————◆————

MR. and Mrs. Openshaw came from Manchester to settle in London.[a] He had been, what is called in Lancashire, a Salesman for a large manufacturing firm, who were extending their business, and opening a warehouse in the city; where Mr. Openshaw was now to superintend their affairs. He rather enjoyed the change; having a kind of curiosity about London, which he had never yet been able to gratify in his brief visits to the metropolis. At the same time, he had an odd, shrewd, contempt for the inhabitants; whom he always pictured to himself as fine, lazy people; caring nothing but for fashion and aristocracy, and lounging away their days in Bond Street, and such places; ruining good English, and ready in their turn to despise him as a provincial. The hours that the men of business kept in the city scandalized him too, accustomed as he was to the early dinners of Manchester folk and the consequently far longer evenings.[1] Still, he was pleased to go to London; though he would not for the world have confessed it, even to himself, and always spoke of the step to his friends as one demanded of him by the interests of his employers, and sweetened to him by a considerable increase of salary. This, indeed,[b] was so liberal that he might have been justified in taking a much larger house than the one he did,[c] had he not thought himself bound to set an example to Londoners of how little a Manchester man of business cared for show. Inside, however, he furnished it with an unusual degree of comfort, and, in the winter-time, he insisted on keeping up as large fires as the grates would allow, in every room where the temperature was in the least chilly. Moreover, his northern sense of hospitality was such, that, if he were at home, he could hardly suffer a visitor to leave the house without forcing meat and drink upon him. Every servant in the house was well warmed, well fed, and kindly treated; for their master scorned all petty saving in aught that conduced to comfort; while he amused himself by following out all his accustomed habits and individual ways, in defiance of what any of his new neighbours might think.

His wife was a pretty, gentle woman, of suitable age and character. He was forty-two, she thirty-five. He was loud and decided; she soft and yielding. They had two children; or rather, I should say, she had two; for the elder, a girl of eleven, was Mrs. Openshaw's child by Frank Wilson, her first husband. The younger was a little boy, Edwin, who could just prattle, and to whom his father delighted to speak in the broadest and most unintelligible Lancashire dialect, in order to keep up what he called the true Saxon accent.[2]

Mrs. Openshaw's Christian-name was Alice, and her first husband had been her own cousin. She was the orphan niece of a sea-captain in Liverpool; a quiet, grave little creature, of great personal attraction when she was fifteen or sixteen, with regular features and a blooming complexion. But she was very shy, and believed herself to be very stupid and awkward; and was frequently scolded by her aunt, her own uncle's second wife. So when her cousin, Frank Wilson, came home from a long absence at sea, and first was kind and protective to her; secondly, attentive, and thirdly, desperately in love with her, she hardly knew how to be grateful enough to him. It is true, she would have preferred his remaining in the first or second stages of behaviour; for his violent love puzzled and frightened her. Her uncle neither helped nor hindered the love affair; though it was going on under his own eyes. Frank's stepmother had such a variable temper, that there was no knowing whether what she liked one day she would like the next, or not. At length she went to such extremes of crossness, that Alice was only too glad to shut her eyes and rush blindly at the chance of escape from domestic tyranny offered her by a marriage with her cousin; and, liking him better than any one in the world, except her uncle (who was at this time at sea), she went off one morning and was married to him; her only bridesmaid being the housemaid at her aunt's. The consequence was, that Frank and his wife went into lodgings, and Mrs. Wilson refused to see them, and turned away Norah, the warm-hearted housemaid, whom they accordingly took into their service. When Captain Wilson returned from his voyage, he was very cordial with the young couple, and spent many an evening at their lodgings, smoking his pipe, and sipping his grog; but he told them that, for quietness' sake, he could not ask them to his own house; for his wife was bitter against them. They were not, however, very unhappy about this.

The seed of future unhappiness lay rather in Frank's vehement, passionate disposition; which led him to resent his wife's shyness and want of demonstrativeness as failures in conjugal duty. He was already tormenting himself, and her too, in a slighter degree, by apprehensions and imaginations of what might befal her during his approaching absence at sea. At last, he went to his father and urged him to insist upon Alice's being once more received under his roof; the more especially as there was now a prospect of her confinement while her husband was away on his voyage. Captain Wilson was, as he himself expressed it, 'breaking up,' and unwilling to undergo the excitement of a scene; yet he felt that what his son said was true. So he went to his wife. And before Frank set sail, he had the comfort of seeing his wife installed in her old little garret in his father's house. To have placed her in the one best spare room, was a step beyond Mrs. Wilson's powers of submission or generosity. The worst part about it, however, was that the faithful

Norah had to be dismissed. Her place as housemaid had been filled up; and, even if it had not,[a] she had forfeited Mrs. Wilson's good opinion for ever. She comforted her young master and mistress by pleasant prophecies of the time when they would have a household of their own; of which, whatever service she might be in meanwhile, she should be sure to form a part.[b] Almost the last action Frank did, before setting sail, was going with Alice to see Norah once more at her mother's house; and then he went away.

Alice's father-in-law grew more and more feeble as winter advanced. She was of great use to her stepmother in nursing and amusing him; and, although there was anxiety enough in the household, there was, perhaps, more of peace than there had been for years; for Mrs. Wilson had not a bad heart, and was softened by the visible approach of death to one whom she loved, and, touched by the lonely condition of the young creature, expecting her first confinement in her husband's absence. To this relenting mood Norah owed the permission to come and nurse Alice when her baby was born, and to remain to attend on Captain Wilson.

Before one letter had been received from Frank (who had sailed for the East Indies and China), his father died. Alice was always glad to remember that he had held her baby in his arms, and kissed and blessed it before his death. After that, and the consequent examination into the state of his affairs, it was found that he had left far less property than people had been led by his style of living to expect; and what money there was, was all settled upon his wife, and at her disposal after her death. This did not signify much to Alice, as Frank was now first mate of his ship, and, in another voyage or two, would be captain. Meanwhile he had left her rather more than two hundred pounds (all his savings) in the bank.

It became time for Alice to hear from her husband. One letter from the Cape[3] she had already received. The next was to announce his arrival in India. As week after week passed over, and no intelligence of the ship having got there reached the office of the owners, and the Captain's wife was in the same state of ignorant suspense as Alice herself, her fears grew most oppressive. At length the day came when, in reply to her inquiry at the Shipping Office, they told her that the owners had given up hope of ever hearing more of the 'Betsy-Jane,' and had sent in their claim upon the Underwriters.[4] Now that he was gone for ever, she first felt a yearning, longing love for the kind cousin, the dear friend, the sympathizing protector, whom she should never see again; – first felt a passionate desire to show him his child, whom she had hitherto rather craved to have all to herself – her own sole possession. Her grief was, however, noiseless, and quiet – rather to the scandal of Mrs. Wilson; who bewailed her stepson as if he and she had always lived together in perfect harmony, and who evidently thought it her duty to burst into fresh tears at every strange face she saw; dwelling on his poor young widow's desolate state, and the helplessness of the fatherless child, with an unction, as if she liked the excitement of the sorrowful story.

So passed away the first days of Alice's widowhood. By-and-by things subsided into their natural and tranquil course. But, as if this young creature was always to be in some heavy trouble, her ewe-lamb[5] began to be ailing, pining, and sickly. The child's mysterious illness turned out to be some affection of the spine, likely to affect health, but not to shorten life – at least, so the doctors said. But the long, dreary suffering of one whom a mother loves as Alice loved her only child, is hard to look forward to. Only Norah guessed what Alice suffered; no one but God knew.

And so it fell out, that when Mrs. Wilson, the elder, came to her one day, in violent distress, occasioned by a very material diminution in the value of the property that her husband had left her, – a diminution which made her income barely enough to support herself, much less Alice – the latter could hardly understand how anything which did not touch health or life could cause such grief; and she received the intelligence with irritating composure. But when, that afternoon, the little sick child was brought in, and the grand-mother – who after all loved it well – began a fresh moan over her losses to its unconscious ears – saying how she had planned to consult this or that doctor, and to give it this or that comfort or luxury in after years, but that now all chance of this had passed away – Alice's heart was touched, and she drew near to Mrs. Wilson with unwonted caresses, and, in a spirit not unlike to that of Ruth,[6] entreated that, come what would, they might remain together. After much discussion in succeeding days, it was arranged that Mrs. Wilson should take a house in Manchester, furnishing it partly with what furniture she had, and providing the rest with Alice's remaining two hundred pounds. Mrs. Wilson was herself a Manchester woman, and naturally longed to return to her native town; some connections of her own, too, at that time required lodgings, for which they were willing to pay pretty handsomely. Alice undertook the active superintendence and superior work of the household; Norah, willing, faithful Norah, offered to cook, scour, do anything in short, so that she might but remain with them.

The plan succeeded. For some years, their first lodgers remained with them, and all went smoothly, – with the one sad exception of the little girl's increasing deformity. How that mother loved that child, it is not for words to tell!

Then came a break of misfortune. Their lodgers left, and no one suc-ceeded to them. After some months, it became necessary to remove to a smaller house; and Alice's tender conscience was torn by the idea that she ought not to be a burden to her mother-in-law, but to go out and seek her own maintenance. And leave her child! The thought came like the sweeping boom of a funeral bell over her heart.

By-and-by, Mr. Openshaw came to lodge with them. He had started in life as the errand-boy and sweeper-out of a warehouse; had struggled up through all the grades of employment in it,[a] fighting his way through the hard striving Manchester life with strong, pushing energy of character. Every spare moment of time had been sternly given up to self-teaching. He was a capital accountant, a good French and German scholar, a keen, far-seeing, tradesman, – understanding markets, and the bearing of events, both near and distant, on trade: and yet, with such vivid attention to present details, that I do not think he ever saw a group of flowers in the fields without thinking whether their colours would, or would not, form harmonious contrasts in the coming spring muslins and prints. He went to debating societies, and threw himself with all his heart and soul into politics; esteeming, it must be owned, every man a fool or a knave who differed from him, and overthrowing his opponents rather by the loud strength of his language than the calm strength of his logic. There was something of the Yankee in all this. Indeed, his theory ran parallel to the famous Yankee motto – 'England flogs creation, and Manchester flogs England.'[7] Such a man, as may be fancied, had had no time for falling in love, or any such nonsense. At the age when most young men go through their courting and matrimony, he had not the means of keeping a wife, and was far too practical to think of having one. And now that he was in easy circumstances, a rising man, he considered women almost as incumbrances to the world, with whom a man had better have as little to do as possible. His first impression of Alice was indistinct, and he did not care enough about her to make it distinct. 'A pretty yea-nay kind of woman,' would have been his description of her, if he had been pushed into a corner. He was rather afraid, in the beginning, that her quiet ways arose from a listlessness and laziness of character, which would have been exceedingly discordant to his active, energetic nature. But, when he found out the punctuality with which his wishes were attended to, and her work was done; when he was called in the morning at the very stroke of the clock, his shaving-water scalding hot, his fire bright, his coffee made exactly as his peculiar fancy dictated, (for he was a man who had his theory about everything based upon what he knew of science, and often perfectly original) – then he began to think: not that Alice had any peculiar merit, but that he had got into remarkably good lodgings; his restlessness wore away, and he began to consider himself as almost settled for life in them.

Mr. Openshaw had been too busy, all his days, to be introspective. He did not know that he had any tenderness in his nature; and if he had become conscious of its abstract existence, he would have considered it as a manifestation of disease in some part of him. But he was decoyed into pity unawares; and pity led on to tenderness. That little helpless child – always carried about by one of the three busy women of the house, or else patiently threading coloured beads in the chair from which, by no effort of its own, could it ever move, – the great grave blue eyes, full of serious, not uncheerful, expression, giving to the small delicate face a look beyond its years, – the soft plaintive voice dropping out but few words, so unlike the continual prattle of a child, – caught Mr. Openshaw's attention in spite of himself. One day – he half scorned himself for doing so – he cut short his dinnerhour to go in search of some toy, which should take the place of those eternal beads. I forget what he bought; but, when he gave the present (which he took care to do in a short, abrupt manner, and when no one was by to see him), he was almost thrilled by the flash of delight that came over that child's face, and he could not help, all through that afternoon, going over and over again the picture left on his memory, by the bright effect of unexpected joy on the little girl's face. When he returned home, he found his slippers placed by his sitting-room fire; and even more careful attention paid to his fancies than was habitual in those model lodgings. When Alice had taken the last of his tea-things away – she had been silent as usual till then – she stood for an instant with the door in her hand. Mr. Openshaw looked as if he were deep in his book, though in fact he did not see a line; but was heartily wishing the woman would go, and not make any palaver of gratitude. But she only said:

'I am very much obliged to you, sir. Thank you very much,' and was gone, even before he could send her away with a 'There, my good woman, that's enough!'

For some time longer he took no apparent notice of the child. He even hardened his heart into disregarding her sudden flush of colour and little timid smile of recognition, when he saw her by chance. But, after all, this could not last for ever; and, having a second time given way to tenderness, there was no relapse. The insidious enemy having thus entered his heart, in the guise of compassion to the child, soon assumed the more dangerous form of interest in the mother. He was aware of this change of feeling, – despised himself for it, – struggled with it; nay, internally yielded to it and cherished it, long before he suffered the slightest expression of it, by word, action, or look to escape him. He watched Alice's docile, obedient ways to her stepmother; the love which she had inspired in the rough Norah (roughened by the wear and tear of sorrow and years); but, above all, he saw the wild, deep, passionate affection existing between her and her child. They spoke little to any one else, or when any one else was by; but, when alone together, they talked, and murmured, and cooed, and chattered so continually, that Mr. Openshaw first wondered what they could find to say to each other, and next became irritated because they were always so grave and silent with him. All this time he was perpetually devising small new pleasures for the child. His thoughts ran, in a pertinacious way, upon the desolate life before her; and often he came back from his day's work loaded with the very thing Alice had been longing for, but had not been able to procure. One

time, it was a little chair for drawing the little sufferer along the streets; and,
many an evening that following summer, Mr. Openshaw drew her along
himself, regardless of the remarks of his acquaintances. One day in autumn,
he put down his newspaper, as Alice came in with the breakfast, and said, in
as indifferent a voice as he could assume: –

'Mrs. Frank, is there any reason why we two should not put up our horses
together?'

Alice stood still in perplexed wonder. What did he mean? He had
resumed the reading of his newspaper, as if he did not expect any answer; so
she found silence her safest course, and went on quietly arranging his breakfast, without another word passing between them. Just as he was leaving the
house, to go to the warehouse as usual, he turned back and put his head into
the bright, neat, tidy kitchen, where all the women breakfasted in the morning: –

'You'll think of what I said, Mrs. Frank' (this was her name with the lodgers), 'and let me have your opinion upon it to-night.'

Alice was thankful that her mother and Norah were too busy talking
together to attend much to this speech. She determined not to think about it
at all through the day; and, of course, the effort not to think, made her think
all the more. At night she sent up Norah with his tea. But Mr. Openshaw
almost knocked Norah down as she was going out at the door, by pushing
past her and calling out, 'Mrs. Frank!' in an impatient voice, at the top of the
stairs.

Alice went up, rather than seem to have affixed too much meaning to his
words.

'Well, Mrs. Frank,' he said, 'what answer? Don't make it too long; for I
have lots of office work to get through to-night.'

'I hardly know what you meant, sir,' said truthful Alice.

'Well! I should have thought you might have guessed. You're not new at
this sort of work, and I am. However, I'll make it plain this time. Will you
have me to be thy wedded husband,[8] and serve me, and love me, and honour me, and all that sort of thing? Because, if you will, I will do as much by
you, and be a father to your child – and that's more than is put in the Prayer-
book.[a] Now, I'm a man of my word; and what I say, I feel; and what I promise, I'll do. Now, for your answer!'

Alice was silent. He began to make the tea, as if her reply was a matter of
perfect indifference to him; but, as soon as that was done, he became
impatient

'Well?' said he.

'How long, sir, may I have to think over it?'

'Three minutes!' (looking at his watch). 'You've had two already – that
makes five. Be a sensible woman, say Yes, and sit down to tea with me, and
we'll talk it over together; for, after tea, I shall be busy; say No' (he hesitated

a moment to try and keep his voice in the same tone), 'and I shan't say another word about it, but pay up a year's rent for my rooms to-morrow, and be off. Time's up! Yes or no?'

'If you please, sir, – you have been so good to little Ailsie –'

'There, sit down comfortably by me on the sofa, and let us have our tea together. I am glad to find you are as good and sensible as I took you for.'

And this was Alice Wilson's second wooing.

Mr. Openshaw's will was too strong, and his circumstances too good, for him not to carry all before him. He settled Mrs. Wilson in a comfortable house of her own, and made her quite independent of lodgers. The little that Alice said with regard to future plans was in Norah's behalf.

'No,' said Mr. Openshaw. 'Norah shall take care of the old lady as long as she lives; and, after that, she shall either come and live with us, or, if she likes it better, she shall have a provision for life – for your sake, missus. No one who has been good to you or the child shall go unrewarded. But even the little one will be better for some fresh stuff about her. Get her a bright, sensible girl as a nurse: one who won't go rubbing her with calf's-foot jelly as Norah does; wasting good stuff outside that ought to go in, but will follow doctors' directions; which, as you must see pretty clearly by this time, Norah won't; because they give the poor little wench pain. Now, I'm not above being nesh for other folks myself. I can stand a good blow, and never change colour; but, set me in the operating-room in the Infirmary,[9a] and I turn as sick as a girl. Yet, if need were, I would hold the little wench on my knees while she screeched with pain, if it were to do her poor back good. Nay, nay, wench! keep your white looks for the time when it comes – I don't say it ever will. But this I know, Norah will spare the child and cheat the doctor, if she can. Now, I say, give the bairn a year or two's chance, and then, when the pack of doctors have done their best – and, maybe, the old lady has gone – we'll have Norah back, or do better for her.'

The pack of doctors could do no good to little Ailsie. She was beyond their power. But her father (for so he insisted on being called, and also on Alice's no longer retaining the appellation of Mamma,[b] but becoming henceforward Mother), by his healthy cheerfulness of manner, his clear decision of purpose, his odd turns and quirks of humour, added to his real strong love for the helpless little girl, infused a new element of brightness and confidence into her life; and, though her back remained the same, her general health was strengthened, and Alice – never going beyond a smile herself – had the pleasure of seeing her child taught to laugh.

As for Alice's own life, it was happier than it had ever been before. Mr. Openshaw required no demonstration, no expressions of affection from her. Indeed, these would rather have disgusted him. Alice could love deeply, but could not talk about it. The perpetual requirement of loving words, looks, and caresses, and misconstruing their absence into absence of love, had been the great trial of her former married life. Now, all went on clear and straight, under the guidance of her husband's strong sense, warm heart, and powerful will. Year by year, their worldly prosperity increased. At Mrs. Wilson's death, Norah came back to them, as nurse to the newly-born little Edwin; into which post she was not installed without a pretty strong oration on the part of the proud and happy father; who declared that if he found out that Norah ever tried to screen the boy by a falsehood, or to make him nesh either in body or mind, she should go that very day. Norah and Mr. Openshaw were not on the most thoroughly cordial terms; neither of them fully recognizing or appreciating the other's best qualities.

This was the previous history of the Lancashire family who had now removed to London.[a]

They had been there about a year, when Mr. Openshaw suddenly informed his wife that he had determined to heal long-standing feuds, and had asked his uncle and aunt Chadwick to come and pay them a visit and see London. Mrs. Openshaw had never seen this uncle and aunt of her husband's. Years before she had married him, there had been a quarrel. All she knew was, that Mr. Chadwick was a small manufacturer in a country town in South Lancashire. She was extremely pleased that the breach was to be healed, and began making preparations to render their visit pleasant.

They arrived at last. Going to see London was such an event to them, that Mrs. Chadwick had made all new linen fresh for the occasion – from night-caps downwards; and as for gowns, ribbons, and collars, she might have been going into the wilds of Canada where never a shop is, so large was her stock. A fortnight before the day of her departure for London, she had formally called to take leave of all her acquaintance; saying she should need every bit of the intermediate time for packing up. It was like a second wedding in her imagination; and, to complete the resemblance which an entirely new wardrobe made between the two events, her husband brought her back from Manchester, on the last market-day before they set off, a gorgeous pearl and amethyst brooch, saying, 'Lunnon should see that Lancashire folks knew a handsome thing when they saw it.'

For some time after Mr. and Mrs. Chadwick arrived at the Openshaws' there was no opportunity for wearing this brooch; but at length they obtained an order to see Buckingham Palace,[10] and the spirit of loyalty demanded that Mrs. Chadwick should wear her best clothes in visiting the abode of her sovereign. On her return, she hastily changed her dress; for Mr. Openshaw had planned that they should go to Richmond, drink tea, and return by moonlight. Accordingly, about five o'clock, Mr. and Mrs. Openshaw and Mr. and Mrs. Chadwick set off.

The housemaid and cook sat[b] below, Norah hardly knew where. She was always engrossed in the nursery, in tending her two children, and in sitting by the restless, excitable Ailsie till she fell asleep. By-and-by, the housemaid

Bessy[11] tapped gently at the door. Norah went to her, and they spoke in whispers.

'Nurse! there's some one down stairs wants you.'

'Wants me! Who is it?'

'A gentleman –'

'A gentleman? Nonsense!'

'Well! a man, then, and he asks for you, and he rang at the front-door[12a] bell, and has walked into the dining-room.'

'You should never have let him,' exclaimed Norah, 'master and missus out –'

'I did not want him to come in; but, when he heard you lived here, he walked past me, and sat down on the first chair, and said, "Tell her to come and speak to me." There is no gas lighted in the room, and supper is all set out.'

'He'll be off with the spoons!' exclaimed Norah, putting the housemaid's fear into words, and preparing to leave the room, first, however, giving a look to Ailsie, sleeping soundly and calmly.

Down stairs she went, uneasy fears stirring in her bosom. Before she entered the dining-room she provided herself with a candle, and, with it in her hand, she went in, looking around her in the darkness for her visitor.

He was standing up, holding by the table. Norah and he looked at each other; gradual recognition coming into their eyes.

'Norah?' at length he asked.

'Who are you?' asked Norah, with the sharp tones of alarm and incredulity. 'I don't know you:' trying, by futile words of disbelief, to do away with the terrible fact before her.

'Am I so changed?' he said, pathetically. 'I dare say I am. But, Norah, tell me!' he breathed hard, 'where is my wife? Is she – is she alive?'

He came nearer to Norah, and would have taken her hand; but she backed away from him; looking at him all the time with staring eyes, as if he were some horrible object. Yet he was a handsome, bronzed, good-looking fellow, with beard and moustache, giving him a foreign-looking aspect; but his eyes! there was no mistaking those eager, beautiful eyes – the very same that Norah had watched not half an hour ago, till sleep stole softly over them.

'Tell me, Norah – I can bear it – I have feared it so often. Is she dead?' Norah still kept silence, 'She is dead!' He hung on Norah's words and looks, as if for confirmation or contradiction.

'What shall I do?' groaned Norah. 'O, sir! why did you come? how did you find me out? where have you been? We thought you dead, we did indeed!' She poured out words and questions to gain time, as if time would help her.

'Norah! answer me this question straight, by yes or no – Is my wife dead?'

'No, she is not!' said Norah, slowly and heavily.

'O, what a relief! Did she receive my letters? But perhaps you don't know. Why did you leave her? Where is she? O, Norah, tell me all quickly!'

'Mr. Frank!' said Norah at last, almost driven to bay by her terror lest her mistress should return at any moment, and find him there – unable to consider what was best to be done or said – rushing at something decisive, because she could not endure her present state: 'Mr. Frank! we never heard a line from you, and the shipowners said you had gone down, you and every one else. We thought you were dead, if ever man was, and poor Miss Alice and her little sick, helpless child! O, sir, you must guess it,' cried the poor creature at last, bursting out into a passionate fit of crying, 'for indeed I cannot tell it. But it was no one's fault. God help us all this night!'

Norah had sat down. She trembled too much to stand. He took her hands in his. He squeezed them hard, as if, by physical pressure, the truth could be wrung out

'Norah.' This time his tone was calm, stagnant as despair. 'She has married again!'

Norah shook her head sadly. The grasp slowly relaxed. The man had fainted.

There was brandy in the room. Norah forced some drops into Mr. Frank's mouth, chafed his hands, and – when mere animal life returned, before the mind poured in its flood of memories and thoughts – she lifted him up, and rested his head against her knees. Then she put a few crumbs of bread taken from the supper-table, soaked in brandy, into his mouth. Suddenly he sprang to his feet.

'Where is she? Tell me this instant.' He looked so wild, so mad, so desperate, that Norah felt herself to be in bodily danger; but her time of dread had gone by. She had been afraid to tell him the truth, and then she had been a coward. Now, her wits were sharpened by the sense of his desperate state. He must leave the house. She would pity him afterwards; but now she must rather command and upbraid; for he must leave the house before her mistress came home. That one necessity stood clear before her.

'She is not here: that is enough for you to know. Nor can I say exactly where she is' (which was true to the letter if not to the spirit). 'Go away, and tell me where to find you to-morrow, and I will tell you all. My master and mistress may come back at any minute, and then what would become of me, with a strange man in the house?'

Such an argument was too petty to touch his excited mind.

'I don't care for your master and mistress. If your master is a man, he must feel for me – poor ship-wrecked sailor that I am – kept for years a prisoner amongst savages, always, always, always thinking of my wife and my home – dreaming of her by night, talking to her, though she could not hear, by day. I loved her more than all heaven and earth put together. Tell me where she is, this instant, you wretched woman, who salved over her wickedness to her, as you to do to me!'

The clock struck ten. Desperate positions require desperate measures.

'If you will leave the house now, I will come to you to-morrow and tell you all. What is more, you shall see your child now. She lies sleeping upstairs. O, sir, you have a child, you do not know that as yet – a little weakly girl – with just a heart and soul beyond her years. We have reared her up with such care![a] We watched her, for we thought for many a year she might die any day, and we tended her, and no hard thing has come near her, and no rough word has ever been said to her. And now you come and will take her life into your hand, and will crush it. Strangers to her have been kind to her; but her own father – Mr. Frank, I am her nurse, and I love her, and I tend her, and I would do anything for her that I could. Her mother's heart beats as hers beats; and, if she suffers a pain, her mother trembles all over. If she is happy, it is her mother that smiles and is glad. If she is growing stronger, her mother is healthy: if she dwindles, her mother languishes. If she dies – well, I don't know: it is not every one can lie down and die when they wish it. Come up stairs, Mr. Frank, and see your child. Seeing her will do good to your poor heart. Then go away, in God's name, just this one night; – to-morrow, if need be, you can do anything – kill us all if you will, or show yourself a great, grand man, whom God will bless for ever and ever. Come, Mr. Frank, the look of a sleeping child is sure to give peace.'

She led him up-stairs; at first almost helping his steps, till they came near the nursery door. She had well-nigh forgotten the existence of little Edwin. It struck upon her with affright as the shaded light fell over the other cot; but she skilfully threw that corner of the room into darkness, and let the light fall on the sleeping Ailsie. The child had thrown down the coverings, and her deformity, as she lay with her back to them,[13] was plainly visible through her slight night-gown. Her little face, deprived of the lustre of her eyes, looked wan and pinched, and had a pathetic expression in it, even as she slept. The poor father looked and looked with hungry, wistful eyes, into which the big tears came swelling up slowly and dropped heavily down, as he stood trembling and shaking all over. Norah was angry with herself, for growing impatient of the length of time that long lingering gaze lasted. She thought that she waited for full half an hour before Frank stirred. And then – instead of going away – he sank down on his knees by the bedside, and buried his face in the clothes. Little Ailsie stirred uneasily. Norah pulled him up in terror. She could afford no more time, even for prayer, in her extremity of fear; for surely the next moment would bring her mistress home. She took him forcibly by the arm: but, as he was going, his eye lighted on the other bed: he stopped. Intelligence came back into his face. His hands clenched.

'His child?' he asked.

'Her child,' replied Norah. 'God watches over him,' said she instinctively; for Frank's looks excited her fears, and she needed to remind herself of the Protector of the helpless.

'God has not watched over me,' he said, in despair; his thoughts apparently recoiling on his own desolate, deserted state. But Norah had no time for pity. To-morrow she would be as compassionate as her heart prompted. At length she guided him down-stairs, and shut the outer door, and bolted it – as if by bolts to keep out facts.

Then she went back into the dining-room, and effaced all traces of his presence, as far as she could. She went up-stairs to the nursery and sat there, her head on her hand, thinking what was to come of all this misery. It seemed to her very long before her master and mistress returned;[a] yet it was hardly eleven o'clock. She heard the loud, hearty Lancashire voices on the stairs; and, for the first time, she understood the contrast of the desolation of the poor man who had so lately gone forth in lonely despair.

It almost put her out of patience to see Mrs. Openshaw come in, calmly smiling, handsomely dressed, happy, easy, to inquire after her children.

'Did Ailsie go to sleep comfortably?' she whispered to Norah.

'Yes.'

Her mother bent over her, looking at her slumbers with the soft eyes of love. How little she dreamed who had looked on her last! Then she went to Edwin, with perhaps less wistful anxiety in her countenance, but more of pride. She took off her things, to go down to supper. Norah saw her no more that night.

Beside having a door into the passage, the sleeping-nursery opened out of Mr. and Mrs. Openshaw's room, in order that they might have the children more immediately under their own eyes. Early the next summer morning, Mrs. Openshaw was awakened by Ailsie's startled call of 'Mother! mother!' She sprang up, put on her dressing-gown, and went to her child. Ailsie was only half awake, and in a not unusual state of terror.

'Who was he mother? Tell me!'

'Who, my darling? No one is here. You have been dreaming, love. Waken up quite. See, it is broad daylight.'

'Yes,' said Ailsie, looking round her; then clinging to her mother, 'but a man was here in the night, mother.'

'Nonsense, little goose. No man has ever come near you!'

'Yes, he did. He stood there. Just by Norah. A man with hair and a beard. And he knelt down and said his prayers. Norah knows he was here, mother' (half angrily, as Mrs. Openshaw shook her head in smiling incredulity).

'Well! we will ask Norah when she comes,' said Mrs. Openshaw, soothingly. 'But we won't talk any more about him now. It is not five o'clock; it is too early for you to get up. Shall I fetch you a book and read to you?'

'Don't leave me, mother,' said the child, clinging to her. So Mrs. Openshaw sat on the bedside talking to Ailsie, and telling her of what they had done at Richmond the evening before, until the little girl's eyes slowly closed and she once more fell asleep.

'What was the matter?' asked Mr. Openshaw, as his wife returned to bed.

'Ailsie wakened up in a fright, with some story of a man having been in the room to say his prayers, – a dream, I suppose.' And no more was said at the time.

Mrs. Openshaw had almost forgotten the whole affair when she got up about seven o'clock. But, by-and-by, she heard a sharp altercation going on in the nursery – Norah speaking angrily to Ailsie, a most unusual thing. Both Mr. and Mrs. Openshaw listened in astonishment.

'Hold your tongue, Ailsie! let me hear none of your dreams; never let me hear you tell that story again!' Ailsie began to cry.

Mr. Openshaw opened the door of communication, before his wife could say a word.

'Norah, come here!'

The nurse stood at the door, defiant. She perceived she had been heard, but she was desperate.

'Don't let me hear you speak in that manner to Ailsie again,' he said sternly, and shut the door.

Norah was infinitely relieved; for she had dreaded some questioning; and a little blame for sharp speaking was what she could well bear, if cross examination was let alone.

Down-stairs they went, Mr. Openshaw carrying Ailsie; the sturdy Edwin coming step by step, right foot foremost, always holding his mother's hand. Each child was placed in a chair by the breakfast-table, and then Mr. and Mrs. Openshaw stood together at the window, awaiting their visitors' appearance and making plans for the day. There was a pause. Suddenly Mr. Openshaw turned to Ailsie, and said:

'What a little goosy somebody is with her dreams, wakening up poor, tired mother in the middle of the night, with a story of a man being in the room.'

'Father! I'm sure I saw him,' said Ailsie, half crying. 'I don't want to make Norah angry; but I was not asleep, for all she says I was. I had been asleep, – and I wakened up quite wide awake, though I was so frightened. I kept my eyes nearly shut, and I saw the man quite plain. A great brown man with a beard. He said his prayers. And then he looked at Edwin. And then Norah took him by the arm and led him away, after they had whispered a bit together.'

'Now, my little woman must be reasonable,' said Mr. Openshaw, who was always patient with Ailsie. 'There was no man in the house last night at all. No man comes into the house, as you know, if you think; much less goes up into the nursery. But sometimes we dream something has happened, and the dream is so like reality, that you are not the first person, little woman, who has stood out that the thing has really happened.'

'But, indeed it was not a dream!' said Ailsie, beginning to cry.

Just then Mr. and Mrs. Chadwick came down, looking grave and discomposed. All during breakfast time, they were silent and uncomfortable. As soon as the breakfast things were taken away, and the children had been carried up-stairs, Mr. Chadwick began, in an evidently preconcerted manner, to inquire if his nephew was certain that all his servants were honest; for, that Mrs. Chadwick had that morning missed a very valuable brooch, which she had worn the day before. She remembered taking it off when she came home from Buckingham Palace. Mr. Openshaw's face contracted into hard lines: grew like what it was before he had known his wife and her child. He rang the bell, even before his uncle had done speaking. It was answered by the housemaid.

'Bessy,[14] was any one here last night, while we were away?'

'A man, sir, came to speak to Norah.'

'To speak to Norah! Who was he? How long did he stay?'

'I'm sure I can't tell, sir. He came – perhaps about nine. I went up to tell Norah in the nursery, and she came down to speak to him. She let him out, sir. She will know who he was, and how long he stayed.'

She waited a moment to be asked any more questions, but she was not, so she went away.

A minute afterwards, Mr. Openshaw made as though he were going out of the room; but his wife laid her hand on his arm:

'Do not speak to her before the children,' she said, in her low, quiet voice. 'I will go up and question her.'

'No! I must speak to her. You must know,' said he, turning to his uncle and aunt, 'my missus has an old servant, as faithful as ever woman was, I do believe, as far as love goes, – but at the same time, who does not always speak truth, as even the missus must allow. Now, my notion is, that this Norah of ours has been come over by some good-for-nothing chap (for she's at the time o' life when they say women pray for husbands – "any, good Lord, any,")[15] and has let him into our house, and the chap has made off with your brooch, and m'appen many another thing beside. It's only saying that Norah is soft-hearted, and doesn't stick at a white lie – that's all, missus.'

It was curious to notice how his tone, his eyes, his whole face was changed, as he spoke to his wife; but he was the resolute man through all. She knew better than to oppose him; so she went up-stairs, and told Norah her master wanted to speak to her, and that she would take care of the children in the meanwhile.

Norah rose to go, without a word. Her thoughts were these:

'If they tear me to pieces, they shall never know through me. He may come, – and then, just Lord have mercy upon us all! for some of us are dead folk to a certainty. But *he*[a] shall do it; not me.'

You may fancy, now, her look of determination, as she faced her master alone in the dining-room; Mr. and Mrs. Chadwick having left the affair in their nephew's hands, seeing that he took it up with such vehemence.

'Norah! Who was that man that came to my house last night?'

'Man, sir!' As if infinitely surprised; but it was only to gain time.

'Yes; the man that Bessy let in; that she went up-stairs to the nursery to tell you about; that you came down to speak to; the same chap, I make no doubt, that you took into the nursery to have your talk out with; the one Ailsie saw, and afterwards dreamed about; thinking, poor wench! she saw him say his prayers, when nothing, I'll be bound, was further from his thoughts; the one that[b] took Mrs. Chadwick's brooch, value ten pounds. Now, Norah! Don't go off. I'm as sure, as my name's Thomas Openshaw, that you knew nothing of this robbery. But I do think you've been imposed on, and that's the truth. Some good-for-nothing chap has been making up to you, and you've been just like all other women, and have turned a soft place in your heart to him; and he came last night a-lovyering, and you had him up in the nursery, and he made use of his opportunities, and made off with a few things on his way down! Come, now, Norah: it's no blame to you, only you must not be such a fool again! Tell us,' he continued, 'what name he gave you, Norah. I'll be bound, it was not the right one; but it will be a clue for the police.'

Norah drew herself up. 'You may ask that question, and taunt me with my being single, and with my credulity, as you will, Master Openshaw. You'll get no answer from me. As for the brooch, and the story of theft and burglary; if any friend ever came to see me (which I defy you to prove, and deny), he'd be just as much above doing such a thing as you yourself, Mr. Openshaw – and more so too; for I'm not at all sure as everything you have is rightly come by, or would be yours long, if every man had his own.' She meant, of course, his wife; but he understood her to refer to his property in goods and chattels.

'Now, my good woman,' said he, 'I'll just tell you truly, I never trusted you out and out; but my wife liked you, and I thought you had many a good point about you. If you once begin to sauce me, I'll have the police to you, and get out the truth in a court of justice, if you'll not tell it me quietly and civilly here. Now, the best thing you can do, is quietly to tell me who the fellow is. Look here! a man comes to my house; asks for you; you take him up-stairs; a valuable brooch is missing next day; we know that you, and Bessy, and cook, are honest; but you refuse to tell us who the man is. Indeed, you've told one lie already about him, saying no one was here last night. Now, I just put it to you, what do you think a policeman would say to this, or a magistrate? A magistrate would soon make you tell the truth, my good woman.'

'There's never the creature born that should get it out of me,' said Norah. 'Not unless I choose to tell.'

'I've a great mind to see,' said Mr. Openshaw, growing angry at the defiance. Then, checking himself, he thought before he spoke again:

'Norah, for your missus's sake I don't want to go to extremities. Be a sensible woman, if you can. It's no great disgrace, after all, to have been taken in. I ask you once more – as a friend – who was this man that you let into my house last night?'

No answer. He repeated the question in an impatient tone. Still no answer. Norah's lips were set in determination not to speak.

'Then there is but one thing to be done. I shall send for a policeman.'

'You will not,' said Norah, starting forward.[a] 'You shall not, sir! No policeman shall touch me. I know nothing of the brooch, but I know this: ever since I was four-and-twenty, I have thought more of your wife than of myself: ever since I saw her, a poor motherless girl, put upon in her uncle's house, I have thought more of serving her than of serving myself! I have cared for her and her child, as nobody ever cared for me. I don't cast blame on you, sir, but I say it's ill giving up one's life to any one; for, at the end, they will turn round upon you, and forsake you. Why does not my missus come herself to suspect me? Maybe, she is gone for the police? But I don't stay here, either for police, or magistrate, or master. You're an unlucky lot. I believe there's a curse on you. I'll leave you this very day. Yes! I'll leave that poor Ailsie, too. I will! No good will ever come to you!'

Mr. Openshaw was utterly astonished at this speech; most of which was completely unintelligible to him, as may easily be supposed. Before he could make up his mind what to say, or what to do, Norah had left the room. I do not think he had ever really intended to send for the police to this old servant of his wife's; for he had never for a moment doubted her perfect honesty. But he had intended to compel her to tell him who the man was, and in this he was baffled. He was, consequently, much irritated. He returned to his uncle and aunt in a state of great annoyance and perplexity, and told them he could get nothing out of the woman; that some man had been in the house the night before; but that she refused to tell who he was. At this moment his wife came in, greatly agitated, and asked what had happened to Norah; for that she had put on her things in passionate haste, and left the house.

'This looks suspicious,' said Mr. Chadwick. 'It is not the way in which an honest person would have acted.'

Mr. Openshaw kept silence. He was sorely perplexed. But Mrs. Openshaw turned round on Mr. Chadwick, with a sudden fierceness no one ever saw in her before.

'You don't know Norah, uncle! She is gone because she is deeply hurt at being suspected. Oh, I wish I had seen her – that I had spoken to her myself. She would have told me anything.' Alice wrung her hands.

'I must confess,' continued Mr. Chadwick to his nephew, in a lower voice, 'I can't make you out. You used to be a word and a blow, and oftenest the blow first; and now, when there is every cause for suspicion, you just do nought. Your missus is a very good woman, I grant; but she may have been put upon as well as other folk, I suppose. If you don't send for the police, I shall.'

'Very well,' replied Mr. Openshaw, surlily. 'I can't clear Norah. She won't clear herself, as I believe she might if she would. Only I wash my hands of it; for I am sure the woman herself is honest, and she's lived a long time with my wife, and I don't like her to come to shame.'

'But she will then be forced to clear herself. That, at any rate, will be a good thing.'

'Very well, very well! I am heart-sick of the whole business. Come, Alice, come up to the babies; they'll be in a sore way. I tell you, uncle,' he said, turning round once more to Mr. Chadwick, suddenly and sharply, after his eye had fallen on Alice's wan, tearful, anxious face; 'I'll have no[a] sending for the police, after all. I'll buy my aunt twice as handsome a brooch this very day; but I'll not have Norah suspected, and my missus plagued. There's for you!'

He and his wife left the room. Mr. Chadwick quietly waited till he was out of hearing, and then said to his wife, 'For all Tom's heroics, I'm just quietly going for a detective, wench. Thou need'st know nought about it.'

He went to the police-station, and made a statement of the case. He was gratified by the impression which the evidence against Norah seemed to make. The men all agreed in his opinion, and steps were to be immediately taken to find out where she was. Most probably, as they suggested, she had gone at once to the man, who, to all appearance, was her lover. When Mr. Chadwick asked how they would find her out, they smiled, shook their heads, and spoke of mysterious but infallible ways and means.[16] He returned to his nephew's house with a very comfortable opinion of his own sagacity. He was met by his wife with a penitent face:

'O master, I've found my brooch! It was just sticking by its pin in the flounce of my brown silk, that I wore yesterday. I took it off in a hurry, and it must have caught in it: and I hung up my gown in the closet. Just now, when I was going to fold it up, there was the brooch! I'm very vexed, but I never dreamt but what it was lost!'

Her husband muttering something very like 'Confound thee and thy brooch too! I wish I'd never given it thee,' snatched up his hat, and rushed back to the station, hoping to be in time to stop the police from searching for Norah. But a detective was already gone off on the errand.

Where was Norah? Half mad with the strain of the fearful secret, she had hardly slept through the night for thinking what must be done. Upon this terrible state of mind had come Ailsie's questions, showing that she had seen the Man, as the unconscious child called her father. Lastly came the suspicion of her honesty. She was little less than crazy as she ran up stairs and dashed on her bonnet and shawl; leaving all else, even her purse, behind her. In that house she would not stay. That was all she knew or was clear about. She would not even see the children again, for fear it should weaken her. She dreaded above everything Mr. Frank's return to claim his wife. She could not tell what remedy there was for a sorrow so tremendous, for her to stay to witness. The desire of escaping from the coming event was a stronger motive for her departure, than her soreness about the suspicions directed against her; although this last had been the final goad to the course she took. She walked away almost at headlong speed; sobbing as she went, as she had not dared to do during the past night for fear of exciting wonder in those who might hear her.[17] Then she stopped. An idea came into her mind that she would leave London altogether, and betake herself to her native town of Liverpool. She felt in her pocket for her purse, as she drew near the Euston Square station with this intention. She had left it at home. Her poor head aching, her eyes swollen with crying, she had to stand still, and think as well as she could, where next she should bend her steps. Suddenly the thought flashed into her mind, that she would go and find out poor Mr. Frank. She had been hardly kind to him the night before, though her heart had bled for him ever since. She remembered his telling her, when she inquired for his address, almost as she had pushed him out of the door, of some hotel in a street not far distant from Euston Square. Thither she went: with what intention she scarcely knew, but to assuage her conscience by telling him how much she pitied him. In her present state she felt herself unfit to counsel, or restrain, or assist, or do aught else but sympathise and weep. The people of the inn said such a person had been there; had arrived only the day before; had gone out soon after his arrival, leaving his luggage in their care; but had never come back. Norah asked for leave to sit down, and await the gentleman's return. The landlady – pretty secure in the deposit of luggage against any probable injury – showed her into a room, and quietly locked the door on the outside. Norah was utterly worn out, and fell asleep – a shivering, starting, uneasy slumber, which lasted for hours.

The detective, meanwhile, had come up with her some time before she entered the hotel, into which he followed her. Asking the landlady to detain her for an hour or so, without giving any reason beyond showing his authority (which made the landlady applaud herself a good deal for having locked her in), he went back to the police-station to report his proceedings. He could have taken her directly; but his object was, if possible, to trace out the man who was supposed to have committed the robbery. Then he heard of the discovery of the brooch; and consequently did not care to return.

Norah slept till even the summer evening began to close in. Then started up. Some one was at the door. It would be Mr. Frank; and she dizzily pushed back her ruffled grey hair, which had fallen over her eyes, and stood looking to see him. Instead, there came in Mr. Openshaw and a policeman.

'This is Norah Kennedy,' said Mr. Openshaw.

'O, sir,' said Norah, 'I did not touch the brooch; indeed I did not. O, sir, I cannot live to be thought so badly of;' and very sick and faint, she suddenly sank down on the ground. To her surprise, Mr. Openshaw raised her up very tenderly. Even the policeman helped to lay her on the sofa; and, at Mr. Openshaw's desire, he went for some wine and sandwiches; for the poor gaunt woman lay there almost as if dead with weariness and exhaustion.

'Norah,' said Mr. Openshaw, in his kindest voice, 'the brooch is found. It was hanging to Mrs. Chadwick's gown. I beg your pardon. Most truly I beg your pardon, for having troubled you about it. My wife is almost broken-hearted. Eat, Norah, – or, stay, first drink this glass of wine,' said he, lifting her head, and pouring a little down her throat.

As she drank, she remembered where she was, and who she was waiting for. She suddenly pushed Mr Openshaw away, saying, 'O, sir, you must go. You must not stop a minute. If he comes back, he will kill you.'

'Alas, Norah! I do not know who "he" is. But some one is gone away who will never come back: some one who knew you, and whom I am afraid you cared for.'

'I don't understand you, sir,' said Norah, her master's kind and sorrowful manner bewildering her yet more than his words. The policeman had left the room at Mr. Openshaw's desire, and they two were alone.

'You know what I mean, when I say some one is gone who will never come back. I mean that he is dead!'

'Who?' said Norah, trembling all over.

'A poor man has been found in the Thames this morning – drowned.'

'Did he drown himself?' asked Norah, solemnly

'God only knows,' replied Mr. Openshaw, in the same tone. 'Your name and address at our house were found in his pocket: that, and his purse, were the only things that were found upon him. I am sorry to say it, my poor Norah; but you are required to go and identify him.'

'To what?' asked Norah.

'To say who it is. It is always done, in order that some reason may be discovered for the suicide – if suicide it was. – I make no doubt, he was the man who came to see you at our house last night. – It is very sad, I know.' He made pauses between each little clause, in order to try and bring back her senses, which he feared were wandering – so wild and sad was her look.

'Master Openshaw,' said she, at last, 'I've a dreadful secret to tell you – only you must never breathe it to any one, and you and I must hide it away for ever. I thought to have done it all by myself, but I see I cannot. Yon poor man – yes! the dead, drowned creature is, I fear, Mr. Frank, my mistress's first husband!'

Mr. Openshaw sat[a] down, as if shot. He did not speak; but, after a while, he signed to Norah to go on.

'He came to me the other night – when – God be thanked! you were all away at Richmond. He asked me if his wife was dead or alive. I was a brute, and thought more of your all coming home than of his sore trial: I spoke out sharp, and said she was married again, and very content and happy: I all but turned him away: and now he lies dead and cold.'

'God forgive me!' said Mr. Openshaw.

'God forgive us all!' said Norah. 'Yon poor man needs forgiveness, perhaps, less than any one among us. He had been among the savages – shipwrecked – I know not what – and he had written letters which had never reached my poor missus.'

'He saw his child!'

'He saw her – yes! I took him up, to give his thoughts another start; for I believed he was going mad on my hands. I came to seek him here, as I more than half promised. My mind misgave me when I heard he never came in. O, sir! it must be him!'

Mr. Openshaw rang the bell. Norah was almost too much stunned to wonder at what he did. He asked for writing materials, wrote a letter, and then said to Norah:

'I am writing to Alice, to say I shall be unavoidably absent for a few days; that I have found you; that you are well, and send her your love, and will come home to-morrow. You must go with me to the Police Court; you must identify the body; I will pay high to keep names and details out of the papers.'

'But where are you going, sir?'

He did not answer her directly. Then he said:

'Norah! I must go with you, and look on the face of the man whom I have so injured, – unwittingly, it is true; but it seems to me as if I had killed him. I will lay his head in the grave, as if he were my only brother: and how he must have hated me! I cannot go home to my wife till all that I can do for him is done. Then I go with a dreadful secret on my mind. I shall never speak of it again, after these days are over. I know you will not, either.' He shook hands with her: and they never named the subject again, the one to the other.

Norah went home to Alice the next day. Not a word was said on the cause of her abrupt departure a day or two before. Alice had been charged by her husband, in his letter, not to allude to the supposed theft of the brooch; so she, implicitly obedient to those whom she loved both by nature and habit, was entirely silent on the subject, only treated Norah with the most tender respect, as if to make up for unjust suspicion.

Nor did Alice inquire into the reason why Mr. Openshaw had been absent during his uncle and aunt's visit, after he had once said that it was unavoidable

He came back grave and quiet; and from that time forth was curiously changed. More thoughtful, and perhaps less active; quite as decided in conduct, but with new and different rules for the guidance of that conduct. Towards Alice he could hardly be more kind than he had always been; but he now seemed to look upon her as some one sacred, and to be treated with reverence, as well as tenderness. He throve in business, and made a large fortune, one half of which was settled upon her.[18]

Long years after these events – a few months after her mother died – Ailsie and her 'father' (as she always called Mr. Openshaw), drove to a cemetery a little way out of town, and she was carried to a certain mound by her maid, who was then sent back to the carriage. There was a head-stone, with F. W. and a date upon it. That[a] was all. Sitting by the grave, Mr. Openshaw told her the story; and for the sad fate of that poor father whom she had never seen,[19] he shed the only tears she ever saw fall from his eyes.

ROUND THE SOFA

When EG published *Round the Sofa* (1859) a volume of stories (and one non-fiction article) she decided to link them together with a frame narrative. Her immediate model was probably Dickens's *HW* Christmas numbers, to which she had contributed, in which a series of stories by different hands were connected together by means of a fairly perfunctory frame story. All the same, the setting in early nineteenth-century Edinburgh, in the circle of an invalid lady possesses some essential features of the Gaskell story, its perennial interest in the provincial, in vanishing cultures, unexpected friendships and the restorative power of affectionate social intercourse. Ellis H. Chadwick, always keen to identify real-life originals for EG's fictional characters, suggests, not wholly implausibly, that Margaret Dawson may have been inspired by EG's friend Eliza Fletcher, *née* Dawson, an old acquaintance of the Stevenson family who met EG for the first time in about 1850, and whose *Autobiography of Mrs. Fletcher, of Edinburgh* (1874) describes her salon in Edinburgh in the early nineteenth century (*Chadwick*, p. 179). See *Early Years*, pp. 70, 150; *Letters*, p. 121.

ROUND THE SOFA.

BY THE AUTHOR OF
'Mary Barton,' 'Life of Charlotte Bronte,' &c. &c.

TWO VOLUMES.

VOL. I.

LONDON:

SAMPSON LOW, SON & CO., 47 LUDGATE HILL.

1859.

LONDON: PRINTED BY WILLIAM CLOWES AND SONS, STAMFORD STREET.

PREFACE.

MOST of these Stories have already appeared in *Household Words*: one, however, has never been published in England, and another has obtained only a limited circulation.

ROUND THE SOFA.

LONG ago I was placed by my parents under the medical treatment of a certain Mr. Dawson, a surgeon in Edinburgh, who had obtained a reputation for the cure of a particular class of diseases. I was sent with my governess into lodgings near his house, in the Old Town. I was to combine lessons from the excellent Edinburgh masters, with the medicines and exercises needed for my indisposition. It was at first rather dreary to leave my brothers and sisters, and to give up our merry out-of-doors life with our country home, for dull lodgings, with only poor grave Miss Duncan for a companion; and to exchange our romps in the garden and rambles through the fields for stiff walks in the streets, the decorum of which obliged me to tie my bonnet-strings neatly, and put on my shawl with some regard to straightness.

The evenings were the worst. It was autumn, and of course they daily grew longer: they were long enough, I am sure, when we first settled down in those gray and drab lodgings. For, you must know, my father and mother were not rich, and there were a great many of us, and the medical expenses to be incurred by my being placed under Mr. Dawson's care were expected to be considerable; therefore, one great point in our search after lodgings was economy. My father, who was too true a gentleman to feel false shame, had named this necessity for cheapness to Mr. Dawson; and in return, Mr. Dawson had told him of those at No. 6 Cromer Street, in which we were finally settled. The house belonged to an old man, at one time a tutor to young men preparing for the University, in which capacity he had become known to Mr. Dawson. But his pupils had dropped off; and when we went to lodge with him, I imagine that his principal support was derived from a few occasional lessons which he gave, and from letting the rooms that we took, a drawing-room opening into a bed-room, out of which a smaller chamber led. His daughter was his housekeeper: a son, whom we never saw, was supposed to be leading the same life that his father had done before him, only we never saw or heard of any pupils; and there was one hard-working, honest little Scottish maiden, square, stumpy, neat, and plain, who might have been any age from eighteen to forty.

Looking back on the household now, there was perhaps much to admire in their quiet endurance of decent poverty; but at this time, their poverty grated against many of my tastes, for I could not recognize the fact, that in a town the simple graces of fresh flowers, clean white muslin curtains, pretty bright chintzes, all cost money, which is saved by the adoption of dust-coloured moreen, and mud-coloured carpets. There was not a penny spent on mere elegance in that room; yet there was everything considered necessary to comfort: but after all, such mere pretences of comfort! a hard, slippery, black horse-hair sofa, which was no place of rest; an old piano, serving as a sideboard; a grate, narrowed by an inner supplement, till it hardly held a handful of the small coal which could scarcely ever be stirred up into a genial blaze. But there were two evils worse than even this coldness and bareness of the rooms: one was that we were provided with a latch-key, which allowed us to open the front door whenever we came home from a walk, and go upstairs without meeting any face of welcome, or hearing the sound of a human voice in the apparently deserted house – Mr. Mackenzie piqued himself on the noiselessness of his establishment; and the other, which might almost seem to neutralize the first, was the danger we were always exposed to on going out, of the old man – sly, miserly, and intelligent – popping out upon us from his room, close to the left hand of the door, with some civility which we learnt to distrust as a mere pretext for extorting more money, yet which it was difficult to refuse: such as the offer of any books out of his library, a great temptation, for we could see into the shelf-lined room; but just as we were on the point of yielding, there was a hint of the 'consideration' to be expected for the loan of books of so much higher a class than any to be obtained at the circulating library, which made us suddenly draw back. Another time he came out of his den to offer us written cards, to distribute among our acquaintance, on which he undertook to teach the very things I was to learn; but I would rather have been the most ignorant woman that ever lived than tried to learn anything from that old fox in breeches. When we had declined all his proposals, he went apparently into dudgeon. Once when we had forgotten our latch-key we rang in vain for many times at the door, seeing our landlord standing all the time at the window to the right, looking out of it in an absent and philosophical state of mind, from which no signs and gestures of ours could arouse him. The women of the household were far better, and more really respectable, though even on them poverty had laid her heavy left hand, instead of her blessing right. Miss Mackenzie kept us as short in our food as she decently could – we paid so much a week for our board, be it observed; and if one day we had less appetite than another, our meals were docked to the smaller standard, until Miss Duncan ventured to remonstrate. The sturdy maid-of-all-work was scrupulously honest, but looked discontented, and scarcely vouchsafed us thanks, when on leaving we gave her what Mrs. Dawson had told us would be considered handsome in most lodgings. I do not believe Phenice ever received wages from the Mackenzies.

But that dear Mrs. Dawson! The mention of her comes into my mind like the bright sunshine into our dingy little drawing-room came on those days; – as a sweet scent of violets greets the sorrowful passer among the woodlands.

Mrs. Dawson was not Mr. Dawson's wife, for he was a bachelor. She was his crippled sister, an old maid, who had, what she called, taken her brevet rank.[1]

After we had been about a fortnight in Edinburgh, Mr. Dawson said, in a sort of half-doubtful manner to Miss Duncan –

'My sister bids me say, that every Monday evening a few friends come in to sit round her sofa for an hour or so, – some before going to gayer parties – and that if you and Miss Greatorex would like a little change, she would only be too glad to see you. Any time from seven to eight to-night; and I must add my injunctions, both for her sake, and for that of my little patient's, here, that you leave at nine o'clock. After all, I do not know if you will care to come; but Margaret bade me ask you;' and he glanced up suspiciously and sharply at us. If either of us had felt the slightest reluctance, however well disguised by manner, to accept this invitation, I am sure he would have at once detected our feelings, and withdrawn it; so jealous and chary was he of anything pertaining to the appreciation of this beloved sister.

But if it had been to spend an evening at a dentist's, I believe I should have welcomed the invitation, so weary was I of the monotony of the nights in our lodgings; and as for Miss Duncan, an invitation to tea was of itself a pure and unmixed honour, and one to be accepted with all becoming form and gratitude: so Mr. Dawson's sharp glances over his spectacles failed to detect anything but the truest pleasure, and he went on.

'You'll find it very dull, I dare say. Only a few old fogies like myself, and one or two good sweet young women: I never know who'll come. Margaret is obliged to lie in a darkened room, – only half-lighted I mean, – because her eyes are weak, – oh, it will be very stupid, I dare say: don't thank me till you've been once and tried it, and then, if you like it, your best thanks will be to come again every Monday, from half-past seven to nine, you know. Good-bye, good-bye.'

Hitherto I had never been out to a party of grown-up people; and no court ball to a London young lady could seem more redolent of honour and pleasure than this Monday evening to me.

Dressed out in new stiff book-muslin, made up to my throat, – a frock which had seemed to me and my sisters the height of earthly grandeur and finery – Alice, our old nurse, had been making it at home, in contemplation of the possibility of such an event during my stay in Edinburgh, but which had then appeared to me a robe too lovely and angelic to be ever worn short of heaven – I went with Miss Duncan to Mr. Dawson's at the appointed time. We entered through one small lofty room, perhaps I ought to call it an antechamber, for the house was old-fashioned, and stately and grand, the large square drawing-room, into the centre of which Mrs. Dawson's sofa was drawn. Behind her a little was placed a table with a great cluster candle-stick upon it, bearing seven or eight wax-lights; and that was all the light in the room, which looked to me very vast and indistinct after our pinched-up apartment at the Mackenzies'. Mrs. Dawson must have been sixty; and yet her face looked very soft and smooth and child-like. Her hair was quite gray: it would have looked white but for the snowiness of her cap, and satin rib-bon. She was wrapped in a kind of dressing-gown of French grey merino: the furniture of the room was deep rose-colour, and white and gold, – the paper which covered the walls was Indian,[2] beginning low down with a pro-fusion of tropical leaves and birds and insects, and gradually diminishing in richness of detail till at the top it ended in the most delicate tendrils and most filmy insects.

Mr. Dawson had acquired much riches in his profession, and his house gave one this impression. In the corners of the rooms were great jars of East-ern china, filled with flower-leaves and spices; and in the middle of all this was placed the sofa, on which poor Mrs. Margaret Dawson passed whole days, and months, and years, without the power of moving by herself. By-and-by Mrs. Dawson's maid brought in tea and macaroons for us, and a little cup of milk and water and a biscuit for her. Then the door opened. We had come very early, and in came Edinburgh professors, Edinburgh beauties, and celebrities, all on their way to some other gayer and later party, but coming first to see Mrs. Dawson, and tell her their *bon-mots*, or their interests, or their plans. By each learned man, by each lovely girl, she was treated as a dear friend, who knew something more about their own individual selves, independent of their reputation and general society-character, than any one else.

It was very brilliant and very dazzling, and gave enough to think about and wonder about for many days.

Monday after Monday we went, stationary, silent; what could we find to say to any one but Mrs. Margaret herself? Winter passed, summer was com-ing, still I was ailing, and weary of my life; but still Mr. Dawson gave hopes of my ultimate recovery. My father and mother came and went; but they could not stay long, they had so many claims upon them. Mrs. Margaret Dawson had become my dear friend, although, perhaps, I had never exchanged as many words with her as I had with Miss Mackenzie, but then with Mrs. Dawson every word was a pearl or a diamond.

People began to drop off from Edinburgh, only a few were left, and I am not sure if our Monday evenings were not all the pleasanter.

There was Mr. Sperano, the Italian exile, banished even from France, where he had long resided, and now teaching Italian with meek diligence in the northern city; there was Mr. Preston, the Westmoreland squire, or, as he preferred to be called, statesman, whose wife had come to Edinburgh for the education of their numerous family, and who, whenever her husband had come over on one of his occasional visits, was only too glad to accompany him to Mrs. Dawson's Monday evenings, he and the invalid lady having been friends from long ago. These and ourselves kept steady visitors, and enjoyed ourselves all the more for having the more of Mrs. Dawson's society.

One evening I had brought the little stool close to her sofa, and was caressing her thin white hand, when the thought came into my head and out I spoke it.

'Tell me, dear Mrs. Dawson,' said I, 'how long you have been in Edinburgh; you do not speak Scotch, and Mr. Dawson says he is not Scotch.'

'No, I am Lancashire – Liverpool-born,' said she, smiling. 'Don't you hear it in my broad tongue?'

'I hear something different to other people, but I like it because it is just you; is that Lancashire?'

'I dare say it is; for, though I am sure Lady Ludlow took pains enough to correct me in my younger days, I never could get rightly over the accent.'

'Lady Ludlow,' said I, 'what had she to do with you? I heard you talking about her to Lady Madeline Stuart the first evening I ever came here; you and she seemed so fond of Lady Ludlow; who is she?'

'She is dead, my child; dead long ago.'

I felt sorry I had spoken about her, Mrs. Dawson looked so grave and sad. I suppose she perceived my sorrow, for she went on and said,

'My dear, I like to talk and to think of Lady Ludlow: she was my true, kind friend and benefactress for many years; ask me what you like about her, and do not think you give me pain.'

I grew bold at this.

'Will you tell me all about her then, please Mrs. Dawson?'

'Nay,' said she, smiling, 'that would be too long a story. Here are Signor Sperano, and Miss Duncan, and Mr. and Mrs. Preston are coming to-night, Mr. Preston told me; how would they like to hear an old-world story which, after all, would be no story at all, neither beginning, nor middle, nor end, only a bundle of recollections.'

'If you speak of me, madame,' said Signor Sperano, 'I can only say you do me one great honour by recounting in my presence anything about any person that has ever interested you.'

Miss Duncan tried to say something of the same kind. In the middle of her confused speech, Mr. and Mrs. Preston came in. I sprang up; I went to meet them.

'Oh,' said I, 'Mrs. Dawson is just going to tell us all about Lady Ludlow, and a great deal more, only she is afraid it won't interest anybody: do say you would like to hear it!'

Mrs. Dawson smiled at me, and in reply to their urgency she promised to tell us all about Lady Ludlow, on condition that each one of us should, after she had ended, narrate something interesting, which we had either heard, or which had fallen within our own experience. We all promised willingly, and then gathered round her sofa to hear what she could tell us about my Lady Ludlow.

'MY LADY LUDLOW'

'My Lady Ludlow' was first published in fourteen parts in *Household Words* between 19 June and 25 September 1858, coming out each week with the exception of the week of 21 August, for which, it appears EG did not submit copy in time (*CD Letters*, 9 August 1858, pp. viii, 620). Each part corresponded to one of the chapters in the volume publication. The pagination of the parts is 19 June, pp. 1–7; 26 June, pp. 29–34; 3 July, pp. 51–6; 10 July, pp. 85–9; 17 July, pp. 99–104; 24 July, pp. 123–8; 31 July, pp. 148–53; 7 August, pp. 175–81; 14 August, pp. 205–11; 28 August, pp. 247–52; 4 September, pp. 277–82; 11 September, pp. 299–305; 18 September, pp. 327–32; 25 September, pp. 341–6. The story was first collected in *Round the Sofa*, 2 vols (London: Sampson Low, 1859), vol. i, pp. 13–340, forming, with the introductory frame, the whole of the first volume. An edition was also published by Harper Bros in America in 1858; as Walter E. Smith, points out, the implication in the Harper accounts that EG had provided advance copy on 10 December 1857 is certainly an error: she was evidently still composing the story in August of the following year (*Smith*, p. 137). For her fury at this piracy see *Further Letters*, p. 194 (Meta Gaskell to C. E. Norton (27 January 1859)). The story was also reprinted, with the *Round the Sofa* frame and links and the other tales in that collection, in *My Lady Ludlow and Other Tales* (London: Sampson Low, 1861). Such differences as there are between *Household Words* and 1859 are generally minor; few are certainly authorial. Not infrequently 1859 substitutes a colon for a semi-colon, and there are some different spellings: it is probable that the publisher is responsible for these.

Chadwick (p. 91), argues, unconvincingly it seems to me, the case that the early chapters are largely autobiographical and based on EG's experience of going to school aged eleven at Barford House, near Warwick, under the headmistress Maria Byerley, whom she sees as the original of Lady Ludlow, who also owes something to anecdotes of the Knutsford eccentric Lady Jane Stanley. The evidence is not compelling. It does seem likely that EG knew the journal of Frances Burney, published as the *Diary and Letters of Madame D'Arblay*, 7 vols (1842, 1846), and derived from it some features of Lady Ludlow's period as a maid of honour to Queen Charlotte and other details of late eighteenth-century life. Although individually the parallels would bear other explanations, cumulatively they are quite striking, and I have therefore recorded them in the notes.

MY LADY LUDLOW.

CHAPTER I.

I AM an old woman now, and things are very different to what they were in my youth. Then we, who travelled, travelled in coaches, carrying six inside, and making a two days' journey out of what people now go over in a couple of hours with a whizz and a flash, and a screaming whistle,[1] enough to deafen one. Then letters came in but three times a week: indeed, in some places in Scotland where I have stayed when I was a girl, the post came in but once a month; – but letters were letters then; and we made great prizes of them, and read them and studied them like books. Now the post comes rattling in twice a day, bringing short jerky notes, some without beginning or end, but just a little sharp sentence, which well-bred folks would think too abrupt to be spoken. Well, well! they may all be improvements, – I dare say they are; but you will never meet with a Lady Ludlow in these days.

I will try and tell you about her. It is no story: it has, as I said, neither beginning, middle, nor end.

My father was a poor clergyman with a large family. My mother was always said to have good blood in her veins; and when she wanted to maintain her position with the people she was thrown among, – principally rich democratic manufacturers, all for liberty and the French Revolution, – she would put on a pair of ruffles, trimmed with real old English point, very much darned to be sure, – but which could not be bought new for love or money, as the art of making it was lost years before. These ruffles showed, as she said, that her ancestors had been Somebodies, when the grandfathers of the rich folk, who now looked down upon her, had been Nobodies, – if, indeed, they had any grandfathers at all. I don't know whether any one out of our own family ever noticed these ruffles, – but we were all taught as children to feel rather proud when my mother put them on, and to hold up our heads as became the descendants of the lady who had first possessed the lace. Not but what my dear father often told us that pride was a great sin; we were never allowed to be proud of anything but my mother's ruffles: and she was so innocently happy when she put them on, – often, poor dear creature, to a very worn and thread-bare gown, – that I still think, even after all my experience of life, they were a blessing to the family. You will think that I am wandering away from my Lady Ludlow. Not at all. The Lady who had owned the lace, Ursula Hanbury, was a common ancestress of both my mother and my Lady Ludlow. And so it fell out, that when my poor father died, and my mother was sorely pressed to know what to do with her nine children, and looked far and wide for signs of willingness to help, Lady Ludlow sent her a letter, proffering aid and assistance. I see that letter now: a large sheet of thick yellow paper, with a straight broad margin left on the left-hand side of the delicate Italian writing, – writing which contained far more in the same space of paper than all the sloping, or masculine hand-writings of the present day. It was sealed with a coat of arms, – a lozenge, – for Lady Ludlow was a widow. My mother made us notice the motto, 'Foy et Loy,' and told us where to look for the quarterings[2] of the Hanbury arms before she opened the letter. Indeed, I think she was rather afraid of what the contents might be; for, as I have said, in her anxious love for her fatherless children, she had written to many people upon whom, to tell truly, she had but little claim; and their cold, hard answers had many a time made her cry, when she thought none of us were looking. I do not even know if she had ever seen Lady Ludlow: all I knew of her was that she was a very grand lady, whose grandmother had been half-sister to my mother's great-grandmother; but of her character and circumstances I had heard nothing, and I doubt if my mother was acquainted with them.

I looked over my mother's shoulder to read the letter; it began, 'Dear Cousin Margaret Dawson,' and I think I felt hopeful from the moment I saw those words. She went on to say, – stay, I think I can remember the very words:

> 'DEAR COUSIN MARGARET DAWSON, – I have been much grieved to hear of the loss you have sustained in the death of so good a husband, and so excellent a clergyman as I have always heard that my late cousin Richard was esteemed to be.'

'There!' said my mother, laying her finger on the passage, 'read that aloud to the little ones. Let them hear how their father's good report travelled far and wide, and how well he is spoken of by one whom he never saw. COUSIN Richard, how prettily her ladyship writes! Go on, Margaret!' She wiped her eyes as she spoke: and laid her finger on her lips, to still my little sister, Cecily, who, not understanding anything about the important letter, was beginning to talk and make a noise.

> 'You say you are left with nine children. I too should have had nine, if mine had all lived. I have none left but Rudolph,[3] the present Lord Ludlow. He is married, and lives, for the most part, in London. But I entertain six young gentlewomen at my house at Connington,[4] who are to me as daughters – save that, perhaps, I restrict them in certain indulgences in dress and diet that might be befitting in young ladies of a higher rank, and of more

probable wealth. These young persons – all of condition, though out[a] of means – are my constant companions, and I strive to do my duty as a Christian lady towards them. One of these young gentlewomen died (at her own home, whither she had gone upon a visit) last May. Will you do me the favour to allow your eldest daughter to supply her place in my household? She is, as I make out, about sixteen years of age. She will find companions here who are but a little older than herself. I dress my young friends myself, and make each of them a small allowance for pocket-money. They have but few opportunities for matrimony, as Connington is far removed from any town. The clergyman is a deaf old widower; my agent is married; and as for the neighbouring farmers, they are, of course, below the notice of the young gentlewomen under my protection. Still, if any young woman wishes to marry, and has conducted herself to my satisfaction, I give her a wedding dinner, her clothes, and her house-linen. And such as remain with me to my death, will find a small competency provided for them in my will. I reserve to myself the option of paying their travelling expenses, – disliking gadding women, on the one hand; on the other, not wishing by too long absence from the family home to weaken natural ties.

'If my proposal pleases you and your daughter – or rather, if it pleases you, for I trust your daughter has been too well brought up to have a will in opposition to yours – let me know, dear cousin Margaret Dawson, and I will make arrangements for meeting the young gentlewoman at Cavistock, which is the nearest point to which the coach will bring her.'

My mother dropped the letter, and sat silent.

'I shall not know what to do without you, Margaret.'

A moment before, like a young untried girl as I was, I had been pleased at the notion of seeing a new place, and leading a new life. But now, – my mother's look of sorrow, and the children's cry of remonstrance: 'Mother; I won't go,' I said.

'Nay! but you had better,' replied she, shaking her head. 'Lady Ludlow has much power. She can help your brothers. It will not do to slight her offer.'

So we accepted it, after much consultation. We were rewarded, – or so we thought, – for, afterwards, when I came to know Lady Ludlow, I saw that she would have done her duty by us, as helpless relations, however we might have rejected her kindness, – by a presentation to Christ's Hospital[5] for one of my brothers.

And this was how I came to know my Lady Ludlow.

I remember well the afternoon of my arrival at Hanbury Court. Her ladyship had sent to meet me at the nearest post-town at which the mail-coach stopped. There was an old groom inquiring for me, the ostler said, if my name was Dawson – from Hanbury Court, he believed. I felt it rather formidable; and first began to understand what was meant by going among strangers, when I lost sight of the guard to whom my mother had intrusted

me. I was perched up in a high gig with a hood to it, such as in those days
was called a chair, and my companion was driving deliberately through the
most pastoral country I had ever yet seen. By-and-by we ascended a long
hill, and the man got out and walked at the horse's head. I should have liked
to walk, too, very much indeed; but I did not know how far I might do it;
and, in fact, I dared not speak to ask to be helped down the deep steps of the
gig. We were at last at the top, – on a long, breezy, sweeping, unenclosed[6]
piece of ground, called, as I afterwards learnt, a Chase.[a] The groom stopped,
breathed, patted his horse, and then mounted again to my side.

'Are we near Hanbury Court?' I asked.

'Near! Why, Miss! we've a matter of ten mile yet to go.'

Once launched into conversation, we went on pretty glibly. I fancy he had
been afraid of beginning to speak to me, just as I was to him; but he got over
his shyness with me sooner than I did mine with him. I let him choose the
subjects of conversation, although very often I could not understand the
points of interest in them: for instance, he talked for more than a quarter of
an hour of a famous race which a certain dog-fox had given him, above
thirty years before; and spoke of all the covers and turns just as if I knew
them as well as he did; and all the time I was wondering what kind of an animal a dog-fox might be.

After we left the Chase, the road grew worse. No one in these days, who
has not seen the byroads[b] of fifty years ago, can imagine what they were. We
had to quarter,[7] as Randal called it, nearly all the way along the deep-rutted,
miry lanes; and the tremendous jolts I occasionally met with made my seat
in the gig so unsteady that I could not look about me at all, I was so much
occupied in holding on. The road was too muddy for me to walk without
dirtying myself more than I liked to do, just before my first sight of my Lady
Ludlow. But by-and-by, when we came to the fields in which the lane ended,
I begged Randal to help me down, as I saw that I could pick my steps among
the pasture grass without making myself unfit to be seen; and Randal, out of
pity for his steaming horse, wearied with the hard struggle through the mud,
thanked me kindly, and helped me down with a springing jump.

The pastures fell gradually down to the lower land, shut in on either side
by rows of high elms, as if there had been a wide grand avenue here in
former times. Down the grassy gorge we went, seeing the sunset[c] sky at the
end of the shadowed descent. Suddenly we came to a long flight of steps.

'If you'll run down there, Miss, I'll go round and meet you, and then
you'd better mount again, for my lady will like to see you drive up to the
house.'

'Are we near the house?' said I, suddenly checked by the idea.

'Down there, Miss,' replied he, pointing with his whip to certain stacks of
twisted chimneys rising out of a group of trees, in deep shadow against the

crimson light, and which lay just beyond a great square lawn at the base of the steep slope of a hundred yards, on the edge of which we stood.

I went down the steps quietly enough. I met Randal and the gig at the bottom; and, falling into a side road to the left, we drove sedately round, through the gateway, and into the great court in front of the house.

The road by which we had come lay right at the back.

Hanbury Court is a vast red-brick house – at least, it is cased in part with red bricks; and the gate-house and walls about the place are of brick, – with stone facings at every corner, and door, and window, such as you see at Hampton Court. At the back are the gables, and arched doorways, and stone mullions, which show (so Lady Ludlow used to tell us) that it was once a priory. There was a prior's parlour, I know – only we called it Mrs. Medlicott's room; and there was a tithe-barn as big as a church, and rows of fish-ponds, all got ready for the monks' fasting-days in old time. But all this I did not see till afterwards. I hardly noticed, this first night, the great Virginian Creeper[8] (said to have been the first planted in England by one of my lady's ancestors) that half-covered the front of the house. As I had been unwilling to leave the guard of the coach, so did I now feel unwilling to leave Randal, a known friend of three hours. But there was no help for it; in I must go; past the grand-looking old gentleman holding the door open for me, on into the great hall on the right hand, into which the sun's last rays were sending in glorious red light, – the gentleman was now walking before me, – up a step on to the dais,[9] as I afterwards learned that it was called, – then again to the left, through a series of sitting-rooms, opening one out of another, and all of them looking into a stately garden, glowing, even in the twilight, with the bloom of flowers. We went up four steps out of the last of these rooms, and then my guide lifted up a heavy silk curtain, and I was in the presence of my Lady Ludlow.

She was very small of stature, and very upright. She wore a great lace cap, nearly half her own height, I should think, that went round her head (caps which tied under the chin, and which we called 'mobs,' came in later, and my lady held them in great contempt, saying people might as well come down in their night-caps). In front of my lady's cap was a great bow of white satin ribbon; and a broad band of the same ribbon was tied tight round her head, and served to keep the cap straight. She had a fine Indian muslin shawl folded over her shoulders and across her chest, and an apron of the same; a black silk mode gown, made with short sleeves and ruffles, and with the tail thereof pulled through the pocket-hole, so as to shorten it to a useful length: beneath it she wore, as I could plainly see, a quilted lavender satin petticoat. Her hair was snowy white, but I hardly saw it, it was so covered with her cap: her skin, even at her age, was waxen in texture and tint; her eyes were large and dark blue, and must have been her great beauty when she was young, for there was nothing particular, as far as I can remember, either in mouth or nose. She had a great gold-headed stick by her chair; but I think it was more as a mark of state and dignity than for use; for she had as light and brisk a step when she chose as any girl of fifteen, and, in her private early walk of meditation in the mornings, would go as swiftly from garden alley to garden alley as any one of us.

She was standing up when I went in. I dropped my curtsy[a] at the door, which my mother had always taught me as a part of good manners, and went up instinctively to my lady. She did not put out her hand, but raised herself a little on tiptoe, and kissed me on both cheeks.

'You are cold, my child. You shall have a dish of tea with me.' She rang a little hand-bell on the table by her, and her waiting-maid came in from a small anteroom; and, as if all had been prepared, and was awaiting my arrival, brought with her a small china-service with tea ready made, and a plate of delicately-cut bread-and-butter,[b] every morsel of which I could have eaten, and been none the better for it, so hungry was I after my long ride. The waiting-maid took off my cloak, and I sat[c] down, sorely alarmed at the silence, the hushed foot-falls of the subdued maiden over the thick carpet, and the soft voice and clear pronunciation of my Lady Ludlow. My teaspoon fell against my cup with a sharp noise, that seemed so out of place and sea-son that I blushed deeply. My lady caught my eye with hers, – both keen and sweet were those dark-blue eyes of her ladyship's: –

'Your hands are very cold, my dear; take off those gloves' (I wore thick serviceable doeskin, and had been too shy to take them off unbidden), 'and let me try and warm them – the evenings are very chilly.' And she held my great red hands in hers, – soft, warm, white, ring-laden. Looking at last a lit-tle wistfully into my face, she said – 'Poor child! And you're the eldest of nine! I had a daughter who would have been just your age; but I cannot fancy her the eldest of nine.' Then came a pause of silence; and then she rang her bell, and desired her waiting-maid, Adams, to show me to my room.

It was so small that I think it must have been a cell. The walls were white-washed stone; the bed was of white dimity. There was a small piece of red stair-carpet on each side of the bed, and two chairs. In a closet adjoining were my washstand and toilet-table. There was a text of Scripture painted on the wall right opposite to my bed; and below hung a print, common enough in those days, of King George and Queen Charlotte, with all their numerous children,[10] down to the little Princess Amelia in a go-cart. On each side hung a small portrait, also engraved: on the left, it was Louis the Sixteenth, on the other, Marie-Antoinette. On the chimney-piece there was a tinder-box and a Prayer-book.[d] I do not remember anything else in the room. Indeed, in those days people did not dream of writing-tables, and inkstands, and portfolios, and easy chairs, and what not. We were taught to go into our bedrooms for the purposes of dressing, and sleeping, and praying.

Presently I was summoned to supper. I followed the young lady who had been sent to call me, down the wide shallow stairs, into the great hall, through which I had first passed on my way to my Lady Ludlow's room. There were four other young gentlewomen, all standing, and all silent, who curtsied[a] to me when I first came in. They were dressed in a kind of uniform: muslin caps bound round their heads with blue ribbons, plain muslin handkerchiefs, lawn aprons, and drab-coloured stuff gowns. They were all gathered together at a little distance from the table, on which were placed a couple of cold chickens, a salad, and a fruit-tart. On the dais there was a smaller round table, on which stood a silver jug filled with milk, and a small roll. Near that was set a carved chair, with a countess's coronet surmounting the back of it. I thought that some one might have spoken to me; but they were shy, and I was shy; or else there was some other reason; but, indeed, almost the minute after I had come into the hall by the door at the lower end, her ladyship entered by the door opening upon the dais; whereupon we all curtsied[b] very low; I, because I saw the others do it. She stood, and looked at us for a moment.

'Young gentlewomen,' said she, 'make Margaret Dawson welcome among you;' and they treated me with the kind politeness due to a stranger, but still without any talking beyond what was required for the purposes of the meal. After it was over, and grace was said by one of our party, my lady rang her hand-bell, and the servants came in and cleared away the supper things: then they brought in a portable reading-desk, which was placed on the dais, and, the whole household trooping in, my lady called to one of my companions to come up and read the Psalms and Lessons for the day. I remember thinking how afraid I should have been had I been in her place. There were no prayers. My lady thought it schismatic[11] to have any prayers excepting those in the Prayer-book;[c] and would as soon have preached a sermon herself in the parish church, as have allowed any one not a deacon at the least to read prayers in a private dwelling-house. I am not sure that even then she would have approved of his reading them in an unconsecrated place.

She had been maid of honour to Queen Charlotte:[12] a Hanbury of that old stock that flourished in the days of the Plantagenets, and heiress of all the land that remained to the family, of the great estates which had once stretched into four separate counties. Hanbury Court was hers by right. She had married Lord Ludlow, and had lived for many years at his various seats, and away from her ancestral home. She had lost all her children but one, and most of them had died at these houses of Lord Ludlow's; and, I dare say, that gave my lady a distaste to the places, and a longing to come back to Hanbury Court, where she had been so happy as a girl. I imagine her girlhood had been the happiest time of her life; for, now I think of it, most of her opinions, when I knew her in later life, were singular enough then, but had been universally prevalent fifty years before. For instance, while I lived at

Hanbury Court, the cry for education was beginning to come up: Mr. Raikes had set up his Sunday Schools;[13] and some clergymen were all for teaching writing and arithmetic, as well as reading. My lady[a] would have none of this; it was levelling and revolutionary, she said. When a young woman came to be hired, my lady would have her in, and see if she liked her looks and her dress, and question her about her family. Her ladyship laid great stress upon this latter point, saying that a girl who did not warm up when any interest or curiosity was expressed about her mother, or the 'baby' (if there was one), was not likely to make a good servant. Then she would make her put out her feet, to see if they were well and neatly shod. Then she would bid her say the Lord's Prayer and the Creed. Then she inquired if she could write. If she could, and she had liked all that had gone before, her face sank – it was a great disappointment, for it was an all but inviolable rule with her never to engage a servant who could write. But I have known her ladyship break through it, although in both cases in which she did so she put the girl's principles to a further and unusual test in asking her to repeat the Ten Commandments.[b] One pert young woman – and yet I was sorry for her too, only she afterwards married a rich draper in Shrewsbury –[14] who had got through her trials pretty tolerably, considering she could write, spoilt all, by saying glibly, at the end of the last Commandment,[c] 'An't please your ladyship, I can cast accounts.'

'Go away, wench,' said my lady in a hurry, 'You're only fit for trade; you will not suit me for a servant.' The girl went away crestfallen: in a minute, however, my lady sent me after her to see that she had something to eat before leaving the house; and, indeed, she sent for her once again, but it was only to give her a Bible, and to bid her beware of French principles, which had led the French to cut off their king's and queen's[d] heads.

The poor, blubbering girl said, 'Indeed, my lady, I wouldn't hurt a fly, much less a king, and I cannot abide the French, nor frogs neither, for that matter.'

But my lady was inexorable, and took a girl who could neither read nor write, to make up for her alarm about the progress of education towards addition and subtraction; and, afterwards, when the clergyman who was at Hanbury parish when I came there, had died, and the bishop had appointed another, and a younger man, in his stead, this was one of the points on which he and my lady did not agree. While good old deaf Mr. Mountford lived, it was my lady's custom, when indisposed for a sermon, to stand up at the door of her large square pew, – just opposite to the reading-desk, – and to say (at that part of the morning service where it is decreed that, in quires and places where they sing,[15] here followeth the Anthem): 'Mr. Mountford, I will not trouble you for a discourse this morning.' And we all knelt down to the Litany with great satisfaction; for Mr. Mountford, though he could not hear, had always his eyes open about this part of the service, for any of my lady's movements. But the new clergyman, Mr. Gray, was of a different stamp. He was very zealous in all his parish work; and my lady, who was just as good as she could be to the poor, was often crying him up as a godsend to the parish, and he never could send amiss to the Court when he wanted broth, or wine, or jelly, or sago for a sick person. But he needs must take up the new hobby of education; and I could see that this put my lady sadly about one Sunday, when she suspected, I know not how, that there was something to be said in his sermon about a Sunday-school[a] which he was planning. She stood up, as she had not done since Mr. Mountford's death, two years and better before this time, and said, –

'Mr. Gray, I will not trouble you for a discourse this morning.'

But her voice was not well-assured and steady; and we knelt down with more of curiosity than satisfaction in our minds. Mr. Gray preached a very rousing sermon, on the necessity of establishing a Sabbath-school[b] in the village. My lady shut her eyes, and seemed to go to sleep; but I don't believe she lost a word of it, though she said nothing about it that I heard until the next Saturday, when two of us, as was the custom, were riding out with her in her carriage, and we went to see a poor bed-ridden woman, who lived some miles away at the other end of the estate and of the parish: and as we came out of the cottage we met Mr. Gray walking up to it, in a great heat, and looking very tired. My lady beckoned him to her, and told him she should wait and take him home with her, adding that she wondered to see him there, so far from his home, for that it was beyond a Sabbath-day's journey,[16] and, from what she had gathered from his sermon the last Sunday, he was all for Judaism against Christianity. He looked as if he did not understand what she meant; but the truth was that, besides the way in which he had spoken up for schools and schooling, he had kept calling Sunday the Sabbath: and, as her ladyship said, 'the Sabbath is the Sabbath, and that's one thing – it is Saturday; and if I keep it, I'm a Jew, which I'm not. And Sunday is Sunday; and that's another thing; and if I keep it, I'm a Christian, which I humbly trust I am.'

But when Mr. Gray got an inkling of her meaning in talking about a Sabbath-day's journey, he only took notice of a part of it: he smiled and bowed, and said no one knew better than her ladyship what were the duties that abrogated all inferior laws regarding the Sabbath; and that he must go in and read to old Betty Brown, so that he would not detain her ladyship.

'But I shall wait for you, Mr. Gray,' said she. 'Or I will take a drive round by Oakfield, and be back in an hour's time.' For, you see, she would not have him feel hurried or troubled with a thought that he was keeping her waiting, while he ought to be comforting and praying with old Betty.

'A very pretty young man, my dears,' said she, as we drove away. 'But I shall have my pew[17] glazed all the same.'

We did not know what she meant at the time; but the next Sunday but one we did. She had the curtains all round the grand old Hanbury family seat taken down, and, instead of them, there was glass up to the height of six or seven feet. We entered by a door, with a window in it that drew up or down just like what you see in carriages. This window was generally down, and then we could hear perfectly; but if Mr. Gray used the word 'Sabbath,' or spoke in favour of schooling and education, my lady stepped out of her corner, and drew up the window with a decided clang and clash.

I must tell you something more about Mr. Gray. The presentation to the living of Hanbury was vested in two trustees, of whom Lady Ludlow was one: Lord Ludlow had exercised this right in the appointment of Mr. Mountford, who had won his lordship's favour by his excellent horseman-ship. Nor was Mr. Mountford a bad clergyman, as clergyman went in those days. He did not drink, though he liked good eating as much as any one. And if any poor person was ill, and he heard of it, he would send them plates from his own dinner of what he himself liked best; sometimes of dishes which were almost as bad as poison to sick people. He meant kindly to everybody except dissenters, whom Lady Ludlow and he united in trying to drive out of the parish; and among dissenters he particularly abhorred Methodists – some one said, because John Wesley had objected to his hunt-ing.[18] But that must have been long ago, for when I knew him he was far too stout and too heavy to hunt; besides, the bishop of the diocese disapproved of hunting, and had intimated his disapprobation to the clergy. For my own part, I think a good run would not have come amiss, even in a moral point of view, to Mr. Mountford. He ate so much, and took so little exercise, that we young women often heard of his being in terrible passions with his servants, and the sexton and clerk. But they none of them minded him much, for he soon came to himself, and was sure to make them some present or other – some said in proportion to his anger; so that the sexton, who was a bit of a wag (as all sextons are, I think), said that the vicar's saying, 'the Devil take you,' was worth a shilling any day, whereas 'the Deuce' was a shabby six-penny speech, only fit for a curate.

There was a great deal of good in Mr. Mountford, too. He could not bear to see pain, or sorrow, or misery of any kind; and, if it came under his notice, he was never easy till he had relieved it, for the time, at any rate. But he was afraid of being made uncomfortable; so, if he possibly could, he would avoid seeing any one who was ill or unhappy; and he did not thank any one for telling him about them.

'What would your ladyship have me to do?' he once said to my Lady Lud-low, when she wished him to go and see a poor man who had broken his leg. 'I cannot piece the leg as the doctor can; I cannot nurse him as well as his wife does; I may talk to him, but he no more understands me than I do the language of the alchemists. My coming puts him out; he stiffens himself

into an uncomfortable posture, out of respect to the cloth, and dare not take
the comfort of kicking, and swearing, and scolding his wife, while I am
there. I hear him, with my figurative ears, my lady, heave a sigh of relief
when my back is turned, and the sermon that he thinks I ought to have kept
for the pulpit, and have delivered to his neighbours (whose case, as he fancies, it would just have fitted, as it seemed to him to be addressed to the
sinful), is all ended, and done for the day. I judge others as myself; I do to
them as I would be done to. That's Christianity, at any rate. I should hate –
saving your ladyship's presence – to have my Lord Ludlow coming and seeing me, if I were ill. 'Twould be a great honour, no doubt; but I should have
to put on a clean nightcap for the occasion; and sham patience, in order to be
polite, and not weary his lordship with my complaints. I should be twice as
thankful to him if he would send me game, or a good fat haunch, to bring
me up to that pitch of health and strength one ought to be in, to appreciate
the honour of a visit from a nobleman. So I shall send Jerry Butler a good
dinner every day till he is strong again; and spare the poor old fellow my
presence and advice.'

My lady would be puzzled by this, and by many other of Mr. Mountford's speeches. But he had been appointed by my lord, and she could not
question her dead husband's wisdom; and she knew that the dinners were
always sent, and often a guinea or two to help to pay the doctor's bills; and
Mr. Mountford was true blue, as we call it, to the back-bone; hated the dissenters and the French; and could hardly drink a dish of tea without giving
out the toast of 'Church and King, and down[a] with the Rump.'[19] Moreover,
he had once had the honour of preaching before the King and Queen, and
two of the Princesses, at Weymouth;[20] and the King had applauded his sermon audibly with, – 'Very good; very good;' and that was a seal put upon his
merit in my lady's eyes.

Besides, in the long winter Sunday evenings, he would come up to the
Court, and read a sermon to us girls, and play a game of picquet with my
lady afterwards; which served to shorten the tedium of the time. My lady
would, on those occasions, invite him to sup with her on the dais; but as her
meal was invariably bread and milk only, Mr. Mountford preferred sitting
down amongst us, and made a joke about its being wicked and heterodox to
eat meagre on Sunday, a festival of the Church. We smiled at this joke just as
much the twentieth time we heard it as we did at the first; for we knew it
was coming, because he always coughed a little nervously before he made a
joke, for fear my lady should not approve: and neither she nor he seemed to
remember that he had ever hit upon the idea before.

Mr. Mountford died quite suddenly at last. We were all very sorry to lose
him. He left some of his property (for he had a private estate) to the poor of
the parish, to furnish them with an annual Christmas dinner of roast-beef

and plum-pudding,[a] for which he wrote out a very good receipt in the codicil to his will.

Moreover, he desired his executors to see that the vault, in which the vicars of Hanbury were interred, was well aired, before his coffin was taken in; for, all his life long, he had had a dread of damp, and latterly he kept his rooms to such a pitch of warmth that some thought it hastened his end.

Then the other trustee, as I have said, presented the living to Mr. Gray, Fellow of Lincoln College, Oxford. It was quite natural for us all, as belonging in some sort to the Hanbury family, to disapprove of the other trustee's choice. But when some ill-natured person circulated the report that Mr. Gray was a Moravian Methodist,[21] I remember my lady said, 'She could not believe anything so bad, without a great deal of evidence.'

CHAPTER II.

BEFORE I tell you about Mr. Gray, I think I ought to make you understand something more of what we did all day long at Hanbury Court. There were five of us at the time of which I am speaking, all young women of good descent, and allied (however distantly) to people of rank. When we were not with my lady, Mrs. Medlicott looked after us; a gentle little woman, who had been companion to my lady for many years, and was indeed, I have been told, some kind of relation to her. Mrs. Medlicott's parents had lived in Germany, and the consequence was, she spoke English with a very foreign accent. Another consequence was, that she excelled in all manner of needlework, such as is not known even by name in these days. She could darn either lace, table-linen, India muslin, or stockings, so that no one could tell where the hole or rent had been. Though a good Protestant, and never missing Guy Faux'[a] day[22] at church, she was as skilful at fine work as any nun in a Paptist convent. She would take a piece of French cambric, and by drawing out some threads, and working in others, it became delicate lace in a very few hours. She did the same by Hollands cloth, and made coarse strong lace, with which all my lady's napkins and table-linen were trimmed. We worked under her during a great part of the day, either in the still-room, or at our sewing in a chamber that opened out of the great hall. My lady despised every kind of work that would now be called Fancy-work.[23] She considered that the use of coloured threads or worsted was only fit to amuse children; but that grown women ought not to be taken with mere blues and reds, but to restrict their pleasure in sewing to making small and delicate stitches. She would speak of the old tapestry in the hall as the work of her ancestresses, who lived before the Reformation, and were consequently unacquainted with pure and simple tastes in work, as well as in religion. Nor would my lady sanction the fashion of the day, which, at the beginning of this century, made all the fine ladies take to making shoes. She said that such work was a consequence of the French Revolution, which had done much to annihilate all distinctions of rank and class, and hence it was, that she saw young ladies of birth and breeding handling lasts, and awls, and dirty cobblers-wax,[b] like shoemakers'[c] daughters.

Very frequently one of us would be summoned to my lady to read aloud to her, as she sat[d] in her small withdrawing-room, some improving book. It was generally Mr. Addison's 'Spectator;'[24] but one year I remember, we had to read 'Sturm's Reflections,'[a] translated from a German book Mrs. Medlicott recommended. Mr. Sturm told us what to think about for every day in the year; and very dull it was. But I believe Queen Charlotte had liked the book very much, and the thought of her royal approbation kept my lady awake during the reading. 'Mrs. Chapone's Letters' and 'Dr. Gregory's Advice to Young Ladies'[25b] composed the rest of our library for week-day reading. I, for one, was glad to leave my fine sewing, and even my reading aloud, (though this last did keep me with my dear lady,) to go to the still-room and potter about among the preserves and the medicated waters. There was no doctor for many miles round, and with Mrs. Medlicott to direct us, and Dr. Buchan[26] to go by for recipes, we sent out many a bottle of physic, which, I dare say, was as good as what comes out of the druggist's shop. At any rate, I do not think we did much harm; for if any of our physics tasted stronger than usual, Mrs. Medlicott would bid us let it down with cochineal and water, to make all safe, as she said. So our bottles of medicine had very little real physic in them at last; but we were careful in putting labels on them, which looked very mysterious to those who could not read, and helped the medicine to do its work. I have sent off many a bottle of salt and water coloured red; and whenever we had nothing else to do in the still-room, Mrs. Medlicott would set us to making bread-pills by way of practice, and, as far as I can say, they were very efficacious, as before we gave out a box Mrs. Medlicott always told the patient what symptoms to expect; and I hardly ever inquired without hearing that they had produced their effect. There was one old man, who took six pills a-night, of any kind we liked to give him, to make him sleep; and if, by any chance, his daughter had forgotten to let us know that he was out of his medicine, he was so restless and miserable that, as he said, he thought he was like to die. I think ours was what would be called homœopathic practice[27] now-a-days. Then we learnt to make all the cakes and dishes of the season in the still-room. We had plum-porridge and mince-pies at Christmas, fritters and pancakes on Shrove Tuesday, furmenty on Mothering Sunday, violet-cakes in Passion Week, tansy-pudding on Easter Sunday, three-cornered cakes on Trinity Sunday, and so on through the year: all made from good old Church receipts, handed down from one of my lady's earliest Protestant ancestresses.[28c] Every one of us passed a portion of the day with Lady Ludlow; and now and then we rode out with her in her coach-and-four. She did not like to go out with a pair of horses, considering this rather beneath her rank; and, indeed, four horses were very often needed to pull her heavy coach through the stiff mud. But it was rather a cumbersome equipage through the narrow Warwickshire lanes; and I used often to think it was well that countesses were not plentiful, or else we might have met another lady of quality in another coach-and-four where there would have been no possibility of turning, or passing each other, and very little chance of backing. Once when the idea of this danger of meeting another countess in a narrow deep-rutted lane was very prominent in my mind, I ventured to ask Mrs. Medlicott what would have to be done on such an occasion; and she told me that 'de latest creation must back,[29] for sure,' which puzzled me a good deal at the time, although I understand it now. I began to find out the use of the 'Peerage,' a book which had seemed to me rather dull before; but, as I was always a coward in a coach, I made myself well acquainted with the dates of creation of our three Warwickshire earls, and was happy to find that Earl Ludlow ranked second, the oldest earl being a hunting widower, and not likely to drive out in a carriage.

All this time I have wandered from Mr. Gray. Of course, we first saw him in church when he read himself in. He was very red-faced, the kind of red-ness which goes with light hair, and a blushing complexion; he looked slight and short, and his bright light frizzy hair had hardly a dash of powder[30] in it. I remember my lady making this observation, and sighing over it; for, though since the famine in seventeen hundred and ninety-nine and eighteen hundred,[31] there had been a tax on hair-powder, yet it was reckoned very revolutionary and Jacobin not to wear a good deal of it. My lady hardly liked the opinions of any man who wore his own hair; but this she would say was rather a prejudice: only in her youth none but the mob had gone wigless, and she could not get over the association of wigs with birth and breeding; a man's own hair with that class of people who had formed the rioters in sev-enteen hundred and eighty, when Lord George Gordon[32] had been one of the bugbears of my lady's life. Her husband and his brothers, she told us, had been put into breeches, and had their heads shaved on their seventh birthday, each of them; a handsome little wig of the newest fashion forming the old Lady Ludlow's invariable birthday present to her sons as they each arrived at that age; and afterwards, to the day of their death, they never saw their own hair. To be without powder, as some underbred people were talk-ing of being now, was in fact to insult the proprieties of life, by being undressed. It was English sans-culottism. But Mr. Gray did wear a little powder, enough to save him in my lady's good opinion; but not enough to make her approve of him decidedly.

The next time I saw him was in the great hall. Mary Mason and I were going to drive out with my lady in her coach, and when we went down-stairs with our best hats and cloaks on, we found Mr. Gray awaiting my lady's coming. I believe he had paid his respects to her before, but we had never seen him; and he had declined her invitation to spend Sunday evening at the Court (as Mr. Mountford used to do pretty regularly, – and play a game of picquet too –),[33] which, Mrs. Medlicott told us, had caused my lady to be not over well pleased with him.

He blushed redder than ever at the sight of us, as we entered the hall, and dropped him our curtsies. He coughed two or three times, as if he would have liked to speak to us, if he could but have found something to say; and every time he coughed, he became hotter-looking than ever. I am ashamed to say, we were nearly laughing at him; half because we, too, were so shy that we understood what his awkwardness meant.

My lady came in, with her quick active step – she always walked quickly when she did not bethink herself of her cane, – as if she were sorry to have kept us waiting, – and, as she entered, she gave us all round one of those graceful sweeping curtsies, of which I think the art must have died out with her, – it implied so much courtesy; – this time it said, as well as words could do, 'I am sorry to have kept you all waiting, – forgive me.'

She went up to the mantelpiece, near which Mr. Gray had been standing until her entrance, and curtsying afresh to him, and pretty deeply this time, because of his cloth, and her being hostess, and he, a new guest. She asked him if he would not prefer speaking to her in her own private parlour, and looked as though she would have conducted him there. But he burst out with his errand, of which he was full even to choking, and which sent the glistening tears into his large blue eyes, which stood farther and farther out with his excitement.

'My lady, I want to speak to you, and to persuade you to exert your kind interest, with Mr. Lathom – Justice Lathom of Hathaway Manor –'

'Harry Lathom?' inquired my lady, – as Mr. Gray stopped to take the breath he had lost in his hurry, – 'I did not know he was in the commission.'[34]

'He is only just appointed; he took the oaths not a month ago, – more's the pity!'

'I do not understand why you should regret it. The Lathoms have held Hathaway since Edward the First, and Mr. Lathom bears a good character, although his temper is hasty –'

'My lady! he has committed Job Gregson for stealing – a fault of which he is as innocent as I – and all the evidence goes to prove it, now that the case is brought before the Bench; only the Squires hang so together that they can't be brought to see justice, and are all for sending Job to gaol, out of compliment to Mr. Lathom, saying it is his first committal,[35] and it won't be civil to tell him there is no evidence against his man. For God's sake, my lady, speak to the gentlemen; they will attend to you, while they only tell me to mind my own business.'

Now my lady was always inclined to stand by her order, and the Lathoms of Hathaway Court were cousins to the Hanburys. Besides, it was rather a point of honour in those days to encourage a young magistrate, by passing a pretty sharp sentence on his first committals; and Job Gregson was the father of a girl who had been lately turned away from her place as scullery-maid for sauciness to Mrs. Adams, her ladyship's own maid; and Mr. Gray had not said a word of the reasons why he believed the man innocent, – for he was in such a hurry, I believe he would have had my lady drive off to the Henley Court-house[36] then and there; – so there seemed a good deal against the man, and nothing but Mr. Gray's bare word for him; and my lady drew herself a little up, and said:

'Mr. Gray! I do not see what reason either you or I have to interfere. Mr. Harry Lathom is a sensible kind of young man, well capable of ascertaining the truth without our help –'

'But more evidence has come out since,' broke in Mr. Gray.

My lady went a little stiffer, and spoke a little more coldly: –

'I suppose this additional evidence is before the justices; men of good family, and of honour and credit, well known in the county. They naturally feel that the opinion of one of themselves must have more weight than the words of a man like Job Gregson, who bears a very indifferent character, – has been strongly suspected of poaching, coming from no one knows where, squatting on Hareman's Common – which, by the way, is extra-parochial,[37] I believe; consequently you, as a clergyman, are not responsible for what goes on there; and, although impolitic, there might be some truth in what the magistrates said, in advising you to mind your own business,' – said her ladyship, smiling, –'and they might be tempted to bid me mind mine, if I interfered, Mr. Gray; might they not?'

He looked extremely uncomfortable; half angry. Once or twice he began to speak, but checked himself, as if his words would not have been wise or prudent. At last he said:

'It may seem presumptuous in me, – a stranger of only a few weeks'[a] standing – to set up my judgment as to men's character against that of residents' –' Lady Ludlow gave a little bow of acquiescence, which was, I think, involuntary on her part, and which I don't think he perceived, – 'but I am convinced that the man is innocent of this offence, – and besides, the justices themselves allege this ridiculous custom of paying a compliment to a newly-appointed magistrate as their only reason.'

That unlucky word 'ridiculous!' It undid all the good his modest beginning had done him with my lady. I knew, as well as words could have told me, that she was affronted at the expression being used by a man inferior in rank to those whose actions he applied it to, – and, truly, it was a great want of tact, considering to whom he was speaking.

Lady Ludlow spoke very gently and slowly; she always did so when she was annoyed; it was a certain sign, the meaning of which we had all learnt.

'I think, Mr. Gray, we will drop the subject. It is one on which we are not likely to agree.'

Mr. Gray's ruddy colour grew purple, and then faded away, and his face became pale. I think both my lady and he had forgotten our presence; and we were beginning to feel too awkward to wish to remind them of it. And yet we could not help watching and listening with the greatest interest.

Mr. Gray drew himself up to his full height, with an unconscious feeling of dignity. Little as was his stature, and awkward and embarrassed as he had been only a few minutes before, I remember thinking he looked almost as grand as my lady when he spoke.

'Your ladyship must remember that it may be my duty to speak to my parishioners on many subjects on which they do not agree with me. I am not at liberty to be silent, because they differ in opinion from me.'

Lady Ludlow's great blue eyes dilated with surprise, and – I do think – anger, at being thus spoken to. I am not sure whether it was very wise in Mr. Gray. He himself looked afraid of the consequences, but as if he was determined to bear them without flinching. For a minute there was silence. Then my lady replied:

'Mr. Gray, I respect your plain speaking, although I may wonder whether a young man of your age and position has any right to assume that he is a better judge than one with the experience which I have naturally gained at my time of life, and in the station I hold.'

'If I, madam, as the clergyman of this parish, am not to shrink from telling what I believe to be the truth to the poor and lowly, no more am I to hold my peace in the presence of the rich and titled.' Mr. Gray's face showed that he was in that state of excitement which in a child would have ended in a good fit of crying. He looked as if he had nerved himself up to doing and saying things, which he disliked above everything, and which nothing short of serious duty could have compelled him to do and say. And at such times every minute circumstance which could add to pain comes vividly before one. I saw that he became aware of our presence, and that it added to his discomfiture.

My lady flushed up. 'Are you aware, sir,' asked she, 'that you have gone far astray from the original subject of conversation? But as you talk of your parish, allow me to remind you that Hareman's Common is beyond the bounds, and that you are really not responsible for the characters and lives of the squatters on that unlucky piece of ground.'

'Madam, I see I have only done harm in speaking to you about the affair at all. I beg your pardon, and take my leave.'

He bowed, and looked very sad. Lady Ludlow caught the expression of his face.

'Good morning!' she cried, in rather a louder and quicker way than that in which she had been speaking. 'Remember, Job Gregson is a notorious poacher and evildoer, and you really are not responsible for what goes on at Hareman's Common.'

He was near the hall-door, and said something – half to himself, which we heard (being nearer to him), but my lady did not; although she saw that he spoke. 'What did he say?' she asked, in a somewhat hurried manner, as soon as the door was closed – 'I did not hear.' We looked at each other, and then I spoke:

'He said, my lady, that "God help him! he was responsible for all the evil he did not strive to overcome."'[a]

My lady turned sharp round away from us, and Mary Mason said afterwards she thought her ladyship was much vexed with both of us, for having been present, and with me for having repeated what Mr. Gray had said. But it was not our fault that we were in the hall, and when my lady asked what Mr. Gray had said, I thought it right to tell her.

In a few minutes she bade us accompany her in her ride in the coach.

Lady Ludlow always sat[b] forwards[38] by herself, and we girls backwards. Somehow this was a rule, which we never thought of questioning. It was true that riding backwards made some of us feel very uncomfortable and faint; and to remedy this my lady always drove with both windows open, which occasionally gave her the rheumatism; but we always went on in the old way. This day she did not pay any great attention to the road by which we were going, and Coachman[c] took his own way. We were very silent, as my lady did not speak, and looked very serious. Or else, in general, she made these rides very pleasant (to those who were not qualmish, with riding backwards), by talking to us in a very agreeable manner, and telling us of the different things which had happened to her at various places, – at Paris and Versailles, where she had been in her youth, – at Windsor and Kew and Weymouth, where she had been with the Queen, when maid-of-honour – and so on. But this day she did not talk at all. All at once she put her head out of the window.

'John Footman,' said she, 'where are we? Surely this is Hareman's Common.'

'Yes, an't please my lady,' said John Footman, and waited for further speech or orders. My lady thought awhile, and then said she would have the steps put down and get out.

As soon as she was gone, we looked at each other, and then without a word began to gaze after her. We saw her pick her dainty way, in the little high-heeled shoes she always wore (because they had been in fashion in her youth), among the yellow pools of stagnant water that had gathered in the clayey soil. John Footman followed, stately, after; afraid too, for all his stateliness of splashing his pure white stockings. Suddenly my lady turned round, and said something to him, and he returned to the carriage with a half-pleased, half-puzzled air.

My lady went on to a cluster of rude mud houses at the higher end of the Common; cottages built, as they were occasionally at that day, of wattles and clay, and thatched with sods. As far as we could make out from dumb show, Lady Ludlow saw enough of the interiors of these places to make her hesitate before entering, or even speaking to any of the children who were playing about in the puddles. After a pause, she disappeared into one of the cottages. It seemed to us a long time before she came out; but I dare say it was not more than eight or ten minutes. She came back with her head hanging down, as if to choose her way, – but we saw it was more in thought and bewilderment than for any such purpose.

She had not made up her mind where we should drive to when she got into the carriage again. John Footman stood, bare-headed, waiting for orders.

'To Hathaway. My dears, if you are tired, or if you have anything to do for Mrs. Medlicott, I can drop you at Barford Corner,[39a] and it is but a quarter of an hour's brisk walk home?'

But luckily we could safely say that Mrs. Medlicott did not want us; and as we had whispered to each other, as we sat alone in the coach, that surely my lady must have gone to Job Gregson's, we were far too anxious to know the end of it all to say that we were tired. So we all set off to Hathaway. Mr. Harry Lathom was a bachelor squire, thirty or thirty-five years of age, more at home in the field than in the drawing-room, and with sporting men than with ladies.

My lady did not alight, of course; it was Mr. Lathom's place to wait upon her, and she bade the butler, – who had a smack of the gamekeeper in him, very unlike our own powdered venerable fine gentleman at Hanbury, – tell his master, with her compliments, that she wished to speak to him. You may think how pleased we were to find that we should hear all that was said; though, I think, afterwards we were half sorry when we saw how our presence confused the squire, who would have found it bad enough to answer my lady's questions, even without two eager girls for audience.

'Pray, Mr. Lathom,' began my lady, something abruptly for her, – but she was very full of her subject, – 'what is this I hear about Job Gregson?'

Mr. Lathom looked annoyed and vexed, but dared not show it in his words

'I gave out a warrant against him, my lady, for theft, that is all. You are doubtless aware of his character; a man who sets nets and springes in long cover, and fishes wherever he takes a fancy. It is but a short step from poaching to thieving.'

'That is quite true,' replied Lady Ludlow (who had a horror of poaching for this very reason): 'but I imagine you do not send a man to gaol[b] on account of his bad character.'

'Rogues and vagabonds,' said Mr. Lathom. 'A man may be sent to prison for being a vagabond;[40] for no specific act, but for his general mode of life.'

He had the better of her ladyship for one moment; but then she answered,

'But in this case, the charge on which you committed him was theft; now his wife tells me he can prove he was some miles distant from Holmwood, where the robbery took place, all that afternoon; she says you had the evidence before you.'

Mr. Lathom here interrupted my lady, by saying, in a somewhat sulky manner, –

'No such evidence was brought before me when I gave the warrant. I am not answerable for the other magistrates' decision, when they had more evidence before them. It was they who committed him to gaol. I am not responsible for that.'

My lady did not often show signs of impatience; but we knew she was feeling irritated by the little perpetual tapping of her high-heeled shoe against the bottom of the carriage. About the same time we, sitting backwards, caught a glimpse of Mr. Gray through the open door, standing in the shadow of the hall. Doubtless Lady Ludlow's arrival had interrupted a conversation between Mr. Lathom and Mr. Gray. The latter must have heard every word of what she was saying; but of this she was not aware, and caught at Mr. Lathom's disclaimer of responsibility with pretty much the same argument which she had heard (through our repetition) that Mr. Gray had used not two hours before.

'And do you mean to say, Mr. Lathom, that you don't consider yourself responsible for all injustice or wrong-doing that you might have prevented, and have not? Nay, in this case the first germ of injustice was your own mistake. I wish you had been with me a little while ago, and seen the misery in that poor fellow's cottage.' She spoke lower, and Mr. Gray drew near, in a sort of involuntary manner; as if to hear all she was saying. We saw him, and doubtless Mr. Lathom heard his footstep, and knew who it was that was listening behind him, and approving of every word that was said. He grew yet more sullen in manner; but still my lady was my lady, and he dared not speak out before her, as he would have done to Mr. Gray. Lady Ludlow, however, caught the look of stubbornness in his face, and it roused her as I had never seen her roused.

'I am sure you will not refuse, sir, to accept my bail. I offer to bail the fellow out, and to be responsible for his appearance at the sessions. What say you to that, Mr. Lathom?'

'The offence of theft is not bailable, my lady.'

'Not in ordinary cases, I dare say. But I imagine this is an extraordinary case. The man is sent to prison out of compliment to you, and against all evidence, as far as I can learn. He will have to rot in gaol[a] for two months, and his wife and children to starve. I, Lady Ludlow, offer to bail him out, and pledge myself for his appearance at next quarter-sessions.'[b]

'It is against the law, my lady.'

'Bah! Bah! Bah! Who makes laws? Such as I, in the House of Lords – such as you, in the House of Commons. We, who make the laws in St. Stephen's,[41] may break the mere forms of them, when we have right on our sides, on our own land, and amongst our own people.'

'The lord-lieutenant[42] may take away my commission, if he heard of it.'

'And a very good thing for the county, Harry Lathom; and for you too, if he did, – if you don't go on more wisely than you have begun. A pretty set you and your brother magistrates are to administer justice through the land! I always said a good despotism[43] was the best form of government; and I am twice as much in favour of it now I see what a quorum[44] is! My dears!' suddenly turning round to us, 'if it would not tire you to walk home, I would beg Mr. Lathom to take a seat in my coach, and we would drive to Henley Gaol, and have the poor man out at once.'

'A walk over the fields at this time of day is hardly fitting for young ladies to take alone,' said Mr. Lathom, anxious no doubt to escape from his tête-à-tête drive with my lady, and possibly not quite prepared to go to the illegal length of prompt measures, which she had in contemplation.

But Mr. Gray now stepped forward, too anxious for the release of the prisoner to allow any obstacle to intervene which he could do away with. To see Lady Ludlow's face when she first perceived whom she had had for auditor and spectator of her interview with Mr. Lathom, was as good as a play. She had been doing and saying the very things she had been so much annoyed at Mr. Gray's saying and proposing only an hour or two ago. She had been setting down Mr. Lathom pretty smartly, in the presence of the very man to whom she had spoken of that gentleman as so sensible, and of such a standing in the county, that it was presumption to question his doings. But before Mr. Gray had finished his offer of escorting us back to Hanbury Court, my lady had recovered herself. There was neither surprise nor displeasure in her manner, as she answered:

'I thank you, Mr. Gray. I was not aware that you were here, but I think I can understand on what errand you came. And seeing you here, recalls me to a duty I owe Mr. Lathom. Mr. Lathom, I have spoken to you pretty plainly, – forgetting, until I saw Mr. Gray, that only this very afternoon I differed from him on this very question; taking completely, at that time, the same view of the whole subject which you have done; thinking that the county would be well rid of such a man as Job Gregson, whether he had committed this theft or not. Mr. Gray and I did not part quite friends,' she continued, bowing towards him; 'but it so happened that I saw Job Gregson's wife and home, – I felt that Mr. Gray had been right and I had been wrong, so, with the famous inconsistency of my sex, I came hither to scold you,' smiling towards Mr. Lathom, who looked half-sulky yet, and did not relax a bit of his gravity at her smile, 'for holding the same opinions that I had done an hour before. Mr. Gray,' (again bowing towards him) 'these young ladies will be very much obliged to you for your escort, and so shall I. Mr. Lathom, may I beg of you to accompany me to Henley?'

Mr. Gray bowed very low, and went very red; Mr. Lathom said something which we none of us heard, but which was, I think, some remonstrance against the course he was, as it were, compelled to take. Lady Ludlow, however, took no notice of his murmur, but sat[a] in an attitude of polite expectancy; and as we turned off on our walk, I saw Mr. Lathom getting into the coach with the air of a whipped hound. I must say, considering my lady's feeling, I did not envy him his ride, – though, I believe, he was quite in the right as to the object of the ride being illegal.

Our walk home was very dull. We had no fears; and would far rather have been without the awkward, blushing young man, into which Mr. Gray had sunk. At every stile he hesitated, – sometimes he half got over it, thinking that he could assist us better in that way; then he would turn back unwilling to go before ladies. He had no ease of manner, as my lady once said of him, though on any occasion of duty, he had an immense deal of dignity.

CHAPTER III.

As far as I can remember, it was very soon after this that I first began to have the pain in my hip, which has ended in making me a cripple for life. I hardly recollect more than one walk after our return under Mr. Gray's escort from Mr. Lathom's. Indeed, at the time, I was not without suspicions (which I never named) that the beginning of all the mischief was a great jump I had taken from the top of one of the stiles on that very occasion.

Well, it is a long while ago, and God disposes of us all, and I am not going to tire you out with telling you how I thought and felt, and how, when I saw what my life was to be, I could hardly bring myself to be patient, but rather wished to die at once. You can every one of you think for yourselves what becoming all at once useless and unable to move, and by-and-by growing hopeless of cure, and feeling that one must be a burden to some one all one's life long, would be to an active, wilful, strong girl of seventeen, anxious to get on in the world, so as, if possible, to help her brothers and sisters. So I shall only say, that one among the blessings which arose out of what seemed at the time a great, black sorrow, was, that Lady Ludlow for many years took me, as it were, into her own especial charge; and now, as I lie still and alone in my old age, it is such a pleasure to think of her!

Mrs. Medlicott was great as a nurse, and I am sure I can never be grateful enough to her memory for all her kindness. But she was puzzled to know how to manage me in other ways. I used to have long, hard fits of crying; and, thinking that I ought to go home – and yet what could they do with me there? – and a hundred and fifty other anxious thoughts, some of which I could tell to Mrs. Medlicott, and others I could not. Her way of comforting me was hurrying away for some kind of tempting or strengthening food – a basin of melted calves'-foot jelly was, I am sure she thought, a cure for every woe.

'There! take it, dear, take it!' she would say; 'and don't go on fretting for what can't be helped.'

But, I think, she got puzzled at length at the non-efficacy of good things to eat; and one day, after I had limped down to see the doctor, in Mrs. Medlicott's sitting room – a room lined with cupboards, containing preserves and dainties of all kinds, which she perpetually made, and never touched

herself – when I was returning to my bed-room to cry away the afternoon,
under pretence of arranging my clothes, John Footman brought me a message from my lady (with whom the doctor had been having a conversation)
to bid me go to her in that private sitting-room at the end of the suite of
apartments, about which I spoke in describing the day of my first arrival at
Hanbury. I had hardly been in it since; as, when we read to my lady, she generally sat[a] in the small withdrawing-room out of which this private room of
hers opened. I suppose great people do not require what we smaller people
value so much, – I mean privacy.[45] I do not think that there was a room
which my lady occupied that had not two doors, and some of them had
three or four. Then my lady had always Adams waiting upon her in her bed-
chamber; and it was Mrs. Medlicott's duty to sit within call, as it were, in a
sort of anteroom that led out of my lady's own sitting-room, on the opposite
side to the drawing-room door. To fancy the house, you must take a great
square, and halve it by a line; at one end of this line was the hall-door, or
public-entrance;[b] at the opposite the private entrance from a terrace, which
was terminated at one end by a sort of postern door in an old gray[c] stone
wall, beyond which lay the farm buildings and offices; so that people could
come in this way to my lady on business, while, if she were going into the
garden from her own room, she had nothing to do but to pass through Mrs.
Medlicott's apartment, out into the lesser hall, and then turning to the right
as she passed on to the terrace, she could go down the flight of broad, shallow steps at the corner of the house into the lovely garden, with stretching,
sweeping lawns, and gay flower-beds, and beautiful, bossy laurels, and other
blooming or massy shrubs, with full-grown beeches, or larches feathering
down to the ground a little farther off. The whole was set in a frame, as it
were, by the more distant woodlands. The house had been modernized in
the days of Queen Anne, I think; but the money had fallen short that was
requisite to carry out all the improvements, so it was only the suite of with-
drawing-rooms and the terrace-rooms, as far as the private entrance, that
had the new, long, high windows put in, and these were old enough by this
time to be draped with roses, and honeysuckles and pyracanthus, winter and
summer long.

Well, to go back to that day when I limped into my lady's sitting-room,
trying hard to look as if I had not been crying, and not to walk as if I was in
much pain. I do not know whether my lady saw how near my tears were to
my eyes, but she told me she had sent for me, because she wanted some help
in arranging the drawers of her bureau, and asked me – just as if it was a
favour I was to do her – if I could sit down in the easy chair near the window
– (all quietly arranged before I came in, with a footstool, and a table quite
near) – and assist her. You will wonder, perhaps, why I was not bidden to sit
or lie on the sofa; but (although I found one there a morning or two afterwards, when I came down) the fact was, that there was none in the room at

this time. I have even fancied that the easy-chair was brought in on purpose for me, for it was not the chair in which I remembered my lady sitting the first time I saw her. That chair was very much carved and gilded, with a countess' coronet at the top. I tried it one day, some time afterwards, when my lady was out of the room, and I had a fancy for seeing how I could move about, and very uncomfortable it was. Now my chair (as I learnt to call it, and to think it) was soft and luxurious, and seemed somehow to give one's body rest just in that part where one most needed it.

I was not at my ease that first day, nor indeed for many days afterwards, notwithstanding my chair was so comfortable. Yet I forgot my sad pain in silently wondering over the meaning of many of the things we turned out of those curious old drawers. I was puzzled to know why some were kept at all; a scrap of writing may-be, with only half-a-dozen common-place words written on it, or a bit of broken riding-whip, and here and there a stone, of which I thought I could have picked up twenty just as good in the first walk I took. But it seems that was just my ignorance; for my lady told me they were pieces of valuable marble, used to make the floors of the great Roman emperors' palaces long ago; and that when she had been a girl, and made the grand tour long ago, her cousin, Sir Horace Mann,[46] the Ambassador or Envoy at Florence, had told her to be sure to go into the fields inside the walls of ancient Rome, when the farmers were preparing the ground for the onion-sowing, and had to make the soil fine, and pick up what bits of marble she could find. She had done so, and meant to have had them made into a table; but somehow that plan fell through, and there they were with all the dirt out of the onion-field upon them; but once when I thought of cleaning them with soap and water, at any rate, she bade me not to do so, for it was Roman dirt – earth, I think, she called it – but it was dirt all the same.

Then, in this bureau, were many other things, the value of which I could understand – locks of hair carefully ticketed, which my lady looked at very sadly; and lockets and bracelets with miniatures in them, – very small pictures to what they make now-a-days, and call miniatures; some of them had even to be looked at through a microscope before you could see the individual expression of the faces, or how beautifully they were painted. I don't think that looking at these made my lady seem so melancholy, as the seeing and touching of the hair did. But, to be sure, the hair was, as it were, a part of some beloved body which she might never touch and caress again, but which lay beneath the turf, all faded and disfigured, except perhaps the very hair, from which the lock she held had been dissevered; whereas the pictures were but pictures after all – likenesses, but not the very things themselves. This is only my own conjecture, mind. My lady rarely spoke out her feelings. For, to begin with, she was of rank: and I have heard her say that people of rank do not talk about their feelings except to their equals, and even to them they conceal them, except upon rare occasions. Secondly, – and this is my own reflection, – she was an only child and an heiress; and as such was more apt to think than to talk, as all well-brought-up heiresses must be, I think. Thirdly, she had long been a widow, without any companion of her own age with whom it would have been natural for her to refer to old associations, past pleasures, or mutual sorrows. Mrs. Medlicott came nearest to her as a companion of this sort; and her ladyship talked more to Mrs. Medlicott, in a kind of familiar way, than she did to all the rest of the household put together. But Mrs. Medlicott was silent by nature, and did not reply at any great length. Adams, indeed, was the only one who spoke much to Lady Ludlow.

After we had worked away about an hour at the bureau, her ladyship said we had done enough for one day; and as the time was come for her afternoon ride, she left me, with a volume of engravings from Mr. Hogarth's pictures on one side of me (I don't like to write down the names of them, though my lady thought nothing of it,[47] I am sure), and upon a stand her great prayer-book open at the evening-psalms for the day, on the other. But as soon as she was gone, I troubled myself little with either, but amused myself with looking round the room at my leisure. The side on which the fire-place stood, was all panelled, – part of the old ornaments of the house, for there was an Indian paper with birds and beasts, and insects on it, on all the other sides. There were coats of arms, of the various families with whom the Hanburys had intermarried, all over these panels, and up and down the ceiling as well. There was very little looking-glass in the room, though one of the great drawing-rooms was called the 'Mirror Room,' because it was lined with glass, which my lady's great-grandfather had brought from Venice when he was ambassador there. There were china jars of all shapes and sizes round and about the room, and some china monsters, or idols, of which I could never bear the sight, they were so ugly, though I think my lady valued them more than all. There was a thick carpet on the middle of the floor, which was made of small pieces of rare wood fitted into a pattern; the doors were opposite to each other, and were composed of two heavy tall wings, and opened in the middle, moving on brass grooves inserted into the floor – they would not have opened over a carpet. There were two windows reaching up nearly to the ceiling, but very narrow, and with deep window-seats in the thickness of the wall. The room was full of scent, partly from the flowers outside, and partly from the great jars of pot-pourri inside. The choice of odours was what my lady piqued herself upon, saying nothing showed birth like a keen susceptibility of smell. We never named musk[48] in her presence, her antipathy to it was so well understood through the household: her opinion on the subject was believed to be, that no scent derived from an animal could ever be of a sufficiently pure nature to give pleasure to any person of good family, where, of course, the delicate perception of the senses had been cultivated for generations. She would instance the way in which sportsmen preserve the breed of dogs who have shown keen scent; and how such gifts descend for generations amongst animals, who cannot be supposed to have anything of ancestral pride, or hereditary fancies about them. Musk, then, was never mentioned at Hanbury Court. No more were bergamot or south-ern-wood, although vegetable in their nature. She considered these two latter as betraying a vulgar taste in the person who chose to gather or wear them. She was sorry to notice sprigs of them in the button-hole of any young man in whom she took an interest, either because he was engaged to a servant of hers or otherwise, as he came out of church on a Sunday after-noon. She was afraid that he liked coarse pleasures; and I am not sure if she did not think that his preference for these coarse sweetnesses did not imply a probability that he would take to drinking. But she distinguished between vulgar and common. Violets, pinks, and sweetbriar[a] were common enough; roses and mignonette, for those who had gardens, honeysuckle for those who walked along the bowery lanes; but wearing them betrayed no vulgarity of taste: the queen upon her throne might be glad to smell at a nosegay of these flowers. A beau-pot (as we called it) of pinks and roses freshly gathered was placed every morning that they were in bloom on my lady's own partic-ular table. For lasting vegetable odours she preferred lavender and sweet-woodroof to any extract whatever. Lavender reminded her of old customs, she said, and of homely cottage-gardens, and many a cottager made his offering to her of a bundle of lavender. Sweet woodroof, again, grew in wild, woodland places, where the soil was fine and the air delicate: the poor chil-dren used to go and gather it for her up in the woods on the higher lands; and for this service she always rewarded them with bright new pennies, of which my lord, her son, used to send her down a bagful fresh from the Mint in London every February.

Attar-of-roses,[b] again, she disliked. She said it reminded her of the city and of merchants' wives, over-rich, over-heavy in its perfume. And lilies-of-the-valley[c] somehow fell under the same condemnation. They were most graceful and elegant to look at (my lady was quite candid about this), flower, leaf, colour – everything was refined about them but the smell. That was too strong. But the great hereditary faculty on which my lady piqued herself, and with reason, for I never met with any other person who possessed it, was the power she had of perceiving the delicious odour arising from a bed of strawberries in the late autumn, when the leaves were all fading and dying. 'Bacon's Essays'[49] was one of the few books that lay about in my lady's room; and if you took it up and opened it carelessly, it was sure to fall apart at his 'Essay on Gardens.'[d] 'Listen,' her ladyship would say, 'to what that great philosopher and statesman says, "Next to that," – he is speaking of violets, my dear, – "is the musk-rose," – of which you remember the great bush, at the corner of the south wall just by the Blue Drawing-room win-dows; that is the old musk-rose, Shakespeare's musk-rose,[50] which is dying out through the kingdom now. But to return to my Lord Bacon: "Then the strawberry leaves, dying with a most excellent cordial smell." Now the Hanburys can always smell this excellent cordial odour, and very delicious and refreshing it is. You see, in Lord Bacon's time, there had not been so many intermarriages between the court and the city as there have been since the needy days of his Majesty Charles the Second; and altogether in the time of Queen Elizabeth, the great, old families of England were a distinct race, just as a cart-horse is one creature, and very useful in its place, and Childers or Eclipse[51] is another creature, though both are of the same species. So the old families have gifts and powers of a different and higher class to what the other orders have. My dear, remember that you try if you can smell the scent of dying strawberry-leaves in this next autumn. You have some of Ursula Hanbury's blood in you, and that gives you a chance.'

But when October came, I sniffed and sniffed, and all to no purpose; and my lady – who had watched the little experiment rather anxiously – had to give me up as a hybrid. I was mortified, I confess, and thought that it was in some ostentation of her own powers that she ordered the gardener to plant a border of strawberries on that side the terrace that lay under her windows.

I have wandered away from time and place. I tell you all the remembrances I have of those years just as they come up, and I hope that, in my old age, I am not getting too like a certain Mrs. Nickleby,[52] whose speeches were once read out aloud to me.

I came by degrees to be all day long in this room which I have been describing; sometimes sitting in the easy chair, doing some little piece of dainty work for my lady, or sometimes arranging flowers, or sorting letters according to their handwriting, so that she could arrange them afterwards, and destroy or keep, as she planned, looking ever onward to her death. Then, after the sofa was brought in, she would watch my face, and if she saw my colour change, she would bid me lie down and rest. And I used to try to walk upon the terrace every day for a short time: it hurt me very much, it is true, but the doctor had ordered it, and I knew her ladyship wished me to obey.

Before I had seen the background of a great lady's life, I had thought it all play and fine doings. But whatever other grand people are, my lady was never idle. For one thing, she had to superintend the agent for the large Hanbury estate. I believe it was mortgaged for a sum of money which had gone to improve the late lord's Scotch lands; but she was anxious to pay off this before her death, and so to leave her own inheritance free of incumbrance to her son, the present Earl; whom, I secretly think, she considered a greater person, as being the heir of the Hanburys (though through a female line), than as being my Lord Ludlow with half-a-dozen other minor titles.

With this wish of releasing her property from the mortgage, skilful care was much needed in the management of it: and as far as my lady could go, she took every pains. She had a great book, in which every page was ruled into three divisions; on the first column was written the date and the name of the tenant who addressed any letter on business to her; on the second was briefly stated the subject of the letter, which generally contained a request of some kind. This request would be surrounded and enveloped in so many words, and often inserted amidst so many odd reasons and excuses, that Mr. Horner (the steward) would sometimes say it was like hunting through a bushel of chaff to find a grain of wheat. Now, in the second column of this book, the grain of meaning was placed, clean and dry, before her ladyship every morning. She sometimes would ask to see the original letter; sometimes she simply answered the request by a 'Yes,' or a 'No;' and often she would send for leases and papers, and examine them well, with Mr. Horner at her elbow, to see if such petitions, as to be allowed to plough up pasture fields, &c., were provided for in the terms of the original agreement. On every Thursday she made herself at liberty to see her tenants, from four to six in the afternoon. Mornings would have suited my lady better, as far as convenience went, and I believe the old custom had been to have these levées (as her ladyship used to call them) held before twelve. But, as she said to Mr. Horner, when he urged returning to the former hours, it spoilt a whole day for a farmer, if he had to dress himself in his best and leave his work in the forenoon (and my lady liked to see her tenants come in their Sunday-clothes; she would not say a word, may-be, but she would take her spectacles slowly out, and put them on with silent gravity, and look at a dirty or raggedly-dressed man so solemnly and earnestly, that his nerves must have been pretty strong if he did not wince, and resolve that, however poor he might be, soap and water, and needle and thread should be used before he again appeared in her ladyship's anteroom). The outlying tenants had always a supper provided for them in the servants'-hall on Thursdays, to which, indeed, all comers were welcome to sit down. For my lady said, though there were not many hours left of a working-man's day when their business with her was ended, yet that they needed food and rest, and that she should be ashamed if they sought either at the Fighting Lion (called at this day the Hanbury Arms). They had as much beer as they could drink while they were eating; and when the food was cleared away, they had a cup a-piece of good ale,[53] in which the oldest tenant present, standing up, gave Madam's health; and after that was drunk, they were expected to set off homewards; at any rate, no more liquor was given them. The tenants one and all called her 'Madam;' for they recognised in her the married heiress of the Hanburys, not the widow of a Lord Ludlow, of whom they and their forefathers knew nothing; and against whose memory, indeed, there rankled a dim unspoken grudge, the cause of which was accurately known to the very few who understood the nature of a mortgage, and were therefore aware that Madam's money had been taken to enrich my lord's poor land in Scotland. I am sure – for you can understand I was behind the scenes, as it were, and had many an opportunity of seeing and hearing, as I lay or sat[a] motionless in my lady's room, with the double doors open between it and the anteroom beyond, where Lady Ludlow saw her steward, and gave audience to her tenants, – I am certain, I say, that Mr. Horner was silently as much annoyed at the money that was swallowed up by this mortgage as any one; and, some time or other, he had probably spoken his mind out to my lady; for there was a sort of offended reference on her part, and respectful submission to blame on his, while every now and then there was an implied protest, – whenever the payments of the interest became due, or whenever my lady stinted herself of any personal expense, such as Mr. Horner thought was only decorous and becoming in the heiress of the Hanburys. Her carriages were old and cumbrous, wanting all the improvements which had been adopted by those of her rank throughout the county. Mr. Horner would fain have had the ordering of a new coach. The carriage-horses, too, were getting past their work; yet all the promising colts bred on the estate were sold for ready money; and so on. My lord, her son, was ambassador at some foreign place; and very proud we all were of his glory and dignity; but I fancy it cost money, and my lady would have lived on bread and water sooner than have called upon him to help her in paying off the mortgage, although he was the one who was to benefit by it in the end.

Mr. Horner was a very faithful steward, and very respectful to my lady; although, sometimes, I thought she was sharper to him than to any one else; perhaps because she knew that, although he never said anything, he disapproved of the Hanburys being made to pay for the Earl Ludlow's estates and state.

The late lord had been a sailor, and had been as extravagant in his habits as most sailors are, I am told, – for I never saw the sea; and yet he had a long sight to his own interests; but whatever he was, my lady loved him and his memory, with about as fond and proud a love as ever wife gave husband, I should think.

For a part of his life Mr. Horner, who was born on the Hanbury property, had been a clerk to an attorney in Birmingham; and these few years had given him a kind of worldly wisdom, which, though always exerted for her benefit, was antipathetic to her ladyship, who thought that some of her steward's maxims savoured of trade and commerce. I fancy that if it had been possible, she would have preferred a return to the primitive system, of living on the produce of the land, and exchanging the surplus for such articles as were needed, without the intervention of money.

But Mr. Horner was bitten with new-fangled notions, as she would say, though his new-fangled notions were what folk at the present day would think sadly behindhand;[b] and some of Mr. Gray's ideas fell on Mr. Horner's mind like sparks on tow, though they started from two different points. Mr.

Horner wanted to make every man useful and active in this world, and to direct as much activity and usefulness as possible to the improvement of the Hanbury estates, and the aggrandisement of the Hanbury family, and therefore he fell into the new cry for education.

Mr. Gray did not care much, – Mr. Horner thought not enough, – for this world, and where any man or family stood in their earthly position; but he would have every one prepared for the world to come, and capable of understanding and receiving certain doctrines, for which latter purpose, it stands to reason, he must have heard of these doctrines; and therefore Mr. Gray wanted education. The answer in the catechism that Mr. Horner was most fond of calling upon a child to repeat, was that to, 'What is thy duty towards thy[a] neighbour?'[54] The answer Mr. Gray liked best to hear repeated with unction, was that to the question, 'What is the inward and spiritual grace?' The reply to which Lady Ludlow bent her head the lowest, as we said our Catechism[b] to her on Sundays, was to, 'What is thy duty towards God?' But neither Mr. Horner nor Mr. Gray had heard many answers[55] to the Catechism[c] as yet.

Up to this time there was no Sunday-school in Hanbury. Mr. Gray's desires were bounded by that object. Mr. Horner looked farther on: he hoped for a day-school at some future time, to train up intelligent labourers for working on the estate. My lady would hear of neither one nor the other: indeed, not the boldest man whom she ever saw would have dared to name the project of a day-school within her hearing.

So Mr. Horner contented himself with quietly teaching a sharp, clever lad to read and write, with a view to making use of him as a kind of foreman in process of time. He had his pick of the farm-lads for this purpose; and, as the brightest and sharpest, although by far the raggedest and dirtiest, singled out Job Gregson's son. But all this – as my lady never listened to gossip, or indeed, was spoken to unless she spoke first – was quite unknown to her, until the unlucky incident took place which I am going to relate.

CHAPTER IV.

I THINK my lady was not aware of Mr. Horner's views on education (as making men into more useful members of society) or the[a] practice to which he was putting his precepts in taking Harry Gregson as pupil and protégé; if, indeed, she were aware of Harry's distinct existence at all, until the following unfortunate occasion. The anteroom, which was a kind of business-place for my lady to receive her steward and tenants in, was surrounded by shelves. I cannot call them book-shelves, though there were many books on them; but the contents of the volumes were principally manuscript, and relating to details connected with the Hanbury property. There were also one or two dictionaries, gazetteers, works of reference on the management of property; all of a very old date (the dictionary was Bailey's,[b] I remember; we had a great Johnson[56] in my lady's room, but where lexicographers differed, she generally preferred Bailey).[c]

In this antechamber a footman generally sat,[d] awaiting orders from my lady; for she clung to the grand old customs, and despised any bells, except her own little hand-bell,[e] as modern inventions; she would have her people always within summons of this silvery bell, or her scarce less silvery voice. This man had not the sinecure you might imagine. He had to reply to the private entrance; what we should call the back door[f] in a smaller house. As none came to the front door[g] but my lady, and those of the county whom she honoured by visiting, and her nearest acquaintance of this kind lived eight miles (of bad road) off, the majority of comers knocked at the nail-studded terrace-door; not to have it opened (for open it stood, by my lady's orders, winter and summer, so that the snow often drifted into the back-hall, and lay there in heaps when the weather was severe), but to summon some one to receive their message, or carry their request to be allowed to speak to my lady. I remember it was long before Mr. Gray could be made to understand that the great door[57] was only opened on state occasions, and even to the last he would as soon come in by that as the terrace entrance. I had been received there on my first setting foot over my lady's threshold; every stranger was led in by that way the first time they came; but after that (with the exceptions I have named) they went round by the terrace, as it were by instinct. It was an assistance to this instinct to be aware that from time immemorial, the magnificent and fierce Hanbury wolf-hounds, which were extinct in every other part of the island, had been and still were kept chained in the front quadrangle, where they bayed through a great part of the day and night, and were always ready with their deep, savage growl at the sight of every person and thing, excepting the man who fed them, my lady's carriage-and-four,[a] and my lady herself. It was pretty to see her small figure go up to the great, crouching brutes, thumping the flags with their heavy, wagging tails, and slobbering in an ecstacy of delight, at her light approach and soft caress. She had no fear of them; but she was a Hanbury born, and the tale went, that they and their kind knew all Hanburys instantly, and acknowledged their supremacy, ever since the ancestors of the breed had been brought from the East by the great Sir Urian Hanbury, who lay with his legs crossed on the altar-tomb in the church. Moreover, it was reported that, not fifty years before, one of these dogs had eaten up a child, which had inadvertently strayed within reach of its chain. So you may imagine how most people preferred the terrace-door. Mr. Gray did not seem to care for the dogs. It might be absence of mind, for I have heard of his starting away from their sudden spring when he had unwittingly walked within reach of their chains; but it could hardly have been absence of mind, when one day he went right up to one of them, and patted him in the most friendly manner, the dog meanwhile looking pleased, and affably wagging his tail, just as if Mr. Gray had been a Hanbury. We were all very much puzzled by this, and to this day I have not been able to account for it.

But now let us go back to the terrace-door, and the footman sitting in the antechamber.

One morning we heard a parleying which rose to such a vehemence, and lasted for so long, that my lady had to ring her hand-bell twice before the footman heard it.

'What is the matter, John?' asked she, when he entered.

'A little boy, my lady, who says he comes from Mr. Horner, and must see your ladyship. Impudent little lad!' (this last to himself.)

'What does he want?'

'That's just what I have asked him, my lady, but he won't tell me, please your ladyship.'

'It is, probably, some message from Mr. Horner,' said Lady Ludlow, with just a shade of annoyance in her manner; for it was against all etiquette to send a message to her, and by such a messenger too!

'No! please your ladyship, I asked him if he had any message, and he said no, he had none; but he must see your ladyship for all that.'

'You had better show him in then, without more words,' said her ladyship, quietly, but still, as I have said, rather annoyed.

As if in mockery of the humble visitor, the footman threw open both battants of the door, and in the opening their stood a lithe, wiry lad, with a thick head of hair, standing out in every direction, as if stirred by some electrical current, a short, brown face, red now from affright and excitement, wide, resolute mouth, and bright, deep-set eyes; which glanced keenly and rapidly round the room, as if taking in everything (and all was new and strange) to be thought and puzzled over at some future time. He knew enough of manners not to speak first to one above him in rank, or else he was afraid.

'What do you want with me?' asked my lady; in so gentle a tone that it seemed to surprise and stun him.

'An't please your ladyship?' said he, as if he had been deaf.

'You come from Mr. Horner's: why do you want to see me?' again asked she, a little more loudly.

'An't please your ladyship, Mr. Horner was sent for all on a sudden to Warwick this morning.'

His face began to work; but he felt it, and closed his lips into a resolute form.

'Well?'

'And he went off all on a sudden-like.'

'Well?'

'And he left a note for your ladyship with me, your ladyship.'

'Is that all? You might have given it to the footman.'

'Please your ladyship, I've clean gone and lost it.'

He never took his eyes off her face. If he had not kept his look fixed, he would have burst out crying.

'That was very careless,' said my lady, gently. 'But I am sure you are very sorry for it. You had better try and find it. It may have been of consequence.'

'Please, Mum – please your ladyship – I can say it off by heart.'

'You! What do you mean?' I was really afraid now. My lady's blue eyes absolutely gave out light, she was so much displeased, and, moreover, perplexed. The more reason he had for affright, the more his courage rose. He must have seen, – so sharp a lad must have perceived her displeasure, but he went on quickly and steadily.

'Mr. Horner, my lady, has taught me to read, write, and cast accounts, my lady. And he was in a hurry, and he folded his paper up, but he did not seal it; and I read it, my lady; and now, my lady, it seems like as if I had got it off by heart;' and he went on with a high pitched voice, saying out very loud what, I have no doubt, were the identical words of the letter, date, signature and all: it was merely something about a deed, which required my lady's signature.

When he had done, he stood almost as if he expected commendation for his accurate memory.

My lady's eyes contracted till the pupils were as needle-points; it was a way she had when much disturbed. She looked at me, and said,

'Margaret Dawson, what will this world come to?' And then she was silent.

The lad, beginning to perceive he had given deep offence, stood stock still – as if his brave will had brought him into this presence, and impelled him to confession, and the best amends he could make, but had now deserted him, or was extinct, and left his body motionless, until some one else with word or deed made him quit the room. My lady looked again at him, and saw the frowning, dumb-foundering[a] terror at his misdeed, and the manner in which his confession had been received.

'My poor lad!' said she, the angry look leaving her face, 'into whose hands have you fallen?'

The boy's lips began to quiver.

'Don't you know what tree we read of in Genesis? – No! I hope you have not got to read so easily as that.' A pause. 'Who has taught you to read and write?'

'Please, my lady, I meant no harm, my lady.' He was fairly blubbering, overcome by her evident feeling of dismay and regret, the soft repression of which was more frightening to him than any strong or violent words would have been.

'Who taught you, I ask?'

'It were Mr. Horner's clerk who learned me, my lady.'

'And did Mr. Horner know of it?'

'Yes, my lady. And I am sure I thought for to please him.'

'Well! perhaps you were not to blame for that. But I wonder at Mr. Horner. However, my boy, as you have got possession of edge-tools, you must have some rules how to use them. Did you never hear that you were not to open letters?'

'Please, my lady, it were open. Mr. Horner forgot for to seal it, in his hurry to be off.'

'But you must not read letters that are not intended for you. You must never try to read any letters that are not directed to you, even if they be open before you.'

'Please, my lady, I thought it were good for practice, all as one as a book.'

My lady looked bewildered as to what way she could farther explain to him the laws of honour as regarded letters.

'You would not listen, I am sure,' said she, 'to anything you were not intended to hear?'

He hesitated for a moment, partly because he did not fully comprehend the question. My lady repeated it. The light of intelligence came into his eager eyes, and I could see that he was not certain if he could tell the truth.

'Please, my lady, I always hearken when I hear folk talking secrets; but I mean no harm.'

My poor lady sighed: she was not prepared to begin a long way off in morals. Honour was, to her, second nature, and she had never tried to find out on what principle its laws were based. So, telling the lad that she wished to see Mr. Horner when he returned from Warwick, she dismissed him with a despondent look; he, meanwhile, right glad to be out of the awful gentleness of her presence.

'What is to be done?' said she, half to herself and half to me. I could not answer, for I was puzzled myself.

'It was a right word,' she continued, 'that I used, when I called reading and writing "edge-tools." If our lower orders have these edge-tools given to them, we shall have the terrible scenes of the French Revolution[a] acted over again in England. When I was a girl, one never heard of the rights of men, one only heard of the duties. Now, here was Mr. Gray, only last night, talking of the right every child had to instruction. I could hardly keep my patience with him, and at length we fairly came to words; and I told him I would have no such thing as a Sunday-school (or a Sabbath-school, as he calls it, just like a Jew) in my village.'

'And what did he say, my lady?' I asked; for the struggle that seemed now to have come to a crisis, had been going on for some time in a quiet way.

'Why, he gave way to temper, and said he was bound to remember he was under the bishop's[b] authority, not under mine; and implied that he should persevere in his designs, notwithstanding my expressed opinion.'

'And your ladyship –' I half inquired.

'I could only rise and curtsy,[c] and civilly dismiss him. When two persons have arrived at a certain point of expression on a subject, about which they differ as materially as I do from Mr. Gray, the wisest course, if they wish to remain friends, is to drop the conversation entirely and suddenly. It is one of the few cases where abruptness is desirable.'

I was sorry for Mr. Gray. He had been to see me several times, and had helped me to bear my illness in a better spirit than I should have done without his good advice and prayers. And I had gathered, from little things he said, how much his heart was set upon this new scheme. I liked him so much, and I loved and respected my lady so well, that I could not bear them to be on the cool terms to which they were constantly getting. Yet I could do nothing but keep silence.

I suppose my lady understood something of what was passing in my mind; for, after a minute or two, she went on: –

'If Mr. Gray knew all I know, – if he had my experience, he would not be so ready to speak of setting up his new plans in opposition to my judgment. Indeed,' she continued, lashing herself up with her own recollections, 'times are changed when the parson of a village comes to beard the liege lady in her own house. Why, in my grandfather's days, the parson was family chaplain too, and dined at the Hall every Sunday. He was helped last, and expected to have done first. I remember seeing him take up his plate and knife and fork, and say, with his mouth full all the time he was speaking: "If you please, Sir Urian, and my Lady, I'll follow the beef into the housekeeper's room;" for, you see, unless he did so, he stood no chance of a second helping. A greedy man, that parson was, to be sure! I recollect his once eating up the whole of some little bird at dinner, and by way of diverting attention from his greediness, he told how he had heard that a rook soaked in vinegar and then dressed in a particular way, could not be distinguished from the bird he was then eating. I saw by the grim look of my grandfather's face that the parson's doing and saying displeased him; and, child as I was, I had some notion what was coming, when, as I was riding out on my little, white pony, by my grandfather's side, the next Friday, he stopped one of the gamekeepers, and bade him shoot one of the oldest rooks he could find. I knew no more about it till Sunday, when a dish was set right before the parson, and Sir Urian said: "Now, Parson Hemming, I have had a rook shot, and soaked in vinegar, and dressed as you described last Sunday. Fall to, man, and eat it with as good an appetite as you had last Sunday. Pick the bones clean, or by —, no more Sunday dinners shall you eat at my table!" I gave one look at poor Mr. Hemming's face, as he tried to swallow the first morsel, and make believe as though he thought it very good; but I could not look again, for shame, although my grandfather laughed, and kept asking us all round if we knew what could have become of the parson's appetite.'

'And did he finish it?' I asked.

'O yes, my dear. What my grandfather said was to be done, was done always. He was a terrible man in his anger! But to think of the difference between Parson Hemming and Mr. Gray! or even of poor, dear Mr. Mountford and Mr. Gray. Mr. Mountford would never have withstood me as Mr. Gray did!'

'And your ladyship really thinks that it would not be right to have a Sunday-school?' I asked, feeling very timid as I put the question.

'Certainly not. As I told Mr. Gray, I consider a knowledge of the Creed, and of the Lord's Prayer, as essential to salvation; and that any child may have, whose parents bring it regularly to church. Then there are the Ten Commandments, which teach simple duties in the plainest language. Of course, if a lad is taught to read and write (as that unfortunate boy has been who was here this morning) his duties become complicated, and his temptations much greater, while, at the same time, he has no hereditary principles and honourable training to serve as safeguards. I might take up my old simile of the race-horse and cart-horse.[a] I am distressed,' continued she, with a break in her ideas, 'about that boy. The whole thing reminds me so much of a story of what happened to a friend of mine – Clément de Créquy. Did I ever tell you about him?'

'No, your ladyship,' I replied.

'Poor Clément! more than twenty years ago, Lord Ludlow and I spent a winter in Paris. He had many friends there; perhaps not very good or very wise men, but he was so kind that he liked every one, and every one liked him. We had an apartment, as they call it there, in the Rue de Lille;[58] we had the first-floor of a grand hôtel, with the basement for our servants. On the floor above us the owner of the house lived, a Marquise de Créquy, a widow. They tell me that the Créquy coat-of-arms is still emblazoned, after all these terrible years, on a shield above the arched porte-cochère, just as it was then, though the family is quite extinct. Madam de Créquy had only one son, Clément, who was just the same age as my Urian – you may see his portrait in the great hall – Urian's, I mean.' I knew that Master Urian had been drowned at sea; and often had I looked at the presentment of his bonny hopeful face, in his sailor's dress, with right hand outstretched to a ship on the sea in the distance, as if he had just said, 'Look at her! all her sails are set, and I'm just off.' Poor Master Urian! he went down in this very ship not a year after the picture was taken! But now I will go back to my lady's story. 'I can see those two boys playing now,' continued she, softly, shutting her eyes, as if the better to call up the vision, 'as they used to do five-and-twenty years ago in those old-fashioned French gardens behind our hôtel. Many a time have I watched them from my windows. It was, perhaps, a better play-place than an English garden would have been, for there were but few flower-beds, and no lawn at all to speak about; but instead, terraces and balustrades and vases and flights of stone steps more in the Italian style; and there were jets-d'eau, and little fountains that could be set playing by turning water-cocks that were hidden here and there. How Clément delighted in turning the water on to surprise Urian, and how gracefully he did the honours, as it were, to my dear, rough, sailor lad! Urian was as dark as a gypsy boy, and cared little for his appearance, and resisted all my efforts at setting off his black eyes and tangled curls; but Clément, without ever showing that he thought about himself and his dress, was always dainty and elegant, even though his clothes were sometimes but threadbare. He used to be dressed in a kind of hunter's green suit, open at the neck and half-way down the chest to beautiful old lace frills; his long golden curls fell behind just like a girl's, and his hair in front was cut over his straight dark eyebrows in a line almost as straight. Urian learnt more of a gentleman's carefulness and propriety of appearance from that lad in two months than he had done in years from all my lectures. I recollect one day, when the two boys were in full romp – and, my window being open, I could hear them perfectly – and Urian was daring Clément to some scrambling or climbing, which Clément refused to undertake, but in a hesitating way, as though he longed to do it if some reason had not stood in the way; and at times, Urian, who was hasty and thoughtless, poor fellow, told Clément that he was afraid. "Fear!" said the French boy, drawing himself up; "you do not know what you say. If you will be here at six to-morrow morning, when it is only just light, I will take that starling's

nest on the top of yonder chimney." "But why not now, Clément?" said
Urian, putting his arm round Clément's neck. "Why then, and not now, just
when we are in the humour for it?" "Because we De Créquys are poor, and
my mother cannot afford me another suit of clothes this year, and yonder
stone carving is all jagged, and would tear my coat and breeches. Now, to-
morrow morning I could go up with nothing on but an old shirt."

"'But you would tear your legs?'"

"'My race do not care for pain," said the boy, drawing himself from
Urian's arm, and walking a few steps away, with a becoming pride and
reserve; for he was hurt at being spoken to as if he were afraid, and annoyed
at having to confess the true reason for declining the feat. But Urian was not
to be thus baffled. He went up to Clément, and put his arm once more
about his neck, and I could see the two lads as they walked down the terrace
away from the hôtel windows: first Urian spoke eagerly, looking with
imploring fondness into Clément's face, which sought the ground, till at last
the French boy spoke, and by-and-by his arm was round Urian too, and they
paced backwards and forwards in deep talk, but gravely, as became men,
rather than boys.

'All at once, from the little chapel at the corner of the large garden belonging to the Missions Etrangères,[59] I heard the tinkle of the little bell,
announcing the elevation of the host. Down on his knees went Clément,
hands crossed, eyes bent down: while Urian stood looking on in respectful
thought.

'What a friendship that might have been! I never dream of Urian without
seeing Clément too, – Urian speaks to me, or does something, – but Clément only flits round Urian, and never seems to see any one else!

'But I must not forget to tell you, that the next morning, before he was
out of his room, a footman of Madame de Créquy's brought Urian the starling's nest.

'Well! we came back to England, and the boys were to correspond; and
Madame de Créquy and I exchanged civilities; and Urian went to sea.

'After that, all seemed to drop away. I cannot tell you all. However, to confine myself to the De Créquys. I had a letter from Clément; I knew he felt
his friend's death deeply; but I should never have learnt it from the letter he
sent. It was formal, and seemed like chaff to my hungering heart. Poor fellow! I dare say he had found it hard to write. What could he – or any one –
say to a mother who has lost her child? The world does not think so, and, in
general, one must conform to the customs of the world; but, judging from
my own experience, I should say that reverent silence at such times is the
tenderest balm.

'Madame de Créquy wrote too. But I knew she could not feel my loss so
much as Clément, and therefore her letter was not such a disappointment.
She and I went on being civil and polite in the way of commissions, and

occasionally introducing friends to each other, for a year or two, and then we ceased to have any intercourse. Then the terrible revolution came. No one who did not live at those times can imagine the daily expectation of news, – the hourly terror of rumours affecting the fortunes and lives of those whom most of us had known as pleasant hosts, receiving us with peaceful welcome in their magnificent houses. Of course, there was sin enough and suffering enough behind the scenes; but we English visitors to Paris had seen little or nothing of that, – and I had sometimes thought, indeed, how even Death seemed loth to choose his victims out of that brilliant throng whom I had known. Madame de Créquy's one boy lived; while three out of my six were gone since we had met! I do not think all lots are equal, even now that I know the end of her hopes; but I do say, that whatever our individual lot is, it is our duty to accept it, without comparing it with that of others.

'The times were thick with gloom and terror. "What next?" was the question we asked of every one who brought us news from Paris. Where were these demons hidden when, so few years ago, we danced and feasted, and enjoyed the brilliant salons and the charming friendships of Paris?

'One evening, I was sitting alone in Saint James' Square; my lord off at the club with Mr. Fox[60] and others: he had left me, thinking that I should go to one of the many places to which I had been invited for that evening; but I had no heart to go anywhere, for it was poor Urian's birthday, and I had not even rung for lights, though the day was fast closing in, but was thinking over all his pretty ways, and on his warm affectionate nature, and how often I had been too hasty in speaking to him, for all I loved him so dearly; and how I seemed to have neglected and dropped his dear friend Clément, who might even now be in need of help in that cruel, bloody Paris. I say I was thinking reproachfully of all this, and particularly of Clément de Créquy in connection with Urian, when Fenwick brought me a note, sealed with a coat-of-arms I knew well, though I could not remember at the moment where I had seen it. I puzzled over it, as one does sometimes, for a minute or more, before I opened the letter. In a moment I saw it was from Clément de Créquy. "My mother is here," he said: "she is very ill, and I am bewildered in this strange country. May I entreat you to receive me for a few minutes?" The bearer of the note was the woman of the house where they lodged. I had her brought up into the anteroom, and questioned her myself, while my carriage was being brought round. They had arrived in London a fortnight or so before: she had not known their quality, judging them (according to her kind) by their dress and their luggage; poor enough, no doubt. The lady had never left her bedroom since her arrival; the young man waited upon her, did everything for her, never left her, in fact; only she (the messenger) had promised to stay within call, as soon as she returned, while he went out somewhere. She could hardly understand him, he spoke English so badly. He had never spoken it, I dare say, since he had talked to my Urian.

CHAPTER V.

'IN the hurry of the moment I scarce knew what I did. I bade the house-keeper put up every delicacy she had, in order to tempt the invalid, whom yet I hoped to bring back with me to our house. When the carriage was ready, I took the good woman with me to show us the exact way, which my coachman professed not to know; for, indeed, they were staying at but a poor kind of place at the back of Leicester Square, of which they had heard, as Clément told me afterwards, from one of the fishermen who had carried them across from the Dutch coast in their disguises as a Friesland peasant and his mother. They had some jewels of value concealed round their persons; but their ready money was all spent before I saw them, and Clément had been unwilling to leave his mother, even for the time necessary to ascertain the best mode of disposing of the diamonds. For, overcome with distress of mind and bodily fatigue, she had reached London only to take to her bed in a sort of low, nervous fever, in which her chief and only idea seemed to be, that Clément was about to be taken from her to some prison or other; and if he were out of her sight, though but for a minute, she cried like a child, and could not be pacified or comforted. The landlady was a kind, good woman, and though she but half understood the case, she was truly sorry for them, as foreigners, and the mother sick in a strange land.

'I sent her forwards to request permission for my entrance. In a moment I saw Clément – a tall, elegant young man, in a curious dress of coarse cloth, standing at the open door of a room, and evidently – even before he accosted me – striving to soothe the terrors of his mother inside. I went towards him, and would have taken his hand, but he bent down and kissed mine.

'"May I come in, madame?" I asked, looking at the poor sick lady, lying in the dark, dingy bed, her head propped up on coarse and dirty pillows, and gazing with affrighted eyes at all that was going on.

'"Clément! Clément! come to me!" she cried; and when he went to the bedside she turned on one side, and took his hand in both of hers, and began stroking it, and looking up in his face. I could scarce keep back my tears.

'He stood there quite still, except that from time to time he spoke to her in a low tone. At last I advanced into the room, so that I could talk to him, without renewing her alarm. I asked for the doctor's address; for I had heard that they had called in some one, at their landlady's recommendation: but I could hardly understand Clément's broken English, and mispronunciation of our proper names, and was obliged to apply to the woman herself. I could not say much to Clément, for his attention was perpetually needed by his mother, who never seemed to perceive that I was there. But I told him not to fear, however long I might be away, for that I would return before night; and, bidding the woman take charge of all the heterogeneous things the housekeeper had put up, and leaving one of my men in the house, who could understand a few words of French, with directions that he was to hold himself at Madame de Créquy's orders until I sent or gave him fresh commands, I drove off to the doctor's. What I wanted was his permission to remove Madame de Créquy to my own house, and to learn how it best could be done; for I saw that every movement in the room, every sound, except Clément's voice, brought on a fresh access of trembling and nervous agitation.

'The doctor was, I should think, a clever man; but he had that kind of abrupt manner which people get who have much to do with the lower orders.

'I told him the story of his patient, the interest I had in her, and the wish I entertained of removing her to my own house.

'"It can't be done," said he. "Any change will kill her."

'"But it must be done," I replied. "And it shall not kill her."

'"Then I have nothing more to say," said he, turning away from the carriage-door, and making as though he would go back into the house.

'"Stop a moment. You must help me; and, if you do, you shall have reason to be glad, for I will give you fifty pounds down with pleasure. If you won't do it, another shall."

'He looked at me, then (furtively) at the carriage, hesitated, and then said: "You do not mind expense, apparently. I suppose you are a rich lady of quality. Such folks will not stick at such trifles as the life or death of a sick woman to get their own way. I suppose, I must e'en help you, for if I don't, another will."

'I did not mind what he said, so that he would assist me. I was pretty sure that she was in a state to require opiates; and I had not forgotten Christopher Sly,[61] you may be sure, so I told him what I had in my head. That in the dead of night, – the quiet time in the streets, – she should be carried in a hospital litter, softly and warmly covered over, from the Leicester Square lodging-house to rooms that I would have in perfect readiness for her. As I planned, so it was done. I let Clément know, by a note, of my design. I had all prepared at home, and we walked about my house as though shod with velvet, while the porter watched at the open door. At last, through the darkness, I saw the lanterns carried by my men, who were leading the little procession. The litter looked like a hearse; on one side walked the doctor, on the other

Clément: they came softly and swiftly along. I could not try any farther experiment; we dared not change her clothes; she was laid in the bed in the landlady's coarse night-gear, and covered over warmly, and left in the shaded, scented room, with a nurse and the doctor watching by her, while I led Clément to the dressing-room adjoining, in which I had had a bed placed for him. Farther than that he would not go; and there I had refreshments brought. Meanwhile, he had shown his gratitude by every possible action (for we none of us dared to speak): he had kneeled at my feet, and kissed my hand, and left it wet with his tears. He had thrown up his arms to Heaven, and prayed earnestly, as I could see by the movement of his lips. I allowed him to relieve himself by these dumb expressions, if I may so call them, – and then I left him, and went to my own rooms to sit up for my lord, and tell him what I had done.

'Of course, it was all right; and neither my lord nor I could sleep for wondering how Madame de Créquy would bear her awakening. I had engaged the doctor, to whose face and voice she was accustomed, to remain with her all night: the nurse was experienced, and Clément was within call. But it was with the greatest relief that I heard from my own woman, when she brought me my chocolate,[a] that Madame de Créquy (Monsieur had said) had awakened more tranquil than she had been for many days. To be sure, the whole aspect of the bed-chamber must have been more familiar to her than the miserable place where I had found her, and she must have intuitively felt herself among friends.

'My lord was scandalized at Clément's dress, which, after the first moment of seeing him, I had forgotten, in thinking of other things, and for which I had not prepared Lord Ludlow. He sent for his own tailor, and bade him bring patterns of stuffs, and engage his men to work night and day till Clément could appear as became his rank. In short, in a few days so much of the traces of their flight were removed, that we had almost forgotten the terrible causes of it, and rather felt as if they had come on a visit to us than that they had been compelled to fly their country. Their diamonds, too, were sold well by my lord's agents, though the London shops were stocked with jewellery, and such portable valuables, some of rare and curious fashion, which were sold for half their real value by emigrants who could not afford to wait. Madame de Créquy was recovering her health, although her strength was sadly gone, and she would never be equal to such another flight, as the perilous one which she had gone through, and to which she could not bear the slightest reference. For some time things continued in this state; – the De Créquys still our honoured visitors, – many houses besides our own, even among our own friends, open to receive the poor flying nobility of France, driven from their country by the brutal republicans, and every freshly-arrived emigrant bringing new tales of horror, as if these revolutionists were drunk with blood, and mad to devise new atrocities.

One day Clément; – I should tell you he had been presented to our good King George and the sweet Queen, and they had accosted him most graciously, and his beauty and elegance, and some of the circumstances attendant on his flight, made him be received in the world quite like a hero of romance: he might have been on intimate terms in many a distinguished house, had he cared to visit much; but he accompanied my lord and me with an air of indifference and languor, which I sometimes fancied, made him be all the more sought after: Monkshaven (that was the title my eldest son bore) tried in vain to interest him in all young men's sports. But no! it was the same through all. His mother took far more interest in the on-dits of the London world, into which she was far too great an invalid to venture, than he did in the absolute events themselves, in which he might have been an actor. One day, as I was saying, an old Frenchman of a humble class presented himself to our servants, several of whom understood French; and, through Medlicott, I learnt that he was in some way connected with the De Créquys; not with their Paris-life; but I fancy he had been intendant of their estates in the country; estates which were more useful as hunting-grounds than as adding to their income. However, there was the old man; and with him, wrapped round his person, he had brought the long parchment rolls, and deeds relating to their property. These he would deliver up to none but Monsieur de Créquy, the rightful owner; and Clément was out with Monkshaven, so the old man waited; and when Clément came in, I told him of the steward's arrival, and how he had been cared for by my people. Clément went directly to see him. He was a long time away, and I was waiting for him to drive out with me, for some purpose or another, I scarce know what, but I remember I was tired of waiting, and was just in the act of ringing the bell to desire that he might be reminded of his engagement with me, when he came in, his face as white as the powder in his hair, his beautiful eyes dilated with horror. I saw that he had heard something that touched him even more closely than the usual tales which every fresh emigrant brought.

"'What is it, Clément?" I asked.

'He clasped his hands, and looked as though he tried to speak, but could not bring out the words.

"'They have guillotined my uncle!" said he at last. Now, I knew that there was a Count de Créquy; but I had always understood that the elder branch held very little communication with him; in fact, that he was a vaurien[62] of some kind, and rather a disgrace than otherwise to the family. So, perhaps, I was hard-hearted; but I was a little surprised at this excess of emotion, till I saw that peculiar look in his eyes that many people have when there is more terror in their hearts than they dare put into words. He wanted me to understand something without his saying it; but how could I? I had never heard of a Mademoiselle de Créquy.

"'Virginie!" at last he uttered. In an instant I understood it all, and remembered that, if Urian had lived, he too might have been in love.

"'Your uncle's daughter?" I inquired.

"'My cousin," he replied.

'I did not say, "your betrothed," but I had no doubt of it. I was mistaken, however.

"'O madame!" he continued, "her mother died long ago – her father now – and she is in daily fear, – alone, deserted – "

"'Is she in the Abbaye?"[63] asked I.

"'No! She is in hiding with the widow of her father's old concierge. Any day they may search the house for aristocrats. They are seeking them every-where. Then, not her life alone, but that of the old woman, her hostess, is sacrificed. The old woman knows this, and trembles with fear. Even if she is brave enough to be faithful, her fears would betray her, should the house be searched. Yet, there is no one to help Virginie to escape. She is alone in Paris."

'I saw what was in his mind. He was fretting and chafing to go to his cousin's assistance; but the thought of his mother restrained him. I would not have kept back Urian from such an errand at such a time. How should I restrain him? And yet, perhaps, I did wrong in not urging the chances of danger more. Still, if it was danger to him, was it not the same or even greater danger to her? – for the French spared neither age nor sex in those wicked days of terror. So I rather fell in with his wish, and encouraged him to think how best and most prudently it might be fulfilled; never doubting, as I have said, that he and his cousin were troth-plighted.

'But when I went to Madame de Créquy – after he had imparted his, or rather our plan to her – I found out my mistake. She, who was in general too feeble to walk across the room save slowly, and with a stick, was going from end to end with quick, tottering steps; and, if now and then she sank upon a chair, it seemed as if she could not rest, for she was up again in a moment, pacing along, wringing her hands, and speaking rapidly to herself. When she saw me, she stopped: "Madame," she said, "you have lost your own boy. You might have left me mine."

'I was so astonished – I hardly knew what to say. I had spoken to Clément as if his mother's consent were secure (as I had felt my own would have been if Urian had been alive to ask it). Of course, both he and I knew that his mother's consent must be asked and obtained, before he could leave her to go on such an undertaking; but, somehow, my blood always rose at the sight or sound of danger; perhaps, because my life had been so peaceful. Poor Madame de Créquy! it was otherwise with her; she despaired while I hoped, and Clément trusted.

"'Dear Madame de Créquy," said I, "he will return safely to us; every pre-caution shall be taken, that either he or you, or my lord, or Monkshaven can think of; but he cannot leave a girl – his nearest relation save you – his betrothed, is she not?"

"'His betrothed!' cried she, now at the utmost pitch of her excitement. "Virginie betrothed to Clément? – no! thank heaven, not so bad as that! Yet it might have been. But Mademoiselle scorned my son! She would have nothing to do with him. Now is the time for him to have nothing to do with her!"

'Clément had entered at the door behind his mother as she thus spoke. His face was set and pale, till it looked as gray[a] and immovable as if it had been carved in stone. He came forward and stood before his mother. She stopped her walk, threw back her haughty head, and the two looked each other steadily in the face. After a minute or two in this attitude, her proud and resolute gaze never flinching or wavering, he went down upon one knee, and, taking her hand – her hard, stony hand, which never closed on his, but remained straight and stiff:

"'Mother," he pleaded, "withdraw your prohibition. Let me go!"

"'What were her words?" Madame de Créquy replied, slowly, as if forcing her memory to the extreme of accuracy. "My cousin," she said, "when I marry, I marry a man, not a petit-maître.[64] I marry a man who, whatever his rank may be, will add dignity to the human race by his virtues, and not be content to live in an effeminate court on the traditions of past grandeur." She borrowed her words from the infamous Jean-Jacques Rousseau,[65] the friend of her scarce less infamous father, – nay! I will say it, – if not her words, she borrowed her principles. And my son to request her to marry him!'

"'It was my father's written wish," said Clément.

"'But did you not love her? You plead your father's words, – words written twelve years before, – and as if that were your reason for being indifferent to my dislike to the alliance. But you requested her to marry you, – and she refused you with insolent contempt; and now you are ready to leave me, – leave me desolate in a foreign land – "

"'Desolate! my mother! and the Countess Ludlow stands there!"

"'Pardon, madame! But all the earth, though it were full of kind hearts, is but a desolation and a desert place to a mother when her only child is absent. And you, Clément, would leave me for this Virginie, – this degenerate De Créquy, tainted with the atheism of the Encyclopédistes![66] She is only reaping some of the fruit of the harvest whereof her friends have sown the seed. Let her alone! Doubtless she has friends – it may be lovers – among these demons, who, under the cry of liberty, commit every licence. Let her alone, Clément! She refused you with scorn: be too proud to notice her now."

"'Mother, I cannot think of myself; only of her."

"'Think of me, then! I, your mother, forbid you to go."

'Clément bowed low, and went out of the room instantly, as one blinded. She saw his groping movement, and, for an instant, I think her heart was touched. But she turned to me, and tried to exculpate her past violence by dilating upon her wrongs, and they certainly were many. The Count, her husband's younger brother, had invariably tried to make mischief between husband and wife. He had been the cleverer man of the two, and had possessed extraordinary influence over her husband. She suspected him of having instigated that clause in her husband's will, by which the Marquis expressed his wish for the marriage of the cousins. The Count had had some interest in the management of the De Créquy property during her son's minority. Indeed, I remembered then, that it was through Count de Créquy that Lord Ludlow had first heard of the apartment which we afterwards took in the Hôtel de Créquy; and then the recollection of a past feeling came distinctly out of the mist, as it were; and I called to mind how, when we first took up our abode in the Hôtel de Créquy, both Lord Ludlow and I imagined that the arrangement was displeasing to our hostess; and how it had taken us a considerable time before we had been able to establish relations of friendship with her. Years after our visit, she began to suspect that Clément (whom she could not forbid to visit at his uncle's house, considering the terms on which his father had been with his brother; though she herself never set foot over the Count de Créquy's threshold) was attaching himself to Mademoiselle, his cousin; and she made cautious inquiries as to the appearance, character, and disposition of the young lady. Mademoiselle was not handsome, they said; but of a fine figure, and generally considered as having a very noble and attractive presence. In character she was daring and wilful (said one set); original and independent (said another). She was much indulged by her father, who had given her something of a man's education, and selected for her intimate friend a young lady below her in rank, one of the Bureaucracie, a Mademoiselle Necker,[67a] daughter of the Minister of Finance. Mademoiselle de Créquy was thus introduced into all the free-thinking salons of Paris; among people who were always full of plans for subverting society. "And did Clément affect such people?" Madame de Créquy had asked, with some anxiety. No! Monsieur de Créquy had neither eyes nor ears, nor thought for anything but his cousin, while she was by. And she? She hardly took notice of his devotion, so evident to every one else. The proud creature! But perhaps that was her haughty way of concealing what she felt. And so Madame de Créquy listened, and questioned, and learnt nothing decided, until one day she surprised Clément with the note in his hand, of which she remembered the stinging words so well, in which Virginie had said, in reply to a proposal Clément had sent her through her father, that "When she married she married a man, not a petit-maître."

'Clément was justly indignant at the insulting nature of the answer Virginie had sent to a proposal, respectful in its tone, and which was, after all, but the cool, hardened lava over a burning heart. He acquiesced in his mother's desire, that he should not again present himself in his uncle's salons; but he did not forget Virginie, though he never mentioned her name.

'Madame de Créquy and her son were among the earliest proscrits, as they were of the strongest possible royalists, and aristocrats, as it was the custom of the horrid Sansculottes to term those who adhered to the habits of expression and action in which it was their pride to have been educated. They had left Paris some weeks before they had arrived in England, and Clément's belief at the time of quitting the Hôtel de Créquy had certainly been, that his uncle was not merely safe, but rather a popular man with the party in power. And, as all communication having relation to private individuals of a reliable kind was intercepted, Monsieur de Créquy had felt but little anxiety for his uncle and cousin, in comparison with what he did for many other friends of very different opinions in politics, until the day when he was stunned by the fatal information that even his progressive uncle was guillotined, and learnt that his cousin was imprisoned by the licence of the mob, whose rights (as she called them) she was always advocating.

'When I had heard all this story, I confess I lost in sympathy for Clément what I gained for his mother. Virginie's life did not seem to me worth the risk that Clément's would run. But when I saw him – sad, depressed, nay, hopeless – going about like one oppressed by a heavy dream which he cannot shake off; caring neither to eat, drink, nor sleep, yet bearing all with silent dignity, and even trying to force a poor, faint smile when he caught my anxious eyes; I turned round again, and wondered how Madame de Créquy could resist this mute pleading of her son's altered appearance. As for my Lord Ludlow and Monkshaven, as soon as they understood the case, they were indignant that any mother should attempt to keep a son out of honourable danger; and it was honourable, and a clear duty (according to them) to try to save the life of a helpless orphan girl, his next of kin. None but a Frenchman, said my lord, would hold himself bound by an old woman's whimsies and fears, even though she were his mother. As it was, he was chafing himself to death under the restraint. If he went, to be sure, the – wretches might make an end of him, as they had done of many a fine fellow; but my lord would take heavy odds that, instead of being guillotined, he would save the girl, and bring her safe to England, just desperately in love with her preserver, and then we would have a jolly wedding down at Monkshaven. My lord repeated his opinion so often, that it became a certain prophecy in his mind of what was to take place; and, one day seeing Clément look even paler and thinner than he had ever done before, he sent a message to Madame de Créquy, requesting permission to speak to her in private.

'"For, by George!" said he, "she shall hear my opinion, and not let that lad of hers kill himself by fretting. He's too good for that. If he had been an

English lad, he would have been off to his sweetheart long before this, without saying with your leave or by your leave; but being a Frenchman, he is all for Æneas and filial piety, – [68] filial fiddle-sticks!" (My lord had run away to sea, when a boy, against his father's consent, I am sorry to say; and, as all had ended well, and he had come back to find both his parents alive, I do not think he was ever as much aware of his fault as he might have been under other circumstances.) "No, my lady," he went on, "don't come with me. A woman can manage a man best when he has a fit of obstinacy, and a man can persuade a woman out of her tantrums, when all her own sex, the whole army of them, would fail. Allow me to go alone to my tête-à-tête with madame."

'What he said, what passed, he never could repeat; but he came back graver than he went. However, the point was gained; Madame de Créquy withdrew her prohibition, and had given him leave to tell Clément as much.

"'But she is an old Cassandra,"[69] said he. "Don't let the lad be much with her; her talk would destroy the courage of the bravest man; she is so given over to superstition." Something that she had said had touched a chord in my lord's nature which he inherited from his Scotch ancestors.[70] Long afterwards, I heard what this was. Medlicott told me.

'However, my lord shook off all fancies that told against the fulfilment of Clément's wishes. All that afternoon we three sat[a] together, planning; and Monkshaven passed in and out, executing our commissions, and preparing everything. Towards nightfall all was ready for Clément's start on his journey towards the coast.

'Madame had declined seeing any of us since my lord's stormy interview with her. She sent word that she was fatigued, and desired repose. But, of course, before Clément set off, he was bound to wish her farewell, and to ask for her blessing. In order to avoid an agitating conversation between mother and son, my lord and I resolved to be present at the interview. Clément was already in his travelling-dress, that of a Norman fisherman, which Monkshaven had, with infinite trouble, discovered in the possession of one of the emigrés who thronged London, and who had made his escape from the shores of France in this disguise. Clément's plan was, to go down to the Coast of Sussex, and get some of the fishing or smuggling boats to take him across to the French Coast near Dieppe. There again he would have to change his dress. O, it was so well planned! His mother was startled by his disguise (of which we had not thought to forewarn her) as he entered her apartment. And either that, or the being suddenly roused from the heavy slumber into which she was apt to fall when she was left alone, gave her manner an air of wildness that was almost like insanity.

"'Go, go!" she said to him, almost pushing him away as he knelt to kiss her hand. "Virginie is beckoning to you, but you don't see what kind of a bed it is – "

"'Clément, make haste!' said my lord, in a hurried manner, as if to inter-rupt madame. "The time is later than I thought, and you must not miss the morning's tide. Bid your mother good-bye at once, and let us be off." For my lord and Monkshaven were to ride with him to an inn near the shore, from whence he was to walk to his destination. My lord almost took him by the arm to pull him away; and they were gone, and I was left alone with Madame de Créquy. When she heard the horses' feet, she seemed to find out the truth, as if for the first time. She set her teeth together. "He has left me for her!" she almost screamed. "Left me for her!" she kept muttering; and then, as the wild look came back into her eyes, she said, almost with exulta-tion, "But I did not give him my blessing!'"

CHAPTER VI.

'ALL night Madame de Créquy raved in delirium. If I could, I would have sent for Clément back again. I did send off one man, but I suppose my directions were confused, or they were wrong, for he came back after my lord's return, on the following afternoon. By this time Madame de Créquy was quieter: she was, indeed, asleep from exhaustion when Lord Ludlow and Monkshaven came in. They were in high spirits, and their hopefulness brought me round to a less dispirited state. All had gone well: they had accompanied Clément on foot along the shore, until they had met with a lugger, which my lord had hailed in good nautical language. The captain had responded to these freemason terms[71] by sending a boat to pick up his passenger, and by an invitation to breakfast sent through a speaking-trumpet. Monkshaven did not approve of either the meal or the company, and had returned to the inn, but my lord had gone with Clément, and breakfasted on board, upon grog, biscuit, fresh-caught fish – "the best breakfast he ever ate," he said, but that was probably owing to the appetite his night's ride had given him. However, his good fellowship had evidently won the captain's heart, and Clément had set sail under the best auspices. It was agreed that I should tell all this to Madame de Créquy, if she inquired; otherwise, it would be wiser not to renew her agitation by alluding to her son's journey.

'I sat[a] with her constantly for many days; but she never spoke of Clément. She forced herself to talk of the little occurrences of Parisian society in former days: she tried to be conversational and agreeable, and to betray no anxiety or even interest in the object of Clément's journey; and, as far as unremitting efforts could go, she succeeded. But the tones of her voice were sharp and yet piteous, as if she were in constant pain; and the glance of her eye hurried and fearful, as if she dared not let it rest on any object.

'In a week we heard of Clément's safe arrival on the French coast. He sent a letter to this effect by the captain of the smuggler, when the latter returned. We hoped to hear again; but week after week elapsed, and there was no news of Clément. I had told Lord Ludlow, in Madame de Créquy's presence, as he and I had arranged, of the note I had received from her son, informing us of his landing in France. She heard, but she took no notice. Yet now, evidently, she began to wonder that we did not mention any further intelligence of him in the same manner before her; and daily I began to fear that her pride would give way, and that she would supplicate for news before I had any to give her.

'One morning, on my awakening, my maid told me that Madame de Cré-quy had passed a wretched night, and had bidden Medlicott (whom, as understanding French, and speaking it pretty well, though with that horrid German accent, I had put about her) request that I would go to madame's room as soon as I was dressed.

'I knew what was coming, and I trembled all the time they were doing my hair, and otherwise arranging me. I was not encouraged by my lord's speeches. He had heard the message, and kept declaring that he would rather be shot than have to tell her that there was no news of her son; and yet he said, every now and then, when I was at the lowest pitch of uneasiness, that he never expected to hear again: that some day soon we should see him walking in, and introducing Mademoiselle de Créquy to us.

'However, at last I was ready, and go I must.

'Her eyes were fixed on the door by which I entered. I went up to the bedside. She was not rouged, – she had left it off now for several days, – she no longer attempted to keep up the vain show of not feeling, and loving, and fearing.

'For a moment or two she did not speak, and I was glad of the respite.

'"Clément?" she said at length, covering her mouth with a handkerchief the minute she had spoken, that I might not see it quiver.

'"There has been no news since the first letter, saying how well the voyage was performed, and how safely he had landed, – near Dieppe, you know," I replied as cheerfully as possible. "My lord does not expect that we shall have another letter; he thinks that we shall see him soon."

'There was no answer. As I looked, uncertain whether to do or say more, she slowly turned herself in bed, and lay with her face to the wall; and, as if that did not shut out the light of day and the busy, happy world enough, she put out her trembling hands, and covered her face with her handkerchief. There was no violence: hardly any sound.

'I told her what my lord had said about Clément's coming in some day, and taking us all by surprise. I did not believe it myself, but it was just possible, – and I had nothing else to say. Pity, to one who was striving so hard to conceal her feelings, would have been impertinent. She let me talk; but she did not reply. She knew that my words were vain and idle, and had no root in my belief, as well as I did myself.

'I was very thankful when Medlicott came in with Madame's breakfast, and gave me an excuse for leaving.

'But I think that conversation made me feel more anxious and impatient than ever. I felt almost pledged to Madame de Créquy for the fulfilment of the vision I had held out. She had taken entirely to her bed by this time; not from illness, but because she had no hope within her to stir her up to the effort of dressing. In the same way she hardly cared for food. She had no appetite, – why eat to prolong a life of despair? But she let Medlicott feed her, sooner than take the trouble of resisting.

'And so it went on, – for weeks, months, – I could hardly count the time, it seemed so long. Medlicott told me she noticed a preternatural sensitiveness of ear in Madame de Créquy, induced by the habit of listening silently for the slightest unusual sound in the house. Medlicott was always a minute watcher of any one whom she cared about; and, one day, she made me notice by a sign madame's acuteness of hearing, although the quick expectation was but evinced for a moment in the turn of the eye, the hushed breath – and then, when the unusual footstep turned into my lord's apartments, the soft quivering sigh, and the closed eyelids.

'At length the intendant of the De Créquy estates, – the old man, you will remember, whose information respecting Virginie de Créquy first gave Clément the desire to return to Paris, – came to St. James's Square, and begged to speak to me. I made haste to go down to him in the housekeeper's room, sooner than that he should be ushered into mine, for fear of madame hearing any sound.

'The old man stood – I see him now – with his hat held before him in both his hands; he slowly bowed till his face touched it when I came in. Such long excess of courtesy augured ill. He waited for me to speak.

'"Have you any intelligence?" I inquired. He had been often to the house before, to ask if we had received any news; and once or twice I had seen him, but this was the first time he had begged to see me.

'"Yes, madame," he replied, still standing with his head bent down, like a child in disgrace.

'"And it is bad!" I exclaimed.

'"It is bad." For a moment I was angry at the cold tone in which my words were echoed; but directly afterwards I saw the large, slow, heavy tears of age falling down the old man's cheeks, and on to the sleeves of his poor, threadbare coat.

'I asked him how he had heard it: it seemed as though I could not all at once bear to hear what it was. He told me that the night before, in crossing Long Acre, he had stumbled upon an old acquaintance of his; one who, like himself, had been a dependant upon the De Créquy family, but had managed their Paris affairs, while Fléchier had taken charge of their estates in the country. Both were now emigrants, and living on the proceeds of such small available talents as they possessed. Fléchier, as I knew, earned a very fair livelihood by going about to dress salads for dinner parties. His compatriot, Le Fèbvre, had begun to give a few lessons as a dancing-master. One of them took the other home to his lodgings; and there, when their most immediate

personal adventures had been hastily talked over, came the inquiry from
Fléchier as to Monsieur de Créquy.

"'Clément was dead – guillotined. Virginie was dead – guillotined.'"

'When Fléchier had told me thus much, he could not speak for sobbing;
and I, myself, could hardly tell how to restrain my tears sufficiently, until I
could go to my own room and be at liberty to give way. He asked my leave to
bring in his friend Le Fèbvre, who was walking in the square, awaiting a possible summons to tell his story. I heard afterwards a good many details,
which filled up the account, and made me feel – which brings me back to
the point I started from – how unfit the lower orders are for being trusted
indiscriminately with the dangerous powers of education. I have made a
long preamble, but now I am coming to the moral of my story.'

My lady was trying to shake off the emotion which she evidently felt in
recurring to this sad history of Monsieur de Créquy's death. She came
behind me, and arranged my pillows, and then, seeing I had been crying –
for, indeed, I was weak-spirited at the time, and a little served to unloose my
tears – she stooped down, and kissed my forehead, and said 'Poor child!'
almost as if she thanked me for feeling that old grief of hers.

'Being once in France, it was no difficult thing for Clément to get into
Paris. The difficulty in those days was to leave, not to enter. He came in
dressed as a Norman peasant, in charge of a load of fruit and vegetables, with
which one of the Seine barges was freighted. He worked hard with his companions in landing and arranging their produce on the quays; and then,
when they dispersed to get their breakfasts at some of the estaminets near
the old Marché aux Fleurs, he sauntered up a street which conducted him,
by many an odd turn, through the Quartier Latin to a horrid back alley, leading out of the Rue l'Ecole de Médécine; some atrocious place, as I have
heard, not far from the shadow of that terrible Abbaye, where so many of the
best blood of France awaited their deaths. But here some old man lived on
whose fidelity Clément thought that he might rely. I am not sure if he had
not been gardener in those very gardens behind the Hôtel Créquy where
Clément and Urian used to play together years before. But, whatever the old
man's dwelling might be, Clément was only too glad to reach it, you may be
sure. He had been kept in Normandy, in all sorts of disguises, for many days
after landing in Dieppe, through the difficulty of entering Paris unsuspected
by the many ruffians who were always on the look-out for aristocrats.

'The old gardener was, I believe, both faithful and tried, and sheltered
Clément in his garret as well as might be. Before he could stir out, it was
necessary to procure a fresh disguise; and one more in character with an
inhabitant of Paris than that of a Norman carter was procured; and, after
waiting in-doors for one or two days, to see if any suspicion was excited,
Clément set off to discover Virginie.

'He found her at the old concièrge's dwelling.

Madame Babette was the name of this woman, who must have been a less faithful – or rather, perhaps I should say, a more interested – friend to her guest than the old gardener Jacques was to Clément.

'I have seen a miniature[72] of Virginie, which a French lady of quality happened to have in her possession at the time of her flight from Paris, and which she brought with her to England unwittingly; for it belonged to the Count de Créquy, with whom she was slightly acquainted. I should fancy from it, that Virginie was taller and of a more powerful figure for a woman than her cousin Clément was for a man. Her dark-brown hair was arranged in short curls – the way of dressing the hair announced the politics of the individual, in those days, just as patches did in my grandmother's time; and Virginie's hair was not to my taste, or according to my principles; it was too classical. Her large, black eyes looked out at you steadily. One cannot judge of the shape of a nose from a full-face miniature, but the nostrils were clearly cut and largely opened. I do not fancy her nose could have been pretty; but her mouth had a character all its own, and which would, I think, have redeemed a plainer face. It was wide and deep set into the cheeks at the corners; the upper lip was very much arched, and hardly closed over the teeth; so that the whole face looked (from the serious, intent look in the eyes, and the sweet intelligence of the month) as if she were listening eagerly to something to which her answer was quite ready, and would come out of those red, opening lips as soon as ever you had done speaking, and you longed to know what she would say.

'Well; this Virginie de Créquy was living with Madame Babette in the concièrgerie of an old French inn, somewhere to the north of Paris, so, far enough from Clément's refuge. The inn had been frequented by farmers from Brittany and such kind of people, in the days when that sort of intercourse went on between Paris and the provinces which had nearly stopped now. Few Bretons came near it now, and the inn had fallen into the hands of Madame Babette's brother, as payment for a bad wine debt of the last proprietor. He put his sister and her child in, to keep it open, as it were, and sent all the people he could to occupy the half-furnished rooms of the house. They paid Babette for their lodging every morning as they went out to breakfast, and returned or not as they chose, at night. Every three days, the wine-merchant or his son came to Madame Babette, and she accounted to them for the money she had received. She and her child occupied the porter's office (in which the lad slept at nights) and a little, miserable bed-room which opened out of it, and received all the light and air that was admitted through the door of communication, which was half glass. Madame Babette must have had a kind of attachment for the De Créquys – her De Créquys, you understand – Virginie's father, the Count; for, at some risk to herself, she had warned both him and his daughter of the danger impending over them. But he, infatuated, would not believe that his dear Human Race could ever do him harm; and, as long as he did not fear, Virginie was not afraid. It was by some ruse, the nature of which I never heard, that Madame Babette induced Virginie to come to her abode at the very hour in which the Count had been recognised in the streets, and hurried off to the Lanterne.[73] It was after Babette had got her there, safe shut up in the little back den, that she told her what had befallen her father. From that day, Virginie had never stirred out of the gates, or crossed the threshold of the porter's lodge. I do not say that Madame Babette was tired of her continual presence, or regretted the impulse which had made her rush to the De Créquy's well-known house – after being compelled to form one of the mad crowds that saw the Count de Créquy seized and hung – and hurry his daughter out, through alleys and back-ways, until at length she had the orphan safe in her own dark sleeping-room, and could tell her tale of horror: but Madame Babette was poorly paid for her porter's work by her avaricious brother; and it was hard enough to find food for herself and her growing boy; and, though the poor girl ate little enough, I dare say, yet there seemed no end to the burthen that Madame Babette had imposed upon herself: the De Créquys were plundered, ruined, had become an extinct race, all but a lonely, friendless girl, in broken health and spirits; and, though she lent no positive encouragement to his suit, yet, at the time, when Clément reappeared in Paris, Madame Babette was beginning to think that Virginie might do worse than encourage the attentions of Monsieur Morin fils, her nephew, and the wine-merchant's son. Of course, he and his father had the entrée into the concièrgerie of the hotel that belonged to them, in right of being both proprietors and relations. The son, Morin, had seen Virginie in this manner. He was fully aware that she was far above him in rank, and guessed from her whole aspect that she had lost her natural protectors by the terrible guillotine; but he did not know her exact name or station, nor could he persuade his aunt to tell him. However, he fell head over ears in love with her, whether she were princess or peasant; and, though at first there was something about her which made his passionate love conceal itself with shy, awkward reserve, and then, made it only appear in the guise of deep, respectful devotion; yet, by-and-by, – by the same process of reasoning I suppose that his aunt had gone through even before him – Jean Morin began to let Hope oust Despair from his heart. Sometimes he thought – perhaps years hence – that solitary, friendless lady, pent up in squalor, might turn to him as to a friend and comforter – and then – and then – . Meanwhile Jean Morin was most attentive to his aunt; whom he had rather slighted before. He would linger over the accounts; would bring her little presents; and, above all, he made a pet and favourite of Pierre, the little cousin who could tell him about all the ways of going on of Mam'selle Cannes, as Virginie was called. Pierre was thoroughly aware of the drift and cause of his cousin's inquiries; and was his ardent partisan,[a] as I have heard, even before Jean Morin had exactly acknowledged his wishes to himself.

'It must have required some patience and much diplomacy, before Clément de Créquy found out the exact place where his cousin was hidden. The old gardener took the cause very much to heart; as, judging from my recollections, I imagine he would have forwarded any fancy, however wild, of Monsieur Clément's. (I will tell you afterwards how I came to know all these particulars so well.)

'After Clement's return, on two succeeding days, from his dangerous search, without meeting with any good result, Jacques entreated Monsieur de Créquy to let him take it in hand. He represented that he, as gardener for the space of twenty years and more at the Hôtel de Créquy, had a right to be acquainted with all the successive concièrges at the Count's house; that he should not go among them as a stranger, but as an old friend, anxious to renew pleasant intercourse; and that if the Intendant's story, which he had told Monsieur de Créquy in England, was true, that Mademoiselle was in hiding at the house of a former concièrge, why, something relating to her would surely drop out in the course of conversation. So he persuaded Clément to remain in-doors, while he set off on his round, with no apparent object but to gossip.

'At night he came home, – having seen Mademoiselle. He told Clément much of the story relating to Madame Babette that I have told to you. Of course, he had heard nothing of the ambitious hopes of Morin Fils, – hardly of his existence, I should think. Madame Babette had received him kindly; although, for some time, she had kept him standing in the carriage gateway outside her door. But, on his complaining of the draught and his rheumatism, she had asked him in: first looking round with some anxiety, to see who was in the room behind her. No one was there when he entered and sat down. But, in a minute or two, a tall, thin young lady, with great, sad eyes, and pale cheeks, came from the inner room, and, seeing him, retired. "It is Mademoiselle Cannes," said Madame Babette, rather unnecessarily; for, if he had not been on the watch for some sign of Mademoiselle de Créquy, he would hardly have noticed the entrance and withdrawal.

'Clément and the good old gardener were always rather perplexed by Madame Babette's evident avoidance of all mention of the De Créquy family. If she were so much interested in one member as to be willing to undergo the pains and penalties of a domiciliary visit, it was strange that she never inquired after the existence of her charge's friends and relations from one who might very probably have heard something of them. They settled that Madame Babette must believe that the Marquise and Clément were dead; and admired her for her reticence in never speaking of Virginie. The truth was, I suspect, that she was so desirous of her nephew's success by this time, that she did not like letting any one into the secret of Virginie's whereabouts who might interfere with their plan. However, it was arranged between Clément and his humble friend, that the former, dressed in the peasant's clothes in which he had entered Paris, but smartened up in one or two particulars, as if, although a countryman, he had money to spare, should go and engage a sleeping-room in the old Bréton Inn; where, as I told you, accommodation for the night was to be had. This was accordingly done, without exciting Madame Babette's suspicions, for she was unacquainted with the Normandy accent, and consequently did not perceive the exaggeration of it which Monsieur de Créquy adopted in order to disguise his pure Parisian. But after he had for two nights slept in a queer, dark closet, at the end of one of the numerous short galleries in the Hôtel Duguesclin, and paid his money for such accommodation each morning at the little bureau under the window of the concièrgerie, he found himself no nearer to his object. He stood outside in the gateway: Madame Babette opened a pane in her window, counted out the change, gave polite thanks, and shut to the pane with a clack, before he could ever find out what to say that might be the means of opening a conversation. Once in the streets, he was in danger from the bloodthirsty mob, who were ready in those days to hunt to death every one who looked like a gentleman, as an aristocrat: and Clément, depend upon it, looked a gentleman, whatever dress he wore. Yet it was unwise to traverse Paris to his old friend the gardener's grénier,[74] so he had to loiter about, where I hardly know. Only he did leave the Hôtel Duguesclin, and he did not go to old Jacques, and there was not another house in Paris open to him. At the end of two days, he had made out Pierre's existence; and he began to try to make friends with the lad. Pierre was too sharp and shrewd not to suspect something from the confused attempts at friendliness. It was not for nothing that the Norman farmer lounged in the court and doorway, and brought home presents of galette.[75] Pierre accepted the galette, reciprocated the civil speeches, but kept his eyes open. Once, returning home pretty late at night, he surprised the Norman studying the shadows on the blind, which was drawn down when Madame Babette's lamp was lighted. On going in, he found Mademoiselle Cannes with his mother, sitting by the table, and helping in the family mending.

'Pierre was afraid that the Norman had some view upon the money which his mother, as concièrge, collected for her brother. But the money was all safe next evening when his cousin, Monsieur Morin fils,[a] came to collect it. Madame Babette asked her nephew to sit down, and skilfully barred the passage to the inner door, so that Virginie, had she been ever so much disposed, could not have retreated. She sat silently sewing. All at once the little party were startled by a very sweet tenor voice, just close to the street window, singing one of the airs out of Beaumarchais' operas,[76] which, a few years before, had been popular all over Paris. But after a few moments of silence, and one or two remarks, the talking went on again. Pierre, however, noticed an increased air of abstraction in Virginie, who, I suppose, was recurring to the last time that she had heard the song, and did not consider, as her cousin had hoped she would have done, what were the words set to the air, which he imagined she would remember, and which would have told her so much. For, only a few years before, Adam's opera of Richard le Roi[77] had made the story of the Minstrel Blondel and our English Cœur de Lion familiar to all the opera-going part of the Parisian public, and Clément had bethought him of establishing a communication with Virginie by some such means.

'The next night, about the same hour, the same voice was singing outside the window again. Pierre, who had been irritated by the proceeding the evening before, as it had diverted Virginie's attention from his cousin, who had been doing his utmost to make himself agreeable, rushed out to the door, just as the Norman was ringing the bell to be admitted for the night. Pierre looked up and down the street; no one else was to be seen. The next day, the Norman mollified him somewhat by knocking at the door of the concièrgerie, and begging Monsieur Pierre's acceptance of some knee-buckles, which had taken the country farmer's fancy the day before, as he had been gazing into the shops, but which, being too small for his purpose, he took the liberty of offering to Monsieur Pierre. Pierre, a French boy, inclined to foppery, was charmed, ravished by the beauty of the present and with monsieur's goodness, and he began to adjust them to his breeches immediately, as well as he could, at least, in his mother's absence. The Norman, whom Pierre kept carefully on the outside of the threshold, stood by, as if amused at the boy's eagerness.

'"Take care," said he, clearly and distinctly; "take care, my little friend, lest you become a fop; and, in that case, some day, years hence, when your heart is devoted to some young lady, she may be inclined to say to you" – here he raised his voice – "No, thank you; when I marry, I marry a man, not a petit-maître; I marry a man, who, whatever his position may be, will add dignity to the human race by his virtues." Farther than that in his quotation Clément dared not go. His sentiments (so much above the apparent occasion) met with applause from Pierre, who liked to contemplate himself in the light of a lover, even though it should be a rejected one, and who hailed the mention of the words "virtues" and "dignity of the human race" as belonging to the cant of a good citizen.

'But Clément was more anxious to know how the invisible lady took his speech. There was no sign at the time. But when he returned at night, he heard a voice, low singing, behind Madame Babette, as she handed him his candle, the very air he had sung without effect for two nights past. As if he had caught it up from her murmuring voice, he sang it loudly and clearly as he crossed the court.

'"Here is our opera-singer!" exclaimed Madame Babette. "Why, the Norman grazier sings like Boupré,"[78] naming a favourite singer at the neighbouring theatre.

'Pierre was struck by the remark, and quietly resolved to look after the Norman; but again, I believe, it was more because of his mother's deposit of money than with any thought of Virginie.

'However, the next morning, to the wonder of both mother and son, Mademoiselle Cannes proposed, with much hesitation, to go out and make some little purchase for herself. A month or two ago, this was what Madame Babette had been never weary of urging. But now she was as much surprised as if she had expected Virginie to remain a prisoner in her rooms all the rest of her life. I suppose she had hoped that her first time of quitting it would be when she left it for Monsieur's Morin's house as his wife.

'A quick look from Madame Babette towards Pierre was all that was needed to encourage the boy to follow her. He went out cautiously. She was at the end of the street. She looked up and down, as if waiting for some one. No one was there. Back she came, so swiftly that she nearly caught Pierre before he could retreat through the porte-cochère. There he looked out again. The neighbourhood was low and wild, and strange; and some one spoke to Virginie, – nay, laid his hand upon her arm, – whose dress and aspect (he had emerged out of a side-street) Pierre did not know; but, after a start, and (Pierre could fancy) a little scream, Virginie recognised the stranger, and the two turned up the side street whence the man had come. Pierre stole swiftly to the corner of this street; no one was there: they had disappeared up some of the alleys. Pierre returned home to excite his mother's infinite surprise. But they had hardly done talking, when Virginie returned, with a colour and a radiance in her face, which they had never seen there since her father's death.

CHAPTER VII.

'I HAVE told you that I heard much of this story from a friend of the Intendant of the De Créquys, whom he met with in London. Some years afterwards – the summer before my lord's death – I was travelling with him in Devonshire, and we went to see the French prisoners of war on Dartmoor.[79] We fell into conversation with one of them, whom I found out to be the very Pierre of whom I had heard before, as having been involved in the fatal story of Clément and Virginie, and by him I was told much of their last days, and thus I learnt how to have some sympathy with all those who were concerned in those terrible events; yes, even with the younger Morin himself, on whose behalf Pierre spoke warmly, even after so long a time had elapsed.

'For when the younger Morin called at the porter's lodge, on the evening of the day when Virginie had gone out for the first time after so many months' confinement to the concièrgerie, he was struck with the improvement in her appearance. It seems to have hardly been that he thought her beauty greater; for, in addition to the fact that she was not beautiful, Morin had arrived at that point of being enamoured when it does not signify whether the beloved one is plain or handsome –[a] she has enchanted one pair of eyes, which henceforward see her through their own medium. But Morin noticed the faint increase of colour and light in her countenance. It was as though she had broken through her thick cloud of hopeless sorrow, and was dawning forth into a happier life. And so, whereas during her grief, he had revered and respected it even to a point of silent sympathy, now that she was gladdened, his heart rose on the wings of strengthened hopes. Even in the dreary monotony of this existence in his Aunt Babette's concièrgerie, Time had not failed in his work, and now, perhaps, soon he might humbly strive to help Time. The very next day he returned – on some pretence of business – to the Hôtel Duguesclin, and made his aunt's room, rather than his aunt herself, a present of roses and geraniums tied up in a bouquet with a tricolor ribbon. Virginie was in the room, sitting at the coarse sewing she liked to do for Madame Babette. He saw her eyes brighten at the sight of the flowers: she asked his aunt to let her arrange them; he saw her untie the ribbon, and with a gesture of dislike, throw it on the ground, and give it a kick with her little foot, and even in this girlish manner of insulting his dearest prejudices, he found something to admire.

'As he was coming out, Pierre stopped him. The lad had been trying to arrest his cousin's attention by futile grimaces and signs played off behind Virginie's back; but Monsieur Morin saw nothing but Mademoiselle Cannes. However, Pierre was not to be baffled, and Monsieur Morin found him in waiting just outside the threshold. With his finger on his lips, Pierre walked on tiptoe by his companion's side till they would have been long past sight or hearing of the concièrgerie, even had the inhabitants devoted themselves to the purposes of spying or listening.

'"Chut!" said Pierre, at last. "She goes out walking."

'"Well?" said Monsieur Morin, half curious, half annoyed at being disturbed in the delicious reverie of the future into which he longed to fall.

'"Well! It is not well. It is bad."

'"Why? I do not ask who she is, but I have my ideas. She is an aristocrat. Do the people about here begin to suspect her?"

'"No, no!" said Pierre. "But she goes out walking. She has gone these two mornings. I have watched her. She meets a man – she is friends with him, for she talks to him as eagerly as he does to her – mamma cannot tell who he is."

'"Has my aunt seen him?"

'"No, not so much as a fly's wing of him. I myself have only seen his back. It strikes me like a familiar back, and yet I cannot think who it is. But they separate with sudden darts, like two birds who have been together to feed their young ones. One moment they are in close talk, their heads together chuckotting the next he has turned up some bye-street, and Mademoiselle Cannes is close upon me – has almost caught me."

'"But she did not see you?" inquired Monsieur Morin, in so altered a voice that Pierre gave him one of his quick penetrating looks. He was struck by the way in which his cousin's features – always coarse and common-place – had become contracted and pinched; struck, too, by the livid look on his sallow complexion. But as if Morin was conscious of the manner in which his face belied his feelings, he made an effort, and smiled, and patted Pierre's head, and thanked him for his intelligence, and gave him a five-franc piece, and bade him go on with his observations of Mademoiselle Cannes' movements, and report all to him.

'Pierre returned home with a light heart, tossing up his five-franc piece as he ran. Just as he was at the concièrgerie door, a great tall man bustled past him, and snatched his money away from him, looking back with a laugh, which added insult to injury. Pierre had no redress; no one had witnessed the impudent theft, and if they had, no one to be seen in the street was strong enough to give him redress. Besides, Pierre had seen enough of the state of the streets of Paris at that time to know that friends, not enemies,

were required, and the man had a bad air about him. But all these considera-
tions did not keep Pierre from bursting out into a fit of crying when he was
once more under his mother's roof; and Virginie, who was alone there
(Madame Babette having gone out to make her daily purchases), might have
imagined him pommeled to death by the loudness of his sobs.

"'What is the matter?" asked she. "Speak, my child. What hast thou
done?"[a]

"'He has robbed me! he has robbed me!" was all Pierre could gulp out.

"'Robbed thee! and of what, my poor boy?" said Virginie, stroking his hair
gently.

"'Of my five-franc piece – of a five-franc piece," said Pierre, correcting
himself, and leaving out the word my, half fearful lest Virginie should
inquire how he became possessed of such a sum, and for what services it had
been given him. But, of course, no such idea came into her head, for it
would have been impertinent, and she was gentle-born.

"'Wait a moment, my lad," and, going to the one small drawer in the inner
apartment, which held all her few possessions, she brought back a little ring
– a ring just with one ruby in it – which she had worn in the days when she
cared to wear jewels. "Take this," said she, "and run with it to a jeweller's. It
is but a poor, valueless thing, but it will bring you in your five francs at any
rate. Go! I desire you."

"'But I cannot," said the boy, hesitating; some dim sense of honour flitting through his misty morals.

"'Yes; you must!" she continued, urging him with her hand to the door.
"Run! if it brings in more than five francs, you shall return the surplus to
me."

'Thus tempted by her urgency, and, I suppose, reasoning with himself to
the effect that he might as well have the money, and then see whether he
thought it right to act as a spy upon her or not – the one action did not
pledge him to the other, nor yet did she make any conditions with her gift –
Pierre went off with her ring; and, after repaying himself his five francs, he
was enabled to bring Virginie back two more, so well had he managed his
affairs. But, although the whole transaction did not leave him bound, in any
way, to discover or forward Virginie's wishes, it did leave him pledged,
according to his code, to act according to her advantage, and he considered
himself the judge of the best course to be pursued to this end. And, moreover, this little kindness attached him to her personally. He began to think
how pleasant it would be to have so kind and generous a person for a relation; how easily his troubles might be borne if he had always such a ready
helper at hand; how much he should like to make her like him, and come to
him for the protection of his masculine power! First of all his duties, as her
self-appointed squire, came the necessity of finding out who her strange
new acquaintance was. Thus, you see, he arrived at the same end, viâ inter-

est. I fancy a good number of us, when any line of action will promote our own interest, can make ourselves believe that reasons exist which compel us to it as a duty.

'In the course of a very few days, Pierre had so circumvented Virginie as to have discovered that her new friend was no other than the Norman farmer in a different dress. This was a great piece of knowledge to impart to Morin. But Pierre was not prepared for the immediate physical effect it had on his cousin. Morin sat[a] suddenly down on one of the seats in the Boulevards – it was there Pierre had met with him accidentally – when he heard who it was that Virginie met. I do not suppose the man had the faintest idea of any relationship or even previous acquaintanceship between Clément and Virginie. If he thought of anything beyond the mere fact presented to him, that his idol was in communication with another, younger, handsomer man than himself, it must have been that the Norman farmer had seen her at the concièrgerie, and had been attracted by her, and, as was but natural, had tried to make her acquintance, and had succeeded. But, from what Pierre told me, I should not think that even this much thought passed through Morin's mind. He seems to have been a man of rare and concentrated attachments; violent, though restrained and undemonstrative passions; and, above all, a capability of jealousy, of which his dark oriental complexion must have been a type. I could fancy that if he had married Virginie, he would have coined his life-blood for luxuries to make her happy; would have watched over and petted her, at every sacrifice to himself, as long as she would have been content to live for him alone. But, as Pierre expressed it to me: 'When I saw what my cousin was, when I learned his nature too late, I perceived that he would have strangled a bird if she whom he loved was attracted by it from him.'

'When Pierre had told Morin of his discovery, Morin sat[b] down, as I have said, quite suddenly, as if he had been shot. He found out that the first meeting between the Norman and Virginie was no accidental, isolated circumstance. Pierre was torturing him with his accounts of daily rendezvous: if but for a moment, they were seeing each other every day, sometimes twice a day. And Virginie could speak to this man, though to himself she was so coy and reserved as hardly to utter a sentence. Pierre caught these broken words while his cousin's complexion grew more and more livid, and then purple, as if some great effect were produced on his circulation by the news he had just heard. Pierre was so startled by his cousin's wandering, senseless eyes, and otherwise disordered looks, that he rushed into a neighbouring cabaret for a glass of absinthe, which he paid for, as he recollected afterwards, with a portion of Virginie's five francs. By-and-by Morin recovered his natural appearance; but he was gloomy and silent; and all that Pierre could get out of him was, that the Norman farmer should not sleep another night at the Hôtel Duguesclin, giving him such opportunities of passing and repassing by the concièrgerie door. He was too much absorbed in his own thoughts to repay Pierre the half-franc he had spent on the absinthe, which Pierre perceived, and seems to have noted down in the ledger of his mind as on Virginie's balance of favour.

'Altogether, he was so much disappointed at his cousin's mode of receiving intelligence, which the lad thought worth another five-franc piece at least; or, if not paid for in money, to be paid for in open-mouthed confidence and expression of feeling, that he was for a time, so far a partisan of Virginie's – unconscious Virginie – against his cousin, as to feel regret when the Norman returned no more to his night's lodging, and when Virginie's eager watch at the crevice of the closely-drawn blind ended only with a sigh of disappointment. If it had not been for his mother's presence at the time, Pierre thought he should have told her all. But how far was his mother in his cousin's confidence as regarded the dismissal of the Norman?[a]

'In a few days, however,[b] Pierre felt almost sure that they had established some new means of communication. Virginie went out for a short time every day; but, though Pierre followed her as closely as he could without exciting her observation, he was unable to discover what kind of intercourse she held with the Norman. She went, in general, the same short round among the little shops in the neighbourhood; not entering any, but stopping at two or three. Pierre afterwards remembered that she had invariably paused at the nosegays displayed in a certain window, and studied them long; but, then, she stopped and looked at caps, hats, fashions, confectionery (all of the humble kind common in that quarter), so how should he have known that any particular attraction existed among the flowers? Morin came more regularly than ever to his aunt's; but Virginie was apparently unconscious that she was the attraction. She looked healthier and more hopeful than she had done for months, and her manners to all were gentler and not so reserved. Almost as if she wished to manifest her gratitude to Madame Babette for her long continuance of a kindness, the necessity for which was nearly ended, Virginie showed an unusual alacrity in rendering the old woman any little service in her power, and evidently tried to respond to Monsieur Morin's civilities, he being Madame Babette's nephew, with the soft graciousness which must have made one of her principal charms; for all who knew her speak of the fascination of her manners,[80] so winning and attentive to others, while yet her opinions, and often her actions, were of so decided a character. For, as I have said, her beauty was by no means great; yet every man who came near her seems to have fallen into the sphere of her influence. Monsieur Morin was deeper than ever in love with her during these last few days: he was worked up into a state capable of any sacrifice, either of himself or others, so that he might obtain her at last. He sat[c] "devouring her with his eyes" (to use Pierre's expression) whenever she could not see him; but, if she looked towards him, he looked to the ground

– anywhere – away from her, and almost stammered in his replies if she addressed any question to him.

'He had been, I should think, ashamed of his extreme agitation on the Boulevards, for Pierre thought that he absolutely shunned him for these few succeeding days. He must have believed that he had driven the Norman (my poor Clément!) off the field, by banishing him from his inn; and thought that the intercourse between him and Virginie, which he had thus interrupted, was of so slight and transient a character as to be quenched by a little difficulty.

'But he appears to have felt that he made but little way, and he awkwardly turned to Pierre for help – not yet confessing his love, though; he only tried to make friends again with the lad after their silent estrangement. And Pierre for some time did not choose to perceive his cousin's advances. He would reply to all the roundabout questions Morin put to him respecting household conversations when he was not present, or household occupations and tone of thought, without mentioning Virginie's name any more than his questioner did. The lad would seem to suppose, that his cousin's strong interest in their domestic ways of going on was all on account of Madame Babette. At last he worked his cousin up to the point of making him a confidant; and then the boy was half frightened at the torrent of vehement words he had unloosed. The lava came down with a greater rush for having been pent up so long. Morin cried out his words in a hoarse, passionate voice, clenched his teeth, his fingers, and seemed almost convulsed, as he spoke out his terrible love for Virginie, which would lead him to kill her sooner than see her another's; and if another stepped in between him and her! –[a] and then he smiled a fierce, triumphant smile, but did not say any more.

'Pierre was, as I said, half-frightened; but also half-admiring. This was really love – a "grande passion," – a really fine, dramatic thing, – like the plays they acted at the little theatre yonder. He had a dozen times the sympathy with his cousin now that he had had before, and readily swore by the infernal gods, for they were far too enlightened to believe in one God, or Christianity, or anything of the kind, – that he would devote himself, body and soul, to forwarding his cousin's views. Then his cousin took him to a shop, and bought him a smart second-hand watch, on which they scratched the word Fidélité, and thus was the compact sealed. Pierre settled in his own mind, that if he were a woman, he should like to be beloved as Virginie was, by his cousin, and that it would be an extremely good thing for her to be the wife of so rich a citizen as Morin fils, –[b] and for Pierre himself, too, for doubtless their gratitude would lead them to give him rings and watches ad infinitum.

'A day or two afterwards, Virginie was taken ill. Madame Babette said it was because she had persevered in going out in all weathers, after confining herself to two warm rooms for so long; and very probably this was really the cause, for, from Pierre's account, she must have been suffering from a fever-ish cold, aggravated, no doubt, by her impatience at Madame Babette's familiar prohibitions of any more walks until she was better. Every day, in spite of her trembling, aching limbs, she would fain have arranged her dress for her walk at the usual time; but Madame Babette was fully prepared to put physical obstacles in her way, if she was not obedient in remaining tran-quil on the little sofa by the side of the fire. The third day, she called Pierre to her, when his mother was not attending (having, in fact, locked up Made-moiselle Cannes' out-of-door things).

"'See, my child," said Virginie. "Thou must do me a great favour. Go to the gardener's shop in the Rue des Bons-Enfans, and look at the nosegays in the window. I long for pinks; they are my favourite flower. Here are two francs. If thou seest a nosegay of pinks displayed in the window, if it be ever so faded, – nay, if thou seest two or three nosegays of pinks, remember, buy them all, and bring them to me, I have so great a desire for the smell." She fell back weak and exhausted. Pierre hurried out. Now was the time; here was the clue to the long inspection of the nosegay in this very shop.

'Sure enough, there was a drooping nosegay of pinks in the window. Pierre went in, and, with all his impatience, he made as good a bargain as he could, urging that the flowers were faded, and good for nothing. At last he purchased them at a very moderate price. And now you will learn the bad consequences of teaching the lower orders anything beyond what is imme-diately necessary to enable them to earn their daily bread! The silly Count de Créquy, – he who had been sent to his bloody rest, by the very canaille[81] of whom he thought so much, – he who had made Virginie (indirectly, it is true) reject such a man as her cousin Clément, by inflating her mind with his bubbles of theories, – this Count de Créquy had long ago taken a fancy to Pierre, as he saw the bright sharp child playing about his court-yard. Monsieur de Créquy had even begun to educate the boy himself, to try to work out certain opinions of his into practice, – but the drudgery of the affair wearied him, and, beside, Babette had left his employment. Still the Count took a kind of interest in his former pupil; and made some sort of arrangement by which Pierre was to be taught reading and writing, and accounts, and Heaven knows what besides, – Latin, I dare say. So Pierre, instead of being an innocent messenger, as he ought to have been – (as Mr. Horner's little lad Gregson ought to have been this morning) – could read writing as well as either you or I. So what does he do, on obtaining the nose-gay, but examine it well. The stalks of the flowers were tied up with slips of matting in wet moss. Pierre undid the strings, unwrapped the moss, and out fell a piece of wet paper, with the writing all blurred with moisture. It was but a torn piece of writing-paper apparently, but Pierre's wicked mischie-vous eyes read what was written on it, – written so as to look like a fragment. – 'Ready, every and any night at nine. All is prepared. Have no fright. Trust one who, whatever hopes he might once have had, is content now to serve you as a faithful cousin,' and a place was named, which I forget, but which Pierre did not, as it was evidently the rendezvous. After the lad had studied every word, till he could say it off by heart, he placed the paper where he had found it, enveloped it in moss, and tied the whole up again carefully. Virginie's face coloured scarlet as she received it. She kept smelling at it, and trembling: but she did not untie it, although Pierre suggested how much fresher it would be if the stalks were immediately put into water. But once, after his back had been turned for a minute, he saw it untied when he looked round again, and Virginie was blushing, and hiding something in her bosom.

'Pierre was now all impatience to set off and find his cousin. But his mother seemed to want him for small domestic purposes even more than usual; and he had chafed over a multitude of errands connected with the Hôtel before he could set off and search for his cousin at his usual haunts.[a] At last the two met; and Pierre related all the events of the morning to Morin. He said the note off word by word. (That lad this morning had something of the magpie look of Pierre – it made me shudder to see him, and hear him repeat the note by heart.) Then Morin asked him to tell him all over again. Pierre was struck by Morin's heavy sighs as he repeated the story. When he came the second time to the note, Morin tried to write the words down; but either he was not a good, ready scholar, or his fingers trembled too much. Pierre hardly remembered, but, at any rate, the lad had to do it, with his wicked reading and writing. When this was done, Morin sat[b] heavily silent. Pierre would have preferred the expected outburst, for this impenetrable gloom perplexed and baffled him. He had even to speak to his cousin to rouse him; and when he replied, what he said had so little apparent connection with the subject which Pierre had expected to find uppermost in his mind, that he was half afraid that his cousin had lost his wits.

'"My Aunt Babette is out of coffee."

'"I am sure I do not know," said Pierre.

'"Yes, she is. I heard her say so. Tell her that a friend of mine has just opened a shop in the Rue Saint Antoine, and that if she will join me there in an hour, I will supply her with a good stock of coffee, just to give my friend encouragement. His name is Antoine Meyer, Number One hundred and Fifty, at the sign of the Cap of Liberty."

'"I could go with you now. I can carry a few pounds of coffee better than my mother," said Pierre, all in good faith. He told me he should never forget the look on his cousin's face, as he turned round, and bade him begone, and give his mother the message without another word. It had evidently sent him home promptly to obey his cousin's command. Morin's message perplexed Madame Babette.

"'How could he know I was out of coffee?" said she. "I am; but I only used the last up this morning. How could Jean[82] know about it?"

"'I am sure I can't tell," said Pierre, who by this time had recovered his usual self-possession. "All I know is, that Monsieur is in a pretty temper, and that if you are not sharp to your time at this Antoine Meyer's you are likely to come in for some of his black looks."

"'Well, it is very kind of him to offer to give me some coffee, to be sure! But how could he know I was out?"

'Pierre hurried his mother off impatiently, for he was certain that the offer of the coffee was only a blind to some hidden purpose on his cousin's part; and he made no doubt that when his mother had been informed of what his cousin's real intention was, he, Pierre, could extract it from her by coaxing or bullying. But he was mistaken. Madame Babette returned home, grave, depressed, silent, and loaded with the best coffee. Some time afterwards he learnt why his cousin had sought for this interview. It was to extract from her, by promises and threats, the real name of Mam'selle Cannes, which would give him a clue to the true appellation of The Faithful Cousin. He concealed this second purpose from his aunt, who had been quite unaware of his jealousy of the Norman farmer, or of his identification of him with any relation of Virginie's. But Madame Babette instinctively shrank from giving him any information: she must have felt that, in the lowering mood in which she found him, – his desire for greater knowledge of Virginie's antecedents boded her no good. And yet he made his aunt his confidante – told her what she had only suspected before – that he was deeply enamoured of Mam'selle Cannes, and would gladly marry her. He spoke to Madame Babette of his father's hoarded riches; and of the share which he, as partner, had in them at the present time; and of the prospect of the succession to the whole, which he had, as an only child. He told his aunt of the provision for her (Madame Babette's) life, which he would make on the day when he married Mam'selle Cannes. And yet – and yet – Babette saw that in his eye and look which made her more and more reluctant to confide in him. By-and-by he tried threats. She should leave the concièrgerie, and find employment where she liked. Still silence. Then he grew angry, and swore that he would inform against her at the bureau of the Directory,[83] for harbouring an aristocrat; an aristocrat he knew Mademoiselle was, whatever her real name might be. His aunt should have a domiciliary visit, and see how she liked that. The officers of the Government were the people for finding out secrets. In vain she reminded him that, by so doing, he would expose to imminent danger the lady whom he had professed to love. He told her, with a sullen relapse into silence after his vehement outpouring of passion, never to trouble herself about that. At last he wearied out the old woman, and, frightened alike of herself, and of him, she told him all, – that Mam'selle Cannes was Mademoiselle Virginie de

Créquy, daughter of the Count of that name. Who was the Count? Younger brother of the Marquis. Where was the Marquis? Dead long ago, leaving a widow and child. A son? (eagerly). Yes, a son. Where was he? Parbleu! how should she know? – for her courage returned a little as the talk went away from the only person of the De Créquy family that she cared about. But, by dint of some small glasses out of a bottle of Antoine Meyer's, she told him more about the De Créquys than she liked afterwards to remember. For the exhilaration of the brandy lasted but a very short time, and she came home, as I have said, depressed, with a presentiment of coming evil.

She would not answer Pierre, but cuffed him about in a manner to which the spoilt boy was quite unaccustomed. His cousin's short, angry words, and sudden withdrawal of confidence, – his mother's unwonted crossness and fault-finding, all made Virginie's kind, gentle treatment more than ever charming to the lad. He half resolved to tell her how he had been acting as a spy upon her actions, and at whose desire he had done it. But he was afraid of Morin, and of the vengeance which he was sure would fall upon him for any breach of confidence. Towards half-past eight that evening – Pierre, watching, saw Virginie arrange several little things – she was in the inner room, but he sat^a where he could see her through the glazed partition. His mother sat –^{b} apparently sleeping – in the great easy chair; Virginie moved about softly, for fear of disturbing her. She made up one or two little parcels of the few things she could call her own: one packet she concealed about herself, – the others she directed, and left on the shelf. "She is going," thought Pierre, and (as he said in giving me the account) his heart gave a spring, to think that he should never see her again. If either his mother or his cousin had been more kind to him, he might have endeavoured to inter-cept her; but as it was, he held his breath, and when she came out he pretended to read, scarcely knowing whether he wished her to succeed in the purpose which he was almost sure she entertained, or not. She stopped by him, and passed her hand over his hair. He told me that his eyes filled with tears at this caress. Then she stood for a moment, looking at the sleep-ing Madame Babette, and stooped down and softly kissed her on the forhead. Pierre dreaded lest his mother should awake (for by this time the wayward, vacillating boy must have been quite on Virginie's side), but the brandy she had drank made her slumber heavily. Virginie went. Pierre's heart beat fast. He was sure his cousin would try to intercept her; but how, he could not imagine. He longed to run out and see the catastrophe, – but he had let the moment slip; he was also afraid of reawakening his mother to her unusual state of anger and violence.'

CHAPTER VIII.

'PIERRE went on pretending to read, but in reality listening with acute tension of ear to every little sound. His perceptions became so sensitive in this respect that he was incapable of measuring[a] time, every moment had seemed so full of noises, from the beating of his heart up to the roll of the heavy carts in the distance. He wondered whether Virginie would have reached the place of rendezvous, and yet he was unable to compute the passage of minutes. His mother slept soundly: that was well. By this time Virginie must have met the "faithful cousin:" if, indeed, Morin had not made his appearance.

'At length, he felt as if he could no longer sit still, awaiting the issue, but must run out and see what course events had taken. In vain his mother, half-rousing herself, called after him to ask whither he was going: he was already out of hearing before she had ended her sentence, and he ran on until stopped by the sight of Mademoiselle Cannes walking along at so swift a pace that it was almost a run; while at her side, resolutely keeping by her, Morin was striding abreast. Pierre had just turned the corner of the street, when he came upon them. Virginie would have passed him without recognising him, she was in such passionate agitation, but for Morin's gesture, by which he would fain have kept Pierre from interrupting them. Then, when Virginie saw the lad, she caught at his arm, and thanked God, as if in that boy of twelve or fourteen she held a protector. Pierre felt her tremble from head to foot, and was afraid lest she would fall, there where she stood, in the hard rough street.

'"Begone, Pierre!" said Morin.

'"I cannot," replied Pierre, who indeed was held firmly by Virginie. "Besides, I won't," he added. "Who has been frightening Mademoiselle in this way?" asked he, very much inclined to brave his cousin at all hazards.

'"Mademoiselle is not accustomed to walk in the streets alone," said Morin, sulkily. "She came upon a crowd attracted by the arrest of an aristocrat, and their cries alarmed her. I offered to take charge of her home. Mademoiselle should not walk in these streets alone. We are not like the cold-blooded people of the Faubourg Saint Germain."

'Virginie did not speak. Pierre doubted if she heard a word of what they were saying. She leant upon him more and more heavily.

"'Will Mademoiselle condescend to take my arm?" said Morin, with sulky, and yet humble, uncouthness. I dare say he would have given worlds if he might have had that little hand within his arm; but, though she still kept silence, she shuddered up away from him, as you shrink from touching a toad. He had said something to her during that walk, you may be sure, which had made her loathe him. He marked and understood the gesture. He held himself aloof while Pierre gave her all the assistance he could in their slow progress homewards. But Morin accompanied her all the same. He had played too desperate a game to be baulked now. He had given information against the çi-devant[84a] Marquis de Créquy, as a returned emigré, to be met with at such a time, in such a place. Morin had hoped that all sign of the arrest would have been cleared away before Virginie reached the spot – so swiftly were terrible deeds done in those days. But Clément defended himself desperately: Virginie was punctual to a second; and, though the wounded man was borne off to the Abbaye, amid a crowd of the unsympathising jeerers who mingled with the armed officials of the Directory, Morin feared lest Virginie had recognised him; and he would have preferred that she should have thought that the "faithful cousin"[b] was faithless, than that she should have seen him in bloody danger on her account. I suppose he fancied that, if Virginie never saw or heard more of him, her imagination would not dwell on his simple disappearance, as it would do if she knew what he was suffering for her sake.

'At any rate, Pierre saw that his cousin was deeply mortified by the whole tenor of his behaviour during their walk home. When they arrived at Madame Babette's, Virginie fell fainting on the floor; her strength had but just sufficed for this exertion of reaching the shelter of the house. Her first sign of restoring consciousness consisted in avoidance of Morin. He had been most assiduous in his efforts to bring her round; quite tender in his way, Pierre said; and this marked, instinctive repugnance to him evidently gave him extreme pain. I suppose Frenchmen are more demonstrative than we are; for Pierre declared that he saw his cousin's eyes fill with tears, as she shrank away from his touch, if he tried to arrange the shawl they had laid under her head like a pillow, or as she shut her eyes when he passed before her. Madame Babette was urgent with her to go and lie down on the bed in the inner room; but it was some time before she was strong enough to rise and do this.

'When Madame Babette returned from arranging the girl comfortably, the three relations sat[c] down in silence; a silence which Pierre thought would never be broken. He wanted his mother to ask his cousin what had happened. But Madame Babette was afraid of her nephew, and thought it more discreet to wait for such crumbs of intelligence as he might think fit to throw to her. But, after she had twice reported Virginie to be asleep, without a word being uttered in reply to her whispers by either of her companions, Morin's powers of self-containment gave way.

"'It is hard!' he said.

"'What is hard?' asked Madame Babette, after she had paused for a time, to enable him to add to, or to finish, his sentence, if he pleased.

"'It is hard for a man to love a woman as I do,' he went on. "I did not seek to love her, it came upon me before I was aware – before I had ever thought about it at all, I loved her better than all the world beside. All my life before I knew her, seems a dull blank. I neither know nor care for what I did before then. And now there are just two lives before me. Either I have her, or I have not. That is all: but that is everything. And what can I do to make her have me? Tell me, aunt," and he caught at Madame Babette's arm, and gave it so sharp a shake, that she half screamed out, Pierre said, and evidently grew alarmed at her nephew's excitement.

"'Hush, Victor!' said she. "There are other women in the world, if this one will not have you."

"'None other for me,' he said, sinking back as if hopeless. "I am plain and coarse, not one of the scented darlings of the aristocrats. Say that I am ugly, brutish; I did not make myself so, any more than I made myself love her. It is my fate. But am I to submit to the consequences of my fate without a struggle? Not I. As strong as my love is, so strong is my will. It can be no stronger," continued he, gloomily. "Aunt Babette, you must help me – you must make her love me." He was so fierce here, that Pierre said he did not wonder that his mother was frightened.

"'I, Victor!' she exclaimed. "I make her love you? How can I? Ask me to speak for you to Mademoiselle Didot, or to Mademoiselle Cauchois even, or to such as they, and I'll do it, and welcome. But to Mademoiselle de Créquy, why you don't know the difference! Those people – the old nobility I mean – why they don't know a man from a dog, out of their own rank! And no wonder, for the young gentlemen of quality are treated differently to us from their very birth. If she had you to-morrow, you would be miserable. Let me alone for knowing the aristocracy. I have not been a concièrge to a duke and three counts for nothing. I tell you, all your ways are different to her ways."

"'I would change 'my ways,' as you call them."

"'Be reasonable, Victor."

"'No, I will not be reasonable, if by that you mean giving her up. I tell you two lives are before me; one with her, one without her. But the latter will be but a short career for both of us. You said, aunt, that the talk went in the concièrgerie of her father's hotel, that she would have nothing to do with this cousin whom I put out of the way to-day?"

"'So the servants said. How could I know? All I know is, that he left off coming to our hotel, and that at one time before then he had never been two days absent."

"'So much the better for him. He suffers now for having come between me and my object – in trying to snatch[a] her away out of my sight. Take you warning, Pierre! I did not like your meddling to-night." And so he went off, leaving Madame Babette rocking herself backwards and forwards, in all the depression of spirits consequent upon the reaction after the brandy, and upon her knowledge of her nephew's threatened purpose combined.

'In telling you most of this, I have simply repeated Pierre's account, which I wrote down at the time. But here what he had to say came to a sudden break; for, the next morning, when Madame Babette rose, Virginie was missing, and it was some time before either she, or Pierre, or Morin, could get the slightest clue to the missing girl.

'And now I must take up the story as it was told to the Intendant Fléchier by the old gardener Jacques, with whom Clément had been lodging on his first arrival in Paris. The old man could not, I dare say, remember half as much of what had happened as Pierre did; the former had the dulled memory of age, while Pierre had evidently thought over the whole series of events as a story – as a play, if one may call it so – during the solitary hours in his after-life, wherever they were passed, whether in lonely camp watches, or in the foreign prison where he had to drag out many years. Clément had, as I said, returned to the gardener's garret after he had been dismissed from the Hôtel Duguesclin. There were several reasons for his thus doubling back. One was, that he put nearly the whole breadth of Paris between him and an enemy; though why Morin was an enemy, and to what extent he carried his dislike or hatred, Clément could not tell, of course. The next reason for returning to Jacques was, no doubt, the conviction that, in multiplying his residences, he multiplied the chances against his being suspected and recognised. And then, again, the old man was in his secret, and his ally, although perhaps but a feeble kind of one. It was through Jacques that the plan of communication, by means of a nosegay of pinks, had been devised; and it was Jacques who procured him the last disguise that Clément was to use in Paris – as he hoped and trusted. It was that of a respectable shop-keeper of no particular class; a dress that would have seemed perfectly suitable to the young man who would naturally have worn it; and yet, as Clément put it on, and adjusted it – giving it a sort of finish and elegance which I always noticed about his appearance, and which I believed was innate in the wearer – I have no doubt it seemed like the usual apparel of a gentleman. No coarseness of texture, nor clumsiness of cut could disguise the nobleman of thirty descents, it appeared; for immediately on arriving at the place of rendezvous, he was recognised by the men placed there on Morin's information to seize him. Jacques, following at a little distance, with a bundle under his arm containing articles of feminine disguise for Virginie, saw four men attempt Clément's arrest – saw him, quick as lightning, draw a sword hitherto concealed in a clumsy stick – saw his agile figure spring to his guard, – and saw him defend himself with the rapidity and art of a man skilled in arms. But what good did it do? as Jacques piteously used to ask, Monsieur Fléchier told me. A great blow from a heavy club on the sword-arm of Monsieur de Créquy laid it helpless and immoveable by his side. Jacques always thought that that blow came from one of the spectators, who by this time had collected round the scene of the affray. The next instant, his master, – his little marquis – was down among the feet of the crowd, and though he was up again before he had received much damage – so active and light was my poor Clément – it was not before the old gardener had hobbled forwards, and, with many an old-fashioned oath and curse, proclaimed himself a partizan of the losing side – a follower of a çi-devant aristocrat. It was quite enough. He received one or two good blows, which were, in fact, aimed at his master; and then, almost before he was aware, he found his arms piniored behind him with a woman's garter, which one of the viragos in the crowd had made no scruple of pulling off in public, as soon as she heard for what purpose it was wanted. Poor Jacques was stunned and unhappy, – his master was out of sight, on before; and the old gardener scarce knew whither they were taking him. His head ached from the blows which had fallen upon it; it was growing dark, – June day though it was, – and when first he seems to have become exactly aware of what had happened to him, it was when he was turned into one of the larger rooms of the Abbaye, in which all were put who had no other allotted place wherein to sleep. One or two iron lamps hung from the ceiling by chains, giving a dim light for a little circle. Jacques stumbled forwards over a sleeping body lying on the ground. The sleeper wakened up enough to complain; and the apology of the old man in reply caught the ear of his master, who, until this time, could hardly have been aware of the straits and difficulties of his faithful Jacques. And there they sat, –[a] against a pillar, the live-long night, holding one another's hands, and each restraining expressions of pain, for fear of adding to the other's distress. That night made them intimate friends, in spite of the difference of age and rank. The disappointed hopes, the acute suffering of the present, the apprehensions of the future, made them seek solace in talking of the past. Monsieur de Créquy and the gardener found themselves disputing with interest in which chimney of the stack the starling used to build, – the starling whose nest Clément sent to Urian, you remember, – and discussing the merits of different espalier-pears which grew, and may grow still, in the old garden of the Hôtel de Créquy. Towards morning both fell asleep. The old man wakened first. His frame was deadened to suffering, I suppose, for he felt relieved of his pain; but Clément moaned and cried in feverish slumber. His broken arm was beginning to inflame his blood. He was, besides, much injured by some kicks from the crowd as he fell. As the old man looked sadly on the white, baked lips, and the flushed cheeks, contorted with suffering even in his sleep, Clément gave a sharp cry, which disturbed his miserable neighbours, all slumbering around in uneasy attitudes. They bade him with curses be silent; and then turning round, tried again to forget their own misery in sleep. For you see, the bloodthirsty canaille had not been sated with guillotining and hanging all the nobility they could find, but were now informing, right and left, even against each other; and when Clément and Jacques were in the prison, there were few of gentle blood in the place, and fewer still of gentle manners. At the sound of the angry words and threats, Jacques thought it best to awaken his master from his feverish uncomfortable sleep, lest he should provoke more enmity; and, tenderly lifting him up, he tried to adjust his own body, so that it should serve as a rest and a pillow for the younger man. The motion aroused Clément, and he began to talk in a strange, feverish way, of Virginie, too, – whose name he would not have breathed in such a place had he been quite himself. But Jacques had as much delicacy of feeling as any lady in the land, although, mind you, he knew neither how to read nor write, – and bent his head low down, so that his master might tell him in a whisper what messages he was to take to Mademoiselle de Créquy, in case – Poor Clément, he knew it must come to that! No escape for him now, in Norman disguise or otherwise! Either by gathering fever or guillotine, death was sure of his prey. Well! when that happened, Jacques was to go and find Mademoiselle de Créquy, and tell her that her cousin loved her at the last as he had loved her at the first; but that she should never have heard another word of his attachment from his living lips; that he knew he was not good enough for her, his queen; and that no thought of earning her love by his devotion had prompted his return to France, only that, if possible, he might have the great privilege of serving her whom he loved. And then he went off into rambling talk about petit-maîtres, and such kind of expressions, said Jacques to Fléchier, the intendant, little knowing what a clue that one word gave to much of the poor lad's suffering.

'The summer morning came slowly on in that dark prison, and when Jacques could look round – his master was now sleeping on his shoulder, still the uneasy, starting sleep of fever, – he saw that there were many women among the prisoners. (I have heard some of those who have escaped from the prisons say, that the look of despair and agony that came into the faces of the prisoners on first wakening, as the sense of their situation grew upon them, was what lasted the longest in the memory of the survivors. This look, they said, passed away from the women's faces sooner than it did from those of the men.)

'Poor old Jacques kept falling asleep, and plucking himself up again for fear lest, if he did not attend to his master, some harm might come to the swollen, helpless arm. Yet his weariness grew upon him in spite of all his efforts, and at last he felt as if he must give way to the irresistible desire, if only for five minutes. But just then there was a bustle at the door. Jacques opened his eyes wide to look.

"'The gaoler is early with breakfast," said some one, lazily.

"'It is the darkness of this accursed place that makes us think it early," said another.

'All this time a parley was going on at the door. Some one came in; not the gaoler – a woman. The door was shut to and locked behind her. She only advanced a step or two; for it was too sudden a change, out of the light into that dark shadow, for any one to see clearly for the first few minutes. Jacques had his eyes fairly open now; and was wide awake. It was Mademoiselle de Créquy, looking bright, clear, and resolute. The faithful heart of the old man read that look like an open page. Her cousin should not die there on her behalf, without at least the comfort of her sweet presence.

"'Here he is," he whispered, as her gown would have touched him in passing, without her perceiving him, in the heavy obscurity of the place.

"'The good God bless you, my friend!" she murmured, as she saw the attitude of the old man, propped against a pillar, and holding Clément in his arms, as if the young man had been a helpless baby, while one of the poor gardener's hands supported the broken limb in the easiest position. Virginie sat down by the old man, and held out her arms. Softly she moved Clément's head to her own shoulder; softly she transferred the task of holding the arm to herself. Clément lay on the floor, but she supported him, and Jacques was at liberty to arise and stretch and shake his stiff, weary old body. He then sat down at a little distance, and watched the pair until he fell asleep. Clément had muttered "Virginie," as they half-roused him by their movements out of his stupor; but Jacques thought he was only dreaming; nor did he seem fully awake when once his eyes opened, and he looked full at Virginie's face bending over him, and growing crimson under his gaze, though she never stirred, for fear of hurting him if she moved. Clément looked in silence, until his heavy eyelids came slowly down, and he fell into his oppressive slumber again. Either he did not recognise her, or she came in too completely as a part of his sleeping visions for him to be disturbed by her appearance there.

'When Jacques awoke it was full daylight – at least as full as it would ever be in that place. His breakfast – the gaol-allowance of bread and vin ordinaire – was by his side. He must have slept soundly. He looked for his master. He and Virginie had recognised each other now, – hearts, as well as appearance. They were smiling into each other's faces, as if that dull, vaulted room in the grim Abbaye were the sunny gardens of Versailles, with music and festivity all abroad. Apparently they had much to say to each other; for whispered questions and answers never ceased.

'Virginie had made a sling for the poor broken arm; nay, she had obtained two splinters of wood in some way, and one of their fellow-prisoners – having, it appeared, some knowledge of surgery – had set it. Jacques felt more desponding by far than they did, for he was suffering from the night he had passed, which told upon his aged frame; while they must have heard some good news, as it seemed to him, so bright and happy did they look. Yet Clément was still in bodily pain and suffering, and Virginie, by her own act and deed, was a prisoner in that dreadful Abbaye, whence the only issue was the guillotine. But they were together: they loved: they understood each other at length.

'When Virginie saw that Jacques was awake, and languidly munching his breakfast, she rose from the wooden stool on which she was sitting, and went to him, holding out both hands, and refusing to allow him to rise, while she thanked him with pretty eagerness for all his kindness to Monsieur. Monsieur himself came towards him, – following Virginie, – but with tottering steps, as if his head was weak and dizzy, to thank the poor old man, who, now on his feet, stood between them, ready to cry while they gave him credit for faithful actions which he felt to have been almost involuntary on his part, – for loyalty was like an instinct in the good old days, before your educational cant had come up. And so two days went on. The only event was the morning call for the victims, a certain number of whom were summoned to trial every day. And to be tried was to be condemned. Every one of the prisoners became grave, as the hour for their summons approached. Most of the victims went to their doom with uncomplaining resignation, and for awhile after their departure there was comparative silence in the prison. But, by-and-by, – so said Jacques, – the conversation or amusements began again. Human nature cannot stand the perpetual pressure of such keen anxiety, without an effort to relieve itself by thinking of something else. Jacques said that Monsieur and Mademoiselle were for ever talking together of the past days, – it was "Do you remember this?" or, "Do you remember that?" perpetually. He sometimes thought they forgot where they were, and what was before them. But Jacques did not, and every day he trembled more and more as the list was called over.

'The third morning of their incarceration, the gaoler brought in a man whom Jacques did not recognise, and therefore did not at once observe; for he was waiting, as in duty bound, upon his master and his sweet young lady (as he always called her in repeating the story). He thought that the new introduction was some friend of the gaoler, as the two seemed well acquainted, and the latter stayed a few minutes talking with his visitor before leaving him in the prison. So Jacques was surprised when, after a short time had elapsed, he looked round, and saw the fierce stare with which the stranger was regarding Monsieur and Mademoiselle de Créquy, as the pair sat at breakfast, – the said breakfast being laid as well as Jacques knew how, on a bench fastened into the prison wall, – Virginie sitting on her low stool, and Clément half lying on the ground by her side, and submitting gladly to be fed by her pretty white fingers; for it was one of her fancies, Jacques said, to do all she could for him, in consideration of his broken arm. And, indeed, Clément was wasting away daily; for he had received other injuries, internal and more serious than that to his arm, during the mélée[a] which had ended in his capture. The stranger made Jacques conscious of his presence by a sigh, which was almost a groan. All three prisoners looked round at the sound. Clément's face expressed little but scornful indifference; but Virginie's face froze into stony hate. Jacques said he never saw such a look, and hoped that he never should again. Yet after that first revelation of feeling, her look was steady and fixed in another direction to that in which the stranger stood, – still motionless – still watching. He came a step nearer at last.

'"Mademoiselle," he said. Not the quivering of an eyelash showed that she heard him. "Mademoiselle!" he said again, with an intensity of beseeching that made Jacques – not knowing who he was – almost pity him, when he saw his young lady's obdurate face.

'There was perfect silence for a space of time which Jacques could not measure. Then again the voice, hesitatingly, saying, "Monsieur!" Clément could not hold the same icy countenance as Virginie; he turned his head with an impatient gesture of disgust; but even that emboldened the man.

'"Monsieur, do ask Mademoiselle to listen to me, – just two words!"

'"Mademoiselle de Créquy only listens to whom she chooses." Very haughtily my Clément would say that, I am sure.

'"But, Mademoiselle," – lowering his voice, and coming a step or two nearer. Virginie must have felt his approach, though she did not see it; for she drew herself a little on one side, so as to put as much space as possible between him and her. "Mademoiselle, it is not too late. I can save you; but to-morrow your name is down on the list. I can save you, if you will listen."

'Still no word or sign. Jacques did not understand the affair. Why was she so obdurate to one who might be ready to include Clément in the proposal, as far as Jacques knew?

'The man withdrew a little, but did not offer to leave the prison. He never took his eyes off Virginie; he seemed to be suffering from some acute and terrible pain as he watched her.

'Jacques cleared away the breakfast-things as well as he could. Purposely, as I suspect, he passed near the man.

'"Hist!" said the stranger. "You are Jacques, the gardener, arrested for assisting an aristocrat. I know the gaoler. You shall escape, if you will. Only take this message from me to Mademoiselle. You heard. She will not listen to me: I did not want her to come here. I never knew she was here, and she will die to-morrow. They will put her beautiful, round throat under the guillotine. Tell her, good old man, tell her how sweet life is; and how I can save her; and how I will not ask for more than just to see her from time to time. She is so young; and death is annihilation, you know.[85] Why does she hate me so? I want to save her; I have done her no harm. Good old man, tell her how terrible death is; and that she will die to-morrow, unless she listens to me."

'Jacques saw no harm in repeating this message. Clément listened in silence, watching Virginie with an air of infinite tenderness.

"Will you not try him, my cherished one?" he said. "Towards you he may mean well" (which makes me think that Virginie had never repeated to Clément the conversation which she had overheard that last night at Madame Babette's); "you would be in no worse a situation than you were before!"

"No worse, Clément! and I should have known what you were, and have lost you. My Clément!" said she, reproachfully.

"Ask him," said she, turning to Jacques, suddenly, "if he can save Monsieur de Créquy as well, – if he can? – O Clément, we might escape to England; we are but young." And she hid her face on his shoulder.

'Jacques returned to the stranger, and asked him Virginie's question. His eyes were fixed on the cousins; he was very pale, and the twitchings or contortions, which must have been involuntary whenever he was agitated, convulsed his whole body.

'He made a long pause. "I will save mademoiselle and monsieur, if she will go straight from prison to the mairie, and be my wife."

"Your wife!" Jacques could not help exclaiming. "That she will never be – never!"

"Ask her!" said Morin, hoarsely.

"But almost before Jacques thought he could have fairly uttered the words, Clément caught their meaning.

"Begone!" said he; "not one word more." Virginie touched the old man as he was moving away. "Tell him he does not know how he makes me welcome Death." And smiling, as if triumphant, she turned again to Clément.

'The stranger did not speak as Jacques gave him the meaning, not the words of their replies. He was going away, but stopped. A minute or two afterwards, he beckoned to Jacques. The old gardener seems to have thought it undesirable to throw away even the chance of assistance from such a man as this, for he went forwards to speak to him.

"Listen! I have influence with the gaoler. He shall let thee pass out with the victims to-morrow. No one will notice it, or miss thee, – . They will be led to trial, – even at the last moment, I will save her, if she sends me word she relents. Speak to her, as the time draws on. Life is very sweet, – tell her how sweet. Speak to him; he will do more with her than thou canst. Let him urge her to live. Even at the last, I will be at the Palais de Justice, – at the Grève.[86] I have followers, – I have interest. Come among the crowd that follow the victims, – I shall see thee. It will be no worse for him, if she escapes" –

"Save my master, and I will do all," said Jacques.

"'Only on my one condition," said Morin, doggedly; and Jacques was hopeless of that condition ever being fulfilled. But he did not see why his own life might not be saved. By remaining in prison until the next day, he should have rendered every service in his power to his master and the young lady. He, poor fellow, shrank from death; and he agreed with Morin to escape, if he could, by the means Morin suggested, and to bring him word if Mademoiselle de Créquy relented. (Jacques had no expectation that she would; but I fancy he did not think it necessary to tell Morin of this conviction of his.) This bargaining with so base a man for so slight a thing as life, was the only flaw that I heard of in the old gardener's behaviour. Of course, the mere reopening of the subject was enough to stir Virginie to displeasure. Clément urged her, it is true; but the light he had gained upon Morin's motions, made him rather try to set the case before her in as fair a manner as possible than use any persuasive arguments. And, even as it was, what he said on the subject made Virginie shed tears – the first that had fallen from her since she entered the prison. So, they were summoned and went together, at the fatal call of the muster-roll of victims the next morning. He, feeble from his wounds and his injured health; she, calm and serene, only petitioning to be allowed to walk next to him, in order that she might hold him up when he turned faint and giddy from his extreme suffering.

'Together they stood at the bar; together they were condemned. As the words of judgment were pronounced, Virginie turned to Clément, and embraced him with passionate fondness. Then, making him lean on her, they marched out towards the Place de la Grève.

'Jacques was free now. He had told Morin how fruitless his efforts at persuasion had been; and, scarcely caring to note the effect of his information upon the man, he had devoted himself to watching Monsieur and Mademoiselle de Créquy. And now he followed them to the Place de la Grève. He saw them mount the platform; saw them kneel down together till plucked up by the impatient officials; could see that she was urging some request to the executioner; the end of which seemed to be, that Clément advanced first to the guillotine, was executed (and just at this moment there was a stir among the crowd, as of a man pressing forward towards the scaffold). Then she, standing with her face to the guillotine, slowly made the sign of the cross, and knelt down.

'Jacques covered his eyes, blinded with tears. The report of a pistol made him look up. She was gone – another victim in her place – and where there had been the little stir in the crowd not five minutes before, some men were carrying off a dead body. A man had shot himself, they said. Pierre told me who that man was.'

CHAPTER IX.

AFTER a pause, I ventured to ask what became of Madame de Créquy, Clément's mother.

'She never made any inquiry about him again,' said my lady. 'She must have known that he was dead; though how, we never could tell. Medlicott remembered afterwards that it was about, if not on – Medlicott to this day declares that it was on the very Monday, June the nineteenth, when her son was executed, that Madame de Créquy left off her rouge, and took to her bed, as one bereaved and hopeless. It certainly was about that time; and Medlicott – who was deeply impressed by that dream of Madame de Créquy's (the relation of which I told you had had such an effect on my lord), in which she had seen the figure of Virginie – as the only light object amid much surrounding darkness as of night, smiling and beckoning Clément on – on – till at length the bright phantom stopped, motionless, and Madame de Créquy's eyes began to penetrate the murky darkness, and to see closing around her the gloomy dripping walls which she had once seen and never forgotten – the walls of the vault of the chapel of the De Créquys in Saint Germain l'Auxerrois;[87] and there the two last of the Créquys laid them down among their forefathers, and Madame de Créquy had wakened to the sound of the great door, which led to the open air, being locked upon her – I say Medlicott, who was predisposed by this dream to look out for the supernatural, always declared that Madame de Créquy was made conscious, in some mysterious way, of her son's death, on the very day and hour when it occurred, and that after that she had no more anxiety, but was only conscious of a kind of stupefying despair.'

'And what became of her, my lady?' asked I, repeating my question.

'What could become of her?' replied Lady Ludlow. 'She never could be induced to rise again, though she lived more than a year after her son's departure. She kept her bed; her room darkened, her face turned towards the wall, whenever any one besides Medlicott was in the room. She hardly ever spoke, and would have died of starvation but for Medlicott's tender care, in putting a morsel to her lips every now and then, feeding her, in fact, just as an old bird feeds her young ones. In the height of summer my lord and I left London. We would fain have taken her with us into Scotland, but the doctor (we had the old doctor from Leicester Square) forbade her removal; and this time he gave such good reasons against it that I acquiesced. Medlicott and a maid were left with her. Every care was taken of her. She survived till our return. Indeed, I thought she was in much the same state as I had left her in, when I came back to London. But Medlicott spoke of her as much weaker; and one morning on awakening, they told me she was dead. I sent for Medlicott, who was in sad distress, she had become so fond of her charge. She said that, about two o'clock, she had been awakened by unusual restlessness on Madame de Créquy's part; that she had gone to her bedside, and found the poor lady feebly but perpetually moving her wasted arm up and down – and saying to herself in a wailing voice: "I did not bless him when he left me – I did not bless him when he left me!" Medlicott gave her a spoonful or two of jelly, and sat[a] by her, stroking her hand, and soothing her till she seemed to fall asleep. But in the morning she was dead.'

'It is a sad story, your ladyship,' said I, after a while.

'Yes it is. People seldom arrive at my age without having watched the beginning, middle, and end of many lives and many fortunes. We do not talk about them, perhaps; for they are often so sacred to us, from having touched into the very quick of our own hearts, as it were, or into those of others who are dead and gone, and veiled over from human sight, that we cannot tell the tale as if it was a mere story. But young people should remember that we have[b] had this solemn experience of life, on which to base our opinions and form our judgments, so that they are not mere untried theories. I am not alluding to Mr. Horner just now, for he is nearly as old as I am – within ten years, I daresay – but I am thinking of Mr. Gray, with his endless plans for some new thing – schools, education, Sabbaths, and what not. Now he has not seen what all this leads to.'

'It is a pity he has not heard your ladyship tell the story of poor Monsieur de Créquy.'

'Not at all a pity, my dear. A young man like him, who, both by position and age must have had his experience confined to a very narrow circle, ought not to set up his opinion against mine; he ought not to require reasons from me, nor to need such explanation of my arguments (if I condescend to argue), as going into relation of the circumstances on which my arguments are based in my own mind, would be.'

'But, my lady, it might convince him,' I said, with perhaps injudicious perseverance.

'And why should he be convinced?' she asked, with gentle inquiry in her tone. 'He has only to acquiesce. Though he is appointed by Mr. Croxton, I am the lady of the manor, as he must know. But it is with Mr. Horner that I must have to do about this unfortunate lad Gregson. I am afraid there will be no method of making him forget his unlucky knowledge. His poor brains will be intoxicated with the sense of his powers, without any counterbalancing principles to guide him. Poor fellow! I am quite afraid it will end in his being hanged!'

The next day Mr. Horner came to apologise and explain. He was evidently – as I could tell from his voice, as he spoke to my lady in the next room – extremely annoyed at her ladyship's discovery of the education he had been giving to this boy. My lady spoke with great authority, and with reasonable grounds of complaint. Mr. Horner was well acquainted with her thoughts on the subject, and had acted in defiance of her wishes. He acknowledged as much, and should on no account have done it, in any other instance, without her leave.

'Which I could never have granted you,' said my lady.

But this boy had extraordinary capabilities; would, in fact, have taught himself much that was bad, if he not been rescued, and another direction given to his powers. And in all Mr. Horner had done, he had had her ladyship's service in view. The business was getting almost beyond his power, so many letters and so much account-keeping was required by the complicated state in which things were.

Lady Ludlow felt what was coming – a reference to the mortgage for the benefit of my lord's Scottish estates, which, she was perfectly aware, Mr. Horner considered as having been a most unwise proceeding – and she hastened to observe: –

'All this may be very true, Mr. Horner, and I am sure I should be the last person to wish you to over-work or distress yourself; but of that we will talk another time. What I am now anxious to remedy is, if possible, the state of this poor little Gregson's mind. Would not hard work in the fields be a wholesome and excellent way of enabling him to forget?'

'I was in hopes, my lady, that you would have permitted me to bring him up to act as a kind of clerk,' said Mr. Horner, jerking out his project abruptly.

'A what?' asked my lady, in infinite surprise.

'A kind of – of assistant, in the way of copying letters and doing up accounts. He is already an excellent penman and very quick at figures.'

'Mr. Horner,' said my lady, with dignity, 'the son of a poacher and vagabond ought never to have been able to copy letters relating to the Hanbury estates; and, at any rate, he shall not. I wonder how it is that, knowing the use he has made of his power of reading a letter, you should venture to propose such an employment for him as would require his being in your confidence, and you the trusted agent of this family. Why, every secret (and every ancient and honourable family has its secrets, as you know, Mr. Horner!) would be learnt off by heart, and repeated to the first comer!'

'I should have hoped to have trained him, my lady, to understand the rules of discretion.'

'Trained! Train a barn-door fowl to be a pheasant, Mr. Horner! That would be the easier task. But you did right to speak of discretion rather than honour. Discretion looks to the consequences of actions – honour looks to the action itself, and is an instinct rather than a virtue. After all, it is possible, you might have trained him to be discreet.'

Mr. Horner was silent. My lady was softened by his not replying, and began, as she always did in such cases, to fear lest she had been too harsh. I could tell that by her voice and by her next speech, as well as if I had seen her face.

'But I am sorry you are feeling the pressure of the affairs; I am quite aware that I have entailed much additional trouble upon you by some of my measures; I must try and provide you with some suitable assistance. Copying letters and doing up accounts, I think you said?'

Mr. Horner had certainly had a distant idea of turning the little boy, in process of time, into a clerk; but he had rather urged this possibility of future usefulness beyond what he had at first intended, in speaking of it to my lady as a palliation of his offence, and he certainly was very much inclined to retract his statement that the letter-writing, or any other business, had increased, or that he was in the slightest want of help of any kind, when my lady, after a pause of consideration, suddenly said:

'I have it. Miss Galindo will, I am sure, be glad to assist you. I will speak to her myself. The payment we should make to a clerk would be of real service to her!'

I could hardly help echoing Mr. Horner's tone of surprise as he said –

'Miss Galindo!'

For, you must be told who Miss Galindo was; at least, told us much as I know. Miss Galindo had lived in the village for many years, keeping house on the smallest possible means, yet always managing to maintain a servant. And this servant was invariably chosen because she had some infirmity that made her undesirable to every one else. I believe Miss Galindo had had lame and blind and hump-backed maids. She had even at one time taken in a girl hopelessly gone in consumption, because if not she would have had to go to the workhouse, and not have had enough to eat. Of course the poor creature could not perform a single duty usually required of a servant, and Miss Galindo herself was both servant and nurse.

Her present maid was scarcely four feet high, and bore a terrible character for ill-temper. Nobody but Miss Galindo would have kept her; but, as it was, mistress and servant squabbled perpetually, and were, at heart, the best of friends. For it was one of Miss Galindo's peculiarities to do all manner of kind and self-denying actions, and to say all manner of provoking things. Lame, blind, deformed, and dwarf, all came in for scoldings without number:[a] it was only the consumptive girl that never had heard a sharp word. I don't think any of her servants liked her the worse for her peppery temper, and passionate odd ways, for they knew her real and beautiful kindness of heart; and, besides, she had so great a turn for humour, that very often her speeches amused as much or more than they irritated; and, on the other side, a piece of witty impudence from her servant would occasionally tickle her so much and so suddenly, that she would burst out laughing in the middle of her passion.

But the talk about Miss Galindo's choice and management of her servants was confined to village gossip, and had never reached my Lady Ludlow's ears, though doubtless Mr. Horner was well acquainted with it. What my lady knew of her amounted to this. It was the custom in those days for the wealthy ladies of the county to set on foot a repository,[88] as it was called, in the assize-town. The ostensible manager of this repository was generally a decayed gentlewoman, a clergyman's widow, or so forth. She was, however, controlled by a committee of ladies; and paid by them in proportion to the amount of goods she sold; and these goods were the small manufactures of ladies of little or no fortune, whose names, if they chose it, were only signified by initials.

Poor water-colour drawings, in indigo and Indian ink; screens, ornamented with moss and dried leaves; paintings on velvet, and such faintly ornamental works were displayed on one side of the shop. It was always reckoned a mark of characteristic gentility in the repository, to have only common heavy framed sash-windows, which admitted very little light, so I never was quite certain of the merit of these Works of Art as they were entitled. But, on the other side, where the Useful Work placard was put up, there was a great variety of articles, of whose unusual excellence every one might judge. Such fine sewing, and stitching, and button-holing! Such bundles of soft delicate knitted stockings and socks; and, above all, in Lady Ludlow's eyes, such hanks of the finest spun flaxen thread!

And the most delicate dainty work of all was done by Miss Galindo, as Lady Ludlow very well knew. Yet, for all their fine sewing, it sometimes happened that Miss Galindo's patterns were of an old-fashioned kind; and the dozen night-caps, may-be, on the materials for which she had expended bonâ-fide money, and on the making-up, no little time and eye-sight, would lie for months in a yellow neglected heap; and at such times, it was said, Miss Galindo was more amusing than usual, more full of dry drollery and humour; just as at the times when an order came in to X. (the initial she had chosen) for a stock of well-paying things, she sat and stormed at her servant as she stitched away. She herself explained her practice in this way: –

'When everything goes wrong, one would give up breathing if one could not lighten one's heart by a joke. But when I've to sit still from morning till night, I must have something to stir my blood, or I should go off into an apoplexy, so I set to, and quarrel with Sally.'

Such were Miss Galindo's means and manner of living in her own house. Out of doors, and in the village, she was not popular, although she would have been sorely missed had she left the place. But she asked too many home questions (not to say impertinent) respecting the domestic economies (for[a] even the very poor like to spend their bit of money their own way), and would open cupboards to find out hidden extravagances, and question closely respecting the weekly amount of butter, till one day she met with what would have been a rebuff to any other person, but which she rather enjoyed than otherwise.

She was going into a cottage, and in the doorway met the good woman chasing out a duck, and apparently unconscious of her visitor.

'Get out, Miss Galindo!' she cried addressing the duck. 'Get out! O, I ask your pardon,' she continued, as if seeing the lady for the first time. 'It's only that weary duck that will come in. Get out, Miss Gal–' (to the duck).

'And so you call it after me, do you?' inquired her visitor.

'O, yes, ma'am, my master would have it so, for he said, sure enough the unlucky bird was always poking herself where she was not wanted.'

'Ha, ha! very good! And so your master is a wit, is he? Well! tell him to come up and speak to me to-night about my parlour chimney, for there is no one like him for chimney doctoring.'

And the master went up, and was so won over by Miss Galindo's merry ways, and sharp insight into the mysteries of his various kinds of business (he was a mason, chimney-sweeper, and ratcatcher), that he came home and abused his wife the next time she called the duck the name by which he himself had christened her.

But odd as Miss Galindo was in general, she could be as well-bred a lady as any one when she chose. And choose she always did when my Lady Ludlow was by. Indeed, I don't know the man, woman, or child, that did not instinctively turn out its best side to her ladyship. So she had no notion of the qualities which, I am sure, made Mr. Horner think that Miss Galindo would be most unmanageable as a clerk, and heartily wish that the idea had never come into my lady's head. But there is was; and he had annoyed her ladyship already more than he liked to-day, so he could not directly contradict her, but only urge difficulties which he hoped might prove insuperable. But every one of them Lady Ludlow knocked down. Letters to copy? Doubtless. Miss Galindo could come up to the hall; she should have a room to herself; she wrote a beautiful hand; and writing would save her eyesight. 'Capability with regard to accounts?' My lady would anwer for that too; and for more than Mr. Horner seemed to think it necessary to inquire about. Miss Galindo was by birth and breeding a lady of the strictest honour, and would, if possible, forget the substance of any letters that passed through her hands; at any rate, no one would ever hear of them again from her. 'Remuneration?' Oh! as for that, Lady Ludlow would herself take care that it was managed in the most delicate manner possible. She would send to invite Miss Galindo to tea at the Hall that very afternoon, if Mr. Horner would only give her ladyship the slightest idea of the average length of time that my lady was to request Miss Galindo to sacrifice to her daily, 'Three hours! Very well.' Mr. Horner looked very grave as he passed the windows of the room where I lay. I don't think he liked the idea of Miss Galindo as a clerk.

Lady Ludlow's invitations were like royal commands. Indeed, the village was too quiet to allow the inhabitants to have many evening engagements of any kind. Now and then, Mr. and Mrs. Horner gave a tea and supper to the principal tenants and their wives, to which the clergyman was invited, and Miss Galindo, Mrs. Medlicott, and one or two other spinsters and widows. The glory of the supper-table on these occasions was invariably furnished by her ladyship:[a] it was a cold roasted peacock, with his tail stuck out as if in life. Mrs. Medlicott would take up the whole morning arranging the feathers in the proper semicircle, and was always pleased with the wonder and admiration it excited. It was considered a due reward and fitting compliment to her exertions that Mr. Horner always took her in to supper, and placed her opposite to the magnificent dish, at which she sweetly smiled all the time they were at table. But since Mrs. Horner had had the paralytic stroke these parties had been given up; and Miss Galindo wrote a note to Lady Ludlow in reply to her invitation, saying that she was entirely disengaged, and would have great pleasure in doing herself the honour of waiting upon her ladyship.

Whoever visited my lady took their meals with her, sitting on the dais, in the presence of all my former companions. So I did not see Miss Galindo until some time after tea; as the young gentlewomen had had to bring her their sewing and spinning, to hear the remarks of so competent a judge. At length her ladyship brought her visitor into the room where I lay, – it was one of my bad days, I remember, – in order to have her little bit of private conversation. Miss Galindo was dressed in her best gown, I am sure, but I had never seen anything like it except in a picture, it was so old-fashioned. She wore a white muslin apron, delicately embroidered, and put on a little crookedly, in order, as she told us, even Lady Ludlow, before the evening was over, to conceal a spot whence the colour had been discharged by a lemon-stain. This crookedness had an odd effect, especially when I saw that it was intentional; indeed, she was so anxious about her apron's right adjustment in the wrong place, that she told us straight out why she wore it so, and asked her ladyship if the spot was properly hidden, at the same time lifting up her apron and showing her how large it was.

'When my father was alive, I always took his right arm, so, and used to remove any spotted or discoloured breadths to the left side, if it was a walking-dress. That's the convenience of a gentleman. But widows and spinsters must do what they can. Ah, my dear (to me)! when you are reckoning up the blessings in your lot, – though you may think it a hard one in some respects, – don't forget how little your stockings want darning, as you are obliged to lie down so much! I would rather knit two pairs of stockings than darn one, any day.'

'Have you been doing any of your beautiful knitting lately?' asked my lady, who had now arranged Miss Galindo in the pleasantest chair, and taken her own little wicker-work one, and, having her work in her hands, was ready to try and open the subject.

'No, and alas! your ladyship. It is partly the hot weather's fault, for people seem to forget that winter must come; and partly, I suppose, that every one is stocked who has the money to pay four-and-sixpence a pair for stockings.'

'Then may I ask if you have any time in your active days at liberty?' said my lady, drawing a little nearer to her proposal, which I fancy she found it a little awkward to make.

'Why, the village keeps me busy, your ladyship, when I have neither knitting nor^a sewing to do. You know I took X. for my letter at the repository, because it stands for Xantippe,[89] who was a great scold in old times, as I have learnt. But I'm sure I don't know how the world would get on without scolding, your ladyship. It would go to sleep, and the sun would stand still.'

'I don't think I could bear to scold, Miss Galindo,' said her ladyship, smiling.

'No! because your ladyship has people to do it for you. Begging your pardon, my lady, it seems to me the generality of people may be divided into saints' scolds, and sinners. Now, your ladyship is a saint, because you have a sweet and holy nature, in the first place; and have people to do your anger and vexation for you, in the second place. And Jonathan Walker is a sinner, because he is sent to prison. But here am I, half way, having but a poor kind of disposition at best, and yet hating sin, and all that leads to it, such as wasting and extravagance, and gossiping, – and yet all this lies right under my nose in the village, and I am not saint enough not to be vexed at it; and so I scold. And though I had rather be a saint, yet I think I do good in my way.'

'No doubt you do, dear Miss Galindo,' said Lady Ludlow. 'But I am sorry to hear that there is so much that is bad going on in the village, – very sorry.'

'O, your ladyship! then I am sorry I brought it out. It was only by way of saying, that when I have no particular work to do at home, I take a turn abroad, and set my neighbours to rights, just by way of steering clear of Satan.

> For Satan finds some mischief still
> For idle hands to do,[90]

you know, my lady.'

There was no leading into the subject by delicate degrees, for Miss Galindo was evidently so fond of talking, that, if asked a question, she made her answer so long, that before she came to an end of it, she had wandered far away from the original starting point. So Lady Ludlow plunged at once into what she had to say.

'Miss Galindo, I have a great favour to ask of you.'

'My lady, I wish I could tell you what a pleasure it is to hear you say so,' replied Miss Galindo, almost with tears in her eyes; so glad were we all to do anything for her ladyship, which could be called a free service and not merely a duty.

'It is this. Mr. Horner tells me that the business-letters, relating to the estate, are multiplying so much that he finds it impossible to copy them all himself, and I therefore require the services of some confidential and discreet person to copy these letters, and occasionally to go through certain accounts. Now, there is a very pleasant little sitting-room very near to Mr. Horner's office (you know Mr. Horner's office? on the other side of the stone hall?) and if I could prevail upon you to come here to breakfast and afterwards sit there for three hours every morning, Mr. Horner should bring or send you the papers –'

Lady Ludlow stopped. Miss Galindo's countenance had fallen. There was some great obstacle in her mind to her wish for obliging Lady Ludlow.

'What would Sally do?' she asked at length. Lady Ludlow had not a notion who Sally was. Nor if she had had a notion, would she have had a conception of the perplexities that poured into Miss Galindo's mind, at the idea of leaving her rough forgetful dwarf without the perpetual monitorship of her mistress. Lady Ludlow, accustomed to a household where everything went on noiselessly, perfectly, and by clock-work, conducted by a number of highly-paid, well-chosen, and accomplished servants, had not a conception of the nature of the rough material from which her servants came. Besides, in her establishment, so that the result was good, no one inquired if the small economies had been observed in the production. Whereas every penny – every halfpenny, was of consequence to Miss Galindo; and visions of squandered drops of milk and wasted crusts of bread filled her mind with dismay. But she swallowed all her apprehensions down, out of her regard for Lady Ludlow, and desire to be of service to her. No one knows how great a trial it was to her when she thought of Sally, unchecked and unscolded for three hours every morning. But all she said was, –

'"Sally, go to the Deuce." I beg your pardon, my lady, if I was talking to myself; it's a habit I have got into of keeping my tongue in practice, and I am not quite aware when I do it. Three hours every morning! I shall be only too proud to do what I can for your ladyship; and I hope Mr. Horner will not be too impatient with me at first. You know, perhaps, that I was nearly being an authoress once, and that seems as if I was destined to "employ my time in writing."'[91]

'No, indeed; we must return to the subject of the clerkship afterwards, if you please. An authoress, Miss Galindo! You surprise me!'

'But, indeed, I was. All was quite ready. Doctor Burney[92] used to teach me music: not that I ever could learn, but it was a fancy of my poor father's. And his daughter wrote a book, and they said she was but a very young lady, and nothing but a music-master's daughter; so why should not I try?'

'Well?'

'Well! I got paper and half-a-hundred good pens, a bottle of ink, all ready –'

'And then –'

'O, it ended in my having nothing to say, when I sat down to write. But sometimes, when I get hold of a book, I wonder why I let such a poor reason stop me. It does not others.'

'But I think it was very well it did, Miss Galindo,' said her ladyship. 'I am extremely against women usurping men's employments, as they are very apt to do. But perhaps, after all, the notion of writing a book improved your hand. It is one of the most legible I ever saw.'

'I despise z's without tails,' said Miss Galindo, with a good deal of gratified pride at my lady's praise. Presently, my lady took her to look at a curious old cabinet, which Lord Ludlow had picked up at the Hague; and while they were out of the room on this errand, I suppose the question of remuneration was settled, for I heard no more of it.

When they came back, they were talking of Mr. Gray. Miss Galindo was unsparing in her expressions of opinion about him: going much farther than my lady – in her language, at least.

'A little blushing man like him, who can't say bo to a goose without hesitating and colouring, to come to this village – which is as good a village as ever lived – and cry us down for a set of sinners, as if we had all committed murder and that other thing! – I have no patience with him, my lady. And then, how is he to help us to heaven, by teaching us our a b, ab – b a, ba? And yet, by all accounts, that's to save poor children's souls. O, I knew your ladyship would agree with me.

I am sure my mother was as good a creature as ever breathed the blessed air; and if she's not gone to heaven, I don't want to go there; and she could not spell a letter decently. And does Mr. Gray think God took note of that?'

'I was sure you would agree with me, Miss Galindo,' said my lady. 'You and I can remember how this talk about education – Rousseau, and his writings – stirred up the French people to their Reign of Terror, and all those bloody scenes.'

'I'm afraid that Rousseau and Mr. Gray are birds of a feather,' replied Miss Galindo, shaking her head. 'And yet there is some good in the young man, too. He sat[a] up all night with Billy Davis, when his wife was fairly worn out with nursing him.'

'Did he, indeed!' said my lady, her face lighting up, as it always did when she heard of any kind or generous action, no matter who performed it.

'What a pity he is bitten with these new revolutionary ideas, and is so much for disturbing the established order of society!'

When Miss Galindo went, she left so favourable an impression of her visit on my lady, that she said to me with a pleased smile:

'I think I have provided Mr. Horner with a far better clerk than he would have made of that lad Gregson in twenty years. And I will send the lad to my lord's grieve,[93] in Scotland, that he may be kept out of harm's way.'

But something happened to the lad before this purpose could be accomplished.

CHAPTER X.

THE next morning, Miss Galindo made her appearance, and, by some mistake, unusual in my lady's well-trained servants, was shown into the room where I was trying to walk; for a certain amount of exercise was prescribed for me, painful although the exertion had become.

She brought a little basket along with her; and while the footman was gone to inquire my lady's wishes (for I[a] don't think that Lady Ludlow expected Miss Galindo so soon to assume her clerkship; nor, indeed, had Mr. Horner any work of any kind ready for his new assistant to do), she launched out into conversation with me.

'It was a sudden summons, my dear! However, as I have often said to myself, ever since an occasion long ago, if Lady Ludlow ever honours me by asking for my right hand, I'll cut it off, and wrap the stump up so tidily she shall never find out it bleeds. But, if I had had a little more time, I could have mended my pens better. You see, I have had to sit up pretty late to get these sleeves made' – and she took out of her basket a pair of brown-holland over-sleeves, very much such as a grocer's apprentice wears – 'and I had only time to make seven or eight pens, out of some quills Farmer Thomson gave me last autumn. As for ink, I'm thankful to say, that's always ready; an ounce of steel filings, an ounce of nut-gall, and a pint of water (tea, if you're extravagant, which, thank Heaven! I'm not), put all in a bottle, and hang it up behind the house door, so that the whole gets a good shaking every time you slam it to – and even if you are in a passion and bang it, as Sally and I often do, it is all the better for it – and there's my ink ready for use; ready to write my lady's will with, if need be.'

'O, Miss Galindo!' said I, 'don't talk so; my lady's will! and she not dead yet.'

'And if she were, what would be the use of talking of making her will! Now, if you were Sally, I should say, "Answer me that, you goose!" But, as you're a relation of my lady's, I must be civil, and only say, "I can't think how you can talk so like a fool!" To be sure, poor thing, you're lame!'

I do not know how long she would have gone on; but my lady came in, and I, released from my duty of entertaining Miss Galindo, made my limping way into the next room. To tell the truth, I was rather afraid of Miss Galindo's tongue, for I never knew what she would say next.

After a while my lady came, and began to look in the bureau for something; and as she looked she said:[a]

'I think Mr. Horner must have made some mistake, when he said he had so much work that he almost required a clerk, for this morning he cannot find anything for Miss Galindo to do; and there she is, sitting with her pen behind her ear, waiting for something to write. I am come to find her my mother's letters, for I should like to have a fair copy made of them. O, here they are! don't trouble yourself, my dear child.'

When my lady returned again, she sat[b] down and began to talk of Mr. Gray.

'Miss Galindo says she saw him going to hold a prayer-meeting in a cottage. Now, that really makes me unhappy, it is so like what Mr. Wesley[94] used to do in my younger days; and since then we have had rebellion in the American colonies and the French revolution. You may depend upon it, my dear, making religion and education common – vulgarising them, as it were – is a bad thing for a nation. A man who hears prayers read in the cottage where he has just supped on bread and bacon, forgets the respect due to a church: he begins to think that one place is as good as another, and, by-and-by, that one person is as good as another; and after that, I always find that people begin to talk of their rights, instead of thinking of their duties. I wish Mr. Gray had been more tractable, and had left well alone. What do you think I heard this morning? Why, that the Home Hill estate, which niches into the Hanbury property, was bought by a Baptist baker from Birmingham!'

'A Baptist baker!' I exclaimed. I had never seen a Dissenter, to my knowledge; but, having always heard them spoken of with horror, I looked upon them almost as if they were rhinoceroses. I wanted to see a live Dissenter, I believe, and yet I wished it were over. I was almost surprised when I heard that any of them were engaged in such peaceful occupations as baking.

'Yes! so Mr. Horner tells me. A Mr. Brooke,[95c] I believe. But, at any rate, he is a Baptist, and has been in trade. What with his schismatism and Mr. Gray's methodism, I am afraid all the primitive character of this place will vanish.'

From what I could hear, Mr. Gray seemed to be taking his own way; at any rate, more than he had done when he first came to the village, when his natural timidity had made him defer to my lady, and seek her consent and sanction before embarking in any new plan. But newness was a quality Lady Ludlow especially disliked. Even in the fashions of dress and furniture, she clung to the old, to the modes which had prevailed when she was young; and, though she had a deep personal regard for Queen Charlotte (to whom, as I have already[d] said, she had been maid-of-honour), yet there was a tinge of Jacobitism[96] about her, such as made her extremely dislike to hear Prince Charles Edward called the Young Pretender, as many loyal people did in those days, and made her fond of telling of the thorn-tree in my lord's park in Scotland, which had been planted by bonny Queen Mary[97] herself, and before which every guest in the Castle of Monkshaven was expected to stand bare-headed, out of respect to the memory and misfortunes of the royal planter.

We might play at cards, if we so chose, on a Sunday; at least, I suppose we might, for my lady and Mr. Mountford used to do so often when I first went. But we must neither play cards, nor read, nor sew on the fifth of November and on the thirtieth of January,[98] but must go to church, and meditate all the rest of the day – and very hard work meditating was. I would far rather have scoured a room. That was the reason, I suppose, why a passive life was seen to be better discipline for me than an active one.

But I am wandering away from my lady, and her dislike to all innovation. Now, it seemed to me, as far as I heard, that Mr. Gray was full of nothing but new things, and that what he first did was to attack all our established institutions, both in the village and the parish, and also in the nation. To be sure, I heard of his ways of going on principally from Miss Galindo, who was apt to speak more strongly than accurately.

'There he goes,' she said, 'clucking up the children just like an old hen, and trying to teach them about their salvation and their souls, and I don't know what – things that it is just blasphemy to speak about out of church. And he potters old people about reading their Bibles. I am sure I don't want to speak disrespectfully about the Holy Scriptures, but I found old Job Horton busy reading his Bible yesterday. Says I, "What are you reading, and where did you get it, and who gave it you?" So he made answer, "That he was reading Susannah and the Elders, for that he had read Bel and the Dragon[99] till he could pretty near say it off by heart, and they were two as pretty stories as ever he had read, and that it was a caution to him what bad old chaps there were in the world." Now, as Job is bed-ridden, I don't think he is likely to meet with the Elders, and I say that I think repeating his Creed, the Commandments, and the Lord's Prayer, and, maybe, throwing in a verse of the Psalms, if he wanted a bit of a change, would have done him far more good than his pretty stories, as he called them. And what's the next thing our young parson does? Why he tries to make us all feel pitiful for the black slaves, and leaves little pictures of negroes about, with the question printed below, "Am I not a man and a brother?"[100] just as if I was to be hail-fellow-well-met with every negro footman. They do say he takes no sugar in his tea,[101] because he thinks he sees spots of blood in it. Now I call that superstition.'

The next day it was a still worse story.

'Well, my dear! and how are you? My lady sent me in to sit a bit with you, while Mr. Horner looks out some papers for me to copy. Between ourselves, Mr. Steward Horner does not like having me for a clerk. It is all very well, he does not; for, if he were decently civil to me, I might want a chaperone, you know, now poor Mrs. Horner is dead.' This was one of Miss Galindo's grim jokes. 'As it is, I try to make him forget I'm a woman, I do everything as ship-shape as a masculine man-clerk. I see he can't find a fault – writing good, spelling correct, sums all right. And then he squints up at me with the tail of his eye, and looks glummer than ever, just because I'm a woman – as if I could help that. I have gone good lengths to set his mind at case. I have stuck my pen behind my ear, I have made him a bow instead of a curtsey, I have whistled – not a tune, I can't pipe up that – nay, if you won't tell my lady, I don't mind telling you that I have said "Confound it!" and "Zounds!" I can't get any farther. For all that, Mr. Horner won't forget I am a lady, and so I am not half the use I might be, and if it were not to please my Lady Ludlow, Mr. Horner and his books might go hang (see how natural that came out!). And there is an order for a dozen nightcaps for a bride, and I am so afraid I shan't have time to do them. Worst of all, there's Mr. Gray taking advantage of my absence to seduce Sally!'

'To seduce Sally! Mr. Gray!'

'Pooh, pooh, child! There's many a kind of seduction. Mr. Gray is seduc-ing Sally to want to go to church. There has he been twice at my house, while I have been away in the mornings, talking to Sally about the state of her soul and that sort of thing. But when I found the meat all roasted to a cinder, I said, "Come, Sally, let's have no more praying when beef is down at the fire. Pray at six o'clock in the morning and nine at night, and I won't hinder you." So she sauced me, and said something about Martha and Mary,[102] implying that, because she had let the beef get so overdone that I declare I could hardly find a bit fit for Nancy Pole's sick grandchild, she had chosen the better part. I was very much put about, I own, and perhaps you'll be shocked at what I said – indeed, I don't know if it was right myself – but I told her I had a soul as well as she, and if it was to be saved by my sitting still and thinking about salvation and never doing my duty, I thought I had as good a right as she had to be Mary, and save my soul. So, that afternoon I sat[a] quite still, and it was really a comfort, for I am often too busy, I know, to pray as I ought. There is first one person wanting me, and then another, and the house and the food and the neighbours to see after. So, when tea-time comes, there enters my maid with her hump on her back, and her soul to be saved. "Please, ma'am, did you order the pound of butter?" – "No, Sally," I said, shaking my head, "this morning I did not go round by Hale's farm, and this afternoon I have been employed in spiritual things."

'Now, our Sally likes tea and bread-and-butter above everything, and dry bread was not to her taste.

"'I'm thankful," said the impudent hussy, "that you have taken a turn towards godliness. It will be my prayers, I trust, that's given it you."

'I was determined not to give her an opening towards the carnal subject of butter, so she lingered still, longing to ask leave to run for it. But I gave her none, and munched my dry bread myself, thinking what a famous cake I could make for little Ben Pole with the bit of butter we were saving; and when Sally had had her butterless tea, and was in none of the best of tempers because Martha had not bethought herself of the butter, I just quietly said:

"'Now, Sally, to-morrow we'll try to hash that beef well, and to remember the butter, and to work out our salvation all at the same time, for I don't see why it can't all be done, as God has set us to do it all." But I heard her at it again about Mary and Martha, and I have no doubt that Mr. Gray will teach her to consider me a lost sheep.'[103]

I had heard so many little speeches about Mr. Gray from one person or another, all speaking against him, as a mischief-maker, a setter-up of new doctrines, and of a fanciful standard of life (and you may be sure that, where Lady Ludlow led, Mrs. Medlicott and Adams were certain to follow, each in their different ways showing the influence my lady had over them), that I believe I had grown to consider him as a very instrument of evil, and to expect to perceive in his face marks of his presumption, and arrogance, and impertinent interference. It was now many weeks since I had seen him, and when he was one morning shown into the blue drawing-room (into which I had been removed for a change), I was quite surprised to see how innocent and awkward a young man he appeared, confused even more than I was at our unexpected tête-à-tête. He looked thinner, his eyes more eager, his expression more anxious, and his colour came and went more than it had done when I had seen him last. I tried to make a little conversation, as I was, to my own surprise, more at my ease than he was; but his thoughts were evidently too much preoccupied for him to do more than answer me with monosyllables.

Presently my lady came in. Mr. Gray twitched and coloured more than ever; but plunged into the middle of his subject at once.

'My lady, I cannot answer it to my conscience, if I allow the children of this village to go on any longer the little heathens that they are. I must do something to alter their condition. I am quite aware that your ladyship disapproves of many of the plans which have suggested themselves to me; but nevertheless I must do something, and I am come now to your ladyship to ask respectfully, but firmly, what you would advise me to do.'

His eyes were dilated, and I could almost have said they were full of tears with his eagerness. But I am sure it is a bad plan to remind people of decided opinions which they have once expressed, if you wish them to modify those opinions. Now, Mr. Gray had done this with my lady; and though I do not mean to say she was obstinate, yet she was not one to retract.

She was silent for a moment or two before she replied.

'You ask me to suggest a remedy for an evil of the existence of which I am not conscious,' was her answer – very coldly, very gently given. 'In Mr. Mountford's time I heard no such complaints: whenever I see the village children (and they are not unfrequent visitors at this house, on one pretext or another), they are well and decently behaved.'

'Oh, madam, you cannot judge,' he broke in. 'They are trained to respect you in word and deed; you are the highest they ever look up to; they have no notion of a higher.'

'Nay, Mr. Gray,' said my lady, smiling, 'they are as loyally disposed as any children can be. They come up here every fourth of June,[104] and drink his Majesty's health, and have buns, and (as Margaret Dawson can testify) they take a great and respectful interest in all the pictures I can show them of the Royal family.'

'But, madam, I think of something higher than any earthly dignities.'

My lady coloured at the mistake she had made; for she herself was truly pious. Yet when she resumed the subject, it seemed to me as if her tone was a little sharper than before.

'Such want of reverence is, I should say, the clergyman's fault. You must excuse me, Mr. Gray, if I speak plainly.'

'My lady, I want plain-speaking. I myself am not accustomed to those ceremonies and forms which are, I suppose, the etiquette in your ladyship's rank of life, and which seem to hedge you in from any power of mine to touch you. Among those with whom I have passed my life hitherto, it has been the custom to speak plainly out what we have felt earnestly. So, instead of needing any apology from your ladyship for straightforward speaking, I will meet what you say at once, and admit that it is the clergyman's fault, in a great measure, when the children of his parish swear, and curse, and are brutal, and ignorant of all saving grace; nay, some of them of the very name of God. And because this guilt of mine, as the clergyman of this parish, lies heavy on my soul, and every day leads but from bad to worse, till I am utterly bewildered how to do good to children who escape from me as if I were a monster, and who are growing up to be men fit for and capable of any crime, but those requiring wit or sense, I come to you, who seem to me all-powerful, as far as material power goes – for your ladyship only knows the surface of things, and barely that, that pass in your village – to help me with advice, and such outward help as you can give.'

Mr. Gray had stood up and sat[a] down once or twice while he had been speaking, in an agitated, nervous kind of way, and now he was interrupted by a violent fit of coughing, after which he trembled all over.

My lady rang for a glass of water, and looked much distressed.

'Mr. Gray,' said she, 'I am sure you are not well; and that makes you exaggerate childish faults into positive evils. It is always the case with us when we are not strong in health. I hear of you exerting yourself in every direction: you over-work yourself, and the consequence is, that you imagine us all worse people than we are.'

And my lady smiled very kindly and pleasantly at him, as he sat,[a] a little panting, a little flushed, trying to recover his breath. I am sure that now they were brought face to face, she had quite forgotten all the offence she had taken at his doings when she heard of them from others; and, indeed, it was enough to soften any one's heart to see that young, almost boyish face, looking in such anxiety and distress.

'O, my lady, what shall I do?' he asked, as soon as he could recover breath, and with such an air of humility that I am sure no one who had seen it could have ever thought him conceited again. 'The evil of this world is too strong for me. I can do so little. It is all in vain. It was only to-day –' And again the cough and agitation returned.

'My dear Mr. Gray,' said my lady (the day before, I could never have believed she could have called him My dear), 'you must take the advice of an old woman about yourself. You are not fit to do anything just now but attend to your own health: rest, and see a doctor (but, indeed, I will take care of that), and when you are pretty strong again, you will find that you have been magnifying evils to yourself.'

'But, my lady, I cannot rest. The evils do exist, and the burden of their continuance lies on my shoulders. I have no place to gather the children together in, that I may teach them the things necessary to salvation. The rooms in my own house are too small; but I have tried them. I have money of my own; and, as your ladyship knows, I tried to get a piece of leasehold property on which to build a school-house at my own expense. Your ladyship's lawyer comes forward, at your instructions, to enforce some old feudal right, by which no building is allowed on leasehold property without the sanction of the Lady of the Manor. It may be all very true; but it was a cruel thing to do, – that is, if your ladyship had known (which I am sure you do not) the real moral and spiritual state of my poor parishioners. And now I come to you to know what I am to do? Rest! I cannot rest, while children whom I could possibly save are being left in their ignorance, their blasphemy, their uncleanness, their cruelty. It is known through the village that your ladyship disapproves of my efforts, and opposes all my plans. If you think them wrong, foolish, ill-digested (I have been a student, living in a college, and eschewing all society but that of pious men, until now: I may not judge for the best, in my ignorance of this sinful human nature), tell me of better plans and wiser projects for accomplishing my end; but do not bid me rest, with Satan compassing me round,[105] and stealing souls away.'

'Mr. Gray,' said my lady, 'there may be some truth in what you have said. I do not deny it, though I think, in your present state of indisposition and excitement, you exaggerate it much. I believe – nay, the experience of a pretty long life has convinced me – that education is a bad thing, if given indiscriminately. It unfits the lower orders for their duties, the duties to which they are called by God, of submission to those placed in authority over them, of contentment with that state of life to which it has pleased God to call them,[106] and of ordering themselves lowly and reverently to all their betters. I have made this conviction of mine tolerably evident to you; and have expressed distinctly my disapprobation of some of your ideas. You may imagine, then, that I was not well pleased when I found that you had taken a rood or more of Farmer Hale's land, and were laying the foundations of a school-house. You had done this without asking for my permission, which, as Farmer Hale's liege lady, ought to have been obtained legally, as well as asked for out of courtesy. I put a stop to what I believed to be calculated to do harm to a village, to a population in which, to say the least of it, I may be supposed to take as much interest as you can do. How can reading and writing, and the multiplication-table (if you choose to go so far), prevent blasphemy, and uncleanness and cruelty? Really, Mr. Gray, I hardly like to express myself so strongly on the subject in your present state of health, as I should do at any other time. It seems to me that books do little; character much; and character is not formed from books.'

'I do not think of character: I think of souls. I must get some hold upon these children, or what will become of them in the next world? I must be found to have some power beyond what they have, and which they are rendered capable of appreciating, before they will listen to me. At present, physical force is all they look up to; and I have none.'

'Nay, Mr. Gray, by your own admission, they look up to me.'

'They would not do anything your ladyship disliked if it was likely to come to your knowledge; but if they could conceal it from you, the knowledge of your dislike to a particular line of conduct would never make them cease from pursuing it.'

'Mr. Gray' – surprise in her air, and some little indignation – 'they and their fathers have lived on the Hanbury lands for generations!'

'I cannot help it, madam. I am telling you the truth, whether you believe me or not.' There was a pause; my lady looking perplexed, and somewhat ruffled; Mr. Gray as though hopeless and wearied out. 'Then, my lady,' said he, at last, rising as he spoke, 'you can suggest nothing to ameliorate the state of things which, I do assure you, does exist on your lands, and among your tenants. Surely, you will not object to my using Farmer Hale's great barn every Sabbath?[a] He will allow me the use of it, if your ladyship will grant your permission.'

'You are not fit for any extra work at present,' (and indeed he had been coughing very much all through the conversation). 'Give me time to consider of it. Tell me what you wish to teach. You will be able to take care of your health and grow stronger while I consider. It shall not be the worse for you, if you leave it in my hands for a time.'

My lady spoke very kindly; but he was in too excited a state to recognise the kindness, while the idea of delay was evidently a sore irritation. I heard him say: 'And I have so little time in which to do my work. Lord! lay not this sin to my charge.'

But my lady was speaking to the old butler, for whom, at her sign, I had rung the bell some little time before. Now she turned round.

'Mr. Gray, I find I have some bottles of Malmsey,[107] of the vintage of seventeen hundred and seventy-eight, yet left. Malmsey, as perhaps you know, used to be considered a specific for coughs arising from weakness. You must permit me to send you half-a-dozen bottles, and, depend upon it, you will take a more cheerful view of life and its duties before you have finished them, especially if you will be so kind as to see Doctor Trevor, who is coming to see me in the course of the week. By the time you are strong enough to work, I will try and find some means of preventing the children from using such bad language, and otherwise annoying you.'

'My lady, it is the sin, and not the annoyance. I wish I could make you understand.' He spoke with some impatience; poor fellow, he was too weak, exhausted, and nervous. 'I am perfectly well; I can set to work to-morrow; I will do anything not to be oppressed with the thought of how little I am doing. I do not want your wine. Liberty to act in the manner I think right, will do me far more good. But it is of no use. It is preordained[a] that I am to be nothing but a cumberer of the ground.[108] I beg your ladyship's pardon for this call.'

He stood up, and then turned dizzy. My lady looked on, deeply hurt, and not a little offended. He held out his hand to her, and I could see that she had a little hesitation before she took it. He then saw me, I almost think, for the first time; and put out his hand once more, drew it back, as if undecided, put it out again, and finally took hold of mine for an instant in his damp, listless hand, and was gone.

Lady Ludlow was dissatisfied with both him and herself, I was sure. Indeed, I was dissatisfied with the result of the interview myself. But my lady was not one to speak out her feelings on the subject; nor was I one to forget myself, and begin on a topic which she did not begin. She came to me, and was very tender with me; so tender, that that, and the thoughts of Mr. Gray's sick, hopeless, disappointed look, nearly made me cry.

'You are tired, little one,' said my lady. 'Go and lie down in my room, and hear what Medlicott and I can decide upon in the way of strengthening dainties for that poor young man, who is killing himself with his over-sensitive conscientiousness.'

'O, my lady!' said I, and then I stopped.

'Well. What?' asked she.

'If you would but let him have Farmer Hale's barn at once, it would do him more good than all.'

'Pooh, pooh, child!' though I don't think she was displeased, 'he is not fit for more work just now. I shall go and write for Doctor Trevor.'

And, for the next half-hour, we did nothing but arrange physical comforts and cures for poor Mr. Gray. At the end of the time, Mrs. Medlicott said:

'Has your ladyship heard that Harry Gregson has fallen from a tree, and broken his thigh-bone, and is like to be a cripple for life?'

'Harry Gregson! That black-eyed lad who read my letter? It all comes from over-education!'

CHAPTER XI.

BUT I don't see how my lady could think it was over-education that made Harry Gregson break his thigh, for the manner in which he met with the accident was this: –

Mr. Horner, who had fallen sadly out of health since his wife's death, had attached himself greatly to Harry Gregson. Now, Mr. Horner had a cold manner to every one, and never spoke more than was necessary, at the best of times. And, latterly, it had not been the best of times with him. I dare say, he had had some causes for anxiety (of which I knew nothing) about my lady's affairs; and he was evidently annoyed by my lady's whim (as he once inadvertently called it) of placing Miss Galindo under him in the position of a clerk. Yet he had always been friends, in his quiet way, with Miss Galindo, and she devoted herself to her new occupation with diligence and punctuality, although more than once she had moaned to me over the orders for needlework which had been sent to her, and which, owing to her occupation in the service of Lady Ludlow, she had been unable to fulfil.

The only living creature to whom the staid Mr. Horner could be said to be attached, was Harry Gregson. To my lady he was a faithful and devoted servant, looking keenly after her interests, and anxious to forward them at any cost of trouble to himself. But the more shrewd Mr. Horner was, the more probability was there of his being annoyed at certain peculiarities of opinion which my lady held with a quiet, gentle pertinacity; against which no arguments, based on mere worldly and business calculations, made any way. This frequent opposition to views which Mr. Horner entertained, although it did not interfere with the sincere respect which the lady and the steward felt for each other, yet prevented any warmer feeling of affection from coming in. It seems strange to say it, but I must repeat it – the only person for whom, since his wife's death, Mr. Horner seemed to feel any love, was the little imp Harry Gregson, with his bright, watchful eyes, his tangled hair hanging right down to his eyebrows, for all the world like a Skye terrier. This lad, half gipsy and whole poacher, as many people esteemed him, hung about the silent, respectable, staid Mr. Horner, and followed his steps with something of the affectionate fidelity of the dog which he resembled. I suspect, this demonstration of attachment to his person on Harry Gregson's part was what won Mr. Horner's regard. In the first instance, the steward had only chosen the lad out as the cleverest instrument he could find for his purpose; and I don't mean to say that, if Harry had not been almost as shrewd as Mr. Horner himself was, both by original disposition and subsequent experience, the steward would have taken to him as he did, let the lad have shown ever so much affection for him.

But even to Harry Mr. Horner was silent. Still, it was pleasant to find himself in many ways so readily understood; to perceive that the crumbs of knowledge he let fall were picked up by his little follower, and hoarded like gold; that here was one to hate the persons and things whom Mr. Horner coldly disliked, and to reverence and admire all those for whom he had any regard. Mr. Horner had never had a child, and unconsciously, I suppose, something of the paternal feeling had begun to develop[a] itself in him towards Harry Gregson. I heard one or two things from different people, which have always made me fancy that Mr. Horner secretly and almost unconsciously hoped that Harry Gregson might be trained so as to be first his clerk, and next his assistant, and finally his successor in his stewardship to the Hanbury estates.

Harry's disgrace with my lady, in consequence of his reading the letter, was a deeper blow to Mr. Horner than his quiet manner would ever have led any one to suppose, or than Lady Ludlow ever dreamed of inflicting, I am sure.

Probably Harry had a short, stern, rebuke from Mr. Horner at the time, for his manner was always hard even to those he cared for the most. But Harry's love was not to be daunted or quelled by a few sharp words. I dare say, from what I heard of them afterwards, that Harry accompanied Mr. Horner in his walk over the farm the very day of the rebuke; his presence apparently unnoticed by the agent, by whom his absence would have been painfully felt nevertheless. That was the way of it, as I have been told. Mr. Horner never bade Harry go with him; never thanked him for going, or being at his heels ready to run on any errands, straight as the crow flies to his point, and back to heel in as short a time as possible. Yet, if Harry were away, Mr. Horner never inquired the reason from any of the men who might be supposed to know whether he was detained by his father, or otherwise engaged; he never asked Harry himself where he had been. But Miss Galindo said that those labourers who knew Mr. Horner well, told her that he was always more quick-eyed to short-comings, more savage-like in fault-finding, on those days when the lad was absent.

Miss Galindo, indeed, was my great authority for most of the village news which I heard. She it was who gave me the particulars of poor Harry's accident.

'You see, my dear,' she said, 'the little poacher has taken some unaccountable fancy to my master.' (This was the name by which Miss Galindo always spoke of Mr. Horner to me, ever since she had been, as she called it, appointed his clerk.)

'Now, if I had twenty hearts to lose, I never could spare a bit of one of them for that good, grey, square severe man. But different people have different tastes, and here is that little imp of a gipsy-tinker ready to turn slave for my master; and, odd enough, my master, – who, I should have said before-hand, would have made short work of imp, and imp's family, and have sent Hall, the Bang-beggar,[109] after them in no time – my master, as they tell me, is in his way quite fond of the lad, and if he could, without vexing my lady too much, he would have made him what the folks here call a Latiner. However, last night, it seems that there was a letter of some importance forgotten (I can't tell you what it was about, my dear, though I know perfectly well, but "*service oblige*,"[a] as well as "noblesse," and you must take my word for it that it was important, and one that I am surprised my master could forget), till too late for the post. (The poor, good, orderly man is not what he was before his wife's death.) Well, it seems that he was sore annoyed by his forgetfulness, and well he might be. And it was all the more vexatious, as he had no one to blame but himself. As for that matter, I always scold somebody else when I'm in fault; but I suppose my master would never think of doing that, else it's a mighty relief. However, he could eat no tea, and was altogether put out and gloomy. And the little faithful imp-lad, perceiving all this, I suppose, got up like a page in an old balled,[110] and said he would run for his life across country to Comberford, and see if he could not get there before the bags were made up. So my master gave him the letter, and nothing more was heard of the poor fellow till this morning, for the father thought his son was sleeping in Mr. Horner's barn, as he does occasionally it seems, and my master, as was very natural, that he had gone to his father's.'

'And he had fallen down the old stone quarry, had he not?'

'Yes, sure enough. Mr. Gray had been up here fretting my lady with some of his new-fangled schemes, and because the young man could not have it all his own way, from what I understand, he was put out, and thought he would go home by the back lane, instead of through the village, where the folks would notice if the parson looked glum. But, however, it was a mercy, and I don't mind saying so, ay, and meaning it too, though it may be like methodism,[111] for, as Mr. Gray walked by the quarry, he heard a groan, and at first he thought it was a lamb fallen down; and he stood still, and then he heard it again; and then, I suppose, he looked down and saw Harry. So he let himself down by the boughs of the trees to the ledge where Harry lay half-dead, and with his poor thigh broken. There he had lain ever since the night before: he had been returning to tell the master that he had safely posted the letter, and the first words he said, when they recovered him from the exhausted state he was in, were' (Miss Galindo tried hard not to whimper, as she said it), "'It was in time, sir. I see'd it put in the bag with my own eyes.'"

'But where is he?' asked I. 'How did Mr. Gray get him out?'

'Ay! there it is, you see. Why the old gentleman (I daren't say Devil in Lady Ludlow's house) is not so black as he is painted; and Mr. Gray must have a deal of good in him, as I say at times; and then at others, when he has gone against me, I can't bear him, and think hanging too good for him. But he lifted the poor lad, as if he had been a baby, I suppose, and carried him up the great ledges that were formerly used for steps; and laid him soft and easy on the wayside grass, and ran home and got help and a door, and had him carried to his house, and laid on his bed; and then somehow, for the first time either he or any one else perceived it, he himself was all over blood – his own blood – he had broken a blood-vessel; and there he lies in the little dressing-room, as white and as still as if he were dead; and the little imp in Mr. Gray's own bed, sound asleep, now his leg is set, just as if linen sheets and a feather bed were his native element, as one may say. Really, now he is doing so well, I've no patience with him, lying there where Mr. Gray ought to be. It is just what my lady always prophesied would come to pass, if there was any confusion of ranks.'

'Poor Mr. Gray!' said I, thinking of his flushed face, and his feverish, restless ways, when he had been calling on my lady not an hour before his exertions on Harry's behalf. And I told Miss Galindo how ill I had thought him.

'Yes,' said she. 'And that was the reason my lady had sent for Doctor Trevor. Well, it has fallen out admirably, for he looked well after that old donkey of a Prince, and saw that he made no blunders.'

Now 'that old donkey of a Prince' meant the village surgeon, Mr. Prince, between whom and Miss Galindo there was war to the knife, as they often met in the cottages, when there was illness, and she had her queer, odd recipes, which he, with his grand pharmacopœia, held in infinite contempt, and the consequence of their squabbling had been, not long before this very time, that he had established a kind of rule, that into whatever sick-room Miss Galindo was admitted, there he refused to visit. But Miss Galindo's prescriptions and visits cost nothing, and were often backed by kitchen-physic;[112] so, though it was true that she never came but she scolded about something or other, she was generally preferred as medical attendant to Mr. Prince.

'Yes, the old donkey is obliged to tolerate me, and be civil to me; for, you see, I got there first, and had possession, as it were, and yet my lord the donkey likes the credit of attending the parson, and being in consultation with so grand a county-town doctor as Doctor Trevor. And Doctor Trevor is an old friend of mine' (she sighed a little, some time I may tell you why), 'and treats me with infinite bowing and respect; so the donkey, not to be out of medical fashion, bows too, though it is sadly against the grain: and he pulled a face as if he had heard a slate-pencil gritting against a slate, when I told Doctor Trevor I meant to sit up with the two lads, for I call Mr. Gray little more than a lad, and a pretty conceited one, too, at times.'

'But why should you sit up, Miss Galindo? It will tire you sadly.'

'Not it. You see, there is Gregson's mother to keep quiet; for she sits by her lad, fretting and sobbing, so that I'm afraid of her disturbing Mr. Gray; and there's Mr. Gray to keep quiet, for Doctor Trevor says his life depends on it; and there is medicine to be given to the one, and bandages to be attended to for the other; and the wild horde of gipsy brothers and sisters to be turned out, and the father to be held in from showing too much gratitude to Mr. Gray, who can't bear it, – and who is to do it all but me? The only servant is old lame Betty, who once lived with me, and *would*[a] leave me because she said I was always bothering – (there was a good deal of truth in what she said, I grant, but she need not have said it; a good deal of truth is best let alone at the bottom of the well), and what can she do, – deaf as ever she can be, too?'

So Miss Galindo went her ways; but not the less was she at her post in the morning; a little crosser and more silent than usual; but the first was not to be wondered at, and the last was rather a blessing.

Lady Ludlow had been extremely anxious both about Mr. Gray and Harry Gregson. Kind and thoughtful in any case of illness and accident, she always was; but somehow, in this, the feeling that she was not quite – what shall I call it? – 'friends' seems hardly the right word to use, as to the possible feeling between the Countess Ludlow and the little vagabond messenger, who had only once been in her presence, – that she had hardly parted from either as she could have wished to do, had death been near, made her more than usually anxious. Doctor Trevor was not to spare obtaining the best medical advice the county could afford; whatever he ordered in the way of diet, was to be prepared under Mrs. Medlicott's own eye, and sent down from the Hall to the Parsonage. As Mr. Horner had given somewhat similar directions, in the case of Harry Gregson at least, there was rather a multiplicity of counsellors and dainties, than any lack of them. And, the second night, Mr. Horner insisted on taking the superintendence of the nursing himself, and sat[b] and snored by Harry's bedside, while the poor, exhausted mother lay by her child, – thinking that she watched him, but in reality fast asleep, as Miss Galindo told us; for, distrusting any one's powers of watching and nursing but her own, she had stolen across the quiet village street in cloak and dressing-gown, and found Mr. Gray in vain trying to reach the cup of barley-water which Mr. Horner had placed just beyond his reach.

In consequence of Mr. Gray's illness, we had to have a strange curate to do duty; a man who dropped his h's, and hurried through the service, and yet had time enough to stand in my lady's way, bowing to her as she came out of church, and so subservient in manner, that I believe that sooner than remain unnoticed by a countess, he would have preferred being scolded, or even cuffed. Now I found out, that great as was my lady's liking and approval of respect, nay, even reverence, being paid to her as a person of quality, – a sort of tribute to her Order, which she had no individual right to remit, or, indeed, not to exact, – yet she, being personally simple, sincere, and holding herself in low esteem, could not endure anything like the servility of Mr. Crosse, the temporary curate. She grew absolutely to loathe his perpetual smiling and bowing; his instant agreement with the slightest opinion she uttered; his veering round as she blew the wind. I have often said that my lady did not talk much, as she might have done had she lived among her equals. But we all loved her so much, that we had learnt to interpret all her little ways pretty truly; and I knew what particular turns of her head, and contractions of her delicate fingers meant, as well as if she had expressed herself in words. I began to suspect that my lady would be very thankful to have Mr. Gray about again, and doing his duty even with a conscientiousness that might amount to worrying himself, and fidgeting others; and although Mr. Gray might hold her opinions in as little esteem as those of any simple gentlewoman, she was too sensible not to feel how much flavour there was in his conversation, compared to that of Mr. Crosse, who was only her tasteless echo.

As for Miss Galindo, she was utterly and entirely a partisan of Mr. Gray's, almost ever since she had begun to nurse him during his illness.

'You know, I never set up for reasonableness, my lady. So I don't pretend to say, as I might do if I were a sensible woman and all that, – that I am convinced by Mr. Gray's arguments of this thing or t'other. For one thing, you see, poor fellow! he has never been able to argue, or hardly indeed to speak, for Doctor Trevor has been very peremptory. So there's been no scope for arguing! But what I mean is this: – When I see a sick man thinking always of others, and never of himself; patient, humble – a trifle too much at times, for I've caught him praying to be forgiven for having neglected his work as a parish priest,' (Miss Galindo was making horrible faces, to keep back tears, squeezing up her eyes in a way which would have amused me at any other time, but when she was speaking of Mr. Gray); 'when I see a downright good, religious man, I'm apt to think he's got hold of the right clue, and that I can do no better than hold on by the tails of his coat and shut my eyes, if we've got to go over doubtful places on our road to Heaven. So, my lady, you must excuse me, if, when he gets about again, he is all agog about a Sunday-school, for if he is, I shall be agog too, and perhaps twice as bad as him, for, you see, I've a strong constitution compared to his, and strong ways of speaking and acting. And I tell your ladyship this now, because I think from your rank – and still more, if I may say so, for all your kindness to me long ago, down to this very day – you've a right to be first told of anything about me. Change of opinion I can't exactly call it, for I don't see the good of schools and teaching A B C, any more than I did before, only Mr. Gray does, so I'm to shut my eyes, and leap over the ditch to the side of education. I've told Sally already, that if she does not mind her work, but stands gossiping with Nelly Mather, I'll teach her her lessons; and I've never caught her with old Nelly since.'

I think Miss Galindo's desertion to Mr. Gray's opinions in this matter hurt my lady just a little bit; but she only said:

'Of course, if the parishioners wish for it, Mr. Gray must have his Sunday-school. I shall, in that case, withdraw my opposition. I am sorry I cannot change my opinions as easily as you.'

My lady made herself smile as she said this. Miss Galindo saw it was an effort to do so. She thought a minute before she spoke again.

'Your ladyship has not seen Mr. Gray as intimately as I have done. That's one thing. But, as for the parishioners, they will follow your ladyship's lead in everything; so there is no chance of their wishing for a Sunday-school.'

'I have never done anything to make them follow my lead, as you call it, Miss Galindo,' said my lady, gravely.

'Yes, you have,' replied Miss Galindo, bluntly. And then, correcting herself, she said, 'Begging your ladyship's pardon, you have. Your ancestors have lived here time out of mind, and have owned the land on which their forefathers have lived ever since there were forefathers. You yourself were born amongst them, and have been like a little queen to them ever since, I might say, and they've never known your ladyship do anything but what was kind and gentle; but I'll leave fine speeches about your ladyship to Mr. Crosse. Only you, my lady, lead the thoughts of the parish; and save some of them a world of trouble, for they could never tell what was right if they had to think for themselves. It's all quite right that they should be guided by you, my lady, – if only you would agree with Mr. Gray.'

'Well,' said my lady, 'I told him only the last day that he was here, that I would think about it. I do believe I could make up my mind on certain subjects better if I were left alone, than while being constantly talked to about them.'

My lady said this in her usual soft tones; but the words had a tinge of impatience about them; indeed, she was more ruffled than I had often seen her; but, checking herself in an instant, she said:

'You don't know how Mr. Horner drags in this subject of education apropos of everything. Not that he says much about it at any time: it is not his way. But he cannot let the thing alone.'

'I know why, my lady,' said Miss Galindo. 'That poor lad, Harry Gregson, will never be able to earn his livelihood in any active way, but will be lame for life. Now, Mr. Horner thinks more of Harry than of any one else in the world, – except, perhaps, your ladyship.' Was it not a pretty companionship for my lady? 'And he has schemes of his own for teaching Harry; and if Mr. Gray could but have his school, Mr. Horner and he think Harry might be school-master, as your ladyship would not like to have him coming to you as steward's clerk. I wish your ladyship would fall into this plan; Mr. Gray has it so at heart.'

Miss Galindo looked wistfully at my lady, as she said this. But my lady only said, drily, and rising at the same time, as if to end the conversation:

'So! Mr. Horner and Mr. Gray seem to have gone a long way in advance of my consent to their plans.'

'There!' exclaimed Miss Galindo, as my lady left the room, with an apology for going away; 'I have gone and done mischief with my long, stupid tongue. To be sure, people plan a long way ahead of to-day; more especially when one is a sick man, lying all through the weary day on a sofa.'

'My lady will soon get over her annoyance,' said I, as it were apologetically. I only stopped Miss Galindo's self-reproaches to draw down her wrath upon myself.

'And has not she a right to be annoyed with me, if she likes, and to keep annoyed as long as she likes? Am I complaining of her, that you need tell me that? Let me tell you, I have known my lady these thirty years; and if she were to take me by the shoulders, and turn me out of the house, I should only love her the more. So don't you think to come between us with any little mincing, peace-making speeches. I have been a mischief-making parrot, and I like her the better for being vexed with me. So good-bye to you, Miss, and wait till you know Lady Ludlow as well as I do, before you next think of telling me she will soon get over her annoyance!' And off Miss Galindo went.

I could not exactly tell what I had done wrong; but I took care never again to come in between my lady and her by any remark about the one to the other; for I saw that some most powerful bond of grateful affection made Miss Galindo almost worship my lady.

Meanwhile, Harry Gregson was limping a little about in the village, still finding his home in Mr. Gray's house; for there he could most conveniently be kept under the doctor's eye, and receive the requisite care, and enjoy the requisite nourishment. As soon as he was a little better, he was to go to Mr. Horner's house; but, as the steward lived some distance out of the way, and was much from home, he had agreed to leave Harry at the house to which he had first been taken, until he was quite strong again; and the more willingly, I suspect, from what I heard afterwards, because Mr. Gray gave up all the little strength of speaking which he had, to teaching Harry in the very manner which Mr. Horner most desired.

As for Gregson the father – he – wild man of the woods, poacher, tinker, jack-of-all-trades – was getting tamed by this kindness to his child. Hitherto his hand had been against every man, as every man's had been against him.

That affair before the justice, which I told you about, when Mr. Gray and even my lady had interested themselves to get him released from unjust imprisonment, was the first bit of justice he had ever met with; it attracted him to the people, and attached him to the spot on which he had but squatted for a time. I am not sure if any of the villagers were grateful to him for remaining in their neighbourhood, instead of decamping as he had often done before, for good reasons, doubtless, of personal safety. Harry was only one out of a brood of ten or twelve children, some of whom had earned for themselves no good character in service: one, indeed, had been actually transported, for a robbery committed in a distant part of the county; and the tale was yet told in the village of how Gregson the father came back from the trial in a state of wild rage, striding through the place, and uttering oaths of vengeance to himself, his great black eyes gleaming out of his matted hair, and his arms working by his side, and now and then tossed up in his impotent despair. As I heard the account, his wife followed him, child-laden and weeping. After this, they had vanished from the country for a time, leaving their mud hovel locked up, and the door-key, as the neighbours said, buried in a hedge bank. The Gregsons had reappeared much about the same time that Mr. Gray came to Hanbury. He had either never heard of their evil character, or considered that it gave them all the more claims upon his Christian care, and the end of it was that this rough, untamed, strong giant of a heathen was loyal slave to the weak, hectic, nervous, self-distrustful parson. Gregson had also a kind of grumbling respect for Mr. Horner: he did not quite like the steward's monopoly of his Harry: the mother submitted to that with a better grace, swallowing down her maternal jealousy in the prospect of her child's advancement to a better and more respectable position than that in which his parents had struggled through life. But Mr. Horner, the steward, and Gregson, the poacher and squatter, had come into disagreeable contact too often in former days for them to be perfectly cordial at any future time. Even now, when there was no immediate cause for anything but gratitude for his child's sake on Gregson's part, he would skulk out of Mr. Horner's way, if he saw him coming; and it took all Mr. Horner's natural reserve and acquired self-restraint to keep him from occasionally holding up his father's life as a warning to Harry. Now Gregson had nothing of this desire for avoidance with regard to Mr. Gray. The poacher had a feeling of physical protection towards the parson; while the latter had shown the moral courage, without which Gregson would never have respected him, in coming right down upon him more than once in the exercise of unlawful pursuits, and simply and boldly telling him he was doing wrong, with such a quiet reliance upon Gregson's better feeling, at the same time, that the strong poacher could not have lifted a finger against Mr. Gray, though it had been to save himself from being apprehended and taken to the lockups the very next hour. He had rather listened to the parson's bold words with an approving smile, much as Mr. Gulliver might have hearkened to a lecture from a Lilliputian.[113] But when brave words passed into kind deeds, Gregson's heart mutely acknowledged its master and keeper. And the beauty of it all was, that Mr. Gray knew nothing of the good work he had done, or recognised himself as the instrument which God had employed. He thanked God, it is true, fervently and often, that the work was done; and loved the wild man for his rough gratitude; but it never occurred to the poor young clergyman, lying on his sick-bed, and praying, as Miss Galindo had told us he did, to be forgiven for his unprofitable life, to think of Gregson's reclaimed soul as anything with which he had had to do. It was now more than three months since Mr. Gray had been at Hanbury Court. During all that time, he had been confined to his house, if not to his sick-bed, and he and my lady had never met since their last discussion and difference about Farmer Hale's barn.

This was not my dear lady's fault; no one could have been more attentive in every way to the slightest possible want of either of the invalids, especially of Mr. Gray. And she would have gone to see him at his own house, as she sent him word, but that her foot had slipped upon the polished oak staircase, and her ancle had been sprained.

So we had never seen Mr. Gray since his illness, when one November day he was announced as wishing to speak to my lady. She was sitting in her room – the room in which I lay now pretty constantly – and I remember she looked startled, when word was brought to her of Mr. Gray's being at the Hall.

She could not go to him, she was too lame for that, so she bade him be shown into where she sat.

'Such a day for him to go out!' she exclaimed, looking at the fog which had crept up to the windows, and was sapping the little remaining life in the brilliant Virginian creeper leaves that draperied the house on the terrace side.

He came in white, trembling, his large eyes wild and dilated. He hastened up to Lady Ludlow's chair, and, to my surprise, took one of her hands and kissed it, without speaking, yet shaking all over.

'Mr. Gray!' said she, quickly, with sharp, tremulous apprehension of some unknown evil. 'What is it? There is something unusual about you.'

'Something unusual has occurred,' replied he, forcing his words to be calm, as with a great effort. 'A gentleman came to my house, not half-an-hour ago – a Mr. Howard. He came straight from Vienna.'

'My son!' said my dear lady, stretching out her arms in dumb questioning attitude.

'The Lord gave and the Lord taketh away. Blessed be the name of the Lord.'

But my poor lady could not echo the words. He was the last remaining child. And once she had been the joyful mother of nine.

CHAPTER XII.

I AM ashamed to say what feeling become strongest in my mind about this time. Next to the sympathy we all of us felt for my dear lady in her deep sorrow, I mean. For that was greater and stronger than anything else, however contradictory you may think it, when you hear all.

It might arise from my being so far from well at the time, which produced a diseased mind in a diseased body; but I was absolutely jealous for my father's memory, when I saw how many signs of grief there were for my lord's death, he having done next to nothing for the village and parish, which now changed, as it were, its daily course of life, because his lordship died in a far-off city. My father had spent the best years of his manhood in labouring hard, body and soul, for the people amongst whom he lived. His family, of course, claimed the first place in his heart; he would have been good for little, even in the way of benevolence, if they had not. But close after them he cared for his parishioners and neighbours. And yet, when he died, though the church-bells tolled, and smote upon our hearts with hard, fresh pain at every beat, the sounds of every-day life still went on, close pressing around us, – carts and carriages, street-cries, distant barrel-organs (the kindly neighbours kept them out of our street): life, active, noisy life, pressed on our acute consciousness of Death, and jarred upon it as on a quick nerve.

And when we went to church, – my father's own church, – though the pulpit-cushions were black, and many of the congregation had put on some humble sign of mourning, yet it did not alter the whole material aspect of the place. And yet what was Lord Ludlow's relation to Hanbury, compared to my father's work and place in – ?

O! it was very wicked in me! I think if I had seen my lady, – if I had dared to ask to go to her, I should not have felt so miserable, so discontented. But she sat[a] in her own room, hung with black, all, even over the shutters. She saw no light but that which was artificial – candles, lamps, and the like, for more than a month. Only Adams went near her. Mr. Gray was not admitted, though he called daily. Even Mrs. Medlicott did not see her for near a fortnight. The sight of my lady's griefs, or rather the recollection of it, made Mrs. Medlicott talk far more than was her wont. She told us, with many tears, and much gesticulation, even speaking German at times, when her English would not flow, that my lady sat[a] there, a white figure in the middle of the darkened room; a shaded lamp near her, the light of which fell on an open Bible, – the great family Bible. It was not opened at any chapter, or consoling verse; but at the page whereon were registered[b] the births of her nine children. Five had died in infancy, – sacrificed to the cruel system which forbade the mother to suckle her babies.[114] Four had lived longer; Urian had been the first to die, Ughtred-Mortimar, Earl Ludlow, the last.

My lady did not cry, Mrs. Medlicott said. She was quite composed; very still, very silent. She put aside everything that savoured of mere business; sent people to Mr. Horner for that. But she was proudly alive to every possible form which might do honour to the last of her race.

In those days, expresses were slow things, and forms still slower. Before my lady's directions could reach Vienna, my lord was buried. There was some talk (so Mrs. Medlicott said) about taking the body up, and bringing him to Hanbury. But his executors, – connections on the Ludlow side, – demurred to this. If he were removed to England, he must be carried on to Scotland, and interred with his Monkshaven forefathers. My lady, deeply hurt, withdrew from the discussion before it degenerated to an unseemly contest. But all the more, for this understood mortification of my lady's, did the whole village and estate of Hanbury assume every outward sign of mourning. The church-bells tolled morning and evening. The church itself was draped in black inside. Hatchments[115] were placed everywhere, where hatchments could be put. All the tenantry spoke in hushed voices for more than a week, scarcely daring to observe that all flesh, even that of an Earl Ludlow, and the last of the Hanburys, was but grass after all. The very Fighting Lion closed its front door, front shutters it had none, and those who needed drink stole in at the back, and were silent and maudlin over their cups, instead of riotous and noisy. Miss Galindo's eyes were swollen up with crying, and she told me, with a fresh burst of tears, that even hump-backed Sally had been found sobbing over her Bible, and using a pocket-handkerchief for the first time in her life; her aprons having hitherto stood her in the necessary stead, but not being sufficiently in accordance with etiquette, to be used when mourning over an earl's premature decease.

If it was in this way out of the Hall, 'you might work it by the rule of three,' as Miss Galindo used to say, and judge what it was in the Hall. We none of us spoke but in a whisper: we tried not to eat; and indeed the shock had been so really great, and we did really care so much for my lady, that for some days we had but little appetite. But after that, I fear our sympathy grew weaker, while our flesh grew stronger. But we still spoke low, and our hearts ached whenever we thought of my lady sitting there alone in the darkened room, with the light ever falling on that one solemn page.

We wished, O how I wished that she would see Mr. Gray! But Adams said, she thought my lady ought to have a bishop come to see her. Still no one had authority enough to send for one.

Mr. Horner all this time was suffering as much as any one. He was too faithful a servant of the great Hanbury family, though now the family had dwindled down to a fragile old lady, not to mourn acutely over its probable extinction. He had, besides, a deeper sympathy and reverence with, and for, my lady in all things, than probably he ever cared to show, for his manners were always measured and cold. He suffered from sorrow. He also suffered from wrong. My lord's executors kept writing to him continually. My lady refused to listen to mere business, saying she intrusted[a] all to him. But the 'all'[b] was more complicated than I ever thoroughly understood. As far as I comprehended the case, it was something of this kind: – There had been a mortgage raised on my lady's property of Hanbury,[116] to enable my lord, her husband, to spend money in cultivating his Scotch estates,[117] after some new fashion that required capital. As long as my lord, her son, lived, who was to succeed to both the estates after her death, this did not signify; so she had said and felt; and she had refused to take any steps to secure the repayment of capital, or even the payment of the interest of the mortgage from the possible representatives and possessors of the Scotch estates, to the possible owner of the Hanbury property; saying it ill became her to calculate on the contingency of her son's death.

But he had died, childless, unmarried. The heir of the Monkshaven property was an Edinburgh advocate, a far-away kinsman of my lord's: the Hanbury property, at my lady's death, would[c] go to the descendants of a third son of the Squire Hanbury in the days of Queen Anne.

This complication of affairs was most grievous to Mr. Horner. He had always been opposed to the mortgage; had hated the payment of the interest, as obliging my lady to practise certain economies which, though she took care to make them as personal as possible, he disliked as derogatory to the family. Poor Mr. Horner! He was so cold and hard in his manner, so curt and decisive in his speech, that I don't think we any of us did him justice. Miss Galindo was almost the first, at this time, to speak a kind word of him, or to take thought of him at all, any farther than to get out of his way when we saw him approaching.

'I don't think Mr. Horner is well,' she said one day, about three weeks after we had heard of my lord's death. 'He sits resting his head on his hand, and hardly hears me when I speak to him.'

But I thought no more of it, as Miss Galindo did not name it again. My Lady came amongst us once more. From elderly she had become old; a little, frail, old lady, in heavy black drapery, never speaking about nor alluding to her great sorrow; quieter, gentler, paler than ever before; and her eyes dim with much weeping, never witnessed by mortal.

She had seen Mr. Gray at the expiration of the month of deep retirement. But I do not think that even to him she had said one word of her own particular individual sorrow. All mention of it seemed buried deep for evermore. One day, Mr. Horner sent word that he was too much indisposed to attend to his usual business at the Hall; but he wrote down some directions and requests to Miss Galindo, saying that he would be at his office early the next morning. The next morning he was dead!

Miss Galindo told my lady. Miss Galindo herself cried plentifully, but my lady, although very much distressed, could not cry. It seemed a physical impossibility, as if she had shed all the tears in her power. Moreover, I almost think her wonder was far greater that she herself lived than that Mr. Horner died. It was almost natural that so faithful a servant should break his heart, when the family he belonged to lost their stay, their heir and their last hope.

Yes! Mr. Horner was a faithful servant. I do not think there are many so faithful now; but, perhaps, that is an old woman's fancy of mine. When his will came to be examined, it was discovered that, soon after Harry Gregson's accident, Mr. Horner had left the few thousands (three, I think,) of which he was possessed, in trust for Harry's benefit, desiring his executors to see that the lad was well educated in certain things, for which Mr. Horner had thought that he had shown especial aptitude; and there was a kind of implied apology to my lady in one sentence, where he stated that Harry's lameness would prevent his being ever able to gain his living by the exercise of any mere bodily faculties, 'as had been wished by a lady whose wishes' he, the testator, 'was[a] bound to regard.'

But there was a codicil to the will, dated since Lord Ludlow's death – feebly written by Mr. Horner himself, as if in preparation only for some more formal manner of bequest; or, perhaps, only as a mere temporary arrangement till he could see a lawyer, and have a fresh will made. In this he revoked his previous bequest to Harry Gregson. He only left two hundred pounds to Mr. Gray to be used, as that gentleman thought best, for Henry Gregson's benefit. With this one exception, he bequeathed all the rest of his savings to my lady, with a hope that they might form a nest-egg, as it were, towards the paying off of the mortgage which had been such a grief to him during his life. I may not repeat all this in lawyer's phrase; I heard it through Miss Galindo, and she might make mistakes. Though, indeed, she was very clear-headed, and soon earned the respect of Mr. Smithson, my lady's lawyer from Warwick. Mr. Smithson knew Miss Galindo a little before, both personally and by reputation; but I don't think he was prepared to find her installed as steward's clerk, and, at first, he was inclined to treat her, in this capacity, with polite contempt. But Miss Galindo was both a lady and a spirited, sensible woman, and she could put aside her self-indulgence in eccentricity of speech and manner whenever she chose. Nay more; she was usually so talkative, that if she had not been amusing and warm-hearted, one might have thought her wearisome occasionally. But, to meet Mr. Smithson, she came out daily in her Sunday gown; she said no more than was required in answer to his questions; her books and papers were in thorough order, and methodically kept; her statements of matters-of-fact accurate, and to be relied on. She was amusingly conscious of her victory over his contempt of a woman-clerk and his preconceived opinion of her unpractical eccentricity.

'Let me alone,' said she, one day when she came in to sit awhile with me. 'That man is a good man – a sensible man – and, I have no doubt, he is a good lawyer; but he can't fathom women yet. I make no doubt he'll go back to Warwick, and never give credit again to those people who made him think me half-cracked to begin with. O, my dear, he did! He showed it twenty times worse than my poor dear master ever did. It was a form to be gone through to please my lady, and, for her sake, he would hear my statements and see my books. It was keeping a woman out of harm's way, at any rate, to let her fancy herself useful. I read the man. And, I am thankful to say, he cannot read me. At least, only one side of me. When I see an end to be gained, I can behave myself accordingly. Here was a man who thought that a woman in a black silk gown was a respectable, orderly kind of person; and I was a woman in a black silk gown. He believed that a woman could not write straight lines, and required a man to tell her that two and two made four. I was not above ruling my books, and had Cocker[118] a little more at my fingers' ends than he had. But my greatest triumph has been holding my tongue. He would have thought nothing of my books, or my sums, or my black silk gown, if I had spoken unasked. So I have buried more sense in my bosom these ten days than ever I have uttered in the whole course of my life before. I have been so curt, so abrupt, so abominably dull, that I'll answer for it he thinks me worthy to be a man. But I must go back to him, my dear, so goodbye to conversation and you.'

But though Mr. Smithson might be satisfied with Miss Galindo, I am afraid she was the only part of the affair with which he was content. Everything else went wrong. I could not say who told me so – but the conviction of this seemed to pervade the house. I never knew how much we had all looked up to the silent, gruff Mr. Horner for decisions, until he was gone. My lady herself was a pretty good woman of business, as women of business go. Her father, seeing that she would be the heiress of the Hanbury property, had given her a training which was thought unusual in those days, and she liked to feel herself queen regnant, and to have to decide in all cases between herself and her tenantry. But, perhaps, Mr. Horner would have done it more wisely; not but what she always attended to him at last. She would begin by saying, pretty clearly and promptly, what she would have done, and what she would not have done. If Mr. Horner approved of it, he bowed, and set about obeying her directly; if he disapproved of it, he bowed, and lingered so long before he obeyed her, that she forced his opinion out of him with her 'Well,

Mr. Horner! and what have you to say against it?' For she always understood
his silence as well as if he had spoken. But the estate was pressed for ready
money, and Mr. Horner had grown gloomy and languid since the death of
his wife, and even his own personal affairs were not in the order in which
they had been a year or two before, for his old clerk had gradually become
superannuated, or, at any rate, unable by the superfluity of his own energy
and wit to supply the spirit that was wanting in Mr. Horner.

Day after day Mr. Smithson seemed to grow more fidgety, more annoyed
at the state of affairs. Like every one else employed by Lady Ludlow, as far as
I could learn, he had an hereditary tie to the Hanbury family. As long as the
Smithsons had been lawyers, they had been lawyers to the Hanburys; always
coming in on all great family occasions, and better able to understand the
characters, and connect the links of what had once been a large and scattered
family, than any individual thereof had ever been.

As long as a man was at the head of the Hanburys, the lawyers had simply
acted as servants, and had only given their advice when it was required. But
they had assumed a different position on the memorable occasion of the
mortgage: they had remonstrated against it. My lady had resented this
remonstrance, and a slight, unspoken coolness had existed between her and
the father of this Mr. Smithson ever since.

I was very sorry for my lady. Mr. Smithson was inclined to blame Mr.
Horner for the disorderly state in which he found some of the outlying
farms, and for the deficiencies in the annual payment of rents. Mr. Smithson
had too much good feeling to put this blame into words; but my lady's quick
instinct led her to reply to a thought, the existence of which she perceived;
and she quietly told the truth, and explained how she had interfered repeatedly to prevent Mr. Horner from taking certain desirable steps, which were
discordant to her hereditary sense of right and wrong between landlord and
tenant. She also spoke of the want of ready money as a misfortune that could
be remedied, by more economical personal expenditure on her own part; by
which individual saving, it was possible that a reduction of fifty pounds a
year might have been accomplished. But as soon as Mr. Smithson touched
on larger economies, such as either affected the welfare of others, or the
honour and standing of the great House of Hanbury, she was inflexible. Her
establishment consisted of somewhere about forty servants, of whom nearly
as many as twenty were unable to perform their work properly, and yet
would have been hurt if they had been dismissed; so they had the credit of
fulfilling duties, while my lady paid and kept their substitutes. Mr. Smithson
made a calculation, and would have saved some hundreds a year by pension-
ing off these old servants. But my lady would not hear of it. Then, again, I
know privately that he urged her to allow some of us to return to our homes.
Bitterly we should have regretted the separation from Lady Ludlow; but we

would have gone back gladly, had we known at the time that her circumstances required it: but she would not listen to the proposal for a moment.

'If I cannot act justly towards every one, I will give up a plan which has been a source of much satisfaction; at least, I will not carry it out to such an extent in future. But to these young ladies, who do me the favour to live with me at present, I stand pledged. I cannot go back from my word, Mr. Smithson. We had better talk no more of this.'

As she spoke, she entered the room where I lay. She and Mr. Smithson were coming for some papers contained in the bureau. They did not know I was there, and Mr. Smithson started a little when he saw me, as he must have been aware that I had overheard something. But my lady did not change a muscle of her face. All the world might overhear her kind, just, pure sayings, and she had no fear of their misconstruction. She came up to me, and kissed me on the forehead, and then went to search for the required papers.

'I rode over the Conington farms yesterday, my lady. I must say I was quite grieved to see the condition they are in; all the land that is not waste is utterly exhausted with working successive white crops. Not a pinch of manure laid on the ground for years. I must say that a greater contrast could never have been presented than that between Harding's farm and the next fields – fences in perfect order, rotation crops, sheep eating down the turnips on the waste lands – everything that could be desired.'

'Whose farm is that?' asked my lady.

'Why, I am sorry to say, it was on none of your ladyship's that I saw such good methods adopted. I hoped it was, I stopped my horse to inquire. A queer-looking man, sitting on his horse like a tailor, watching his men with a couple of the sharpest eyes I ever saw, and dropping his h's at every word, answered my question, and told me it was his. I could not go on asking him who he was; but I fell into conversation with him, and I gathered that he had earned some money in trade in Birmingham, and had bought the estate (five hundred acres, I think he said,) on which he was born, and now was setting himself to cultivate it in downright earnest, going to Holkham and Woburn,[119] and half the country over, to get himself up on the subject.'

'It would be Brooke, that dissenting baker from Birmingham,' said my lady in her most icy tone. 'Mr. Smithson, I am sorry I have been detaining you so long, but I think these are the letters you wished to see.'

If her ladyship thought by this speech to quench Mr. Smithson she was mistaken. Mr. Smithson just looked at the letters, and went on with the old subject.

'Now, my lady, it struck me that if you had such a man to take poor Horner's place, he would work the rents and the land round most satisfactorily. I should not despair of inducing this very man to undertake the work. I should not mind speaking to him myself on the subject, for we got capital friends over a snack of luncheon that he asked me to share with him.'

Lady Ludlow fixed her eyes on Mr. Smithson as he spoke, and never took them off his face until he had ended. She was silent a minute before she answered.

'You are very good, Mr. Smithson, but I need not trouble you with any such arrangements. I am going to write this afternoon to Captain James, a friend of one of my sons, who has, I hear, been severely wounded at Trafalgar,[120] to request him to honour me by accepting Mr. Horner's situation.'

'A Captain James! A captain in the navy! going to manage your ladyship's estate!'

'If he will be so kind. I shall esteem it a condescension on his part; but I hear that he will have to resign his profession, his state of health is so bad, and a country life is especially prescribed for him. I am in some hopes of tempting him here, as I learn he has but little to depend on if he gives up his profession.'

'A Captain James! an invalid captain!'

'You think I am asking too great a favour,' continued my lady. (I never could tell how far it was simplicity, or how far a kind of innocent malice, that made her misinterpret Mr. Smithson's words and looks as she did.) 'But he is not a post-captain, only a commander, and his pension will be but small. I may be able, by offering him country air and a healthy occupation, to restore him to health.'

'Occupation! My lady, may I ask how a sailor is to manage land? Why, your tenants will laugh him to scorn.'

'My tenants, I trust, will not behave so ill as to laugh at any one I choose to set over them. Captain James has had experience in managing men. He has remarkable practical talents, and great common sense, as I hear from every one. But, whatever he may be, the affair rests between him and myself. I can only say I shall esteem myself fortunate if he comes.'

There was no more to be said, after my lady spoke in this manner. I had heard her mention Captain James before, as a middy who had been very kind to her son Urian. I thought I remembered then, that she had mentioned that his family circumstances were not very prosperous. But, I confess, that little as I knew of the management of land, I quite sided with Mr. Smithson. He, silently prohibited from again speaking to my lady on the subject, opened his mind to Miss Galindo, from whom I was pretty sure to hear all the opinions and news of the household and village. She had taken a great fancy to me, because she said I talked so agreeably. I believe it was because I listened so well.

'Well, have you heard the news,' she began, 'about this Captain James? A sailor, – with a wooden leg, I have no doubt. What would the poor, dear, deceased master have said to it, if he had known who was to be his successor?

My dear, I have often thought of the postman's bringing me a letter as one of the pleasures I shall miss in heaven. But, really, I think Mr. Horner may be thankful he has got out of the reach of news; or else he would hear of Mr. Smithson's having made up to the Birmingham baker, and of this one-legged Captain, coming to dot-and-go-one over the estate. I suppose he will look after the labourers through a spy-glass. I only hope he won't stick in the mud with his wooden leg; for I, for one, won't help him out. Yes, I would,' said she, correcting herself; 'I would, for my lady's sake.'

'But are you sure he has a wooden leg?' asked I. 'I heard Lady Ludlow tell Mr. Smithson about him, and she only spoke of him as wounded.'

'Well, sailors are almost always wounded in the leg. Look at Greenwich Hospital![121] I should say there were twenty one-legged pensioners to one without an arm there. But say he has got half-a-dozen legs, what is he to do with managing land? I shall think him very impudent if he comes, taking advantage of my lady's kind heart.'

However, come he did. In a month from that time, the carriage was sent to meet Captain James; just as three years before it had been sent to meet me. His coming had been so much talked about that we were all as curious as possible to see him, and to know how so unusual an experiment, as it seemed to us, would answer. But, before I tell you anything about our new agent, I must speak of something quite as interesting, and I really think quite as important. And this was my lady's making friends with Harry Gregson. I do believe she did it for Mr. Horner's sake; but, of course, I can only conjecture why my lady did anything. But I heard one day, from Mary Legard, that my lady had sent for Harry to come and see her, if he was well enough to walk so far; and the next day he was shown into the room he had been in once before under such unlucky circumstances.

The lad looked pale enough, as he stood propping himself up on his crutch, and the instant my lady saw him, she bade John Footman place a stool for him to sit down upon while she spoke to him. It might be his paleness that gave his whole face a more refined and gentle look; but I suspect it was that the boy was apt to take impressions, and that Mr. Horner's grave, dignified ways, and Mr. Gray's tender and quiet manners, had altered him; and then the thoughts of illness and death seem to turn many of us into gentlemen, and gentlewomen, as long as such thoughts are in our minds. We cannot speak loudly or angrily at such times; we are not apt to be eager about mere worldly things, for our very awe at our quickened sense of the nearness of the invisible world, makes us calm and serene about the petty trifles of to-day. At least, I know that was the explanation Mr. Gray once gave me of what we all thought the great improvement in Harry Gregson's way of behaving.

My lady hesitated so long about what she had best say, that Harry grew a little frightened at her silence. A few months ago it would have surprised me more than it did now; but since my lord her son's death, she had seemed altered in many ways, – more uncertain and distrustful of herself, as it were.

At last she said, and I think the tears were in her eyes: 'My poor little fellow, you have had a narrow escape with your life since I saw you last.'

To this there was nothing to be said but 'Yes;' and again there was silence.

'And you have lost a good, kind friend, in Mr. Horner.'

The boy's lips worked, and I think he said, 'Please, don't.' But I can't be sure; at any rate, my lady went on:

'And so have I, – a good, kind friend, he was to both of us; and to you he wished to show his kindness in even a more generous way than he has done. Mr. Gray has told you about his legacy to you, has he not?'

There was no sign of eager joy on the lad's face, as if he realised the power and pleasure of having what to him must have seemed like a fortune.

'Mr. Gray said as how he had left me a matter of money.'

'Yes, he has left you two hundred pounds.'

'But I would rather have had him alive, my lady,' he burst out, sobbing as if his heart would break.

'My lad, I believe you. We would rather have had our dead alive, would we not? and there is nothing in money that can comfort us for their loss. But you know – Mr. Gray has told you – who has appointed us all our times to die. Mr. Horner was a good, just man; and has done well and kindly, both by me and you. You perhaps do not know' (and now I understood what my lady had been making up her mind to say to Harry, all the time she was hesitating how to begin) 'that Mr. Horner, at one time, meant to leave you a great deal more; probably all he had, with the exception of a legacy to his old clerk, Morrison. But he knew that this estate – on which my forefathers had lived for six hundred years – was in debt, and that I had no immediate chance of paying off this debt; and yet he felt that it was a very sad thing for an old property like this to belong in part to those other men, who had lent the money. You understand me, I think, my little man?' said she, questioning Harry's face.

He had left off crying, and was trying to understand, with all his might and main; and I think he had got a pretty good general idea of the state of affairs; though probably he was puzzled by the term 'the estate being in debt.' But he was sufficiently interested to want my lady to go on; and he nodded his head at her, to signify this to her.

'So Mr. Horner took the money which he once meant to be yours, and has left the greater part of it to me, with the intention of helping me to pay off this debt I have told you about. It will go a long way, and I shall try hard to save the rest, and then I shall die happy in leaving the land free from debt.' She paused. 'But I shall not die happy in thinking of you. I do not know if having money, or even having a great estate and much honour, is a good thing for any of us. But God sees fit that some of us should be called to this condition, and it is our duty then to stand by our posts, like brave soldiers. Now, Mr. Horner intended you to have this money first. I shall only call it borrowing it from you, Harry Gregson, if I take it and use it to pay off the debt. I shall pay Mr. Gray interest on this money, because he is to stand as your guardian, as it were, till you come of age; and he must fix what ought to be done with it, so as to fit you for spending the principal rightly when the estate can repay it you. I suppose, now, it will be right for you to be educated. That will be another snare that will come with your money. But have courage, Harry. Both education and money may be used rightly, if we only pray against the temptations they bring with them.'

Harry could make no answer, though I am sure he understood it all. My lady wanted to get him to talk to her a little, by way of becoming acquainted with what was passing in his mind; and she asked him what he would like to have done with his money, if he could have part of it now? To such a simple question, involving no talk about feelings, his answer came readily enough.

'Build a cottage for father, with stairs in it, and give Mr. Gray a school-house. O, father does so want Mr. Gray for to have his wish! Father saw all the stones lying quarried and hewn on Farmer Hale's land; Mr. Gray had paid for them all himself. And father said he would work night and day, and little Tommy should carry mortar, if the parson would let him, sooner than that he should be fretted and frabbed[122] as he was, with no one giving him a helping hand or a kind word.'

Harry knew nothing of my lady's part in the affair; that was very clear. My lady kept silence.

'If I might have a piece of my money, I would buy land from Mr. Brooke: he has got a bit to sell just at the corner of Hendon Lane, and I would give it to Mr. Gray; and, perhaps, if your ladyship thinks I may be learned again, I might grow up into the schoolmaster.'

'You are a good boy,' said my lady. 'But there are more things to be thought of, in carrying out such a plan, than you are aware of. However, it shall be tried.'

'The school, my lady?' I exclaimed, almost thinking she did not know what she was saying.

'Yes, the school. For Mr. Horner's sake, for Mr. Gray's sake, and last, not least, for this lad's sake, I will give the new plan a trial. Ask Mr. Gray to come up to me this afternoon about the land he wants. He need not go to a Dissenter[a] for it. And tell your father he shall have a good share in the building of it, and Tommy shall carry the mortar.'

'And I may be schoolmaster?' asked Harry, eagerly.

'We'll see about that,' said my lady, amused. 'It will be some time before that plan comes to pass, my little fellow.'

And now to return to Captain James. My first account of him was from Miss Galindo.

'He's not above thirty; and I must just pack up my pens and my paper, and be off; for it would be the height of impropriety for me to be staying here as his clerk. It was all very well in the old master's days. But here am I, not fifty till next May, and this young, unmarried man, who is not even a widower! O, there would be no end of gossip. Besides, he looks as askance at me as I do at him. My black silk gown had no effect. He's afraid I shall marry him. But I won't; he may feel himself quite safe from that. And Mr. Smithson has been recommending a clerk to my lady. She would far rather keep me on; but I can't stop. I really could not think it proper.'

'What sort of a looking man is he?'

'O, nothing particular. Short, and brown, and sunburnt. I did not think it became me to look at him. Well, now for the nightcaps. I should have grudged any one else doing them, for I have got such a pretty pattern!'

But, when it came to Miss Galindo's leaving, there was a great misunderstanding between her and my lady. Miss Galindo had imagined that my lady had asked her as a favour to copy the letters, and enter the accounts, and had agreed to do the work without a notion of being paid for so doing. She had, now and then, grieved over a very profitable order for needlework passing out of her hands on account of her not having time to do it, because of her occupation at the Hall; but she had never hinted this to my lady, but gone on cheerfully at her writing as long as her clerkship was required. My lady was annoyed that she had not made her intention of paying Miss Galindo more clear, in the first conversation she had had with her; but I suppose that she had been too delicate to be very explicit with regard to money matters; and now Miss Galindo was quite hurt at my lady's wanting to pay her for what she had done in such right-down goodwill.

'No,' Miss Galindo said; 'my own dear lady, you may be as angry with me as you like, but don't offer me money. Think of six-and-twenty years ago, and poor Arthur, and as you were to me then! Besides, I wanted money – I don't disguise it – for a particular purpose; and when I found that (God bless you for asking me!) I could do you a service, I turned it over in my mind, and I gave up one plan and took up another, and it's all settled now. Bessy is to leave school and come and live with me. Don't, please, offer me money again. You don't know how glad I have been to do anything for you. Have not I, Margaret Dawson? Did you not hear me say, one day, I would cut off my hand for my lady; for am I a stock or a stone,[123] that I should forget kindness? O, I have been so glad to work for you. And now Bessy is coming here; and no one knows anything about her – as if she had done anything wrong, poor child!'

'Dear Miss Galindo,' replied my lady, 'I will never ask you to take money again. Only I thought it was quite understood between us. And, you know, you have taken money for a set of morning wrappers, before now.'

'Yes, my lady; but that was not confidential. Now I was so proud to have something to do for you confidentially.'

'But who is Bessy?' asked my lady. 'I do not understand who she is, or why she is to come and live with you. Dear Miss Galindo, you must honour me by being confidential with me in your turn!'

CHAPTER XIII.

I HAD always understood that Miss Galindo had once been in much better circumstances, but I had never liked to ask any questions respecting her. But about this time many things came out respecting her former life, which I will try and arrange; not, however, in the order in which I heard them, but rather as they occurred.

Miss Galindo was the daughter of a clergyman in Westmoreland. Her father was the younger brother of a baronet, his ancestor having been one of those of James the First's creation.[124] This baronet-uncle of Miss Galindo was one of the queer, out-of-the-way people who were bred at that time, and in that northern district of England. I never heard much of him from any one, besides this one great fact: that he had early disappeared from his family, which indeed only consisted of a brother and sister who died unmarried, and lived no one knew where, – somewhere on the Continent it was supposed, for he had never returned from the grand tour which he had been sent to make, according to the general fashion of the day, as soon as he left Oxford. He corresponded occasionally with his brother the clergyman; but the letters passed through a banker's hands; the banker being pledged to secrecy, and, as he told Mr. Galindo, having the penalty, if he broke his pledge, of losing the whole profitable business, and of having the management of the baronet's affairs taken out of his hands' without any advantage accruing to the inquirer, for Sir Lawrence had told Messrs. Graham that, in case his place of residence was revealed by them, not only would he cease to bank with them, but instantly take measures to baffle any future inquiries as to his whereabouts, by removing to some distant country.

Sir Lawrence paid a certain sum of money to his brother's account every year; but the time of this payment varied, and it was sometimes eighteen or nineteen months between the deposits; then, again, it would not be above a quarter of the time, showing that he intended it to be annual, but, as this intention was never expressed in words, it was impossible to rely upon it, and a great deal of this money was swallowed up by the necessity Mr. Galindo felt himself under of living in the large, old, rambling family mansion, which had been one of Sir Lawrence's rarely expressed desires. Mr. and Mrs. Galindo often planned to live upon their own small fortune and the income derived from the living (a vicarage, of which the great tithes went to Sir Lawrence as lay impropriator),[125] so as to put-by the payments made by the baronet, for the benefit of Laurentia – our Miss Galindo. But I suppose they found it difficult to live economically in a large house, even though they had it rent free. They had to keep up with hereditary neighbours and friends, and could hardly help doing it in the hereditary manner.

One of these neighbours, a Mr. Gibson, had a son a few years older than Laurentia. The families were sufficiently intimate for the young people to see a good deal of each other: and I was told that this young Mr. Mark Gibson was an unusually prepossessing man (he seemed to have impressed every one who spoke of him to me as being a handsome, manly, kind-hearted fellow), just what a girl would be sure to find most agreeable. The parents either forgot that their children were growing up to man's and woman's estate, or thought that the intimacy and probable attachment would be no bad thing, even if it did lead to a marriage. Still, nothing was ever said by young Gibson till later on, when it was too late, as it turned out. He went to and from Oxford; he shot and fished with Mr. Galindo, or came to the Mere to skate in winter-time; was asked to accompany Mr. Galindo to the Hall, as the latter returned to the quiet dinner with his wife and daughter; and so, and so, it went on, nobody much knew how, until one day, when Mr. Galindo received a formal letter from his brother's bankers, announcing Sir Lawrence's death, of malaria fever, at Albano, and congratulating Sir Hubert on his accession to the estates and the baronetcy. 'The king is dead – Long live the king!' as I have since heard that the French express it.

Sir Hubert and his wife were greatly surprised. Sir Lawrence was but two years older than his brother; and they had never heard of any illness till they heard of his death. They were sorry; very much shocked; but still a little elated at the succession to the baronetcy and estates. The London bankers had managed everything well. There was a large sum of ready money in their hands, at Sir Hubert's service, until he should touch his rents, the rent-roll being eight thousand a-year. And only Laurentia to inherit it all! Her mother, a poor clergyman's daughter, began to plan all sorts of fine marriages for her; nor was her father much behind his wife in his ambition. They took her up to London, when they went to buy new carriages, and dresses, and furniture. And it was then and there she made my lady's acquaintance.

How it was that they came to take a fancy to each other, I cannot say. My lady was of the old nobility, – grand, composed, gentle, and stately in her ways. Miss Galindo must always have been hurried in her manner, and her energy must have shown itself in inquisitiveness and oddness even in her youth. But I don't pretend to account for things: I only narrate them. And the fact was this: – that the elegant, fastidious Countess was attracted to the country girl, who on her part almost worshipped my lady. My lady's notice of their daughter made her parents think, I suppose, that there was no match that she might not command; she, the heiress of eight thousand a-year, and visiting about among earls and dukes. So when they came back to their old Westmoreland Hall, and Mark Gibson rode over to offer his hand

and his heart, and prospective estate of nine hundred a-year to his old companion and playfellow, Laurentia, Sir Hubert and Lady Galindo made very
short work of it. They refused him plumply themselves, and when he
begged to be allowed to speak to Laurentia, they found some excuse for
refusing him the opportunity of so doing, until they had talked to her themselves, and brought up every argument and fact in their power to convince
her – a plain girl, and conscious of her plainness – that Mr. Mark Gibson had
never thought of her in the way of marriage till after her father's accession to
his fortune; and that it was the estate – not the young lady – that he was in
love with. I suppose it will never be known in this world how far this supposition of theirs was true. My Lady Ludlow had always spoken as if it was; but
perhaps events, which came to her knowledge about this time, altered her
opinion. At any rate, the end of it was, Laurentia refused Mark, and almost
broke her heart in doing so. He discovered the suspicions of Sir Hubert and
Lady Galindo, and that they had persuaded their daughter to share in them.
So he flung off with high words, saying that they did not know a true heart
when they met with one; and that, although he had never offered till after
Sir Lawrence's death, yet that his father knew all along that he had been
attached to Laurentia, only that he, being the eldest of five children, and having as yet no profession, had had to conceal, rather than to express, an
attachment, which, in those days, he had believed was reciprocated. He had
always meant to study for the bar, and the end of all he had hoped for had
been to earn a moderate income, which he might ask Laurentia to share.
This, or something like it, was what he said. But his reference to his father
cut two ways. Old Mr. Gibson was known to be very keen about money. It
was just as likely that he would urge Mark to make love to the heiress, now
she was an heiress, as that he would have restrained him previously, as Mark
said he had done. When this was repeated to Mark, he became proudly
reserved, or sullen, and said that Laurentia, at any rate, might have known
him better. He left the country, and went up to London to study law soon
afterwards; and Sir Hubert and Lady Galindo thought they were well rid of
him. But Laurentia never ceased reproaching herself, and never did to her
dying day, as I believe. The words, 'she might have known me better,' told to
her by some kind friend or other, rankled in her mind, and were never forgotten. Her father and mother took her up to London the next year; but she
did not care to visit – dreaded going out even for a drive, lest she should see
Mark Gibson's reproachful eyes – pined and lost her health. Lady Ludlow
saw this change with regret, and was told the cause by Lady Galindo, who, of
course, gave her own version of Mark's conduct and motives. My lady never
spoke to Miss Galindo about it, but tried constantly to interest and please
her. It was at this time that my lady told Miss Galindo so much about her
own early life, and about Hanbury, that Miss Galindo resolved, if ever she

could, she would go and see the old place which her friend loved so well. The end of it all was, that she came to live there, as we know.

But a great change was to come first. Before Sir Hubert and Lady Galindo had left London on this, their second visit, they had a letter from the lawyer, whom they employed, saying that Sir Lawrence had left an heir, his legitimate child by an Italian woman of low rank; at least, legal claims to the title and property had been sent into him on the boy's behalf. Sir Lawrence had always been a man of adventurous and artistic, rather than of luxurious tastes; and it was supposed, when all came to be proved at the trial, that he was captivated by the free, beautiful life they lead in Italy, and had married this Neapolitan fisherman's daughter, who had people about her shrewd enough to see that the ceremony was legally performed. She and her husband had wandered about the shores of the Mediterranean for years, leading a happy, careless, irresponsible life, unencumbered by any duties except those connected with a rather numerous family. It was enough for her that they never wanted money, and that her husband's love was always continued to her. She hated the name of England – wicked, cold, heretic England – and avoided the mention of any subjects connected with her husband's early life. So that, when he died at Albano, she was almost roused out of her vehement grief to anger with the Italian doctor, who declared that he must write to a certain address to announce the death of Lawrence Galindo. For some time, she feared lest English barbarians might come down upon her, making a claim to the children. She hid herself and them in the Abruzzi, living upon the sale of what furniture and jewels Sir Lawrence had died possessed of. When these failed, she returned to Naples, which she had not visited since her marriage. Her father was dead; but her brother inherited some of his keenness. He interested the priests, who made inquiries and found that the Galindo succession was worth securing to an heir of the true faith. They stirred about it, obtained advice at the English Embassy; and hence that letter to the lawyers, calling upon Sir Hubert to relinquish title and property, and to refund what money he had expended. He was vehement in his opposition to this claim. He could not bear to think of his brother having married a foreigner – a papist, a fisherman's daughter; nay, of his having become a papist himself. He was in despair at the thought of his ancestral property going to the issue of such a marriage. He fought tooth and nail, making enemies of his relations, and losing almost all his own private property; for he would go on against the lawyer's advice, long after every one was convinced except himself and his wife. At last he was conquered. He gave up his living in gloomy despair. He would have changed his name if he could, so desirous was he to obliterate all tie between himself and the mongrel papist baronet and his Italian mother, and all the succession of children and nurses who came to take possession of the Hall soon after Mr. Hubert Galindo's departure, stayed[a] there one winter, and then flitted back to Naples with gladness and delight. Mr. and Mrs. Hubert Galindo lived in London. He had obtained a curacy somewhere in the city. They would have been thankful now if Mr. Mark Gibson had renewed his offer. No one could accuse him of mercenary motives if he had done so. Because he did not come forward, as they wished, they brought his silence up as a justification of what they had previously attributed to him. I don't know what Miss Galindo thought herself; but Lady Ludlow has told me how she shrank from hearing her parents abuse him. Lady Ludlow supposed that he was aware that they were living in London. His father must have known the fact, and it was curious if he had never named it to his son. Besides, the name was very uncommon; and it was unlikely that it should never come across him, in the advertisements of charity sermons which the new and rather eloquent curate of Saint Mark's East was asked to preach. All this time Lady Ludlow never lost sight of them, for Miss Galindo's sake. And when the father and mother died, it was my lady who upheld Miss Galindo in her determination not to apply for any provision to her cousin, the Italian baronet,[126] but rather to live upon the hundred a-year which had been settled on her mother and the children of his son Hubert's marriage by the old grandfather, Sir Lawrence.

Mr. Mark Gibson had risen to some eminence as a barrister on the Northern Circuit; but had died unmarried in the lifetime of his father, a victim (so people said) to intemperance. Doctor Trevor, the physician who had been called in to Mr. Gray and Harry Gregson, had married a sister of his. And that was all my lady knew about the Gibson family. But who was Bessy?

That mystery and secret came out, too, in process of time. Miss Galindo had been to Warwick, some years before I arrived at Hanbury, on some kind of business or shopping, which can only be transacted in a county town. There was an old Westmoreland connection between her and Mrs. Trevor, though I believe the latter was too young to have been made aware of her brother's offer to Miss Galindo at the time when it took place; and such affairs, if they are unsuccessful, are seldom spoken about in the gentleman's family afterwards. But the Gibsons and Galindos had been county neighbours too long for the connection not to be kept up between two members settled far away from their early homes. Miss Galindo always desired her parcels to be sent to Doctor Trevor's, when she went to Warwick for shopping purchases. If she were going any journey, and the coach did not come through Warwick as soon as she arrived (in my lady's coach or otherwise) from Hanbury, she went to Doctor Trevor's to wait. She was as much expected to sit down to the household meals as if she had been one of the family; and in after-years it was Mrs. Trevor who managed her repository business for her.

So, on the day I spoke of, she had gone to Doctor Trevor's to rest, and possibly to dine. The post in those times came in at all hours of the morning; and Doctor Trevor's letters had not arrived until after his departure on his morning round. Miss Galindo was sitting down to dinner with Mrs. Trevor and her seven children,[127] when the Doctor came in. He was flurried and uncomfortable, and hurried the children away as soon as he decently could. Then (rather feeling Miss Galindo's presence an advantage, both as a present restraint on the violence of his wife's grief, and as a consoler when he was absent on his afternoon round), he told Mrs. Trevor of her brother's death. He had been taken ill on circuit, and had hurried back to his chambers in London, only to die. She cried terribly; but Doctor Trevor said afterwards, he never noticed that Miss Galindo cared much about it one way or another. She helped him to soothe his wife, promised to stay with her all the afternoon instead of returning to Hanbury, and afterwards offered to remain with her while the Doctor went to attend the funeral. When they heard of the old love-story between the dead man and Miss Galindo, – brought up by mutual friends in Westmoreland, in the review which we are all inclined to take of the events of a man's life when he comes to die, – they tried to remember Miss Galindo's speeches and ways of going on during this visit. She was a little pale, a little silent; her eyes were sometimes swollen, and her nose red; but she was at an age when such appearances are generally attributed to a bad cold in the head, rather than to any more sentimental reason. They felt towards her as towards an old friend, a kindly, useful, eccentric old maid. She did not expect more, or wish them to remember that she might once have had other hopes, and more youthful feelings. Doctor Trevor thanked her very warmly for staying with his wife, when he returned home from London (where the funeral had taken place). He begged Miss Galindo to stay with them, when the children were gone to bed, and she was preparing to leave the husband and wife by themselves. He told her and his wife many particulars – then paused – then went on –

'And Mark has left a child – a little girl –'

'But he never was married,' exclaimed Mrs. Trevor.

'A little girl,' continued her husband, 'whose mother, I conclude, is dead. At any rate, the child was in possession of his chambers; she and an old nurse, who seemed to have the charge of everything, and has cheated poor Mark, I should fancy, not a little.'

'But the child!' asked Mrs. Trevor, still almost breathless with astonishment. 'How do you know it is his?'

'The nurse told me it was, with great appearance of indignation at my doubting it. I asked the little thing her name, and all I could get was "Bessy!" and a cry of "Me wants papa!" The nurse said the mother was dead, and she knew no more about it than that Mr. Gibson had engaged her to take care of the little girl, calling it his child. One or two of his lawyer friends, whom I met with at the funeral, told me they were aware of the existence of the child.'

'What is to be done with her?' asked Mrs. Trevor.[128]

'Nay, I don't know,' replied he. 'Mark has hardly left assets enough to pay his debts, and your father is not inclined to come forward.'

That night, as Doctor Trevor sat[a] in his study, after his wife had gone to bed, Miss Galindo knocked at his door. She and he had a long conversation. The result was that he accompanied Miss Galindo up to town the next day; that they took possession of the little Bessy, and she was brought down, and placed at nurse at a farm in the country near Warwick, Miss Galindo under-taking to pay one-half the expense, and to furnish her with clothes, and Dr. Trevor undertaking that the remaining half should be furnished by the Gibson family, or by himself in their default.

Miss Galindo was not fond of children, and I daresay she dreaded taking this child to live with her for more reasons than one. My Lady Ludlow could not endure any mention of illegitimate children. It was a principle of hers that society ought to ignore them. And I believe Miss Galindo had always agreed with her until now, when the thing came home to her womanly heart. Still she shrank from having this child of some strange woman under her roof. She went over to see it from time to time; she worked at its clothes long after every one thought she was in bed; and, when the time came for Bessy to be sent to school, Miss Galindo laboured away more diligently than ever, in order to pay the increased expense. For the Gibson family had, at first, paid their part of the compact, but with unwillingness and grudging hearts; then they had left it off altogether, and it fell hard on Doctor Trevor with his twelve children; and, latterly, Miss Galindo had taken upon herself almost all the burden. One can hardly live and labour, and plan and make sacrifices, for any human creature, without learning to love it. And Bessy loved Miss Galindo, too, for all the poor girl's scanty pleasures came from her, and Miss Galindo had always a kind word, and, latterly, many a kind caress, for Mark Gibson's child; whereas, if she went to Doctor Trevor's for her holiday, she was overlooked and neglected in that bustling family, who seemed to think that if she had comfortable board and lodging under their roof, it was enough.

I am sure, now, that Miss Galindo had often longed to have Bessy to live with her; but, as long as she could pay for her being at school, she did not like to take so bold a step as bringing her home, knowing what the effect of the consequent explanation would be on my lady. And as the girl was now more than seventeen, and past the age when young ladies are usually kept at school, and as there was no great demand for governesses in those days, and as Bessy had never been taught any trade by which to earn her own living, why I don't exactly see what could have been done but for Miss Galindo to bring her to her own home in Hanbury. For, although the child had grown up lately, in a kind of unexpected manner, into a young woman, Miss Galindo might have kept her at school for a year longer, if she could have afforded it; but this was impossible when she became Mr. Horner's clerk, and relinquished all the payment of her repository work; and perhaps, after all, she was not sorry to be compelled to take the step she was longing for. At any rate, Bessy came to live with Miss Galindo, in a very few weeks from the time when Captain James set Miss Galindo free to superintend her own domestic economy again.

For a long time, I knew nothing about this new inhabitant of Hanbury. My lady never mentioned her in any way. This was in accordance with Lady Ludlow's well-known principles. She neither saw nor heard, nor was in any way cognisant of the existence of those who had no legal right to exist at all. If Miss Galindo had hoped to have an exception made in Bessy's favour, she was mistaken. My lady sent a note inviting Miss Galindo herself to tea one evening, about a month after Bessy came; but Miss Galindo 'had a cold and could not come.' The next time she was invited, she 'had an engagement at home' – a step nearer to the absolute truth. And the third time, she 'had a young friend staying with her whom she was unable to leave.' My lady accepted every excuse as bonâ fide, and took no further notice. I missed Miss Galindo very much; we all did; for, in the days when she was clerk, she was sure to come in and find the opportunity of saying something amusing to some of us before she went away. And I, as an invalid, or perhaps from natural tendency, was particularly fond of little bits of village gossip. There was no Mr. Horner – he even had come in, now and then, with formal, stately pieces of intelligence – and there was no Miss Galindo, in these days. I missed her much. And so did my lady, I am sure. Behind all her quiet, sedate manner, I am certain her heart ached sometimes for a few words from Miss Galindo, who seemed to have absented herself altogether from the Hall now Bessy was come.

Captain James might be very sensible, and all that; but not even my lady could call him a substitute for the old familiar friends. He was a thorough sailor, as sailors were in those days – swore a good deal, drank a good deal (without its ever affecting him in the least), and was very prompt and kindhearted in all his actions; but he was not accustomed to women, as my lady once said, and would judge in all things for himself. My lady had expected, I think, to find some one who would take his notions on the management of her estate from her ladyship's own self; but he spoke as if he were responsible for the good management of the whole, and must, consequently, be allowed full liberty of action. He had been too long in command over men at sea to like to be directed by a woman in anything he undertook, even though that woman was my lady. I suppose this was the common-sense my lady spoke of; but when common-sense goes against us, I don't think we value it quite so much as we ought to do.

Lady Ludlow was proud of her personal superintendence of her own estate. She liked to tell us how her father used to take her with him in his rides, and bid her observe this and that, and on no account to allow such and such things to be done. But I have heard that the first time she told all this to Captain James, he told her point-blank that he had heard from Mr. Smithson that the farms were much neglected and the rents sadly behind-hand, and that he meant to set to in good earnest and study agriculture, and see how he could remedy the state of things. My lady would, I am sure, be greatly surprised, but what could she do? Here was the very man she had chosen herself, setting to with all his energy to conquer the defect of ignorance, which was all that those who had presumed to offer her ladyship advice had ever had to say against him. Captain James read Arthur Young's 'Tours'[129a] in all his spare time, as long as he was an invalid; and shook his head at my lady's accounts as to how the land had been cropped or left fallow from time immemorial. Then he set to, and tried too many new experiments at once. My lady looked on in dignified silence; but all the farmers and tenants were in an uproar, and prophesied a hundred failures. Perhaps fifty did occur; they were only half as many as Lady Ludlow had feared; but they were twice as many, four, eight times as many as the captain had anticipated. His openly-expressed disappointment made him popular again. The rough country people could not have understood silent and dignified regret at the failure of his plans; but they sympathised with a man who swore at his ill success – sympathised, even while they chuckled over his discomfiture. Mr. Brooke, the retired tradesman, did not cease blaming him for not succeeding, and for swearing. 'But what could you expect from a sailor?' Mr. Brooke asked, even in my lady's hearing; though he might have known Captain James was my lady's own personal choice, from the old friendship Mr. Urian had always shown for him. I think it was this speech of the Birmingham baker's that made my lady determine to stand by Captain James, and encourage him to try again. For she would not allow that her choice had been an unwise one, at the bidding (as it were) of a Dissenting tradesman; the only person in the neighbourhood, too, who had flaunted about in coloured clothes, when all the world was in mourning for my lady's only son.

Captain James would have thrown the agency up at once, if my lady had not felt herself bound to justify the wisdom of her choice, by urging him to stay. He was much touched by her confidence in him, and swore a great oath, that the next year he would make the land such as it had never been before for produce. It was not my lady's way to repeat anything she had heard, especially to another person's disadvantage. So I don't think she ever told Captain James of Mr. Brooke's speech about a sailor's being likely to mismanage the property; and the captain was too anxious to succeed in this, the second year of his trial, to be above going to the flourishing, shrewd Mr. Brooke, and asking for his advice as to the best method of working the estate. I dare say, if Miss Galindo had been as intimate as formerly at the Hall, we should all of us have heard of this new acquaintance of the agent's long before we did. As it was, I am sure my lady never dreamed that the captain, who held opinions that were even more Church and King than her own, could ever have made friends with a Baptist baker from Birmingham, even to serve her ladyship's own interests in the most loyal manner.

We heard of it first from Mr. Gray, who came now often to see my lady, for neither he nor she could forget the solemn tie which the fact of his being the person to acquaint her with my lord's death had created between them. For true and holy words spoken at that time, though having no reference to aught below the solemn subjects of life and death, had made her withdraw her opposition to Mr. Gray's wish about establishing a village school. She had sighed a little, it is true, and was even yet more apprehensive than hopeful as to the result; but, almost as if as a memorial to my lord, she had allowed a kind of rough schoolhouse to be built on the green, just by the church; and had gently used the power she undoubtedly had, in expressing her strong wish that the boys might only be taught to read and write, and the first four rules of arithmetic;[130] while the girls were only to learn to read, and to add up in their heads, and the rest of the time to work at mending their own clothes, knitting stockings and spinning. My lady presented the school with more spinning-wheels than there were girls, and requested that there might be a rule that they should have spun so many hanks of flax, and knitted so many pairs of stockings, before they ever were taught to read at all. After all, it was but making the best of a bad job with my poor lady – but life was not what it had been to her. I remember well the day that Mr. Gray pulled some delicately fine yarn (and I was a good judge of those things) out of his pocket, and laid it and a capital pair of knitted stockings before my lady, as the first-fruits, so to say, of his school. I recollect seeing her put on her spectacles, and carefully examine both productions. Then she passed them to me.

'This is well, Mr. Gray. I am much pleased. You are fortunate in your schoolmistress. She has had both proper knowledge of womanly things and much patience. Who is she? One out of our village?'

'My lady,' said Mr. Gray, stammering and colouring in his old fashion, 'Miss Bessy is so very kind as to teach all those sorts of things – Miss Bessy, and Miss Galindo, sometimes.'

My lady looked at him over her spectacles: but she only repeated the words 'Miss Bessy,' and paused, as if trying to remember who such a person could be; and he, if he had then intended to say more, was quelled by her manner, and dropped the subject. He went on to say, that he had thought it his duty to decline the subscription to his school offered by Mr. Brooke, because he was a Dissenter; that he (Mr. Gray) feared that Captain James, through whom Mr. Brooke's offer of money had been made, was offended at his refusing to accept it from a man who held heterodox opinions; nay, whom Mr. Gray suspected of being infected by Dodwell's heresy.[131]

'I think there must be some mistake,' said my lady, 'or I have misunderstood you. Captain James would never be sufficiently with a schismatic to be employed by that man Brooke in distributing his charities. I should have doubted, until now, if Captain James knew him.'

'Indeed, my lady, he not only knows him, but is intimate with him, I regret to say. I have repeatedly seen the captain and Mr. Brooke walking together; going through the fields together; and people do say –'

My lady looked up in interrogation at Mr. Gray's pause.

'I disapprove of gossip, and it may be untrue; but people do say that Captain James is very attentive to Miss Brooke.'

'Impossible!' said my lady, indignantly. 'Captain James is a loyal and religious man. I beg your pardon, Mr. Gray, but it is impossible.'

CHAPTER XIV.

LIKE many other things which have been declared to be impossible, this report of Captain James being attentive to Miss Brooke turned out to be very true.

The mere idea of her agent being on the slightest possible terms of acquaintance with the Dissenter, the tradesman, the Birmingham democrat, who had come to settle in our good, orthodox, aristocratic, and agricultural Hanbury, made my lady very uneasy. Miss Galindo's misdemeanor in having taken Miss Bessy to live with her, faded into a mistake, a mere error of judgment, in comparison with Captain James's intimacy at Yeast House, as the Brookes called their ugly square-built farm. My lady talked herself quite into complacency with Miss Galindo, and even Miss Bessy was named by her, the first time I had ever been aware that my lady recognised her existence; but – I recollect it was a long rainy afternoon, and I sat[a] with her ladyship, and we had time and opportunity for a long uninterrupted talk – whenever we had been silent for a little while, she began again, with something like a wonder how it was that Captain James could ever have commenced an acquaintance with 'that man Brooke.' My lady recapitulated all the times she could remember, that anything had occurred, or been said by Captain James which she could now understand as throwing light upon the subject.

'He said once that he was anxious to bring in the Norfolk system of cropping,[132] and spoke a good deal about Mr. Coke of Holkham (who, by the way, was no more a Coke than I am –[133] collateral in the female line – which counts for little or nothing among the great old commoners' families of pure blood), and his new ways of cultivation; of course new men bring in new ways, but it does not follow that either are better than the old ways. However, Captain James has been very anxious to try turnips and bone manure, and he really is a man of such good sense and energy, and was so sorry last year about the failure, that I consented; and now I begin to see my error. I have always heard that town bakers adulterate their flour with bone-dust; and, of course, Captain James would be aware of this, and go to Brooke to inquire where the article was to be purchased.'

My lady always ignored the fact which had sometimes, I suspect, been brought under her very eyes during her drives, that Mr. Brooke's few fields were in a state of far higher cultivation than her own; so she could not, of course, perceive that there was any wisdom to be gained from asking the advice of the tradesman turned farmer.

But by-and-by this fact of her agent's intimacy with the person whom in the whole world she most disliked (with that sort of dislike in which a large amount of uncomfortableness is combined – the dislike which conscientious people sometimes feel to another without knowing why, and yet which they cannot indulge in with comfort to themselves without having a moral reason why), came before my lady in many shapes. For, indeed, I am sure that Captain James was not a man to conceal or be ashamed of one of his actions. I cannot fancy his ever lowering his strong loud clear voice, or having a confidential conversation with any one. When his crops had failed, all the village had known it. He complained, he regretted, he was angry, or owned himself a — fool, all down the village street; and the consequence was that, although he was a far more passionate man than Mr. Horner, all the tenants liked him far better. People, in general, take a kindlier interest in any one, the workings of whose mind and heart they can watch and understand, than in a man who only lets you know what he has been thinking about and feeling, by what he does. But Harry Gregson was faithful to the memory of Mr. Horner. Miss Galindo has told me that she used to watch him hobble out of the way of Captain James, as if to accept his notice, however good-naturedly given, would have been a kind of treachery to his former benefactor. But Gregson (the father) and the new agent rather took to each other; and one day, much to my surprise, I heard that the 'poaching, tinkering vagabond,' as people used to call Gregson when I first had come to live at Hanbury, had been appointed gamekeeper; Mr. Gray standing godfather, as it were, to his trustworthiness, if he were trusted with anything; which I thought at the time was rather an experiment, only it answered, as many of Mr. Gray's deeds of daring did. It was curious how he was growing to be a kind of autocrat in the village; and how unconscious he was of it. He was as shy and awkward and nervous as ever in any affair that was not of some moral consequence to him. But as soon as he was convinced that a thing was right, he 'shut his eyes and ran and butted at it like a ram,' as Captain James once expressed it, in talking over something Mr. Gray had done. People in the village said, 'they never knew what the parson would be at next;' or they might have said 'where his reverence would next turn up.'

For I have heard of his marching right into the middle of a set of poachers, gathered together for some desperate midnight enterprise, or walking into a public-house that lay just beyond the bounds of my lady's estate, and in that extra-parochial piece of ground I named long ago, and which was considered the rendezvous of all the ne'er-do-weel characters for miles round, and where a parson and a constable were held in much the same kind of esteem, as unwelcome visitors. And yet Mr. Gray had his long fits of depression, in which he felt as if he were doing nothing, making no way in his work, useless and unprofitable, and better out of the world than in it. In comparison with the work he had set himself to do, what he did seemed to be nothing. I suppose it was constitutional, those attacks of lowness of spirits which he had about this time; perhaps a part of the nervousness which made him always so awkward when he came to the Hall. Even Mrs. Medlicott, who almost worshipped the ground he trod on, as the saying is, owned that Mr. Gray never entered one of my lady's rooms without knocking down something, and too often breaking it. He would much sooner have faced a desperate poacher than a young lady any day. At least so we thought.

I do not know how it was that it came to pass that my lady became reconciled to Miss Galindo about this time. Whether it was that her ladyship was weary of the unspoken coolness with her old friend; or that the specimens of delicate sewing and fine spinning at the school had mollified her towards Miss Bessy; but I was surprised to learn one day that Miss Galindo and her young friend were coming that very evening to tea at the Hall. This information was given me by Mrs. Medlicott, as a message from my lady, who further went on to desire that certain little preparations should be made in her own private sitting-room, in which the greater part of my days were spent. From the nature of these preparations, I became quite aware that my lady intended to do honour to her expected visitors. Indeed Lady Ludlow never forgave by halves, as I have known some people do. Whoever was coming as a visitor to my lady, peeress, or poor nameless girl, there was a certain amount of preparation required, in order to do them fitting honour. I do not mean to say that the preparation was of the same degree of importance in each case. I dare say, if a peeress had come to visit us at the Hall, the covers would have been taken off the furniture in the white drawing-room (they never were uncovered all the time I stayed at the Hall), because my lady would wish to offer her the ornaments and luxuries which this grand visitor (who never came – I wish she had! I did so want to see that furniture uncovered!) was accustomed to at home, and to present them to her in the best order in which my lady could. The same rule, modified, held good with Miss Galindo. Certain things, in which my lady knew she took an interest, were laid out ready for her to examine on this very day; and, what was more, great books of prints were laid out, such as I remembered my lady had had brought forth to beguile my own early days of illness, – Mr. Hogarth's works, and the like, – which I was sure were put out for Miss Bessy.

No one knows how curious I was to see this mysterious Miss Bessy – twenty times more mysterious, of course, for want of her surname. And then again (to try and account for my great curiosity, of which in recollection I am more than half ashamed), I had been leading the quiet monotonous life of a crippled invalid for many[a] years, – shut up from any sight of new faces;

and this was to be the face of one whom I had thought about so much and so long, – Oh! I think I might be excused.

Of course, they drank tea in the great hall, with the four young gentle-women, who, with myself, formed the small bevy now under her ladyship's charge. Of those who were at Hanbury when first I came, none remained; all were married, or gone once more to live at some home which could be called their own, whether the ostensible head were father or brother. I myself was not without some hopes of a similar kind. My brother Harry was now a curate in Westmoreland, and wanted me to go and live with him, as eventually I did for a time. But that is neither here nor there at present. What I am talking about is Miss Bessy.

After a reasonable time had elapsed, occupied as I well knew by the meal in the great hall, – the measured, yet agreeable conversation afterwards, – and a certain promenade around the hall, and through the drawing-rooms, with pauses before different pictures, the history or subject of each of which was invariably told by my lady to every new visitor, – a sort of giving them the freedom of the old family-seat, by describing the kind and nature of the great progenitors who had lived there before the narrator, – I heard the steps approaching my lady's room where I lay. I think I was in such a state of nerv-ous expectation, that if I could have moved easily, I should have got up and run away. And yet I need not have been, for Miss Galindo was not in the least altered (her nose a little redder, to be sure, but then that might only have had a temporary cause in the private crying I know she would have had before coming to see her dear Lady Ludlow once again.) But I could almost have pushed Miss Galindo away, as she intercepted me in my view of the mysterious Miss Bessy.

Miss Bessy was, as I knew, only about eighteen, but she looked older. Dark hair, dark eyes, a tall, firm figure, a good, sensible face, with a serene expression, not in the least disturbed by what I had been thinking must be such awful circumstances as a first introduction to my lady, who had so dis-approved of her very existence: those are the clearest impressions I remember of my first interview with Miss Bessy. She seemed to observe us all, in her quiet manner, quite as much as I did her; but she spoke very little; occupied herself, indeed, as my lady had planned, with looking over the great books of engravings. I think I must have (foolishly) intended to make her feel at her ease, by my patronage; but she was seated far away from my sofa, in order to command the light, and really seemed so unconcerned at her unwonted circumstances, that she did not need my countenance or kindness. One thing I did like – her watchful look at Miss Galindo from time to time: it showed that her thoughts and sympathy were ever at Miss Galindo's service, as indeed they well might be. When Miss Bessy spoke, her voice was full and clear, and what she said, to the purpose, though there was a slight provincial accent in her way of speaking. After a while, my lady set us

two to play at chess, a game which I had lately learnt at Mr. Gray's suggestion. Still we did not talk much together, though we were becoming
attracted towards each other, I fancy.

'You will play well,' said she. 'You have only learnt about six months, have
you? And yet you can nearly beat me, who have been at it as many years.'

'I began to learn last November. I remember Mr. Gray's bringing me
"Philidor on Chess,"[134a] one very foggy, dismal day.'

What made her look up so suddenly, with bright inquiry in her eyes?
What made her silent for a moment, as if in thought, and then go on with
something, I know not what, in quite an altered tone?

My lady and Miss Galindo went on talking, while I sat thinking. I heard
Captain James's name mentioned pretty frequently; and at last my lady put
down her work, and said, almost with tears in her eyes:

'I could not – I cannot believe it. He must be aware she is a schismatic; a
baker's daughter; and he is a gentleman by virtue and feeling, as well as by
his profession, though his manners may be at times a little rough. My dear
Miss Galindo, what will this world come to?'

Miss Galindo might possibly be aware of her own share in bringing the
world to the pass which now dismayed my lady, – for, of course, though all
was now over and forgiven, yet Miss Bessy's being received into a respectable maiden lady's house, was one of the portents as to the world's future
which alarmed her ladyship; and Miss Galindo knew this, – but, at any rate,
she had too lately been forgiven herself not to plead for mercy for the next
offender against my lady's delicate sense of fitness and propriety, – so she
replied:

'Indeed, my lady, I have long left off trying to conjecture what makes Jack
fancy Gill, or Gill Jack.[135] It's best to sit down quiet under the belief that
marriages are made for us, somewhere out of this world, and out of the
range of this world's reasons and laws. I'm not so sure that I should settle it
down that they were made in Heaven; t'other place seems to me as likely a
workshop; but, at any rate, I've given up troubling my head as to why they
take place. Captain James is a gentleman; I make no doubt of that ever since
I saw him stop to pick up old Goody Blake (when she tumbled down on the
slide last winter) and then swear at a little lad who was laughing at her, and
cuff him till he tumbled down crying; but we must have bread somehow,
and though I like it better baked at home in a good sweet brick oven, yet, as
some folks never can get it to rise, I don't see why a man may not be a baker.
You see, my lady, I look upon baking as a simple trade, and as such lawful.
There is no machine comes in to take away a man's or woman's power of
earning their living, like the spinning-jenny[136] (the old busybody that she
is), to knock up all our good old women's livelihood, and send them to their
graves before their time. There's an invention of the enemy, if you will!'

'That's very true!' said my lady, shaking her head.

'But baking bread is wholesome, straight-forward elbow-work. They have not got to inventing any contrivance for that yet, thank Heaven! It does not seem to me natural, nor according to Scripture, that iron and steel (whose brows can't sweat) should be made to do man's work. And so I say, all those trades where iron and steel do the work ordained to man at the Fall, are unlawful, and I never stand up for them. But say this baker Brooke did knead his bread, and make it rise, and then that people, who had, perhaps, no good ovens, came to him, and bought his good light bread, and in this manner he turned an honest penny, and got rich; why, all I say, my lady, is this, – I dare say he would have been born a Hanbury, or a lord, if he could; and if he was not, it is no fault of his, that I can see, that he made good bread (being a baker by trade), and got money, and bought his land. It was his misfortune, not his fault, that he was not a person of quality by birth.'

'That's very true,' said my lady, after a moment's pause for consideration. 'But, although he was a baker, he might have been a Churchman. Even your eloquence, Miss Galindo, shan't convince me that that is not his own fault.'

'I don't see even that, begging your pardon, my lady,' said Miss Galindo, emboldened by the first success of her eloquence. 'When a Baptist is a baby, if I understand their creed aright, he is not baptized;[a] and, consequently, he can have no godfathers and godmothers to do anything for him in his baptism; you agree to that, my lady?'

My lady would rather have known what her acquiescence would lead to, before acknowledging that she could not dissent from this first proposition; still she gave her tacit agreement by bowing her head.

'And, you know, our godfathers and godmothers are expected to promise and vow three things in our name, when we are little babies, and can do nothing but squall for ourselves. It is a great privilege, but don't let us be hard upon those who have not had the chance of godfathers and godmothers. Some people, we know, are born with silver spoons, – that's to say, a godfather to give one things, and teach one one's catechism, and see that we're confirmed into good church-going Christians, – and others with wooden ladles in their mouths. These poor last folks must just be content to be godfatherless orphans, and Dissenters,[b] all their lives: and if they are tradespeople into the bargain, so much the worse for them; but let us be humble Christians, my dear lady, and not hold our heads too high because we were born orthodox quality.'

'You go on too fast, Miss Galindo! I can't follow you. Besides, I do believe dissent to be an invention of the Devil's. Why can't they believe as we do? It's very wrong. Besides, it's schism and heresy, and, you know, the Bible says that's as bad as witchcraft.'

My lady was not convinced, as I could see. After Miss Galindo had gone, she sent Mrs. Medlicott for certain books out of the great old library up stairs, and had them made up into a parcel under her own eye.

'If Captain James comes to-morrow, I will speak to him about these Brookes. I have not hitherto liked to speak to him, because I did not wish to hurt him, by supposing there could be any truth in the reports about his intimacy with them. But now I will try and do my duty by him and them. Surely, this great body of divinity will bring them back to the true church.'

I could not tell, for though my lady read me over the titles, I was not any the wiser as to their contents. Besides, I was much more anxious to consult my lady as to my own change of place. I showed her the letter I had that day received from Harry; and we once more talked over the expediency of my going to live with him, and trying what entire change of air would do to re-establish my failing health. I could say anything to my lady, she was so sure to understand me rightly. For one thing, she never thought of herself, so I had no fear of hurting her by stating the truth. I told her how happy my years had been while passed under her roof; but that now I had begun to wonder whether I had not duties elsewhere, in making a home for Harry, – and whether the fulfilment of these duties, quiet ones they must needs be in the case of such a cripple as myself, would not prevent my sinking into the querulous habit of thinking and talking into which I found myself occasion-ally falling. Add to which, there was the prospect of benefit from the more bracing air of the north.

It was then settled that my departure from Hanbury, my happy home for so long, was to take place before many weeks had passed. And as, when one period of life is about to be shut up for ever, we are sure to look back upon it with fond regret, so I, happy enough in my future prospects, could not avoid recurring to all the days of my life in the Hall, from the time when I came to it, a shy, awkward girl, scarcely past childhood, to now, when a grown woman, – past childhood – almost, from the very character of my illness, past youth, – I was looking forward to leaving my lady's house (as a resi-dence) for ever. As it has turned out, I never saw either her or it again. Like a piece of sea-wrack,[137] I have drifted away from those days: quiet, happy, eventless days, very happy to remember!

I thought of good, jovial Mr. Mountford, – and his regrets that he might not keep a pack, 'a very small pack,' of harriers, and his merry ways, and his love of good eating; of the first coming of Mr. Gray, and my lady's attempt to quench his sermons, when they tended to enforce any duty connected with education. And now we had an absolute school-house in the village; and since Miss Bessy's drinking tea at the Hall, my lady had been twice inside it, to give directions about some fine yarn she was having spun for table-napery. And her ladyship had so outgrown her old custom of dispensing with ser-mon or discourse, that even during the temporary preaching of Mr. Crosse, she had never had recourse to it, though I believe she would have had all the congregation on her side if she had.

And Mr. Horner was dead, and Captain James reigned in his stead. Good, steady, severe, silent Mr. Horner! with his clock-like regularity, and his snuff-coloured clothes, and silver buckles! I have often wondered which one misses most when they are dead and gone, – the bright creatures full of life, who are hither and thither and everywhere, so that no one can reckon upon their coming and going, with whom stillness and the long quiet of the grave seems utterly irreconcilable, so full are they of vivid motion and passion, – or the slow, serious people, whose movements – nay, whose very words, seem to go by clock-work; who never appear much to affect the course of our life while they are with us, but whose methodical ways show themselves, when they are gone, to have been intertwined with our very roots of daily existence. I think I miss these last the most, although I may have loved the former best. Captain James never was to me what Mr. Horner was, though the latter had hardly changed a dozen words with me at the day of his death. Then Miss Galindo! I remembered the time, as if it had been only yesterday, when she was but a name – and a very odd one – to me; then she was a queer, abrupt, disagreeable, busy old maid. Now I loved her dearly, and I found out that I was almost jealous of Miss Bessy.

Mr. Gray I never thought of with love; the feeling was almost reverence with which I looked upon him. I have not wished to speak much of myself, or else I could have told you how much he had been to me during these long, weary years of illness. But he was almost as much to every one, rich and poor, from my lady down to Miss Galindo's Sally.

The village, too, had a different look about it. I am sure I could not tell you what caused the change; but there were no more lounging young men to form a group at the cross-road, at a time of day when young men ought to be at work. I don't say this was all Mr. Gray's doing, for there really was so much to do in the fields that there was but little time for lounging now-a days. And the children were hushed up in school, and better behaved out of it, too, than in the days when I used to be able to go my lady's errands in the village. I went so little about now, that I am sure I can't tell who Miss Galindo found to scold; and yet she looked so well and so happy that I think she must have had her accustomed portion of that wholesome exercise.

Before I left Hanbury, the rumour that Captain James was going to marry Miss Brooke, Baker Brooke's eldest daughter, who had only a sister to share his property with her,[a] was confirmed. He himself announced it to my lady; nay, more, with a courage, gained, I suppose, in his former profession, where, as I have heard, he had led his ship into many a post of danger, he asked her ladyship, the Countess Ludlow, if he might bring his bride elect (the Baptist baker's daughter!) and present her to my lady!

I am glad I was not present when he made this request; I should have felt so much ashamed for him, and I could not have helped being anxious till I heard my lady's answer, if I had been there. Of course she acceded; but I can fancy the grave surprise of her look. I wonder if Captain James noticed it.

I hardly dared ask my lady, after the interview had taken place, what she thought of the bride elect; but I hinted my curiosity, and she told me, that if the young person had applied to Mrs. Medlicott, for the situation of cook, and Mrs. Medlicott had engaged her, she thought that it would have been a very suitable arrangement. I understood from this how little she thought a marriage with Captain James, R.N., suitable.

About a year after I left Hanbury, I received a letter from Miss Galindo, I think I can find it. – Yes, this is it.[a]

'Hanbury, May 4, 1811.

'DEAR MARGARET,

'You ask for news of us all. Don't you know there is no news in Hanbury? Did you ever hear of an event here? Now, if you have answered "Yes," in your own mind to these questions, you have fallen into my trap, and never were more mistaken in your life. Hanbury is full of news; and we have more events on our hands than we know what to do with. I will take them in the order of the newspapers – births, deaths, and marriages. In the matter of births, Jenny Lucas has had twins not a week ago. Sadly too much of a good thing, you'll say. Very true: but then they died; so their birth did not much signify. My cat has kittened, too; she has had three kittens, which again you may observe is too much of a good thing; and so it would be, if it were not for the next item of intelligence I shall lay before you. Captain and Mrs. James have taken the old house next Pearson's; and the house is overrun with mice, which is just as fortunate for me as the King of Egypt's rat-ridden kingdom was to Dick Whittington. For my cat's kittening decided me to go and call on the bride,[138] in hopes she wanted a cat; which she did, like a sensible woman, as I do believe she is, in spite of Baptism, Bakers, Bread, and Birmingham, and something worse than all, which you shall hear about, if you'll only be patient. As I had got my best bonnet on – the one I bought when poor Lord Ludlow was last at Hanbury in '99 – I thought it a great condescension in myself (always remembering the date of the Galindo Baronetcy) to go and call on the bride; though I don't think so much of myself in my every-day clothes, as you know. But who should I find there but my Lady Ludlow! She looks as frail and delicate as ever, but is, I think, in better heart ever since that old city merchant of a Hanbury[139] took it into his head that he was a cadet of the Hanburys of Hanbury, and left her that handsome legacy. I'll warrant you the mortgage was paid off pretty fast; and Mr. Horner's money – or my lady's money, or Harry Gregson's money, call it which you will, – is invested in his name, all right and tight, and they do talk of his being captain of his school, or Grecian,[140] or something, and going to college, after all! Harry Gregson the poacher's son! Well! to be sure, we are living in strange times!

'But I have not done with the marriages yet. Captain James's is all very well, but no one cares for it now, we are all so full of Mr. Gray's. Yes, indeed, Mr. Gray is going to be married, and to nobody else but my little Bessy! I tell her she will have to nurse him half the days of her life, he is such a frail little body.

But she says she does not care for that, so that his body holds his soul, it is enough for her. She has a good spirit, and a brave heart, has my Bessy! It is a great advantage that she won't have to mark her clothes over again; for when she had knitted herself her last set of stockings, I told her to put G for Galindo, if she did not choose to put it for Gibson, for she should be my child if she was no one else's. And now, you see, it stands for Gray. So there are two marriages, and what more would you have? And she promises to take another of my kittens.

'Now,[a] as to deaths, old Farmer Hale is dead – poor old man, I should think his wife thought it a good riddance, for he beat her every day that he was drunk, and he never was sober, in spite of Mr. Gray. I don't think (as I tell him) that Mr. Gray would ever have found courage to speak to Bessy as long as Farmer Hale lived, he took the old gentleman's sins so much to heart, and seemed to think it was all his fault for not being able to make a sinner into a saint. The parish bull is dead too. I never was so glad in my life. But they say we are to have a new one in his place. In the meantime I cross the common in peace, which is convenient just now, when I have so often to go to Mr. Gray's to see about furnishing.

'Now you think I have told you all the Hanbury news, don't you? Not so. The very[b] greatest thing of all is to come. I won't tantalize[c] you, but just out with it, for you would never guess it. My Lady Ludlow has given a party, just like any plebeian amongst us. We had tea and toast in the blue drawing-room, old John Footman waiting, with Tom Diggles, the lad that used to frighten away crows in Farmer Hale's fields, following in my lady's livery, hair powdered[141] and everything. Mrs. Medlicott made tea in my lady's own room. My lady looked like a splendid fairy queen of mature age, in black velvet, and the old lace, which I have never seen her wear before since my lord's death. But the company?[d] you'll say. Why we had the parson of Clover, and the parson of Headleigh, and the parson of Merribank, and the three parsonesses; and Farmer Donkin and two Miss Donkins; and Mr. Gray (of course), and myself and Bessy; and Captain and Mrs. James; yes, and Mr. and Mrs. Brooke: think of that! I am not so sure the parsons liked it; but he was there. For he has been helping Captain James to get my lady's land into order; and then his daughter married the agent; and Mr. Gray (who ought to know) says, after all, Baptists are not such bad people; and he was right against them at one time, as you may remember. Mrs. Brooke is a rough diamond, to be sure. People have said that of me, I know. But, being a Galindo, I learnt manners in my youth, and can take them up when I choose. But Mrs. Brooke never learnt manners, I'll be bound. When John Footman handed her the tray with the tea-cups, she looked up at him as if she were sorely puzzled by that way of going on. I was sitting next to her, so I pretended not to see her perplexity, and put her cream and sugar in for her, and was all ready to pop it into her hands, – when who should come up, but that impudent lad Tom Diggles (I call him lad, for all his hair is powdered, for you know that it is not natural grey hair), with his tray full of cakes and what not, all as good as Mrs. Medlicott could make them. By this time, I should tell you, all the parsonesses were looking at Mrs. Brooke, for she had shown her want of breeding before; and the parsonesses, who were just a step above her in manners, were very much inclined to smile at her doings and sayings. Well! what does she do but pull out a clean Bandanna[142] pocket-hand-kerchief, all red and yellow silk, and spread it over her best silk gown; it was, like enough, a new one, for I had it from Sally, who had it from her cousin Molly, who is dairy-woman at the Brookes', that the Brookes were mighty set-up with an invitation to drink tea at the Hall. There we were, Tom Diggles even on the grin (I wonder how long it is since he was own brother to a scare-crow, only not so decently dressed) and Mrs. Parsoness of Headleigh, – I forget her name, and it's no matter, for she's an ill-bred creature, I hope Bessy will behave herself better, – was right-down bursting with laughter, and as near a hee-haw as ever a donkey was, when what does my lady do? Ay![a] there's my own dear Lady Ludlow, God bless her! She takes out her own pocket-handker-chief, all snowy cambric, and lays it softly down on her velvet lap, for all the world as if she did it every day of her life, just like Mrs. Brooke, the baker's wife; and when the one got up to shake the crumbs into the fire-place, the other did just the same. But with such a grace! and such a look at us all! Tom Diggles went red all over; and Mrs. Parsoness of Headleigh scarce spoke for the rest of the evening; and the tears came into my old silly eyes; and Mr. Gray, who was before silent and awkward, in a way which I tell Bessy she must cure him of, was made so happy by this pretty action of my lady's, that he talked away all the rest of the evening, and was the life of the company.

'Oh! Margaret Dawson, I sometimes wonder if you're the better off for leaving us. To be sure, you're with your brother, and blood is blood. But when I look at my lady and Mr. Gray, for all they're so different, I would not change places with any in England.'

Alas! alas! I never saw my dear lady again. She died in eighteen hundred and fourteen, and Mr. Gray did not long survive her. As I dare say you know the Reverend Henry Gregson[143] is now vicar of Hanbury, and his wife is the daughter of Mr. Gray and Miss Bessy.

As any one may guess, it had taken Mrs. Dawson several Monday eve-nings to narrate all this history of the days of her youth. Miss Duncan thought it would be a good exercise for me, both in memory and composi-tion, to write out on Tuesday mornings all that I had heard the night before; and thus it came to pass that I have the manuscript of 'My Lady Ludlow' now lying by me.

END OF VOL. I.

LONDON : PRINTED BY WILLIAM CLOWES AND SONS, STAMFORD STREET.

ROUND THE SOFA.

MR. DAWSON had often come in and out of the room during the time that his sister had been telling us about Lady Ludlow. He would stop, and listen a little, and smile or sigh as the case might be. The Monday after the dear old lady had wound up her tale (if tale it could be called), we felt rather at a loss what to talk about, we had grown so accustomed to listen to Mrs. Dawson. I remember I was saying, 'Oh, dear! I wish some one would tell us another story!' when her brother said, as if in answer to my speech, that he had drawn up a paper all ready for the Philosophical Society, and that perhaps we might care to hear it before it was sent off: it was in a great measure compiled from a French book, published by one of the Academies,[1] and rather dry in itself; but to which Mr. Dawson's attention had been directed, after a tour he had made in England during the past year, in which he had noticed small walled-up doors in unusual parts of some old parish churches, and had been told that they had formerly been appropriated to the use of some half-heathen race, who, before the days of gipsies, held the same outcast parish position in most of the countries of western Europe. Mr. Dawson had been recommended to the French book which he named, as containing the fullest and most authentic account of this mysterious race, the Cagots. I did not think I should like hearing this paper as much as a story; but, of course, as he meant it kindly, we were bound to submit, and I found it, on the whole, more interesting than I anticipated.

'AN ACCURSED RACE'

'An Accursed Race' was first published in *Household Words*, 12 (25 August 1855), pp. 73–80. It was reprinted in *Round the Sofa*, 2 vols (London: Sampson Low, 1859), vol. ii, pp. 1–30. The differences between the two texts are not numerous but there are some corrections of punctuation and phrasing. It was also reprinted in *My Lady Ludlow and Other Tales* (1861).

On the contents page of volume ii of *Round the Sofa* the title appears as 'The Accursed Race'. Thereafter at the opening of the story (p. 3) and in the running title it is 'An Accursed Race', as it is throughout *HW*.

Though it belongs properly to the non-fiction volume it is included here to preserve the arrangement of *Round the Sofa* made by EG. Like most of her non-fiction articles, it has not been extensively discussed by her critics, but Julian Wolfreys, *Being English*, pp. 84–7, has an interesting passage on its relation to the unity and diversity of the *Round the Sofa* collection. The extent of EG's debt to Francisque Michel, *Histoire des races maudites de la France et de l'Espagne* (1847), of which the story is basically a précis, is recorded in the explanatory notes below.

AN ACCURSED RACE.

———•———

WE have our prejudices in England. Or, if that assertion offends any of my
readers, I will modify it: we[a] have had our prejudices in England. We have
tortured Jews; we have burnt Catholics and Protestants, to say nothing of a
few witches and wizards. We have satirised Puritans, and we have dressed-up
Guys.[1] But, after all, I do not think we have been so bad as our Continental
friends. To be sure, our insular position has kept us free, to a certain degree,
from the inroads of alien races; who, driven from one land of refuge, steal
into another equally unwilling to receive them; and where, for long centuries, their presence is barely endured, and no pains is taken to conceal the
repugnance which the natives of 'pure blood' experience towards them.

There yet remains a remnant of the miserable people called Cagots in the
valleys of the Pyrenees; in the Landes near Bourdeaux; and, stretching up on
the west side of France, their numbers become larger in Lower Brittany.
Even now, the origin of these families is a word of shame to them among
their neighbours; although they are protected by the law, which confirmed
them in the equal rights of citizens about the end of the last century.[2] Before
then they had lived, for hundreds of years, isolated from all those who
boasted of pure blood, and they had been, all this time, oppressed by cruel
local edicts. They were truly what they were popularly called, The Accursed
Race.

All distinct traces of their origin are lost. Even at the close of that period
which we call the Middle Ages, this was a problem which no one could
solve; and as the traces, which even then were faint and uncertain, have vanished away one by one, it is a complete mystery at the present day. Why they
were accursed in the first instance, why isolated from their kind, no one
knows. From the earliest accounts of their state that are yet remaining to us,
it seems that the names which they gave each other were ignored by the
population they lived amongst, who spoke of them as Crestiaa, or Cagots,
just as we speak of animals by their generic names. Their houses or huts
were always placed at some distance out of the villages of the country-folk,
who unwillingly called in the services of the Cagots as carpenters, or tilers,
or slaters – trades which seemed appropriated by this unfortunate race –
who were forbidden to occupy land, or to bear arms, the usual occupations
of those times. They had some small right of pasturage on the common

lands, and in the forests: but the number of their cattle and livestock was strictly limited by the earliest laws relating to the Cagots. They were forbidden by one act to have more than twenty sheep, a pig, a ram, and six geese. The pig was to be fattened and killed for winter food; the fleece of the sheep was to clothe them; but, if the said sheep had lambs, they were forbidden to eat them. Their only privilege arising from this increase was, that they might choose out the strongest and finest in preference to keeping the old sheep. At Martinmas[3] the authorities of the commune came round, and counted over the stock of each Cagot. If he had more than his appointed number, they were forfeited; half went to the commune, and half to the baillie, or chief magistrate of the commune. The poor beasts were limited as to the amount of common land which they might stray over in search of grass. While the cattle of the inhabitants of the commune might wander hither and thither in search of the sweetest herbage, the deepest shade, or the coolest pool in which to stand on the hot days, and lazily switch their dappled sides, the Cagot sheep and pig had to learn imaginary bounds, beyond which if they strayed, any one might snap them up, and kill them, reserving a part of the flesh for his own use, but graciously restoring the inferior parts to their original owner. Any damage done by the sheep was, however, fairly appraised, and the Cagot paid no more for it than any other man would have done.

Did a Cagot leave his poor cabin, and venture into the towns, even to render services required of him in the way of his trade, he was bidden, by all the municipal laws, to stand by and remember his rude old state. In all the towns and villages in the large districts extending on both sides of the Pyrenees – in all that part of Spain – they were forbidden to buy or sell anything eatable, to walk in the middle (esteemed the better) part of the streets, to come within the gates before sunrise,[a] or to be found after sunset[b] within the walls of the town. But still, as the Cagots were good-looking men, and (although they bore certain natural marks of their caste, of which I shall speak by-and-by) were not easily distinguished by casual passers-by from other men, they were compelled to wear some distinctive peculiarity which should arrest the eye; and, in the greater number of towns, it was decreed that the outward sign of a Cagot should be a piece of red cloth sewed conspicuously on the front of his dress. In other towns, the mark of Cagoterie was the foot of a duck[4] or a goose hung over their left shoulder, so as to be seen by any one meeting them. After a time, the more convenient badge of a piece of yellow cloth cut out in the shape of a duck's foot, was adopted. If any Cagot was found in any town or village without his badge, he had to pay a fine of five sous, and to lose his dress. He was expected to shrink away from any passer-by, for fear that their clothes should touch each other; or else to stand still in some corner or by-place. If the Cagots were thirsty during the days which they passed in those towns where their presence was barely suffered, they had no means of quenching their thirst, for they were forbidden to enter into the little cabarets or taverns. Even the water gushing out of the common fountain was prohibited to them. Far away, in their own squalid village, there was the Cagot fountain, and they were not allowed to drink of any other water.[a] A Cagot woman having to make purchases in the town, was liable to be flogged out of it if she went to buy anything except on a Monday – a day on which all other people who could, kept their houses for fear of coming in contact with the accursed race.

In the Pays Basque, the prejudices – and for some time the laws – ran stronger against them than any which I have hitherto mentioned. The Basque Cagot was not allowed to possess sheep.[5] He might keep a pig for provision, but his pig had no right of pasturage. He might cut and carry grass for the ass, which was the only other animal he was permitted to own; and this ass was permitted, because its existence was rather an advantage to the oppressor, who constantly availed himself of the Cagot's[b] mechanical skill, and was glad to have him and his tools easily conveyed from one place to another.

The race was[c] repulsed by the State. Under the small local governments they could hold no post whatsoever. And they were barely tolerated by the Church, although they were good Catholics,[d] and zealous frequenters of the mass. They might only enter the churches by a small door set apart for them, through which no one of the pure race ever passed. This door was low, so as to compel them to make an obeisance. It was occasionally surrounded by sculpture, which invariably represented an oak-branch with a dove above it. When they were once in, they might not go to the holy water used by others. They had a bénitier[6] of their own; nor were they allowed to share in the consecrated bread when that was handed round to the believers of the pure race. The Cagots stood afar off, near the door. There were certain boundaries – imaginary lines – on the nave and in the aisles which they might not pass. In one or two of the more tolerant of the Pyrenean villages, the blessed bread was offered to the Cagots, the priest standing on one side of the boundary, and giving the pieces of bread on a long wooden fork to each person successively.

When the Cagot died, he was interred apart, in a plot of burying-ground on the north side of the cemetery. Under such laws and prescriptions as I have described, it is no wonder that he was generally too poor to have much property for his children to inherit; but certain descriptions of it were forfeited to the commune. The only possession which all who were not of his own race refused to touch, was his furniture. That was tainted, infectious, unclean – fit for none but Cagots.

When such were, for at least three centuries, the prevalent usages and opinions with regard to this oppressed race, it is not surprising[e] that we read of occasional outbursts of ferocious violence on their part. In the Basses-Pyrénées, for instance, it is only about a hundred years since, that the Cagots of Rehouilhes[7] rose up against the inhabitants of the neighbouring town of Lourdes, and got the better of them, by their magical powers, as it is said. The people of Lourdes were conquered and slain, and their ghastly, bloody heads served the triumphant Cagots for balls to play at nine-pins with! The local parliaments had begun, by this time, to perceive how oppressive was the ban of public opinion under which the Cagots lay, and were not inclined to enforce too severe a punishment. Accordingly, the decree of the parliament of Toulouse condemned only the leading Cagots concerned in this affray to be put to death, and that henceforward and for ever no Cagot was to be permitted to enter the town of Lourdes by any gate but that called Capdet-pourtet: they were only to be allowed to walk under the rain-gutters, and neither to sit, eat, nor drink in[a] the town. If they failed in observing any of these rules, the parliament decreed, in the spirit of Shylock, that the disobedient Cagots should have two strips of flesh, weighing never more than two ounces a-piece,[b] cut out from each side of their spines.

In the fourteenth, fifteenth, and sixteenth centuries, it was considered no more a crime to kill a Cagot than to destroy obnoxious vermin. A 'nest of Cagots,' as the old accounts phrase it, had assembled in a deserted castle of Mauvezin,[8] about the year sixteen hundred; and, certainly, they made themselves not very agreeable neighbours, as they seemed to enjoy their reputation of magicians; and, by some acoustic secrets which were known to them, all sorts of moanings and groanings were heard in the neighbouring forests, very much to the alarm of the good people of the pure race; who could not cut off a withered branch for firewood, but some unearthly sound seemed to fill the air, nor[c] drink water which was not poisoned, because the Cagots would persist in filling their pitchers at the same running stream. Added to these grievances, the various pilferings perpetually going on in the neighbourhood made the inhabitants of the adjacent towns and hamlets believe that they had a very sufficient cause for wishing to murder all the Cagots in the Château de Mauvezin. But it was surrounded by a moat, and only accessible by a drawbridge; besides which, the Cagots were fierce and vigilant. Some one, however, proposed to get into their confidence; and for this purpose he pretended to fall ill close to their path, so that on returning to their stronghold they perceived him, and took him in, restored him to health, and made a friend of him. One day, when they were all playing at nine-pins in the woods, their treacherous friend left the party on pretence of being thirsty, and went back into the castle, drawing up the bridge after he had passed over it, and so cutting off their means of escape into safety. Then, going up to the highest part of the castle, he blew a horn, and the pure race, who were lying in wait on the watch for some such signal, fell upon the Cagots at their games, and slew them all. For this murder I find no punishment decreed in the parliament of Toulouse, or elsewhere.

As any intermarriage with the pure race was strictly forbidden, and as there were books kept in every commune in which the names and habitations of the reputed Cagots were written, these unfortunate people had no hope of ever becoming blended with the rest of the population. Did a Cagot marriage take place, the couple were serenaded with satirical songs.[9] They also had minstrels, and many of their romances are still current in Brittany; but they did not attempt to make any reprisals of satire or abuse. Their disposition was amiable, and their intelligence great. Indeed, it required both these qualities, and their great love of mechanical labour, to make their lives tolerable.

At last, they began to petition that they might receive some protection from the laws; and, towards the end of the seventeenth century, the judicial power took their side. But they gained little by this. Law could not prevail against custom: and, in the ten or twenty years just preceding the first French revolution, the prejudice in France against the Cagots amounted to fierce and positive abhorrence.

At the beginning of the sixteenth century, the Cagots of Navarre complained to the Pope,[a] that they were excluded from the fellowship of men, and accursed by the Church, because their ancestors had given help to a certain Count Raymond of Toulouse[10] in his revolt against the Holy See. They entreated his holiness not to visit upon them the sins of their fathers. The Pope issued a bull – on the thirteenth of May, fifteen hundred and fifteen – ordering them to be well-treated and to be admitted to the same privileges as other men. He charged Don Juan de Santa Maria of Pampeluna to see to the execution of this bull. But Don Juan was slow to help, and the poor Spanish Cagots grew impatient, and resolved to try the secular power. They accordingly applied to the cortes of Navarre, and were opposed on a variety of grounds. First, it was stated that their ancestors had had 'nothing to do with Raymond Count of Toulouse, or with any such knightly personage; that they were in fact descendants of Gehazi,[11] servant of Elisha (second book of Kings, fifth chapter, twenty-seventh verse), who had been accursed by his master for his fraud upon Naaman, and doomed, he and his descendants, to be lepers for evermore. Name, Cagots or Gahets; Gahets, Gehazites. What can be more clear? And if that is not enough, and you tell us that the Cagots are not lepers now; we reply that there are two kinds of leprosy, one perceptible and the other imperceptible, even to the person suffering from it. Besides, it is the country talk, that where the Cagot treads, the grass withers, proving the unnatural heat of his body. Many credible and trustworthy witnesses will also tell you that, if a Cagot holds a freshly-gathered apple in his hand, it will shrivel and wither up in an hour's time as much as if it had been kept for a whole winter in a dry room. They are born with tails; although the parents are cunning enough to pinch them off immediately. Do you doubt this? If it is not true, why do the children of the pure race delight in sewing on sheep's tails to the dress of any Cagot who is so absorbed in his work as not to perceive them? And[a] their bodily smell is so horrible and detestable that it shows that they must be heretics of some vile and pernicious description, for do we not read of the incense of good workers, and the fragrance of holiness?'

Such were literally the arguments by which the Cagots were thrown back into a worse position than ever, as far as regarded their rights as citizens. The Pope insisted that they should receive all their ecclesiastical privileges. The Spanish priests said nothing; but tacitly refused to allow the Cagots to mingle with the rest of the faithful, either dead or alive. The accursed race obtained laws in their favour from the Emperor Charles the Fifth;[12] which, however, there was no one to carry into[b] effect. As a sort of revenge for their want of submission, and for their impertinence in daring to complain, their tools were all taken away from them by the local authorities: an old man and all his family died of starvation, being no longer allowed to fish.

They could not emigrate. Even to remove their poor mud habitations, from one spot to another, excited anger and suspicion. To be sure, in sixteen hundred and ninety-five, the Spanish government ordered the alcaldes[13] to search out all the Cagots, and to expel them before two months had expired, under pain of having fifty ducats to pay for every Cagot remaining in Spain at the expiration of that time. The inhabitants of the villages rose up and flogged out any of the miserable race who might be in their neighbourhood; but the French were on their guard against this enforced irruption, and refused to permit them to enter France. Numbers were hunted up into the inhospitable Pyrenees, and there died of starvation, or became a prey to wild beasts. They were obliged to wear both gloves and shoes when they were thus put to flight, otherwise the stones and herbage they trod upon, and the balustrades of the bridges that they handled in crossing, would, according to popular belief, have become poisonous.

And all this time, there was nothing remarkable or disgusting in the outward appearance of this unfortunate people. There was nothing about them to countenance the idea of their being lepers – the most natural mode of accounting for the abhorrence in which they were held. They were repeatedly examined by learned doctors, whose experiments, although singular and rude, appear to have been made in a spirit of humanity. For instance, the surgeons of the king of Navarre, in sixteen hundred, bled twenty-two Cagots, in order to examine and analyse their blood. They were young and healthy people of both sexes; and the doctors seem to have expected that they should have been able to extract some new kind of salt from their blood which might account for the wonderful heat of their bodies. But their blood was just like that of other people. Some of these medical men have left us a description of the general appearance of this unfortunate race, at a time when they were more numerous and less intermixed than they are now. The families existing in the south and west of France, who are reputed to be of Cagot descent at this day, are, like their ancestors, tall, largely made, and powerful in frame; fair and ruddy[14] in complexion, with gray-blue[a] eyes, in which some observers see a pensive heaviness of look. Their lips are thick, but well-formed. Some of the reports name their sad expression of countenance with surprise and suspicion – 'They are not gay, like other folk.' The wonder would be if they were. Dr. Guyon,[15] the medical man of the last century who has left the clearest report on the health of the Cagots, speaks of the vigorous old age they attain to. In one family alone, he found a man of seventy-four years of age; a woman as old, gathering cherries; and another woman, aged eighty-three, was lying on the grass, having her hair combed by her great-grandchildren. Dr. Guyon and other surgeons examined into the subject of the horribly infectious smell which the Cagots were said to leave behind them, and upon everything they touched; but they could perceive nothing unusual on this head. They also examined their ears, which, according to common belief (a belief existing to this day), were differently shaped from those of other people; being round and gristly, without the lobe of flesh into which the earring is inserted. They decided that most of the Cagots whom they examined had the ears of this round shape; but they gravely added, that they saw no reason why this should exclude them from the good-will of men, and from the power of holding office in Church and State.[b] They recorded the fact, that the children of the towns ran baaing after any Cagot who had been compelled to come into the streets to make purchases, in allusion to this peculiarity of the shape of the ear, which bore some resemblance to the ears of the sheep as they are cut by the shepherds in this district. Dr. Guyon names the case of a beautiful Cagot girl, who sang most sweetly, and prayed to be allowed to sing canticles in the organ-loft. The organist, more musician than bigot, allowed her to come; but the indignant congregation, finding out whence proceeded that clear, fresh voice, rushed up to the organ-loft, and chased the girl out, bidding her 'remember her ears,' and not commit the sacrilege of singing praises to God along with the pure race.

But this medical report of Dr. Guyon's – bringing facts and arguments to confirm his opinion, that there was no physical reason why the Cagots should not be received on terms of social equality by the rest of the world – did no more for his clients than the legal decrees promulgated two centuries before had done. The French proved the truth of the saying in Hudibras,

> He[c] that's convinced against his will
> Is of the same opinion still.[16]

And, indeed, the being convinced by Dr. Guyon that they ought to receive Cagots as fellow-creatures, only made them more rabid in declaring that they would not.

One or two little occurrences which are recorded, show that the bitterness of the repugnance to the Cagots was in full force at the time just preceding the first French revolution. There was a M. d'Abedos, the curate of Lourbes,[17] and brother to the seigneur of the neighbouring castle, who was living in seventeen hundred and eighty; he was well-educated for the time, a travelled man, and sensible and moderate in all respects but that of his abhorrence of the Cagots: he would insult them from the very altar, calling out to them, as they stood afar off, 'Oh! ye Cagots, damned for evermore!' One day, a half-blind Cagot stumbled and touched the censer borne before this Abbé de Lourbes. He was immediately turned out of the church, and forbidden ever to re-enter it. One does not know how to account for the fact, that the very brother of this bigoted abbé, the seigneur of the village, went and married a Cagot girl; but so it was, and the abbé brought a legal process against him, and had his estates taken from him, solely on account of his marriage, which reduced him to the condition of a Cagot, against whom the old law was[a] still in force. The descendants of this Seigneur de Lourbes are simple peasants at this very day, working on the lands which belonged to their grandfather.

This prejudice against mixed marriages remained prevalent until very lately. The tradition of the Cagot descent lingered among[b] the people, long after the laws against the accursed race were abolished. A Breton girl,[18] within the last few years, having two lovers each of reputed Cagot descent, employed a notary to examine their pedigrees, and see which of the two had least Cagot in him; and to that one she gave her hand. In Brittany the prejudice seems to have been more virulent than anywhere else. M. Emile Souvestre[19] records proofs of the hatred borne to them in Brittany so recently as in eighteen hundred and thirty-five. Just lately a baker at Hennebon, having married a girl of Cagot descent, lost all his custom. The godfather and godmother of a Cagot child became Cagots themselves by the Breton laws, unless, indeed, the poor little baby died before attaining a certain number of days. They had to eat the butchers' meat condemned as unhealthy; but, for some unknown reason, they were considered to have a right to every cut loaf turned upside down, with its cut side towards the door, and might enter any house in which they saw a loaf in this position, and carry it away with them. About thirty years ago, there was the skeleton of a hand[20] hanging up as an offering in a Breton Church near Quimperle, and the tradition was, that it was the hand of a rich Cagot who had dared to take holy water out of the usual bénitier, some time at the beginning of the reign of Louis the Sixteenth;[21] which an old soldier witnessing, he lay[c] in wait, and the next time the offender approached the bénitier he cut off his hand, and hung it up, dripping with blood, as an offering to the patron saint of the church. The poor Cagots in Brittany petitioned against their opprobrious name, and begged to be distinguished by the appellation of

Malandrins. To English ears one is much the same as the other, as neither conveys any meaning; but, to this day, the descendants of the Cagots do not like to have this name applied to them, preferring that of Malandrin.

The French Cagots tried to destroy all the records of their pariah descent, in the commotions of seventeen hundred and eighty-nine;[22] but if writings have disappeared, the tradition yet remains, and points out such and such a family as Cagot, or Malandrin, or Oiselier, according to the old terms of abhorrence.

There are various ways in which learned men have attempted to account for the universal repugnance in which this well-made, powerful race are held. Some say that the antipathy to them took its rise in the days when leprosy was a dreadfully prevalent disease; and that the Cagots are more liable than any other[a] men to a kind of skin disease,[23] not precisely leprosy, but resembling it in some of its symptoms; such as dead whiteness of complexion, and swellings of the face and extremities. There was also some resemblance to the ancient Jewish custom in respect to lepers, in the habit of the people; who, on meeting a Cagot, called out, 'Cagote? Cagote?' to which they were bound to reply, 'Perlute! perlute!' Leprosy is not properly an infectious complaint, in spite of the horror in which the Cagot furniture, and the cloth woven by them, are[b] held in some places; the disorder is hereditary, and hence (say this body of wise men, who have troubled themselves to account for the origin of Cagoterie) the reasonableness and the justice of preventing any mixed marriages, by which this terrible tendency to leprous complaints might be spread far and wide. Another authority says, that though the Cagots are fine-looking men, hard-working, and good mechanics, yet they[c] bear in their faces, and show in their actions, reasons for the detestation in which they are held: their glance, if you meet it, is the jettatura, or evil-eye, and they are spiteful, and cruel, and deceitful above all other men. All these qualities they derive from their ancestor Gehazi, the servant of Elisha, together with their tendency to leprosy.

Again, it is said that they are descended from the Arian Goths, who were permitted to live in certain places in Guienne and Languedoc, after their defeat by King Clovis,[24] on condition that they abjured their heresy, and kept themselves separate from all other men for ever. The principal reason alleged in support of this supposition of their Gothic descent, is the specious one of derivation, – Chiens Gots, Cans Gots, Cagots, equivalent to Dogs of Goths.

Again, they were thought to be Saracens, coming from Syria. In confirmation of this idea, was the belief that all Cagots were possessed by a horrible smell.[25] The Lombards, also, were an unfragrant race, or so reputed among the Italians: witness Pope Stephen's letter to Charlemagne,[26] dissuading him from marrying Bertha, daughter of Didier, King of Lombardy. The Lombards boasted of Eastern descent, and were noisome. The Cagots were noisome, and therefore must be of Eastern descent. What could be clearer? In addition, there was the proof to be derived from the name Cagot, which those maintaining the opinion of their Saracen descent held to be Chiens, or Chasseurs des Gots, because the Saracens chased the Goths out of Spain. Moreover, the Saracens were originally Mahometans, and as such obliged to bathe seven times a-day: whence the badge of the duck's foot. A duck was a water-bird: Mahometans bathed in the water. Proof upon proof!

In Brittany the common idea was, they were of Jewish descent. Their unpleasant smell was again pressed into the service. The Jews, it was well known, had this physical infirmity, which might be cured either by bathing in a certain fountain in Egypt – which was a long way from Brittany – or by anointing themselves with the blood of a Christian child. Blood gushed out of the body of every Cagot on Good Friday. No wonder, if they were of Jewish descent. It was the only way of accounting for so portentous a fact. Again; the Cagots were capital carpenters, which gave the Bretons every reason to believe that their ancestors were the very Jews who made the cross. When first the tide of emigration set from Brittany to America, the oppressed Cagots crowded to the ports, seeking to go to some new country, where their race might be unknown. Here was another proof of their descent from Abraham and his nomadic people; and, the forty years' wandering in the wilderness and the Wandering Jew himself, were pressed into the service to prove that the Cagots derived their restlessness and love of change from their ancestors, the Jews. The Jews, also, practised arts-magic, and the Cagots sold bags of wind to the Breton sailors, enchanted maidens to love them – maidens who never would have cared for them, unless they had been previously enchanted – made hollow rocks and trees give out strange and unearthly noises, and sold the magical herb called bon-succès. It is true enough that, in all the early acts of the fourteenth century, the same laws apply to Jews as to Cagots, and the appellations seem used indiscriminately; but their fair complexions, their remarkable devotion to all the ceremonies of the Catholic Church, and many other circumstances, conspire to forbid our believing them to be of Hebrew descent.

Another very plausible idea is, that they are the descendants of unfortunate individuals afflicted with goîtres,[27] which is, even to this day, not an uncommon disorder in the gorges and valleys of the Pyrenees. Some have even derived the word goître from Got, or Goth; but their name, Crestiaa, is not unlike Cretin, and the same symptoms of idiotism were not unusual among the Cagots; although sometimes, if old tradition is to be credited, their malady of the brain took rather the form of violent delirium, which attacked them at new and full moons. Then the workmen laid down their tools, and rushed off from their labour to play mad pranks up and down the country. Perpetual[a] motion was required to alleviate the agony of fury that seized upon the Cagots at such times. In this desire for rapid movement, the attack resembled the Neapolitan tarantella;[28] while in the mad deeds they performed during such attacks, they were not unlike the northern Berserker.[29] In Béarn especially, those suffering from this madness were dreaded by the pure race; the Béarnais, going to cut their wooden clogs in the great forests that lay around the base of the Pyrenées,[a] feared above all things to go too near the periods when the Cagoutelle seized on the oppressed and accursed people; from whom it was then the oppressors' turn to fly. A man was living within the memory of some, who had married a Cagot wife; he used to beat her right soundly when he saw the first symptoms of the Cagoutelle, and, having reduced her to a wholesome state of exhaustion and insensibility, he locked her up until the moon had altered her shape in the heavens. If he had not taken such decided steps, say the oldest inhabitants, there is no knowing what might have happened.

From the thirteenth to the end of the nineteenth century, there are facts enough to prove the universal abhorrence in which this unfortunate race was held; whether called Cagots, or Gahets in Pyrenean districts, Caqueaux in Brittany, or Vaqueros in Asturias. The great French revolution brought some good out of its fermentation of the people: the more intelligent among them tried to overcome the prejudice against the Cagots.

In seventeen hundred and eighteen, there was a famous cause tried at Biarritz relating to Cagot rights and privileges. There was a wealthy miller, Etienne Arnauld[30] by name, of the race of Gotz, Quagotz, Bisigotz, Astragotz, or Gahetz, as his people are described in the legal documeut. He married an heiress a Gotte (or Cagot) of Biarritz; and the newly-married, well-to-do couple saw no reason why they should stand near the door in the church, nor why he should not hold some civil office in the commune, of which he was the principal inhabitant. Accordingly, he petitioned the law that he and his wife might be allowed to sit in the gallery of the church, and that he might be relieved from his civil disabilities. This wealthy white miller,[31] Etienne Arnauld, pursued his rights with some vigour against the Baillie of Labourd, the dignitary of the neighbourhood. Whereupon the inhabitants of Biarritz met in the open air, on the eighth of May, to the number of one hundred and fifty; approved of the conduct of the Baillie in rejecting Arnauld, made a subscription, and gave all power to their lawyers to defend the cause of the pure race against Etienne Arnauld – 'that stranger,' who, having married a girl of Cagot blood, ought also to be expelled from the holy places. This lawsuit was carried through all the local courts, and ended by an appeal to the highest court in Paris; where a decision was given against Basque superstitions; and Etienne Arnauld was thenceforward entitled to enter the gallery of the church.

Of course, the inhabitants of Biarritz were all the more ferocious for having been conquered; and, four years later, a carpenter, Miguel Legaret, suspected of Cagot descent, having placed himself in church among other people, was dragged out by the abbé and two of the jurats of the parish. Legaret defended himself with a sharp knife at the time, and went to law afterwards; the end of which was, that the abbé and his two accomplices were condemned to a public confession of penitence, to be uttered while on their knees at the church door, just after high-mass. They appealed to the parliament of Bourdeaux against this decision, but met with no better success than the opponents of the miller Arnauld. Legaret was confirmed in his right of standing where he would in the parish church. That a living Cagot had equal rights with other men in the town of Biarritz seemed now ceded to them; but a dead Cagot was a different thing. The inhabitants of pure blood struggled long and hard to be interred apart from the abhorred race. The Cagots were equally persistent in claiming to have a common burying-ground. Again the texts of the old Testament were referred to, and the pure blood quoted triumphantly the precedent of Uzziah the leper (twenty-sixth chapter of the second book of Chronicles), who was buried in the field of the Sepulchres of the Kings, not in the sepulchres themselves. The Cagots pleaded that they were healthy and able-bodied; with no taint of leprosy near them. They were met by the strong argument so difficult to be refuted, which I have quoted before. Leprosy was of two kinds, perceptible and imperceptible. If the Cagots were suffering from the latter kind, who could tell whether they were free from it or not? That decision must be left to the judgment of others.

One sturdy Cagot family alone, Belone by name, kept up a lawsuit, claiming the privilege of common sepulture, for forty-two years; although the curé of Biarritz had to pay one hundred livres for every Cagot not interred in the right place. The inhabitants indemnified the curate for all these fines.

M. de Romagne, Bishop of Tarbes,[32] who died in seventeen hundred and sixty-eight, was the first to allow a Cagot to fill any office in the Church. To be sure, some were so spiritless as to reject office when it was offered to them, because, by so claiming their equality, they had to pay the same taxes as other men, instead of the Rancale or poll-tax levied on the Cagots; the collector of which had also a right to claim a piece of bread of a certain size for his dog at every Cagot dwelling.

Even in the present century, it has been necessary in some churches for the archdeacon of the district, followed by all his clergy, to pass out of the small door previously appropriated to the Cagots, in order to mitigate the superstition which, even so lately, made the people refuse to mingle with them in the house of God. A Cagot once played the congregation at Larroque a trick[a] suggested by what I have just named. He slily locked the great parish-door of the church, while the greater part of the inhabitants were assisting at mass inside; put gravel into the lock itself, so as to prevent the use of any duplicate key, – and had the pleasure of seeing the proud pure-blooded people file out with bended head, through the small low door used by the abhorred Cagots.

We are naturally shocked at discovering, from facts such as these, the causeless rancour with which innocent and industrious people were so recently persecuted. The moral of the history of the accursed race may, perhaps, be[a] best conveyed in the words of an epitaph on Mrs. Mary Hand,[b] who lies buried in the churchyard of Stratford-on-Avon.

> What faults you saw in me,
> Pray strive to shun;
> And look at home: there's
> Something to be done.

FOR some time past I had observed that Miss Duncan made a good deal of occupation for herself in writing, but that she did not like me to notice her employment. Of course, this made me all the more curious; and many were my silent conjectures – some of them so near the truth that I was not much surprised when, after Mr. Dawson had finished reading his Paper to us, she hesitated, coughed, and abruptly introduced a little formal speech, to the effect that she had noted down an old Welsh story, the particulars of which had often been told her in her youth, as she lived close to the place where the events occurred. Everybody pressed her to read the manuscript, which she now produced from her reticule; but, when on the point of beginning, her nervousness seemed to overcome her, and she made so many apologies for its being the first and only attempt she had ever made at that kind of composition, that I began to wonder if we should ever arrive at the story at all. At length, in a high-pitched, ill-assured voice, she read out the title:

'THE DOOM OF THE GRIFFITHS.'

'THE DOOM OF THE GRIFFITHS'

'The Doom of the Griffiths' was first published in *Harper's New Monthly Magazine*, 16 (January 1858), pp. 220–34. It was collected in *Round the Sofa*, 2 vols (1859), vol. ii, pp. 32–95. It was also published in *My Lady Ludlow and Other Tales* (1861) and *Lois the Witch and Other Tales* (Leipzig: Tauchnitz 1861). A few changes were made to the text of 1859, some of which relate to the fact that the *Harper's* text was aimed at an American audience; these are probably authorial.

EG's uncle Samuel Holland and his son and namesake had a house, Plas Penrhyn, at Minffordd, near Penrhyndeudraeth, which she visited frequently from 1827. She described the story to Charles Eliot Norton as 'an old rubbishy one, – begun when Marianne was a baby, – the only merit whereof is that it is founded on fact' (*Letters*, p. 488). This would date the beginning of its composition to 1834–5. A letter to the publisher Sampson Low (2 October 1857), acting on behalf of Harper's, says:

> I have had no time to finish copying the 'Doom of the Griffiths', which being written upwards of 12 years ago, required some alterations. I will indeed send it as soon as possible. (*Further Letters*, pp. 175, 179n3)

One can only speculate as to the extent of these alterations. *Uglow*, p. 125 argues for a connection between this tale and 'The Well of Pen-Morfa'. It shares with 'Morton Hall' and 'The Poor Clare' its focus on an hereditary curse and a decaying gentry family.

THE DOOM OF THE GRIFFITHS.

———•———

CHAPTER I.

I HAVE always been much interested by the traditions which are scattered up and down North Wales relating to Owen Glendower[1] (Owain Glendwr is the national spelling of the name), and I fully enter into the feeling which makes the Welsh peasant still look upon him as the hero of his country. There was great joy among many of the inhabitants of the principality, when the subject of the Welsh prize poem at Oxford,[2] some fifteen or sixteen years ago, was announced to be 'Owain Glendwr.' It was the most proudly national subject that had been given for years.

Perhaps, some[a] may not be aware that this redoubted chieftain is, even in the present days of enlightenment, as famous[b] among his illiterate country-men for his magical powers as for his patriotism. He says himself – or Shakspeare says it for him, which is much the same thing –

> 'At my nativity
> The front of heaven was full of fiery shapes
> Of burning cressets . . . . .
>   . . . . I can call spirits from the vasty deep.'

And few among the lower orders in the principality would think of asking Hotspur's irreverent question[3] in reply.

Among other traditions preserved relative to this part of the Welsh hero's character, is the old family prophecy which gives a title to this tale. When Sir David Gam,[4] 'as black a traitor as if he had been born in Builth,'[5] sought to murder Owen at Machynlleth, there was one with him whose name Glendwr little dreamed of having associated with his enemies. Rhys ap Gryfydd, his 'old familiar friend,' his relation, his more than brother, had consented unto his blood.[6] Sir David Gam might be forgiven, but one whom he had loved, and who had betrayed him, could never be forgiven. Glendwr was too deeply read in the human heart to kill him. No, he let him live on, the loathing and scorn of his compatriots, and the victim of bitter remorse. The mark of Cain[7] was upon him.

But before he went forth – while yet he stood a prisoner, cowering beneath his conscience before Owain Glendwr – that chieftain passed a doom upon him and his race:

'I doom thee to live, because I know thou wilt pray for death. Thou shalt live on beyond the natural term of the life of man, the scorn of all good men. The very children shall point to thee with hissing tongue, and say, "There goes one who would have shed a brother's blood!" For I loved thee more than a brother, oh Rhys ap Gryfydd! Thou shalt live on to see all of thy house, except the weakling in arms, perish by the sword. Thy race shall be accursed. Each generation shall see their lands melt away like snow; yea, their wealth shall vanish, though they may labour night and day to heap up gold. And when nine generations have passed from the face of the earth, thy blood shall no longer flow in the veins of any human being. In those days the last male of thy race shall avenge me. The son shall slay the father.'

Such was the traditional account of Owain Glendwr's speech to his once-trusted friend. And it was declared that the doom had been fulfilled in all things; that, live in as miserly a manner as they would, the Griffiths never were wealthy and prosperous – indeed, that their worldly stock diminished without any visible cause.

But the lapse of many years had almost deadened the wonder-inspiring power of the whole curse. It was only brought forth from the hoards of Memory when some untoward event happened to the Griffiths family; and in the eighth generation the faith in the prophecy was nearly destroyed, by the marriage of the Griffiths of that day, to a Miss Owen, who, unexpectedly, by the death of a brother, became an heiress – to no considerable amount, to be sure, but enongh to make the prophecy appear reversed. The heiress and her husband removed from his small patrimonial estate in Merionethshire, to her heritage in Caernarvonshire, and for a time the prophecy lay dormant.

If you go from Tremadoc to Criccaeth[8] you pass by the parochial church of Ynysynhanarn, situated in a boggy valley running from the mountains, which shoulder up to the Rivals, down to Cardigan Bay. This tract of land has every appearance of having been redeemed at no distant period of time from the sea, and has all the desolate rankness often attendant upon such marshes. But the valley beyond, similar in character, had yet more of gloom at the time of which I write. In the higher part there were large plantations of firs, set too closely to attain to any size, and remaining stunted in height and scrubby in appearance. Indeed, many of the smaller and more weakly had died, and the bark had fallen down on the brown soil neglected and unnoticed. These trees had a ghastly appearance, with their white trunks, seen by the dim light which struggled through the thick boughs above. Nearer to the sea, the valley assumed a more open, though hardly a more cheerful character; it looked dank and overhung by sea-fog through the greater part of the year, and even a farm-house, which usually imparts something of cheerfulness to a landscape, failed to do so here. This valley formed the greater part of the estate to which Owen Griffiths became entitled by right of his wife. In the higher part of the valley was situated the family mansion, or rather dwelling-house, for 'mansion,' is too grand a word to apply to the clumsy, but substantially-built Bodowen. It was square and heavy-looking, with just that much pretension to ornament necessary to distinguish it from the mere farm-house.

In this dwelling Mrs. Owen Griffiths bore her husband two sons – Llewellyn, the future Squire, and Robert, who was early destined for the Church. The only difference in their situation, up to the time when Robert was entered at Jesus College,[9] was that the elder was invariably indulged by all around him, while Robert was thwarted and indulged by turns; that Llewellyn never learned anything from the poor Welsh parson who was nominally his private tutor; while occasionally Squire Griffiths made a great point of enforcing Robert's diligence, telling him that, as he had his bread to earn, he must pay attention to his learning. There is no knowing how far the very irregular education he had received would have carried Robert through his college examinations; but, luckily for him in this respect, before such a trial of his learning came round, he heard of the death of his elder brother, after a short illness, brought on by a hard-drinking bout. Of course, Robert was summoned home, and it seemed quite as much of course, now that there was no necessity for him to 'earn his bread by his learning,' that he should not return to Oxford. So the half-educated, but not unintelligent, young man continued at home, during the short remainder of his parent's lifetime.

His was not an uncommon character. In general he was mild, indolent, and easily managed; but once thoroughly roused, his passions were vehement and fearful. He seemed, indeed, almost afraid of himself, and in common hardly dared to give way to justifiable anger – so much did he dread losing his self-control. Had he been judiciously educated, he would, probably, have distinguished himself in those branches of literature which call for taste and imagination, rather than any exertion of reflection or judgment. As it was, his literary taste showed itself in making collections of Cambrian antiquities of every description, till his stock of Welsh MSS. would have excited the envy of Dr. Pugh[10] himself, had he been alive at the time of which I write.

There is one characteristic of Robert Griffiths which I have omitted to note, and which was peculiar among his class. He was no hard drinker; whether it was that his head was very easily affected, or that his partially-refined taste led him to dislike intoxication and its attendant circumstances, I cannot say; but at five-and-twenty Robert Griffiths was habitually sober – a thing so rare in Llyn,[11] that he was almost shunned as a churlish, unsocial being, and passed much of his time in solitude.

About this time, he had to appear in some case that was tried at the Caernarvon assizes; and while there, was a guest at the house of his agent, a shrewd, sensible Welsh attorney, with one daughter, who had charms enough to captivate Robert Griffiths. Though he remained only a few days at her father's house, they were sufficient to decide his affections, and short was the period allowed to elapse before he brought home a mistress to Bod-owen. The new Mrs. Griffiths was a gentle, yielding person, full of love toward her husband, of whom, nevertheless, she stood something in awe, partly arising from the difference in their ages, partly from his devoting much time to studies of which she could understand nothing.

She soon made him the father of a blooming little daughter, called Augharad after her mother. Then there came several uneventful years in the household of Bodowen; and when the old women had one and all declared that the cradle would not rock again, Mrs. Griffiths bore the son and heir. His birth was soon followed by his mother's death: she had been ailing and low-spirited during her pregnancy, and she seemed to lack the buoyancy of body and mind requisite to bring her round after her time of trial. Her husband, who loved her all the more from having few other claims on his affections, was deeply grieved by her early death, and his only comforter was the sweet little boy whom she had left behind. That part of the Squire's character, which was so tender, and almost feminine, seemed called forth by the helpless situation of the little infant, who stretched out his arms to his father with the same earnest cooing that happier children make use of to their mother alone. Augharad was almost neglected, while the little Owen was king of the house; still, next to his father, none tended him so lovingly as his sister. She was so accustomed to give way to him that it was no longer a hardship. By night and by day Owen was the constant companion of his father, and increasing years seemed only to confirm the custom. It was an unnatural life for the child, seeing no bright little faces peering into his own (for Augharad was, as I said before, five or six years older, and her face, poor motherless girl, was often anything but bright), hearing no din of clear ring-ing voices, but day after day sharing the otherwise solitary hours of his father, whether in the dim room, surrounded by wizard-like antiquities, or pattering his little feet to keep up with his 'tada' in his mountain rambles or shooting excursions. When the pair came to some little foaming brook, where the stepping-stones were far and wide, the father carried his little boy across with the tenderest care; when the lad was weary, they rested, he cra-dled in his father's arms, or the Squire would lift him up and carry him to his home again. The boy was indulged (for his father felt flattered by the desire) in his wish of sharing his meals and keeping the same hours. All this indulgence did not render Owen unamiable, but it made him wilful,[a] and not a happy child. He had a thoughtful look, not common to the face of a young boy. He knew no games, no merry sports; his information was of an imaginative and speculative character. His father delighted to interest him in his own studies, without considering how far they were healthy for so young a mind.

Of course Squire Griffiths was not unaware of the prophecy which was to be fulfilled in his generation. He would occasionally refer to it when among his friends, with sceptical[a] levity; but in truth it lay nearer to his heart than he chose to acknowledge. His strong imagination rendered him peculiarly impressible on such subjects; while his judgment, seldom exercised or fortified by severe thought, could not prevent his continually recurring to it. He used to gaze on the half-sad countenance of the child, who sat looking up into his face with his large dark eyes, so fondly yet so inquiringly, till the old legend swelled around his heart, and became too painful for him not to require sympathy. Besides, the overpowering love he bore to the child seemed to demand fuller vent than tender words; it made him like, yet dread, to upbraid its object for the fearful contrast foretold. Still Squire Griffiths told the legend, in a half-jesting manner, to his little son, when they were roaming over the wild heaths in the autumn days, 'the saddest of the year,' or while they sat in the oak-wainscoted room, surrounded by mysterious relics that gleamed strangely forth by the flickering fire-light. The legend was wrought into the boy's mind, and he would crave, yet tremble to hear it told over and over again, while the words were intermingled with caresses and questions as to his love. Occasionally his loving words and actions were cut short by his father's light yet bitter speech – 'Get thee away, my lad; thou knowest what is to come of all this love.'

When Augharad was seventeen, and Owen eleven or twelve, the rector of the parish in which Bodowen was situated, endeavoured to prevail on Squire Griffiths to send the boy to school. Now, this rector had many congenial tastes with his parishioner, and was his only intimate; and, by repeated arguments, he succeeded in convincing the Squire that the unnatural life Owen was leading was in every way injurious. Unwillingly was the father wrought to part from his son; but he did at length send him to the Grammar School at Bangor, then under the management of an excellent classic. Here Owen showed that he had more talents than the rector had given him credit for, when he affirmed that the lad had been completely stupified[b] by the life he led at Bodowen. He bade fair to do credit to the school in the peculiar branch of learning for which it was famous. But he was not popular among his schoolfellows. He was wayward, though, to a certain degree, generous and unselfish; he was reserved but gentle, except when the tremendous bursts of passion (similar in character to those of his father) forced their way.

On his return from school one Christmas time, when he had been a year or so at Bangor, he was stunned by hearing that the undervalued Augharad was about to be married to a gentleman of South Wales, residing near Aberystwith. Boys seldom appreciate their sisters; but Owen thought of the many slights with which he had requited the patient Augharad, and he gave way to bitter regrets, which, with a selfish want of control over his words, he kept expressing to his father, until the Squire was thoroughly hurt and chagrined at the repeated exclamations of 'What shall we do when Augharad is gone?' 'How dull we shall be when Augharad is married!' Owen's holidays were prolonged a few weeks, in order that he might be present at the wedding; and when all the festivities were over, and the bride and bridegroom had left Bodowen, the boy and his father really felt how much they missed the quiet, loving Augharad. She had performed so many thoughtful, noiseless little offices, on which their daily comfort depended; and now she was gone, the household seemed to miss the spirit that peacefully kept it in order; the servants roamed about in search of commands and directions, the rooms had no longer the unobtrusive ordering of taste to make them cheerful, the very fires burned dim, and were always sinking down into dull heaps of gray ashes. Altogether Owen did not regret his return to Bangor, and this also the mortified parent perceived. Squire Griffiths was a selfish parent.

Letters in those days were a rare occurrence. Owen usually received one during his half-yearly absences from home, and occasionally his father paid him a visit. This half-year the boy had no visit, nor even a letter, till very near the time of his leaving school, and then he was astounded by the intelligence that his father was married again.

Then came one of his paroxysms of rage; the more disastrous in its effects upon his character because it could find no vent in action. Independently of the slight to the memory of the first wife, which children are so apt to fancy such an action implies, Owen had hitherto considered himself (and with justice) the first object of his father's life. They had been so much to each other; and now a shapeless, but too real something had come between him and his father there for ever. He felt as if his permission should have been asked, as if he should have been consulted. Certainly he ought to have been told of the intended event. So the Squire felt, and hence his constrained letter, which had so much increased the bitterness of Owen's feelings.

With all this anger, when Owen saw his stepmother, he thought he had never seen so beautiful a woman for her age; for she was no longer in the bloom of youth, being a widow when his father married her. Her manners, to the Welsh lad, who had seen little of female grace among the families of the few antiquarians with whom his father visited, were so fascinating that he watched her with a sort of breathless admiration. Her measured grace, her faultless movements, her tones of voice, sweet, till the ear was sated with their sweetness, made Owen less angry at his father's marriage. Yet he felt, more than ever, that the cloud was between him and his father; that the hasty letter he had sent in answer to the announcement of his wedding was not forgotten, although no allusion was ever made to it. He was no longer his father's confidant – hardly ever his father's companion, for the newly-married wife was all in all to the Squire, and his son felt himself almost a cipher, where he had so long been everything. The lady herself had ever the softest consideration for her stepson; almost too obtrusive was the attention

paid to his wishes, but still he fancied that the heart had no part in the winning advances. There was a watchful glance of the eye that Owen once or
twice caught when she had imagined herself unobserved, and many other
nameless little circumstances, that gave him a strong feeling of want of sin-
cerity in his stepmother. Mrs. Owen brought with her into the family her
little child by her first husband, a boy nearly three years old. He was one of
those elfish, observant, mocking children, over whose feelings you seem to
have no control: agile and mischievous, his little practical jokes, at first performed in ignorance of the pain he gave, but afterward proceeding to a
malicious pleasure in suffering, really seemed to afford some ground to the
superstitious notion of some of the common people that he was a fairy
changeling.

Years passed on; and as Owen grew older he became more observant. He
saw, even in his occasional visits at home (for from school he had passed on
to college), that a great change had taken place in the outward manifestations
of his father's character; and, by degrees, Owen traced this change to the
influence of his stepmother; so slight, so imperceptible to the common
observer, yet so resistless in its effects. Squire Griffiths caught up his wife's
humbly advanced opinions, and, unawares to himself, adopted them as his
own, defying all argument and opposition. It was the same with her wishes;
they met with their fulfilment,[a] from the extreme and delicate art with
which she insinuated them into her husband's mind, as his own. She sacrificed the show of authority for the power. At last, when Owen perceived
some oppressive act in his father's conduct toward his dependants, or some
unaccountable thwarting of his own wishes, he fancied he saw his stepmother's secret influence thus displayed, however much she might regret
the injustice of his father's actions in her conversations with him when they
were alone. His father was fast losing his temperate habits, and frequent
intoxication soon took its usual effect upon the temper. Yet even here was
the spell of his wife upon him. Before her he placed a restraint upon his passion, yet she was perfectly aware of his irritable disposition, and directed it
hither and thither with the same apparent ignorance of the tendency of her
words.

Meanwhile Owen's situation became peculiarly mortifying to a youth
whose early remembrances afforded such a contrast to his present state. As a
child, he had been elevated to the consequence of a man before his years
gave any mental check to the selfishness which such conduct was likely to
engender; he could remember when his will was law to the servants and
dependants, and his sympathy necessary to his father: now he was as a cipher
in his father's house; and the Squire, estranged in the first instance by a feeling of the injury he had done his son in not sooner acquainting him with his
purposed marriage, seemed rather to avoid than to seek him as a companion,
and too frequently showed the most utter indifference to the feelings and

wishes which a young man of a high and independent spirit might be supposed to indulge.

Perhaps Owen was not fully aware of the force of all these circumstances;
for an actor in a family drama is seldom unimpassioned enough to be perfectly observant. But he became moody and soured; brooding over his
unloved existence, and craving with a human heart after sympathy.

This feeling took more full possession of his mind when he had left college, and returned home to lead an idle and purposeless life. As the heir,
there was no worldly necessity for exertion: his father was too much of a
Welsh squire to dream of the moral necessity, and he himself had not sufficient strength of mind to decide at once upon abandoning a place and mode
of life which abounded in daily mortifications; yet to this course his judgment was slowly tending, when some circumstances occurred to detain him
at Bodowen.

It was not to be expected that harmony would long be preserved, even in
appearance, between an unguarded and soured young man, such as Owen,
and his wary stepmother, when he had once left college, and come, not as a
visitor, but as the heir to his father's house.

Some cause of difference occurred, where the woman subdued her hidden anger sufficiently to become convinced that Owen was not entirely the
dupe she had believed him to be. Henceforward there was no peace between
them. Not in vulgar altercations did this show itself; but in moody reserve
on Owen's part, and in undisguised and contemptuous pursuance of her
own plans by his stepmother. Bodowen was no longer a place where, if
Owen was not loved or attended to, he could at least find peace, and care for
himself: he was thwarted at every step, and in every wish, by his father's
desire apparently, while the wife sat by with a smile of triumph on her beautiful lips.

So Owen went forth at the early day dawn, sometimes roaming about on
the shore or the upland, shooting or fishing, as the season might be, but
oftener 'stretched in indolent repose'[12] on the short, sweet grass, indulging
in gloomy and morbid reveries. He would fancy that this mortified state of
existence was a dream, a horrible dream, from which he should awake and
find himself again the sole object and darling of his father. And then he
would start up and strive to shake off the incubus. There was the molten
sunset of his childish memory; the gorgeous crimson piles of glory in the
west, fading away into the cold, calm light of the rising moon, while here
and there a cloud floated across the western heaven, like a seraph's wing, in
its flaming beauty; the earth was the same as in his childhood's days, full of
gentle evening sounds, and the harmonies of twilight – the breeze came
sweeping low over the heather and blue-bells by his side, and the turf was
sending up its evening incense of perfume. But life, and heart, and hope
were changed for ever since those bygone days!

Or he would seat himself in a favourite niche of the rocks on Moel Gêst, hidden by a stunted growth of the whitty, or mountain-ash, from general observation, with a rich-tinted cushion of stone-crop for his feet, and a straight precipice of rock rising just above. Here would he sit for hours, gazing idly at the bay below with its back-ground of purple hills, and the little fishing-sail on its bosom, showing white in the sunbeam, and gliding on in such harmony with the quiet beauty of the glassy sea; or he would pull out an old school-volume, his companion for years, and in morbid accordance with the dark legend that still lurked in the recesses of his mind – a shape of gloom in those innermost haunts awaiting its time to come forth in distinct outline – would he turn to the old Greek dramas which treat of a family foredoomed by an avenging Fate. The worn page opened of itself at the play of the Œdipus Tyrannus,[13] and Owen dwelt with the craving of disease upon the prophecy so nearly resembling that which concerned himself. With his consciousness of neglect, there was a sort of self-flattery in the consequence which the legend gave him. He almost wondered how they durst, with slights and insults, thus provoke the Avenger.

The days drifted onward. Often he would vehemently pursue some sylvan sport, till thought and feeling were lost in the violence of bodily exertion. Occasionally his evenings were spent at a small public-house, such as stood by the unfrequented wayside, where the welcome, hearty though bought, seemed so strongly to contrast with the gloomy negligence of home – unsympathizing home.

One evening (Owen might be four or five-and-twenty), wearied with a day's shooting on the Clenneny[a] Moors, he passed by the open door of 'The Goat' at Penmorfa.[14] The light and the cheeriness within tempted him, poor self-exhausted man, as it has done many a one more wretched in worldly circumstances, to step in, and take his evening meal where at least his presence was of some consequence. It was a busy day in that little hostel. A flock of sheep, amounting to some hundreds, had arrived at Penmorfa, on their road to England, and thronged the space before the house. Inside was the shrewd, kind-hearted hostess, bustling to and fro, with merry greetings for every tired drover who was to pass the night in her house, while the sheep were penned in a field close by. Ever and anon, she kept attending to the second crowd of guests, who were celebrating a rural wedding in her house. It was busy work to Martha Thomas, yet her smile never flagged; and when Owen Griffiths had finished his evening meal she was there, ready with a hope that it had done him good, and was to his mind, and a word of intelligence that the wedding-folk were about to dance in the kitchen, and the harper was the famous Edward of Corwen.[15]

Owen, partly from good-natured compliance with his hostess's implied wish, and partly from curiosity, lounged to the passage which led to the kitchen – not the every-day, working, cooking kitchen which was beyond, but a good-sized room where the mistress sat when her work was done, and where the country people were commonly entertained at such merry-makings as the present. The lintels of the door formed a frame for the animated picture which Owen saw within, as he leaned against the wall in the dark passage. The red light of the fire, with every now and then a falling piece of turf sending forth a fresh blaze, shone full upon four young men who were dancing a measure something like a Scotch reel, keeping admirable time in their rapid movements to the capital tune the harper was playing. They had their hats on when Owen first took his stand, but as they grew more and more animated they flung them away, and presently their shoes were kicked off with like disregard to the spot where they might happen to alight. Shouts of applause followed any remarkable exertion of agility, in which each seemed to try to excel his companions. At length, wearied and exhausted, they sat down, and the harper gradually changed to one of those wild, inspiring national airs for which he was so famous. The thronged audience sat earnest and breathless, and you might have heard a pin drop, except when some maiden passed hurriedly, with flaring candle and busy look, through to the real kitchen beyond. When he had finished playing his beautiful theme on 'The march of the men of Harlech,' he changed the measure again to 'Tri chant o' bunnan'[16] (Three hundred pounds), and immediately a most unmusical-looking man began chanting 'Pennillion,'[17] or a sort of recitative stanzas, which were soon taken up by another, and this amusement lasted so long that Owen grew weary, and was thinking of retreating from his post by the door, when some little bustle was occasioned, on the opposite side of the room, by the entrance of a middle-aged man, and a young girl, apparently his daughter. The man advanced to the bench occupied by the seniors of the party, who welcomed him with the usual pretty Welsh greeting, 'Pa sut mae dy galon?'[18] ('How is thy heart?') and drinking his health, passed on to him the cup of excellent *cwrw*.[19] The girl, evidently a village belle, was as warmly greeted by the young men, while the girls eyed her rather askance with a half-jealous look, which Owen set down to the score of her extreme prettiness. Like most Welsh women, she was of middle size as to height, but beautifully made, with the most perfect yet delicate roundness in every limb. Her little mob-cap was carefully adjusted to a face which was excessively pretty, though it never could be called handsome. It also was round, with the slightest tendency to the oval shape, richly coloured,[a] though somewhat olive in complexion, with dimples in cheek and chin, and the most scarlet lips Owen had ever seen, that were too short to meet over the small pearly teeth. The nose was the most defective feature; but the eyes were splendid. They were so long, so lustrous, yet at times so very soft under their thick fringe of eyelash! The nut-brown hair was carefully braided beneath the border of delicate lace: it was evident the little village beauty knew how to make the most of all her attractions, for the gay colours which were displayed in her neckerchief were in complete harmony with the complexion.

Owen was much attracted, while yet he was amused, by the evident coquetry the girl displayed, collecting around her a whole bevy of young fellows, for each of whom she seemed to have some gay speech, some attractive look or action. In a few minutes, young Griffiths of Bodowen was at her side, brought thither by a variety of idle motives, and as her undivided attention was given to the Welsh heir, her admirers, one by one, dropped off, to seat themselves by some less facinating but more attentive fair one. The more Owen conversed with the girl, the more he was taken; she had more wit and talent than he had fancied possible; a self-abandon and thoughtfulness,[a] to boot, that seemed full of charms; and then her voice was so clear and sweet, and her actions so full of grace, that Owen was fascinated before he was well aware, and kept looking into her bright, blushing face, till her uplifted flashing eye fell beneath his earnest gaze.

While it thus happened that they were silent – she from confusion at the unexpected warmth of his admiration, he from an unconsciousness of anything but the beautiful changes in her flexile countenance – the man whom Owen took for her father came up and addressed some observation to his daughter, from whence he glided into some common-place yet respectful remark to Owen, and at length engaging him in some slight, local conversation, he led the way to the account of a spot on the peninsula of Penthryn where teal abounded, and concluded with begging Owen to allow him to show him the exact place, saying that whenever the young Squire felt so inclined, if he would honour him by a call at his house, he would take him across in his boat. While Owen listened, his attention was not so much absorbed as to be unaware that the little beauty at his side was refusing one or two who endeavoured to draw her from her place by invitations to dance. Flattered by his own construction of her refusals, he again directed all his attention to her, till she was called away by her father, who was leaving the scene of festivity. Before he left he reminded Owen of his promise, and added,

'Perhaps, Sir, you do not know me. My name is Ellis Pritchard, and I live at Ty Glas, on this side of Moel Gêst;[20] any one can point it out to you.'

When the father and daughter had left, Owen slowly prepared for his ride home; but, encountering the hostess, he could not resist asking a few questions relative to Ellis Pritchard and his pretty daughter. She answered shortly but respectfully, and then said rather hesitatingly –

'Master Griffiths, you know the triad, "Tri pheth tebyg y naill i'r llall, ysgnbwr heb yd, mail deg heb ddiawd, a merch deg heb ei geirda"[21] (Three things are alike: a fine barn without corn, a fine cup without drink, a fine woman without her reputation.)' She hastily quitted him, and Owen rode slowly to his unhappy home.

Ellis Pritchard, half farmer and half fisherman, was shrewd, and keen, and worldly; yet he was good-natured, and sufficiently generous to have become rather a popular man among his equals. He had been struck with the young Squire's attention to his pretty daughter, and was not insensible to the advantages to be derived from it. Nest would not be the first peasant girl, by any means, who had been transplanted to a Welsh manor-house as its mistress; and, accordingly, her father had shrewdly given the admiring young man some pretext for further opportunities of seeing her.

As for Nest herself, she had somewhat of her father's worldliness, and was fully alive to the superior station of her new admirer, and quite prepared to slight all her old sweethearts on his account. But then she had something more of feeling in her reckoning; she had not been insensible to the earnest yet comparatively refined homage which Owen paid her; she had noticed his expressive and occasionally handsome countenance with admiration, and was flattered by his so immediately singling her out from her companions. As to the hint which Martha Thomas had thrown out, it is enough to say that Nest was very giddy, and that she was motherless. She had high spirits and a great love of admiration, or, to use a softer term, she loved to please; men, women, children, all, she delighted to gladden with her smile and her voice. She coquetted, and flirted, and went to the extreme lengths of Welsh courtship, till the seniors of the village shook their heads, and cautioned their daughters against her acquaintance. If not absolutely guilty, she had too frequently been on the verge of guilt.

Even at the time, Martha Thomas's hint made but little impression on Owen, for his senses were otherwise occupied; but in a few days the recollection thereof had wholly died away, and one warm glorious summer's day, he bent his steps toward Ellis Pritchard's with a beating heart; for, except some very slight flirtations at Oxford, Owen had never been touched; his thoughts, his fancy had been otherwise engaged.

Ty Glas was built against one of the lower rocks of Moel Gêst, which, indeed, formed a side to the low, lengthy house. The materials of the cottage were the shingly stones which had fallen from above, plastered rudely together, with deep recesses for the small oblong windows. Altogether, the exterior was much ruder than Owen had expected; but inside there seemed no lack of comforts. The house was divided into two apartments, one large, roomy, and dark, into which Owen entered immediately; and before the blushing Nest came from the inner chamber (for she had seen the young Squire coming, and hastily gone to make some alteration in her dress), he had had time to look around him, and note the various little particulars of the room. Beneath the window (which commanded a magnificent view) was an oaken dresser, replete with drawers and cupboards, and brightly polished to a rich dark colour. In the farther part of the room, Owen could at first distinguish little, entering as he did from the glaring sunlight, but he soon saw that there were two oaken beds, closed up after the manner of the Welsh:[22] in fact, the dormitories of Ellis Pritchard and the man who served under him, both on sea and on land. There was the large wheel used for spinning wool, left standing on the middle of the floor, as if in use only a few minutes before; and around the ample chimney hung flitches of bacon, dried kids'-flesh, and fish, that was in process of smoking for winter's store.

Before Nest had shyly dared to enter, her father, who had been mending his nets down below, and seen Owen winding up[a] to the house, came in and gave him a hearty yet respectful welcome; and then Nest, downcast and blushing, full of the consciousness which her father's advice and conversation had not failed to inspire, ventured to join them. To Owen's mind this reserve and shyness gave her new charms.

It was too bright, too hot, too anything, to think of going to shoot teal till later in the day, and Owen was delighted to accept a hesitating invitation to share the noonday meal. Some ewe-milk cheese, very hard and dry, oat-cake, slips of the dried kids'-flesh broiled, after having been previously soaked in water for a few minutes, delicious butter and fresh buttermilk, with a liquor called 'diod griafol'[23] (made from the berries of the *Sorbus aucuparia*, infused in water and then fermented), composed the frugal repast; but there was something so clean and neat, and withal such a true welcome, that Owen had seldom enjoyed a meal so much. Indeed, at that time of day the Welsh squires differed from the farmers more in the plenty and rough abundance of their manner of living than in the refinement of style of their table.

At the present day, down in Llyn, the Welsh gentry are not a whit behind their Saxon equals in the expensive elegances of life; but then (when there was but one pewter-service in all Northumberland) there was nothing in Ellis Pritchard's mode of living that grated on the young Squire's sense of refinement.

Little was said by that young pair of wooers during the meal: the father had all the conversation to himself, apparently heedless of the ardent looks and inattentive mien of his guest. As Owen became more serious in his feelings, he grew more timid in their expression, and at night, when they returned from their shooting-excursion, the caress he gave Nest was almost as bashfully offered as received.

This was but the first of a series of days devoted to Nest in reality, though at first he thought some little disguise of his object was necessary. The past, the future, was all forgotten in those happy days of love.

And every worldly plan, every womanly wile was put in practice by Ellis Pritchard and his daughter, to render his visits agreeable and alluring. Indeed, the very circumstance of his being welcome was enough to attract the poor young man, to whom the feeling so produced was new and full of charms. He left a home where the certainty of being thwarted made him chary in expressing his wishes, where no tones of love ever fell on his ear, save those addressed to others, where his presence or absence was a matter of utter indifference; and when he entered Ty Glas, all, down to the little cur which, with clamorous barkings, claimed a part of his attention, seemed to rejoice. His account of his day's employment found a willing listener in Ellis; and when he passed on to Nest, busy at her wheel or at her churn, the deepened colour, the conscious eye, and the gradual yielding of herself up to his lover-like caress, had worlds of charms. Ellis Pritchard was a tenant on the Bodowen estate, and therefore had reasons in plenty for wishing to keep the young Squire's visits secret; and Owen, unwilling to disturb the sunny calm of these halcyon days by any storm at home, was ready to use all the artifice which Ellis suggested as to the mode of his calls at Ty Glas. Nor was he unaware of the probable, nay, the hoped-for termination of these repeated days of happiness. He was quite conscious that the father wished for nothing better than the marriage of his daughter to the heir of Bodowen; and when Nest had hidden her face in his neck, which was encircled by her clasping arms, and murmured into his ear her acknowledgment of love, he felt only too desirous of finding some one to love him for ever. Though not highly principled, he would not have tried to obtain Nest on other terms save those of marriage: he did so pine after enduring love, and fancied he should have bound her heart for evermore to his, when they had taken the solemn oaths of matrimony.

There was no great difficulty attending a secret marriage at such a place and at such a time. One gusty autumn day, Ellis ferried them round Penthryn to Llandutrwyn,[24] and there saw his little Nest become future lady of Bodowen.

How often do we see giddy, coquetting, restless girls become sobered by marriage! A great object in life is decided; one on which their thoughts have been running in all their vagaries, and they seem to verify the beautiful fable of Undine.[25] A new soul beams out in the gentleness and repose of their future lives. An indescribable softness and tenderness takes place of the wearying vanity of their former endeavours to attract admiration. Something of this sort took place in Nest Pritchard. If at first she had been anxious to attract the young Squire of Bodowen, long before her marriage this feeling had merged into a truer love than she had ever felt before; and now that he was her own, her husband, her whole soul was bent toward making him amends, as far as in her lay, for the misery which, with a woman's tact, she saw that he had to endure at his home. Her greetings were abounding in delicately-expressed love; her study of his tastes unwearying, in the arrangement of her dress, her time, her very thoughts.

No wonder that he looked back on his wedding-day with a thankfulness which is seldom the result of unequal marriages. No wonder that his heart beat aloud as formerly when he wound up the little path to Ty Glas, and saw – keen though the winter's wind might be – that Nest was standing out at the door to watch for his dimly-seen approach, while the candle flared in the little window as a beacon to guide him aright.

The angry words and unkind actions of home fell deadened on his heart; he thought of the love that was surely his, and of the new promise of love that a short time would bring forth, and he could almost have smiled at the impotent efforts to disturb his peace.

A few more months, and the young father was greeted by a feeble little cry, when he hastily entered Ty Glas, one morning early, in consequence of a summons conveyed mysteriously to Bodowen; and the pale mother, smiling, and feebly holding up her babe to its father's kiss, seemed to him even more lovely than the bright gay Nest who had won his heart at the little inn of Penmorfa.

But the curse was at work! The fulfilment of the prophecy was nigh at hand!

CHAPTER II.

IT was the autumn after the birth of their boy: it had been a glorious summer, with bright, hot, sunny weather; and now the year was fading away as
seasonably into mellow days, with mornings of silver mists and clear frosty
nights. The blooming look of the time of flowers was past and gone; but
instead there were even richer tints abroad in the sun-coloured[a] leaves, the
lichens, the golden-blossomed furze: if it was the time of fading, there was a
glory in the decay.

Nest, in her loving anxiety to surround her dwelling with every charm
for her husband's sake, had turned gardener, and the little corners of the
rude court before the house were filled with many a delicate mountain-
flower, transplanted more for its beauty than its rarity. The sweetbrier bush
may even yet be seen, old and gray, which she and Owen planted a green sli-
pling beneath the window of her little chamber.

In those moments Owen forgot all besides the present; all the cares and
griefs he had known in the past, and all that might await him of woe and
death in the future. The boy, too, was as lovely a child as the fondest parent
was ever blessed with; and crowed with delight, and clapped his little hands,
as his mother held him in her arms at the cottage-door to watch his father's
ascent up the rough path that led to Ty Glas, one bright autumnal morning;
and when the three entered the house together, it was difficult to say which
was the happiest. Owen carried his boy, and tossed and played with him,
while Nest sought out some little article of work, and seated herself on the
dresser beneath the window, where now busily plying the needle, and then
again looking at her husband, she eagerly told him the little pieces of domestic intelligence, the winning ways of the child, the result of yesterday's
fishing, and such of the gossip of Penmorfa as came to the ears of the now
retired Nest. She noticed that, when she mentioned any little circumstance
which bore the slightest reference to Bodowen, her husband appeared chafed
and uneasy, and at last avoided anything that might in the least remind him of
home. In truth, he had been suffering much of late from the irritability of his
father, shown in trifles to be sure, but not the less galling on that account.

While they were thus talking, and caressing each other and the child, a
shadow darkened the room, and before they could catch a glimpse of the

object that had occasioned it, it vanished, and Squire Griffiths lifted the door-latch and stood before them. He stood and looked – first on his son, so different, in his buoyant expression of content and enjoyment, with his noble child in his arms, like a proud and happy father, as he was, from the depressed, moody young man he too often appeared at Bodowen; then on Nest – poor, trembling, sickened Nest! – who dropped her work, but yet durst not stir from her seat on the dresser, while she looked to her husband as if for protection from his father.

The Squire was silent, as he glared from one to the other, his features white with restrained passion. When he spoke, his words came most distinct in their forced composure. It was to his son he addressed himself:

'That woman! who is she?'

Owen hesitated one moment, and then replied, in a steady, yet quiet voice:

'Father, that woman is my wife.'

He would have added some apology for the long concealment of his marriage; have appealed to his father's forgiveness; but the foam flew from Squire Owen's lips as he burst forth with invective against Nest: –

'You have married her! It is as they told me! Married Nest Pritchard yr buten![26] And you stand there as if you had not disgraced yourself for ever and ever[a] with your accursed wiving! And the fair harlot sits there, in her mocking modesty, practising the mimming airs that will become her state as future lady of Bodowen. But I will move heaven and earth before that false woman darken the doors of my father's house as mistress!'

All this was said with such rapidity that Owen had no time for the words that thronged to his lips. 'Father!' (he burst forth at length) 'Father, whosoever told you that Nest Pritchard was a harlot told you a lie as false as hell! Ay! a lie as false as hell!' he added, in a voice of thunder, while he advanced a step or two nearer to the Squire. And then, in a lower tone, he said:

'She is as pure as your own wife; nay, God help me! as the dear, precious mother who brought me forth, and then left me – with no refuge in a mother's heart – to struggle on through life alone. I tell you Nest is as pure as that dear, dead mother!'

'Fool – poor fool!'[27b]

At this moment the child – the little Owen – who had kept gazing from one angry countenance to the other, and with earnest look, trying to understand what had brought the fierce glare into the face where till now he had read nothing but love, in some way attracted the Squire's attention, and increased his wrath.

'Yes!' he continued, 'poor, weak fool that you are, hugging the child of another as if it were your own offspring!' Owen involuntarily caressed the affrighted child, and half smiled at the implication of his father's words.

This the Squire perceived, and raising his voice to a scream of rage, he went on:

'I bid you, if you call yourself my son, to cast away that miserable, shameless woman's offspring; cast it away this instant – this instant!'

In his ungovernable rage, seeing that Owen was far from complying with his command, he snatched the poor infant from the loving arms that held it, and throwing it to its mother, left the house inarticulate with fury.

Nest – who had been pale and still as marble during this terrible dialogue, looking on and listening as if fascinated by the words that smote her heart – opened her arms to receive and cherish her precious babe; but the boy was not destined to reach the white refuge of her breast. The furious action of the Squire had been almost without aim, and the infant fell against the sharp edge of the dresser down on to the stone floor.

Owen sprang up to take the child, but he lay so still, so motionless, that the awe of death came over the father, and he stooped down to gaze more closely. At that moment, the upturned, filmy eyes rolled convulsively – a spasm passed along the body – and the lips, yet warm with kissing, quivered into everlasting rest.

A word from her husband told Nest all. She slid down from her seat, and lay by her little son as corpse-like as he, unheeding all the agonizing endearments and passionate adjurations of her husband. And that poor, desolate husband and father! Scarce one little quarter of an hour, and he had been so blessed in his consciousness of love! the bright promise of many years on his infant's face, and the new, fresh soul beaming forth in its awakened intelligence. And there it was; the little clay image, that would never more gladden up at the sight of him, nor stretch forth to meet his embrace; whose inarticulate, yet most eloquent cooings might haunt him in his dreams, but would never more be heard in waking life again! And by the dead babe, almost as utterly insensate, the poor mother had fallen in a merciful faint – the slandered, heart-pierced Nest! Owen struggled against the sickness that came over him, and busied himself in vain attempts at her restoration.

It was now near noon-day, and Ellis Pritchard came home, little dreaming of the sight that awaited him; but, though stunned, he was able to take more effectual measures for his poor daughter's recovery than Owen had done.

By-and-by she showed symptoms of returning sense, and was placed in her own little bed in a darkened room, where, without ever waking to complete consciousness, she fell asleep. Then it was that her husband, suffocated by pressure of miserable thought, gently drew his hand from her tightened clasp, and printing one long soft kiss on her white waxen forehead, hastily stole out of the room, and out of the house.

Near the base of Moel Gêst – it might be a quarter of a mile from Ty Glas – was a little neglected solitary copse, wild and tangled with the trailing branches of the dog-rose and the tendrils of the white bryony. Toward the middle of this thicket lay a deep crystal pool – a clear mirror for the blue heavens above – and round the margin floated the broad green leaves of the water-lily, and when the regal sun shone down in his noonday glory the flowers arose from their cool depths to welcome and greet him. The copse was musical with many sounds; the warbling of birds rejoicing in its shades, the ceaseless hum of the insects that hovered over the pool, the chime of the distant waterfall, the occasional bleating of the sheep from the mountain-top, were all blended into the delicious harmony of nature.

It had been one of Owen's favourite resorts when he had been a lonely wanderer – a pilgrim in search of love in the years gone by. And thither he went, as if by instinct, when he left Ty Glas; quelling the uprising agony till he should reach that little solitary spot.

It was the time of day when a change in the aspect of the weather so frequently takes place; and the little pool was no longer the reflection of a blue and sunny sky; it sent back the dark and slaty clouds above, and, every now and then, a rough gust shook the painted autumn leaves from their branches, and all other music was lost in the sound of the wild winds piping down from the moorlands, which lay up and beyond the clefts in the mountain-side. Presently the rain came on and beat down in torrents.

But Owen heeded it not. He sat on the dank ground, his face buried in his hands, and his whole strength, physical and mental, employed in quelling the rush of blood, which rose and boiled and gurgled in his brain as if it would madden him.

The phantom of his dead child rose ever before him, and seemed to cry aloud for vengeance. And when the poor young man thought upon the victim whom he required in his wild longing for revenge, he shuddered, for it was his father!

Again and again he tried not to think; but still the circle of thought came round, eddying through his brain. At length he mastered his passions, and they were calm; then he forced himself to arrange some plan for the future.

He had not, in the passionate hurry of the moment, seen that his father had left the cottage before he was aware of the fatal accident that befell the child. Owen thought he had seen all; and once he planned to go to the Squire and tell him of the anguish of heart he had wrought, and awe him, as it were, by the dignity of grief. But then again he durst not – he distrusted his self-control – the old prophecy rose up in its horror – he dreaded his doom.

At last he determined to leave his father for ever; to take Nest to some distant country where she might forget her first-born, and where he himself might gain a livelihood by his own exertions.

But when he tried to descend to the various little arrangements which were involved in the execution of this plan, he remembered that all his money (and in this respect Squire Griffiths was no niggard) was locked up in his escritoire at Bodowen. In vain he tried to do away with this matter-of-fact difficulty; go to Bodowen he must; and his only hope – nay his determination – was to avoid his father.

He rose and took a by-path to Bodowen. The house looked even more gloomy and desolate than usual in the heavy down-pouring rain, yet Owen gazed on it with something of regret – for sorrowful as his days in it had been, he was about to leave it for many, many years, if not for ever. He entered by a side-door, opening into a passage that led to his own room, where he kept his books, his guns, his fishing-tackle, his writing-materials, etc.

Here he hurriedly began to select the few articles he intended to take; for, besides the dread of interruption, he was feverishly anxious to travel far that very night, if only Nest was capable of performing the journey. As he was thus employed, he tried to conjecture what his father's feelings would be on finding that his once-loved son was gone away for ever. Would he then awaken to regret for the conduct which had driven him from home, and bitterly think on the loving and caressing boy who haunted his footsteps in former days?

Or, alas! would he only feel that an obstacle to his daily happiness – to his contentment with his wife, and his strange, doting affection for her child – was taken away? Would they make merry over the heir's departure? Then he thought of Nest – the young childless mother, whose heart had not yet realized her fullness of desolation. Poor Nest! so loving as she was, so devoted to her child – how should he console her? He pictured her away in a strange land, pining for her native mountains, and refusing to be comforted because her child was not.

Even this thought of the home-sickness that might possibly beset Nest hardly made him hesitate in his determination; so strongly had the idea taken possession of him that only by putting miles and leagues between him and his father could he avert the doom which seemed blending itself with the very purposes of his life as long as he stayed[a] in proximity with the slayer of his child.

He had now nearly completed his hasty work of preparation, and was full of tender thoughts of his wife, when the door opened, and the elfish Robert peered in, in search of some of his brother's possessions. On seeing Owen he hesitated, but then came boldly forward, and laid his hand on Owen's arm, saying,

'Nesta yr buten! How is Nest yr buten?'

He looked maliciously into Owen's face to mark the effect of his words, but was terrified at the expression he read there. He started off and ran to the door, while Owen tried to check himself, saying continually, 'He is but a child. He does not understand the meaning of what he says. He is but a child!' Still Robert, now in fancied security, kept calling out his insulting words, and Owen's hand was on his gun, grasping it as if to restrain his rising fury.

But when Robert passed on daringly to mocking words relating to the poor dead child, Owen could bear it no longer; and before the boy was well aware, Owen was fiercely holding him in an iron clasp with one hand, while he struck him hard with the other.

In a minute he checked himself. He paused, relaxed his grasp, and, to his horror, he saw Robert sink to the ground; in fact, the lad was half-stunned, half-frightened, and thought it best to assume insensibility.

Owen – miserable Owen – seeing him lie there prostrate, was bitterly repentant, and would have dragged him to the carved settle, and done all he could to restore him to his senses, but at this instant the Squire came in.

Probably, when the household at Bodowen rose that morning, there was but one among them ignorant of the heir's relation to Nest Pritchard and her child; for secret as he had tried to make his visits to Ty Glas, they had been too frequent not to be noticed, and Nest's altered conduct – no longer frequenting dances and merry-makings – was a strongly corroborative circumstance. But Mrs. Griffiths' influence reigned paramount, if unacknowledged, at Bodowen, and till she sanctioned the disclosure, none would dare to tell the Squire.

Now, however, the time drew near when it suited her to make her husband aware of the connection his son had formed; so, with many tears, and much seeming reluctance, she broke the intelligence to him – taking good care, at the same time, to inform him of the light character Nest had borne. Nor did she confine this evil reputation to her conduct before her marriage, but insinuated that even to this day she was a 'woman of the grove and brake' –[28] for centuries the Welsh term of opprobrium for the loosest female characters.

Squire Griffiths easily tracked Owen to Ty Glas; and without any aim but the gratification of his furious anger, followed him to upbraid as we have seen. But he left the cottage even more enraged against his son than he had entered it, and returned home to hear the evil suggestions of the stepmother. He had heard a slight scuffle in which he caught the tones of Robert's voice, as he passed along the hall, and an instant afterwards he saw the apparently lifeless body of his little favourite[a] dragged along by the culprit Owen – the marks of strong passion yet visible on his face. Not loud, but bitter and deep were the evil words which the father bestowed on the son; and as Owen stood proudly and sullenly silent, disdaining all exculpation of himself in the presence of one who had wrought him so much graver – so fatal an injury – Robert's mother entered the room. At sight of her natural emotion the wrath of the Squire was redoubled, and his wild suspicions that this violence of Owen's to Robert was a premeditated act appeared like the proven truth through the mists of rage. He summoned domestics as if to guard his own

and his wife's life from the attempts of his son; and the servants stood wondering around – now gazing at Mrs. Griffiths, alternately scolding and
sobbing, while she tried to restore the lad from his really bruised and half-
unconscious state; now at the fierce and angry Squire; and now at the sad and
silent Owen. And he – he was hardly aware of their looks of wonder and terror; his father's words fell on a deadened ear; for before his eyes there rose a
pale dead babe, and in that lady's violent sounds of grief he heard the wailing
of a more sad, more hopeless mother. For by this time the lad Robert had
opened his eyes, and though evidently suffering a good deal from the effects
of Owen's blows, was fully conscious of all that was passing around him.

Had Owen been left to his own nature, his heart would have worked
itself to doubly love the boy whom he had injured; but he was stubborn
from injustice, and hardened by suffering. He refused to vindicate himself;
he made no effort to resist the imprisonment the Squire had decreed, until a
surgeon's opinion of the real extent of Robert's injuries was made known. It
was not until the door was locked and barred, as if upon some wild and furious beast, that the recollection of poor Nest, without his comforting
presence, came into his mind. Oh! thought he, how she would be wearying,
pining for his tender sympathy; if, indeed, she had recovered the shock of
mind sufficiently to be sensible of consolation! What would she think of his
absence? Could she imagine he believed his father's words, and had left her,
in this her sore trouble and bereavement? The thought maddened him, and
he looked around for some mode of escape.

He had been confined in a small unfurnished room on the first floor,
wainscoted, and carved all round, with a massy door, calculated to resist the
attempts of a dozen strong men, even had he afterward been able to escape
from the house unseen, unheard. The window was placed (as is common in
old Welsh houses) over the fire-place; with branching chimneys on either
hand, forming a sort of projection on the outside. By this outlet his escape
was easy, even had he been less determined and desperate than he was. And
when he had descended, with a little care, a little winding, he might elude all
observation and pursue his original intention of going to Ty Glas.

The storm had abated, and watery sunbeams were gilding the bay, as
Owen descended from the window, and, stealing along in the broad afternoon shadows, made his way to the little plateau of green turf in the garden
at the top of a steep precipitous rock, down the abrupt face of which he had
often dropped, by means of a well-secured rope, into the small sailing-boat
(his father's present, alas! in days gone by) which lay moored in the deep
sea-water below. He had always kept his boat there, because it was the nearest available spot to the house; but before he could reach the place – unless,
indeed, he crossed a broad sun-lighted piece of ground in full view of the
windows on that side of the house, and without the shadow of a single shel-
tering tree or shrub – he had to skirt round a rude semicircle of underwood,

which would have been considered as a shrubbery had any one taken pains with it. Step by step he stealthily moved along – hearing voices now, again seeing his father and stepmother in no distant walk, the Squire evidently caressing and consoling his wife, who seemed to be urging some point with great vehemence, again forced to crouch down to avoid being seen by the cook, returning from the rude kitchen-garden with a handful of herbs. This was the way the doomed heir of Bodowen left his ancestral house for ever, and hoped to leave behind him his doom. At length he reached the plateau – he breathed more freely. He stooped to discover the hidden coil of rope, kept safe and dry in a hole under a great round flat piece of rock: his head was bent down; he did not see his father approach, nor did he hear his foot-step for the rush of blood to his head in the stooping effort of lifting the stone; the Squire had grappled with him before he rose up again, before he fully knew whose hands detained him, now, when his liberty of person and action seemed secure. He made a vigorous struggle to free himself; he wres-tled with his father for a moment – he pushed him hard, and drove him on to the great displaced stone, all unsteady in its balance.

Down went the Squire, down into the deep waters below – down after him went Owen, half consciously, half unconsciously, partly compelled by the sudden cessation of any opposing body, partly from a vehement irre-pressible impulse to rescue his father. But he had instinctively chosen a safer place in the deep sea-water pool than that into which his push had sent his father. The Squire had hit his head with much violence against the side of the boat, in his fall; it is, indeed, doubtful whether he was not killed before ever he sank into the sea. But Owen knew nothing save that the awful doom seemed even now present. He plunged down, he dived below the water in search of the body which had none of the elasticity of life to buoy it up; he saw his father in those depths, he clutched at him, he brought him up and cast him, a dead weight, into the boat, and, exhausted by the effort, he had begun himself to sink again before he instinctively strove to rise and climb into the rocking boat. There lay his father, with a deep dent in the side of his head where the skull had been fractured by his fall; his face blackened by the arrested course of the blood. Owen felt his pulse, his heart – all was still. He called him by his name.

'Father, father!' he cried, 'come back! come back! You never knew how I loved you! how I could love you still – if – oh God!'

And the thought of his little child rose before him. 'Yes, father,' he cried afresh, 'you never knew how he fell – how he died! Oh, if I had but had patience to tell you! If you would but have borne with me and listened! And now it is over! Oh father! father!'

Whether she had heard this wild wailing voice, or whether it was only that she missed her husband and wanted him for some little every-day ques-tion, or, as was perhaps more likely, she had discovered Owen's escape, and come to inform her husband of it, I do not know, but on the rock, right above his head, as it seemed, Owen heard his stepmother calling her husband.

He was silent, and softly pushed the boat right under the rock till the sides grated against the stones, and the overhanging branches concealed him and it from all not on a level with the water. Wet as he was, he lay down by his dead father the better to conceal himself; and, somehow, the action recalled those early days of childhood – the first in the Squire's widowhood – when Owen had shared his father's bed, and used to waken him in the morning to hear one of the old Welsh legends. How long he lay thus – body chilled, and brain hard-working through the heavy pressure of a reality as terrible as a nightmare – he never knew; but at length he roused himself up to think of Nest.

Drawing out a great sail, he covered up the body of his father with it where he lay in the bottom of the boat. Then with his numbed hands he took the oars, and pulled out into the more open sea toward Criccaeth. He skirted along the coast till he found a shadowed cleft in the dark rocks; to that point he rowed, and anchored his boat close in land. Then he mounted, staggering, half longing to fall into the dark waters and be at rest – half instinctively finding out the surest foot-rests on that precipitous face of rock, till he was high up, safe landed on the turfy summit. He ran off, as if pursued, toward Penmorfa; he ran with maddened energy. Suddenly he paused, turned, ran again with the same speed, and threw himself prone on the summit, looking down into his boat with straining eyes to see if there had been any movement of life – any displacement of a fold of sail-cloth. It was all quiet deep down below, but as he gazed the shifting light gave the appearance of a slight movement. Owen ran to a lower part of the rock, stripped, plunged into the water, and swam to the boat. When there, all was still – awfully still! For a minute or two, he dared not lift up the cloth. Then reflecting that the same terror might beset him again – of leaving his father unaided while yet a spark of life lingered – he removed the shrouding cover. The eyes looked into his with a dead stare! He closed the lids and bound up the jaw. Again he looked. This time he raised himself out of the water and kissed the brow.

'It was my doom, father! It would have been better if I had died at my birth!'

Daylight was fading away. Precious daylight! He swam back, dressed, and set off afresh for Penmorfa. When he opened the door of Ty Glas, Ellis Pritchard looked at him reproachfully, from his seat in the darkly-shadowed chimney corner.

'You're come at last,' said he. 'One of our kind (*i.e.*, station) would not have left his wife to mourn by herself[a] over her dead child; nor would one of our kind have let his father kill his own true son. I've a good mind to take her from you for ever.'

'I did not tell him,' cried Nest, looking piteously at her husband; 'he made me tell him part, and guessed the rest.'

She was nursing her babe on her knee as if it was alive. Owen stood before Ellis Pritchard.

'Be silent,' said he, quietly. 'Neither words nor deeds but what are decreed can come to pass. I was set to do my work, this[a] hundred years and more. The time waited for me, and the man waited for me. I have done what was foretold of me for generations!'

Ellis Pritchard knew the old tale of the prophecy, and believed in it in a dull, dead kind of way, but somehow never thought it would come to pass in his time. Now, however, he understood it all in a moment, though he mistook Owen's nature so much as to believe that the deed was intentionally done, out of revenge for the death of his boy; and viewing it in this light, Ellis thought it little more than a just punishment for the cause of all the wild despairing sorrow he had seen his only child suffer during the hours of this long afternoon. But he knew the law would not so regard it. Even the lax Welsh law of those days could not fail to examine into the death of a man of Squire Griffiths' standing. So the acute Ellis thought how he could conceal the culprit for a time.

'Come,' said he; 'don't look so scared! It was your doom, not your fault;' and he laid a hand on Owen's shoulder.

'You're wet,' said he, suddenly. 'Where have you been? Nest, your husband is dripping, drookit wet. That's what makes him look so blue and wan.'

Nest softly laid her baby in its cradle; she was half stupified with crying, and had not understood to what Owen alluded, when he spoke of his doom being fulfilled, if indeed she had heard the words.

Her touch thawed Owen's miserable heart.

'Oh, Nest!' said he, clasping her in his arms; 'do you love me still – can you love me, my own darling?'

'Why not?' asked she, her eyes filling with tears.

'I only love you more than ever, for you were my poor baby's father!'

'But, Nest – Oh, tell her, Ellis! *you* know.'

'No need, no need!' said Ellis. 'She's had enough to think on. Bustle, my girl, and get out my Sunday clothes.'

'I don't understand,' said Nest, putting her hand up to her head. 'What is to tell? and why are you so wet? God help me for a poor crazed thing, for I cannot guess at the meaning of your words and your strange looks! I only know my baby is dead!' and she burst into tears.

'Come, Nest! go and fetch him a change, quick!' and as she meekly obeyed, too languid to strive further to understand, Ellis said rapidly to Owen, in a low, hurried voice,

'Are you meaning that the Squire is dead? Speak low, lest she hear! Well, well, no need to talk about how he died. It was sudden, I see; and we must all of us die; and he'll have to be buried. It's well the night is near. And I should not wonder now if you'd like to travel for a bit; it would do Nest a power of good; and then – there's many a one goes out of his own house and never comes back again; and – I trust he's not lying in his own house – and there's a stir for a bit, and a search, and a wonder – and, by-and-by, the heir just steps in, as quiet as can be. And that's what you'll do, and bring Nest to Bodowen after all. Nay, child, better stockings nor those; find the blue woollens I bought at Llanrwst fair. Only don't lose heart. It's done now and can't be helped. It was the piece of work set you to do from the days of the Tudors, they say. And he deserved it. Look in yon cradle. So tell us where he is, and I'll take heart of grace and see what can be done for him.'

But Owen sat wet and haggard, looking into the peat fire as if for visions of the past, and never heeding a word Ellis said. Nor did he move when Nest brought the armful of dry clothes.

'Come, rouse up, man!' said Ellis, growing impatient.

But he neither spoke nor moved.

'What is the matter, father?' asked Nest, bewildered.

Ellis kept on watching Owen for a minute or two, till, on his daughter's repetition of the question, he said,

'Ask him yourself, Nest.'

'Oh, husband, what is it?' said she, kneeling down and bringing her face to a level with his.

'Don't you know?' said he, heavily. 'You won't love me when you do know. And yet it was not my doing. It was my doom.'

'What does he mean, father?' asked Nest, looking up; but she caught a gesture from Ellis urging her to go on questioning her husband.

'I will love you, husband, whatever has happened. Only let me know the worst.'

A pause, during which Nest and Ellis hung breathless.

'My father is dead, Nest.'

Nest caught her breath with a sharp gasp.

'God forgive him!' said she, thinking on her babe.

'God forgive *me*!' said Owen.

'You did not –' Nest stopped.

'Yes, I did. Now you know it. It was my doom. How could I help it? The devil helped me – he placed the stone so that my father fell. I jumped into the water to save him. I did, indeed, Nest. I was nearly drowned myself. But he was dead – dead – killed by the fall!'

'Then he is safe at the bottom of the sea?' said Ellis, with hungry eagerness.

'No, he is not; he lies in my boat,' said Owen, shivering a little, more at the thought of his last glimpse at his father's face than from cold.

'Oh, husband, change your wet clothes!' pleaded Nest, to whom the death of the old man was simply a horror with which she had nothing to do, while her husband's discomfort was a present trouble.

While she helped him to take off the wet garments which he would never have had energy enough to remove of himself, Ellis was busy[a] preparing food, and mixing a great tumbler of spirits and hot water. He stood over the unfortunate young man and compelled him to eat and drink, and made Nest too taste some mouthfuls – all the while planning in his own mind how best to conceal what had been done, and who had done it; not altogether without a certain feeling of vulgar triumph in the reflection that Nest, as she stood there, carelessly dressed, dishevelled[b] in her grief, was in reality the mistress of Bodowen, than which Ellis Pritchard had never seen a grander house, though he believed such might exist.

By dint of a few dexterous[c] questions he found out all he wanted to know from Owen, as he ate and drank. In fact, it was almost a relief to Owen to dilute the horror by talking about it. Before the meal was done, if meal it could be called, Ellis knew all he cared to know.

'Now, Nest, on with your cloak and haps.[29] Pack up what needs to go with you, for you and your husband must be half way to Liverpool by to-morrow's morn. I'll take you past Rhyl Sands in my fishing-boat, with yours in tow; and, once over the dangerous part, I'll return with my cargo of fish, and learn how much stir there is at Bodowen. Once safe hidden in Liverpool, no one will know where you are, and you may stay quiet till your time comes for returning.'

'I will never come home again,' said Owen, doggedly. 'The place is accursed!'

'Hoot! be guided by me, man. Why, it was but an accident, after all! And we'll land at the Holy Island, at the Point of Llyn; there is an old cousin of mine, the parson, there – for the Pritchards have known better days, Squire – and we'll bury him there. It was but an accident, man. Hold up your head! You and Nest will come home yet and fill Bodowen with children, and I'll live to see it.'

'Never!' said Owen. 'I am the last male of my race, and the son has murdered his father!'

Nest came in laden and cloaked. Ellis was for hurrying them off. The fire was extinguished, the door was locked.

'Here, Nest, my darling, let me take your bundle while I guide you down the steps.' But her husband bent his head, and spoke never a word. Nest gave her father the bundle (already loaded with such things as he himself had seen fit to take), but clasped another softly and tightly.

'No one shall help me with this,' said she, in a low voice.

Her father did not understand her; her husband did, and placed his strong helping arm round her waist, and blessed her.

'We will all go together, Nest,' said he. 'But where?' and he looked up at the storm-tossed clouds coming up from windward.

'It is a dirty night,' said Ellis, turning his head round to speak to his companions at last. 'But never fear, we'll weather it!' And he made for the place where his vessel was moored. Then he stopped and thought a moment.

'Stay here!' said he, addressing his companions. 'I may meet folk, and I shall, maybe, have to hear and to speak. You wait here till I come back for you.' So they sat down close together in a corner of the path.

'Let me look at him, Nest!' said Owen.

She took her little dead son out from under her shawl; they looked at his waxen face long and tenderly; kissed it, and covered it up reverently and softly.

'Nest,' said Owen, at last, 'I feel as though my father's spirit had been near us, and as if it had bent over our poor little one. A strange chilly air met me as I stooped over him. I could fancy the spirit of our pure, blameless child guiding my father's safe over the paths of the sky to the gates of heaven, and escaping those accursed dogs of hell that were darting up from the north in pursuit of souls not five minutes since.'

'Don't talk so, Owen,' said Nest, curling up to him in the darkness of the copse. 'Who knows what may be listening?'

The pair were silent, in a kind of nameless terror, till they heard Ellis Pritchard's loud whisper. 'Where are ye? Come along, soft and steady. There were folk about even now, and the Squire is missed, and madam in a fright.'

They went swiftly down to the little harbour, and embarked on board Ellis's boat. The sea heaved and rocked even there; the torn clouds went hurrying overhead in a wild tumultuous manner.

They put out into the bay; still in silence, except when some word of command was spoken by Ellis, who took the management of the vessel. They made for the rocky shore, where Owen's boat had been moored. It was not there. It had broken loose and disappeared.

Owen sat[a] down and covered his face. This last event, so simple and natural in itself, struck on his excited and superstitious mind in an extraordinary manner. He had hoped for a certain reconciliation, so to say, by laying his father and his child both in one grave. But now it appeared to him as if there was to be no forgiveness; as if his father revolted even in death against any such peaceful union. Ellis took a practical view of the case. If the Squire's body was found drifting about in a boat known to belong to his son, it would create terrible suspicion as to the manner of his death. At one time in the evening, Ellis had thought of persuading Owen to let him bury the Squire in a sailor's grave; or, in other words, to sew him up in a spare sail, and weighting it well, sink it for ever. He had not broached the subject, from a certain fear of Owen's passionate repugnance to the plan; otherwise, if he had consented, they might have returned to Penmorfa, and passively awaited the course of events, secure of Owen's succession to Bodowen, sooner or later; or if Owen was too much overwhelmed by what had happened, Ellis would have advised him to go away for a short time, and return when the buzz and the talk was over.

Now it was different. It was absolutely necessary that they should[a] leave the country for a time. Through those stormy waters they must plough[b] their way that very night. Ellis had no fear – would have had no fear, at any rate, with Owen as he had been a week, a day ago; but with Owen wild, despairing, helpless, fate-pursued, what could he do?

They sailed into the tossing darkness, and were never more seen of men.

The house of Bodowen has sunk into damp, dark ruins; and a Saxon stranger holds the lands of the Griffiths.

'HALF A LIFE-TIME AGO'

'Half a Life-Time Ago' was first published in three parts as 'Half a Life-Time Ago: In Five Chapters', *Household Words*, 12 (6, 13, 20 October 1855), pp. 229–37, 253–7, 276–82. The first part consisted of Chapters I and II; the second part of Chapter III; and the third part of Chapters IV and V. The story was first collected in *Round the Sofa*, 2 vols (London: Sampson Low, 1859), vol. ii, pp. 97–176. It was also published in the American periodicals *Littell's Living Age*, 11 (24 Nov 1855), pp. 478–96, and *Harper's New Monthly Magazine*, 12 (January 1856), pp. 185–202. It was reprinted in *My Lady Ludlow and Other Tales* (1861) and in *Lois the Witch and Other Tales* (Leipzig: Tauchnitz, 1861). The differences between the *HW* text and 1859 are slight; the latter is more heavily punctuated; there are a few insignificant changes of phrase.

'Half a Life-Time Ago' is a substantial rewriting of an early story, 'Martha Preston', which appeared in *Sartain's Union Magazine*, 6 (February 1850), pp. 133–8, and which EG never republished. However, although both stories are about a young woman who makes the choice between marriage and looking after her idiot brother, there are significant differences of plot and characterisation, nor did EG re-use passages of text. Though both are set in the Lake District the localities are precise and distinct. It is perhaps more accurate, therefore, to describe 'Martha Preston' and 'Half a Life-Time Ago' as two distinct stories with marked resemblances of plot and theme than to call the latter a revision of the former. In 'Martha Preston' there are references to a recent visit paid by EG to the Lake District, and to her acquaintance with Wordsworth and his family. There seems no reason to doubt that her original inspiration derived from the several holidays in the Lake District, and her reading of Wordsworth. In its revised form it is generally regarded as one of EG's most successful stories; high claims have been made for it: see for example *Easson*, pp. 211–12, and Stephen Gill, *Wordsworth and the Victorians* (Oxford: Oxford University Press, 1997), pp. 136–7.

The story was the occasion of Dickens's often-quoted comment: 'Mrs. Gaskell, fearful-fearful. If I were Mr G. O Heaven how I would beat her!' (*CD Letters*, vol. vii, p. 700 (11 September 1855)). The issue was probably the division of the story into parts for serial publication, as is suggested by a subsequent letter (*CD Letters*, vol vii, p. 710 (25 September 1855)), also to his colleague W. H. Wills:

Half a Life Time Ago will be well divided, I think, as you propose. I have marked a place at page 235 where the effect would be obviously served by making a new chapter. Is such a thing to be done with that lady? If so, do it.

HALF A LIFE-TIME AGO.

———•———

CHAPTER I.

HALF a life-time ago, there lived in one of the Westmoreland dales a single woman,[a] of the name of Susan Dixon. She was owner of the small farm-house where she resided, and of some thirty or forty acres of land by which it was surrounded. She had also an hereditary right to a sheep-walk, extend-ing to the wild fells that overhang Blea Tarn. In the language of the country, she was a Stateswoman. Her house is yet to be seen on the Oxenfell road, between Skelwith and Coniston.[1] You go along a moorland track, made by the carts that occasionally came for turf from the Oxenfell. A brook babbles and brattles[2] by the way-side, giving you a sense of companionship, which relieves the deep solitude in which this way is usually traversed. Some miles on this side of Coniston there is a farmstead – a gray stone house, and a square of farm-buildings surrounding a green space of rough turf, in the midst of which stands a mighty, funereal, umbrageous yew, making a solemn shadow, as of death, in the very heart and centre of the light and heat of the brightest summer day. On the side away from the house, this yard slopes down to a dark-brown pool, which is supplied with fresh water from the overflowings of a stone cistern, into which some rivulet of the brook before mentioned continually and melodiously falls bubbling. The cattle drink out of this cistern. The household bring their pitchers and fill them with drink-ing-water by a dilatory, yet pretty, process. The water-carrier brings with her a leaf of the hound's-tongue fern, and, inserting it in the crevice of the gray rock, makes a cool, green spout for the sparkling stream.

The house is no specimen, at the present day, of what it was in the life-time of Susan Dixon.[3] Then, every small diamond-pane in the windows glittered with cleanliness. You might have eaten off the floor; you could see yourself in the pewter plates and the polished oaken awmry, or dresser, of the state kitchen into which you entered. Few strangers penetrated further than this room. Once or twice, wandering tourists, attracted by the lonely picturesqueness of the situation, and the exquisite cleanliness of the house itself, made their way into this house-place, and offered money enough (as they thought) to tempt the hostess to receive them as lodgers. They would give no trouble, they said; they would be out rambling or sketching all day

long; would be perfectly content with a share of the food which she provided for herself; or would procure what they required from the Waterhead
Inn at Coniston. But no liberal sum – no fair words – moved her from her
stony manner, or her monotonous tone of indifferent refusal. No persuasion could induce her to show any more of the house than that first room;
no appearance of fatigue procured for the weary an invitation to sit down
and rest; and if one more bold and less delicate did so[a] without being asked,
Susan stood by, cold and apparently deaf, or only replying by the briefest
monosyllables, till the unwelcome visitor had departed. Yet those with
whom she had dealings, in the way of selling her cattle or her farm produce,
spoke of her as keen after a bargain – a hard one to have to do with; and she
never spared herself exertion or fatigue, at market or in the field, to make the
most of her produce. She led the hay-makers with her swift, steady rake, and
her noiseless evenness of motion. She was about among the earliest in the
market, examining samples of oats, pricing them, and then turning with
grim satisfaction to her own cleaner corn.

She was served faithfully and long by those who were rather her fellow-
labourers than her servants. She was even and just in her dealing with them.
If she was peculiar and silent, they knew her, and knew that she might be
relied on. Some of them had known her from her childhood; and deep in
their hearts was an unspoken – almost unconscious – pity for her; for they
knew her story, though they never spoke of it.

Yes; the time had been when that tall, gaunt, hard-featured, angular
woman – who never smiled, and hardly ever spoke an unnecessary word –
had been a fine-looking girl, bright-spirited and rosy; and when the hearth at
the Yew Nook had been as bright as she, with family love and youthful hope
and mirth. Fifty or fifty-one years ago, William Dixon and his wife Margaret
were alive; and Susan, their daughter, was about eighteen years old – ten
years older than the only other child, a boy named after his father. William
and Margaret Dixon were rather superior people, of a character belonging –
as far as I have seen – exclusively to the class of Westmoreland and Cumberland statesmen – just, independent, upright; not given to much speaking;
kind-hearted, but not demonstrative; disliking change, and new ways, and
new people; sensible and shrewd; each household self-contained, and its
members having[b] little curiosity as to their neighbours, with whom they
rarely met for any social intercourse, save at the stated times of sheep-shearing and Christmas; having a certain kind of sober pleasure in amassing
money, which occasionally made them miserable (as they call miserly people
up in the north) in their old age; reading no light or ephemeral literature;
but the grave, solid books brought round by the pedlars (such as the 'Paradise Lost' and 'Regained,' 'The Death of Abel,' 'The Spiritual Quixote,' and
'The Pilgrim's Progress')[4] were to be found in nearly every house: the men
occasionally going off laking, *i.e.* playing, *i.e.* drinking for days together, and

having to be hunted up by anxious wives, who dared not leave their husbands to the chances of the wild precipitous roads, but walked miles and
miles, lantern in hand, in the dead of night, to discover and guide the sol-
emnly-drunken husband home; who had a dreadful headache the next day,
and the day after that came forth as grave, and sober, and virtuous-looking as
if there were no such things as malt and spirituous liquors in the world; and
who were seldom reminded of their misdoings by their wives, to whom
such occasional outbreaks were as things of course, when once the immediate anxiety produced by them was over. Such were – such are – the
characteristics of a class now passing away from the face of the land, as their
compeers, the yeomen, have done before them. Of such was William Dixon.
He was a shrewd, clever farmer, in his day and generation, when shrewdness
was rather shown in the breeding and rearing of sheep and cattle than in the
cultivation of land. Owing to this character of his, statesmen from a distance,
from beyond Kendal, or from Borrowdale, of greater wealth than he, would
send their sons to be farm-servants for a year or two with him, in order to
learn some of his methods before setting up on land of their own. When
Susan, his daughter, was about seventeen, one Michael Hurst was farm-
servant at Yew Nook. He worked with the master, and lived with the family,
and was in all respects treated as an equal, except in the field. His father was
a wealthy statesman at Wythburne, up beyond Grasmere;[5] and through
Michael's servitude the families had become acquainted, and the Dixons
went over to the High Beck sheep-shearing, and the Hursts came down by
Red Bank and Loughrig Tarn and across the Oxenfell when there was the
Christmas-tide feasting at Yew Nook. The fathers strolled round the fields
together, examined cattle and sheep, and looked knowing over each other's
horses. The mothers inspected the dairies and household arrangements,
each openly admiring the plans of the other, but secretly preferring their
own. Both fathers and mothers cast a glance from time to time at Michael
and Susan, who were thinking of nothing less than farm or dairy, but whose
unspoken attachment was, in all ways, so suitable and natural a thing that
each parent rejoiced over it, although with characteristic reserve it was never
spoken about – not even between husband and wife.

Susan had been a strong, independent, healthy girl; a clever help to her
mother, and a spirited companion to her father; more of a man in her (as he
often said) than her delicate little brother ever would have. He was his
mother's darling, although she loved Susan well. There was no positive
engagement between Michael and Susan – I doubt whether even plain
words of love had been spoken; when one winter-time Margaret Dixon was
seized with inflammation consequent upon a neglected cold. She had always
been strong and notable,[6] and had been too busy to attend to the earliest
symptoms of illness. It would go off, she said to the woman who helped in
the kitchen; or if she did not feel better when they had got the hams and

bacon out of hand, she would take some herb-tea and nurse up a bit. But Death could not wait till the hams and bacon were cured: he came on with rapid strides, and shooting arrows of portentous agony. Susan had never seen illness – never knew how much she loved her mother till now, when she felt a dreadful, instinctive certainty that she was losing her. Her mind was thronged with recollections of the many times she had slighted her mother's wishes; her heart was full of the echoes of careless and angry replies that she had spoken. What would she not now give to have opportunities of service and obedience, and trials of her patience and love, for that dear mother who lay gasping in torture! And yet Susan had been a good girl and an affectionate daughter.

The sharp pain went off, and delicious ease came on; yet still her mother sunk. In the midst of this languid peace she was dying. She motioned Susan to her bedside, for she could only whisper; and then, while the father was out of the room, she spoke as much to the eager, hungering eyes of her daughter by the motion of her lips, as by the slow, feeble sounds of her voice.

'Susan, lass, thou must not fret. It is God's will, and thou wilt have a deal to do. Keep father straight if thou canst; and if he goes out Ulverstone ways, see that thou meet him before he gets to the Old Quarry. It's a dree bit for a man who has had a drop. As for lile Will' – here the poor woman's face began to work and her fingers to move nervously as they lay on the bed-quilt – 'lile Will will miss me most of all. Father's often vexed with him because he's not a quick, strong lad; he is not, my poor lile chap. And father thinks he's saucy, because he cannot always stomach oat-cake and porridge. There's better than three pound in th' old black teapot on the top shelf of the cupboard. Just keep a piece of loaf-bread by you, Susan dear, for Will to come to when he's not taken his breakfast. I have, may be, spoilt him; but there'll be no one to spoil him now.'

She began to cry a low, feeble cry, and covered up her face that Susan might not see her. That dear face! those precious moments while yet the eyes could look out with love and intelligence. Susan laid her head down close by her mother's ear.

'Mother, I'll take tent[7] of Will. Mother, do you hear? He shall not want ought I can give or get for him, least of all the kind words which you had ever ready for us both. Bless you! bless you! my own mother.'

'Thou'lt promise me that, Susan, wilt thou? I can die easy if thou'lt take charge of him. But he's hardly like other folk; he tries father at times, though I think father'll be tender of him when I'm gone, for my sake. And, Susan, there's one thing more. I never spoke on it for fear of the bairn being called a tell-tale, but I just comforted him up. He vexes Michael at times, and Michael has struck him before now. I did not want to make a stir; but he's not strong, and a word from thee, Susan, will go a long way with Michael.'

Susan was as red now as she had been pale before; it was the first time that her influence over Michael had been openly acknowledged by a third person, and a flash of joy came athwart the solemn sadness of the moment. Her mother had spoken too much, and now came on the miserable faintness. She never spoke again coherently; but when her children and her husband stood by her bedside, she took lile Will's hand and put it into Susan's, and looked at her with imploring eyes. Susan clasped her arms round Will, and leaned her head upon his curly little one, and vowed within herself to be as a mother to him.

Henceforward she was all in all to her brother. She was a more spirited and amusing companion to him than his mother had been, from her greater activity, and perhaps, also, from her originality of character, which often prompted her to perform her habitual actions in some new and racy manner. She was tender to lile Will when she was prompt and sharp with everybody else – with Michael most of all; for somehow the girl felt that, unprotected by her mother, she must keep up her own dignity, and not allow her lover to see how strong a hold he had upon her heart. He called her hard and cruel, and left her so; and she smiled softly to herself, when his back was turned, to think how little he guessed how deeply he was loved. For Susan was merely comely and fine-looking; Michael was strikingly handsome, admired by all the girls for miles round, and quite enough of a country coxcomb to know it and plume himself accordingly. He was the second son of his father; the eldest would have High Beck farm, of course, but there was a good penny in the Kendal bank in store for Michael. When harvest was over, he went to Chapel Langdale to learn to dance; and at night, in his merry moods, he would do his steps on the flag-floor of the Yew Nook kitchen, to the secret admiration of Susan, who had never learned dancing, but who flouted him perpetually, even while she admired, in accordance with the rule she seemed to have made for herself about keeping him at a distance so long as he lived under the same roof with her. One evening he sulked at some saucy remark of hers; he sitting in the chimney-corner with his arms on his knees, and his head bent forwards, lazily gazing into the wood-fire on the hearth, and luxuriating in rest after a hard day's labour; she sitting among the geraniums on the long, low window-seat, trying to catch the last slanting rays of the autumnal light to enable her to finish stitching a shirt-collar for Will, who lounged full length on the flags at the other side of the hearth to Michael, poking the burning wood from time to time with a long hazel-stick to bring out the leap of glittering sparks.

'And if you can dance a threesome reel, what good does it do ye?' asked Susan, looking askance at Michael, who had just been vaunting his proficiency. 'Does it help you plough, or reap, or even climb the rocks to take a raven's nest? If I were a man, I'd be ashamed to give in to such softness.'

'If you were a man, you'd be glad to do anything which made the pretty girls stand round and admire.'

'As they do to you, eh! Ho, Michael, that would not be my way o' being a man!'

'What would then?' asked he, after a pause, during which he had expected in vain that she would go on with her sentence. No answer.

'I should not like you as a man, Susy; you'd be too hard and headstrong.'

'Am I hard and headstrong?' asked she, with as indifferent a tone as she could assume, but which yet had a touch of pique in it. His quick ear detected the inflexion.

'No, Susy! You're wilful at times, and that's right enough. I don't like a girl without spirit. There's a mighty pretty girl comes to the dancing-class; but she is all milk and water. Her eyes never flash like yours[a] when you're put out; why, I can see them flame across the kitchen like a cat's in the dark. Now, if you were a man, I should feel queer before those looks of yours;[b] as it is, I rather like them, because –'

'Because what?' asked she, looking up and perceiving that he had stolen close up to her.

'Because I can make all right in this way,' said he, kissing her suddenly.

'Can you?' said she, wrenching herself out of his grasp and panting, half with rage. 'Take that, by way of proof that making right is none so easy.' And she boxed his ears pretty sharply. He went back to his seat discomfited and out of temper. She could no longer see to look, even if her face had not burnt and her eyes dazzled, but she did not choose to move her seat, so she still preserved her stooping attitude and pretended to go on sewing.

'Eleanor Hebthwaite may be milk-and-water,' muttered he, 'but – Confound thee, lad! what art doing?' exclaimed Michael, as a great piece of burning wood was cast into his face by an unlucky poke of Will's. 'Thou great lounging, clumsy chap, I'll teach thee better!' and with one or two good, round kicks he sent the lad whimpering away into the back-kitchen. When he had a little recovered himself from his passion, he saw Susan standing before him, her face looking strange and almost ghastly by the reversed position of the shadows, arising from the fire-light shining upwards right under it.

'I tell thee what, Michael,' said she, 'that lad's motherless, but not friendless.'

'His own father leathers him, and why should not I, when he's given me such a burn on my face?' said Michael, putting up his hand to his cheek as if in pain.

'His father's his father, and there is nought more to be said. But if he did burn thee, it was by accident, and not o' purpose, as thou kicked him; it's a mercy if his ribs are not broken.'

'He howls loud enough, I'm sure. I might ha' kicked many a lad twice as hard and they'd ne'er ha' said ought but "damn ye;" but yon lad must needs cry out like a stuck pig if one touches him,' replied Michael, sullenly.

Susan went back to the window-seat, and looked absently out of the window at the drifting clouds for a minute or two, while her eyes filled with tears. Then she got up and made for the outer door which led into the back-kitchen. Before she reached it, however, she heard a low voice, whose music made her thrill, say –

'Susan, Susan!'

Her heart melted within her, but it seemed like treachery to her poor boy, like faithlessness to her dead mother, to turn to her lover while the tears which he had caused to flow were yet unwiped on Will's cheeks. So she seemed to take no heed, but passed into the darkness, and, guided by the sobs, she found her way to where Willie sat crouched among disused tubs and churns.

'Come out wi' me, lad;' and they went into the orchard, where the fruit-trees were bare of leaves, but ghastly in their tattered covering of gray moss: and the soughing November wind came with long sweeps over the fells till it rattled among the crackling boughs, underneath which the brother and sister sat in the dark; he in her lap, and she hushing his head against her shoulder.

'Thou should'st na' play wi' fire. It's a naughty trick. Thou't suffer for it in worse ways nor this before thou'st done, I'm afeared. I should ha' hit thee twice as lungeous kicks as Mike, if I'd been in his place. He did na' hurt thee, I am sure,' she assumed, half as a question.

'Yes! but he did. He turned me quite sick.'

And he let his head fall languidly down on his sister's breast.

'Come lad! come lad!' said she, anxiously. 'Be a man. It was not much that I saw. Why, when first the red cow came, she kicked me far harder for offering to milk her before her legs were tied. See thee! here's a peppermint-drop, and I'll make thee a pasty to-night; only don't give way so, for it hurts me sore to think that Michael has done thee any harm, my pretty.'

Willie roused himself up, and put back the wet and ruffled hair from his heated face; and he and Susan rose up, and hand-in-hand went towards the house, walking slowly and quietly except for a kind of sob which Willie could not repress. Susan took him to the pump and washed his tear-stained face, till she thought she had obliterated all traces of the recent disturbance, arranging his curls for him, and then she kissed him tenderly, and led him in, hoping to find Michael in the kitchen, and make all straight between them. But the blaze had dropped down into darkness; the wood was a heap of gray[a] ashes in which the sparks ran hither and thither; but, even in the groping darkness, Susan knew by the sinking at her heart that Michael was not there. She threw another brand on the hearth and lighted the candle, and sat[a] down to her work in silence. Willie cowered on his stool by the side of the fire, eyeing his sister from time to time, and sorry and oppressed, he knew not why, by the sight of her grave, almost stern face. No one came. They two were in the house alone. The old woman who helped Susan with the household work had gone out for the night to some friend's dwelling. William Dixon, the father, was up on the fells seeing after his sheep. Susan had no heart to prepare the evening meal.

'Susy, darling, are you angry with me?' said Willie, in his little piping, gentle voice. He had stolen up to his sister's side. 'I won't never play with fire again; and I'll not cry if Michael does kick me. Only don't look so like dead mother – don't – don't – please don't!' he exclaimed, hiding his face on her shoulder.

'I'm not angry, Willie,' said she. 'Don't be feared on me. You want your supper, and you shall have it; and don't you be feared on Michael. He shall give reason for every hair of your head that he touches – he shall.'

When William Dixon came home, he found Susan and Willie sitting together, hand-in-hand, and apparently pretty cheerful. He bade them go to bed, for that he would sit up for Michael; and the next morning, when Susan came down, she found that Michael had started an hour before with the cart for lime. It was a long day's work; Susan knew it would be late, perhaps later than on the preceding night, before he returned – at any rate, past her usual bed-time; and on no account would she stop up a minute beyond that hour in the kitchen, whatever she might do in her bed-room. Here she sat and watched till past midnight; and when she saw him coming up the brow with the carts, she knew full well, even in that faint moonlight, that his gait was the gait of a man in liquor. But though she was annoyed and mortified to find in what way he had chosen to forget her, the fact did not disgust or shock her as it would have done many a girl, even at that day, who had not been brought up as Susan had, among a class who considered it no crime, but rather a mark of spirit, in a man to get drunk occasionally. Nevertheless, she chose to hold herself very high all the next day when Michael was, perforce, obliged to give up any attempt to do heavy work, and hung about the out-buildings and farm in a very disconsolate and sickly state. Willie had far more pity on him than Susan. Before evening, Willie and he were fast, and on his side, ostentatious friends. Willie rode the horses down to water; Willie helped him to chop wood. Susan sat[b] gloomily at her work, hearing an indistinct but cheerful conversation going on in the shippon, while the cows were being milked. She almost felt irritated with her little brother, as if he were a traitor, and had gone over to the enemy in the very battle that she was fighting in his cause. She was alone with no one to speak to, while they prattled on, regardless if she were glad or sorry.

Soon Willie burst in. 'Susan! Susan! come with me; I've something so pretty to show you. Round the corner of the barn – run! run –' (He was dragging her along, half reluctant, half desirous of some change in that weary day.) Round the corner of the barn; and caught hold of by Michael, who stood there awaiting her.

'O Willie!' cried she, 'you naughty boy. There is nothing pretty – what have you brought me here for? Let me go; I won't be held.'

'Only one word. Nay, if you wish it so much, you may go,' said Michael, suddenly loosing his hold as she struggled. But now she was free, she only drew off a step or two, murmuring something about Willie.

'You are going, then?' said Michael, with seeming sadness. 'You won't hear me say a word of what is in my heart.'

'How can I tell whether it is what I should like to hear?' replied she, still drawing back.

'That is just what I want you to tell me; I want you to hear it, and then to tell me whether you like it or not.'

'Well, you may speak,' replied she, turning her back, and beginning to plait the hem of her apron.

He came close to her ear.

'I'm sorry I hurt Willie the other night. He has forgiven me. Can you?'

'You hurt him very badly,' she replied. 'But you are right to be sorry. I forgive you.'

'Stop, stop!' said he, laying his hand upon her arm. 'There is something more I've got to say. I want you to be my – what is it they call it, Susan?'

'I don't know,' said she, half-laughing, but trying to get away with all her might now; and she was a strong girl, but she could not manage it.

'You do. My – what is it I want you to be?'

'I tell you I don't know, and you had best be quiet, and just let me go in, or I shall think you're as bad now as you were last night.'

'And how did you know what I was last night? It was past twelve when I came home. Were you watching? Ah, Susan! be my wife, and you shall never have to watch for a drunken husband. If I were your husband, I would come straight home, and count every minute an hour till I saw your bonny face. Now you know what I want you to be. I ask you to be my wife. Will you, my own dear Susan?'

She did not speak for some time. Then she only said, 'Ask father.' And now she was really off like a lapwing round the corner of the barn, and up in her own little room, crying with all her might, before the triumphant smile had left Michael's face where he stood.

The 'Ask father' was a mere form to be gone through. Old Daniel Hurst and William Dixon had talked over what they could respectively give their children long before this; and that was the parental way of arranging such matters. When the probable amount of worldly gear that he could give his child had been named by each father, the young folk, as they said, might take their own time in coming to the point which the old men, with the prescience of experience, saw that they were drifting to; no need to hurry them, for they were both young, and Michael, though active enough, was too thoughtless, old Daniel said, to be trusted with the entire management of a farm. Meanwhile, his father would look about him, and see after all the farms that were to be let.

Michael had a shrewd notion of this preliminary understanding between the fathers, and so felt less daunted than he might otherwise have done at making the application for Susan's hand. It was all right, there was not an obstacle; only a deal of good advice, which the lover thought might have as well been spared, and which it must be confessed he did not much attend to, although he assented to every part of it. Then Susan was called down stairs, and slowly came dropping into view down the steps which led from the two family apartments into the house-place. She tried to look composed and quiet, but it could not be done. She stood side by side with her lover, with her head drooping, her cheeks burning, not daring to look up or move, while her father made the newly-betrothed a somewhat formal address in which he gave his consent, and many a piece of worldly wisdom beside. Susan listened as well as she could for the beating of her heart; but when her father solemnly and sadly referred to his own lost wife, she could keep from sobbing no longer; but throwing her apron over her face, she sat down on the bench by the dresser, and fairly gave way to pent-up tears. Oh, how strangely sweet to be comforted as she was comforted, by tender caress, and many a low-whispered promise of love![a] Her father sat[b] by the fire, thinking of the days that were gone; Willie was still out of doors; but Susan and Michael felt no one's presence or absence – they only knew they were together as betrothed husband and wife.

In a week, or two, they were formally told of the arrangements to be made in their favour. A small farm in the neighbourhood happened to fall vacant; and Michael's father offered to take it for him, and be responsible for the rent for the first year, while William Dixon was to contribute a certain amount of stock, and both fathers were to help towards the furnishing of the house. Susan received all this information in a quiet, indifferent way; she did not care much for any of these preparations, which were to hurry her through the happy hours; she cared least of all for the money amount of dowry and of substance. It jarred on her to be made the confidant of occasional slight repinings of Michael's, as one by one his future father-in-law set aside a beast or a pig for Susan's portion, which were not always the best animals of their kind upon the farm. But he also complained of his own father's stinginess, which somewhat, though not much, alleviated Susan's dislike to being awakened out of her pure dream of love to the consideration of worldly wealth.

But in the midst of all this bustle, Willie moped and pined. He had the same chord of delicacy running through his mind that made his body feeble and weak. He kept out of the way, and was apparently occupied in whittling and carving uncouth heads on hazel-sticks in an out-house. But he positively avoided Michael, and shrunk away even from Susan. She was too much occupied to notice this at first. Michael pointed it out to her, saying, with a laugh, –

'Look at Willie! he might be a cast-off lover and jealous of me, he looks so dark and downcast at me.' Michael spoke this jest out loud, and Willie burst into tears, and ran out of the house.

'Let me go. Let me go!' said Susan (for her lover's arm was round her waist). 'I must go to him if he's fretting. I promised mother I would!' She pulled herself away, and went in search of the boy. She sought in byre and barn, through the orchard, where indeed in this leafless winter-time there was no great concealment, up into the room where the wool was usually stored in the later summer, and at last she found him, sitting at bay, like some hunted creature, up behind the wood-stack.

'What are ye gone for, lad, and me seeking you everywhere?' asked she, breathless.

'I did not know you would seek me. I've been away many a time, and no one has cared to seek me,' said he, crying afresh.

'Nonsense,' replied Susan, 'don't be so foolish, ye little good-for-nought.' But she crept up to him in the hole he had made underneath the great, brown sheafs of wood, and squeezed herself down by him. 'What for should folk seek after you, when you get away from them whenever you can?' asked she.

'They don't want me to stay. Nobody wants me. If I go with father, he says I hinder more than I help. You used to like to have me with you. But now, you've taken up with Michael, and you'd rather I was away; and I can just bide away; but I cannot stand Michael jeering at me. He's got you to love him and that might serve him.'

'But I love you, too, dearly, lad!' said she, putting her arm round his neck.

'Which on us do you like best?' said he, wistfully, after a little pause, putting her arm away, so that he might look in her face, and see if she spoke truth.

She went very red.

'You should not ask such questions. They are not fit for you to ask, nor for me to answer.'

'But mother bade you love me!' said he, plaintively.

'And so I do. And so I ever will do. Lover nor husband shall come betwixt thee and me, lad – ne'er a one of them. That I promise thee (as I promised mother before),[a] in the sight of God and with her hearkening now, if ever she can hearken to earthly word again. Only I cannot abide to have thee fretting, just because my heart is large enough for two.'

'And thou'lt love me always?'

'Always, and ever. And the more – the more thou'lt love Michael,' said she, dropping her voice.

'I'll try,' said the boy, sighing, for he remembered many a harsh word and blow of which his sister knew nothing. She would have risen up to go away, but he held her tight, for here and now she was all his own, and he did not know when such a time might come again. So the two sat[a] crouched up and silent, till they heard the horn blowing at the field-gate, which was the summons home to any wanderers belonging to the farm, and at this hour of the evening, signified that supper was ready. Then the two went in.

CHAPTER II.

SUSAN and Michael were to be married in April. He had already gone to take possession of his new farm, three or four miles away from Yew Nook – but that is neighbouring, according to the acceptation of the word in that thinly-populated district, – when William Dixon fell ill. He came home one evening, complaining of head-ache and pains in his limbs, but seemed to loathe the posset which Susan prepared for him; the treacle-posset which was the homely country remedy against an incipient cold. He took to his bed with a sensation of exceeding weariness, and an odd, unusual looking-back to the days of his youth, when he was a lad living with his parents, in this very house.

The next morning he had forgotten all his life since then, and did not know his own children; crying, like a newly-weaned baby, for his mother to come and soothe away his terrible pain. The doctor from Coniston said it was the typhus-fever, and warned Susan of its infectious character, and shook his head over his patient. There were no friends near to come and share her anxiety; only good, kind old Peggy, who was faithfulness itself, and one or two labourers' wives, who would fain have helped her, had not their hands been tied by their responsibility to their own families. But, somehow, Susan neither feared nor flagged. As for fear, indeed, she had no time to give way to it, for every energy of both body and mind was required. Besides, the young have had too little experience of the danger of infection to dread it much. She did indeed wish, from time to time, that Michael had been at home to have taken Willie over to his father's at High Beck; but then, again, the lad was docile and useful to her, and his fecklessness in many things might make him be harshly treated by strangers; so, perhaps, it was as well that Michael was away at Appleby fair, or even beyond that – gone into York-shire after horses.

Her father grew worse; and the doctor insisted on sending over a nurse from Coniston. Not a professed nurse – Coniston could not have supported such a one; but a widow who was ready to go where the doctor sent her for the sake of the payment. When she came, Susan suddenly gave way; she was felled by the fever herself, and lay unconscious for long weeks. Her con-sciousness returned to her one spring afternoon; early spring; April, her wedding-month. There was a little fire burning in the small corner-grate, and the flickering of the blaze was enough for her to notice in her weak state. She felt that there was some one sitting on the window-side of her bed, behind the curtain, but she did not care to know who it was; it was even too great a trouble for her languid mind to consider who it was likely to be. She would rather shut her eyes, and melt off again into the gentle luxury of sleep. The next time she wakened, the Coniston nurse perceived her movement, and made her a cup of tea, which she drank with eager relish; but still they did not speak, and once more Susan lay motionless – not asleep, but strangely, pleasantly conscious of all the small chamber and household sounds; the fall of a cinder on the hearth, the fitful singing of the half-empty kettle, the cattle tramping out to field again after they had been milked, the aged step on the creaking stair – old Peggy's, as she knew. It came to her door; it stopped; the person outside listened for a moment, and then lifted the wooden latch, and looked in. The watcher by the bedside arose, and went to her. Susan would have been glad to see Peggy's face once more, but was far too weak to turn, so she lay and listened.

'How is she?' whispered one trembling, aged voice.

'Better,' replied the other. 'She's been awake, and had a cup of tea. She'll do now.'

'Has she asked after him?'

'Hush! No; she has not spoken a word.'

'Poor lass! poor lass!'

The door was shut. A weak feeling of sorrow and self-pity came over Susan. What was wrong? Whom had she loved? And dawning, dawning, slowly rose the sun of her former life, and all particulars were made distinct to her. She felt that some sorrow was coming to her, and cried over it before she knew what it was, or had strength enough to ask. In the dead of night, – and she had never slept again, – she softly called to the watcher, and asked,

'Who?'

'Who what?' replied the woman, with a conscious affright, ill-veiled by a poor assumption of ease. 'Lie still, there's a darling, and go to sleep. Sleep's better for you than all the doctor's stuff.'

'Who?' repeated Susan. 'Something is wrong. Who?'

'Oh, dear!' said the woman. 'There's nothing wrong. Willie has taken the turn, and is doing nicely.'

'Father?'

'Well! he's all right now,' she answered, looking another way, as if seeking for something.

'Then it's Michael! Oh, me! oh, me!' She set up a succession of weak, plaintive, hysterical cries before the nurse could pacify her, by declaring that Michael had been at the house not three hours before to ask after her, and looked as well and as hearty as ever man did.

'And you heard of no harm to him since?' inquired Susan.

'Bless the lass, no, for sure! I've ne'er heard his name named since I saw him go out of the yard as stout a man as ever trod shoe-leather.'

'It was well, as the nurse said afterwards to Peggy, that Susan had been so easily pacified by the equivocating answer in respect to her father. If she had pressed the questions home in his case as she did in Michael's, she would have learnt that he was dead and buried more than a month before. It was well, too, that in her weak state of convalescence (which lasted long after this first day of consciousness) her perceptions were not sharp enough to observe the sad change that had taken place in Willie. His bodily strength returned, his appetite was something enormous, but his eyes wandered continually; his regard could not be arrested; his speech became slow, impeded, and incoherent. People began to say, that the fever had taken away the little wit Willie Dixon had ever possessed, and that they feared that he would end in being a 'natural,'[a] as they call an idiot in the Dales.

The habitual affection and obedience to Susan lasted longer than any other feeling that the boy had had previous to his illness; and, perhaps, this made her be the last to perceive what every one else had long anticipated. She felt the awakening rude when it did come. It was in this wise: –

One June evening, she sat out of doors under the yew-tree, knitting. She was pale still from her recent illness; and her languor, joined to the fact of her black dress, made her look more than usually interesting. She was no longer the buoyant self-sufficient Susan, equal to every occasion. The men were bringing in the cows to be milked, and Michael was about in the yard giving orders and directions with somewhat the air of a master, for the farm belonged of right to Willie, and Susan had succeeded to the guardianship of her brother. Michael and she were to be married as soon as she was strong enough – so, perhaps, his authoritative manner was justified; but the labourers did not like it, although they said little. They remembered him a stripling on the farm, knowing far less than they did, and often glad to shelter his ignorance of all agricultural matters behind their superior knowledge. They would have taken orders from Susan with far more willingness; nay! Willie himself might have commanded them; and from the old hereditary feeling toward the owners of land, they would have obeyed him with far greater cordiality then they now showed to Michael. But Susan was tired with even three rounds of knitting, and seemed not to notice, or to care, how things went on around her; and Willie – poor Willie! – there he stood lounging against the door-sill, enormously grown and developed, to be sure, but with restless eyes and ever-open mouth, and every now and then setting up a strange kind of howling cry, and then smiling vacantly to himself at the sound he had made. As the two old labourers passed him, they looked at each other ominously, and shook their heads.

'Willie, darling,' said Susan, 'don't make that noise – it makes my head ache.'

She spoke feebly, and Willie did not seem to hear; at any rate, he continued his howl from time to time.

'Hold thy noise, wilt'a?' said Michael, roughly, as he passed near him, and threatening him with his fist. Susan's back was turned to the pair. The expression of Willie's face changed from vacancy to fear, and he came shambling up to Susan, and put her arm round him, and, as if protected by that shelter, he began making faces at Michael. Susan saw what was going on, and, as if now first struck by the strangeness of her brother's manner, she looked anxiously at Michael for an explanation. Michael was irritated at Willie's defiance of him, and did not mince the matter.

'It's just that the fever has left him silly – he never was as wise as other folk, and now I doubt if he will ever get right.'

Susan did not speak, but she went very pale, and her lip quivered. She looked long and wistfully at Willie's face, as he watched the motion of the ducks in the great stable-pool. He laughed softly to himself every now and then.

'Willie likes to see the ducks go overhead,' said Susan, instinctively adopting the form of speech she would have used to a young child.

'Willie, boo! Willie, boo!' he replied, clapping his hands, and avoiding her eye.

'Speak properly, Willie,' said Susan, making a strong effort at self-control, and trying to arrest his attention.

'You know who I am – tell me my name!' She grasped his arm almost painfully tight to make him attend. Now he looked at her, and, for an instant, a gleam of recognition quivered over his face; but the exertion was evidently painful, and he began to cry at the vainness of the effort to recall her name. He hid his face upon her shoulder with the old affectionate trick of manner. She put him gently away, and went into the house into her own little bedroom. She locked the door, and did not reply at all to Michael's calls for her, hardly spoke to old Peggy, who tried to tempt her out to receive some homely sympathy, and through the open casement there still came the idiotic sound of 'Willie, boo! Willie, boo!'

CHAPTER III.

AFTER the stun of the blow came the realisation of the consequences. Susan would sit for hours trying patiently to recall and piece together fragments of recollection and consciousness in her brother's mind. She would let him go and pursue some senseless bit of play, and wait until she could catch his eye or his attention again, when she would resume her self-imposed task. Michael complained that she never had a word for him, or a minute of time to spend with him now; but she only said she must try, while there was yet a chance, to bring back her brother's lost wits. As for marriage in this state of uncertainty, she had no heart to think of it. Then Michael stormed, and absented himself for two or three days; but it was of no use. When he came back, he saw that she had been crying till her eyes were all swollen up, and he gathered from Peggy's scoldings (which she did not spare him) that Susan had eaten nothing since he went away. But she was as inflexible as ever.

'Not just yet. Only not just yet. And don't say again that I do not love you,' said she, suddenly hiding herself in his arms.

And so matters went on through August. The crop of oats was gathered in; the wheat-field was not ready as yet, when one fine day Michael drove up in a borrowed shandry, and offered to take Willie a ride. His manner, when Susan asked him where he was going to, was rather confused; but the answer was straight and clear enough.

'He had business in Ambleside. He would never lose sight of the lad, and have him back safe and sound before dark.' So Susan let him go.

Before night they were at home again: Willie in high delight at a little rattling, paper windmill that Michael had bought for him in the street, and striving to imitate this new sound with perpetual buzzings. Michael, too, looked pleased. Susan knew the look, although afterwards she remembered that he had tried to veil it from her, and had assumed a grave appearance of sorrow whenever he caught her eye. He put up his horse; for, although he had three miles further to go, the moon was up – the bonny harvest-moon – and he did not care how late he had to drive on such a road by such a light. After the supper which Susan had prepared for the travellers was over, Peggy went up-stairs to see Willie safe in bed; for he had to have the same care taken of him that a little child of four years old requires.

Michael drew near to Susan.

'Susan,' said he, 'I took Will to see Dr. Preston, at Kendal. He's the first doctor in the county. I thought it were better for us – for you – to know at once what chance there were for him.'

'Well!' said Susan, looking eagerly up. She saw the same strange glance of satisfaction, the same instant change to apparent regret and pain. 'What did he say?' said she. 'Speak! can't you?'

'He said he would never get better of his weakness.'

'Never!'

'No; never. It's a long word, and hard to bear. And there's worse to come, dearest. The doctor thinks he will get badder from year to year. And he said, if he was us – you – he would send him off in time to Lancaster Asylum. They've ways there both of keeping such people in order and making them happy. I only tell you what he said,' continued he, seeing the gathering storm in her face.

'There was no harm in his saying it,' she replied, with great self-constraint, forcing herself to speak coldly instead of angrily. 'Folk is welcome to their opinions.'

They sat silent for a minute or two, her breast heaving with suppressed feeling.

'He's counted a very clever man,' said Michael, at length.

'He may be. He's none of my clever men, nor am I going to be guided by him, whatever he may think. And I don't thank them that went and took my poor lad to have such harsh notions formed about him. If I'd been there, I could have called out the sense that is in him.'

'Well! I'll not say more to-night, Susan. You're not taking it rightly, and I'd best be gone, and leave you to think it over. I'll not deny they are hard words to hear, but there's sense in them, as I take it; and I reckon you'll have to come to 'em. Anyhow, it's a bad way of thanking me for my pains, and I don't take it well in you, Susan,' said he, getting up, as if offended.

'Michael, I'm beside myself with sorrow. Don't blame me, if I speak sharp. He and me is the only ones, you see. And mother did so charge me to have a care of him! And this is what he's come to, poor lile chap!' She began to cry, and Michael to comfort her with caresses.

'Don't,' said she. 'It's no use trying to make me forget poor Willie is a natural. I could hate myself for being happy with you, even for just a little minute. Go away, and leave me to face it out.'

'And you'll think it over, Susan, and remember what the doctor says?'

'I can't forget it,' said she. She meant she could not forget what the doctor had said about the hopelessness of her brother's case; Michael[a] had referred to the plan of sending Willie away to an asylum, or madhouse, as they were called in that day and place. The idea had been gathering force in Michael's mind for some time; he had talked it over with his father, and secretly rejoiced over the possession of the farm and land which would then be his in fact, if not in law, by right of his wife. He had always considered the good penny her father could give her in his catalogue of Susan's charms and attractions. But of late he had grown to esteem her as the heiress of Yew Nook. He, too, should have land like his brother – land to possess, to cultivate, to make profit from, to bequeath. For some time he had wondered that Susan had been so much absorbed in Willie's present, that she had never seemed to look forward to his future, state. Michael had long felt the boy to be a trouble; but of late he had absolutely loathed him. His gibbering, his uncouth gestures, his loose, shambling gait, all irritated Michael inexpressibly. He did not come near the Yew Nook for a couple of days. He thought that he would leave her time to become anxious to see him and reconciled to his plan. They were strange, lonely days to Susan. They were the first she had spent face to face with the sorrows that had turned her from a girl into a woman; for hitherto Michael had never let twenty-four hours pass by without coming to see her since she had had the fever. Now that he was absent, it seemed as though some cause of irritation was removed from Will, who was much more gentle and tractable than he had been for many weeks. Susan thought that she observed him making efforts at her bidding, and there was something piteous in the way in which he crept up to her, and looked wistfully in her face, as if asking her to restore him the faculties that he felt to be wanting.

'I never will let thee go, lad. Never! There's no knowing where they would take thee to, or what they would do with thee. As it says in the Bible, "Nought but death shall part thee and me!"'[8]

The country-side was full, in those days, of stories of the brutal treatment offered to the insane; stories that were, in fact, but too well founded, and the truth of one of which only would have been a sufficient reason for the strong prejudice existing against all such places. Each succeeding hour that Susan passed, alone, or with the poor affectionate lad for her sole companion, served to deepen her solemn resolution never to part with him. So, when Michael came, he was annoyed and surprised by the calm way in which she spoke, as if following Dr. Preston's advice was utterly and entirely out of the question. He had expected nothing less than a consent, reluctant it might be, but still a consent; and he was extremely irritated. He could have repressed his anger, but he chose rather to give way to it; thinking that he could thus best work upon Susan's affection, so as to gain his point. But, somehow, he over-reached himself; and now he was astonished in his turn at the passion of indignation that she burst into.

'Thou wilt not bide in the same house with him, say'st thou? There's no need for thy biding, as far as I can tell. There's solemn reason why I should bide with my own flesh and blood, and keep to the word I pledged my mother on her death-bed; but, as for thee, there's no tie that I know on to keep thee fro'[a] going to America or Botany Bay this very night, if that were thy inclination. I will have no more of your threats to make me send my bairn away. If thou marry me, thou'lt help me to take charge of Willie. If thou doesn't choose to marry me on those terms – why! I can snap my fingers at thee, never fear. I'm not so far gone in love as that. But I will not have thee, if thou say'st in such a hectoring way that Willie must go out of the house – and the house his own too – before thou'lt set foot in it. Willie bides here, and I bide with him.'

'Thou hast may-be spoken a word too much,' said Michael, pale with rage. 'If I am free, as thou say'st, to go to Canada or Botany Bay, I reckon I'm free to live where I like, and that will not be with a natural who may turn into a madman some day, for aught I know. Choose between him and me, Susy, for I swear to thee, thou shan't have both.'

'I have chosen,' said Susan, now perfectly composed and still. 'Whatever comes of it, I bide with Willie.'

'Very well,' replied Michael, trying to assume an equal composure of manner. 'Then I'll wish you a very good night.' He went out of the house-door, half-expecting to be called back again; but, instead, he heard a hasty step inside, and a bolt drawn.

'Whew!' said he to himself, 'I think I must leave my lady alone for a week or two, and give her time to come to her senses. She'll not find it so easy as she thinks to let me go.'

So he went past the kitchen-window in nonchalant style, and was not seen again at Yew Nook for some weeks. How did he pass the time? For the first day or two, he was unusually cross with all things and people that came athwart him. Then wheat-harvest began, and he was busy, and exultant about his heavy crop. Then a man came from a distance to bid for the lease of his farm, which, by his father's advice, had been offered for sale, as he himself was so soon likely to remove to the Yew Nook. He had so little idea that Susan really would remain firm to her determination, that he at once began to haggle with the man who came after his farm, showed him the crop just got in, and managed skilfully enough to make a good bargain for himself. Of course, the bargain had to be sealed at the public-house; and the companions he met with there soon became friends enough to tempt him into Langdale, where again he met with Eleanor Hebthwaite.

How did Susan pass the time? For the first day or so, she was too angry and offended to cry. She went about her household duties in a quick, sharp, jerking, yet absent way; shrinking one moment from Will, overwhelming him with remorseful caresses the next. The third day of Michael's absence, she had the relief of a good fit of crying; and after that, she grew softer and more tender; she felt how harshly she had spoken to him, and remembered how angry she had been.

She made excuses for him. 'It was no wonder,' she said to herself, 'that he had been vexed with her; and no wonder he would not give in, when she had never tried to speak gently or to reason with him. She was to blame, and she would tell him so, and tell him once again all that her mother had bade her be to Willie, and all the horrible stories she had heard about madhouses, and he would be on her side at once.'

And so she watched for his coming, intending to apologise as soon as ever she saw him. She hurried over her household work, in order to sit quietly at her sewing, and hear the first distant sound of his well-known step or whistle. But even the sound of her flying needle seemed too loud – perhaps she was losing an exquisite instant of anticipation; so she stopped sewing, and looked longingly out through the geranium leaves, in order that her eye might catch the first stir of the branches in the wood-path by which he generally came. Now and then a bird might spring out of the covert; otherwise the leaves were heavily still in the sultry weather of early autumn. Then she would take up her sewing, and, with a spasm of resolution, she would determine that a certain task should be fulfilled before she would again allow herself the poignant luxury of expectation. Sick at heart was she when the evening closed in, and the chances of that day diminished. Yet she stayed up longer than usual, thinking that if he were coming – if he were only passing along the distant road – the sight of a light in the window might encourage him to make his appearance even at that late hour, while seeing the house all darkened and shut up might quench any such intention.

Very sick and weary at heart, she went to bed; too desolate and despairing to cry, or make any moan. But in the morning hope came afresh. Another day – another chance! And so it went on for weeks. Peggy understood her young mistress's sorrow full well, and respected it by her silence on the subject. Willie seemed happier now that the irritation of Michael's presence was removed; for the poor idiot had a sort of antipathy to Michael, which was a kind of heart's echo to the repugnance in which the latter held him. Altogether, just at this time, Willie was the happiest of the three.

As Susan went into Coniston, to sell her butter, one Saturday, some inconsiderate person told her that she had seen Michael Hurst the night before. I said inconsiderate, but I might rather have said unobservant; for any one who had spent half-an-hour in Susan Dixon's company might have seen that she disliked having any reference made to the subjects nearest her heart, were they joyous or grievous. Now she went a little paler than usual (and she had never recovered her colour since she had had the fever), and tried to keep silence. But an irrepressible pang forced out the question –

'Where?'

'At Thomas Applethwaite's, in Langdale. They had a kind of harvest-home, and he were there among the young folk, and very thick wi' Nelly

Hebthwaite, old Thomas's niece. Thou'lt have to look after him a bit, Susan!'

She neither smiled nor sighed. The neighbour who had been speaking to her was struck with the gray stillness of her face. Susan herself felt how well her self-command was obeyed by every little muscle, and said to herself in her Spartan manner, 'I can bear it without either wincing or blenching.' She went home early, at a tearing, passionate pace, trampling and breaking through all obstacles of briar or bush. Willie was moping in her absence – hanging listlessly on the farm-yard gate to watch for her. When he saw her, he set up one of his strange, inarticulate cries, of which she was now learning the meaning, and came towards her with his loose, galloping run, head and limbs all shaking and wagging with pleasant excitement. Suddenly she turned from him, and burst into tears. She sat[a] down on a stone by the way-side, not a hundred yards from home, and buried her face in her hands, and gave way to a passion of pent-up sorrow; so terrible and full of agony were her low cries, that the idiot stood by her, aghast and silent. All his joy gone for the time, but not, like her joy, turned into ashes. Some thought struck him. Yes! the sight of her woe made him think, great as the exertion was. He ran, and stumbled, and shambled home, buzzing with his lips all the time. She never missed him. He came back in a trice, bringing with him his cherished paper windmill, bought on that fatal day when Michael had taken him into Kendal to have his doom of perpetual idiotcy pronounced. He thrust it into Susan's face, her hands, her lap, regardless of the injury his frail plaything thereby received. He leapt before her to think how he had cured all heart-sorrow, buzzing louder than ever. Susan looked up at him, and that glance of her sad eyes sobered him. He began to whimper, he knew not why: and she now, comforter in her turn, tried to soothe him by twirling his windmill. But it was broken; it made no noise; it would not go round. This seemed to afflict Susan more than him. She tried to make it right, although she saw the task was hopeless; and while she did so, the tears rained down unheeded from her bent head on the paper toy.

'It won't do,' said she, at last. 'It will never do again.' And, somehow, she took the accident and her words as omens of the love that was broken, and that she feared could never be pieced together more. She rose up and took Willie's hand, and the two went slowly in to the house.

To her surprise, Michael Hurst sat in the house-place. House-place is a sort of better kitchen, where no cookery is done, but which is reserved for state occasions. Michael had gone in there because he was accompanied by his only sister, a woman older than himself, who was well married beyond Keswick, and who now came for the first time to make acquaintance with Susan. Michael had primed his sister with his wishes regarding Will,[b] and the position in which he stood with Susan; and arriving at Yew Nook in the absence of the latter, he had not scrupled to conduct his sister into the guest-room, as he held Mrs. Gale's worldly position in respect and admiration, and therefore wished her to be favourably impressed with all the signs of property which he was beginning to consider as Susan's greatest charms. He had secretly said to himself, that if Eleanor Hebthwaite and Susan Dixon were equal in point of riches,[a] he would sooner have Eleanor by far. He had begun to consider Susan as a termagant; and when he thought of his intercourse with her, recollections of her somewhat warm and hasty temper came far more readily to his mind than any remembrance of her generous, loving nature.

And now she stood face to face with him; her eyes tear-swollen, her garments dusty, and here and there torn in consequence of her rapid progress through the bushy by-paths. She did not make a favourable impression on the well-clad Mrs. Gale, dressed in her best silk gown, and therefore unusually susceptible to the appearance of another. Nor were Susan's[b] manners gracious or cordial. How could they be, when she remembered what had passed between Michael and herself the last time they met? For her penitence had faded away under the daily disappointment of these last weary weeks.

But she was hospitable in substance. She bade Peggy hurry on the kettle, and busied herself among the tea-cups, thankful that the presence of Mrs. Gale, as a stranger, would prevent the immediate recurrence to the one subject which she felt must be present in Michael's mind as well as in her own. But Mrs. Gale was withheld by no such feelings of delicacy. She had come ready-primed with the case, and had undertaken to bring the girl to reason. There was no time to be lost. It had been prearranged between the brother and sister that he was to stroll out into the farm-yard before his sister introduced the subject; but she was so confident in the success of her arguments, that she must needs have the triumph of a victory as soon as possible; and, accordingly, she brought a hail-storm of good reasons to bear upon Susan. Susan did not reply for a long time; she was so indignant at this intermeddling of a stranger in the deep family sorrow and shame. Mrs. Gale thought she was gaining the day, and urged her arguments more pitilessly. Even Michael winced for Susan, and wondered at her silence. He shrunk out of sight, and into the shadow, hoping that his sister might prevail, but annoyed at the hard way in which she kept putting the case.

Suddenly Susan turned round from the occupation she had pretended to be engaged in, and said to him in a low voice, which yet not only vibrated itself, but made its hearers thrill through all their obtuseness:

'Michael Hurst! does your sister speak truth, think you?'

Both women looked at him for his answer; Mrs. Gale without anxiety, for had she not said the very words they had spoken together before; had she not used the very arguments that he himself had suggested? Susan, on the contrary, looked to his answer as settling her doom for life; and in the gloom of her eyes you might have read more despair than hope.

He shuffled his position. He shuffled in his words.

'What is it you ask? My sister has said many things.'

'I ask you,' said Susan, trying to give a crystal clearness both to her expressions and her pronunciation, 'if, knowing as you do how Will is afflicted, you will help me to take that charge of him which I promised my mother on her death-bed that I would do; and which means, that I shall keep him always with me, and do all in my power to make his life happy. If you will do this, I will be your wife; if not, I remain unwed.'

'But he may get dangerous; he can be but a trouble; his being here is a pain to you, Susan, not a pleasure.'

'I ask you for either yes or no,' said she, a little contempt at his evading her question mingling with her tone. He perceived it, and it nettled him.

'And I have told you. I answered your question the last time I was here. I said I would ne'er keep house with an idiot; no more I will. So now you've gotten your answer.'

'I have,' said Susan. And she sighed deeply.

'Come, now,' said Mrs. Gale, encouraged by the sigh; 'one would think you don't love Michael, Susan, to be so stubborn in yielding to what I'm sure would be best for the lad.'

'Oh! she does not care for me,' said Michael. 'I don't believe she ever did.'

'Don't I? Haven't I?' asked Susan, her eyes blazing out fire. She left the room directly, and sent Peggy in to make the tea; and catching at Will, who was lounging about in the kitchen, she went up-stairs with him and bolted herself in, straining the boy to her heart, and keeping almost breathless, lest any noise she made might cause him to break out into the howls and sounds which she could not bear that those below should hear.

A knock at the door. It was Peggy.

'He wants for to see you, to wish you good-bye.'

'I cannot come. Oh, Peggy, send them away.'

It was her only cry for sympathy; and the old servant understood it. She sent them away, somehow; not politely, as I have been given to understand.

'Good go with them,' said Peggy, as she grimly watched their retreating figures. 'We're rid of bad rubbish, anyhow.'[9] And she turned into the house, with the intention of making ready some refreshment for Susan, after her hard day at the market, and her harder evening. But in the kitchen, to which she passed through the empty house-place, making a face of contemptuous dislike at the used tea-cups and fragments of a meal yet standing there, she found Susan, with her sleeves tucked up and her working apron on, busied in preparing to make clap-bread,[10] one of the hardest and hottest domestic tasks of a Daleswoman.[a] She looked up, and first met and then avoided

Peggy's eye; it was too full of sympathy. Her own cheeks were flushed, and her own eyes were dry and burning.

'Where's the board, Peggy? We need clap-bread; and, I reckon, I've time to get through with it to-night.' Her voice had a sharp, dry tone in it, and her motions a jerking angularity about them.

Peggy said nothing, but fetched her all that she needed. Susan beat her cakes thin with vehement force. As she stooped over them, regardless even of the task in which she seemed so much occupied, she was surprised by a touch on her mouth of something – what she did not see at first. It was a cup of tea, delicately sweetened and cooled, and held to her lips, when exactly ready, by the faithful old woman. Susan held it off a hand's breath, and looked into Peggy's eyes, while her own filled with the strange relief of tears.

'Lass!' said Peggy, solemnly, 'thou hast done well. It is not long to bide, and then the end will come.'

'But you are very old, Peggy,' said Susan, quivering.

'It is but a day sin' I were young,' replied Peggy; but she stopped the conversation by again pushing the cup with gentle force to Susan's dry and thirsty lips. When she had drunken she fell again to her labour, Peggy heating the hearth, and doing all that she knew would be required, but never speaking another word. Willie basked close to the fire, enjoying the animal luxury of warmth, for the autumn evenings were beginning to be chilly. It was one o'clock before they thought of going to bed on that memorable night.

CHAPTER IV.

THE vehemence with which Susan Dixon threw herself into occupation could not last for ever. Times of languor and remembrance would come – times when she recurred with a passionate yearning to bygone days, the recollection of which was so vivid and delicious, that it seemed as though it were the reality, and the present bleak bareness the dream. She smiled anew at the magical sweetness of some touch or tone which in memory she felt and heard, and drank the delicious cup of poison, although at the very time she knew what the consequences[a] of racking pain would be.

'This time, last year,' thought she, 'we went nutting together – this very day last year; just such a day as to-day. Purple and gold were the lights on the hills; the leaves were just turning brown; here and there on the sunny slopes the stubble-fields looked tawny; down in a cleft of yon purple slate-rock the beck fell like a silver glancing thread; all just as it is to-day. And he climbed the slender, swaying nut-trees, and bent the branches for me to gather; or made a passage through the hazel copses, from time to time claiming a toll. Who could have thought he loved me so little? – who? – who?'

Or, as the evening closed in, she would allow herself to imagine that she heard his coming step, just that she might recall the feeling of exquisite delight which had passed by without the due and passionate relish at the time. Then she would wonder how she could have had strength, the cruel, self-piercing strength, to say what she had done; to stab herself with that stern resolution, of which the scar would remain till her dying day. It might have been right; but, as she sickened, she wished she had not instinctively chosen the right. How luxurious a life haunted by no stern sense of duty must be! And many led this kind of life; why could not she? O, for one hour again of his sweet company! If he came now, she would agree to whatever he proposed.

It was a fever of the mind. She passed through it, and came out healthy, if weak. She was capable once more of taking pleasure in following an unseen guide through briar and brake. She returned with tenfold affection to her protecting care of Willie. She acknowledged to herself that he was to be her all-in-all in life. She made him her constant companion. For his sake, as the real owner of Yew Nook, and she as his steward and guardian, she began that course of careful saving, and that love of acquisition, which afterwards gained for her the reputation of being miserly. She still thought that he might regain a scanty portion of sense – enough to require some simple pleasures and excitement, which would cost money. And money should not be wanting. Peggy rather assisted her in the formation of her parsimonious habits than otherwise; economy was the order of the district, and a certain degree of respectable avarice the characteristic of her age.[a] Only Willie was never stinted nor hindered of anything that the two women thought could give him pleasure, for want of money.

There was one gratification which Susan felt was needed for the restoration of her mind to its more healthy state, after she had passed through the whirling fever, when duty was as nothing, and anarchy reigned; a gratification – that, somehow, was to be her last burst of unreasonableness; of which she knew and recognised pain as the sure consequence. She must see him once more, – herself unseen.

The week before the Christmas of this memorable year, she went out in the dusk of the early winter evening, wrapped close[b] in shawl and cloak. She wore her dark shawl under her cloak, putting it over her head in lieu of a bonnet; for she knew that she might have to wait long in concealment. Then she tramped over the wet fell-path, shut in by misty rain for miles and miles, till she came to the place where he was lodging; a farm-house in Langdale, with a steep, stony lane leading up to it: this lane was entered by a gate out of the main road, and by the gate were a few bushes – thorns; but of them the leaves had fallen, and they offered no concealment: an old wreck of a yew-tree grew among them, however, and underneath that Susan cowered down, shrouding her face, of which the colour might betray her, with a corner of her shawl. Long did she wait; cold and cramped she became, too damp and stiff to change her posture readily. And after all, he might never come! But, she would wait till daylight, if need were; and she pulled out a crust, with which she had providently supplied herself. The rain had ceased, – a dull, still, brooding weather had succeeded; it was a night to hear distant sounds. She heard horses' hoofs striking and plashing in the stones, and in the pools of the road at her back. Two horses; not well-ridden, or evenly guided, as she could tell.

Michael Hurst and a companion drew near; not tipsy, but not sober. They stopped at the gate to bid each other a maudlin farewell. Michael stooped forward to catch the latch with the hook of the stick which he carried; he dropped the stick, and it fell with one end close to Susan, – indeed, with the slightest change of posture she could have opened the gate for him. He swore a great oath, and struck his horse with his closed fist, as if that animal had been to blame; then he dismounted, opened the gate, and fumbled about for his stick. When he had found it (Susan had touched the other end) his first use of it was to flog his horse well, and she had much ado to avoid its kicks and plunges. Then, still swearing, he staggered up the lane, for it was evident he was not sober enough to remount.

By daylight Susan was back and at her daily labours at Yew Nook. When the spring came, Michael Hurst was married to Eleanor Hebthwaite. Others, too, were married, and christenings made their firesides merry and glad; or they travelled, and came back after long years with many wondrous tales. More rarely, perhaps, a Dalesman changed his dwelling. But to all households more change came than to Yew Nook. There the seasons came round with monotonous sameness; or, if they brought mutation, it was of a slow, and decaying, and depressing kind. Old Peggy died. Her silent sympathy, concealed under much roughness, was a loss to Susan Dixon. Susan was not yet thirty when this happened, but she looked a middle-aged, not to say an elderly woman. People affirmed that she had never recovered her complexion since that fever, a dozen years ago, which killed her father, and left Will Dixon an idiot. But besides her gray sallowness, the lines in her face were strong, and deep, and hard. The movements of her eyeballs were slow and heavy; the wrinkles at the corners of her mouth and eyes were planted firm and sure; not an ounce of unnecessary flesh was there on her bones – every muscle started strong and ready for use. She needed all this bodily strength, to a degree that no human creature, now Peggy was dead, knew of: for Willie had grown up large and strong in body, and, in general, docile enough in mind; but, every now and then, he became first moody, and then violent. These paroxysms lasted but a day or two; and it was Susan's anxious care to keep their very existence hidden and unknown. It is true, that occasional passers-by on that lonely road heard sounds at night of knocking about of furniture, blows, and cries, as of some tearing demon within the solitary farm-house; but these fits of violence usually occurred in the night; and whatever had been their consequence, Susan had tidied and redded[a] up all signs of aught unnsual before the morning. For, above all, she dreaded lest some one might find out in what danger and peril she occasionally was, and might assume a right to take away her brother from her care. The one idea of taking charge of him had deepened and deepened with years. It was graven into her mind as the object for which she lived. The sacrifice she had made for this object only made it more precious to her. Besides, she separated the idea of the docile, affectionate, loutish, indolent Will, and kept it distinct from the terror which the demon that occasionally possessed him inspired her with. The one was her flesh and her blood, – the child of her dead mother; the other was some fiend who came to torture and convulse the creature she so loved. She believed that she fought her brother's battle in holding down those tearing hands, in binding whenever she could those uplifted restless arms prompt and prone to do mischief. All the time she subdued him with her cunning or her strength, she spoke to him in pitying murmurs, or abused the third person, the fiendish enemy, in no unmeasured tones. Towards morning the paroxysm was exhausted, and he would fall asleep, perhaps only to waken with evil and renewed vigour. But when he was laid down, she would sally out to taste the fresh air, and to work off her wild sorrow in cries and mutterings to herself. The early labourers saw her gestures at a distance, and thought her as crazed as the idiot-brother who made the neighbourhood a haunted place. But did any chance person call at Yew Nook later on in the day, he would find Susan Dixon cold, calm, collected; her manner curt, her wits keen.

Once this fit of violence lasted longer than usual. Susan's strength both of mind and body was nearly worn out; she wrestled in prayer that somehow it might end before she, too, was driven mad; or, worse, might be obliged to give up life's aim, and consign Willie to a madhouse. From that moment of prayer (as she afterwards superstitiously thought) Willie calmed – and then he drooped – and then he sank – and, last of all, he died, in reality from physical exhaustion.

But he was so gentle and tender as he lay on his dying bed; such strange, child-like gleams of returning intelligence came over his face, long after the power to make his dull, inarticulate sounds had departed, that Susan was attracted to him by a stronger tie than she had ever felt before. It was something to have even an idiot loving her with dumb, wistful, animal affection; something to have any creature looking at her with such beseeching eyes, imploring protection from the insidious enemy stealing on. And yet she knew that to him death was no enemy, but a true friend, restoring light and health to his poor clouded mind. It was to her that death was an enemy; to her, the survivor, when Willie died; there was no one to love her. Worse doom still, there was no one left on earth for her to love.

You now know why no wandering tourist could persuade her to receive him as a lodger; why no tired traveller could melt her heart to afford him rest and refreshment; why long habits of seclusion had given her a moroseness of manner, and how care[a] for the interests of another had rendered her keen and miserly.

But there was a third act in the drama of her life.

CHAPTER V.

IN spite of Peggy's prophecy that Susan's life should not seem long, it did seem wearisome and endless, as the years slowly uncoiled their monotonous circles. To be sure, she might have made change for herself, but she did not care to do it. It was, indeed, more than 'not caring,' which merely implies a certain degree of *vis inertiæ*[a] to be subdued before an object can be attained, and that the object itself does not seem to be of sufficient importance to call out the requisite energy. On the contrary, Susan exerted herself to avoid change and variety. She had a morbid dread of new faces, which originated in her desire to keep poor dead Willie's state a profound secret. She had a contempt for new customs; and, indeed, her old ways prospered so well under her active hand and vigilant eye, that it was difficult to know how they could be improved upon. She was regularly present in Coniston market with the best butter and the earliest chickens of the season. Those were the common farm produce that every farmer's wife about had to sell; but Susan, after she had disposed of the more feminine articles, turned to on the man's side. A better judge of a horse or cow there was not in all the country round. Yorkshire itself might have attempted to jockey her, and would have failed. Her corn was sound and clean; her potatoes well preserved to the latest spring. People began to talk of the hoards of money Susan Dixon must have laid up somewhere; and one young ne'er-do-weel[b] of a farmer's son undertook to make love to the woman of forty, who looked fifty-five, if a day. He made up to her by opening a gate on the road-path home, as she was riding on a bare-backed horse, her purchase not an hour ago. She was off before him, refusing his civility; but the remounting was not so easy, and rather than fail she did not choose to attempt it. She walked, and he walked alongside, improving his opportunity, which, as he vainly thought, had been consciously granted to him. As they drew near Yew Nook, he ventured on some expression of a wish to keep company with her. His words were vague and clumsily arranged. Susan turned round and coolly asked him to explain himself. He took courage, as he thought of her reputed wealth, and expressed his wishes this second time pretty plainly. To his surprise, the reply she made was in a series of smart strokes across his shoulders, administered through the medium of a supple hazel-switch. A 'Take that!' said she, almost breathless, 'to teach thee how thou darest make a fool of an honest woman old enough to be thy mother. If thou com'st a step nearer the house, there's a good horse-pool, and there's two stout fellows who'll like no better fun than ducking thee. Be off wi' thee.'

And she strode into her own premises, never looking round to see whether he obeyed her injunction or not.

Sometimes three or four years would pass over without her hearing Michael Hurst's name mentioned. She used to wonder at such times whether he were dead or alive. She would sit for hours by the dying embers of her fire on a winter's evening, trying to recall the scenes of her youth; trying to bring up living pictures of the faces she had then known – Michael's most especially. She thought it was possible, so long had been the lapse of years, that she might now pass by him in the street unknowing and unknown. His outward form she might not recognise, but himself she should feel in the thrill of her whole being. He could not pass her unawares.

What little she did hear about him, all testified a downward tendency. He drank – not at stated times when there was no other work to be done, but continually, whether it was seed-time or harvest. His children were all ill at the same time; then one died, while the others recovered, but were poor sickly things. No one dared to give Susan any direct intelligence of her former lover; many avoided all mention of his name in her presence; but a few spoke out either in indifference to, or ignorance of, those bygone days. Susan heard every word, every whisper, every sound that related to him. But her eye never changed, nor did a muscle of her face move.

Late one November night she sat[a] over her fire; not a human being besides herself in the house; none but she had ever slept there since Willie's death. The farm-labourers had foddered the cattle and gone home hours before. There were crickets chirping all round the warm hearth-stones; there was the clock ticking with the peculiar beat Susan had known from her childhood, and which then and ever since she had oddly associated with the idea of a mother and child talking together, one loud tick, and quick – a feeble, sharp one following.

The day had been keen, and piercingly cold. The whole lift of heaven seemed a dome of iron. Black and frost-bound was the earth under the cruel east wind. Now the wind had dropped, and as the darkness had gathered in, the weather-wise old labourers prophesied snow. The sounds in the air arose again, as Susan sat[b] still and silent. They were of a different character to what they had been during the prevalence of the east wind. Then they had been shrill and piping; now they were like low distant growling; not unmusical, but strangely threatening. Susan went to the window, and drew aside the little curtain. The whole world was white – the air was blinded with the swift and heavy fall[c] of snow. At present it came down straight, but Susan knew those distant sounds in the hollows and gulleys[d] of the hills portended a driving wind and a more cruel storm. She thought of her sheep; were they all folded? the new-born calf, was it bedded well? Before the drifts were formed too deep for her to pass in and out – and by the morning she judged that they would be six or seven feet deep – she would go out and see after the comfort of her beasts. She took a lantern, and tied a shawl over her head, and went out into the open air. She had tenderly provided for all her animals, and was returning, when, borne on the blast as if some spirit-cry – for it seemed to come rather down from the skies than from any creature standing on earth's level – she heard a voice of agony; she could not distinguish words; it seemed rather as if some bird of prey was being caught in the whirl of the icy wind, and torn and tortured by its violence. Again! up high above! Susan put down her lantern, and shouted loud in return; it was an instinct, for if the creature were not human, which she had doubted but a moment before, what good could her responding cry do? And her cry was seized on by the tyrannous wind, and borne farther away in the opposite direction to that from which the call of agony had proceeded. Again she listened; no sound: then again it rang through space; and this time she was sure it was human. She turned into the house, and heaped turf and wood on the fire, which, careless of her own sensations, she had allowed to fade and almost die out. She put a new candle in her lantern; she changed her shawl for a maud,[11] and leaving the door on latch, she sallied out. Just at the moment when her ear first encountered the weird noises of the storm, on issuing forth into the open air, she thought she heard the words, 'O God! O help!' They were a guide to her, if words they were, for they came straight from a rock not a quarter of a mile from Yew Nook, but only to be reached, on account of its precipitous character, by a round-about path. Thither she steered, defying wind and snow; guided by here a thorn-tree, there an old, doddered oak, which had not quite lost their identity under the whelming mask of snow. Now and then she stopped to listen; but never a word or sound heard she, till right from where the copse-wood grew thick and tangled at the base of the rock, round which she was winding, she heard a moan. Into the brake – all snow in appearance – almost a plain of snow looked on from the little eminence where she stood – she plunged, breaking down the bush, stumbling, bruising herself, fighting her way; her lantern held between her teeth, and she herself using head as well as hands to butt away a passage, at whatever cost of bodily injury. As she climbed or staggered, owing to the unevenness of the snow-covered ground, where the briars and weeds of years were tangled and matted together, her foot felt something strangely soft and yielding. She lowered her lantern; there lay a man, prone on his face, nearly covered by the fast-falling flakes; he must have fallen from the rock above, as, not knowing of the circuitous path, he had tried to descend its steep, slippery face. Who could tell? it was no time for thinking. Susan lifted him up with her wiry strength; he gave no help –

no sign of life; but for all that he might be alive: he was still warm; she tied her maud round him; she fastened the lantern to her apron-string; she held him tight: half-carrying, half-dragging –[a] what did a few bruises signify to him, compared to dear life, to precious life! She got him through the brake, and down the path. There, for an instant, she stopped to take breath; but, as if stung by the Furies, she pushed on again with almost superhuman strength. Clasping him round the waist, and leaning his dead weight against the lintel of the door, she tried to undo the latch; but now, just at this moment, a trembling faintness came over her, and a fearful dread took possession of her – that here, on the very threshold of her home, she might be found dead, and buried under the snow, when the farm-servants came in the morning. This terror stirred her up to one more effort. Then she and her companion were in the warmth of the quiet haven of that kitchen; she laid him on the settle, and sank on the floor by his side. How long she remained in this swoon[b] she could not tell; not very long she judged by the fire, which was still red and sullenly glowing when she came to herself. She lighted the candle, and bent over her late burden to ascertain if indeed he were dead. She stood long gazing. The man lay dead. There could be no doubt about it. His filmy eyes glared at her, unshut. But Susan was not one to be affrighted by the stony aspect of death. It was not that; it was the bitter, woeful recognition of Michael Hurst![c]

She was convinced he was dead; but after a while she refused to believe in her conviction. She stripped off his wet outer-garments with trembling, hurried hands. She brought a blanket down from her own bed; she made up the fire. She swathed him in fresh, warm wrappings, and laid him on the flags before the fire, sitting herself at his head, and holding it in her lap, while she tenderly wiped his loose, wet hair, curly still, although its colour had changed from nut-brown to iron-gray since she had seen it last. From time to time she bent over the face afresh, sick, and fain to believe that the flicker of the fire-light was some slight convulsive motion. But the dim, staring eyes struck chill to her heart. At last she ceased her delicate, busy cares; but she still held the head softly, as if caressing it. She thought over all the possibilities and chances in the mingled yarn of their lives that might, by so slight a turn, have ended far otherwise. If her mother's cold had been early tended, so that the responsibility as to her brother's weal or woe had not fallen upon her; if the fever had not taken such rough, cruel hold on Will; nay, if Mrs. Gale, that hard, worldly sister, had not accompanied him on his last visit to Yew Nook – his very last before this fatal, stormy night; if she had heard his cry, – cry uttered by those pale, dead lips with such wild, despairing agony, not yet three hours ago! – O! if she had but heard it sooner, he might have been saved before that blind, false step had precipitated him down the rock! In going over this weary chain of unrealised possibilities, Susan learnt the force of Peggy's words. Life was short, looking back upon it. It seemed but yesterday since all the love of her being had been poured out, and run to waste. The intervening years – the long monotonous years that had turned her into an old woman before her time – were but a dream.

The labourers coming in the dawn of the winter's day were surprised to see the fire-light through the low kitchen-window. They knocked, and hearing a moaning answer, they entered, fearing that something had befallen their mistress. For all explanation they got these words:

'It is Michael Hurst. He was belated, and fell down the Raven's Crag. Where does Eleanor, his wife, live?'

How Michael Hurst got to Yew Nook no one but Susan ever knew. They thought he had dragged himself there, with some sore, internal bruise sapping away his minuted life. They could not have believed the superhuman exertion which had first sought him out, and then dragged him hither. Only Susan knew of that.

She gave him into the charge of her servants, and went out and saddled her horse. Where the wind had drifted the snow on one side, and the road was clear and bare, she rode, and rode fast; where the soft, deceitful heaps were massed up, she dismounted and led her steed, plunging in deep, with fierce energy, the pain at her heart urging her onwards with a sharp, digging spur.

The gray, solemn, winter's noon was more night-like than the depth of summer's night; dim-purple brooded the low skies over the white earth, as Susan rode up to what had been Michael Hurst's abode while living. It was a small farm-house, carelessly kept outside, slatternly tended within. The pretty Nelly Hebthwaite was pretty still; her delicate face had never suffered from any long-enduring feeling. If anything, its expression was that of plaintive sorrow; but the soft, light hair had scarcely a tinge of gray; the wood-rose tint of complexion yet remained, if not so brilliant as in youth; the straight nose, the small mouth were untouched by time. Susan felt the contrast even at that moment. She knew that her own skin was weather-beaten, furrowed, brown, – that her teeth were gone, and her hair gray and ragged. And yet she was not two years older than Nelly, – she had not been, in youth, when she took account of these things.

Nelly stood wondering at the strange-enough horsewoman, who stopped and panted at the door, holding her horse's bridle, and refusing to enter.

'Where is Michael Hurst?' asked Susan, at last.

'Well, I can't rightly say. He should have been at home last night, but he was off, seeing after a public-house to be let at Ulverstone, for our farm does not answer, and we were thinking –'

'He did not come home last night?' said Susan, cutting short the story, and half-affirming, half-questioning, by way of letting in a ray of the awful light before she let it full in, in its consuming wrath.

'No! he'll be stopping somewhere out Ulverstone ways. I'm sure we've need of him at home, for I've no one but lile Tommy to help me tend the beasts. Things have not gone well with us, and we don't keep a servant now. But you're trembling all over, ma'am. You'd better come in, and take something warm, while your horse rests. That's the stable-door, to your left.'

Susan took her horse there; loosened his girths, and rubbed him down with a wisp of straw. Then she looked about her for hay; but the place was bare of food, and smelt damp and unused. She went to the house, thankful for the respite, and got some clapbread, which she mashed up in a pailful of luke-warm water. Every moment was a respite, and yet every moment made her dread the more the task that lay before her. It would be longer than she thought at first. She took the saddle off, and hung about her horse, which seemed, somehow, more like a friend than anything else in the world. She laid her cheek against its neck, and rested there, before returning to the house for the last time.

Eleanor had brought down one of her own gowns, which hung on a chair against the fire, and had made her unknown visitor a cup of hot tea. Susan could hardly bear all these little attentions: they choked her, and yet she was so wet, so weak with fatigue and excitement, that she could neither resist by voice or by action. Two children stood awkwardly about, puzzled at the scene, and even Eleanor began to wish for some explanation of who her strange visitor was.

'You've, may-be, heard him speaking of me? I'm called Susan Dixon.'

Nelly coloured, and avoided meeting Susan's eye.

'I've heard other folk speak of you. He never named your name.'

This respect of silence came like balm to Susan: balm not felt or heeded at the time it was applied, but very grateful in its effects for all that.

'He is at my house,' continued Susan, determined not to stop or quaver in the operation – the pain which must be inflicted.

'At your house? Yew Nook?' questioned Eleanor, surprised. 'How came he there?' – half jealously. 'Did he take shelter from the coming storm? Tell me, – there is something – tell me, woman!'

'He took no shelter. Would to God he had!'

'O! would to God! would to God!' shrieked out Eleanor, learning all from the woful import of those dreary eyes. Her cries thrilled through the house; the children's piping wailings and passionate cries on 'Daddy! Daddy!' pierced into Susan's very marrow. But she remained as still and tearless as the great round face upon the clock.

At last, in a lull of crying, she said, – not exactly questioning – but as if partly to herself –

'You loved him, then?'

'Loved him! he was my husband! He was the father of three bonny bairns that lie dead in Grasmere Churchyard. I wish you'd go, Susan Dixon, and let me weep without your watching me! I wish you'd never come near the place.'

'Alas! alas! it would not have brought him to life. I would have laid down my own to save his. My life has been so very sad! No one would have cared if I had died. Alas! alas!'

The tone in which she said this was so utterly mournful and despairing that it awed Nelly into quiet for a time. But by-and-by she said, 'I would not turn a dog out to do it harm; but the night is clear, and Tommy shall guide you to the Red Cow. But, O! I want to be alone. If you'll come back tomorrow, I'll be better, and I'll hear all, and thank you for every kindness you have shown him, – and I do believe you've showed him kindness, – though I don't know why.'

Susan moved heavily and strangely.

She said something – her words came thick and unintelligible. She had had a paralytic stroke since she had last spoken. She could not go, even if she would. Nor did Eleanor, when she became aware of the state of the case, wish her to leave. She had her laid on her own bed, and weeping silently all the while for her lost husband, she nursed Susan like a sister. She did not know what her guest's worldly position might be; and she might never be repaid. But she sold many a little trifle to purchase such small comforts as Susan needed. Susan, lying still and motionless, learnt much. It was not a severe stroke; it might be the forerunner of others yet to come, but at some distance of time. But for the present she recovered, and regained much of her former health.

On her sick-bed she matured her plans. When she returned to Yew Nook, she took Michael Hurst's widow and children with her to live there, and fill up the haunted hearth with living forms that should banish the ghosts.

And so it fell out that the latter days of Susan Dixon's life were better than the former.

WHEN this narrative was finished, Mrs. Dawson called on our two gentle-men, Signor Sperano and Mr. Preston, and told them that they had hitherto been amused or interested, but that it was now their turn to amuse or inter-est. They looked at each other as if this application of hers took them by surprise, and seemed altogether as much abashed as well-grown men can ever be. Signor Sperano was the first to recover himself: after thinking a lit-tle, he said: –

'Your will, dear Lady, is law. Next Monday evening, I will bring you an old, old story, which I found among the papers of the good old Priest who first welcomed me to England. It was but a poor return for his generous kindness; but I had the opportunity of nursing him through the cholera, of which he died. He left me all that he had – no money – but his scanty furni-ture, his book of prayers, his crucifix and rosary, and his papers. How some of those papers came into his hands I know not. They had evidently been written many years before the venerable man was born; and I doubt whether he had ever examined the bundles, which had come down to him from some old ancestor, or in some strange bequest. His life was too busy to leave any time for the gratification of mere curiosity; I, alas! have only had too much leisure.'

Next Monday, Signor Sperano read to us the story which I will call 'The Poor Clare.'

'THE POOR CLARE'

'The Poor Clare' was first published in three parts as 'The Poor Clare: In Three Chapters' in *Household Words*, 14 (13, 20, 27 December 1856), pp. 510–15, 532–44, 559–65. Each part contained one chapter. It was collected in *Round the Sofa*, 2 vols (London: Sampson Low, 1859), vol. ii, pp. 179–275. It also appeared in the American periodical *Harper's Weekly Magazine*, 1 (10, 17, 24 January 1857), pp. 26–7, 44–7, 58–9. It was collected in *My Lady Ludlow and Other Tales* (1861).

The story had evidently been intended for publication the previous Christmas, for Dickens wrote to EG (2 January 1856) expressing his enthusiasm to know the end of 'the story you could not finish … in time for Christmas' (*CD Letters*, vol. viii, p. 4). For the inspiration of the story, see Chapple, 'Elizabeth Gaskell's "Morton Hall" and "The Poor Clare"', pp. 47–9. He cites an extract from a letter from EG to Caroline, Lady Hatherton, which he dates c. February 1857, preserved in the notebook of Jane Adeane in the Brotherton Library, Leeds: it is printed in *Further Letters*, pp. 168–9:

> but I did not mean any one to know it, because people are always so scandalized at the reopening of Superstition.
>
> Two years ago we used to see the Dowr Lady Elgin at Paris a good deal; & she delighted in wild stories. It was in her vast half lighted room that I heard the germ of that story from a M. Bonette – He told it as having happened to some one he knew in the South of France, as far as the Man's falling in love with a mysterious Girl at a watering place, & her telling him of the Fiendish Double by which she was haunted for some sin of her Father's.
>
> The Grandmother Witch is a pure invention: The History of the poor Clares & their ringing the bell in extremity of famine I heard this year from a Flemish Lady in {Belgium} Antwerp who had a Sister a poor Clare.

Mary Mohl had introduced EG to Elizabeth, Dowager Countess of Elgin (d. 1860), widow of the purchaser of the Elgin marbles, in February 1855 (*Uglow*, p. 388).

The above letter tends to contradict, though it does not totally disprove, the hypothesis advanced by Ellen M. Laun, 'A Missing Gaskell Tale Found',

Studies in Short Fiction, 15 (Spring 1978), pp. 178–183, who argues that the story mentioned in the 'Preface' to *Mary Barton* (1848), 'a tale, the period of which was more than a century ago, and the place, on the borders of Yorkshire' is 'The Poor Clare'. Laun suggests that Chapter II was written at a different and much earlier time than Chapter I, citing the fact that where Bridget's cottage is near Starkey Manor House and carefully furnished (though a primitive hut) in Chapter I, by Chapter II it is in Coldholme village, and other stylistic variations and discontinuities. It might also be argued that there are certain resemblances of plot and mood between 'The Poor Clare' and the slightly melodramatic and humourless 'The Doom of the Griffiths': the possibility that in origin they belong to the same phase of EG's development cannot be entirely excluded.

The historical details of the story are rather vague although a number of the names used in it are those of real families, including the Starkies; as *Sharps*, p. 250, points out, EG's account of the life of the Catholic gentry in Lancashire no doubt drew largely on T. D. Whitaker, *An History of the Original Parish of Whalley and Honor of Clitheroe in the Counties of Lancaster and York*, 2 vols (Blackburn: Hemingway and Crook, 1800, 1801) and *The History and Antiquities of the Deanery of Craven in the County of York* (London: Nichols, 1805).

THE POOR CLARE.

———•———

CHAPTER I.

DECEMBER 12th,[a] 1747. –[1] My life has been strangely bound up with extraordinary incidents, some of which occurred before I had any connection with the principal actors in them, or, indeed, before I even knew of their existence. I suppose, most old men are, like me, more given to looking back upon their own career with a kind of fond interest and affectionate remembrance, than to watching the events – though these may have far more interest for the multitude – immediately passing before their eyes. If this should be the case with the generality of old people, how much more so with me! . . . . If I am to enter upon that strange story connected with poor Lucy, I must begin a long way back. I myself only came to the knowledge of her family history after I knew her; but, to make the tale clear to any one else, I must arrange events in the order in which they occurred – not that in which I became acquainted with them.

There is a great old hall in the north-east of Lancashire, in a part they call the Trough of Bolland,[2] adjoining that other district named Craven. Starkey Manor-House is rather like a number of rooms clustered round a gray, massive, old keep than a regularly-built hall. Indeed, I suppose that the house only consisted of the great tower in the centre, in the days when the Scots made their raids terrible as far south as this; and that after the Stuarts came in, and there was a little more security of property in those parts, the Starkeys of that time added the lower building, which runs, two stories high, all round the base of the keep. There has been a grand garden laid out in my days, on the southern slope near the house; but when I first knew the place, the kitchen-garden at the farm was the only piece of cultivated ground belonging to it. The deer used to come within sight of the drawing-room windows, and might have browsed quite close up to the house if they had not been too wild and shy. Starkey Manor-House itself stood on a projection or peninsula of high land, jutting out from the abrupt hills that form the sides of the Trough of Bolland. These hills were rocky and bleak enough towards their summit; lower down they were clothed with tangled copsewood and green depths of fern, out of which a gray giant of an ancient forest-tree would tower here and there, throwing up its ghastly white branches, as if in imprecation, to the sky. These trees, they told me, were the remnants of that forest which existed in the days of the Heptarchy,[3a] and were even then noted as landmarks. No wonder that their upper and more exposed branches were leafless, and that the dead bark had peeled away, from sapless old age.

Not far from the house there were a few cottages, apparently of the same date as the keep; probably built for some retainers of the family, who sought shelter – they and their families and their small flocks and herds – at the hands of their feudal lord. Some of them had pretty much fallen to decay. They were built in a strange fashion. Strong beams had been sunk firm in the ground at the requisite distance, and their other ends had been fastened together, two and two, so as to form the shape of one of those rounded wag-gon-headed gipsy-tents, only very much larger. The spaces between were filled with mud, stones, osiers, rubbish, mortar – anything to keep out the weather. The fires were made in the centre of these rude dwellings, a hole in the roof forming the only chimney. No Highland hut or Irish cabin could be of rougher construction.

The owner of this property, at the beginning of the present century, was a Mr. Patrick Byrne Starkey. His family had kept to the old faith, and were staunch Roman Catholics, esteeming it even a sin to marry any one of Prot-estant descent, however willing he or she might have been to embrace the Romish religion. Mr. Patrick Starkey's father had been a follower of James the Second;[4] and, during the disastrous Irish campaign of that monarch, he had fallen in love with an Irish beauty, a Miss Byrne, as zealous for her reli-gion and for the Stuarts as himself. He had returned to Ireland after his escape to France, and married her, bearing her back to the court at St. Ger-mains. But some licence on the part of the disorderly gentlemen who surrounded King James in his exile, had insulted his beautiful wife, and dis-gusted him; so he removed from St. Germains to Antwerp, whence, in a few years' time, he quietly returned to Starkey Manor-House – some of his Lan-cashire neighbours having lent their good offices[5] to reconcile him to the powers that were. He was as firm a Roman Catholic as ever, and as staunch an advocate for the Stuarts and the divine right of kings; but his religion almost amounted to asceticism, and the conduct of those with whom he had been brought in such close contact at St. Germains would little bear the inspection of a stern moralist. So he gave his allegiance where he could not give his esteem, and learned to respect sincerely the upright and moral char-acter of one whom he yet regarded as an usurper. King William's[6] government had little need to fear such a one. So he returned, as I have said, with a sobered heart and impoverished fortunes, to his ancestral house, which had fallen sadly to ruin while the owner had been a courtier, a soldier, and an exile. The roads into the Trough of Bolland were little more than cart-ruts; indeed, the way up to the house lay along a ploughed field before you came to the deer-park. Madam, as the country-folk used to call Mrs. Starkey, rode on a pillion behind her husband, holding on to him with a light hand by his leather riding-belt. Little master (he that was afterwards Squire Patrick Byrne Starkey) was held on to his pony by a serving-man. A woman past middle age walked, with a firm and strong step, by the cart that held much of the baggage; and, high up on the mails and boxes, sat[a] a girl of dazzling beauty, perched lightly on the topmost trunk, and swaying herself fearlessly to and fro, as the cart rocked and shook in the heavy roads of late autumn. The girl wore the Antwerp faille,[7] or black Spanish mantle over her head, and altogether her appearance was such that the old cottager, who described the procession to me many years after, said that all the country-folk took her for a foreigner. Some dogs, and the boy who held them in charge, made up the company. They rode silently along, looking with grave, serious eyes at the people, who came out of the scattered cottages to bow or curtsy[b] to the real Squire, 'come back at last,' and gazed after the little procession with gaping wonder, not deadened by the sound of the foreign language in which the few necessary words that passed among them were spoken. One lad, called from his staring by the Squire to come and help about the cart, accompanied them to the Manor-House. He said that when the lady had descended from her pillion, the middle-aged woman whom I have described as walking while the others rode, stepped quickly forward, and taking Madam Starkey (who was of a slight and delicate figure) in her arms, she lifted her over the threshold, and set[c] her down in her husband's house, at the same time uttering a passionate and outlandish blessing. The Squire stood by, smiling gravely at first; but when the words of blessing were pronounced, he took off his fine feathered hat, and bent his head. The girl with the black mantle stepped onward into the shadow of the dark hall, and kissed the lady's hand; and that was all the lad could tell to the group that gathered round him on his return, eager to hear everything, and to know how much the Squire had given him for his services.

From all I could gather, the Manor-House, at the time of the Squire's return, was in the most dilapidated state. The stout gray walls remained firm and entire; but the inner chambers had been used for all kinds of purposes. The great withdrawing-room had been a barn; the state tapestry-chamber had held wool, and so on. But, by-and-by, they were cleared out; and if the Squire had no money to spend on new furniture, he and his wife had the knack of making the best of the old. He was no despicable joiner; she had a kind of grace in whatever she did, and imparted an air of elegant pictur-esqueness to whatever she touched. Besides, they had brought many rare things from the Continent; perhaps I should rather say, things that were rare in that part of England – carvings, and crosses, and beautiful pictures. And then, again, wood was plentiful in the Trough of Bolland, and great log-fires danced and glittered in all the dark, old rooms, and gave a look of home and comfort to everything.

Why do I tell you all this? I have little to do with the Squire and Madam Starkey; and yet I dwell upon them, as if I were unwilling to come to the real people with whom my life was so strangely mixed up. Madam had been nursed in Ireland by the very woman who lifted her in her arms, and welcomed her to her husband's home in Lancashire. Excepting for the short period of her own married life, Bridget Fitzgerald had never left her nursling. Her marriage – to one above her in rank – had been unhappy. Her husband had died, and left her in even greater poverty than that in which she was when he had first met with her. She had one child, the beautiful daughter who came riding on the waggon-load of furniture that was brought to the Manor-House. Madam Starkey had taken her again into her service when she became a widow. She and her daughter had followed 'the mistress' in all her fortunes; they had lived at St. Germains and at Antwerp, and were now come to her home in Lancashire. As soon as Bridget had arrived there, the Squire gave her a cottage of her own, and took more pains in furnishing it for her than he did in anything else out of his own house. It was only nominally her residence. She was constantly up at the great house; indeed, it was but a short cut across the woods from her own home to the home of her nursling. Her daughter Mary, in like manner, moved from one house to the other at her own will. Madam loved both mother and child dearly. They had great influence over her, and, through her, over her husband. Whatever Bridget or Mary willed was sure to come to pass. They were not disliked; for, though wild and passionate, they were also generous by nature. But the other servants were afraid of them, as being in secret the ruling spirits of the household. The Squire had lost his interest in all secular things; Madam was gentle, affectionate, and yielding. Both husband and wife were tenderly attached to each other and to their boy; but they grew more and more to shun the trouble of decision on any point; and hence it was that Bridget could exert such despotic power. But if every one else yielded to her 'magic of a superior mind,' her daughter not unfrequently rebelled. She and her mother were too much alike to agree. There were wild quarrels between them, and wilder reconciliations. There were times when, in the heat of passion, they could have stabbed each other. At all other times they both – Bridget especially – would have willingly laid down their lives for one another. Bridget's love for her child lay very deep – deeper than that daughter ever knew; or I should think she would never have wearied of home as she did, and prayed her mistress to obtain for her some situation – as waiting-maid – beyond the seas, in that more cheerful continental life, among the scenes of which so many of her happiest years had been spent. She thought, as youth thinks, that life would last for ever, and that two or three years were but a small portion of it to pass away from her mother, whose only child she was. Bridget thought differently, but was too proud ever to show what she felt. If her child wished to leave her, why – she should go. But people said Bridget became ten years older in the course of two months at this time. She took it that Mary wanted to leave her. The truth was, that Mary wanted for a time to leave the place, and to seek some change, and would thankfully have taken her mother with her. Indeed, when Madam Starkey had gotten her a situation with some grand lady abroad, and the time drew near for her to go, it was Mary who clung to her mother with passionate embrace, and, with floods of tears, declared that she would never leave her; and it was Bridget, who at last loosened her arms, and, grave and tearless herself, bade her keep her word, and go forth into the wide world. Sobbing aloud, and looking back continually, Mary went away. Bridget was still as death, scarcely drawing her breath, or closing her stony eyes; till at last she turned back into her cottage, and heaved a ponderous old settle against the door. There she sat, motionless, over the gray[a] ashes of her extinguished fire, deaf to Madam's sweet voice, as she begged leave to enter and comfort her nurse. Deaf, stony, and motionless, she sat for more than twenty hours; till, for the third time, Madam came across the snowy path from the great house, carrying with her a young spaniel, which had been Mary's pet up at the hall, and which had not ceased all night long to seek for its absent mistress, and to whine and moan after her. With tears Madam told this story, through the closed door – tears excited by the terrible look of anguish, so steady, so immovable – so the same to-day as it was yesterday – on her nurse's face. The little creature in her arms began to utter its piteous cry, as it shivered with the cold. Bridget stirred; she moved – she listened. Again that long whine; she thought it was for her daughter; and what she had denied to her nursling and mistress she granted to the dumb creature that Mary had cherished. She opened the door, and took the dog from Madam's arms. Then Madam came in, and kissed and comforted the old woman, who took but little notice of her or anything. And sending up Master Patrick to the hall for fire and food, the sweet young lady never left her nurse all that night. Next day, the Squire himself came down, carrying a beautiful foreign picture: Our Lady of the Holy Heart, the Papists call it. It is a picture of the Virgin, her heart pierced with arrows, each arrow representing one of her great woes. That picture hung in Bridget's cottage when I first saw her; I have that picture now.

Years went on. Mary was still abroad. Bridget was still and stern, instead of active and passionate. The little dog, Mignon, was indeed her darling. I have heard that she talked to it continually; although, to most people, she was so silent. The Squire and Madam treated her with the greatest consideration, and well they might; for to them she was as devoted and faithful as ever. Mary wrote pretty often, and seemed satisfied with her life. But at length the letters ceased – I hardly know whether before or after a great and terrible sorrow came upon the house of the Starkeys. The Squire sickened of a putrid fever; and Madam caught it in nursing him, and died. You may be sure, Bridget let no other woman tend her but herself; and in the very arms that had received her at her birth, that sweet young woman laid her head down, and gave up her breath. The Squire recovered, in a fashion. He was never strong – he had never the heart to smile again. He fasted and prayed more than ever; and people did say that he tried to cut off the entail, and leave all the property away to found a monastery abroad, of which he prayed that some day little Squire Patrick might be the reverend father. But he could not do this, for the strictness of the entail and the laws against the Papists.[8] So he could only appoint gentlemen of his own faith as guardians to his son, with many charges about the lad's soul, and a few about the land, and the way it was to be held while he was a minor. Of course, Bridget was not forgotten. He sent for her as he lay on his death-bed, and asked her if she would rather have a sum down, or have a small annuity settled upon her. She said at once she would have a sum down; for she thought of her daughter, and how she could bequeath the money to her, whereas an annuity[9] would have died with her. So the Squire left her her cottage for life, and a fair sum of money. And then he died, with as ready and willing a heart as, I suppose, ever any gentleman took out of this world with him. The young Squire was carried off by his guardians, and Bridget was left alone.

I have said that she had not heard from Mary for some time. In her last letter, she had told of travelling about with her mistress, who was the English wife of some great foreign officer, and had spoken of her chances of making a good marriage, without naming the gentleman's name, keeping it rather back as a pleasant surprise to her mother; his station and fortune being, as I had afterwards reason to know, far superior to anything she had a right to expect. Then came a long silence; and Madam was dead, and the Squire was dead; and Bridget's heart was gnawed by anxiety, and she knew not whom to ask for news of her child. She could not write, and the Squire had managed her communication with her daughter. She walked off to Hurst;[10] and got a good priest there – one whom she had known at Antwerp – to write for her. But no answer came. It was like crying into the awful stillness of night.

One day, Bridget was missed by those neighbours who had been accustomed to mark her goings-out and comings-in.[a] She had never been sociable with any of them; but the sight of her had become a part of their daily lives, and slow wonder arose in their minds, as morning after morning came, and her house-door remained closed, her window dead from any glitter, or light of fire within. At length, some one tried the door; it was locked. Two or three laid their heads together, before daring to look in through the blank, unshuttered window. But, at last, they summoned up courage; and then saw that Bridget's absence from their little world was not the result of accident or death, but of premeditation. Such small articles of furniture as could be secured from the effects of time and damp by being packed up, were stowed away in boxes. The picture of the Madonna was taken down, and gone. In a word, Bridget had stolen away from her home, and left no trace whither she was departed. I knew afterwards, that she and her little dog had wandered off on the long search for her lost daughter. She was too illiterate to have faith in letters, even had she had the means of writing and sending many. But she had faith in her own strong love, and believed that her passionate instinct would guide her to her child. Besides, foreign travel was no new thing to her, and she could speak enough of French to explain the object of her journey, and had, moreover, the advantage of being, from her faith, a welcome object of charitable hospitality at many a distant convent. But the country people round Starkey Manor-House knew nothing of all this. They wondered what had become of her, in a torpid, lazy fashion, and then left off thinking of her altogether. Several years passed. Both Manor-House and cottage were deserted. The young Squire lived far away under the direction of his guardians. There were inroads of wool and corn into the sitting-rooms of the Hall; and there was some low talk, from time to time, among the hinds and country people, whether it would not be as well to break into old Bridget's cottage, and save such of her goods as were left from the moth and rust which must be making sad havoc. But this idea was always quenched by the recollection of her strong character and passionate anger; and tales of her masterful spirit, and vehement force of will, were whispered about, till the very thought of offending her, by touching any article of hers, became invested with a kind of horror: it was believed that, dead or alive, she would not fail to avenge it.

Suddenly she came home; with as little noise or note of preparation as she had departed. One day, some one noticed a thin, blue curl of smoke, ascending from her chimney. Her door stood open to the noon-day sun; and, ere many hours had elapsed, some one had seen an old travel-and-sorrow-stained[a] woman dipping her pitcher in the well; and said, that the dark, solemn eyes that looked up at him were more like Bridget Fitzgerald's than any one else's in this world; and yet, if it were she, she looked as if she had been scorched in the flames of hell, so brown, and scarred, and fierce a creature did she seem. By-and-by many saw her; and those who met her eye once cared not to be caught looking at her again. She had got into the habit of perpetually talking to herself; nay, more, answering herself, and varying her tones according to the side she took at the moment. It was no wonder that those who dared to listen outside her door at night, believed that she held converse with some spirit; in short, she was unconsciously earning for herself the dreadful reputation of a witch.

Her little dog, which had wandered half over the Continent with her, was her only companion; a dumb remembrancer of happier days. Once he was ill; and she carried him more than three miles, to ask about his management from one who had been groom to the last Squire, and had then been noted for his skill in all diseases of animals. Whatever this man did, the dog recovered; and they who heard her thanks, intermingled with blessings (that were rather promises of good fortune than prayers), looked grave at his good luck when, next year, his ewes twinned, and his meadow-grass was heavy and thick.

Now it so happened that, about the year seventeen hundred and eleven, one of the guardians of the young Squire, a certain Sir Philip Tempest,[11] bethought him of the good shooting there must be on his ward's property; and, in consequence, he brought down four or five gentlemen, of his friends, to stay for a week or two at the Hall. From all accounts, they roystered and spent pretty freely. I never heard any of their names but one, and that was Squire Gisborne's. He was hardly a middle-aged man then; he had been much abroad, and there, I believe, he had known Sir Philip Tempest, and done him some service. He was a daring and dissolute fellow in those days: careless and fearless, and one who would rather be in a quarrel than out of it. He had his fits of ill-temper beside, when he would spare neither man nor beast. Otherwise, those who knew him well, used to say he had a good heart, when he was neither drunk, nor angry, nor in any way vexed. He had altered much when I came to know him.

One day, the gentlemen had all been out shooting, and with but little success, I believe; anyhow, Mr. Gisborne had had none, and was in a black humour accordingly. He was coming home, having his gun loaded, sportsman-like, when little Mignon crossed his path, just as he turned out of the wood by Bridget's cottage. Partly for wantonness, partly to vent his spleen upon some living creature, Mr. Gisborne took his gun, and fired – he had better have never fired gun again, than aimed that unlucky shot. He hit Mignon; and at the creature's sudden cry, Bridget came out, and saw at a glance what had been done. She took Mignon up in her arms, and looked hard at the wound; the poor dog looked at her with his glazing eyes, and tried to wag his tail and lick her hand, all covered with blood. Mr. Gisborne spoke in a kind of sullen penitence:

'You should have kept the dog out of my way – a little poaching varmint.'

At this very moment, Mignon stretched out his legs, and stiffened in her arms – her lost Mary's dog, who had wandered and sorrowed with her for years. She walked right into Mr. Gisborne's path, and fixed his unwilling, sullen look with her dark and terrible eye.

'Those never throve that did me harm,' said she. 'I'm alone in the world, and helpless; the more do the Saints in Heaven hear my prayers. Hear me, ye blessed ones! hear me while I ask for sorrow on this bad, cruel man. He has killed the only creature that loved me – the dumb beast that I loved. Bring down heavy sorrow on his head for it, O ye Saints! He thought that I was helpless, because he saw me lonely and poor; but are not the armies of Heaven for the like of me?'

'Come, come,' said he, half-remorseful, but not one whit afraid. 'Here's a crown to buy thee another dog. Take it, and leave off cursing! I care none for thy threats.'

'Don't you?' said she, coming a step closer, and changing her imprecatory cry for a whisper which made the gamekeeper's lad, following Mr. Gisborne, creep all over. 'You shall live to see the creature you love best, and who alone loves you – ay, a human creature, but as innocent and fond as my poor, dead darling – you shall see this creature, for whom death would be too happy, become a terror and a loathing to all, for this blood's sake. Hear me, O holy Saints, who never fail them that have no other help!'

She threw up her right hand, filled with poor Mignon's life-drops; they spirted, one or two of them, on his shooting-dress, – an ominous sight to the follower. But the master only laughed a little, forced, scornful laugh, and went on to the Hall. Before he got there, however, he took out a gold piece, and bade the boy carry it to the old woman on his return to the village. The lad was 'afeared,' as he told me in after years; he came to the cottage, and hovered about, not daring to enter. He peeped through the window at last; and by the flickering wood-flame, he saw Bridget kneeling before the picture of our Lady of the Holy Heart, with dead Mignon lying between her and the Madonna. She was praying wildly, as her outstretched arms betokened. The lad shrank away in redoubled terror; and contented himself with slipping the gold-piece under the ill-fitting door. The next day it was thrown out upon the midden; and there it lay, no one daring to touch it.

Meanwhile Mr. Gisborne, half curious, half uneasy, thought to lessen his uncomfortable feelings by asking Sir Philip who Bridget was? He could only describe her – he did not know her name. Sir Philip was equally at a loss. But an old servant of the Starkeys, who had resumed his livery at the Hall on this occasion – a scoundrel whom Bridget had saved from dismissal more than once during her palmy days – said: –

'It will be the old witch, that his worship means. She needs a ducking, if ever woman did, does that Bridget Fitzgerald.'

'Fitzgerald!' said both the gentlemen at once. But Sir Philip was the first to continue: –

'I must have no talk of ducking her, Dickon. Why, she must be the very woman poor Starkey bade me have a care of; but when I came here last she was gone, no one knew where. I'll go and see her tomorrow. But mind you, sirrah, if any harm comes to her, or any more talk of her being a witch – I've a pack of hounds at home, who can follow the scent of a lying knave as well as ever they followed a dog-fox; so take care how you talk about ducking a faithful old servant of your dead master's.'

'Had she ever a daughter?' asked Mr. Gisborne, after a while.

'I don't know – yes! I've a notion she had; a kind of waiting-woman to Madam Starkey.'

'Please your worship,' said humbled Dickon, 'Mistress Bridget had a daughter – one Mistress Mary – who went abroad, and has never been heard on since; and folk do say that has crazed her mother.'

Mr. Gisborne shaded his eyes with his hand.

'I could wish she had not cursed me,' he muttered. 'She may have power – no one else could.' After a while, he said aloud, no one understanding rightly what he meant, 'Tush! it's impossible!' – and called for claret; and he and the other gentlemen set-to to a drinking-bout.

CHAPTER II.

I NOW come to the time in which I myself was mixed up with the people that I have been writing about. And to make you understand how I became connected with them, I must give you some little account of myself. My father was the younger son of a Devonshire gentleman of moderate property; my eldest uncle succeeded to the estate of his forefathers, my second became an eminent attorney in London, and my father took orders. Like most poor clergymen, he had a large family; and I have no doubt was glad enough when my London uncle, who was a bachelor, offered to take charge of me, and bring me up to be his successor in business.

In this way I came to live in London, in my uncle's house, not far from Gray's Inn, and to be treated and esteemed as his son, and to labour with him in his office. I was very fond of the old gentleman. He was the confidential agent of many country squires, and had attained to his present position as much by knowledge of human nature as by knowledge of law; though he was learned enough in the latter. He used to say his business was law, his pleasure heraldry. From his intimate acquaintance with family history, and all the tragic courses of life therein involved, to hear him talk, at leisure times, about any coat of arms that came across his path was as good as a play or a romance. Many cases of disputed property, dependent on a love of genealogy, were brought to him, as to a great authority on such points. If the lawyer who came to consult him was young, he would take no fee, only give him a long lecture on the importance of attending to heraldry; if the lawyer was of mature age and good standing, he would mulct him pretty well, and abuse him to me afterwards as negligent of one great branch of the profession. His house was in a stately new street called Ormond Street, and in it he had a handsome library; but all the books treated of things that were past; none of them planned or looked forward into the future. I worked away – partly for the sake of my family at home, partly because my uncle had really taught me to enjoy the kind of practice in which he himself took such delight. I suspect I worked too hard; at any rate, in seventeen hundred and eighteen I was far from well,[12] and my good uncle was disturbed by my ill looks.

One day, he rang the bell twice into the clerk's room at the dingy office in Gray's Inn Lane. It was the summons for me, and I went into his private room just as a gentleman – whom I knew well enough by sight as an Irish lawyer of more reputation than he deserved – was leaving.

My uncle was slowly rubbing his hands together and considering. I was there two or three minutes before he spoke. Then he told me that I must pack up my portmanteau that very afternoon, and start that night by post-horse for West Chester.[13] I should get there, if all went well, at the end of five days' time, and must then wait for a packet to cross over to Dublin; from thence I must proceed to a certain town named Kildoon, and in that neighbourhood I was to remain, making certain inquiries as to the existence of any descendants of the younger branch of a family to whom some valuable estates had descended in the female line. The Irish lawyer whom I had seen was weary of the case, and would willingly have given up the property, without further ado, to a man who appeared to claim them; but on laying his tables and trees before my uncle, the latter had foreseen so many possible prior claimants, that the lawyer had begged him to undertake the management of the whole business. In his youth, my uncle would have liked nothing better than going over to Ireland himself, and ferreting out every scrap of paper or parchment, and every word of tradition respecting the family. As it was, old and gouty, he deputed me.

Accordingly, I went to Kildoon. I suspect I had something of my uncle's delight in following up a genealogical scent, for I very soon found out, when on the spot, that Mr. Rooney, the Irish lawyer, would have got both himself and the first claimant into a terrible scrape, if he had pronounced his opinion that the estates ought to be given up to him. There were three poor Irish fellows, each nearer of kin to the last possessor; but, a generation before, there was a still nearer relation, who had never been accounted for, nor his existence ever discovered by the lawyers, I venture to think, till I routed him out from the memory of some of the old dependants of the family. What had become of him? I travelled backwards and forwards; I crossed over to France, and came back again with a slight clue, which ended in my discovering that, wild and dissipated himself, he had left one child, a son, of yet worse character than his father; that this same Hugh Fitzgerald had married a very beautiful serving-woman of the Byrnes – a person below him in hereditary rank, but above him in character; that he had died soon after his marriage, leaving one child, whether a boy or a girl I could not learn, and that the mother had returned to live in the family of the Byrnes. Now, the chief of this latter family was serving in the Duke of Berwick's regiment,[14] and it was long before I could hear from him; it was more than a year before I got a short, haughty letter – I fancy he had a soldier's contempt for a civilian, an Irishman's hatred for an Englishman, an exiled Jacobite's jealousy of one who prospered and lived tranquilly under the government he looked upon as an usurpation. 'Bridget Fitzgerald,' he said, 'had been faithful to the fortunes of his sister – had followed her abroad, and to England when Mrs.

Starkey had thought fit to return. Both her sister and her husband were dead; he knew nothing of Bridget Fitzgerald at the present time: probably Sir Philip Tempest, his nephew's guardian, might be able to give me some information.' I have not given the little contemptuous terms; the way in which faithful service was meant to imply more than it said – all that has nothing to do with my story. Sir Philip, when applied to, told me that he paid an annuity[15] regularly to an old woman named Fitzgerald, living at Coldholme (the village near Starkey Manor-House). Whether she had any descendants he could not say.

One bleak March evening, I came in sight of the places described at[a] the beginning of my story. I could hardly understand the rude dialect in which the direction to old Bridget's house was given.

'Yo' see yon furleets,' all run together, gave me no idea that I was to guide myself by the distant lights that shone in the windows of the Hall, occupied for the time by a farmer who held the post of steward, while the Squire, now four or five and twenty, was making the grand tour. However, at last, I reached Bridget's cottage – a low, moss-grown place; the palings that had once surrounded it were broken and gone; and the underwood of the forest came up to the walls, and must have darkened the windows. It was about seven o'clock – not late to my London notions – but, after knocking for some time at the door and receiving no reply, I was driven to conjecture that the occupant of the house was gone to bed. So I betook myself to the nearest church I had seen, three miles back on the road I had come, sure that close to that I should find an inn of some kind; and early the next morning I set off back to Coldholme, by a field-path which my host assured me I should find a shorter cut than the road I had taken the night before. It was a cold, sharp morning; my feet left prints in the sprinkling of hoar-frost that covered the ground; nevertheless, I saw an old woman, whom I instinctively suspected to be the object of my search, in a sheltered covert on one side of my path. I lingered and watched her. She must have been considerably above the middle size in her prime, for when she raised herself from the stooping position in which I first saw her, there was something fine and commanding in the erectness of her figure. She drooped again in a minute or two, and seemed looking for something on the ground, as, with bent head, she turned off from the spot where I gazed upon her, and was lost to my sight. I fancy I missed my way, and made a round in spite of the landlord's directions; for by the time I had reached Bridget's cottage she was there, with no semblance of hurried walk or discomposure of any kind. The door was slightly ajar. I knocked, and the majestic figure stood before me, silently awaiting the explanation of my errand. Her teeth were all gone, so the nose and chin were brought near together; the gray eyebrows were straight, and almost hung over her deep, cavernous eyes, and the thick white hair lay in silvery masses over the low, wide, wrinkled forehead. For a moment, I stood uncertain how to shape my answer to the solemn questioning of her silence.

'Your name is Bridget Fitzgerald, I believe?' She bowed her head in assent.

'I have something to say to you. May I come in? I am unwilling to keep you standing.'

'You cannot tire me,' she said, and at first she seemed inclined to deny me the shelter of her roof. But the next moment – she had searched the very soul in me with her eyes during that instant – she led me in, and dropped the shadowing hood of her gray, draping cloak, which had previously hid part of the character of her countenance. The cottage was rude and bare enough. But before that picture of the Virgin, of which I have made mention, there stood a little cup filled with fresh primroses. While she paid her reverence to the Madonna, I understood why she had been out seeking through the clumps of green in the sheltered copse. Then she turned round, and bade me be seated. The expression of her face, which all this time I was studying, was not bad, as the stories of my last night's landlord had led me to expect; it was a wild, stern, fierce, indomitable countenance, seamed and scarred by agonies of solitary weeping; but it was neither cunning nor malignant.

'My name is Bridget Fitzgerald,' said she, by way of opening our conversation.

'And your husband was Hugh Fitzgerald, of Knock-Mahon, near Kildoon, in Ireland?'

A faint light came into the dark gloom of her eyes.

'He was.'

'May I ask if you had any children by him?'

The light in her eyes grew quick and red. She tried to speak, I could see; but something rose in her throat, and choked her, and until she could speak calmly, she would fain not speak at all before a stranger. In a minute or so she said:

'I had a daughter – one Mary Fitzgerald,' – then her strong nature mastered her strong will, and she cried out, with a trembling, wailing cry: 'Oh, man! what of her? – what of her?'

She rose from her seat, and came and clutched at my arm, and looked in my eyes. There she read, as I suppose, my utter ignorance of what had become of her child; for she went blindly back to her chair, and sat rocking herself and softly moaning, as if I were not there; I not daring to speak to the lone and awful woman. After a little pause, she knelt down before the picture of our Lady of the Holy Heart, and spoke to her by all the fanciful and poetic names of the Litany.

'O Rose of Sharon! O Tower of David! O Star of the Sea! have you no comfort for my sore heart? Am I for ever to hope? Grant me at least despair!'

– and so on she went, heedless of my presence. Her prayers grew wilder and wilder, till they seemed to me to touch on the borders of madness and blasphemy. Almost involuntarily, I spoke as if to stop her.

'Have you any reason to think that your daughter is dead?'

She rose from her knees, and came and stood before me.

'Mary Fitzgerald is dead,' said she. 'I shall never see her again in the flesh. No tongue ever told me. But I know she is dead. I have yearned so to see her, and my heart's will is fearful and strong: it would have drawn her to me before now, if she had been a wanderer on the other side of the world. I wonder often it has not drawn her out of the grave to come and stand before me, and hear me tell her how I loved her. For, sir, we parted unfriends.'

I knew nothing but the dry particulars needed for my lawyer's quest, but I could not help feeling for the desolate woman; and she must have read the unusual sympathy with her wistful eyes.

'Yes, sir, we did. She never knew how I loved her; and we parted unfriends; and I fear me that I wished her voyage might not turn out well, only meaning, – O, blessed Virgin! you know I only meant that she should come home to her mother's arms as to the happiest place on earth; but my wishes are terrible – their power goes beyond my thought – and there is no hope for me, if my words brought Mary harm.'

'But,' I said, 'you do not know that she is dead. Even now, you hoped she might be alive. Listen to me,' and I told her the tale I have already told you, giving it all in the driest manner, for I wanted to recall the clear sense that I felt almost sure she had possessed in her younger days, and by keeping up her attention to details, restrain the vague wildness of her grief.

She listened with deep attention, putting from time to time such questions as convinced me I had to do with no common intelligence, however dimmed and shorn by solitude and mysterious sorrow. Then she took up her tale; and in few brief words, told me of her wanderings abroad in vain search after her daughter; sometimes in the wake of armies, sometimes in camp, sometimes in city. The lady, whose waiting-woman Mary had gone to be, had died soon after the date of her last letter home; her husband, the foreign officer, had been serving in Hungary, whither Bridget had followed him, but too late to find him. Vague rumours reached her that Mary had made a great marriage; and this sting of doubt was added, – whether the mother might not be close to her child under her new name, and even hearing of her every day, and yet never recognising the lost one under the appellation she then bore. At length the thought took possession of her, that it was possible that all this time Mary might be at home at Coldholme, in the Trough of Bolland, in Lancashire, in England; and home came Bridget, in that vain hope, to her desolate hearth, and empty cottage. Here she had thought it safest to remain; if Mary was in life, it was here she would seek for her mother.

I noted down one or two particulars out of Bridget's narrative that I thought might be of use to me; for I was stimulated to further search in a strange and extraordinary manner. It seemed as if it were impressed upon me, that I must take up the quest where Bridget had laid it down; and this for no reason that had previously influenced me (such as my uncle's anxiety on the subject, my own reputation as a lawyer, and so on), but from some strange power which had taken possession of my will only that very morning, and which forced it in the direction it chose.

'I will go,' said I. 'I will spare nothing in the search. Trust to me. I will learn all that can be learnt. You shall know all that money, or pains, or wit can discover. It is true she may be long dead: but she may have left a child.'

'A child!' she cried, as if for the first time this idea had struck her mind. 'Hear him, Blessed Virgin! he says she may have left a child. And you have never told me, though I have prayed so for a sign, waking or sleeping!'

'Nay,' said I, 'I know nothing but what you tell me. You say you heard of her marriage.'

But she caught nothing of what I said. She was praying to the Virgin in a kind of ecstacy,[a] which seemed to render her unconscious of my very presence.

From Coldholme I went to Sir Philip Tempest's. The wife of the foreign officer had been a cousin of his father's, and from him I thought I might gain some particulars as to the existence of the Count de la T'our d'Auvergne,[16] and where I could find him; for I knew questions *de vive voix*[b] aid the flagging recollection, and I was determined to lose no chance for want of trouble. But Sir Philip had gone abroad, and it would be some time before I could receive an answer. So I followed my uncle's advice, to whom I had mentioned how wearied I felt, both in body and mind, by my will-o'-the-wisp search. He immediately told me to go to Harrogate, there to await Sir Philip's reply. I should be near to one of the places connected with my search, Coldholme; not far from Sir Philip Tempest, in case he returned, and I wished to ask him any further questions; and, in conclusion, my uncle bade me try to forget all about my business for a time.

This was far easier said than done. I have seen a child on a common blown along by a high wind, without power of standing still and resisting the tempestuous force. I was somewhat in the same predicament as regarded my mental state. Something resistless seemed to urge my thoughts on, through every possible course by which there was a chance of attaining to my object. I did not see the sweeping moors when I walked out: when I held a book in my hand, and read the words, their sense did not penetrate to my brain. If I slept, I went on with the same ideas, always flowing in the same direction. This could not last long without having a bad effect on the body. I had an illness, which, although I was racked with pain, was a positive relief to me, as it compelled me to live in the present suffering, and not in the visionary researches I had been continually making before. My kind uncle came to nurse me; and after the immediate danger was over, my life seemed to slip away in delicious languor for two or three months. I did not ask – so much did I dread falling into the old channel of thought – whether any reply had been received to my letter to Sir Philip. I turned my whole imagination right away from all that subject. My uncle remained with me until high summer, and then returned to his business in London; leaving me perfectly well, although not completely strong. I was to follow him in a fortnight; when, as he said, 'we would look over letters, and talk about several things.' I knew what this little speech alluded to, and shrank from the train of thought it suggested, which was so intimately connected with my first feelings of illness. However, I had a fortnight more to roam on those invigorating Yorkshire moors.

In those days, there was one large, rambling inn at Harrogate, close to the Medicinal Spring; but it was already becoming too small for the accommodation of the influx of visitors, and many lodged round about, in the farmhouses of the district. It was so early in the season, that I had the inn pretty much to myself; and, indeed, felt rather like a visitor in a private house, so intimate had the landlord and landlady become with me during my long illness. She would chide me for being out so late on the moors, or for having been too long without food, quite in a motherly way; while he consulted me about vintages and wines, and taught me many a Yorkshire wrinkle about horses. In my walks I met other strangers from time to time. Even before my uncle had left me, I had noticed, with half-torpid curiosity, a young lady of very striking appearance, who went about always accompanied by an elderly companion, – hardly a gentlewoman, but with something in her look that prepossessed me in her favour. The younger lady always put her veil down when any one approached; so it had been only once or twice, when I had come upon her at a sudden turn in the path, that I had even had a glimpse of her face. I am not sure if it was beautiful, though in after-life I grew to think it so. But it was at this time overshadowed by a sadness that never varied: a pale, quiet, resigned look of intense suffering, that irresistibly attracted me, – not with love, but with a sense of infinite compassion for one so young yet so hopelessly unhappy. The companion wore something of the same look: quiet, melancholy, hopeless, yet resigned. I asked my landlord who they were. He said they were called Clarke, and wished to be considered as mother and daughter; but that, for his part, he did not believe that to be their right name, or[a] that there was any such relationship between them. They had been in the neighbourhood of Harrogate for some time, lodging in a remote farm-house. The people there would tell nothing about them; saying that they paid handsomely, and never did any harm; so why should they be speaking of any strange things that might happen? That, as the landlord shrewdly observed, showed there was something out of the common way:

he had heard that the elderly woman was a cousin of the farmer's where they lodged, and so the regard existing between relations might help to keep them quiet.

'What did he think, then, was the reason for their extreme seclusion?' asked I.

'Nay, he could not tell, not he. He had heard that the young lady, for all as quiet as she seemed, played strange pranks at times.' He shook his head when I asked him for more particulars, and refused to give them, which made me doubt if he knew any, for he was in general a talkative and communicative man. In default of other interests, after my uncle left, I set myself to watch these two people. I hovered about their walks, drawn towards them with a strange fascination, which was not diminished by their evident annoyance at so frequently meeting me. One day, I had the sudden good fortune to be at hand when they were alarmed by the attack of a bull, which, in those unenclosed grazing districts, was a particularly dangerous occurrence. I have other and more important things to relate, than to tell of the accident which gave me an opportunity of rescuing them; it is enough to say, that this event was the beginning of an acquaintance, reluctantly acquiesced in by them, but eagerly prosecuted by me. I can hardly tell when intense curiosity became merged in love, but in less than ten days after my uncle's departure I was passionately enamoured of Mrs.[a] Lucy, as her attendant called her; carefully – for this I noted well – avoiding any address which appeared as if there was an equality of station between them. I noticed also that Mrs. Clarke, the elderly woman, after her first reluctance to allow me to pay them any attentions had been overcome, was cheered by my evident attachment to the young girl; it seemed to lighten her heavy burden of care, and she evidently favoured my visits to the farm-house where they lodged. It was not so with Lucy. A more attractive person I never saw, in spite of her depression of manner, and shrinking avoidance of me. I felt sure at once, that whatever was the source of her grief, it rose from no fault of her own. It was difficult to draw her into conversation; but when at times, for a moment or two, I beguiled her into talk, I could see a rare intelligence in her face, and a grave, trusting look in the soft, gray eyes that were raised for a minute to mine. I made every excuse I possibly could for going there. I sought wild flowers for Lucy's sake; I planned walks for Lucy's sake; I watched the heavens by night, in hopes that some unusual beauty of sky would justify me in tempting Mrs. Clarke and Lucy forth upon the moors, to gaze at the great purple dome above.

It seemed to me that Lucy was aware of my love; but that, for some motive which I could not guess, she would fain have repelled me; but then again I saw, or fancied I saw, that her heart spoke in my favour, and that there was a struggle going on in her mind, which at times (I loved so dearly) I could have begged her to spare herself, even though the happiness of my whole life should have been the sacrifice; for her complexion grew paler, her aspect of sorrow more hopeless, her delicate frame yet slighter. During this period I had written, I should say, to my uncle, to beg to be allowed to prolong my stay at Harrogate, not giving any reason; but such was his tenderness towards me, that in a few days I heard from him, giving me a willing permission, and only charging me to take care of myself, and not use too much exertion during the hot weather.

One sultry evening I drew near the farm. The windows of their parlour were open, and I heard voices when I turned the corner of the house, as I passed the first window (there were two windows in their little ground-floor room). I saw Lucy distinctly; but when I had knocked at their door – the house-door stood always ajar – she was gone, and I saw only Mrs. Clarke, turning over the work-things lying on the table, in a nervous and purposeless manner. I felt by instinct that a conversation of some importance was coming on, in which I should be expected to say what was my object in paying these frequent visits. I was glad of the opportunity. My uncle had several times alluded to the pleasant possibility of my bringing home a young wife, to cheer and adorn the old house in Ormond Street. He was rich, and I was to succeed him, and had, as I knew, a fair reputation for so young a lawyer. So on my side I saw no obstacle. It was true that Lucy was shrouded in mystery; her name (I was convinced it was not Clarke), birth, parentage, and previous life were unknown to me. But I was sure of her goodness and sweet innocence, and although I knew that there must be something painful to be told, to account for her mournful sadness, yet I was willing to bear my share in her grief, whatever it might be.

Mrs. Clarke began, as if it was a relief to her to plunge into the subject.

'We have thought, sir – at least I have thought – that you know very little of us, nor we of you, indeed; not enough to warrant the intimate acquaintance we have fallen into. I beg your pardon, sir,' she went on, nervously; 'I am but a plain kind of woman, and I mean to use no rudeness; but I must say straight out that I – we – think it would be better for you not to come so often to see us. She is very unprotected, and –'

'Why should I not come to see you, dear madam?' asked I, eagerly, glad of the opportunity of explaining myself. 'I come, I own, because I have learnt to love Mistress Lucy, and wish to teach her to love me.'

Mistress Clarke shook her head, and sighed.

'Don't, sir – neither love her, nor, for the sake of all you hold sacred, teach her to love you! If I am too late, and you love her already, forget her, – forget these last few weeks. O! I should never have allowed you to come!' she went on, passionately; 'but what am I to do? We are forsaken by all, except the great God, and even He permits a stranger and evil power to afflict us – what am I to do? Where is it to end?' She wrung her hands in her distress; then she turned to me: 'Go away, sir; go away, before you learn to care any more for her. I ask it for your own sake – I implore. You have been good and kind to us, and we shall always recollect you with gratitude; but go away now, and never come back to cross our fatal path!'

'Indeed, madam,' said I, 'I shall do no such thing.

You urge it for my own sake. I have no fear, so urged – nor wish, except to hear more – all. I cannot have seen Mistress Lucy in all the intimacy of this last fortnight, without acknowledging her goodness and innocence; and without seeing – pardon me, madam – that for some reason you are two very lonely women, in some mysterious sorrow and distress. Now, though I am not powerful myself, yet I have friends who are so wise and kind, that they may be said to possess power. Tell me some particulars. Why are you in grief – what is your secret – why are you here? I declare solemnly that nothing you have said has daunted me in my wish to become Lucy's husband; nor will I shrink from any difficulty that, as such an aspirant, I may have to encounter. You say you are friendless – why cast away an honest friend? I will tell you of people to whom you may write, and who will answer any questions as to my character and prospects. I do not shun inquiry.'ª

She shook her head again. 'You had better go away, sir. You know nothing about us.'

'I know your names,' said I, 'and I have heard you allude to the part of the country from which you came, which I happen to know as a wild and lonely place. There are so few people living in it that, if I chose to go there, I could easily ascertain all about you; but I would rather hear it from yourself.' You see I wanted to pique her into telling me something definite.

'You do not know our true names, sir,' said she, hastily.

'Well, I may have conjectured as much. But tell me, then, I conjure you. Give me your reasons for distrusting my willingness to stand by what I have said with regard to Mistress Lucy.'

'Oh, what can I do?' exclaimed she. 'If I am turning away a true friend as he says? – Stay!' coming to a sudden decision – 'I will tell you something – I cannot tell you all – you would not believe it. But, perhaps, I can tell you enough to prevent your going on in your hopeless attachment. I am not Lucy's mother.'

'So I conjectured,' I said. 'Go on.'

'I do not even know whether she is the legitimate or illegitimate child of her father.[17] But he is cruelly turned against her; and her mother is long dead; and, for a terrible reason, she has no other creature to keep constant to her but me. She – only two years ago – such a darling and such a pride in her father's house!ᵇ Why, sir, there is a mystery that might happen in connection with her any moment; and then you would go away like all the rest; and, when you next heard her name, you would loathe her. Others, who have loved her longer, have done so before now. My poor child, whom neither God nor man has mercy upon – or, surely, she would die!'

The good woman was stopped by her crying. I confess, I was a little stunned by her last words; but only for a moment. At any rate, till I knew definitely what was this mysterious stain upon one so simple and pure, as Lucy seemed, I would not desert her, and so I said; and she made answer: –

'If you are daring in your heart to think harm of my child, sir, after knowing her as you have done, you are no good man yourself; but I am so foolish and helpless in my great sorrow, that I would fain hope to find a friend in you. I cannot help trusting that, although you may no longer feel towards her as a lover, you will have pity upon us; and perhaps, by your learning, you can tell us where to go for aid.'

'I implore you to tell me what this mystery is,' I cried, almost maddened by this suspense.

'I cannot,' said she, solemnly. 'I am under a deep vow of secrecy. If you are to be told, it must be by her.' She left the room, and I remained to ponder over this strange interview. I mechanically turned over the few books, and with eyes that saw nothing at the time, examined the tokens of Lucy's frequent presence in that room.

When I got home at night, I remembered how all these trifles spoke of a pure and tender heart and innocent life. Mistress Clarke returned; she had been crying sadly.

'Yes,' said she, 'it is as I feared: she loves you so much that she is willing to run the fearful risk of telling you all herself – she acknowledges it is but a poor chance; but your sympathy will be a balm, if you give it. To-morrow, come here at ten in the morning; and, as you hope for pity in your hour of agony, repress all show of fear or repugnance you may feel towards one so grievously afflicted.'

I half smiled. 'Have no fear,' I said. It seemed too absurd to imagine my feeling dislike to Lucy.

'Her father loved her well,' said she, gravely, 'yet he drove her out like some monstrous thing.'

Just at this moment came a peal of ringing laughter from the garden. It was Lucy's voice; it sounded as if she were standing just on one side of the open casement – and as though she were suddenly stirred to merriment – merriment verging on boisterousness, by the doings or sayings of some other person. I can scarcely say why, but the sound jarred on me inexpressibly. She knew the subject of our conversation, and must have been at least aware of the state of agitation her friend was in: she herself usually so gentle and quiet. I half rose to go to the window, and satisfy my instinctive curiosity as to what had provoked this burst of ill-timed laughter; but Mrs. Clarke threw her whole weight and power upon the hand with which she pressed and kept me down.

'For God's sake!' she said, white and trembling all over, 'sit still; be quiet. Oh! be patient. To-morrow you will know all. Leave us, for we are all sorely afflicted. Do not seek to know more about us.'

Again that laugh – so musical in sound, yet so discordant to my heart. She
held me tight – tighter; without positive violence I could not have risen. I
was sitting with my back to the window, but I felt a shadow pass between the
sun's warmth and me, and a strange shudder ran through my frame. In a
minute or two she released me.

'Go,' repeated she. 'Be warned, I ask you once more. I do not think you
can stand this knowledge that you seek. If I had had my own way, Lucy
should never have yielded, and promised to tell you all. Who knows what
may come of it?'

'I am firm in my wish to know all. I return at ten to-morrow morning,
and then expect to see Mistress Lucy herself.'

I turned away; having my own suspicions, I confess, as to Mistress
Clarke's sanity.

Conjectures as to the meaning of her hints, and uncomfortable thoughts
connected with that strange laughter, filled my mind. I could hardly sleep. I
rose[a] early; and long before the hour I had appointed, I was on the path over
the common that led to the old farm-house where they lodged. I suppose
that Lucy had passed no better a night than I; for there she was also, slowly
pacing with her even step, her eyes bent down, her whole look most saintly
and pure. She started when I came close to her, and grew paler as I reminded
her of my appointment, and spoke with something of the impatience of
obstacles that, seeing her once more, had called up afresh in my mind. All
strange and terrible hints, and giddy merriment were forgotten. My heart
gave forth words of fire, and my tongue uttered them. Her colour went and
came, as she listened; but, when I had ended my passionate speeches, she
lifted her soft eyes to me, and said –

'But you know that you have something to learn about me yet. I only
want to say this: I shall not think less of you – less well of you, I mean – if
you, too, fall away from me when you know all. Stop!' said she, as if fearing
another burst of mad words. 'Listen to me. My father is a man of great
wealth. I never knew my mother; she must have died when I was very
young. When first I remember anything, I was living in a great, lonely house
with my dear and faithful Mistress Clarke. My father, even, was not there;
he was – he is – a soldier, and his duties lie abroad. But he came, from time
to time, and every time I think he loved me more and more. He brought me
rarities from foreign lands, which prove to me now how much he must have
thought of me during his absences. I can sit down and measure the depth of
his lost love now, by such standards as these. I never thought whether he
loved me or not, then; it was so natural, that it was like the air I breathed. Yet
he was an angry man at times, even then; but never with me. He was very
reckless, too; and, once or twice, I heard a whisper among the servants that a
doom was over him, and that he knew it, and tried to drown his knowledge
in wild activity, and even sometimes, sir, in wine. So I grew up in this grand

mansion, in that lonely place. Everything around me seemed at my disposal, and I think every one loved me; I am sure I loved them. Till about two years ago – I remember it well – my father had come to England, to us; and he seemed so proud and so pleased with me and all I had done. And one day his tongue seemed loosened with wine, and he told me much that I had not known till then, – how dearly he had loved my mother, yet how his wilful usage had caused her death; and then he went on to say how he loved me better than any creature on earth, and how, some day, he hoped to take me to foreign places, for that he could hardly bear these long abscences from his only child. Then he seemed to change suddenly, and said, in a strange, wild way, that I was not to believe what he said; that there was many a thing he loved better – his horse – his dog –[18] I know not what.

'And 'twas only the next morning that, when I came into his room to ask his blessing as was my wont, he received me with fierce and angry words. "Why had I," so he asked, "been delighting myself in such wanton mischief – dancing over the tender plants in the flower-beds, all set with the famous Dutch bulbs he had brought from Holland?" I had never been out of doors that morning, sir, and I could not conceive what he meant, and so I said; and then he swore at me for a liar, and said I was of no true blood, for he had seen me doing all that mischief himself – with his own eyes. What could I say? He would not listen to me, and even my tears seemed only to irritate him. That day was the beginning of my great sorrows. Not long after, he reproached me for my undue familiarity – all unbecoming a gentlewoman – with his grooms. I had been in the stable-yard, laughing and talking, he said. Now, sir, I am something of a coward by nature, and I had always dreaded horses; besides that, my father's servants – those whom he brought with him from foreign parts – were wild fellows, whom I had always avoided, and to whom I had never spoken, except as a lady must needs from time to time speak to her father's people. Yet my father called me by names of which I hardly know the meaning, but my heart told me they were such as shame any modest woman; and from that day he turned quite against me; – nay, sir, not many weeks after that, he came in with a riding-whip in his hand; and, accusing me harshly of evil doings, of which I knew no more than you, sir, he was about to strike me, and I, all in bewildering tears, was ready to take his stripes as great kindness compared to his harder words, when suddenly he stopped his arm mid-way, gasped and staggered, crying out, "The curse– the curse!" I looked up in terror. In the great mirror opposite I saw myself, and, right behind, another wicked, fearful self, so like me that my soul seemed to quiver within me, as though not knowing to which similitude of body it belonged. My father saw my double at the same moment, either in its dreadful reality, whatever that might be, or in the scarcely less terrible reflection in the mirror; but what came of it at that moment I cannot say, for I suddenly swooned away; and when I came to myself I was lying in my bed, and my faithful Clarke sitting by me. I was in my bed for days; and even while I lay there my double was seen by all, flitting about the house and gardens, always about some mischievous or detestable work. What wonder that every one shrank from me in dread – that my father drove me forth at length, when the disgrace of which I was the cause was past his patience to bear. Mistress Clarke came with me; and here we try to live such a life of piety and prayer as may in time set me free from the curse.'

All the time she had been speaking, I had been weighing her story in my mind. I had hitherto put cases of witchcraft on one side, as mere superstitions; and my uncle and I had had many an argument, he supporting himself by the opinion of his good friend Sir Matthew Hale.[19] Yet this sounded like the tale of one bewitched; or was it merely the effect of a life of extreme seclusion telling on the nerves of a sensitive girl? My scepticism inclined me to the latter belief, and when she paused I said:

'I fancy that some physician could have disabused your father of his belief in visions –'

Just at that instant, standing as I was opposite to her in the full and perfect morning light, I saw behind her another figure – a ghastly resemblance, complete in likeness, so far as form and feature and minutest touch of dress could go, but with a loathsome demon soul looking out of the gray eyes, that were in turns mocking and voluptuous. My heart stood still within me; every hair rose up erect; my flesh crept with horror. I could not see the grave and tender Lucy – my eyes were fascinated by the creature beyond. I know not why, but I put out my hand to clutch it; I grasped nothing but empty air, and my whole blood curdled to ice. For a moment I could not see; then my sight came back, and I saw Lucy standing before me, alone, deathly pale, and, I could have fancied, almost, shrunk in size.

'IT has been near me?' she said, as if asking a question.

The sound seemed taken out of her voice; it was husky as the notes on an old harpsichord when the strings have ceased to vibrate. She read her answer in my face, I suppose, for I could not speak. Her look was one of intense fear, but that died away into an aspect of most humble patience. At length she seemed to force herself to face behind and around her: she saw the purple moors, the blue distant hills, quivering in the sunlight, but nothing else.

'Will you take me home?' she said, meekly.

I took her by the hand, and led her silently through the budding heather – we dared not speak; for we could not tell but that the dread creature was listening, although unseen, – but that IT might appear and push us asunder. I never loved her more fondly than now when – and that was the unspeakable misery – the idea of her was becoming so inextricably blended with the shuddering thought of IT. She seemed to understand what I must be feeling. She let go my hand, which she had kept clasped until then, when we reached the garden gate, and went forwards to meet her anxious friend, who was standing by the window looking for her. I could not enter the house: I needed silence, society, leisure, change – I knew not what – to shake off the sensation of that creature's presence. Yet I lingered about the garden – I hardly know why; I partly suppose, because I feared to encounter the resemblance again on the solitary common, where it had vanished, and partly from a feeling of inexpressible compassion for Lucy. In a few minutes Mistress Clarke came forth and joined me. We walked some paces in silence.

'You know all now,' said she, solemnly.

'I saw IT,' said I, below my breath.

'And you shrink from us, now,' she said, with a hopelessness which stirred up all that was brave or good in me.

'Not a whit,' said I. 'Human flesh shrinks from encounter with the powers of darkness: and, for some reason unknown to me, the pure and holy Lucy is their victim.'

'The sins of the fathers[20] shall be visited upon the children,' she said.

'Who is her father?' asked I. 'Knowing as much as I do, I may surely know more – know all. Tell me, I entreat you, madam, all that you can conjecture respecting this demoniac persecution of one so good.'

'I will; but not now. I must go to Lucy now. Come this afternoon, I will see you alone; and oh, sir! I will trust that you may yet find some way to help us in our sore trouble!'

I was miserably exhausted by the swooning affright which had taken possession of me. When I reached the inn, I staggered in like one overcome by wine. I went to my own private room. It was some time before I saw that the weekly post had come in, and brought me my letters. There was one from my uncle, one from my home in Devonshire, and one, re-directed over the first address, sealed with a great coat of arms. It was from Sir Philip Tempest: my letter of inquiry respecting Mary Fitzgerald had reached him at Liège, where it so happened that the Count de la Tour d'Auvergne was quartered at the very time. He remembered his wife's beautiful attendant; she had had high words with the deceased countess, respecting her intercourse with an English gentleman of good standing, who was also in the foreign service. The countess augured evil of his intentions; while Mary, proud and vehement, asserted that he would soon marry her, and resented her mistress's warnings as an insult. The consequence was, that she had left Madame de la Tour d'Auvergne's service, and, as the Count believed, had gone to live with the Englishman; whether he had married her, or not, he could not say. 'But,' added Sir Philip Tempest, 'you may easily hear what particulars you wish to know respecting Mary Fitzgerald from the Englishman himself, if, as I suspect, he is no other than my neighbour and former acquaintance, Mr. Gisborne, of Skipford Hall, in the West Riding.[21] I am led to the belief that he is no other by several small particulars, none of which are in themselves conclusive, but which, taken together, make a mass of presumptive

evidence. As far as I could make out from the Count's foreign pronunciation, Gisborne was the name of the Englishman: I know that Gisborne of
Skipford was abroad and in the foreign service at that time – he was a likely
fellow enough for such an exploit, and, above all, certain expressions recur
to my mind which he used in reference to old Bridget Fitzgerald, of Coldholme, whom he once encountered while staying with me at Starkey
Manor-House. I remember that the meeting seemed to have produced some
extraordinary effect upon his mind, as though he had suddenly discovered
some connection which she might have had with his previous life. I beg you
to let me know if I can be of any further service to you. Your uncle once rendered me a good turn, and I will gladly repay it, so far as in me lies, to his
nephew.'

I was now apparently close on the discovery which I had striven so many
months to attain. But success had lost its zest. I put my letters down, and
seemed to forget them all in thinking of the morning I had passed that very
day. Nothing was real but the unreal presence, which had come like an evil
blast across my bodily eyes, and burnt itself down upon my brain. Dinner
came, and went away untouched. Early in the afternoon I walked to the
farm-house. I found Mistress Clarke alone, and I was glad and relieved. She
was evidently prepared to tell me all I might wish to hear.

'You asked me for Mistress Lucy's true name; it is Gisborne,' she began.

'Not Gisborne of Skipford?' I exclaimed, breathless with anticipation.

'The same,' said she, quietly, not regarding my manner. 'Her father is a
man of note; although, being a Roman Catholic, he cannot take that rank in
this country to which his station entitles him. The consequence is that he
lives much abroad – has been a soldier, I am told.'

'And Lucy's mother?' I asked.

She shook her head. 'I never knew her,' said she. 'Lucy was about three
years old when I was engaged to take charge of her. Her mother was dead.'

'But you know her name? – you can tell if it was Mary Fitzgerald?'

She looked astonished. 'That was her name. But, sir, how came you to be
so well acquainted with it? It was a mystery to the whole household at Skipford Court. She was some beautiful young woman whom he lured away
from her protectors while he was abroad. I have heard said he practised
some terrible deceit upon her, and when she came to know it, she was neither to have nor to hold, but rushed off from his very arms, and threw
herself into a rapid stream and was drowned. It stung him deep with
remorse, but I used to think the remembrance of the mother's cruel death
made him love the child yet dearer.'

I told her, as briefly as might be, of my researches after the descendant
and heir of the Fitzgeralds of Kildoon, and added – something of my old
lawyer spirit returning into me for the moment – that I had no doubt but

that we should prove Lucy to be by[a] right possessed of large estates in Ireland.

No flush came over her gray[b] face; no light into her eyes. 'And what is all the wealth in the whole world to that poor girl?' she said. 'It will not free her from the ghastly bewitchment which persecutes her. As for money, what a pitiful thing it is; it cannot touch her.'

'No more can the Evil Creature harm her,' I said. 'Her holy nature dwells apart, and cannot be defiled or stained by all the devilish arts in the whole world.'

'True! but it is a cruel fate to know that all shrink from her, sooner or later, as from one possessed – accursed.'

'How came it to pass?' I asked.

'Nay, I know not. Old rumours there are, that were bruited through the household at Skipford.'

'Tell me,' I demanded.

'They came from servants, who would fain account for everything. They say that, many years ago, Mr. Gisborne killed a dog belonging to an old witch at Coldholme; that she cursed, with a dreadful and mysterious curse, the creature, whatever it might be, that he should love best; and that it struck so deeply into his heart that for years he kept himself aloof from my any temptation to love aught. But who could help loving Lucy?'

'You never heard the witch's name?' I gasped.

'Yes – they called her Bridget; they said he would never go near the spot again for terror of her. Yet he was a brave man!'

'Listen,' said I, taking hold of her arm, the better to arrest her full attention; 'if what I suspect holds true, that man stole Bridget's only child – the very Mary Fitzgerald who was Lucy's mother; if so, Bridget cursed him in ignorance of the deeper wrong he had done her.[22] To this hour she yearns after her lost child, and questions the saints whether she be living or not. The roots of that curse lie deeper than she knows: she unwittingly banned him for a deeper guilt than that of killing a dumb beast. The sins of the fathers are indeed visited upon the children.'

'But,' said Mistress Clarke, eagerly, 'she would never let evil rest on her own grandchild? Surely, sir, if what you say be true, there are hopes for Lucy. Let us go – go at once, and tell this fearful woman all that you suspect, and beseech her to take off the spell she has put upon her innocent grandchild.'

It seemed to me, indeed, that something like this was the best course we could pursue. But first it was necessary to ascertain more than what mere rumour or careless hearsay could tell. My thoughts turned to my uncle – he could advise me wisely – he ought to know all. I resolved to go to him without delay; but I did not choose to tell Mistress Clarke of all the visionary plans that flitted through my mind. I simply declared my intention of proceeding straight to London on Lucy's affairs. I bade her believe that my interest on the young lady's behalf was greater than ever, and that my whole time should be given up to her cause. I saw that Mistress Clarke distrusted me, because my mind was too full of thoughts for my words to flow freely. She sighed and shook her head, and said, 'Well, it is all right!' in such a tone that it was an implied reproach. But I was firm and constant in my heart, and I took confidence from that.

I rode to London. I rode long days drawn out into the lovely summer nights: I could not rest. I reached London. I told my uncle all, though in the stir of the great city the horror had faded away, and I could hardly imagine that he would believe the account I gave him of the fearful double of Lucy which I had seen on the lonely moor-side. But my uncle had lived many years, and learnt many things; and, in the deep secrets of family history that had been confided to him, he had heard of cases of innocent people bewitched and taken possession of by evil spirits yet more fearful than Lucy's. For, as he said, to judge from all I told him, that resemblance had no power over her – she was too pure and good to be tainted by its evil, haunting presence. It had, in all probability, so my uncle conceived, tried to suggest wicked thoughts and to tempt to wicked actions; but she, in her saintly maidenhood, had passed on undefiled by evil thought or deed. It could not touch her soul: but true, it set her apart from all sweet love or common human intercourse. My uncle threw himself with an energy more like six-and-twenty than sixty into the consideration of the whole case. He undertook the proving Lucy's descent, and volunteered to go and find out Mr. Gisborne, and obtain, firstly, the legal proofs of her descent from the Fitzgeralds of Kildoon, and, secondly, to try and hear all that he could respecting the working of the curse, and whether any and what means had been taken to exorcise that terrible appearance. For he told me of instances where, by prayers and long fasting, the evil possessor had been driven forth with howling and many cries from the body which it had come to inhabit; he spoke of those strange New England cases[23] which had happened not so long before; of Mr. Defoe, who had written a book,[24] wherein he had named many modes of subduing apparitions, and sending them back whence they came; and, lastly, he spoke low of dreadful ways of compelling witches to undo their witchcraft. But I could not endure to hear of those tortures and burnings. I said that Bridget was rather a wild and savage woman than a malignant witch; and, above all, that Lucy was of her kith and kin; and that, in putting her to the trial, by water or by fire, we should be torturing – it might be to the death – the ancestress of her we sought to redeem.

My uncle thought awhile, and then said, that in this last matter I was right – at any rate, it should not be tried, with his consent, till all other modes of remedy had failed; and he assented to my proposal that I should go myself and see Bridget, and tell her all.

In accordance with this, I went down once more to the wayside inn near Coldholme. It was late at night when I arrived there; and, while I supped, I inquired of the landlord more particulars as to Bridget's ways. Solitary and savage had been her life for many years. Wild and despotic were her words and manner to those few people who came across her path. The country-folk did her imperious bidding, because they feared to disobey. If they pleased her, they prospered; if, on the contrary, they neglected or traversed her behests, misfortune, small or great, fell on them and theirs. It was not detestation so much as an indefinable terror that she excited.

In the morning I went to see her. She was standing on the green outside her cottage, and received me with the sullen grandeur of a throneless queen. I read in her face that she recognised me, and that I was not unwelcome; but she stood silent till I had opened my errand.

'I have news of your daughter,' said I, resolved to speak straight to all that I knew she felt of love, and not to spare her. 'She is dead!'

The stern figure scarcely trembled, but her hand sought the support of the door-post.

'I knew that she was dead,' said she, deep and low, and then was silent for an instant. 'My tears that should have flowed for her were burnt up long years ago. Young man, tell me about her.'

'Not yet,' said I, having a strange power given me of confronting one, whom, nevertheless, in my secret soul I dreaded.

'You had once a little dog,' I continued. The words called out in her more show of emotion than the intelligence of her daughter's death. She broke in upon my speech: –

'I had! It was hers – the last thing I had of hers – and it was shot for wantonness! It died in my arms. The man who killed that dog rues it to this day. For that dumb beast's blood, his best-beloved stands accursed.'

Her eyes distended, as if she were in a trance and saw the working of her curse. Again I spoke:

'O, woman!' I said, 'that best-beloved, standing accursed before men, is your dead daughter's child.'

The life, the energy, the passion came back to the eyes with which she pierced through me, to see if I spoke truth; then, without another question or word, she threw herself on the ground with fearful vehemence, and clutched at the innocent daisies with convulsed hands.

'Bone of my bone! flesh of my flesh! have I cursed thee – and art thou accursed?'

So she moaned, as she lay prostrate in her great agony. I stood aghast at my own work. She did not hear my broken sentences; she asked no more, but the dumb confirmation which my sad looks had given that one fact, that her curse rested on her own daughter's child. The fear grew on me lest she should die in her strife of body and soul; and then might not Lucy remain under the spell as long as she lived?

Even at this moment, I saw Lucy coming through the woodland path that led to Bridget's cottage; Mistress Clarke was with her: I felt at my heart that it was she, by the balmy peace which the look of her sent over me, as she slowly advanced, a glad surprise shining out of her soft quiet eyes. That was as her gaze met mine. As her looks fell on the woman lying stiff, convulsed on the earth, they became full of tender pity; and she came forward to try and lift her up. Seating herself on the turf, she took Bridget's head into her lap; and, with gentle touches, she arranged the dishevelled gray hair streaming thick and wild from beneath her mutch.

'God help her!' murmured Lucy. 'How she suffers!'

At her desire we sought for water; but when we returned, Bridget had recovered her wandering senses, and was kneeling with clasped hands before Lucy, gazing at that sweet sad face as though her troubled nature drank in health and peace from every moment's contemplation. A faint tinge on Lucy's pale cheeks showed me that she was aware of our return; otherwise it appeared as if she was conscious of her influence for good over the passionate and troubled woman kneeling before her, and would not willingly avert her grave and loving eyes from that wrinkled and careworn countenance.

Suddenly – in the twinkling of an eye – the creature appeared, there, behind Lucy; fearfully the same as to outward semblance, but kneeling exactly as Bridget knelt, and clasping her hands in jesting mimicry as Bridget clasped hers in her ecstasy that was deepening into a prayer. Mistress Clarke cried out – Bridget arose slowly, her gaze fixed on the creature beyond: drawing her breath with a hissing sound, never moving her terrible eyes, that were steady as stone, she made a dart at the phantom, and caught, as I had done, a mere handful of empty air. We saw no more of the creature – it vanished as suddenly as it came, but Bridget looked slowly on, as if watching some receding form. Lucy sat still, white, trembling, drooping – I think she would have swooned if I had not been there to uphold her. While I was attending to her, Bridget passed us, without a word to any one, and, entering her cottage, she barred herself in, and left us without.

All our endeavours were now directed to get Lucy back to the house where she had tarried the night before. Mistress Clarke told me that, not hearing from me (some letter must have miscarried), she had grown impatient and despairing, and had urged Lucy to the enterprise of coming to seek her grandmother; not telling her, indeed, of the dread reputation she possessed, or how we suspected her of having so fearfully blighted that innocent girl; but, at the same time, hoping much from the mysterious stirring of blood, which Mistress Clarke trusted in for the removal of the curse. They had come, by a different route from that which I had taken, to a village inn

not far from Coldholme, only the night before. This was the first interview
between ancestress and descendant.

All through the sultry noon I wandered along the tangled wood-paths of
the old neglected forest, thinking where to turn for remedy in a matter so
complicated and mysterious. Meeting a countryman, I asked my way to the
nearest clergyman, and went, hoping to obtain some counsel from him. But
he proved to be a coarse and common-minded man, giving no time or attention to the intricacies of a case, but dashing out a strong opinion involving
immediate action. For instance, as soon as I named Bridget Fitzgerald, he
exclaimed: –

'The Coldholme witch! the Irish papist! I'd have had her ducked long
since but for that other papist, Sir Philip Tempest. He had had to threaten
honest folk about here over and over again, or they'd have had her up before
the justices for her black doings. And it's the law of the land that witches
should be burnt! Ay, and of Scripture, too, sir! Yet you see a papist, if he's a
rich squire, can overrule both law and Scripture. I'd carry a faggot myself to
rid the country of her!'

Such a one could give me no help. I rather drew back what I had already
said; and tried to make the parson forget it, by treating him to several pots of
beer, in the village inn, to which we had adjourned for our conference at his
suggestion. I left him as soon as I could, and returned to Coldholme, shap-
ing my way past deserted Starkey Manor-House, and coming upon it by the
back. At that side were the oblong remains of the old moat, the waters of
which lay placid and motionless under the crimson rays of the setting sun;
with the forest-trees lying straight along each side, and their deep-green foli-
age mirrored to blackness in the burnished surface of the moat below – and
the broken sun-dial at the end nearest the hall – and the heron, standing on
one leg at the water's edge, lazily looking down for fish – the lonely and desolate house scarce needed the broken windows, the weeds on the door-sill,
the broken shutter softly flapping to and fro in the twilight breeze, to fill up
the picture of desertion and decay. I lingered about the place until the growing darkness warned me on. And then I passed along the path, cut by the
orders of the last lady of Starkey Manor-House, that led me to Bridget's cottage. I resolved at once to see her; and, in spite of closed doors – it might be
of resolved will – she should see me. So I knocked at her door, gently, loudly,
fiercely. I shook it so vehemently that at length the old hinges gave way, and
with a crash it fell inwards, leaving me suddenly face to face with Bridget – I,
red, heated, agitated with my so long-baffled efforts – she, stiff as any stone,
standing right facing me, her eyes dilated with terror, her ashen lips trembling, but her body motionless. In her hands she held her crucifix, as if by
that holy symbol she sought to oppose my entrance. At sight of me, her
whole frame relaxed, and she sank back upon a chair. Some mighty tension
had given way. Still her eyes looked fearfully into the gloom of the outer air,

made more opaque by the glimmer of the lamp inside, which she had placed before the picture of the Virgin.

'Is she there?' asked Bridget, hoarsely.

'No! Who? I am alone. You remember me.'

'Yes,' replied she, still terror-stricken. 'But she – that creature – has been looking in upon me through that window all day long. I closed it up with my shawl; and then I saw her feet below the door, as long as it was light, and I knew she heard my very breathing – nay, worse, my very prayers; and I could not pray, for her listening choked the words ere they rose to my lips. Tell me, who is she? – what means that double girl I saw this morning? One had a look of my dead Mary; but the other curdled my blood, and yet it was the same!'

She had taken hold of my arm, as if to secure herself some human companionship. She shook all over with the slight, never-ceasing tremor of intense terror. I told her my tale, as I have told it you, sparing none of the details.

How Mistress Clarke had informed me that the resemblance had driven Lucy forth from her father's house – how I had disbelieved, until, with mine own eyes, I had seen another Lucy standing behind my Lucy, the same in form and feature, but with the demon-soul looking out of the eyes. I told her all, I say, believing that she – whose curse was working so upon the life of her innocent grandchild – was the only person who could find the remedy and the redemption. When I had done, she sat silent for many minutes.

'You love Mary's child?' she asked.

'I do, in spite of the fearful working of the curse – I love her. Yet I shrink from her ever since that day on the moor-side. And men must shrink from one so accompanied; friends and lovers must stand afar off. Oh, Bridget Fitzgerald! loosen the curse! Set her free!'

'Where is she?'

I eagerly caught at the idea that her presence was needed, in order that, by some strange prayer or exorcism, the spell might be reversed.

'I will go and bring her to you,' I exclaimed. But Bridget tightened her hold upon my arm.

'Not so,' said she, in a low, hoarse voice. 'It would kill me to see her again as I saw her this morning. And I must live till I have worked my work. Leave me!' said she, suddenly, and again taking up the cross. 'I defy the demon I have called up. Leave me to wrestle with it!'

She stood up, as if in an ecstasy of inspiration, from which all fear was banished. I lingered – why, I can hardly tell – until once more she bade me begone. As I went along the forest way, I looked back, and saw her planting the cross in the empty threshold, where the door had been.

The next morning Lucy and I went to seek her, to bid her join her prayers with ours. The cottage stood open and wide to our gaze. No human being was there: the cross remained on the threshold, but Bridget was gone.

CHAPTER III.

WHAT was to be done next? was the question that I asked myself. As for Lucy, she would fain have submitted to the doom that lay upon her. Her gentleness and piety, under the pressure of so horrible a life, seemed over-passive to me. She never complained. Mrs. Clarke complained more than ever. As for me, I was more in love with the real Lucy than ever; but I shrunk from the false similitude with an intensity proportioned to my love. I found out by instinct that Mrs. Clarke had occasional temptations to leave Lucy. The good lady's nerves were shaken, and, from what she said, I could almost have concluded that the object of the Double was to drive away from Lucy this last and almost earliest friend. At times, I could scarcely bear to own it, but I myself felt inclined to turn recreant; and I would accuse Lucy of being too patient – too resigned. One after another, she won the little children of Coldholme. (Mrs. Clarke and she had resolved to stay there, for was it not as good a place as any other to such as they? and did not all our faint hopes rest on Bridget – never seen or heard of now, but still we trusted to come back, or give some token?) So, as I say, one after another, the little children came about my Lucy, won by her soft tones, and her gentle smiles, and kind actions. Alas! one after another they fell away, and shrunk from her path with blanching terror; and we too surely guessed the reason why. It was the last drop. I could bear it no longer. I resolved no more to linger around the spot, but to go back to my uncle, and among the learned divines of the city of London, seek for some power whereby to annul the curse.

My uncle, meanwhile, had obtained all the requisite testimonials relating to Lucy's descent and birth, from the Irish lawyers, and from Mr. Gisborne. The latter gentleman had written from abroad (he was again serving in the Austrian army), a letter alternately passionately self-reproachful and stoically repellent. It was evident that when he thought of Mary – her short life – how he had wronged her, and of her violent death, he could hardly find words severe enough for his own conduct; and from this point of view, the curse that Bridget had laid upon him and his was regarded by him as a pro-phetic doom, to the utterance of which she was moved by a Higher Power, working for the fulfilment of a deeper vengeance than for the death of the poor dog. But then, again, when he came to speak of his daughter, the repugnance which the conduct of the demoniac creature had produced in his mind, was but ill disguised under a show of profound indifference as to Lucy's fate. One almost felt as if he would have been as content to put her out of existence, as he would have been to destroy some disgusting reptile that had invaded his chamber or his couch.

The great Fitzgerald property was Lucy's; and that was all – was nothing.

My uncle and I sat in the gloom of a London November evening, in our house in Ormond Street. I was out of health, and felt as if I were in an inextricable coil of misery. Lucy and I wrote to each other, but that was little; and we dared not see each other for dread of the fearful Third, who had more than once taken her place at our meetings. My uncle had, on the day I speak of, bidden prayers to be put up, on the ensuing Sabbath, in many a church and meeting-house[25] in London, for one grievously tormented by an evil spirit. He had faith in prayers – I had none; I was fast losing faith in all things. So we sat – he trying to interest me in the old talk of other days, I oppressed by one thought – when our old servant, Anthony, opened the door, and, without speaking, showed in a very gentlemanly and prepossessing man, who had something remarkable about his dress, betraying his profession to be that of the Roman Catholic priesthood. He glanced at my uncle first, then at me. It was to me he bowed.

'I did not give my name,' said he, 'because you would hardly have recognised it; unless, sir, when in the north, you heard of Father Bernard, the chaplain at Stoney Hurst?'[26]

I remembered afterwards that I had heard of him, but at the time I had utterly forgotten it; so I professed myself a complete stranger to him; while my ever-hospitable uncle, although hating a papist as much as it was in his nature to hate anything, placed a chair for the visitor, and bade Anthony bring glasses and a fresh jug of claret.

Father Bernard received this courtesy with the graceful ease and pleasant acknowledgment which belongs to the man of the world. Then he turned to scan me with his keen glance. After some slight conversation, entered into on his part, I am certain, with an intention of discovering on what terms of confidence I stood with my uncle, he paused, and said gravely –

'I am sent here with a message to you, sir, from a woman to whom you have shown kindness, and who is one of my penitents, in Antwerp – one Bridget Fitzgerald.'

'Bridget Fitzgerald!' exclaimed I. 'In Antwerp? Tell me, sir, all that you can about her.'

'There is much to be said,' he replied. 'But may I inquire if this gentleman – if your uncle is acquainted with the particulars of which you and I stand informed?'

'All that I know, he knows,' said I, eagerly laying my hand on my uncle's arm, as he made a motion as if to quit the room.

'Then I have to speak before two gentlemen who, however they may differ from me in faith, are yet fully impressed with the fact, that there are evil powers going about continually to take cognizance of our evil thoughts; and, if their Master gives them power, to bring them into overt action. Such is my theory of the nature of that sin, of which I dare not disbelieve – as some sceptics would have us do – the sin of witchcraft. Of this deadly sin, you and I are aware Bridget Fitzgerald has been guilty. Since you saw her last, many prayers have been offered in our churches, many masses sung, many penances undergone, in order that, if God and the Holy Saints so willed it, her sin might be blotted out. But it has not been so willed.'

'Explain to me,' said I, 'who you are, and how you come connected with Bridget. Why is she at Antwerp? I pray you, sir, tell me more. If I am impatient, excuse me; I am ill and feverish, and in consequence bewildered.'

There was something to me inexpressibly soothing in the tone of voice with which he began to narrate, as it were from the beginning, his acquaintance with Bridget.

'I had known Mr. and Mrs. Starkey during their residence abroad, and so it fell out naturally that, when I came as chaplain to the Sherburnes at Stoney Hurst, our acquaintance was renewed; and thus I became the confessor of the whole family, isolated as they were from the offices of the Church, Sherburne being their nearest neighbour who professed the true faith. Of course, you are aware that facts revealed in confession are sealed as in the grave; but I learnt enough of Bridget's character to be convinced that I had to do with no common woman; one powerful for good as for evil. I believe that I was able to give her spiritual assistance from time to time, and that she looked upon me as a servant of that Holy Church, which has such wonderful power of moving men's hearts, and relieving them of the burden of their sins. I have known her cross the moors on the wildest nights of storm, to confess and be absolved; and then she would return, calmed and subdued, to her daily work about her mistress, no one witting where she had been during the hours that most passed in sleep upon their beds. After her daughter's departure – after Mary's mysterious disappearance – I had to impose many a long penance, in order to wash away the sin of impatient repining that was fast leading her into the deeper guilt of blasphemy. She set out on that long journey of which you have possibly heard – that fruitless journey in search of Mary – and during her absence, my superiors ordered my return to my former duties at Antwerp, and for many years I heard no more of Bridget.

'Not many months ago, as I was passing homewards in the evening, along one of the streets near St. Jacques, leading into the Meer Straet, I saw a woman sitting crouched up under the shrine of the Holy Mother of Sorrows. Her hood was drawn over her head, so that the shadow caused by the light of the lamp above fell deep over her face; her hands were clasped round her knees. It was evident that she was some one in hopeless trouble, and as such it was my duty to stop and speak. I naturally addressed her first in Flemish, believing her to be one of the lower class of inhabitants. She shook her head, but did not look up. Then I tried French, and she replied in that language, but speaking it so indifferently, that I was sure she was either English or Irish, and consequently spoke to her in my own native tongue. She recognised my voice; and, starting up, caught at my robes, dragging me before the blessed shrine, and throwing herself down, and forcing me, as much by her evident desire as by her action, to kneel beside her, she exclaimed:

"'O Holy Virgin! you will never hearken to me again, but hear him; for you know him of old, that he does your bidding, and strives to heal broken hearts. Hear him!'"

'She turned to me.

"'She will hear you, if you will only pray. She never hears me: she and all the saints in Heaven cannot hear my prayers, for the Evil One carries them off, as he carried that first away. O, Father Bernard, pray for me!'"

'I prayed for one in sore distress, of what nature I could not say; but the Holy Virgin would know. Bridget held me fast, gasping with eagerness at the sound of my words. When I had ended, I rose, and, making the sign of the Cross over her, I was going to bless her in the name of the Holy Church, when she shrank away like some terrified creature, and said:

"'I am guilty of deadly sin, and am not shriven.'"

"'Arise, my daughter,' said I, "and come with me." And I led the way into one of the confessionals of St. Jacques.

'She knelt; I listened. No words came. The evil powers had stricken her dumb, as I heard afterwards they had many a time before, when she approached confession.

'She was too poor to pay for the necessary forms of exorcism; and hitherto those priests to whom she had addressed herself were either so ignorant of the meaning of her broken French, or her Irish-English, or else esteemed her to be one crazed – as, indeed, her wild and excited manner might easily have led any one to think – that they had neglected the sole means of loosening her tongue, so that she might confess her deadly sin, and after due penance, obtain absolution. But I knew Bridget of old, and felt that she was a penitent sent to me. I went through those holy offices appointed by our church for the relief of such a case. I was the more bound to do this, as I found that she had come to Antwerp for the sole purpose of discovering me, and making confession to me. Of the nature of that fearful confession I am forbidden to speak. Much of it you know; possibly all.

'It now remains for her to free herself from mortal guilt, and to set others free from the consequences thereof. No prayers, no masses, will ever do it, although they may strengthen her with that strength by which alone acts of deepest love and purest self-devotion may be performed. Her words of passion, and cries for revenge – her unholy prayers could never reach the ears of the Holy Saints! Other powers intercepted them, and wrought so that the curses thrown up to Heaven have fallen on her own flesh and blood; and so, through her very strength of love, have bruised and crushed her heart. Henceforward her former self must be buried, – yea, buried quick, if need be, – but never more to make sign, or utter cry on earth! She has become a Poor Clare,[27] in order that, by perpetual penance and constant service of others, she may at length so act as to obtain final absolution and rest for her soul. Until then, the innocent must suffer. It is to plead for the innocent that I come to you; not in the name of the witch, Bridget Fitzgerald, but of the penitent and servant of all men, the Poor Clare, Sister Magdalen.'

'Sir,' said I, 'I listen to your request with respect; only I may tell you it is not needed to urge me to do all that I can on behalf of one, love for whom is part of my very life. If for a time I have absented myself from her, it is to think and work for her redemption. I, a member of the English Church – my uncle, a Puritan – pray morning and night for her by name: the congregations of London, on the next Sabbath, will pray for one unknown, that she may be set free from the Powers of Darkness. Moreover, I must tell you, sir, that those evil ones touch not the great calm of her soul. She lives her own pure and loving life, unharmed and untainted, though all men fall off from her. I would I could have her faith!'

My uncle now spoke.

'Nephew,' said he, 'it seems to me that this gentleman, although professing what I consider an erroneous creed, has touched upon the right point in exhorting Bridget to acts of love and mercy, whereby to wipe out her sin of hate and vengeance. Let us strive after our fashion, by almsgiving and visiting of the needy and fatherless, to make our prayers acceptable. Meanwhile, I myself will go down into the north, and take charge of the maiden. I am too old to be daunted by man or demon. I will bring her to this house as to a home; and let the Double come if it will! A company of godly divines shall give it the meeting, and we will try issue.'

The kindly, brave old man! But Father Bernard sat on musing.

'All hate,' said he, 'cannot be quenched in her heart; all Christian forgiveness cannot have entered into her soul, or the demon would have lost its power. You said, I think, that her grandchild was still tormented?'

'Still tormented!' I replied, sadly, thinking of Mistress Clarke's last letter.

He rose to go. We afterwards heard that the occasion of his coming to London was a secret political mission on behalf of the Jacobites.[28] Nevertheless, he was a good and a wise man.

Months and months passed away without any change. Lucy entreated my uncle to leave her where she was, – dreading, as I learnt, lest if she came, with her fearful companion, to dwell in the same house with me, that my love could not stand the repeated shocks to which I should be doomed. And this she thought from no distrust of the strength of my affection, but from a kind of pitying sympathy for the terror to the nerves which she observed that the demoniac visitation caused in all.

I was restless and miserable. I devoted myself to good works; but I performed them from no spirit of love, but solely from the hope of reward and payment, and so the reward was never granted. At length, I asked my uncle's leave to travel; and I went forth, a wanderer, with no distincter end than that of many another wanderer – to get away from myself. A strange impulse led me to Antwerp, in spite of the wars and commotions then raging in the Low Countries –[29] or rather, perhaps, the very craving to become interested in something external, led me into the thick of the struggle then going on with the Austrians. The cities of Flanders were all full at that time of civil disturbances and rebellions, only kept down by force, and the presence of an Austrian garrison in every place.

I arrived in Antwerp, and made inquiry for Father Bernard. He was away in the country for a day or two. Then I asked my way to the Convent of Poor Clares; but, being healthy and prosperous, I could only see the dim, pent-up, gray walls, shut closely in by narrow streets, in the lowest part of the town. My landlord told me, that had I been stricken by some loathsome disease, or in desperate case of any kind, the Poor Clares would have taken me, and tended me. He spoke of them as an order of mercy of the strictest kind, dressing scantily in the coarsest materials, going barefoot, living on what the inhabitants of Antwerp chose to bestow, and sharing even those fragments and crumbs with the poor and helpless that swarmed all around; receiving no letters or communication with the outer world; utterly dead to everything but the alleviation of suffering. He smiled at my inquiring whether I could get speech of one of them; and told me that they were even forbidden to speak for the purposes of begging their daily food; while yet they lived, and fed others upon what was given in charity.

'But,' exclaimed I, 'supposing all men forgot them! Would they quietly lie down and die, without making sign of their extremity?'

'If such were their rule, the Poor Clares would willingly do it; but their founder appointed a remedy for such extreme case as you suggest. They have a bell – 'tis but a small one, as I have heard, and has yet never been rung in the memory of man: when the Poor Clares have been without food for twenty-four hours, they may ring this bell, and then trust to our good people of Antwerp for rushing to the rescue of the Poor Clares, who have taken such blessed care of us in all our straits.'

It seemed to me that such rescue would be late in the day; but I did not say what I thought. I rather turned the conversation, by asking my landlord if he knew, or had ever heard, anything of a certain Sister Magdalen.'

'Yes,' said he, rather under his breath; 'news will creep out, even from a convent of Poor Clares. Sister Magdalen is either a great sinner or a great saint. She does more, as I have heard, than all the other nuns put together; yet, when last month they would fain have made her mother-superior, she begged rather that they would place her below all the rest, and make her the meanest servant of all.'

'You never saw her?' asked I.

'Never,' he replied.

I was weary of waiting for Father Bernard, and yet I lingered in Antwerp. The political state of things became worse than ever, increased to its height by the scarcity of food consequent on many deficient harvests. I saw groups of fierce, squalid men, at every corner of the street, glaring out with wolfish eyes at my sleek skin and handsome clothes.

At last Father Bernard returned. We had a long conversation, in which he told me that, curiously enough, Mr. Gisborne, Lucy's father, was serving in one of the Austrian regiments, then in garrison at Antwerp. I asked Father Bernard if he would make us acquainted; which he consented to do. But, a day or two afterwards, he told me that, on hearing my name, Mr. Gisborne had declined responding to any advances on my part, saying he had abjured his country, and hated his countrymen.

Probably he recollected my name in connection with that of his daughter Lucy. Anyhow, it was clear enough that I had no chance of making his acquaintance. Father Bernard confirmed me in my suspicions of the hidden fermentation, for some coming evil, working among the 'blouses'[30] of Antwerp, and he would fain have had me depart from out the city; but I rather craved the excitement of danger, and stubbornly refused to leave.

One day, when I was walking with him in the Place Verte, he bowed to an Austrian officer, who was crossing towards the cathedral.

'That is Mr. Gisborne,' said he, as soon as the gentleman was past.

I turned to look at the tall, slight figure of the officer. He carried himself in a stately manner, although he was past middle age, and from his years, might have had some excuse for a slight stoop. As I looked at the man, he turned round, his eyes met mine, and I saw his face. Deeply lined, sallow, and scathed was that countenance; scarred by passion as well as by the fortunes of war. 'Twas but a moment our eyes met. We each turned round, and went on our separate way.

But his whole appearance was not one to be easily forgotten; the thorough appointment of the dress, and evident thought bestowed on it, made but an incongruous whole with the dark, gloomy expression of his countenance. Because he was Lucy's father, I sought instinctively to meet him everywhere. At last he must have become aware of my pertinacity, for he gave me a haughty scowl whenever I passed him. In one of these encounters, however, I chanced to be of some service to him. He was turning the corner of a street, and came suddenly on one of the groups of discontented Flemings of whom I have spoken. Some words were exchanged, when my gentleman out with his sword, and with a slight but skilful cut drew blood from one of those who had insulted him, as he fancied, though I was too far off to hear the words. They would all have fallen upon him had I not rushed forwards and raised the cry, then well known in Antwerp, of rally, to the Austrian soldiers who were perpetually patrolling the streets, and who came in numbers to the rescue. I think that neither Mr. Gisborne nor the mutinous group of plebeians owed me much gratitude for my interference. He had planted himself against a wall, in a skilful attitude of fence, ready with his bright glancing rapier to do battle with all the heavy, fierce, unarmed men, some six or seven in number. But when his own soldiers came up, he sheathed his sword; and, giving some careless word of command, sent them away again, and continued his saunter all alone down the street, the workmen snarling in his rear, and more than half-inclined to fall on me for my cry for rescue. I cared not if they did, my life seemed so dreary a burden just then; and, perhaps, it was this daring loitering among them that prevented their attacking me.

Instead, they suffered me to fall into conversation with them; and I heard some of their grievances. Sore and heavy to be borne were they, and no wonder the sufferers were savage and desperate.

The man whom Gisborne had wounded across his face would fain have got out of me the name of his aggressor, but I refused to tell it. Another of the group heard his inquiry, and made answer:

'I know the man. He is one Gisborne, aide-de-camp to the General-Commandant. I know him well.'

He began to tell some story in connection with Gisborne in a low and muttering voice; and while he was relating a tale, which I saw excited their evil blood, and which they evidently wished me not to hear, I sauntered away and back to my lodgings.

That night Antwerp was in open revolt. The inhabitants rose in rebellion against their Austrian masters. The Austrians, holding the gates of the city, remained at first pretty quiet in the citadel; only, from time to time, the boom of a great cannon swept sullenly over the town. But, if they expected the disturbance to die away, and spend itself in a few hours' fury, they were mistaken. In a day or two, the rioters held possession of the principal municipal buildings. Then the Austrians poured forth in bright flaming array, calm and smiling, as they marched to the posts assigned, as if the fierce mob were no more to them than the swarms of buzzing summer flies. Their practised manœuvres, their well-aimed shot, told with terrible effect; but in the place of one slain rioter, three sprang up of his blood to avenge his loss. But a deadly foe, a ghastly ally of the Austrians, was at work. Food, scarce and dear for months, was now hardly to be obtained at any price. Desperate efforts were being made to bring provisions into the city, for the rioters had friends without. Close to the city port nearest to the Scheldt, a great struggle took place. I was there, helping the rioters, whose cause I had adopted. We had a savage encounter with the Austrians. Numbers fell on both sides; I saw them lie bleeding for a moment; then a volley of smoke obscured them; and when it cleared away, they were dead – trampled upon or smothered, pressed down and hidden by the freshly-wounded whom those last guns had brought low. And then a gray-robed and gray-veiled figure came right across the flashing guns, and stooped over some one, whose life-blood was ebbing away; sometimes it was to give him drink from cans which they carried slung at their sides, sometimes I saw the cross held above a dying man, and rapid prayers were being uttered, unheard by men in that hellish din and clangour, but listened to by One above. I saw all this as in a dream: the reality of that stern time was battle and carnage. But I knew that these gray figures, their bare feet all wet with blood, and their faces hidden by their veils, were the Poor Clares – sent forth now because dire agony was abroad and imminent danger at hand. Therefore, they left their cloistered shelter, and came into that thick and evil mêlée.

Close to me – driven past me by the struggle of many fighters – came the Antwerp burgess with the scarce-healed scar upon his face; and in an instant more, he was thrown by the press upon the Austrian officer Gisborne, and ere either had recovered the shock, the burgess had recognised his opponent.

'Ha! the Englishman Gisborne!' he cried, and threw himself upon him with redoubled fury. He had struck him hard – the Englishman was down; when out of the smoke came a dark-gray figure, and threw herself right under the uplifted flashing sword. The burgess's arm stood arrested. Neither Austrians nor Anversois willingly harmed the Poor Clares.

'Leave him to me!' said a low stern voice. 'He is mine enemy – mine for many years.'

Those words were the last I heard. I myself was struck down by a bullet. I remember nothing more for days. When I came to myself, I was at the extremity of weakness, and was craving for food to recruit my strength. My landlord sat watching me. He, too, looked pinched and shrunken; he had heard of my wounded state, and sought me out. Yes! the struggle still continued, but the famine was sore; and some, he had heard, had died for lack of food. The tears stood in his eyes as he spoke. But soon he shook off his weakness, and his natural cheerfulness returned. Father Bernard had been to see me – no one else. (Who should, indeed?) Father Bernard would come back that afternoon – he had promised. But Father Bernard never came, although I was up and dressed, and looking eagerly for him.

My landlord brought me a meal which he had cooked himself: of what it was composed he would not say, but it was most excellent, and with every mouthful I seemed to gain strength. The good man sat looking at my evident enjoyment with a happy smile of sympathy; but, as my appetite became satisfied, I began to detect a certain wistfulness in his eyes, as if craving for the food I had so nearly devoured – for, indeed, at that time I was hardly aware of the extent of the famine. Suddenly, there was a sound of many rushing feet past our window. My landlord opened one of the sides of it, the better to learn what was going on. Then we heard a faint, cracked, tinkling bell, coming shrill upon the air, clear and distinct from all other sounds. 'Holy Mother!' exclaimed my landlord, 'the Poor Clares!'

He snatched up the fragments of my meal, and crammed them into my hands, bidding me follow. Down-stairs he ran, clutching at more food, as the women of his house eagerly held it out to him; and in a moment we were in the street, moving along with the great current, all tending towards the Convent of the Poor Clares. And still, as if piercing our ears with its inarticulate cry, came the shrill tinkle of the bell. In that strange crowd were old men trembling and sobbing, as they carried their little pittance of food; women with the tears running down their cheeks, who had snatched up what provisions they had in the vessels in which they stood, so that the burden of these was in many cases much greater than that which they contained; children, with flushed faces, grasping tight the morsel of bitten cake or bread, in their eagerness to carry it safe to the help of the Poor Clares; strong men – yea, both Anversois and Austrians – pressing onwards with set teeth, and no word spoken; and over all, and through all, came that sharp tinkle – that cry for help in extremity.

We met the first torrent of people returning with blanched and piteous faces: they were issuing out of the convent to make way for the offerings of others. 'Haste, haste!' said they. 'A Poor Clare is dying! A Poor Clare is dead for hunger! God forgive us, and our city!'

We pressed on. The stream bore us along where it would. We were carried through refectories, bare and crumbless; into cells over whose doors the conventual name of the occupant was written. Thus it was that I, with others, was forced into Sister Magdalen's cell. On her couch lay Gisborne, pale unto death, but not dead. By his side was a cup of water, and a small morsel of mouldy bread, which he had pushed out of his reach, and could not move to obtain. Over against his bed were these words, copied in the English version: 'Therefore, if thine enemy hunger, feed him; if he thirst, give him drink.'[31]

Some of us gave him of our food, and left him eating greedily, like some famished wild animal. For now it was no longer the sharp tinkle, but that one solemn toll, which in all Christian countries tells of the passing of the spirit out of earthly life into eternity; and again a murmur gathered and grew, as of many people speaking with awed breath, 'A Poor Clare is dying! a Poor Clare is dead!'

Borne along once more by the motion of the crowd, we were carried into the chapel belonging to the Poor Clares. On a bier before the high altar, lay a woman – lay sister Magdalen – lay Bridget Fitzgerald. By her side stood Father Bernard, in his robes of office, and holding the crucifix on high while he pronounced the solemn absolution of the Church, as to one who had newly confessed herself of deadly sin. I pushed on with passionate force, till I stood close to the dying woman, as she received extreme unction amid the breathless and awed hush of the multitude around. Her eyes were glazing, her limbs were stiffening; but when the rite was over and finished, she raised her gaunt figure slowly up, and her eyes brightened to a strange intensity of joy, as, with the gesture of her finger and the trance-like gleam of her eye, she seemed like one who watched the disappearance of some loathed and fearful creature.

'She is freed from the curse!' said she, as she fell back dead.

Now, of all our party who had first listened to my Lady Ludlow, Mr. Preston was the only one who had not told us something, either of information, tradition, history, or legend. We naturally turned to him; but we did not like asking him directly for his contribution, for he was a grave, reserved, and silent man.

He understood us, however, and, rousing himself as it were, he said:

'I know you wish me to tell you, in my turn, of something which I have learnt or heard during my life. I could tell you something of my own life, and of a life dearer still to my memory; but I have shrunk from narrating anything so purely personal. Yet, shrink as I will, no other but those sad recollections will present themselves to my mind. I call them sad when I think of the end of it all. However, I am not going to moralize. If my dear brother's life and death does not speak for itself, no words of mine will teach you what may be learnt from it.'

'THE HALF-BROTHERS'

'The Half-Brothers' was first published, as J. G. Sharps has recently discovered, in an almanac and anthology, *Fulcher's Ladies' Memorandum Book and Poetical Miscellany 1856* (Sudbury: Fulcher, 1856), pp. i–xii. It was collected in *Round the Sofa*, 2 vols (London: Sampson Low, 1859), vol. ii, pp. 277–97. It was also printed in *My Lady Ludlow and Other Tales* (1861) and in *Lois the Witch and Other Tales* (Leipzig: Tauchnitz, 1861).

The publication record of this story has been confused by the fact that although EG stated in the Preface to *Round the Sofa*, that it had been previously published, she said that it had 'obtained only a limited circulation' without particularising. With this information to go on, Ward, in *Knutsford*, vol. v, p. xii (followed, *inter alia*, by the *Wellesley Index*) stated incorrectly that it had previously been published in the *Dublin University Magazine*, 52 (November 1858), pp. 587–98. That was a different story of the same name by another, unknown, writer.

Differences between *Fulcher* and *1859* are minor, and the pattern of changes resembles that of the other stories: heavier punctuation in the collected text, replacement of semi-colon with colon; substitution of 'sat' for 'sate'. However the punctuation in *Fulcher* is particularly light, probably representing EG's manuscript.

THE HALF-BROTHERS.

———·———

MY mother was twice married. She never spoke of her first husband,[1] and it is only from other people that I have learnt what little I know about him. I believe, she was scarcely seventeen when she was married to him: and he was barely one-and-twenty. He rented a small farm up in Cumberland, somewhere towards the sea-coast; but he was perhaps too young and inexperienced to have the charge of land and cattle: anyhow, his affairs did not prosper, and he fell into ill health, and died of consumption before they had been three years man and wife, leaving my mother a young widow of twenty, with a little child only just able to walk, and the farm on her hands for four years more by the lease, with[a] half the stock on it dead, or sold off one by one to pay the more pressing debts, and with no[b] money to purchase more, or even to buy the provisions needed for the small consumption of every day. There was another child coming, too; and sad and sorry, I believe, she was to think of it. A dreary winter she must have had in her lonesome dwelling, with never another near it for miles around; her sister came to bear her company, and they two planned and plotted how to make every penny they could raise go as far as possible. I can't tell you how it happened[c] that my little sister, whom I never saw, came to sicken and die; but, as if my poor mother's cup was not full enough, only[d] a fortnight before Gregory was born the little girl took ill of scarlet fever, and in a week she lay dead. My mother was, I believe, just stunned with this last blow. My aunt has told me that she did not cry; aunt[e] Fanny would have been thankful if she had; but she sat[f] holding the poor wee lassie's hand, and looking in her pretty, pale, dead face, without so much as shedding a tear. And it was all the same, when they had to take her away to be buried. She just kissed the child, and sat[g] her down in the window-seat to watch the little black train of people (neighbours – my aunt, and one far-off cousin, who were[h] all the friends they could muster) go winding away amongst the snow, which had fallen thinly over the country the night before. When my aunt came back from the funeral, she found my mother in the same place, and as dry-eyed as ever. So she continued until after Gregory was born; and, somehow, his coming seemed to loosen the tears, and she cried day and night, day and night, till my aunt and the other watcher looked at each other in dismay, and would fain have stopped her if they had but known how. But she bade them let her alone, and not be over-anxious, for every drop she shed eased her brain, which had been in a terrible state before for want of the power to cry. She seemed after that to think of nothing but her new little baby; she hardly appeared to remember either her husband or her little daughter that lay dead in Brigham[2] churchyard – at[a] least so aunt Fanny said; but she was a great talker, and my mother was very silent by nature, and I think aunt Fanny may have been mistaken in believing that my mother never thought of her husband and child just because she never spoke about them. Aunt Fanny was older than my mother, and had a way of treating her like a child; but, for all that, she was a kind, warm-hearted creature, who thought more of her sister's welfare than she did of her own; and it was on her bit of money that they principally lived, and on what the two could earn by working for the great Glasgow sewing-merchants.[3b] But by-and-by my mother's eye-sight began to fail. It was not that she was exactly blind, for she could see well enough to guide herself about the house, and to do a good deal of domestic work; but she could no longer do fine sewing and earn money. It must have been with the heavy crying she had had in her day, for she was but a young creature at this time, and as pretty a young woman, I have heard people say, as any on the country side. She took it sadly to heart that she could no longer gain anything towards the keep of herself and her child. My aunt Fanny would fain have persuaded her that she had enough to do in managing their cottage and minding Gregory; but my mother knew that they were pinched, and that aunt Fanny herself had not as much to eat, even of the commonest kind of food, as she could have done with; and as for Gregory, he was not a strong lad, and needed, not more food – for he always had enough, whoever went short – but better nourishment, and more flesh-meat. One day – it was aunt Fanny who told me all this about my poor mother, long after her death – as the sisters were sitting together, aunt Fanny working, and my mother hushing Gregory to sleep, William Preston,[c] who was afterwards my father, came in. He was reckoned an old bachelor; I suppose he was long past forty, and he was one of the wealthiest farmers thereabouts, and had known my grandfather well, and my mother and my aunt in their more prosperous days. He sat[d] down, and began to twirl his hat by way of being agreeable; my aunt Fanny talked, and he listened and looked at my mother. But he said very little, either on that visit, or on many another that he paid before he spoke out what had been the real purpose of his calling so often all along, and from the very first time he came to their house. One Sunday, however, my aunt Fanny stayed away from church, and took care of the child, and my mother went alone. When she came back, she ran straight up-stairs, without going into the kitchen to look at Gregory or speak any word to her sister, and aunt Fanny heard her cry as if her heart was breaking; so she went up and scolded her right well through the bolted door, till at last she got her to open it. And then she threw herself on my aunt's neck, and told her that William

Preston[a] had asked her to marry him, and had promised to take good charge of her boy, and to let him want for nothing, neither in the way of keep nor of education, and that she had consented. Aunt Fanny was a good deal shocked at this; for, as I have said, she had often thought that my mother had forgotten her first husband very quickly, and now here was proof positive of it, if she could so soon think of marrying again. Besides, as aunt Fanny used to say, she herself would have been a far more suitable match for a man of William Preston's[b] age than Helen, who, though she was a widow, had not seen her four-and-twentieth summer. However, as aunt Fanny said, they had not asked her advice; and there was much to be said on the other side of the question. Helen's eyesight would never be good for much again, and as William Preston's[c] wife she would never need to do anything, if she chose to sit with her hands before her; and a boy was a great charge to a widowed mother; and now there would be a decent, steady man to see after him. So, by-and-by, aunt Fanny seemed to take a brighter view of the marriage than did my mother herself, who hardly ever looked up, and never smiled after the day when she promised William Preston[d] to be his wife. But much as she had loved Gregory before, she seemed to love him more now. She was continually talking to him when they were alone, though he was far too young to understand her moaning words, or give her any comfort, except by his caresses.

At last William Preston[e] and she were wed; and she went to be mistress of a well-stocked house, not above half-an-hour's walk from where aunt Fanny lived. I believe she did all that she could to please my father; and a more dutiful wife, I have heard him himself say, could never have been. But she did not love him, and he soon found it out. She loved Gregory, and she did not love him. Perhaps, love would have come in time, if he had been patient enough to wait; but it just turned him sour to see how her eye brightened and her colour came at the sight of that little child, while for him who had given her so much, she had only gentle words as cold as ice. He got to taunt her with the difference in her manner, as if that would bring love: and he took a positive dislike to Gregory, – he was so jealous of the ready love that always gushed out like a spring of fresh water when he came near. He wanted her to love him more, and perhaps that was all well and good; but he wanted her to love her child less, and that was an evil wish. One day, he gave way to his temper, and cursed and swore at Gregory, who had got into some mischief, as children will; my mother made some excuse for him; my father said it was hard enough to have to keep another man's child, without having it perpetually held up in its naughtiness by his wife, who ought to be always in the same mind that he was; and so from little they got to more; and the end of it was, that my mother took to her bed before her time, and I was born that very day. My father was glad, and proud, and sorry, all in a breath; glad and proud that a son was born to him; and sorry for his poor wife's state, and to think how his angry words had brought it on. But he was a man who liked better to be angry than sorry, so he soon found out that it was all Gregory's fault, and owed him an additional grudge for having hastened my birth. He had another grudge against him before long. My mother began to sink the day after I was born. My father sent to Carlisle for doctors, and would have coined his heart's blood into gold to save her, if that could have been; but it could not. My aunt Fanny used to say sometimes, that she thought that Helen did not wish to live, and so just let herself die away without trying to take hold on life; but when I questioned her, she owned that my mother did all the doctors bade her do, with the same sort of uncomplaining patience with which she had acted through life. One of her last requests was to have Gregory laid in her bed by my side, and then she made him take hold of my little hand. Her husband came in while she was looking at us so, and when he bent tenderly over her to ask her how she felt now, and seemed to gaze on us two little half-brothers, with a grave sort of kindliness, she looked up in his face and smiled, almost her first smile at him; and such a sweet smile! as more besides aunt Fanny have said. In an hour she was dead. Aunt Fanny came to live with us. It was the best thing that could be done. My father would have been glad to return to his old mode of bachelor life, but what could he do with two little children? He needed a woman to take care of him, and who so fitting as his wife's elder sister? So she had the charge of me from my birth; and for a time I was weakly, as was but natural, and she was always beside me, night and day watching over me, and my father nearly as anxious as she. For his land had come down from father to son for more than three hundred years, and he would have cared for me merely as his flesh and blood that was to inherit the land after him. But he needed something to love, for all that, to most people, he was a stern, hard man, and he took to me as, I fancy, he had taken to no human being before – as he might have taken to my mother, if she had had no former life for him to be jealous of. I loved him back again right heartily. I loved all around me, I believe, for everybody was kind to me. After a time, I overcame my original weakliness of constitution, and was just a bonny, strong-looking lad whom every passer-by noticed, when my father took me with him to the nearest town.

At home I was the darling of my aunt, the tenderly-beloved of my father, the pet and plaything of the old domestic, the 'young master' of the farm-labourers, before whom I played many a lordly antic, assuming a sort of authority which sat[a] oddly enough, I doubt not, on such a baby as I was.

Gregory was three years older than I. Aunt Fanny was always kind to him in deed and in action, but she did not often think about him, she had fallen so completely into the habit of being engrossed by me, from the fact of my having come into her charge as a delicate baby. My father never got over his grudging dislike to his stepson, who had so innocently wrestled with him for the possession of my mother's heart. I mistrust me, too, that my father always considered him as the cause of my mother's death and my early delicacy; and utterly unreasonable as this may seem, I believe my father rather cherished his feeling of alienation to my brother as a duty, than strove to repress it. Yet not for the world would my father have grudged him anything that money could purchase. That was, as it were, in the bond when he had wedded my mother. Gregory was lumpish and loutish, awkward and ungainly, marring whatever he meddled in, and many a hard word and sharp scolding did he get from the people about the farm, who hardly waited till my father's back was turned before they rated the stepson. I am ashamed – my heart is sore to think how I fell into the fashion of the family, and slighted my poor orphan step-brother. I don't think I ever scouted him, or was wilfully ill-natured to him; but the habit of being considered in all things, and being treated as something uncommon and superior, made me insolent in my prosperity, and I exacted more than Gregory was always willing to grant, and then, irritated, I sometimes repeated the disparaging words I had heard others use with regard to him, without fully understanding their meaning. Whether he did or not I cannot tell. I am afraid he did. He used to turn silent and quiet – sullen and sulky my father thought it; stupid, aunt Fanny used to call it. But every one said he was stupid and dull, and this stupidity and dullness grew upon him. He would sit without speaking a word, sometimes, for hours; then my father would bid him rise and do some piece of work, maybe, about the farm. And he would take three or four tellings before he would go. When we were sent to school, it was all the same. He could never be made to remember his lessons; the school-master grew weary of scolding and flogging, and at last advised my father just to take him away, and set him to some farm-work that might not be above his comprehension. I think he was more gloomy and stupid than ever after this, yet he was not a cross lad; he was patient and good-natured, and would try to do a kind turn for any one, even if they had been scolding or cuffing him not a minute before. But very often his attempts at kindness ended in some mischief to the very people he was trying to serve, owing to his awkward, ungainly ways. I suppose I was a clever lad; at any rate, I always got plenty of praise; and was, as we called it, the cock of the school. The schoolmaster said I could learn anything I chose, but my father, who had no great learning himself, saw little use in much for me, and took me away betimes, and kept me with him about the farm. Gregory was made into a kind of shepherd, receiving his training under old Adam, who was nearly past his work. I think old Adam was almost the first person who had a good opinion of Gregory. He stood to it that my brother had good parts, though he did not rightly know how to bring them out; and, for knowing the bearings of the Fells,[a] he said he had never seen a lad like him. My father would try to bring Adam round to speak of Gregory's faults and shortcomings; but, instead of that, he would praise him twice as much as soon as he found out what my father's object was.

One winter-time, when I was about sixteen, and Gregory nineteen, I was sent by my father on an errand to a place about seven miles distant by the road, but only about four by the Fells.[a] He bade me return by the road, whichever way I took in going, for the evenings closed in early, and were often thick and misty; besides which, old Adam, now paralytic and bedridden, foretold a downfall of snow before long. I soon got to my journey's end, and soon had done my business; earlier by an hour, I thought, than my father had expected, so I took the decision of the way by which I would return into my own hands, and set off back again over the Fells,[b] just as the first shades of evening began to fall. It looked dark and gloomy enough; but everything was so still that I thought I should have plenty of time to get home before the snow came down. Off I set at a pretty quick pace. But night came on quicker. The right path was clear enough in the day-time, although at several points two or three exactly similar diverged from the same place; but when there was a good light, the traveller was guided by the sight of distant objects, – a piece of rock, – a fall in the ground – which were quite invisible to me now. I plucked up a brave heart, however, and took what seemed to me the right road. It[c] was wrong, however, and led me whither I knew not, but to some wild boggy moor where the solitude seemed painful, intense,[d] as if never footfall of man had come thither to break the silence. I tried to shout, – with the dimmest possible hope of being heard – rather to reassure myself by the sound of my own voice; but my voice came husky and short, and yet it dismayed me; it seemed so weird and strange in that noiseless expanse of black darkness. Suddenly the air was filled thick[e] with dusky flakes, my face and hands were wet with snow. It cut me off from the slightest knowledge of where I was, for I lost every idea of the direction from which I had come, so that I could not even retrace my steps; it hemmed me in, thicker, thicker, with a darkness that might be felt. The boggy soil on which I stood quaked under me if I remained long in one place, and yet I dared[f] not move far. All my youthful hardiness seemed to leave me at once. I was on the point of crying, and only very shame seemed to keep it[g] down. To save myself from shedding tears, I shouted – terrible, wild shouts for bare life they were. I turned sick as I paused to listen; no answering sound came but the unfeeling[h] echoes. Only the noiseless, pitiless snow kept falling thicker, thicker – faster, faster! I was growing numb and sleepy. I tried to move about, but I dared not go far, for fear of the precipices which, I knew, abounded in certain places on the Fells. Now and then, I stood still and shouted again; but my voice was getting choked with tears, as I thought of the desolate, helpless death I was to die, and how little they at home, sitting round the warm, red, bright[i] fire, wotted what was become of me, – and how my poor father would grieve for me – it would surely kill him – it would break his heart, poor old man! Aunt Fanny too – was this to be the end of all her cares for me? I began to review my life in a strange kind of vivid dream, in which the various scenes of my few boyish years passed before me like visions. In a pang of agony, caused by such remembrance of my short life, I gathered up my strength and called out once more, a long, despairing, wailing cry, to which I had no hope of obtaining any answer, save from the echoes around, dulled as the sound might be by the thickened air. To my surprise, I heard a cry – almost as long, as wild as mine – so wild that it seemed unearthly, and I almost thought it must be the voice of some of the mocking spirits of the Fells, about whom I had heard so many tales. My heart suddenly began to beat fast and loud. I could not reply for a minute or two. I nearly fancied[a] I had lost the power of utterance. Just at this moment a dog barked. Was it Lassie's bark – my brother's collie? – an ugly enough brute, with a white, ill-looking face, that my father always kicked whenever he saw it, partly for its own demerits, partly because it belonged to my brother. On such occasions, Gregory would whistle Lassie away, and go off and sit with her in some out-house. My father had once or twice been ashamed of himself, when the poor collie had yowled out with the suddenness of the pain, and had relieved himself of his self-reproach by blaming my brother, who, he said, had no notion of training a dog, and was enough to ruin any collie in Christendom with his stupid way of allowing them to lie by the kitchen fire. To all which Gregory would answer nothing, nor even seem to hear, but go on looking absent and moody.

Yes! there again! It was Lassie's bark! Now or never! I lifted up my voice and shouted 'Lassie! Lassie! For God's sake, Lassie!' Another moment, and the great white-faced Lassie was curving and gambolling with delight round my feet and legs, looking, however, up in my face with her intelligent, apprehensive eyes, as if fearing lest I might greet her with a blow, as I had done oftentimes before. But I cried with gladness, as I stooped down and patted her. My mind was sharing in my body's weakness, and I could not reason, but I knew that help was at hand. A gray[b] figure came more and more distinctly out of the thick, close-pressing darkness. It was Gregory wrapped in his maud.[4]

'Oh, Gregory!' said I, and I fell upon his neck, unable to speak another word. He never spoke much, and made me no answer for some little time.

Then he told me we must move, we must walk for the dear life – we must find our road home, if possible; but we must move or we should be frozen to death.

'Don't you know the way home?' asked I.

'I thought I did when I set out, but I am doubtful now. The snow blinds me, and I am feared that in moving about just now, I have lost the right gait homewards.'

He had his shepherd's staff with him, and by dint of plunging it before us at every step we took – clinging close to each other, we went on safely enough, as far as not falling down any of the steep rocks, but it was slow, dreary work. My brother, I saw, was more guided by Lassie and the way she took than anything else, trusting to her instinct. It was too dark to see far before us; but he called her back continually, and noted from what quarter she returned, and shaped our slow steps accordingly. But the tedious motion scarcely kept my very blood from freezing. Every bone, every fibre in my body seemed first to ache, and then to swell, and then to turn numb with the intense cold. My brother bore it better than I, from having been more out upon the hills. He did not speak, except to call Lassie. I strove to be brave, and not complain; but now I felt the deadly fatal sleep stealing over me.

'I can go no farther,' I said, in a drowsy tone. I remember, I suddenly became dogged and resolved. Sleep I would, were it only for five minutes. If death were to be the consequence, sleep I would. Gregory stood still. I suppose, he recognised the peculiar phase of suffering to which I had been brought by the cold.

'It is of no use,' said he, as if to himself. 'We are no nearer home than we were when we started, as far as I can tell. Our only chance is in Lassie. Here! roll thee in my maud, lad, and lay thee down on this sheltered side of this bit of rock. Creep close under it, lad, and I'll lie by thee, and strive to keep the warmth in us. Stay! hast gotten aught about thee they'll know at home?'

I felt him unkind thus to keep me from slumber, but on his repeating the question, I pulled out my pocket-handkerchief, of some showy pattern, which Aunt Fanny had hemmed for me – Gregory took it, and tied it round Lassie's neck.

'Hie thee, Lassie, hie thee home!' And the white-faced, ill-favoured brute was off like a shot in the darkness. Now I might lie down – now I might sleep. In my drowsy stupor I felt that I was being tenderly covered up by my brother; but what with I neither knew nor cared – I was too dull, too selfish, too numb to think and reason, or I might have known that in that bleak bare place there was nought to wrap me in, save what was taken off another. I was glad enough when he ceased his cares and lay down by me. I took his hand.

'Thou canst not remember, lad, how we lay together thus by our dying mother. She put thy small, wee hand in mine – I reckon, she sees us now; and belike we shall soon be with her. Anyhow, God's will be done.'

'Dear Gregory,' I muttered, and crept nearer to him for warmth. He was talking still, and again about our mother, when I fell asleep. In an instant – or so it seemed – there were many voices about me – many faces hovering round me – the sweet luxury of warmth was stealing into every part of me. I was in my own little bed at home. I am thankful to say, my first word was 'Gregory?'

A look passed from one to another – my father's stern old face strove in vain to keep its sternness; his mouth quivered, his eyes filled slowly with unwonted tears.

'I would have given him half my land – I would have blessed him as my son, – oh God! I would have knelt at his feet, and asked him to forgive my hardness of heart.'

I heard no more. A whirl came through my brain, catching me back to death.

I came slowly to my consciousness, weeks afterwards. My father's hair was white when I recovered, and his hands shook as he looked into my face.

We spoke no more of Gregory. We could not speak of him; but he was strangely in our thoughts. Lassie came and went with never a word of blame; nay, my father would try to stroke her, but she shrank away; and he, as if reproved by the poor dumb beast, would sigh, and be silent and abstracted for a time.

Aunt Fanny – always a talker – told me all. How, on that fatal night, my father, irritated by my prolonged absence, and probably more anxious than he cared to show, had been fierce and imperious, even beyond his wont, to Gregory: had upbraided him with his father's poverty, his own stupidity which made his services good for nothing – for so, in spite of the old shepherd, my father always chose to consider them. At last, Gregory had risen up, and whistled Lassie out with him – poor Lassie, crouching underneath his chair for fear of a kick or a blow. Some time before, there had been some talk between my father and my aunt[a] respecting my return; and when Aunt Fanny told me all this, she said she fancied that Gregory might have noticed the coming storm, and gone out silently to meet me. Three hours afterwards, when all were running about in wild alarm, not knowing whither to go in search of me – not even missing Gregory, or heeding his absence, poor fellow – poor, poor fellow! –[b] Lassie came home, with my handkerchief tied round her neck. They knew and understood, and the whole strength of the farm was turned out to follow her, with wraps, and blankets, and brandy, and everything that could be thought of. I lay in chilly sleep, but still alive, beneath the rock that Lassie guided them to. I was covered over with my brother's plaid, and his thick shepherd's coat was carefully wrapped round my feet. He was in his shirt-sleeves – his arm thrown over me – a quiet smile (he had hardly ever smiled in life) upon his still, cold face.

My father's last words were, 'God forgive me my hardness of heart towards the fatherless child!'[c]

And what marked the depth of his feeling of repentance, perhaps more than all, considering the passionate love he bore my mother, was this: we found a paper of directions after his death, in which he desired that he might lie at the foot of the grave, in which, by his desire, poor Gregory had been laid with OUR MOTHER.

THE END.

EXPLANATORY NOTES

'The Old Nurse's Story'

1   *up in Westmoreland,*] The story is located in the far north-west of England. The modern county of Cumbria, which includes the Lake District and the area north to the Scots border, was divided until 1974 between three counties. The Lake District area was mainly in Westmorland, with the eastern section part of Lancashire. The northern section was in Cumberland. Rosamond and her nurse move north from the Lakes to 'the foot of the Cumberland fells' (p. 4), that is, to another very remote and thinly-populated district.

2   *not so well to do … afterwards,*] Rosamond's middle-class uncle has evidently risen in life since the events described. This detail is evidently included to explain his not taking the child, although he is her uncle and Lord Furnivall only her first cousin once removed.

3   *My lord's gentleman,*] Lord Furnivall's valet.

4   *a great-aunt of my lord's,*] But see note 13 below.

5   *Agnes they called her;*] She is again Agnes on p. 13, but on p. 18 EG wrote 'Bessy, the kitchen-maid' which has been silently corrected to Agnes in this edition, as have all further instances of 'Bessy'.

6   *Miss Grace … the younger sister.*] The seniority of the eldest unmarried sister in a family was expressed in her use of the surname alone; her sisters used their Christian names to distinguish themselves from her: compare Miss Jenkyns, Miss Matty Jenkyns, in *Cranford*.

7   *beaver,*] Beaver fur was commonly used for hats.

8   *Flesh is grass,*] Isaiah 40:6.

9   *Agnes, the kitchen maid,*] EG wrote 'Bessy' for Agnes. See note 5, above.

10   *Crosthwaite Church*] The implication is probably that the setting of the story is near Crosthwaite, the parish church of Keswick in Cumberland, between the Cumbrian Mountains and Derwentwater 'at the foot of the Cumberland fells'. Or possibly Crosthwaite near Windermere is intended, in Westmorland which is the narrator's native place. It contains the church of the parish of Heversham, which answers the description of Rosamond's father's parish: 'very wide, and scattered all abroad over the Westmoreland Fells' (p. 3).

11 *without their ... be busy at.*] Miss Furnivall and Mrs Stark do not sew on Sundays, in accordance with the Fourth Commandment: 'Remember that thou keep holy the Sabbath-day ... thou shalt do no manner of work.'

12 *wrapped in his maud.*] his shepherd's plaid, or cloak.

13 *present Lord Furnivall's father* –] If the present Lord Furnivall was Miss Furnivall's great-nephew, as is stated earlier, he would have been her brother's grandson rather than his son. EG was evidently undecided whether her story includes three or four proud Lord Furnivalls.

14 *the army in America,*] This seems to date the earlier part of the story during the American War of Independence (1775–1783).

'Morton Hall'

1 *Repeal of the Corn Laws.*'] Bridget Sidebotham deplores the transfer of power from the landowning interest to the mercantile middle class. The Corn Laws had discouraged the import of cheap foreign corn, keeping the price high for the benefit of farmers, but also keeping up the cost of bread, and hence the cost of labour. After widespread campaigning, supported by factory owners, they were repealed in 1846. The Sidebothams' political viewpoint is thus a comic version of Tabby Aykroyd's.

2 *the Morton ... Lord Monteagle*] The Gunpowder Plot of 5 November 1605, was a conspiracy among English Catholics to depose James I by blowing up the Houses of Parliament. It was revealed by William Parker, Lord Monteagle (1575–1622), who was brother-in-law of one of the conspirators. I have not traced a Morton who was with Monteagle. It is recorded of Thomas Morton (1564–1659), Bishop of Durham and anti-Catholic polemicist, that he was at school with Guy Fawkes, but he was not otherwise involved in the Gunpowder Plot.

3 *that terrible ... Cardinals in Rome?*] Evidently a myth of anti-Catholic propaganda, here mocked by EG. I have not traced a reference which identifies this book, but there was a widely-disseminated story of the Secret Archives of the Vatican, which were supposed to contain hideous revelations to discredit the papacy; and indeed the legend is still current though the archives were opened by Leo XIII in 1879.

4 *the Female Jesuit.*] Jemima Luke, *The Female Jesuit, or, The Spy in the Family* (1851), a novel. The wave of anti-Catholic feeling which swept the country in response to the so-called Papal Aggression (the appointment of Catholic bishops in England in 1850) produced many such works.

5 *we did know ... Jesuit's second cousin,*] This is a puzzling reference which looks like a private joke. Jemima Luke (1813–1906), the author of *The*

Female Jesuit, was the daughter of Thomas Thompson (1785–1865), a prominent evangelical layman, much involved with the promotion of Sunday schools and lay readers, and his wife Elizabeth Pinckney. He does not seem to have been related to Meta Gaskell's friend Isabel Thompson, who was a granddaughter of the Methodist MP Thomas Thompson (1754–1828), but possibly EG knew some of Luke's relations. See *The Blackwell Dictionary of Evangelical Biography, 1730–1860,* 2 vols (1995), vol. ii, pp. 1097–8; Frederick Boase, *Modern English Biography,* 6 vols (1892–1926), vol. iii, p. 941 and vol. vi, p. 682.

6 *Drumble.*] EG gives this name to Manchester in *Cranford.*

7 *where Liverpool Street runs now;*] a real street in present-day Salford, perhaps locating the hall west of Manchester, where a Tudor manor house, Ordsall Hall, survives.

8 *some time about the Restoration.*] The English Civil War had ended in the execution of Charles I (1649), the exile of his son and many of his Royalist followers, and the establishment of the Commonwealth under Oliver Cromwell. Many Royalist estates were confiscated. The Restoration of Charles II took place in 1660.

9 *General Monk,*] George Monk or Monck (1608–1670) was one of the most successful of the parliamentarian generals. His decision to change sides in 1660 and support the restoration of Charles II was decisive, and he was rewarded by being made Duke of Albemarle. He also became a landowner in Lancashire, and figures largely in Thomas Whitaker's *History of Whalley* (1801) a book which EG is thought to have drawn on in writing 'The Poor Clare'. Monk's generosity to his family is recorded, although the Mortons and the Carrs are of course fictitious.

10 *had calves' head ... January;*] The anniversary of the execution of Charles I on 30 January 1649 was commemorated after the Restoration as the Feast Day of King Charles the Martyr, and between 1661 and 1859 services were held in parish churches. In defiance of this, the date was also celebrated in grotesque parody by some republicans, who dined on roast calf's head. The latter custom is recorded from 1693, and it survived into the nineteenth century. See *The Oxford Book of Days,* ed. by B. Blackburn and L. Holford-Strevens (2000).

11 *the first twenty-ninth of May*] Charles II instituted in 1661 the celebration of Restoration Day or Oak Apple Day, the anniversary of his restoration to the throne, his own birthday, and of the day he had hidden in the Royal Oak at Boscobel. Between 1661 and 1859 it was officially commemorated on this date with religious services in Anglican churches. Oak leaves were worn and used for decoration (and in some places still are).

12   *as if she had … Charles, Solomon,*] Although the biblical analogy (1 Kings
      10) is ostensibly used to emphasise the ceremoniousness of the
      request, EG is probably implying that the notoriously profligate
      Charles II wished to add Alice Carr to his harem, as Solomon did the
      Queen of Sheba. In Dryden's *Absalom and Achitophel* (1681) Charles is
      likened to King David, father of Solomon, and also possessor of many
      wives and concubines.

13   *somewhere in the Virginian plantations;*] Many Royalists lived as exiles in
      Virginia during the Commonwealth.

14   *Old Noll,*] Oliver Cromwell (1599–1658), leader of the opposition to
      Charles I, and ruler of the country as Lord Protector from 1653 to his
      death.

15   *the French witch*] It is implied in the preceding paragraph that Sir John
      has taken a mistress in London; here we learn she is French. The
      French influence on Charles II and his court was widely considered to
      be corrupting both at the time and by subsequent historians; his
      French mistress Louise de Kéroualle, Duchess of Portsmouth (1649–
      1734) was especially unpopular.

16   *cade-lambs*] A cade lamb is one brought up by hand, either as a pet or
      because it has been abandoned by its mother. In this context it is evi-
      dently equivalent to house lamb (see note 23 below): an expensive
      delicacy available before grass lamb was in season.

17   *he had been at Worcester*] The Battle of Worcester (1651) at which
      Cromwell had defeated the royalists.

18   *killed at the battle of the Boyne*] Charles II died in 1685 and was succeeded
      by his brother James II, who was a Catholic. In 1688 the Dutch ruler,
      William of Orange, who was James's nephew and son-in-law, invaded
      England and James fled to France. This transfer of power ('the Glori-
      ous Revolution') was held by several Victorian historians to be the
      decisive moment in the settlement of a secure Protestant parliamentary
      democracy in England. The Battle of the Boyne (1690), in which Wil-
      liam defeated James in northern Ireland, was a major blow to the
      Catholic cause. In terms of the story's symbolic structure, therefore,
      Sir John dies fighting for the Catholic James II against the Protestant
      William III, fighting for tradition, loyalty and despotism against mod-
      ernisation and democracy (the fact that this is an over-simplification of
      the historical events is immaterial).

19   *there's a strict entail now.*] An entail was a legal form used to ensure prop-
      erty remained in a family. A landed estate such as Morton Hall would
      often be entailed on the eldest male heir, and after him his son, or if he
      had none his younger brother, or perhaps the son of a daughter. Each
      successive inheritor would thus only receive the use of the property for
      his life, and would not be able to dispose of it, or to divide it between

several children, or give it out of the family. Such arrangements, which were very common among the English landed gentry and nobility from the seventeenth century, were not invariably successful in maintaining the grandeur of a dynasty. As the story illustrates, the life-tenant could still dispose of his income, including his future income, and might not have an interest in long-term investment in the underlying assets of the estate.

20 *Prince William … George the Third.*] Prince William Frederick of Gloucester (1776–1834), after his father's death in 1805 called the Duke of Gloucester, married in 1816 his cousin Princess Mary, daughter of George III. This would seem to set the period of Miss Phillis's debut about 1796.

21 *making cheeses*] 'Turning rapidly round and then suddenly sinking down, so that the petticoats are inflated all round somewhat in the form of a cheese' (*OED*).

22 *slop and bread-and-butter*] Slop was a term, often contemptuous, which embraced liquid and semi-liquid foods mainly eaten by invalids, children and women. Here the primary meaning is probably tea; but the term might also refer to gruel, porridge, bread and milk, or brewis (bread and water).

23 *house-lamb,*] House lamb, as opposed to grass lamb, was fed by hand; it was thus available in winter, and was more expensive. Isabella Beeton, *Beeton's Book of Household Management* (London: Beeton, 1861), p. 329: 'When the sheep lambs in mid-winter … it is customary to rear the lambs within-doors, and under the shelter of stables or barns, where, foddered on soft hay, and part fed on cow's milk, the little creatures thrive rapidly: to such it is customary to give the name of House Lamb, to distinguish it from that reared in the open air, or grass-fed.' She also says (p. 354) that house lamb is in season from Christmas to March; grass lamb from Easter to Michaelmas.

24 *our own pheasant hen,*] *OED* under Pheasant 3 gives some reason to suppose this refers to a dark breed of chicken rather than to a hen pheasant.

25 *house-place.*] In 'Half a Life-Time Ago' EG gave this definition: 'House-place is a sort of better kitchen, where no cookery is done, but which is reserved for state occasions.' However, it sometimes, as probably here, meant simply 'kitchen' (*OED*).

26 *Grey wood ashes*] Wood could be collected; coal had to be bought: this is a sign of poverty.

27 *some Miss Burrells … of,*] EG probably gestures here towards Maria (1733–1760) and Elizabeth Gunning (1734–1790), two poor Irish beauties who in 1752 married the Earl of Coventry and the Duke of Hamilton respectively.

28 *the rule of three,*] In mathematics, a method of finding a number when it is known to be in the same proportion to a given number as two other numbers are to each other; for example: as 2 is to 4, so 3 is to x.

29 *an honourable*] The sons and daughters of barons and viscounts, and the younger sons of earls, bear the courtesy title 'the Honourable' before their names.

30 *'The Female Chesterfield ... to her niece.'*] Miss Sophronia is evidently writing a courtesy book based on one of the most famous of all such works: *Letters written by the late Right Honourable Philip Dormer Stanhope, Earl of Chesterfield, to his son* (1774).

31 *Pomfret cakes,*] Liquorice sweets, a speciality of Pomfret or Pontefract in Yorkshire.

32 *what the right word was,*] genealogy, not geography.

33 *Santo Sebastiano ... Protector,*] Catharine Cuthbertson, *Santo Sebastiano, or, The Young Protector,* 5 vols (1806), a Gothic novel which EG described to Maria James (*Further Letters,* p. 58) as:

> so funny and so ridiculous, that it carries one on through all that quantity of reading. I do not mean that it is *meant* to be funny, for it is rather highflown, and very sentimental; but the heroine speaks broken English all throughout, and faints so often &c &C, and yet there is a degree of interest in the story to carry one along. It is a very old novel, written by one of Geo. 3rd's daughters I forget which; and I knew a very clever, sensible lady who read it over and over again in each of her 14 confinements.

She also refers to it in *Cranford,* Chapter IX.

34 *less like a Cousin Betty than a hat;*] The idea that a bonnet was more respectable than a hat, which survived right to the end of the nineteenth century, was probably associated with the fact that it concealed more of the face. The wearing of hats (rather than bonnets) by older women, or by married women, by widows, or in church, was at various times discouraged.

35 *called by a worse name still*] belly-ache.

36 *the strange household ... was cast.*] The moral which is conveyed to Miss Cordelia recalls the Church of England catechism 'My duty towards my neighbour is ... to submit myself to all my governors, teachers, spiritual pastors and masters ...to do my duty in that state of life, unto which it shall please God to call me.'

37 *He carried his sisters off to Cheltenham;*] Cheltenham was a genteel spa town to which many army officers retired; it would have offered more entertainment than Morton Hall.

'My French Master'

1 *he gave up his commission … half-pay.*] The implication seems to be that the narrator's father is especially scrupulous, since the half-pay system, which effectively created a reserve of officers not currently employed, was informally used by many as a retirement and disability pension.

2 *an old-fashioned routine… stitching.*] Charles Rollin, *Histoire ancienne*, 13 vols (1730–8), Oliver Goldsmith, *An History of England*, 2 vols (1764) and Lindley Murray, *English Grammar* (1795) were all well-known textbooks which went into many editions. It has been assumed by EG's biographers (*Chadwick*, p. 30, *Gérin*, p. 20, *Uglow*, p. 28) that she knew them from her own childhood, and it supports this theory that she anachronistically implies here that Murray's book could have been read by the narrator's mother in the 1770s, suggesting that they were associated in her mind as the dull schoolbooks of an older generation. There may be a distinction between 'sewing' and 'stitching', though they are synonymous in *OED*: possibly EG means that the girls were taught both how to sew seams (the bulk of domestic needlework) and also learnt different stitches for other purposes such as embroidery.

3 *one of the forest rangers,*] The story seems to be set in the New Forest in Hampshire, which because of its nearness to Southampton was a likely place for both retired naval officers and French emigrants to settle. This was one of the Royal Forests, with which various lucrative crown appointments were associated, such as Rangerships and Keeperships. In 1795 the Warden and Keeper of the New Forest was the King's brother, the Duke of Gloucester. General Ashburton evidently holds an appointment under the Keeper in respect of his distinguished military service. In *North and South* Hampshire symbolises the rural beauties of the south of England, and the curious episode of EG's purchase of a retirement home in the district indicates that it had for her a powerful appeal.

4 *once in January … October.*] Louis XVI was executed on 21 January 1793 and his widow Marie Antoinette on 16 October 1793.

5 *Martia,*] Evidently the nickname is chosen because of its associations with the word 'martial'.

6 *the Iris*] The fleur de lys, or iris, is depicted in stylised form on the Royal Arms of France, and thus symbolises Louis XVI.

7 *the White Lily's*] Marie Antoinette, celebrated for her beauty.

8 *'preux chevalier'*] a 'gallant knight' (French), a hackneyed phrase indicating someone emulating romantic standards of chivalry.

9 *the peace of 1814*] The treaty of Paris (1814) temporarily ended the Napoleonic Wars. Napoleon was exiled to Elba, and the Comte de Provence, younger brother of Louis XVI, was restored to the throne as

Louis XVIII (the child dauphin, who died in captivity, counting as Louis XVII).

10   *the 'Gazette'*] The *London Gazette*, a newspaper which carried official news.

11   *holds a court … Grillon's Hotel;*] 'Yesterday the King of FRANCE received the congratulations of a great number of persons at Grillon's Hotel, Albemarle street. All the visitors came in full court dresses' (*The Times* (22 April 1814), p. 3). EG was probably familiar with Frances Burney's account of this reception in the *Diary and Letters of Madame D'Arblay*, 7 vols (London, 1842, 1846), vol. vii, pp. 23–39.

12   *Gardes du Corps,*] The king's personal bodyguard of noblemen, a regiment in which M. de Chalabre served before the Revolution.

13   *Miss Mary,*] EG wrote 'Fanny', apparently having forgotten that the narrator's sister was earlier named Mary. All other instances have been silently corrected.

14   *the Duc de Duras*] Amédée-Bretagne-Malo de Durfort de Duras, duc de Duras (1771–1838), royalist politician, husband of the novelist Claire de Duras. Duras himself had joined the Gardes du Corps at the age of twelve. The Duras were members of the circle of Chateaubriand, which Mary Mohl had frequented as a young woman, and they also figure in *D'Arblay*, vol. vi, p. 353 and vol. vii, pp. 29, 34, 128.

15   *I turn it … at Chalabre.*] Isaiah 2:4: 'they shall beat their swords into plowshares, and their spears into pruninghooks: nation shall not lift up sword against nation, neither shall they learn war any more.'

16   *the Cent Suisses … Mousquetaires,*] other court regiments guarding the royal family.

17   *Malta,*] The Mediterranean island of Malta was garrisoned by the British, and its cheapness and pleasant climate encouraged naval and military families to settle there. EG's uncle Swinton Holland had lived there for two years in 1808–10.

18   *the foreign … shaking Europe*] the still unsettled state of the new constitution in France.

19   *M. du Fay, Fils,*] M. du Fay, the son.

20   *the return from Elba* –] The so-called 'Hundred Days' between Napoleon's escape on 26 February 1815 from Elba, the Italian island to which he had been exiled, and his defeat at the battle of Waterloo on 18 June 1815 were a time of great political uncertainty throughout Europe.

21   *the Duc de Feltre*] Henri Clarke, duc de Feltre (1765–1818), formerly a successful general under Napoleon; he joined the Bourbons and in 1815 was Louis XVIII's minister of war.

22   *the 'de' was dropped*] The 'de' indicated that the bearer was a member of the nobility.

23   *the two principal county towns*] Southampton and Winchester.

24   *their Jupiter-ship.*] The analogy is ironic since Jupiter, the supreme god in Greek mythology, does not always exercise his authority sensibly, nor is his wife Hera submissive.

25   marraine] godmother (French).

26   *Valetta.*] the principal city in the island of Malta.

27   esprit.] wit, cleverness (French).

28   *a Sister of Charity,*] St Vincent de Paul and St Louise de Marillac founded the order of the Filles de Charité in Paris in 1633. The community specialised in active social work among the poor, and made many recruits from the nobility. Shortly after EG's visit to Paris, Florence Nightingale, aged thirty-two, who had been attempting to train with the Sisters of Charity, caught measles after only a fortnight, and in June 1853 left to recuperate at the Mohls' home, where EG had been staying a few weeks earlier (*Uglow,* p. 347); Martha Vicinus and Bea Nergaard (eds), *Ever Yours, Florence Nightingale* (London: Virago, 1989), p. 69. There is no evidence that EG met Nightingale at this time, but it is likely that she heard of her ambitions from the Mohls. The order seems to have been interchangeably known as Daughters of Charity and Sisters of Charity, and both terms are still used today.

29   *An English friend … German professor,*] This is a recognisable description of EG's friend Mary Mohl, wife since 1847 of Julius Mohl (1800–1876), professor of Persian at the Collège de France.

30   *Ary Scheffer's sacred pictures.*] The sentimental and religiose paintings of Ary Scheffer (1795–1858) had great contemporary popularity, and engravings of them circulated widely. EG met him in 1855, and Mary Mohl knew him well. One of his most frequently reproduced works was 'St. Augustine and St. Monica', now in the Louvre.

'The Squire's Story'

1   *on the outskirts of Barford … Derby.*] The imaginary town of Barford is quite precisely located in the story as between Derby and Kegworth, close to the border with Leicestershire but inside Derbyshire. (Kegworth is in Leicestershire, and from Derby to the boundary is only seven miles.) In reality it was a good deal less isolated than EG implies: the post road from Leicester to Derby crossed the post road from Ashby to Nottingham three miles north-west of Kegworth. The fast stage coaches from Manchester to London went through Derby, Aston-on-Trent, Kegworth, Loughborough and Leicester, so it is possible that EG's sense of the area's bleakness and loneliness derives from the long cold journeys of her youth. See J. D. Welding, *Leicestershire in 1777* (Leicester: Leicester Libraries, 1984), p. 11; Alan Bates (ed.),

Directory of Stage Coach Services, 1836 (Newton Abbot: David and Charles, 1969), p. 34.

2   *'townspeople' and 'county people'*] The sense of this is that the professional middle-class people who live in the town are glad to have the opportunity of associating on terms of equality with the higher status landed gentry who live in the surrounding country.

3   *Mr Bickerstaff's ward.*] Richard Steele's magazine the *Tatler* (1709–11), written under the name Isaac Bickerstaffe, has a reference to a young woman who 'held up her head higher than ordinary and [took] an air that showed a secret satisfaction in herself, mixed with scorn of others' (151, 25 March 1710) when wearing striped garters. EG may also have been remembering Dame Martin in Walter Scott's *Redgauntlet* (1824), Letter 12, who 'bounded from the floor like a tennis-ball, – aye, till the colour of her garters was no particular mystery. She made the less secret of this, perhaps, that they were sky-blue, and fringed with silver.'

4   *to make the mixture thick and slab,*] In *Macbeth*, IV.i.30–2 the witches chant as they brew their potion:

> Finger of birth-strangl'd babe
> Ditch-deliver'd by a drab, –
> Make the gruel thick and slab

5   *the Roman Emperor*] Caligula, who made his horse Incitatus a consul.

6   *Doncaster or Newmarket.*] towns well known as centres of racing.

7   *Leicestershire*] The hunting in the flat country in Leicestershire was considered the finest.

8   aut *a huntsman* aut nullus.] from the expression 'Aut Caesar aut nullus': 'either Caesar or nothing' (Latin).

9   *'length of his fork'*] The length of his legs: *OED* sense 12b, citing the *Examiner* (12 October 1812) 'You are not long enough in the fork for the — dragoons.'

10   *not as a subscriber … amateur.*] The hunt was maintained by the subscriptions of his members, though other riders could follow it. To join the hunt involved some degree of social acknowledgment by fellow-members; hence Higgins shows his *savoir-faire* by modestly demonstrating his skills as a rider before seeking admission.

11   *as he hacked off … fox;*] Higgins receives the fox's brush because he was the first rider to reach the kill.

12   *the poor deceased Reynard,*] the fox.

13   *the Cropper-gate,*] To come a cropper is a hunting term (now used figuratively) meaning to take a heavy fall. The sense of this is therefore that Higgins has succeeded in jumping some dangerous local obstacle.

14   *his only child,*] EG contradicts herself in the next few sentences when we learn that Catherine has a brother.

15   *Gretna Green,*] After the 1754 tightening of the marriage law in England and Wales, the first village on the Scots side of the border was the traditional destination of those attempting to be married according to the laxer law of Scotland, where it was not necessary for persons under twenty-one to obtain parental consent, where a marriage could be celebrated by a lay person rather than a Church of England clergyman, and where it could take place immediately without having banns read.

16   *every form of law and of ceremony*] Unlike his sister's wedding, Nathaniel's will be preceded by the signing of legal settlements, settling property or income on the wife during marriage and in case of widowhood; conveying the capital of her fortune to trustees, thus protecting her interests against his, and that of any daughters and younger sons against an eldest son (privileged by the law of real property and by any entail on the estate); making provision for her after a possible remarriage; and settling the disposition of her income and property should she predecease him or die childless. It will take place after the banns of marriage have been read out on three successive Sundays in both her parish church and his, to maximise the chances that gossip will stop the marriage in the case of an existing marriage or misbehaviour on the part of either. It will take place in church and in public, surrounded by a number of respectable witnesses. These were the normal methods whereby the upper classes protected women against the danger of matrimonial exploitation and financial disaster. By persuading Catherine to run away to Gretna, Higgins has avoided the enquiries into his financial affairs and his family which would have been necessary had the usual marriage settlements been made, and has acquired total control over the £10,000 her mother left her.

17   *buffo stories* –] A buffo was a comedian.

18   *Miss Pratt was a dissenter,*] The term 'dissenter' was loosely used to embrace all the non-Anglican Protestant sects, including Unitarians like EG herself, Methodists, Baptists and Presbyterians.

19   *this female Mordecai,*] Esther 3:5: 'And when Haman saw that Mordecai bowed not, nor did him reverence, then was Haman full of wrath.'

20   *there were no stage-coaches … Barford,*] In this respect Barford was not like either Knutsford, Kegworth or Aston-on-Trent.

21   *a part of the wild heath … enclosed*] The process of enclosure, which accelerated during the eighteenth century, involved the legal transfer of common land to individuals. Moor and heath, which had been used, if at all, by the local population for grazing, were divided up, hedged, drained, fertilised and farmed, or in this instance, gardened. Although contemporaries often saw enclosure as a progressive procedure, in which agricultural science was used to make barren land productive, and dangerous no-mans-lands were civilised, many historians have

emphasised that the poorer farmers were dispossessed of their customary rights and turned into landless labourers. EG here focuses,
however, on the ruthless way in which the huntsmen trample over Mr
Dudgeon's garden as if it were still trackless heath.

22 *a masculine Griselda;*] The story of patient Griselda is the subject of
Chaucer's 'Clerk's Tale'; it is a mediaeval legend in which the heroine
endures frightful suffering at the hands of her husband with incredible
equanimity.

23 *Dogberries and Verges*] Dogberry and Verges are the comic and incompe-
tent parish constables in Shakespeare's *Much Ado About Nothing*.

24 *to play at whist,*] It is mildly surprising that EG should attribute the
habit of playing cards to a Dissenting minister.

25 *the 'Gentleman's Magazine;'*] A popular periodical, founded in 1731,
which carried many articles on antiquarian subjects.

26 *Charity covereth a multitude of sins."*] 1 Peter 4:8: 'And above all things
have fervent charity among yourselves: for charity shall cover the multitude of sins.'

27 *my answer to Philologus ... Urban.'*] Sylvanus Urban was the pseudonym
of the successive editors of the *Gentleman's Magazine*. Mr Davis has evidently written a response to an article signed 'Philologus' or 'Word
Lover', presumably on an etymological subject.

28 *of a comfortable jolly turn;*] The connection between ginger and convivial-
ity recalls *Twelfth Night*, II.iii.110–3: 'SIR TOBY: Dost thou think
because thou art virtuous there shall be no more cakes and ale?
FESTE: Yes, by Saint Anne, and ginger shall be hot i' th' mouth too.'

29 *set by to work;*] left for the yeast to ferment.

30 *Kegworth.*] a real town in Leicestershire. See note 1, above.

31 *Church-and-King-and-down-with-the-Rump."*] The racehorse has been
named after a toast used by Royalists to express their contempt for the
Commonwealth during the Civil Wars. The Rump Parliament (1648–
3) was the body which condemned Charles I to death and created the
Commonwealth of England.

32 *Claude Duval.*] Claude Duval (1643–1670), hanged for highway robbery, celebrated for his gallant behaviour to women victims (*DNB*).

'Right at Last'

1 *Edinburgh,*] Among the many doctors EG knew who had trained at the
celebrated medical school of Edinburgh University were her cousin
Sir Henry Holland (1788–1873) and Dr Anthony Todd Thomson
(1778–1849), her stepmother's brother.

2   *natural guardian)*] Her parents are dead but she is over twenty-one. She is not obliged to obey the uncle (he is not her legal guardian), but as an orphan and a woman she looks to him for support.

3   *a Frazer of Lovat!*] Professor Frazer claims to be related to Lord Lovat, the head of the Fraser clan.

4   *Simon Lord Lovat … great-uncle*] EG is careful not to imply that Margaret is descended from Simon Fraser, Lord Lovat (c. 1667–1747). Found guilty of kidnapping his cousin's widow and forcing her to marry him, he intrigued with both sides in the Jacobite conspiracies, fought on the Hanoverian side in the 1715 rebellion and with the Jacobites in 1745; and was executed for high treason, his title being attainted. His male line of descendants died out in 1815, and the lands were inherited by a distant cousin, who in 1857 got an act of parliament passed to reverse the attainder, perhaps thus drawing the subject to EG's attention.

5   *Admirable Crichton*] This is a stock phrase for a multi-talented person, first applied to the polymath James Crichton (1560–c. 85).

6   *marmelade and mutton hams.*] These are both typically Scots dishes; the latter is a salted and spiced leg of mutton.

7   *rep in preference to moreen?*] different types of upholstery fabric.

8   *the old proverb … scolding wife;*] 'Three things drive a man out of his house – smoke, rain, and a scolding wife', in *The Oxford Dictionary of English Proverbs*, ed. by F. P. Wilson (Oxford: Oxford University Press, 1970), p. 817, which also cites several variants.

9   *'sat all poured out … Germans say;*] The German expression is 'Er lag wie hingegossen'.

10 *'Must I prosecute?'*] At this date criminal prosecutions were still usually brought by private individuals rather than by the Crown.

'The Manchester Marriage'

1   *the early dinners… longer evenings.*] The subject of mealtimes is a complex one, since there were class as well as regional variations, and there was also a shift over time so that by the end of the nineteenth century the evening meal of the middle and upper classes was generally eaten later than it had been in the 1830s. EG herself mentions having dinner at times ranging between about 4.30 p.m. with the Hollands in Wales in 1848 (*Letters*, p. 61) and 7 p.m. while staying with the Nightingales in Derbyshire in 1854 (*Letters*, p. 307).

2   *the true Saxon accent.*] This may be a dig at WG, who certainly held this opinion. In his *Two Lectures on the Lancashire Dialect* (London: Chapman and Hall, 1854), pp. 13–14 (also reproduced in Volume 5 of this edition), he says:

> There are many forms of speech and peculiarities of pronunciation in Lancashire that would yet sound strange, and, to use a Lancashire

expression, strangely 'potter' a southern; but these are often not, as some ignorantly suppose, mere vulgar corruptions of modern English, but genuine relics of the old mother tongue.

3   *the Cape*] the Cape of Good Hope. Capetown, South Africa, was a port of call on the journey to India.

4   *the Underwriters.*] the insurers.

5   *her ewe-lamb*] 2 Samuel 12:3: 'The poor man had nothing, save one little ewe lamb.'

6   *not unlike to that of Ruth,*] Ruth 1:16: 'And Ruth said, Intreat me not to leave thee, or to return from following after thee: for whither thou goest, I will go; and where thou lodgest, I will lodge: thy people shall be my people, and thy God my God.'

7   *the famous Yankee … flogs England.'*] 'Everybody knows that America, at least that favoured portion comprised under the shadow of the stripes and stars, flogs creation' (*The Times* (3 December 1853), p. 6).

8   *Will you have me … husband,*] From the Anglican service for the Solemnisation of Matrimony, the form used at EG's own wedding.

9   *the Infirmary,*] the Manchester Royal Infirmary, founded 1752.

10   *an order to see Buckingham Palace,*] Under its entry for Buckingham Palace, *Murray's Handbook for Modern London* (London: Murray, 1851), p. 3, has 'Mode of Admission to View the Pictures; order from the Lord Chamberlain, granted only when the Court is absent.'

11   *the housemaid Bessy*] EG later forgot her name and she becomes 'Mary' on p. 123, see note 14, below

12   *he rang at the front-door*] This indicates he is a gentleman; a tradesman would ring at the back door.

13   *her deformity … back to them,*] Her back is hunched or twisted.

14   *Bessy,*] EG wrote 'Mary'. This and all other examples of 'Mary' have been silently corrected.

15   *the time o' life… good Lord, any",)*] According to Robert Holland, *Glossary of Words Used in the County of Chester*, English Dialect Society, 16 (London: Trubner, 1886), p. 444, the saying derives from the story of a spinster praying for a husband, overheard by a thatcher in her roof who asks whether a thatcher would do. Taking the question to come from God she answers 'Any, good Lord, before none.'

16   *mysterious but infallible ways and means.*] EG's faith in the detective powers of the Metropolitan Police is expressed in 'Disappearances', first published in *Household Words*, 3 (7 June 1851), see Volume 1 of this edition.

17   *wonder in those who might hear her.*] In such households at this period it was usual for servants to share beds.

18   *one half of which …upon her.*] Openshaw takes legal steps to ensure that his wife will never suffer from the fact that their marriage is invalid

because her first husband was still living. Since their marriage is fictitious (though she does not know it) she has no legal status as his wife
and he could desert her and leave her penniless. Rather than reveal the
truth and remarry her, he does his utmost to render her financially
independent by giving a fortune to trustees for her benefit. EG's apparent endorsement of his silence is interesting as a reflection of her views
on the sacredness of the marriage tie. There are few mainstream mid-
Victorian fictions which permit unwed couples to live together unpun-
ished. It is conceivable that for some readers the implications of
Openshaw's new 'reverence' for his wife could have included absti-
nence from sexual intercourse.

19 *whom she had never seen,*] This looks like a piece of typical carelessness
on EG's part, since Ailsie had seen her father when Norah brought her
into her bedroom. It is just possible that EG meant to write 'whom he
had never seen' (though this theory receives no support from the *HW*
text, which is identical).

Round the Sofa (vol. i)

1 *taken her brevet rank.*] The custom of middle-aged spinsters adopting
the title Mrs rather than Miss was dying out in the early nineteenth
century. The unmarried writers Hannah More (1745–1833) and Har-
riet Martineau (1802–76) both called themselves Mrs, but the latter
was eccentric in so doing.

2 *the paper ... was Indian,*] Hand-painted scenic wallpapers imported
from China, called Indian, were a popular fashion in the late eighteenth century.

'My Lady Ludlow'

1 *a whizz and a flash ... whistle,*] The gulf between the pre-railway age and
the present is a recurring theme for EG and other novelists (such as
Dickens and Thackeray) who lived through the revolution in communications in the 1830s and 1840s which reduced the duration of
journeys across England from days to hours.

2 *a coat of arms ... quarterings*] A spinster or a widow bears arms on a lozenge; a man's arms are displayed on a shield, and a married woman
uses her husband's shield. As heiress of the Hanbury family Lady Ludlow has brought her husband's family the right to quarter the arms of
her family with theirs (though in fact EG makes a technical error since
Lady Ludlow herself would correctly have displayed the Hanbury arms
on an inescutcheon of pretence).

3 *Rudolph,*] The name of Lady Ludlow's only surviving son later (p. 259)
becomes 'Ughtred-Mortimar'. Although the policy of this edition is to

regularise such slips by EG, I have not done so in this case, on the grounds that more is involved in the use of these uncommon names than in the 'Mary/Bessy/Fanny' slips which are common in her work.

4   *I entertain six young gentlewomen*] Such an arrangement was unusual at this date; EG may have taken a hint from James Boswell, *A Tour to the Hebrides* (1786), 'Saturday, 2d October':

> Dr Johnson said, that 'a chief and his lady should make their house like a court. They should have a certain number of the gentlemen's daughters to receive their education in the family, to learn pastry and such things from the housekeeper, and manners from my lady. That was the way in the great families in Wales; at Lady Salisbury's, Mrs Thrale's grand-mother, and at Lady Philips's.

By p. 154 the villages of Connington has been renamed 'Hanbury'.

5   *a presentation to Christ's Hospital*] Christ's Hospital was a charitable school for poor boys in London. Nominations were much sought after, and were obtainable from the Lord Mayor and Aldermen of the City of London and the governors of the school.

6   *unenclosed*] without hedges or fences. See 'The Squire's Story', note 21.

7   *to quarter,*] A quarter is 'one of four parts into which a road is divided by the horse-track and the wheel-ruts' (*OED*, sense 24). The verb 'to quarter' therefore means 'to drive a cart … so that the right and left wheels are on two of the quarters of the road, with a rut between.' *OED* considers it a dialect word.

8   *a great Virginian Creeper*] Virginia Creeper, *parthenocissus quinquefolia*, was growing in Great Britain by 1629.

9   *a step on to the dais,*] The great hall retains the mediaeval arrangement of a raised high table at one end, and long tables for the rest of the house-hold to eat at, as in the colleges at Oxford and Cambridge. The step up onto the dais thus symbolises Lady Ludlow's association with a feudal sense of mutual obligation between the lord of the manor and his serv-ants, a feudalism which is outdated, but which has some admirable features.

10 *a print … her numerous children,*] George III (1738–1820), King of Eng-land 1760–1820, married (1761) Sophie Charlotte of Mecklenburg-Strelitz (1744–1818) and had nine sons (of whom two died in child-hood) and six daughters. The print referred to is probably that by Richard Earlom after Johann Zoffany's group portrait.

11 *schismatic*] Prayers other than those in the Anglican *Book of Common Prayer* would have implied dissatisfaction with the Church of England, of the kind which led some sects, for example the Methodists, to secede from it.

12 *maid of honour to Queen Charlotte:*] Maids of honour were single women of high rank who waited on the Queen. The novelist Frances Burney had been a Woman of the Bedchamber (a lower grade of attendant) to

Queen Charlotte, and EG probably drew on the account of this period in *D'Arblay*, vols ii–v.

13 *Mr. Raikes ... Sunday Schools;*] Robert Raikes (1735–1811) started Sunday Schools in Gloucester in 1780. Without actually being the originator of the idea he was important in publicising it and is generally credited with being the founder of the Sunday School movement. Frances Burney described a visit to his schools in *D'Arblay*, vol. iv., p. 179.

14 *in Shrewsbury –*] perhaps a relic of an original scheme to set the story in Shropshire rather than Warwickshire. Shrewsbury and Ludlow are both towns in the former county, but, unlike Warwickshire, it was not much affected by industrialisation, and social change, not rural tranquillity, is EG's focus here.

15 *in quires and places where they sing,*] In the orders for Morning and Evening Prayer in the *Book of Common Prayer*, the collects are followed by the rubric: 'In Quires and Places where they sing here followeth the Anthem.'

16 *beyond a Sabbath-day's journey,*] Travelling on Sunday, especially the use of horses and carriages, was deprecated by many religious people, who would not go further than they could walk and return in the same day.

17 *my pew*] One of the biggest changes to English parish churches during the Victorian period was the almost total elimination of private pews, which were owned or rented by individuals, and the substitution of benches which were free to all. Private and comfortable pews, often surrounded by high partitions, were considered inconveniently large and inegalitarian; as EG was writing in the 1850s they were the target of every reforming clergyman, and Lady Ludlow's decision to glaze her pew therefore reflects her opposition to the forces of reform.

18 *John Wesley had objected to his hunting.*] The hunting parson was a stock target of reformers. Wesley's journal for 16 July 1756 refers to moral objections to hunting (see *The Journal of the Rev. John Wesley A. M.* (London: Bennett, 1830), p. 399).

19 *'Church and King, and down with the Rump.'*] See 'The Squire's Story', note 31.

20 *at Weymouth;*] Frances Burney describes a visit of George III and Queen Charlotte to Weymouth in *D'Arblay*, vol. v, p. 32.

21 *a Moravian Methodist,*] In the early eighteenth century a contingent of Protestants migrated from Moravia (now in the Czech Republic) to Germany, where, under the leadership of Count Nicholas von Zinzendorf (1700–60), they founded a community, known as the Moravian brethren, which sent out missions to various countries, including England, where some members became associated with the Wesleyan

Methodist movement. There is a reference to Moravian Methodists in *D'Arblay*, vol. ii, pp. 333–4.

22   *never missing Guy Faux' day*] Between 1606 and 1859 there was a special service in Anglican churches on 5 November in commemoration of the Catholic plot against James I on 5 November 1605. A Catholic sympathiser would be expected to absent himself or herself from an anti-Catholic service. The service was abolished in 1859 along with those on 30 January and 29 May commemorating the Martyrdom of Charles I and the Restoration of Charles II (see 'Morton Hall', notes 10 and 11).

23   *Fancy-work.*] In a domestic context the word 'work' often meant needlework, and the term 'fancy-work' referred to its ornamental branches, such as embroidery, and also stretched to cover other ladylike handicrafts such as leatherwork. EG here seems to be associating it particularly with the brightly-coloured Berlin woolwork on canvas which was so popular in the mid-Victorian period.

24   *Mr. Addison's 'Spectator;'*] Joseph Addison (1672–1719) was the main contributor to the *Spectator*, a daily periodical published 1711–12 and in 1714, which was hugely influential on eighteenth-century taste in literature and manners.

25   *'Sturm's Reflections … Young Ladies'*] Christoph Christian Sturm, *Reflections on the Works of God and of His Providence Throughout All Nature for Every Day in the Year*, 3 vols (1788); Hester Chapone, *Letters on the Improvement of the Mind*, 2 vols (1773); John Gregory, *A Father's Legacy to his Daughters* (1774). EG's authority for Queen Charlotte's approval of Sturm is no doubt *D'Arblay*, vol. v, pp. 107–8; Burney also mentions Gregory in vol. i, p. 118 and Chapone in vol. vi, p. 43.

26   *Dr. Buchan*] William Buchan, *Domestic Medicine, or, The Family Physician: Being an Attempt to Render the Medical Art More Generally Useful by Shewing People What is in Their Own Power Both With Respect to the Prevention and Cure of Diseases, Chiefly Calculated to Recommend a Proper Attention to Regimen and Simple Medicines* (1769).

27   *would be called homœpathic practice*] EG is expressing scepticism about the efficacy of homoepathy, in which active ingredients are administered to patients only in extremely dilute form.

28   *plum-porridge … ancestresses.*] EG is joking at the expense of traditionalists who refuse to acknowledge the real origins of customs with obvious roots in the pre-Reformation church calendar. Plum porridge, a Christmas dish, was a precursor of plum or Christmas pudding: a recipe in *Cassell's Household Guide*, 4 vols (1869–71), vol. iv, p. 350 is for a rich spiced meat broth thickened with bread and dried fruit. Furmenty, frumenty or furmity, the dish which was the undoing of Hardy's Mayor of Casterbridge, is a porridge made of whole wheat

grains hulled, soaked and simmered until soft and jellied: it too was sometimes also spiced and enriched with dried fruit, and it was variously eaten on Christmas Eve, Mothering Sunday, in Lent, and at Easter. Violet cakes were perhaps embellished with crystallised flowers; the colour, associated with mourning, was used for church vestments in Passion Week. For tansy pudding and its association with Easter see Alan Davidson, *The Oxford Companion to Food* (1999), p. 781. The three-cornered cakes probably resembled the Coventry Godcakes, triangular mince pies, described by Davidson, *Companion to Food*, p. 220, though those were eaten at Easter. See also Florence White, *Good Things in England* (London: Cape, 1932), pp. 26, 363; and Davidson, *Companion to Food*, pp. 323, 184, 220.

29 *de latest creation must back,*] In the Order of Precedence, countesses ranked according to the date the earldom had originally been given to their husband's family.

30 *hardly a dash of powder*] The custom of wearing the hair powdered was dealt successive blows by the imposition of Hair Powder Taxes in 1786 and 1795. The latter was not, however, as the passage implies, a purchase tax which raised the price of the article, it was a personal tax, and individuals certified to have paid a guinea could wear as much hair powder as they liked for a year.

31 *famine in seventeen hundred ... hundred,*] The story is evidently set in the early 1800s. There is an account of the famine in *Early Years*, p. 61.

32 *Lord George Gordon*] Lord George Gordon (1751–93), an opponent of the Catholic Relief Act (1778), organised a mass protest which degenerated into a week of rioting in London in June 1780.

33 *a game of picquet –),*] The implication is that Mr Gray disapproves of playing cards on a Sunday.

34 *in the commission.'*] The lowest level of criminal justice was administered by unpaid lay magistrates, drawn from the gentry, clergy and professional class, who were known as Justices of the Peace.

35 *his first committal,*] It was necessary for a prisoner to be committed to jail by a Justice of the Peace; he would then later be tried by a bench of magistrates or by a higher court.

36 *Henley Court-house*] Henley-in-Arden is a picturesque market town in rural Warwickshire, less than twenty miles south of the centre of Birmingham, a city which expanded rapidly during the Industrial Revolution and was a centre of technological innovation. EG indicates precisely a locality where rural feudalism and and modern ideas were likely to confront each other.

37 *squatting on Hareman's ... extra-parochial,*] Squatters were those who built themselves homes on unclaimed or common land; if undisturbed for a certain period they eventually acquired rights of abode but until

then their legal position was precarious. The parish was the smallest unit of civil, as well as of ecclesiastical, administration and although most of England was divided into parishes, there were a few extra-parochial areas, usually because at some historical period the land had been regarded as wasteland or forest. Social outcasts were more likely to be permitted to squat outside parish boundaries because the rate-payers would not then be obliged to support them, see note 109, below.

38   *forwards*] Facing the horses and the direction of travel. Sitting with one's back to the horses was considered uncomfortable. Compare Walter Scott, *The Antiquary*, 3 vols (Edinburgh: Constable,1816), vol. ii, p. 30: 'the front seat of the carriage, which is usually conferred upon dependents or inferiors.' Frances Burney's sufferings during carriage journeys with the windows open are a constant theme in *D'Arblay*; see for example vol. iii, pp. 458–61.

39   *Barford Corner,*] Barford was the name of a school EG had attended.

40   *Rogues … a vagabond;*] The Vagrant Act (1743) provided that 'all persons wandering about, or lodging in alehouses, barns, outhouses, or in the open air, not giving a good account of themselves … all other persons wandering abroad and begging, shall be deemed rogues and vaga-bonds.' They could be sent by a Justice of the Peace to be publicly whipped or to be imprisoned until the next meeting of the higher court or for a shorter period. See Richard Burn, *The Justice of the Peace and Parish Officer*, 23rd edition (1820).

41   *St. Stephen's,*] the Houses of Parliament. From 1547–1834 the House of Commons had met in the former Chapel of St Stephen, and it was therefore sometimes referred to as St Stephen's.

42   *The lord-lieutenant*] Each county had a Lord Lieutenant who was the King's representative.

43   *a good despotism*] Despotism, or the absolute rule of a monarch, was associated by eighteen-century thinkers with the tyrannical regimes of the East. Good, or benevolent, despotism (as distinct from the limited monarchies of Europe) was thus a paradox, and the question of whether an absolute ruler could rule over a free, contented and pros-perous people was a topic of much debate. See H. M. Scott, 'The Problem of Enlightened Absolutism' in *Enlightened Absolutism*, ed. by H. M. Scott (London : Macmillan 1990), pp. 1–35.

44   *a quorum*] Lady Ludlow puns on the two meanings of the word: *OED* sense 1, now obsolete, meaning 'justices of the peace', and *OED* sense 2, 'the number of members of a committee or group who are permit-ted to transact business on its behalf'. In opposing 'despotism' to 'quorum' she makes the latter term stand for 'those who act for a larger number of others', and, by implication, contrasts government by elected representatives unfavourably with hereditary despotism.

45   *privacy.*] This is a persistent theme in Frances Burney's account of her
      life at the court of Queen Charlotte, see for example *D'Arblay*, vol. ii,
      pp. 28–31.

46   *Sir Horace Mann,*] Sir Horace Mann (1701–86), best-known as the
      friend and correspondent of Horace Walpole, was the British ambassa-
      dor to the court of the Duke of Tuscany in Florence.

47   *Mr. Hogarth's pictures … nothing of it,*] William Hogarth (1697–1764)
      published a large number of hugely popular prints. Though the pic-
      tures are often shocking, the titles are not usually so, but Margaret
      Dawson perhaps scrupled to write the names of 'A Harlot's Progress'
      (1732) or 'A Rake's Progress' (1735). EG is drawing the reader's atten-
      tion to the difference in taste which permitted so delicate a person as
      Lady Ludlow to show Hogarth's prints to a girl.

48   *musk*] a substance secreted by the male musk deer, *Moschus moschiferus,*
      used in perfumery.

49   *'Bacon's Essays'*] Francis Bacon, *Essayes, or Counsels, Civill and Moral*
      (1625), 'Of Gardens':

>   That which above all others yields the sweetest smell in the air is the vio-
>   let, specially the white double violet, which comes twice a year; about
>   the middle of April, and about Bartholomew-tide. Next to that is the
>   musk-rose. Then the strawberry-leaves dying, which [yield] a most
>   excellent cordial smell.

50   *Shakespeare's musk-rose,*] There are several references to the musk rose
      in *A Midsummer Night's Dream*, the most memorable probably being
      II.i.251–2:

>   Quite over-canopied with luscious woodbine,
>   With sweet musk-roses, and with eglantine.

      Garden historians divide on the question of whether Shakespeare was
      referring to the musk rose, *Rosa moschata,* or another species.

51   *Childers or Eclipse*] Childers (b. 1714) and Eclipse (b. 1764) are two of
      the most famous eighteenth-century racehorses, not only because of
      the races they won, but because of the crucial place of their progeny in
      the breeding of the English thoroughbred.

52   *a certain Mrs. Nickleby,*] the foolish chattering mother of the hero of
      Dickens's *Nicholas Nickleby* (1839).

53   *beer … good ale,*] The distinction is one of strength; small beer would be
      what the servants normally drank at meals, ale a stronger brew fla-
      voured with hops.

54   *'What is thy duty … neighbour?'*] The relevant parts of the Church of
      England catechism run:

>   Question. What is thy duty towards God? Answer. My duty towards
>   God, is to believe in him, to fear him, and to love him with all my heart,
>   with all my mind, with all my soul, and with all my strength; to worship
>   him, to give him thanks, to put my whole trust in him, to call upon him,

to honour his holy Name and his Word, and to serve him truly all the days of my life.

Question. What is thy duty towards thy Neighbour? Answer. My duty towards my Neighbour, is to love him as myself, and to do to all men, as I would they should do unto me: To love, honour, and succour my father and mother: To honour and obey the Queen, and all that are put in authority under her: To submit myself to all my governors, teachers, spiritual pastors and masters: To order myself lowly and reverently to all my betters: To hurt no body by word nor deed: To be true and just in all my dealing: To bear no malice nor hatred in my heart: To keep my hands from picking and stealing, and my tongue from evilspeaking, lying, and slandering: To keep my body in temperance, soberness, and chastity: Not to covet nor desire other men's goods; but to learn and labour truly to get mine own living, and to do my duty in that state of life, unto which it shall please God to call me.

Question. What is the inward and spiritual grace? Answer. A death unto sin, and a new birth unto righteousness: for being by nature born in sin, and the children of wrath, we are hereby made the children of grace.

55 *had heard many answers*] The catechism was commonly taught at Sunday School.

56 *the dictionary was Bailey's; … Johnson*] Nathan Bailey, *An Universal Etymological English Dictionary* (1721); Samuel Johnson, *A Dictionary of the English Language* (1755).

57 *Mr. Gray … the great door*] The point here is probably not Mr Gray's social maladroitness but his concern for the dignity of his office. In the *Autobiography of Henry Taylor, 1800–1875*, 2 vols (London: Longmans, 1885), vol. i, p. 30, Taylor illustrates the change in the social status of the clergy during his lifetime by saying that in his childhood in the north of England the clergyman's wife and daughters came to the back door of his father's house, although the clergyman himself came to the front door.

58 *Rue de Lille;*] The Rue de Lille, which still contains several 'grands hôtels', is in the seventh arrondissement of Paris, runs parallel to the Seine, and intersects at right angles with the Rue du Bac, where EG stayed with the Mohls.

59 *the Missions Etrangères,*] The office of the Missions Etrangères is still (2004) at 128 Rue du Bac, as it was when EG stayed with Mary Mohl at 120 Rue du Bac.

60 *Mr. Fox*] Charles James Fox (1749–1806), liberal politician notorious for his rackety private life.

61 *Christopher Sly,*] in *The Taming of the Shrew*, a drunken tinker who is moved while unconscious and wakes up to find himself treated like a lord.

62 *vaurien*] rogue, good-for-nothing.

63 *the Abbaye?'*] a former convent in which many aristocrats were imprisoned.

64 *petit-maître.*] dandy.

65 *Jean-Jacques Rousseau*] The philosopher Jean-Jacques Rousseau (1712–78), author of *Discours sur l'origine et les fondements de l'inegalité parmi les hommes* (1753) and *Du contrat social* (1762) was a major influence on those who brought about the French Revolution. I have not found a particular passage which this refers to, but the sentiment is similar to that expressed in *Discours sur les sciences et les arts* (1750): 'La richesse de la parure peut annoncer un homme de goût; l'homme sain et robuste se reconnaît à d'autres marques: c'est sous l'habit rustique d'un laboureur, et non sous la dorure d'un courtisan, qu'on trouvera la force et la vigueur du corps.'

66 *Encyclopédistes!*] In mid-eighteenth-century France an attempt was made to codify all knowledge in the form of a great encyclopaedia, *L'Encyclopédie, ou Dictionnaire raisonné des sciences, des Arts et des Métiers*, 28 volumes (1751–72). It was the work of a group of intellectuals, including Rousseau, Denis Diderot (1713–1784) and Jean-le-Rond D'Alembert (1717–81), who were at the forefront of European political debate, and their circle was generally held to have been a breeding ground for revolutionary ideas.

67 *Mademoiselle Necker*] Anne Louise Germaine Necker (1766–1817), daughter of the finance minister Jacques Necker (1732–1804), married Baron de Staël-Holstein in 1786, and, as Madame de Staël, became well-known, first for a salon which was a centre of progressive thought, and subsequently as a novelist and cultural critic. Her novel *Corinne* (1807) analysed the difficulties of a woman writer and was important to many nineteenth-century women novelists. EG refers in *Cranford* to a print of Madame de Staël in a turban (after the painting by François Gérard) and the physical description she gives (see note 72, below) of Virginie de Créquy may derive from the same image.

68 *Æneas and filial piety* –] In Virgil's *Aeneid* the hero is so devoted to his father that he carries him on his back as he flees from burning Troy; he is frequently described as 'pius Æneas'.

69 *an old Cassandra,"*] Priam's daughter Cassandra is a character in both the *Iliad* and the *Aeneid*; she always prophesies disaster but is never believed. Although Lord Ludlow means to stigmatise her as a doom-monger, Madame de Créquy resembles Cassandra both in her fears and in their accuracy.

70 *a chord … Scotch ancestors.*] Belief in the 'second sight' was widespread in Scotland, and the power was held to be hereditary in some families.

71 *these freemason terms*] The sense is that the captain recognises from Lord Ludlow's language that he has been a seaman, and therefore treats him

as a comrade, in the same way that a freemason does who recognises another member of the order.

72 *a miniature*] See note 67, above, for the suggestion that EG is describing the face of Madame de Staël.

73 *the Lanterne.*] The phrase 'les aristocrates à la lanterne' occurs in the song 'Ça ira!', popular during the French Revolution. Enemies of the Revolution are to be hurried to the nearest lamp-post and hanged. Carlyle was to use the expression as a kind of refrain in his *The French Revolution* (1837).

74 *grénier,*] attic, loft (French).

75 *galette.*] cake, biscuit (French).

76 *one of the airs ...Beaumarchais' operas,*] Pierre-Augustin Caron de Beaumarchais (1732–99) was a playwright, whose popular plays *Le barbier de Seville* (1775) and *La folle journée ou le mariage de Figaro* (1778) were notorious, especially the latter, for their critique of aristocratic privilege. However, EG's use of the word opera suggests that she was really thinking of Mozart's *Le nozze di Figaro* (1786), based on *La folle journée*, or even perhaps of one of the operas called *Il barbiere di Siviglia,* either that (1782) by Giovanni Paisiello, or the better-known version (1816) by Gioacchino Rossini.

77 *Adam's opera of Richard le Roi*] In legend King Richard I of England (1157–99), 'the Lionheart', had been rescued from captivity by his minstrel Blondel, who had discovered him by playing his favourite tune in all the possible castles. The story had been popularised in France by the opera *Richard Coeur de Lion* (1784) by André Grétry (1741–1813). Its most famous aria was taken up by Royalists during the French Revolution, and is frequently mentioned by Carlyle in his *The French Revolution* (1837):

> O Richard! O mon roi!
> L'univers t'abandonne;
> Sur la terre il n'est donc que moi
> Qui m'interesse à ta personne!

EG has made a mistake in crediting the French composer Adolphe Adam (1803–56), who had adapted the opera as *Richard en Palestine* (1844), instead of Grétry.

78 *Boupré,'*] Not recorded by Henri Lyonnet, *Dictionnaire des comédiens français* (1910) or Max Fuchs, *Lexique des troupes de comédiens au XVIIIe siècle* (1944).

79 *the French prisoners of war on Dartmoor.*] Dartmoor Prison, at Princetown in Devon, was built in 1806–9 to house French prisoners during the Napoleonic wars.

80 *all who knew her speak ... manners,*] Again, possibly EG was thinking of Germaine de Staël, of whom Frances Burney wrote 'I find her impossible to resist' and Charles Burney 'I am not at all surprised at your

account of the captivating powers of Madame de Staël' (*D'Arblay*, vol. v, pp. 398, 403).

81 *canaille*] scum, riffraff (French).

82 *Jean*] EG wrote 'Victor', forgetting that he had been named 'Jean' on p. 201 above.

83 *the bureau of the Directory,*] The Directoire was the five-man executive council which ruled France between October 1795 and November 1799. The events of the story are thus placed slightly after the most violent period of the Revolution, the Reign of Terror of 1793–4.

84 *ci-devant*] The French term, meaning 'former', applied to ex-nobles after the abolition of the hereditary nobility and its many legal privileges from 1790.

85 *death is annihilation, you know.*] Morin reveals his atheism, which to EG and others was one of the most alarming aspects of French revolutionary culture.

86 *the Palais de Justice ... the Grève.*] The sense of this is that he will be at her trial, and at her place of execution, that is, at the Palais de Justice on the Île de la Cité and at the Place de Grève (now the Place de l'Hôtel de Ville) where the guillotine is.

87 *Saint Germain l'Auxerrois;*] The church of St Germain d'Auxerre in the Place du Louvre in Paris.

88 *a repository,*] *OED* sense 1c: 'A place where things are kept or offered for sale.'

89 *Xantippe,*] The wife of Socrates was traditionally said to have been a scold.

90 *For Satan finds some mischief ... to do,*] From 'Against Idleness and Mischief', ll. 11–12, by Isaac Watts (1674–1748), one of his bestselling *Divine Songs . . for the Use of Children* (1715).

91 *"employ my time in writing."'*] untraced.

92 *Doctor Burney*] Charles Burney (1726–1814), historian of music and father of the novelist Frances Burney (1752–1840).

93 *grieve,*] steward, estate manager.

94 *Mr. Wesley*] The Revd John Wesley (1703–91), the founder of the Methodist movement.

95 *Brooke,*] EG wrote 'Lambe' but later (p. 264) changed the Baptist baker's name to 'Brooke'.

96 *tinge of Jacobitism*] Between the exile of James II in 1688 and the death of his grandson Henry, Cardinal York (1725–1807) there was a Catholic Stuart claimant to the throne of Great Britain with significant support in Britain, although after the battle of Culloden (1746) the threat to the Hanoverian kings was much reduced. Lady Ludlow's Jacobitism is associated with her respect for tradition and loyalty to the overlord, and with her dislike of revolution or any kind of change.

97   *thorn-tree … Queen Mary*] It is claimed of several Scots trees that they
     were planted by Mary, Queen of Scots (1542–87); the best-known of
     these is probably the thorn tree in the grounds of the University of St
     Andrews.

98   *fifth of November … January,*] In commemoration of the discovery of the
     Gunpowder Plot of 5 November 1605 and the execution of Charles I
     on 30 January 1649.

99   *Susannah and the Elders … Dragon*] two stories from Daniel, 13 and 14
     respectively, which appear in the Apocrypha in the Authorised Version
     of the Bible. Daniel vindicates Susannah from a charge of adultery, of
     which she has been accused by the elders who failed to seduce her; he
     subsequently reveals Bel and the dragon to be false gods. In both sto-
     ries those in authority are shown to be wicked and deceitful.

100 *Am I not a man and a brother?"*] The best-known image of the anti-slav-
     ery campaign was the emblem of the Society for Effecting the
     Abolition of the Slave Trade, depicting a kneeling African with this
     motto, which circulated in large numbers in the form of ceramic
     plaques manufactured by Josiah Wedgwood from 1787.

101 *no sugar in his tea,*] William Fox, *An address to the People of Great Britain on
     the propriety of abstaining from West India sugar and rum* (1791), had argued
     for the use of economic as well as moral pressure in the anti-slavery
     campaign.

102 *Martha and Mary,*] Luke 10:38–42. Martha was 'cumbered about much
     serving' while her sister 'sat at Jesus' feet'. When Martha complained
     Jesus said 'Mary hath chosen that good part, which shall not be taken
     away from her'. The story is interpreted as a celebration of spiritual
     contemplation rather than practical good works, but Miss Galindo
     characteristically reads it against the grain.

103 *a lost sheep.'*] Luke 15:4–7. The allusion is to the passage introducing
     the parable of the Prodigal Son: 'What man of you, having an hundred
     sheep, if he lose one of them, doth not leave the ninety and nine in the
     wilderness, and go after that which is lost, until he find it?' There is a
     close parallel to this passage in *Ruth*, Chapter XXVI.

104 *every fourth of June,*] George III's birthday.

105 *Satan compassing me round,*] Perhaps a reminiscence of Job 16:13: 'His
     archers compass me round about, he cleaveth my reins asunder, and
     doth not spare; he poureth out my gall upon the ground.'

106 *submission … God to call them,*] The phrases recall the Church of Eng-
     land catechism, see 'Morton Hall', note 36, above.

107 *Malmsey,*] a sweet fortified wine from Madeira.

108 *preordained … of the ground.*] The implication is that Mr Gray is inclined
     towards the Calvinist doctrine of predestination. This provides a con-
     text for his depression and self-flagellation. It also relates to the story's

interest in good works, since the Protestant churches were divided on the question of whether virtuous conduct had any effect on an individual's chances of salvation, Calvinists believing it did not and Arminians (including the 'High' end of the Church of England with which Lady Ludlow is associated) that it did. The phrase 'cumberer of the ground' alludes to the parable of the fig tree, Luke 13:7: 'why cumbereth the ground?'

109 *Hall, the Bang-beggar,*] Before the Poor Law Amendment Act (1834) it was the responsibility of each parish to support poverty-stricken natives, defined as those born or settled within its limits, under Elizabethan legislation aimed at preventing vagrancy. It was therefore not in the interests of ratepayers to allow poor travellers to stay longer than necessary, for fear they should acquire a settlement and become a charge on the parish. In some places a parish official, the Bang Beggar, was employed to chase away the potentially destitute towards their birthplaces.

110 *got up like a page in an old ballad,*] The allusion is perhaps to 'Prince Robert':

> 'O where will I get a little boy
> That will rin hose and shoon,
> To rin sae fast to Darlinton,
> And bid fair Eleanor come?'

> Then up and spake a little boy,
> That wad win hose and shoon,
> 'Oh I'll away to Darlinton,
> And bid fair Eleanor come.'

The ballad is printed in Walter Scott, *Minstrelsy of the Scottish Border* (1802–3) a copy of which was sold in Meta Gaskell's sale.

111 *may be like methodism,*] Belief in a special providence is associated here with Methodism.

112 *kitchen-physic;*] invalid food (*OED*).

113 *a Lilliputian.*] in Jonathan Swift, *Gulliver's Travels* (1726).

114 *forbade a mother … babies.*] There was much debate in the eighteenth century about the medical benefits to children of being breastfed by their own mothers rather than, as was the custom among the rich, by paid wet nurses; wet-nursing remained not uncommon well into the Victorian period.

115 *Hatchments*] On the death of a member of the upper class it was customary to display a wooden board painted with the coat of arms of the deceased over his or her front door and in church.

116 *my lady's property of Hanbury,*] Whereas it is clear that the Ludlow estates in Scotland are settled on the heir of the title, who will enjoy a life tenancy while the estate is vested in trustees, EG seems to imply that the

Hanbury estate belongs outright to Lady Ludlow, who has the power and the intention to leave it to the next heir of her family. This side-steps the question of how she could have remained its owner during her marriage. It would not have suited EG's purpose, though it might have been more historically plausible, to have had Lady Ludlow acting through the trustees of her marriage settlement, or of her husband's will trust.

117   *cultivating his Scotch estates,*] The application of scientific principles to agriculture was fashionable among the landowning classes by the end of the eighteenth century. In northern Scotland, drainage, fertiliser and large-scale sheep farming brought to an end a peasant economy, lead-ing to the mass emigration known as the Highland Clearances, which thus form a dark counterpart to Lady Ludlow's benevolent feudal rule.

118   *Cocker*] Edward Cocker, *The Tutor to Writing and Arithmetic* (1664) was a standard textbook which went into many later editions, usually with the title *Cocker's Arithmetic*. The phrase 'according to Cocker', meaning above board and accurate, became proverbial.

119   *Holkham and Woburn,*] Holkham Hall, in Norfolk, was the seat of the agricultural reformer Thomas William Coke (1752–1842), later (1837) Earl of Leicester. Woburn Abbey, in Bedfordshire, was the seat of Fran-cis Russell, 5th Duke of Bedford (1765–1802), who established an experimental farm there.

120   *wounded at Trafalgar,*] The British navy defeated the French at the battle of Trafalgar on 21 October 1805.

121   *Greenwich Hospital!*] the Royal Greenwich Hospital, founded in 1694 as a home for elderly and disabled sailors.

122   *frabbed*] worried, irritated.

123   *am I a stock or a stone,*] an inanimate object. A catch phrase, probably deriving from Milton's reference in, 'On the Late Massacre in Pied-mont' to the time when 'all our fathers worshipped stocks and stones', and ultimately from Jeremiah 2:27.

124   *James the First's creation.*] James I founded the order of baronets in 1611. Since the seniority of a baronet depends on the date his title was cre-ated, the baronets created by James I rank above all later creations.

125   *great tithes … impropriator),*] In theory each English parish had a rector, who was paid out of a ten percent tax, the tithe. However, in many cases, the right to collect the great tithes (on corn, hay and wood) was alienated during the Middle Ages to a bishop, a Cathedral chapter, a college or an abbey, who appointed a paid deputy, or vicar, who did not collect the great tithes. At the Dissolution of the Monasteries in the sixteenth century some of these tithes had been acquired by laymen, and subsequently bought and sold as property, in a way which was deplored as an abuse by Victorian reformers for several different rea-

sons, secular as well as religious. Since the compulsory payment of tithes was especially resented by Dissenters (who were obliged to support the Anglican clergyman as well as their own minister), EG was probably familiar with the arguments against them, and against lay impropriation of tithes in particular.

126 *not to apply for … Italian baronet,*] Miss Galindo's situation is akin to that of EG's Knutsford friend, Mrs Granville, whose 'sole dependence' was 'an annual 10£ sent to her by the present possessor of Otterden Place, which had descended in the male line to a distant cousin' (*Letters*, p. 265).

127 *seven children,*] but below, p. 277, 'twelve children'.

128 *Mrs. Trevor.*] The name appears as 'Mrs. Gibson' in both *HW* and *1859*; no doubt either EG or the printer substituted the last mentioned name for that of the doctor's wife, to whom he is talking. It has been silently corrected here.

129 *Arthur Young's 'Tours'*] Arthur Young (1741–1820), Secretary to the Board of Agriculture and author of *The Farmer's Tour Through the East of England*, 4 vols (1771), *A Six Months' Tour Through the North of England*, 3 vols (1770), *A Six Weeks' Tour Through the Southern Counties of England and Wales* (1768) and *A Tour in Ireland*, 2 vols (1780), was the most influential writer in connection with the movement known as the Agricultural Revolution.

130 *the first four rules of arithmetic;*] addition, subtraction, multiplication and division.

131 *Dodwell's heresy.*] The slur on the Baptist baker is probably that he believes that the unbaptised soul is not immortal, as argued by Henry Dodwell (1641–1711), the nonjuror, in *An Epistolary Discourse proving from the Scriptures and the first Fathers, that the Soul is a principle naturally mortal* (1706). In the context this seems more likely than Edgar Wright's suggestion (in his edition of *My Lady Ludlow and Other Stories*, 1989, p. 193) that the allusion is to his son Henry Dodwell the younger (d. 1784), the author of a notorious deist pamphlet, *Christianity Not Founded on Argument* (1742).

132 *the Norfolk system of cropping,*] Crop rotation (turnips, clover, barley and wheat) was a key element in the agricultural reforms popularised by Thomas Coke of Holkham.

133 *no more a Coke than I am –*] Thomas William Coke was the son of Wenman Roberts (d. 1776) who had changed his name to Coke in 1759 on inheriting the estates of his maternal uncle.

134 *Philidor on Chess,'"*] François-André Danican, known as Philidor, *L'analyze des échecs* (1749), a well-known guide. It is mentioned by Frances Burney, *D'Arblay*, vol. vii, p. 280.

135 *Jack fancy Gill, or Gill Jack.*] The ancient proverb 'Every Jack shall have his Jill' was reinforced by Shakespeare's allusion to it in *A Midsummer Night's Dream*, III.ii.461 and *Love's Labour's Lost*, V.ii.885. See Burton Stevenson, *Book of Proverbs* (London: Routledge, 1949), pp. 1262–3.

136 *spinning-jenny*] The invention in 1764 by James Hargreaves of the spinning jenny (a machine for spinning thread on six bobbins simultaneously) paved the way for the mechanisation of the textile industry, a development whose social consequences surrounded EG in Victorian Manchester. It stands here as a symbol for technology in general.

137 *sea-wrack,*] sea-weed.

138 *call on the bride,*] It was customary to call on a newly-married lady to indicate that one wished to welcome her to the neighbourhood.

139 *that old city merchant of a Hanbury*] EG may have had a real case in mind. She cannot, however, have been inspired by Beriah Botfield's bequest to the Marquess of Bath, in similar circumstances, which did not take place until 1863.

140 *captain of his school, or Grecian,*] He is head boy, or top scholar, probably at Christ's Hospital (where the scholarship boys were called Grecians). The significance of this is that it will enable him to gain a scholarship to Oxford or Cambridge, and thereafter perhaps a fellowship, ordination, and an appointment as clergyman of a parish in the patronage of his college: this was the classic route whereby a clever poor boy who belonged to the Church of England could rise in society.

141 *hair powdered*] Long after hair powder had ceased to be worn by gentlemen it remained a status symbol to have liveried footmen with powdered hair.

142 *Bandanna*] a tie-dyed handkerchief, usually brightly-coloured, imported from India.

143 *the Reverend Henry Gregson*] From this it is evident that Harry Gregson has been ordained as a Church of England clergyman, thus acquiring the status of a gentleman. EG leaves the reader with an image of the transformation of Lady Ludlow's rank-ordered universe by social mobility fuelled by education.

Round the Sofa (vol. ii)

1 *a French book … Academies,*] Ward, in *Knutsford*, identifies this as Francisque Michel, *Histoire des races maudites de la France et de l'Espagne*, 2 vols (Paris: A. Franck, 1847). It does not seem to have been published by any of the several academies of the Institut de France, nor was the author a member of one.

'An Accused Race'

1 *dressed-up Guys.*] The widespread custom of burning straw effigies of Guy Fawkes on 5 November to commemorate the failure of the Gunpowder Plot was once accompanied by demonstrations of anti-Catholic feeling.

2 *about the end of the last century.*] i.e., as a result of the French Revolution; the source for this statement is *Michel*, p. 5, see *Round the Sofa* (vol. ii), note 1 above.

3 *Martinmas*] The feast of St Martin on 11 November traditionally marked the beginning of winter, when cows and pigs were slaughtered and salted down; therefore it was an appropriate time for stocktaking.

4 *the foot of a duck*] *Michel*, p. 4.

5 *not allowed to possess sheep,*] *Michel*, p. 125.

6 *bénitier*] a stoup, a container for holy water (French).

7 *the Cagots of Rehouilhes*] *Michel*, p. 85.

8 *Mauvezin,*] *Michel*, p. 90.

9 *satirical songs.*] *Michel*, p. 4.

10 *Count Raymond of Toulouse*] *Michel*, pp. 189–90.

11 *Gehazi,*] 2 Kings 5:27: 'The leprosy therefore of Naaman shall cleave unto thee, and unto thy seed forever.'

12 *the Emperor Charles the Fifth;*] *Michel*, pp. 191–2. Charles V, King of Spain and Holy Roman Emperor, reigned 1516–56.

13 *alcaldes*] a local official, a mayor.

14 *fair and ruddy*] *Michel*, p. 86.

15 *Dr. Guyon,*] The passage is quoted by *Michel*, p. 111.

16 *He that's ... same opinion still.*] Samuel Butler, *Hudibras* (1663–78), III.iii.547–8: 'He that complies against his will, / Is of his own opinion still.'

17 *d'Abedos ... Lourbes,*] *Michel*, pp. 133–4, but he has 'd'Abidos ... Lurbe', which raises the possibility that EG may have had the book read aloud to her.

18 *A Breton girl,*] The story of the girl choosing the less Cagot of two suitors is given by *Michel*, p. 135, but the location is in south-western France.

19 *M. Emile Souvestre*] Émile Souvestre (1806–76), French novelist. His article 'Industrie et commerce de la Bretagne', *Revue des deux mondes*, 4:4 (1835), p. 400, is cited by *Michel*, p. 62. EG had met him with the Mohls in 1853.

20 *the skeleton of a hand*] *Michel*, p. 156

21 *the beginning ... Louis the Sixteenth;*] Louis XVI, King of France, reigned 1774–1793.

22 *in the commotions ... eighty-nine;*] *Michel*, p. 5.

23 *skin disease,*] *Michel*, pp. 6–7.

24 *their defeat by King Clovis,*] Clovis, King of the Franks, reigned 481–511; he defeated Alaric, King of the Visigoths, at Vouillé in 507.

25 *horrible smell.*] *Michel*, p. 7.

26 *Pope Stephen's letter to Charlemagne,*] EG's source is probably Edward Gibbon, *The History of the Decline and Fall of the Roman Empire*, 6 vols (1776–88), vol. v, p. 117, n. 53: 'Pope Stephen IV had most furiously opposed the alliance of a noble Frank – cum perfida, horrida nec dicenda, foetentissima natione Longobardorum – to whom he imputes the first stain of leprosy.'

27 *goîtres,*] *Michel*, pp. 50–2.

28 *the Neapolitan tarantella;*] a whirling dance which takes its name from Taranto in southern Italy.

29 *Berserker.*] a Viking warrior in a state of frenzy.

30 *Etienne Arnauld*] *Michel*, pp. 235–7

31 *This wealthy white miller,*] Millers were covered in flour from the nature of their work. There is however something awkward in the phrase, and EG's use of the word here may also gesture towards the subtext in which this article connects with the current debate about slavery in the United States.

32 *Bishop of Tarbes,*] *Michel*, p. 242.

'The Doom of the Griffiths'

1 *Owen Glendower*] Owain Glyndwr was a Welsh landowner who led a series of uprisings against Henry IV and Henry V between 1400 and 1412, proclaiming himself at one point Prince of Wales. He figures in many Welsh legends as a magician, and as a pioneering Welsh nationalist.

2 *the Welsh prize poem at Oxford,*] This is a puzzling allusion. Although prizes were given for Latin and English poems written by undergraduates at Oxford University, there seem to have been none for Welsh, and the subject 'Glendower' does not seem to have been set for the English prize poem. However, the competitive performance of poetry is congenial to Welsh literary tradition, and prizes were given at eisteddfods. EG might have seen, and been misled by, a copy of John Lloyd Vaughan, *Glyndwr: A Poem* (Ruthin: Robert Jones, 1826), in which the poem (in English) is described as a 'Prize Poem', and the author as 'of Jesus College, Oxford'. It includes a reference (p. 25) to David Gam's attempt to assassinate Glyndwr at his coronation (see note 4, below).

3 *At my nativity . . question*] *Henry IV*, III.i.13–17:

> GLENDOWER   At my nativity
> The front of heaven was full of fiery shapes
> Of burning cressets, and at my birth
> The frame and huge foundation of the earth

Shak'd like a coward.
Later in the same scene, ll. 51–3:
> GLENDOWER   I can call spirits from the vasty deep.
> HOTSPUR   Why, so can I, or so can any man,
> But will they come when you do call for them?

4   *Sir David Gam,*] David Gam or Dafydd ap Llewelyn (d. 1415), was rewarded for his loyalty to the crown during the rebellion of Owain Glyndwr, though there is doubt about the legend that he tried to assassinate him. He is supposed to have been knighted just before his death at the battle of Agincourt. He is mentioned, as Davy Gam, in *Henry V,* IV.viii, and has also been suggested as a model for the character of Fluellen (*DNB*).

5   *as black a traitor … Builth,'*] The death of Llewelyn ap Gruffydd, the last Prince of Wales, at the battle of Irfon Bridge near Builth in 1282, was traditionally ascribed to treachery.

6   *Rhys ap Gryfydd … his blood.*] Psalms 41:9: 'Yea, mine own familiar friend, in whom I trusted, which did eat of my bread, hath lifted up his heel against me.'

7   *The mark of Cain*] Genesis 4:9: 'And the LORD set a mark upon Cain, lest any finding him should kill him.'

8   *If you go from Tremadoc to Criccaeth*] It is only a few miles from Tremadog to Criccieth. The village of Wern seems to occupy the position described.

9   *Jesus College,*] Jesus College, Oxford, had many affiliations with Wales and would therefore be the natural destination of a Welshman. The first university in Wales, St David's College, Lampeter, was not founded until 1822.

10   *Dr. Pugh*] William Owen Pughe (1759–1835), scholar, editor and historian.

11   *Llyn,*] The Lleyn peninsula, where this story is set, is even now one of the remotest parts of Wales.

12   *'stretched in indolent repose'*] Wordsworth, *The Excursion,* IV.851–3:
> In that fair clime the lonely herdsman, stretched
> On the soft grass through half a summer's day,
> With music lulled his indolent repose;

13   *Œdipus Tyrannus,*] Sophocles, *Oedipus the King* (c. 420 BC), a tragedy in which a son is doomed by a prophecy to murder his father. Oedipus marries and has children with his mother, Jocasta.

14   *Clenneny Moors … Penmorfa.*] Clennenney is a remote upland hamlet north of Penmorfa, which is a village west of Tremadog. Penmorfa also figures in EG's story 'The Well of Pen-Morfa'.

15   *the harper … Edward of Corwen.*] Perhaps Edward Jones (1752–1824), harpist to the Prince of Wales, music teacher and collector, who won a

medal at the 1789 Corwen eisteddfod. He was editor of *The Musical and Poetical Relicks of the Welsh Bards*, 3 vols (1784–1820).

16 *The march of the men … o' bunnan'*] 'Men of Harlech' or 'Rhyfelgyrch Gwyr Harlech' is a Welsh folksong with a glorious tune; there are several sets of bellicose lyrics in circulation, variously associated with the rising of Owain Glyndwr or the siege of Harlech in 1468. 'Tri chant o' bunnan' means 'Three hundred pounds'.

17 *'Pennillion,'*] Penillion is a complex Welsh song form in which a singer improvises verses and music to accompany a harpist, without duplicating the harp's tune.

18 *'Pa sut mae dy galon?'*] 'How is your heart?' (Welsh).

19 cwrw.] beer (Welsh).

20 *Moel Gêst;*] Moel-y-gest is a small mountain just south of Wern.

21 *"Tri pheth tebyg y … ei geirda"*] 'Three things are alike: a fine barn without corn, a fine cup without drink, a fine woman without her reputation' (Welsh).

22 *closed up after the manner of the Welsh:*] The beds are built into the wall with doors like cupboards, like the bed in which Lockwood sleeps in *Wuthering Heights*.

23 *'diod griafol'*] literally, rowan drink (Welsh): a drink made from the berries of the rowan or mountain ash, *Sorbus acuparia*.

24 *Penthryn to Llandutrwyn,*] The sense of this seems to be that Ellis takes them round the Portmeirion peninsula and lands them on the other side of the river Cynfal, but the place names are at least obsolete and probably imaginary.

25 *Undine.*] Friedrich, Baron de la Motte Fouqué, *Undine: eine Erzählung* (1811) is the tragic tale of a water nymph adopted by a human family who acquires a soul when she marries the knight Huldbrand.

26 *yr buten!*] In Welsh *putain* is a whore.

27 *'Fool – poor fool!'*] The *Harper's* text has 'Fool – poor wittol fool.' A wittol is a man who knowingly lets his wife be unfaithful.

28 *'woman of the grove and brake' –*] I have not traced this idiom.

29 *cloak and haps.*] OED defines hap as a northern dialect term for a covering (especially one of coarse cloth), a shawl or overcoat.

'Half a Life-Time Ago'

1 *on the Oxenfell road … Coniston.*] The present A593. This carefully specified place is distinct from that in 'Martha Preston', which is set on Loughrigg Fell, above Grasmere, to the north-east.

2 *brattles*] OED defines the verb brattle as 'to rush with rattling noise, as a mountain brook over a stony bed' and considers it mainly a Scots term.

3   *in the lifetime of Susan Dixon.*] In 'Martha Preston' the heroine is still alive as the story is being told.

4   *'Paradise Lost'* ... *'The Pilgrim's Progress')*] John Milton, *Paradise Lost: A Poem Written in Ten Books* (1667) and *Paradise Regain'd: A Poem in Four Books* (1671); Mary Collyer's 1761 translation of Salomon Gessner's *Der Tod Abels* (1759); Richard Graves, *The Spiritual Quixote, or, The summer's ramble of Mr Geoffry Wildgoose, A comic romance* (1772), a satire against Methodism; and John Bunyan, *The Pilgrim's Progress from this World to That Which is to Come* (1678). For the availability and popular readership of cheap editions of Milton see R. D. Altick, *The English Common Reader: A Social History of the Mass Reading Public, 1800–1900* (Chicago and London: Phoenix Books, 1957), p. 40; Louis James, *Fiction for the Working Man, 1830–1850* (London: OUP, 1963), p. 77. See also Charlotte Yonge, *History of Christian Names*, 2 vols (London: Parker, 1863), vol. i, p. 100, who comments 'Thirza, the name of Abel's wife in Gessners's idyll of the *Death of Abel*, a great favourite among the lower classes in England, whence Thyrza has become rather a favourite in English cottages.'

5   *Wythburne, up beyond Grasmere;*] Wythburn is a village on Thirlmere, north of Grasmere.

6   *notable,*] The word is used as in the phrase 'a notable housewife'; the implication is that her pride in her domestic good management prevented her admitting to weakness.

7   *take tent*] Pay attention to, take care of. *OED* says by this date the expression is used only in northern dialect.

8   *"Nought but death shall part thee and me!"'*] Ruth 1:17: 'Where thou diest, will I die, and there will I be buried: the LORD do so to me, and more also, if ought but death part thee and me.'

9   *'We're rid of bad rubbish, anyhow.'*] an allusion to the proverbial phrase 'Good riddance to bad rubbish'.

10   *clap-bread,*] This is a kind of oatcake made very thin by slapping it repeatedly on a round and slightly concave board. When sufficiently flattened it is baked on a griddle until crisp, in which condition it will keep until wanted. Elizabeth David, *English Bread and Yeast Cookery* (1979), p. 531.

11   *maud,*] see, 'The Old Nurse's Story', note 12, above.

'The Poor Clare'

1   *1747. –*] If the narrator is an old man looking back on his youth in this year, the events of the story must be presumed to have taken place at least twenty or thirty years previously.

2   *a part they call the Trough of Bolland,*] The Forest of Bowland is a large thinly populated area of hill and moorland in Lancashire and Yorkshire. The Trough of Bowland, near its centre, is the pass through which the one road crosses the hills. Sydney Moorhouse, *The Forest of Bowland* (London: Saint Catherine Press, 1948), p. viii, says: 'Bolland as it was originally called (and as it is still pronounced by the local folk).'

3   *the days of the Heptarchy,*] The seven or more Anglo-Saxon kingdoms which existed in eastern and northern England before the ninth-century unification under the kings of Wessex.

4   *a follower of James the Second;*] In 1688 the Catholic James II was ousted from the throne by his daughter Mary and her husband, his nephew William of Orange. The elder Starkey evidently joined James in the Irish campaign which ended in defeat at the battle of the Boyne (1690). James II fled to France with many of his followers and had a court in exile at St Germain near Paris.

5   *having lent their good offices*] As a traitor to the crown, he would have had to make his peace with the government; and as a practising Catholic he would have been subject to several legal penalties, the effects of which could be mitigated by the good offices of friendly Protestants, and intensified if the neighbours were hostile.

6   *King William's*] This puts the date of the Starkeys' return to England before the death of William III in 1702.

7   *the Antwerp faille,*] a silk mantilla.

8   *the strictness of the entail ... Papists.*] For entails, see 'Morton Hall', note 19. Catholics were legally disabled from owning land, and the son, on whom the land was entailed, could have claimed it as next of kin, had he been of age and a Protestant. But it was anyway not usually possible to break an entail without the consent of the heir, which he could not give until he was of age.

9   *rather have a sum ... an annuity*] This is contradicted below, p. 397, when she appears to have an annuity after all.

10   *Hurst;*] It is clear from pp. 418–19 below that EG means Stonyhurst, near Clitheroe, on the south-eastern border of the Forest of Bowland, an Elizabethan mansion inhabited by a Catholic gentry family, the Sherburnes, who died out in 1717. In 1794 the house was leased by their heirs as a refuge for the school for English Catholic boys founded at St Omer in 1592, which still exists there as Stonyhurst College; it is in this guise that EG would have known of it.

11   *Sir Philip Tempest,*] Although Sir Philip is imaginary, EG here uses the name of a real family of Catholic Lancashire gentry, the Tempests of Broughton Hall, Skipton-in-Craven, members of which served in foreign regiments during the eighteenth century: T. D. Whitaker, *The*

History and Antiquities of the Deanery of Craven in the County of York (London: Nicols, 1805), pp. 74–87.

12 *far from well,*] The same rather unexpected prescription of genealogical research as a cure for the illness of a young trainee solicitor occurs in *The Autobiography of William Jerdan*, 4 vols (1852–3), vol. i, pp. 68–9, which is a possible influence here.

13 *West Chester.*] By the 1850s the port of Chester had long been superseded by Liverpool as the main departure point for boats to Ireland; EG may have intended to give the journey a period flavour.

14 *the Duke of Berwick's regiment,*] James II's illegitimate son James Fitzjames, Duke of Berwick (1670–1734) commanded a regiment in the French army whose officers were substantially recruited from Irish and English Jacobites. It is possible that EG heard about the regiment from her French translator, Louise Swanton Belloc, whose father James Swanton (d.1828) had served in it.

15 *paid an annuity*] For this inconsistency see note 9, above. The implication that the Starkey heir is not yet of age is awkward for dating purposes: he was born several years before Lucy.

16 *the Count de la T'our d'Auvergne,*] Like Sir Philip Tempest, an imaginary member of a real family.

17 *legitimate or illegitimate child of her father.*] This is a question to which we never learn the answer; probably because it is fudged for the sake of the plot: see note 22 below.

18 *many a thing he loved ... his dog –*] This is a folk tale motif which occurs in some versions of the *Beauty and the Beast* story.

19 *Sir Matthew Hale.*] Sir Matthew Hale (1609–1676), judge, presided at the trial of Rose Cullender and Amy Drury for witchcraft in 1661–2; and saw them convicted and executed. Hale was a puritan in religion and a royalist in politics, famously upright and a great legal scholar (*DNB*). There is some anachronism in the implication that he and the narrator's uncle were contemporaries, since this scene can hardly be supposed to take place earlier than about 1725.

20 *The sins of the fathers*] From the Second Commandment in the version of the catechism in the *Book of Common Prayer*: 'for I the Lord thy God am a jealous God, and visit the sins of the fathers upon the children unto the third and fourth generation of them that hate me ...' The Authorised Version of the Bible (Exodus 20:5) has 'the iniquity of the fathers'.

21 *Skipford Hall, in the West Riding.*] The West Riding of Yorkshire is the part nearest Lancashire. By p. 410 the house is named 'Skipford Court'.

22 *in ignorance of the deeper ... done her.*] The implication seems to be that Gisborne has seduced Mary Fitzgerald by a false marriage, since

merely to marry Mary was hardly to do Bridget wrong. Mary has evidently committed suicide on discovering that she was not really his wife (see p. 410). However, if this is so, the other half of the plot, in which Lucy Gisborne inherits the Fitzgerald property in Ireland as heir-at-law of her maternal grandfather, does not work, since an illegitimate child is not heir to its mother or its father. It may have been EG's awareness of this inconsistency, as much as prudery, which led her to play down the seduction of Mary.

23   *those strange New England cases*] EG had published her first story under the name 'Cotton Mather Mills', and therefore certainly knew at least by reputation the Revd Cotton Mather's several books which describe the Salem trials, such as *The wonders of the invisible world: being an account of the tryals of several witches, lately excuted in New-England* (1693). Easson (in his edition of *Cousin Phillis and Other Tales* (Oxford: Oxford University Press, 1981, p. 358) notes that in writing 'Lois the Witch' (1859) she drew on Charles Upham, *Lectures on Witchcraft* (1831).

24   *Mr. Defoe, who had written a book,*] Daniel Defoe, *A True Relation of the Apparition of one Mrs. Veal, the next day after her death* (1706).

25   *church and meeting-house*] It becomes clear below that the narrator's uncle is not a member of the Church of England. He would therefore attend a meeting-house rather than a church. EG thus emphasises the religious diversity of her characters.

26   *the chaplain at Stoney Hurst?*] See note 10, above.

27   *a Poor Clare,*] an order of nuns founded about 1219 under the inspiration of St Clare, the friend of St Francis of Assisi.

28   *on behalf of the Jacobites.*] The events of the story take place in the 1720s or 1730s, between the two Jacobite risings of 1715 and 1745, since Lucy must have been born about 1705, and has had time to grow to adulthood.

29   *then raging in the Low Countries –*] EG describes a rebellion by the population of Antwerp against their Austrian rulers. Antwerp was the biggest city in what was then the Austrian Netherlands and is now (roughly) modern Belgium. The time is evidently approximately that of the war of Polish Succession 1733–5, which saw fighting in the Austrian Netherlands. However, the historical details are vague, and it may be that, rather than taking the idea from a particular historical event, EG was inspired by a paragraph in the last chapter of Walter Scott, *The Antiquary* (1816), which describes the death, during a revolutionary uprising in 1793, in a convent in 'French Flanders', of a Spanish woman, formerly a nurse in a noble family, who has assisted in the concealment of the birth of a supposedly illegitimate child:

> We were attacked by the enemy, and driven from the town, which was pillaged with savage ferocity by the republicans. The religious orders

were the particular objects of their hate and cruelty. The convent was burned, and several nuns perished, among others Teresa – and with her all chance of knowing the story of my birth ...

30   *the 'blouses'*] The expression 'les blouses', which translates as 'the overalls' or 'the smocks', is used in French to mean 'the workers'.

31   *'Therefore, if thine ... give him drink.'*] Romans 12:20: 'Therefore if thine enemy hunger, feed him; if he thirst, give him drink: for in so doing thou shalt heap coals of fire on his head.'

'The Half-Brothers'

1   *never spoke of her first husband,*] Since it subsequently appears that the narrator's mother died shortly after his birth this comment seems rather misleading; although there is nothing particularly uncharacteristic about this slip it may indicate that the story was not carefully revised for publication.

2   *Brigham*] a village near Cockermouth, Cumberland, within five miles of the sea.

3   *the great Glasgow sewing-merchants.*] White muslin embroidery, known as Ayrshire work, was a cottage industry in many rural areas of Scotland and the north of England; a *broderie anglaise*, resembling lace, it was made into collars, cuffs, christening robes and similar garments, and was immensely fine, enough to give anyone eye strain.

4   *maud.*] See 'The Old Nurse's Story', note 12.

TEXTUAL NOTES

The text of stories in this volume has in each case been prepared from the text in the first publication in volume form in Great Britain, which has been collated with the story's first periodical publication. This decision has been taken for the sake of consistency, despite the fact that in some cases the periodical text seems marginally preferable. But in no case is there much difference, and in the case of the stories included in *Round the Sofa* it seemed desirable to include the frame and links, which forced the choice of the volume text. The notes that follow mention all significant discrepancies between the copy-text and the periodical text. In accordance with editorial policy throughout this edition, EG's use of different names for the same character has been regularised, and this has been recorded in the notes. The headnote to each story includes the details of all its other publications in EG's lifetime. Corrections to the copy-texts made in this edition are recorded in the list of Silent Corrections below. Errors in the accents on French words have not been corrected.

'The Old Nurse's Story'

8a   her lesson I'll] her lesson, I'll *HW*

'Morton Hall'

24a   1460] Fourteen hundred and sixty *HW*
38a   stayed] staid *HW*
41a   poor Aunt Phillis.] *HW adds line space*
45a   develop] develope *HW*

'My French Master'

56a   the fatal 21st of January, 1793;] the fatal January twenty-first, seventeen hundred and ninety-three; *HW*
58a   hard, and] hard and *HW*
62a   1814] eighteen hundred and fourteen *HW*
64a   1791.] seventeen hundred and ninety-one. *HW*
65a   1815,] eighteen hundred and fifteen, *HW*

69a   Anne-Marguérite] Anne-Marguerite *HW*

'The Squire's Story'

75a   1769,] seventeen hundred and sixty-nine, *HW*
75b   yourselves, the] yourselves the *HW*
76a   the 'gentleman'] 'the gentleman' *HW*
76b   the 'gentleman'] 'the gentleman' *HW*
78a   of the Barford] of Barford *HW*
78b   down, the day] down the day *HW*
86a   1775.] seventeen hundred and seventy-five. *HW*

'Right at Last'

91a   RIGHT AT LAST.] THE SIN OF A FATHER. *HW*
91b   dances and evening] dances, evening *HW*
91c   him, – and] him, and *HW*
91d   uncle'.] Uncle.' *HW*
91e   Ay!] Aye!] *HW*
92a   married?'] married.' *HW*
96a   secrétaire] secretaire *HW*
97a   City] city *HW*
98a   'sat all … chair,' as] sat all poured out into his chair, as *HW*
104a   in what way the] how the *HW*

'The Manchester Marriage'

109a   to settle in London.] to London and took the House to Let. *HW*
109b   This, indeed,] His salary indeed, *HW*
109c   house than the one he did,] House than this one, *HW*
111a   even if it had not,] even had it not, *HW*
111b   in meanwhile … form a part.] in the meantime, she should be sure to form part. *HW*
113a   in it,] in the place, *HW*
115a   Prayer-book.] prayer-book. *HW*
116a   Infirmary,] infirmary, *HW*
116b   Mamma,] Mama *HW*
117a   London.] London, and come to occupy the House. *HW*
117b   sat] sate *HW*
118a   he rang … front-door] he rung at the front door *HW*
120a   care!] care. *HW*
121a   before her master … returned;] before they did return; *HW*
124a   *he*] he *HW*
124b   thoughts; the one that] from his thoughts who *HW*
125a   forward.] forwards. *HW*

126a no] none *HW*
129a sat] sate *HW*
130a date upon it. That] date. That *HW*

'My Lady Ludlow'

147a out] not *HW*
148a Chase.] Chace. *HW*
148b byroads] bye-roads *HW*
148c sunset] sun-set *HW*
150a curtsy] curtsey *HW*
150b delicately-cut bread-and-butter,] delicately cut bread and butter, *HW*
150c sat] sate *HW*
150d Prayer-book.] prayer book. *HW*
151a curtsied] curtseyed *HW*
151b curtsied] curtseyed *HW*
151c Prayer-book;] prayer-book; *HW*
152a lady] Lady *HW*
152b Ten Commandments.] ten commandments. *HW*
152c Commandment,] commandment, *HW*
152d king's and queen's] kings' and queens' *HW*
153a Sunday-school] Sunday school *HW*
153b Sabbath-school] Sabbath school *HW*
155a down] Down *HW*
156a roast-beef and plum-pudding,] roast beef and plum pudding, *HW*
157a Faux'] Faux *HW*
157b cobblers-wax,] cobbler's-wax, *HW*
157c shoemakers'] shoe-makers *HW*
157d sat] sate *HW*
158a 'Sturm's Reflections,'] Sturm's Reflections, *HW*
158b 'Mrs. Chapone's … Young Ladies'] Mrs. Chapone's Letters and Dr.
      Gregory's Advice to Young Ladies *HW*
158c ancestresses.] ancestors. *HW*
161a weeks'] weeks *HW*
163a that "God help … to overcome.'"] that God help him! he was respon-
      sible for all the evil he did not strive to overcome.' *HW*
163b sat] sate *HW*
163c Coachman] coachman *HW*
164a Barford Corner,] Barford-Corner, *HW*
164b gaol] jail *HW*
165a gaol] jail *HW*
165b quarter-sessions.'] quarter sessions.' *HW*
167a sat]sate *HW*
169a sat] sate *HW*

169b   public-entrance;] public entrance; *HW*
169c   gray] grey *HW*
172a   sweetbriar] sweet-briar *HW*
172b   Attar-of-roses,] Attar of roses,
172c   lilies-of-the-valley] lilies of the valley *HW*
172d   his 'Essay on Gardens.'] his essay on gardens. *HW*
175a   sat] sate *HW*
175b   behindhand;] behind-hand; *HW*
176a   thy] my *HW*
176b   Catechism] catechism *HW*
176c   Catechism] catechism *HW*
177a   or the] or of the *HW*
177b   Bailey's,] Bayley's,
177c   Bailey).] Bayley). *HW*
177d   sat,] sate, *HW*
177e   hand-bell,] handbell, *HW*
177f   back door] back-door *HW*
177g   front door] front-door *HW*
178a   carriage-and-four,] carriage and four, *HW*
180a   dumb-foundering] dumfoundering *HW*
181a   Revolution] revolution *HW*
181b   bishop's] Bishop's *HW*
181c   curtsy,] curtsey, *HW*
182a   race-horse and cart-horse.] racehorse and carthorse. *HW*
188a   chocolate,] coffee, *HW*
191a   gray] grey *HW*
192a   Necker,] Neckar, *HW*
194a   sat] sate *HW*
196a   sat] sate *HW*
201a   partisan,] partisan, *HW*
206a   handsome –] lovely – *HW*
208a   hast thou done?"] hast thou?" *HW*
209a   sat] sate *HW*
209b   sat] sate *HW*
210a   Norman?] Norman!' *HW*
210b   'In a few days, however,] 'But, in a few days, *HW*
210c   sat] sate
211a   her! –] her: – *HW*
213a   his usual haunts.] his haunts. *HW*
213b   sat] sate *HW*
215a   sat] sate *HW*
215b   sat –] sate – *HW*
216a   incapable of measuring] unable to measure *HW*

217a   çi-devant] ci-devant *HW*
217b   "faithful cousin"] faithful cousin *HW*
217c   sat] sate *HW*
219a   snatch] take *HW*
220a   sat, –] sate, – *HW*
224a   mélée] mêlée *HW*
228a   sat] sate *HW*
228b   have] had *HW*
230a   number:] number! *HW*
232a   (for] (and *HW*
233a   ladyship:] ladyship! *HW*
234a   or] nor
236a   sat] sate *HW*
238a   for I] for, indeed, I *HW*
239a   said:] spoke to me: *HW*
239b   sat] sate down *HW*
239c   Brooke] Lambe *HW, 1859* [see explanatory note 95]
239d   have already] have perhaps already *HW*
241a   sat] sate *HW*
243a   sat] sate *HW*
244a   sat,] sate, *HW*
245a   Sabbath?] Sabbath. *HW*
246a   preordained] pre-ordained *HW*
249a   develop] develope *HW*
250a   *service oblige,"*] service oblige," *HW*
252a   *would*] would *HW*
252b   sat] sate *HW*
258a   sat] sate *HW*
259a   sat] sate *HW*
259b   were registered] was marked *HW*
260a   intrusted] entrusted *HW*
260b   'all'] all *HW*
260c   The heir of the … death, would] The heirs of both estates were, in
       the case of the Monkshaven property, an Edinburgh advocate, a far-
       away kinsman of my lord's: the Hanbury property would go to the
       descendants *HW*
261a   wishes' he … was] whose wishes he, the testator, was *HW*
268a   Dissenter] dissenter *HW*
274a   stayed] staid *HW*
277a   sat] sate *HW*
279a   'Tours'] Tours *HW*
282a   sat] sate *HW*
284a   for many] for now many *HW*

286a   'Philidor on Chess,'] Philidor on Chess *HW*
287a   baptized;] baptised; *HW*
287b   Dissenters,] dissenters, *HW*
289a   who had only … her,] and her father's co-heiress, *HW*
290a   – Yes, this is it.] *HW omits*
291a   kittens. / 'Now,] kittens. 'Now, *HW*
291b   The very] I think the very] *HW*
291c   tantalize] tantalise *HW*
291d   company?] company, *HW*
292a   Ay!] 'Aye! *HW*

'An Accursed Race'

297a   it: we] it. We *HW*
298a   sunrise,] sun-rise, *HW*
298b   sunset] sun-set *HW*
299a   and they were … water.] and to drink of any other water, was forbid-
        den to the Cagoterie. *HW*
299b   himself of the Cagot's] themselves of the Cagot *HW*
299c   The race was] They were *HW*
299d   Catholics,] catholics, *HW*
299e   not surprising] no wonder *HW*
300a   nor] or drink *HW*
300b   ounces a-piece,] ounces each, *HW*
300c   nor drink in] or drink water in *HW*
301a   Pope,] pope, *HW*
302a   And] and *HW*
302b   Fifth; which however … into] Fifth; but there was no one to carry
        these laws into *HW*
303a   gray-blue] grey-blue *HW*
303b   Church and State.] church and state. *HW*
303c   proved the truth … Hudibras, / He] held with Hudibras that – / He
        HW
304a   law was] laws were *HW*
304b   among] amongst the people *HW*
304c   lay] laid *HW*
305a   than any other] than other *HW*
305b   are] is *HW*
305c   yet they] yet that they *HW.*
306a   country. Perpetual] country; perpetual *HW*
307a   Pyrenées] Pyrenees HW
308a   Larroque a trick] Larroque tricks *HW*

309a The moral of the ...be] Gentle reader, am I not rightly representing your feelings? If so, perhaps the moral of the history of the accursed races may be *HW*

309b Hand,] Haud, *HW*

'The Doom of the Griffiths'

313a some] the American reader *Harper's*

313b is, even in ... famous] is as famous, even at the present day of enlightenment, *Harper's*

316a wilful,] willful, *Harper's*

317a sceptical] skeptical *Harper's*

317b stupified] stupefied *Harper's*

319a fulfilment,] fulfillment, *Harper's*

321a Clenneny] Cleuneny *Harper's*

322a coloured,] colored, *Harper's*

323a thoughtfulness,] thoughtlessness, *Harper's*

325a winding up] mounting *Harper's*

328a sun-coloured] sun-colored *Harper's*

329a for ever and ever] forever *Harper's*

329b poor fool!'] poor wittol fool!' *Harper's*

332a stayed] staid *Harper's*

333a favourite] favorite *Harper's*

336a by herself] mourn her lane *Harper's*

337a this] for a *Harper's*

339a was busy] busied himself *Harper's*

339b dishevelled] disheveled *Harper's*

339c dexterous] dextrous *Harper's*

340a sat] sate *Harper's*

341a should] must *Harper's*.

341b plough] plow *Harper's*

'Half a Life-Time Ago'

345a in one of ... single woman,] a single woman, of the name of Susan Dixon, in one of the Westmoreland dales. *HW*

346a did so] sate down *HW*

346b its members having] and having *HW*

350a yours] your's *HW*

350b yours;] your's; *HW*

351a gray] grey *HW*

352a sat] sate *HW*

352b sat] sate *HW*

354a love!] love. *HW*

354b sat] sate *HW*
355a thee (as I ... before),] thee, as I promised mother before, *HW*
356a sat] sate *HW*
359a a 'natural,'] a natural, *HW*
362a Michael] he *HW*
364a fro'] fra *HW*
366a sat] sate *HW*
366b regarding Will,] with regard to Will, *HW*
367a in point of riches,] as to riches, *HW*
367b Susan's] her *HW*
368a Daleswoman.] daleswoman. *HW*
370a consequences] consequence *HW*
371a of her age.] of age. *HW*
371b close] up *HW*
372a redded] redd *HW*
373a and how care] manner, and care *HW*
374a *vis inertiæ*] vis inertiae *HW*
374b ne'er-do-weel] ne'er-do-well *HW*
375a sat] sate *HW*
375b sat] sat *HW*
375c fall] downfal *HW*
375d gulleys] gullies *HW*
377a half-carrying, half-dragging –] half-dragging, half-carrying – *HW*
377b in this swoon] in swoon *HW*
377c Hurst!] Hurst. *HW*

'The Poor Clare'

385a 12th,] 12, *HW*
386a Heptarchy,] heptarchy, *HW*
387a sat] sate *HW*
387b curtsy] curtsey *HW*
387c set] sat *HW*
389a gray] grey *HW*
390a goings-out and comings-in.] out-goings and in-comings. *HW*
391a travel-and-sorrow stained] travel and sorrow-stained *HW*
397a at] in *HW*
400a ecstacy,] ecstasy *HW*
400b *de vive voix*] de vive voix *HW*
401a or] nor *HW*
402a Mrs.] Mistress *HW*
404a inquiry.'] enquiry.' *HW*
404b house!] house? *HW*

406a   rose] arose *HW*
411a   by] of *HW*
411b   gray] grey *HW*

'The Half-Brothers'

431a   with] and *F*
431b   and with no] and no *F*
431c   happened] came to pass *F*
431d   only] not *F*
431e   aunt] Aunt *F*
431f   sat] sate *F*
431g   sat] sate *F*
431h   far-off cousin ... were] far-away cousin, which was *F*
432a   churchyard – at] churchyard. At *F*
432b   sewing-merchants.] Sewing Merchants. *F*
432c   Preston,] Maxwell, *F*
432d   sat] sate *F*
433a   Preston] Maxwell *F*
433b   Preston's] Maxwell's *F*
433c   Preston's] Maxwells's *F*
433d   Preston] Maxwell *F*
433e   Preston] Maxwell *F*
434a   sat] sate F
435a   Fells,] fells, *F*
436a   Fells.] fells. *F*
436b   Fells,] fells, *F*
436c   road. It] road; it *F*
436d   painful, intense,] painfully intense, *F*
436e   filled thick] filled and thick *F*
436f   dared] dare *F*
436g   it] me *F*
436h   unfeeling] pitiless *F*
436i   warm, red, bright] warm red bright *F*
437a   nearly fancied] almost thought *F*
437b   gray] grey *F*
439a   aunt] Aunt *F*
439b   fellow! –] fellow – *F*
439c   child!'] child.' *F*

SILENT CORRECTIONS

3	at once. I was] at once I was
6	watchful, to make] watchful to make
8	Agnes, the kitchen-maid,] Bessy, the kitchen-maid,
8	ran away pretty quickly] run away pretty quickly
9	little lady and I] little lady, and I
9	more and more stormily] more, and more stormily
27	He came to stay] He come to stay
36	said, 'Mrs. Jones] said, Mrs. Jones
41	Ethelinda and I] Ethelinda, and I
58	Mary and I] Mary, and I
58	circumstance that] circumstance, that
63	Ah! Miss Mary,] Ah! Miss Fanny,
79	Higgins if he] Higgins, if he
123	'Bessy, was any one] 'Mary, was any one
126	infallible ways] infallible weys
140	at the Mackenzies'.] at the Mackenzie's.
184	footman of Madame] footman of Madam
201	Morin fils,] Morin Fils,
203	Morin fils,] Morin Fils,
210	an unusual alacrity] an unnusual alacrity
211	Morin fils, –] Morin Fils, –
214	How could Jean] How could Victor
219	naturally have worn] naturedly have worn
221	of the men.)] of the men.
234	enough not to be] enough to be
249	as the crow flies] as the crows flies
272	'The king … the king!'] The king is dead – 'Long live the king!'
272	her parents think] her parent's think
276	asked Mrs. Trevor] asked Mrs. Gibson
277	Ludlow] Ludow
283	turn up.'] turn up.
285	so disapproved] so dissapproved
288	piece of sea-wrack,] piece of sea-wreck,
292	silk, and spread] silk, spread it
314	heritage in Caernarvonshire,] heritage in Caenarvonshire,
345	funereal, umbrageous] funereal umbrageous
391	brown, and scarred] brown, and scared